Strategic Entrepreneurship

Pearson
Education

SECOND EDITION

Strategic Entrepreneurship

A decision-making approach to new venture creation and management

Philip A. Wickham

An imprint of Pearson Education

Harlow, England · London · New York · Reading, Massachusetts · San Francisco · Toronto · Don Mills, Ontario · Sydney
Tokyo · Singapore · Hong Kong · Seoul · Taipei · Cape Town · Madrid · Mexico City · Amsterdam · Munich · Paris · Milan

To Louise

Pearson Education Limited

Edinburgh Gate
Harlow
Essex CM20 2JE
United Kingdom

and Associated Companies throughout the world

Visit us on the World Wide Web at
www.pearsoneduc.com

First published in Great Britain in 1998
Second edition published in 2001

ISBN 0-273 65115-3

British Library Cataloguing in Publication Data
A CIP catalogue record for this book can be obtained from the British Library

10 9 8 7 6 5 4 3 2
04 03 02 01 00

Typeset by TA Tek-Art, Croydon, Surrey
Printed and bound in Great Britain by TJ International Ltd., Padstow, Cornwall

Contents

Part 2 CHOOSING A DIRECTION

Part 3 INITIATING THE NEW VENTURE

Preface to second edition

Over the past ten years, the subject of entrepreneurship has moved from the periphery to the centre of management thinking and education. As we enter the new millennium, an entrepreneurial approach is no longer seen as *an* option but as the *only* option for managers seeking to enhance the performance of their organisations. This is so whether the organisation be a new start-up striving to establish itself in the marketplace, an established business seeking to reinvigorate itself or a governmental or non-profit organisation meeting the opportunity and the challenge of the shifting boundaries between the public and private sectors.

The approach taken by this book is founded on a belief that entrepreneurship should be demystified. It is not, as many of its advocates suggest, a process that is rooted in hidden intuitive processes of a few select individuals and that, in its practice, rises above the restrictive and mundane approach of 'over-formal' strategic management decision making.

The book takes the view that entrepreneurship is a type of management, particularly a form of *strategic management*. It is a very effective form of management to be sure, but one which is transparent in the decisions entrepreneurs identify, the way they approach making those decisions and the skills that entrepreneurs bring in order to make those decisions happen in real, challenging business environments. This means that entrepreneurship should be regarded as a style of management that can be learnt if managers are dedicated to discovering its secrets and developing its skills. The book aims to contribute to this by providing a logical exploration of the decisions entrepreneurs face, the development of conceptual models that assist in making these decisions effectively and by offering an agenda for developing the managerial skills necessary to put them into practice.

This second edition provides an opportunity to enhance the book's contribution to this programme. It takes on board the new trends in the world of entrepreneurial activity (particularly those as resulting from the Internet revolution), new ideas on entrepreneurial practice and decision making and from new studies into entrepreneurial behaviour and strategy. These studies have been drawn from the rapidly growing literature into entrepreneurship that, reflecting the traditional eclecticism of the field and its relevance to a wide range of disciplines, is appearing in the management, economic, sociological and psychological journals.

The original framework, the core of which is the 'strategic window' sequence of the entrepreneurial process, is retained. Around this framework there is an extended discussion of the conceptual framework for understanding entrepreneurship, more extensive discussion of the decisions entrepreneurs face and greater coverage of specific issues relating to those decisions. In particular, the book features new material on the definition of entrepreneurship, cognitive aspects of entrepreneurial decision making, entrepreneurial motivation, entrepreneurial innovation and strategy. I have also taken the opportunity to clarify some of the ideas presented in the first edition. These changes reflect the considerable positive feedback the first edition of this book has received and advice offered from users and reviewers. I am very grateful for these comments.

It is hoped that this new edition will improve the utility of the book for academics seeking a grounding in this fast-growing field, students undertaking and tutors delivering courses in entrepreneurship and managers seeking to develop their entrepreneurial approach. A new series of *Financial Times* articles (with suggested review questions) have been included at the end of each chapter to provide a basis for focused, up-to-date, discussion of the issues raised in the text.

I would like to thank all the team at Pearson Education who have not only made the challenging project of producing this text easier to manage but have also made it enjoyable. In particular, I would like to offer special thanks to Liz Johnson, Sadie McClelland, Jane Powell and Penelope Woolf.

Philip A. Wickham
January 2000

Preface to first edition

Learning outcomes

This book is about entrepreneurship as a *style* of management. It aims to provide an insight into entrepreneurship and entrepreneurial management from a *strategic* perspective. It is suitable for undergraduates, postgraduates and post-experience students on full-time, part-time or distance learning-based courses in entrepreneurship, small business management and strategic management. It provides a useful supplementary source of information about entrepreneurship for specialist courses in areas such as organisational behaviour and organisational change management.

The book also aims to give practising managers, whatever the size, type and sector of their organisation or their position within it, an opportunity to explore the potential for approaching their managerial tasks in a more entrepreneurial style and of undertaking entrepreneurial projects more successfully.

These are challenging aims and obviously no book can 'make' somebody into an entrepreneur on its own. It may inform them; it may highlight the issues that are involved in entrepreneurial success; it may inspire them and give them a sense of direction; but at the end of the day, only the individual can turn themself into an entrepreneur.

However, we must not lose sight of the fact that learning to be entrepreneurial is like learning to do anything else. It is, as we shall see, just a form of *behaviour*, and behaviour is learnt. Being entrepreneurial is certainly a complex and demanding form of behaviour requiring knowledge and skill. Proficiency cannot be acquired overnight, but then few valuable skills can be learnt that quickly.

Learning to be entrepreneurial means learning to *manage* in an *entrepreneurial* way. This means recognising the potential of a situation: the *opportunities* it presents, how *changes* may be made for the better and how *new value* can be created from it. This means being able to spot new possibilities, to recognise the decisions which need to be made and knowing how to follow them through. This book aims to give students and managers who want to understand entrepreneurial possibilities access to those decisions in order to understand how those decisions present themselves and the shape they take. To make this learning effective, this book takes an *active learning* approach.

An active learning strategy

This book, like any management text, can be only a part of the process of discovering and exploring the entrepreneurial option, but it aspires to be a valuable tool in that discovery. It aims to do this in four ways:

1 By being about decisions, not just knowledge

Every entrepreneur has his or her personal store of knowledge. This knowledge is a critical aspect of business venturing. Successful entrepreneurship demands a good knowledge of a particular business, the people who make it up, the industry it is in, the customers it serves and its competitors.

Having knowledge is a *necessary*, but not a *sufficient* condition for entrepreneurial success. What matters is what is *done* with that knowledge, that is how it is used to inform and aid decision making. While every entrepreneur will call upon a different repertoire of knowledge and use it in a wide variety of business situations, all use it to address a remarkably similar set of decisions.

The key learning outcome of the book is an understanding of entrepreneurship not as an abstract subject, but as the pattern of decisions that the entrepreneurial manager must identify, analyse, resolve and follow through. By clarifying these decisions, individual entrepreneurs become aware of the knowledge they have, the knowledge they need and the learning they must undertake, in a way which is specific to the venture they are managing.

2 By presenting frameworks for thinking, not just theories

A framework for thinking is just that: a guide to help us think. It is a conceptual device which highlights certain issues, suggests which factors might be important, draws attention to the way in which they are connected and links together things that might influence one another. A framework for thinking provides a scheme for clarifying the issues that are important in a business situation, helps to indicate the decisions that might be relevant to it and identifies the information needed before a good decision can be made.

A framework for thinking is not intended to reveal fundamental truths. It is intended as an *aide-mémoire* to help decision making, that is as a reminder of what needs to be understood and addressed. This book will develop a number of frameworks for thinking which can be used to aid entrepreneurial decision making. Usually, the best way of presenting a framework for thinking is in a *visual* rather than written format. This makes the elements in the framework explicit and is efficient at depicting their interrelationships. So, whenever possible, this book will use visual representations.

'Theory' is often met with a great deal of suspicion, especially in the world of business. Some draw a hard line between 'theory' and 'practice'. Surely, it is often suggested, what matters is *practice*: being able to do the job rather than being able to speculate about it. To say that someone 'takes a theoretical view' is a double-edged compliment. It can be downright pejorative and suggest an inability to put ideas into action.

This is unfortunate and arises from a misunderstanding about what theory is and how it works. In fact, we all use theories all the time. A theory is just an expectation that a certain set of circumstances will lead to a particular outcome. For example, we all subscribe to the 'theory' that if we step off a cliff we will fall; and if we fall we will injure ourselves. This influences our behaviour: we do not step off cliffs. We constantly make theories about the world and test them. If they are useful, that is if their predictions are good, then we will hold on to them. If their predictions turn out to be false, then we will reject them and look for a better theory. We still do this even in situations where our theories must constantly adapt and evolve to make sense of a changing world. This is what the process of learning is all about. In this sense *experience*, including experience in business, is, in part, a matter of having access to a lot of 'good' theories.

3 By taking a strategic, rather than a tactical approach

This book considers that the decisions faced by an entrepreneur must be recognised as *strategic decisions*. The idea of strategy is a very important one in business. In essence, strategy relates to the *actions* that a business takes in order to achieve its *goals*. The idea of something being strategic touches on several things:

- it refers to issues which affect the *whole* organisation, not just some small part of it;
- it concerns the way in which the organisation interacts with its *environment*, not just its internal affairs;
- it concerns not merely what the company does – the business it is 'in' – but also how it *competes*;
- it involves consideration of how the business is performing not only in absolute terms but in *relation* to its competitors.

Tactical issues are still important though. To be successful, an entrepreneurial venture must be effective in its marketing, it must manage its finances competently and it must be proficient in its operations. What a strategic approach means is that entrepreneurs must think of all of these things not as isolated functions but as different facets of the venture as a *whole*. They must be seen to function in unison enabling the venture to deliver value to its customers, to attract investors' money and to grow in the face of competition.

4 By inviting active, not passive, learning

We all learn continually. Formal learning, when we sit down and deliberately acquire new knowledge, is only one, albeit a special, way in which we learn about the world. We learn quite naturally, often without realising we are doing it, particularly when we are motivated and interested in something. (Think about your hobby and consider how much knowledge and skill you bring to it. How much of that was 'deliberately' learnt?) Effective learning occurs when we are called upon not only to retain knowledge but also to *use* it, and then to challenge and *revise* it in the light of experience.

This forms the basis of the *active learning* cycle. The first stage is to set up a framework for thinking, like the ones that will be developed in this book. Once this is in place, the next stage is to use it to *analyse* some situation facing us. The framework for thinking helps make sense of that situation, indicates the factors involved, highlights the important factors and suggests a direction to move forward.

In the third stage we apply the analysis by responding to the situation and taking *action*. A decision is made and followed through. In the fourth stage we examine the *consequences* of that action. We see if the outcomes are the ones we wanted. Did the decision produce the results we wanted? If not, how did they differ from what we wanted? What went right? What went wrong? As a result, we reflect on the framework for thinking that we used, and the actions we took based on it. This leads to a consideration of how useful it was.

We can then revise the framework in the light of our experience, or adjust the actions it suggests to us. This gives us a new framework for thinking which we can use to make new actions. And so we go round the cycle again. Eventually, we will get a framework for thinking that works for us, in our given situation. Then we begin to forget about it! We quickly learn to make decisions without constant reference to this process. At this point we have become experienced. Our knowledge is manifest as an 'unconscious' skill.

Performing as a business decision maker, and putting the resulting decisions into practice through initiative and leadership is a matter of learning. But that learning must be *active* – see Fig. A. Active learning of entrepreneurship involves setting up *frameworks* to aid decision making, using them to *guide action* and *revising* them in the light of *experience*.

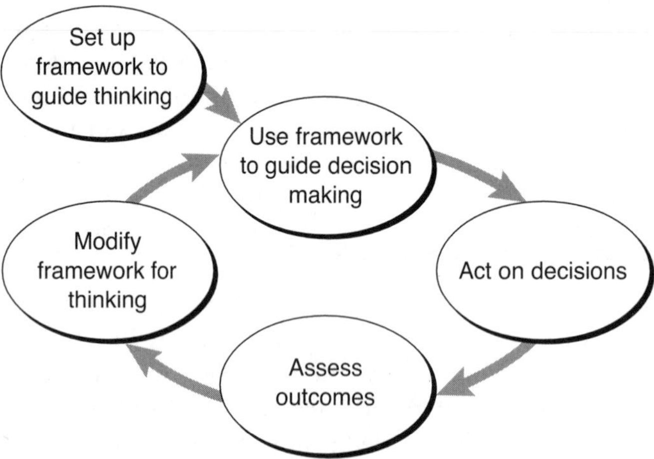

Fig. A The active learning cycle

Layout of the text

The material in this book is arranged so that ideas are presented in a logical order and accessible format. The book is organised into four parts.

Part 1 develops some introductory concepts that will be of use later in the book. The aim of this section is twofold. First, it provides a 'tool-kit' of ideas which will facilitate discussion about the entrepreneur. Second, it aims to put entrepreneurs into their proper *context*. It explores the nature of the entrepreneur and the process by which entrepreneurs create new value. This section is at pains to dispel some common myths about the entrepreneur, in particular, that an entrepreneur is born to be an entrepreneur or that to be a successful entrepreneur one must have a particular type of personality. The emphasis is on the fact that the entrepreneur is just a *manager*, albeit a very effective one.

Part 2 deals with the decisions the entrepreneur faces in giving the venture a direction, that is, deciding what the business will 'be about' and the *strategy* it will adopt. Also considered at this stage is the driving force behind the venture, that is, the *entrepreneurial vision*; what it is, how it might be developed, and how it might be used to give the venture direction and provide a foundation for leadership behaviour.

Part 3 is concerned with the initiation of the venture. This addresses how the entrepreneur can develop a detailed understanding of the opportunity that has presented itself to the business and the ways in which the venture can begin to exploit it. It also deals with the issues of attracting the financial and human investment that is needed to actually start up the business.

Part 4 addresses the issues and decisions that the entrepreneur must consider in successfully managing the growth of the venture and its eventual consolidation. Options for growing the business are explored and the issues that growth creates for the business are highlighted. The book concludes by considering how success may be continued as the venture matures and how the role of the entrepreneur changes.

This follows the process of creating a new venture from planning, through initiation and growth to consolidation. It provides a logical framework for ordering the decisions that the entrepreneur must make and makes them accessible. However, the entrepreneur does not face decisions in a simple order. The entrepreneurial venture constantly faces new possibilities and challenges. It may often have to revisit old decisions. Decisions impact on one another. Making one decision leads to a cascade of others. Managing an entrepreneurial venture is not like planning the journey of a space probe where everything can be calculated in advance. It is more like sailing a yacht, where there is a need for constant tacking of the sails. While planning is an important tool for making sure that the venture stays on course, it does not alleviate the need for continuous assessment of the business's situation or adjustments to respond to the possibilities presented.

A book is constrained by the need to present ideas one after the other in a linear progression. Unfortunately, the world of business does not allow decision making to be linear. Having considered the decisions relating to, say, the initiation of the venture, the entrepreneur cannot then forget about them. There may be a need to go back and reconsider them and their implications. Decisions interrelate and interconnect with one another over time. The shape of one decision will have implications for all the others that must be made.

This indicates that the order in which ideas are presented, although a useful one, is not the *only* one possible. Developing and running an entrepreneurial venture is not like following a recipe. It cannot be reduced to a unique sequence of decisions which must be followed. It is more like painting a picture, where selecting colours from a pallet can form an infinite variety of images. Entrepreneurship is a *creative* process.

This book aims to be self-contained. All the ideas are developed from the ground up and no extensive prior knowledge is assumed. The contents aspire to give a thorough grounding in the strategy of entrepreneurial management. Other than information needed to support the active learning exercises (see below), no reading around the text is required. However, entrepreneurship is a fast growing subject. The suggestions for further reading at the end of each chapter aim to give the student who wishes to explore the discipline further a key starting point from which to do so. The list is not intended to be an exhaustive review of the themes developed in the chapter. Rather, the articles are chosen for their practical style and the scope and accessibility of their approach.

The active learning exercises

As well as presenting frameworks for thinking, this book invites you to apply them and draw them into your own active learning cycle. Two projects are suggested as a way of doing this.

1 Analysing a venture as a role-model

The first exercise is an analysis of a practising entrepreneur and the venture they have developed. This will reveal how the frameworks for thinking can be used to make sense of the entrepreneurial process and the decisions that underlie it.

Though you are free to chose any entrepreneur you like, perhaps someone well-known in the public domain or possibly someone less famous whom you know personally, two caveats are advised:

- First, it should be someone who you find inspiring and whose skills you admire. The idea of this exercise is not that you learn the details of the frameworks for thinking, but rather that you gain an understanding of the entrepreneur and a venture to act as a motivating *role model* for you. This does not mean that you must follow their path slavishly, but that you should recognise the decisions that they had to face and understand how they were addressed.

- Second, you must be able to get hold of some information on the particular entrepreneur and their venture. Clearly, information is needed before the analysis can be performed. Such information is not hard to find. The lives and businesses of numerous entrepreneurs are related in biographies. The financial papers regularly report on entrepreneurs and their businesses. Local libraries will have indexes of key articles. Many management text books summarise well-known entrepreneurial ventures in the form of case studies. You will not need a great deal of information, or anything which might be considered commercially sensitive to make good use of this exercise. What matters is the *quality* of analysis performed rather than the *quantity* of information gathered.

2 Developing your own venture

The second exercise is to develop an idea for a business venture of your own. It may be one you have already started or with which you are working closely. If you are not in the position of running your own venture, then developing a plan for a new venture is a very good alternative. This plan may be one you have had in mind for some time, or it may be one that has been suggested to you or that you have come up with specially for the exercise. Do not worry if it is not a particularly well-developed idea at this stage. The point of the exercise is that the business idea should be shaped and refined. It will evolve as the exercise progresses. It should, however, be something you consider to be a good idea, something that has possibility and that you feel will be *worth* developing.

It is advised that both these exercises are undertaken as the book progresses. In this way you will get to apply the frameworks for thinking as they are encountered, and it will allow your ideas to evolve. Remember, these exercises are suggested to give you an opportunity to use the frameworks presented as tools to make sense of your own situation.

A positive approach to active learning can, in time, help to make an entrepreneurial style of decision making second nature. If these activities inspire you to start your own venture then so much the better.

Good luck!

Philip A. Wickham
September 1997

PART 1
Introductory themes

Entrepreneurship in the modern world

Of all the players who feature in the management of the modern world economy, it is entrepreneurs who most attract our attention. We all have some view of them. We may see entrepreneurs as heroes: as self-starting individuals who take great personal risk in order to bring the benefits of new products to wider world markets. We may express concern at the pace of economic and social change entrepreneurs bring and of the uncertainty they create. We may admire their talents, or we may question the rewards they get for their efforts. Whatever our instinctive reaction to them, we cannot ignore the impact of entrepreneurs.

The modern world is characterised by *change*. Every day we hear of shifts in political orders, developments in economic relationships and new technological advancements. These changes feed off each other and they are global. Developments in information technology allow capital to seek new business investment opportunities ever more efficiently. Success is sought out more quickly; failure punished more ruthlessly. Customers expect continuous improvement in the products and services they consume.

As a result, businesses are having to become more responsive. In order to keep their place in their markets they are having to innovate more quickly. In order to compete, they are having to become more agile. This is not just an issue for profit-making organisations but for all corporate bodies. The boundary between the world of the 'market' and the public domain is being pushed back and blurred.

Consequently, the world is demanding both more entrepreneurs and more *of* entrepreneurs. In the mature economies of the Western world they provide economic dynamism. The fast-growing businesses they create are now the main source of new job opportunities. The vibrant economies of the Pacific Rim are driven by the successes of thousands of new ventures. It is individual entrepreneurs who must restructure the post-modern Communist countries of eastern and central Europe and provide them with vibrant market economies. In the developing world entrepreneurs are increasingly responsible for the creation of new wealth and for making its distribution more equitable.

Change presents both opportunities and challenges. The opportunities come in the shape of new possibilities, and the chance for a better future. The challenges lie in managing the uncertainty these possibilities create. By way of a response to this challenge, we must aim to take advantage of the opportunities while controlling and responding to the uncertainties. This response must be reflected in the way we manage our organisations. In short: we must become more *entrepreneurial*. To do this we must understand *entrepreneurship.*

This book aims to provide an insight into entrepreneurship that will be valuable to both practising managers and to students of management (who will become the entrepreneurial managers of the future). It is for the manager who wants not only to be more informed about entrepreneurism, but who also wants to be more entrepreneurial. It does this by taking a particular perspective on entrepreneurism. This perspective is easily summarised as follows:

- entrepreneurship is a *style* of management;
- entrepreneurial management aims at pursuing *opportunity* and driving *change*;

- entrepreneurial management is *strategic* management: that is, management of the whole organisation; and that, critically:
- entrepreneurism is an approach to management that can be *learnt*.

As we will discover, it is not easy to define, exactly, what an entrepreneur is, or is not.

This book takes a straightforward view. It contends that entrepreneurs are just *managers* who make *entrepreneurial decisions*. This book explores these decisions, what they are, what they involve, and the actions necessary to see them through.

Understanding is as much about recognising our misconceptions as it is about gaining knowledge. There are many myths which surround the entrepreneur. If we are to get to grips with entrepreneurship and recognise the potential to be entrepreneurial these myths must be dispelled. For example, this book rejects the notion that the entrepreneur is someone who is 'born' to achieve greatness. It also dismisses the idea that they are driven by psychological forces beyond their control, or that the entrepreneur must have a particular type of personality to be successful. Rather we will regard the entrepreneur simply as a manager who knows how to make entrepreneurial decisions and how to follow them through.

Discussion will not be limited to the issues of owning businesses or starting new ones. These issues may be an important part of entrepreneurship but they are not its entirety. Nor are they an essential component of entrepreneurship: what makes someone an entrepreneur is not their historical or legal relationship to an organisation but the *changes* they create both with it and within it.

In addition to exploring entrepreneurial management, this book also intends to 'demystify' the entrepreneur. This is not an attempt to devalue them or the work they do. In fact, the opposite is intended. It recognises entrepreneurial success as the result of personal application, hard work and learning, not as some innate imperative. What this book does aim to do, above all else, is make entrepreneurship *accessible* by demonstrating that good entrepreneurship is based on management skill, and that the entrepreneurial path can be opened by managers who wish to follow it and to recognise that success follows from personal effort, knowledge and practice, rather than a pre-ordained destiny.

Suggestions for further reading

Bettis, R.A. and **Hitt, M.A.** (1995) 'The new competitive landscape', *Strategic Management Journal*, Vol. 16, pp. 7–19.

Carroll, G.R. (1994) 'Organizations . . . the smaller they get', *California Management Review*, Vol. 37, No. 1, pp. 28–41.

Moore, J.F. (1993) 'Predators and pray: A new ecology of competition', *Harvard Business Review*, May-June, pp. 75–86.

Thompson, J.L. (1999) 'A strategic perspective of entrepreneurship', *International Journal of Entrepreneurial Behaviour and Research*, Vol. 5, No. 6, pp. 279–96.

1 The nature of entrepreneurship

Chapter overview

*This chapter is concerned with developing an overarching and integrated perspective of the entrepreneur and entrepreneurship. It reviews the great variety of approaches that have been taken to characterise the entrepreneur, highlighting the lack of agreement on a fundamental definition. Three broad approaches are considered. The first defines the entrepreneur as a **manager** undertaking particular **tasks**. The second regards the entrepreneur in **economic** terms and concentrates on the function they have in facilitating **economic processes**. The third regards the entrepreneur in **psychological** terms as an individual with a particular **personality**.*

*This chapter also examines the approaches that have been taken to classifying entrepreneurs. The conclusion of the chapter is that the entrepreneur is best regarded as a **manager** and that entrepreneurship is a **style of management**.*

1.1 What is entrepreneurship?

KEY LEARNING OUTCOME

An understanding of the main approaches to understanding the nature of entrepreneurship. In particular, the distinction between the entrepreneur as a performer of *managerial tasks*, as an *agent of economic change* and as a *personality*.

The word 'entrepreneur' is widely used, both in everyday conversation and as a technical term in management and economics. Its origin lies in seventeenth-century France, where an entrepreneur was an individual commissioned to undertake a particular commercial project. A number of concepts have been derived from the idea of the entrepreneur such as *entrepreneurial, entrepreneurship* and *entrepreneurial process*. The idea that the entrepreneur is someone who undertakes certain projects offers an opening to developing an understanding of the nature of entrepreneurship. Undertaking particular projects demands that particular tasks be engaged in with the objective of achieving specific outcomes and that an individual take charge of the project. *Entrepreneurship* is then what the entrepreneur does. *Entrepreneurial* is an adjective describing how the entrepreneur undertakes what he or she does. The *entrepreneurial process* in which the entrepreneur engages is the means through which new value is created as a result of the project: the *entrepreneurial venture*.

But this is very general. Offering a specific and unambiguous definition of the entrepreneur presents a challenge. This is not because definitions are not available, but because there are so many. The management and economics literature is well served with suggested definitions for the term 'entrepreneur'. The problem arises because these definitions rarely agree with each other on the essential characteristics of the entrepreneur. Economists have long recognised the importance of the entrepreneur. Even in this discipline, known for its rigour, the entrepreneur remains an illusive beast. The difficulty lies not so much in giving entrepreneurs a role, but in giving them a role that is distinct from that of 'conventional' employed managers. Clearly, this is a distinction that is important but the difficulty is a long-standing one. Reviews of the issue by Arthur Cole, William Baumol, Harvey Leibenstein and James Soltow (all 1968) are still pertinent today.

William Gartner (1990) undertook a detailed investigation of this matter. He surveyed academics, business leaders and politicians, asking what they felt was a good definition of entrepreneurship. From the responses he summarised 90 different attributes associated with the entrepreneur. These were not just variations on a theme. Many pairs of definitions shared no common attributes at all!

This suggested that the quest for a universal definition had not moved on since 1971 when Peter Kilby noted that the entrepreneur had a lot in common with the 'Heffalump', a character in A.A. Milne's *Winnie-the-Pooh*, described as:

> **...a rather large and important animal. He has been hunted by many individuals using various trapping devices, but no one so far has succeeded in capturing him. All who claim to have caught sight of him report that that he is enormous, but disagree on his particulars.**

Gartner (1985) is led to conclude that 'Differences among entrepreneurs and among their ventures are as great as the variations between entrepreneurs and non-entrepreneurs and between new and established firms'.

While many definitions of the entrepreneur, or entrepreneurship, might be offered, any one definition is likely to result, in some cases at least, in a mismatch with our expectations. Intuitively, we know who is, or is not an entrepreneur. A particular definition will sometimes exclude those we feel from our experience are entrepreneurs or it will include those we do not think are entrepreneurs. This is illustrated when we consider the attributes associated with the entrepreneur.

For example, the notion of risk is one that is often associated with the entrepreneur. But this fails to distinguish between entrepreneurs who progress ventures and the *investors* who accept financial risk in backing those ventures. Actually founding a new business has been suggested as a defining characteristic. However, many well-known entrepreneurs have revitalised an existing organisation rather than building a new one from scratch. Some definitions emphasise the importance of entrepreneurship in providing the economic efficiency that maximises investors' returns. Rewarding investors is important, but it is not the only objective that entrepreneurs pursue. Effective entrepreneurs work to reward all the stakeholders in their ventures, not just investors. Innovation has also been suggested as a critical characteristic. However, innovation is an important factor in the success of all business ventures, not just the entrepreneurial. These points will be expanded upon in the discussion that follows.

We should not be disheartened by this apparent failure. Entrepreneurship is a rich and complex phenomenon. We should not expect, or even desire, that it be pinned down by a single, universal definition. Its variety presents endless possibilities and offers meaning to specific ventures. It is this that makes it so useful and inviting an idea. In any case, being able to define something is not the same as *understanding* it. This book will not offer a definitive definition of entrepreneurship as a starting point. A better approach is to develop a broad picture of the entrepreneur, to characterise entrepreneurs and explore the process they engage in and then move on to create an understanding of how entrepreneurship provides a route to new wealth creation.

As well as a managerial phenomenon, entrepreneurship has economic and social dimensions. The entrepreneur is an individual who lives and functions within a social setting. Entrepreneurs are not characterised by every action they take, but by a particular set of actions aimed at the creation of new wealth with their ventures. Wealth creation is a general managerial activity. Entrepreneurship is characterised by a particular approach to wealth creation. Recognising this gives us three directions from which we can develop an understanding of it. The entrepreneur can be considered as:

- a **manager** undertaking an activity – i.e. in terms of the particular tasks they perform and the way they undertake them;
- an **agent of economic change** – i.e. in terms of the effects they have on economic systems and the changes they drive; and as
- an **individual** – i.e. in terms of their psychology, personality and personal characteristics.

Each of these three aspects is reflected in the variety of definitions offered for entrepreneurship. The function of each perspective is not merely to characterise entrepreneurs but also to distinguish them from other types of people involved in the generation of wealth such as investors and 'ordinary' managers. The next three sections will explore each of these perspectives in detail.

1.2 The entrepreneur's tasks

KEY LEARNING OUTCOME
An understanding of the tasks that are undertaken by, and which characterise the work of, the entrepreneur.

We recognise entrepreneurs, first and foremost, by what they actually *do* – by the *tasks* they undertake. This aspect provides a starting point for understanding the entrepreneur and the way in which they are different from other types of manager. A number of tasks have been associated with the entrepreneur. Some of the more important are discussed below.

Owning organisations

Most people would be able to give an example of an entrepreneur and would probably claim to be able to recognise an entrepreneur 'if they saw one'. A key element in this common perception is *ownership* of the organisation.

While many entrepreneurs do indeed own their own organisations, using ownership as a defining feature of entrepreneurship can be very restricting. Modern market economies are characterised by a differentiation between the ownership and the running of organisations. Ownership lies with those who invest in the business and own its stock: the *principals*, while the actual running is delegated to professional agents or *managers*. These two roles are quite distinct. Therefore if an entrepreneur actually owns the business then he or she is in fact undertaking two roles at the same time: that of an investor and that of a manager. This is a distinction noticed as far back as 1803 by the classical French Economist J.B. Say (Say, 1964 reprint).

So, we recognise many people as entrepreneurs even if they do not own the venture they are managing. In developed economies, sophisticated markets exist to give investors access to new ventures and most entrepreneurs are active in taking advantage of these to attract investors. For example, when Frederick Smith started the distribution company Federal Express he only put in around ten per cent of the initial capital. Institutional investors provided the rest. We do not think less of him as an entrepreneur because he diluted his ownership in this way. In fact, most would regard the ability to present the venture and to attract the support of investors as an important entrepreneurial skill.

It should also be noted that 'ordinary' managers (whatever that means!) are increasingly being given a means of owning part of their companies through share option schemes which are often linked to the company's performance. While this may encourage them to be more entrepreneurial it does not, in itself, make them into entrepreneurs.

Founding new organisations

The idea that the entrepreneur is someone who has established a new business organisation is one which would fit in with most people's notion of an entrepreneur. The entrepreneur is recognised as the person who undertakes the task of bringing together the different elements of the organisation (people, property, productive resources, etc.) and giving them a separate legal identity. Many thinkers regard this as an essential characteristic for the entrepreneur (e.g. Bygrave and Hofer, 1991). The Indian academic, R.A. Sharma (1980), sees it as particularly important for entrepreneurship in developing economies. However, such a basis for defining the entrepreneur is sensitive to what we mean by 'organisation' and what we would consider to constitute a 'new' organisation.

Many people we recognise as entrepreneurs 'buy into' organisations that have been already founded and then extend them (as Ray Kroc did with McDonald's), develop them (as George and Liz Davis did with Hepworth's, converting it into Next) or absorb them into existing organisations (as Alan Sugar did with Sinclair Scientific). Increasingly, management buy-outs of parts of existing organisations are providing a vehicle for ordinary managers to exhibit their entrepreneurial talent.

A more meaningful, though less precise, idea is that the entrepreneur *makes major changes in their organisational world*. Making a major change is a broad notion, but it goes beyond merely founding the organisation, and it differentiates the entrepreneur from managers who manage within existing organisational structures or make only minor or incremental changes to them.

Bringing innovations to market

Innovation is a crucial part of the entrepreneurial process. The Austrian School Economist J.A. Schumpeter saw innovation as fundamental to the entrepreneurial process of wealth creation. A concise summary of his ideas can be found in a paper he wrote for the *Economic Journal* in 1928. Peter Drucker proposed that innovation is the central task for the entrepreneur-manager in his seminal book *Innovation and Entrepreneurship* (1985). Entrepreneurs must do something new or there would be no point in their entering a market. However, we must be careful here with the idea of innovation. Innovation, in a business sense, can mean a lot more than merely developing a new product or technology. The idea of innovation encompasses any new way of doing something so that value is created. Innovation *can* mean a new product or service, but it can also include a new way of delivering an existing product or service (so that it is cheaper or more convenient for the user, for example), new methods of informing the consumer about a product and promoting it to them, new ways of organising the company, or even new approaches to managing relationships with other organisations. These are all sources of innovation which have been successfully exploited by entrepreneurs.

The entrepreneur's task goes beyond simply *inventing* something new. It also includes bringing that innovation to the marketplace and using it to deliver value to consumers. The innovated product or service must be produced profitably, in addition to being distributed, marketed and defended from the attentions of competitors by a well-run and well-led organisation.

No matter how important innovation might be to the entrepreneurial process, it is not *unique* to it. Most managers are encouraged to be innovative in some way or other. Being successful at developing and launching new products and services is not something that is only witnessed in entrepreneurial organisations. The difference between entrepreneurial innovation and 'ordinary innovation' is, at best, one of degree, not substance.

Identification of market opportunity

An opportunity is a gap in a market where the potential exists to do something better and create value. New opportunities exist all the time, but they do not necessarily present themselves. If they are to be exploited, they must be *actively* sought out. The identification of new opportunities is one of the key tasks of entrepreneurs. They must constantly scan the business landscape watching for the gaps left by existing players (including themselves!) in the marketplace.

As with innovation, no matter how important identifying opportunity is to the entrepreneurial process, it cannot be all that there is to it, nor can it characterise it uniquely. The entrepreneur cannot stop at simply identifying opportunities. Having identified them, the entrepreneur must pursue them with a suitable innovation. An opportunity is simply the 'mould' against which the market tests new ideas. In fact, actually spotting the opportunity may be delegated to specialist market researchers. The real value is created when that opportunity is exploited by something new which fills the market gap.

All organisations are active, to some degree or other, in spotting opportunities. They may call upon specialist managers to do this, or they may encourage everyone in the organisation to be on the look-out for new possibilities. Like innovation, entrepreneurial opportunity scanning differs from that of ordinary managers in degree, not substance.

Application of expertise

It has been suggested that entrepreneurs are characterised by the way that they bring some sort of expertise to their jobs. As discussed above, this expertise may be thought to lie in their ability to innovate or spot new opportunities. A slightly more technical notion is that they have a special ability in deciding how to *allocate scarce resources* in situations where *information is limited*. It is their expertise in doing this that makes entrepreneurs valuable to investors.

While investors will certainly look for evidence of an ability to make proper business decisions and judge entrepreneurs on their record in doing so, the idea that the entrepreneur is an 'expert' in this respect raises a question, namely whether the entrepreneur has a skill *as an entrepreneur* rather than just as a particularly skilful and effective manager in their own particular area. Does, for example, Rupert Murdoch have a knowledge of how to make investment decisions which is *distinct* from his intimate and detailed knowledge of the media industry, backed up by good management and attributes such as confidence, decisiveness and leadership? Is it meaningful to imagine someone developing a skill in (rather than just knowing the principles of) 'resource allocation decision making' other than it being demonstrated in relation to some specific area of business activity?

It is not clear whether such a disembodied skill exists separately from conventional management skills. In any case, such a skill could not be unique to the entrepreneur. Many managers, most of whom would not be called entrepreneurial, make decisions about resource allocation every day.

Provision of leadership

One special skill that entrepreneurs would seem to contribute to their ventures is leadership. Leadership is increasingly recognised as a critical part of managerial success. Entrepreneurs can rarely drive their innovation to market on their own. They need the support of other people, both from within their organisations and from people outside such as investors, customers and suppliers.

If all these people are to pull in the same direction, to be focused on the task in hand and to be motivated, then they must be supported and directed. This is a task that falls squarely on the shoulders of the entrepreneur. If it is to be performed effectively, then the entrepreneur must show leadership. In fact, performing this task well *is* leadership.

Leadership is an important factor in entrepreneurial success and it is often a skill that is exhibited particularly well by the entrepreneur, but it is a *general* management skill rather than one which is specific to the entrepreneur. That said, an entrepreneurial path may give the manager a particularly rich opportunity to develop and express leadership skills.

The entrepreneur as manager

What can we make of all this? It would seem that the entrepreneur takes on no task that is different from the tasks performed by ordinary managers at some time or other. We should not be surprised by this. At the end of the day, the entrepreneur is a *manager*. We may wish to draw a distinction between an entrepreneur and an 'ordinary' manager but if we do so it must be in terms of *what* the entrepreneur manages, *how* they manage, their *effectiveness* and the *effect* they have as a manager, not the particular tasks they undertake.

1.3 The role of the entrepreneur

KEY LEARNING OUTCOME
An understanding of the economic effects of entrepreneurial activity.

Entrepreneurs are significant because they have an important effect on world economies. They play a critical role in maintaining and developing the economic order we live under. We have already noted that entrepreneurs create new value. Understanding *how* they do this is of central importance if we are to draw general conclusions about entrepreneurship. Some important economic effects of entrepreneurial activity are listed below.

Combination of economic factors

Economists generally recognise three primary *economic factors*: the *raw materials* nature offers up, the physical and mental *labour* people provide and *capital* (money). All the products (and services) bought and sold in an economy are a mix of these three things. Value is created by combining these three things together in a way which satisfies human needs.

Factors do not combine themselves, however. They have to be brought together by individuals working together and undertaking different tasks. The co-ordination of these tasks takes place within *organisations*. Some economists regard entrepreneurship as a kind of fourth factor which acts on the other three to combine them in productive ways. In this view, *innovation* is simply finding new combinations of economic factors.

Other economists object to this view, arguing that it does not distinguish entrepreneurship sufficiently from any other form of economic activity. While entrepreneurs do affect the combination of productive factors, so does everyone who is active in an economy. It is not clear in this view why entrepreneurship is a *special* form of economic activity.

Providing market efficiency

Economic theory suggests that the most efficient economic system is one in which unimpeded markets determine the price at which goods are bought and sold. Here, *efficient* means that resources are distributed in an *optimal* way, that is the satisfaction that people can gain from them is *maximised*.

An economic system can only reach this state if there is *competition* between different suppliers. Entrepreneurs provide that efficiency. If a supplier is not facing competition then they will tend to demand profits in excess of what the market would allow and so reduce the overall efficiency of the system. Entrepreneurs, so the theory goes, are on the look-out for such excess profits. Being willing to accept a lower profit themselves (one nearer the true market rate) they will enter the market and offer the goods at a lower price. By so doing entrepreneurs ensure that markets are efficient and that prices are kept down to their lowest possible level.

Classical economics provides a good starting point for understanding the effects that entrepreneurs have on an economic system. However, business life is generally much more complex than this simple picture gives it credit for. As we will discover, the most successful entrepreneurs are often those that avoid competition (at least *direct* competition) with established suppliers.

Accepting risk

We do not know exactly what the future will bring. This lack of knowledge we call *uncertainty*. No matter how well we plan, there is always the possibility that some chance event will result in outcomes we neither expected or wanted. This is *risk*. Some economists have suggested that the primary function of the entrepreneur is to accept risk on behalf of other people. There is, in this view, a *market* for risk. Risk is something that people, generally, want to avoid. Entrepreneurs provide a service by taking this risk off people's hands.

An example should make this clear. We may all appreciate the benefits a new technology, for example the video recording of television images, can bring. However, there is a risk in developing this new technology. Financial investment in its development is very high. There is also a great deal of uncertainty. Competition between different suppliers' formats is intense. There is no guarantee that the investment will be returned. Yet, we now enjoy the benefits of video technology and we, as consumers, have not, personally, had to face the risks inherent in creating it. In effect, we have delegated that risk to the entrepreneurs who *were* active in developing it. Of course, entrepreneurs expect that in return for taking the risk they will be rewarded. This reward, the profit stream from their ventures, is the *price* that customers have

'agreed' to pay so that they can have the benefits
risk of developing it.

The idea that entrepreneurs are risk-takers is one whi
The idea of accepting risk was important to the conce
developed by the classical English economist John Stuart Mi
must be very careful to distinguish between *personal* risk and *ec*
face personal risk by exposing ourselves to dangerous situations, cli
for example, but this is not risk as an economist understands it. To an e
results from making an *investment*. Risk is the possibility that the retu
investment may be *less* than expected. Or, to be exact, might be less than co
been obtained from an alternative investment that was available. As was pointed o
section 1.2, the role of the entrepreneur who manages the venture, and the investor w
puts their money into it, is quite distinct.

So, acceptance of risk is something that *investors* do, not *entrepreneurs* as such. However, the popular impression that the entrepreneur is a risk-taker is not completely inappropriate. It recognises that entrepreneurs are good at managing in situations where risk is high; that is, when faced with a situation of high uncertainty they are able to keep their heads, to continue to communicate effectively and to carry on making effective decisions.

Maximising investors' returns

Some commentators have suggested that the primary role of an entrepreneur is one of maximising the returns that shareholders get from their investments. In effect, the suggestion is that they create and run organisations which maximise long-term profits on behalf of the investors. In a sense, this is another aspect of the entrepreneur's role in generating overall economic efficiency.

Investors will certainly look around for entrepreneurs who create successful and profitable ventures although the view that entrepreneurs in the real world act simply to maximise shareholders' returns is questionable. Entrepreneurship, like all management activity, takes into account the interests of a wide variety of stakeholder groups, not just those of investors. Nor is it evident that investors demand that a firm maximise their returns whatever the social cost might be. Whereas Lord Hanson openly placed maximising shareholder returns at the top of his agenda, Anita Roddick would argue for a much broader range of concerns for The Body Shop.

Processing of market information

Classical economics makes the assumption that all the relevant information about a market is available to and is used by producers and consumers. However, human beings are not perfect information-processors. In practice, markets work without all possible information being made available or being used. One view of the entrepreneur is that they keep an eye out for information that is not being exploited. By taking advantage of this information, they make markets more efficient and are rewarded out of the revenues generated. This information is information about *opportunities*. The idea

-processors is in essence a sophisticated version of opportunities and provide competitive efficiency.
er organisations may be more successful than larger more adept at spotting, and taking advantage of

early play an important economic function. It is is to a single economic process in which the m that of other economic actors.

ersonality

onal characteristics have been seen to influence performance.

We are all different, not only in the way we look, but in the way we *act* and the way we *react* to different situations. We talk of people having *personalities*. Personality can be defined as the consistent, and persistent, profile of beliefs, feelings and actions which makes one person distinct from another. Psychologists have long had an interest in personality and have developed a number of conceptual schemes and exploratory devices to investigate it. The personality of the entrepreneur has been an important theme in this research. A number of perspectives on the entrepreneur may be considered under the broad heading of personality.

The 'great person'

An immediate reaction when faced with an entrepreneur, or indeed anyone with influence and social prominence such as a leading statesman, an important scientist or a successful artist, is to regard them simply as being special: as a 'great person' who is destined by virtue of his or her 'nature' to rise above the crowd. Such people are born to be great and will achieve greatness, one way or another. Such a view often underlies the approach biographers take to important people.

Entrepreneurs can certainly be inspiring, and may provide motivating role models. Generally though, the great person view, however passionate, is not particularly useful. For a start it is self-justifying. If an entrepreneur achieves success, it is because they are great; if they fail then they are not. It has no predictive power. It can only tell us who will become an entrepreneur after they have achieved success. Furthermore, it offers no role for the wider world in offering people the chance to achieve success. Most damaging, however, is the way it denies the possibility of entrepreneurial success to those who are not born to be great persons.

Social misfit

Another view which forms a marked contrast to the great person view but which also has a great deal of currency is the idea that entrepreneurs are *social misfits* at heart. In this view someone is an entrepreneur for an essentially negative reason: they are unable to fit into existing social situations. As a result the entrepreneur is driven to create his or her own situation. It is this that provides the motivation to innovate and build new organisations.

Advocates of this view look towards both anecdotal and psychological evidence for support. Many entrepreneurs achieve success after comparatively unhappy and lacklustre careers working as professional managers. Often they relate their inability to fit into the established firm as a factor in driving them to start their own venture.

Some researchers who have studied the childhood and family backgrounds of entrepreneurs have noted that they are often characterised by privation and hardship which left the person with a lack of self-esteem, a feeling of insecurity and a repressed desire for control. This leads to rebellious and 'deviant' behaviour which limits the person's ability to fit into established organisations. Entrepreneurial activity, it is concluded, is a way of coming to terms with this. It provides not only a means of economic survival but also an activity which enables a reaction against anxiety left by psychological scars.

While the idea of the social misfit may provide insights into the motivations of *some* entrepreneurs, any generalisation of this sort is dangerous. For every entrepreneur whose childhood was unhappy and involved privation, another can be found who was quite comfortable and happy. Many successful entrepreneurs recall being dissatisfied when working within established organisations. However, this is not necessarily because they are misfits in a negative sense. Rather it may be because the organisation did not provide sufficient scope for their abilities and ambitions. This in itself may be demotivating, and therefore managerial performance in an established firm is not necessarily a good indicator of how someone will perform later as an entrepreneur.

Personality type

The conceptual basis for the personality type view of entrepreneurship is that the way people act in a given situation can be categorised into one of a relatively limited number of responses. As a result, individuals can be grouped into a small number of categories based on this response. For example, we may classify people as *extrovert* or *introvert, aggressive* or *passive, spontaneous* or *reserved, internally* or *externally orientated,* etc. Each of these types represents a fixed category.

There is a common impression that entrepreneurs tend to be flamboyant extroverts who are spontaneous in their approach and rely on instinct rather than calculation. Certainly, they are often depicted this way in literature and on film. Detailed studies, however, have shown that all types of personality perform equally well as entrepreneurs. Personality type does not correlate with entrepreneurial performance and success. For example, introverts are as just likely to be entrepreneurs as are extroverts.

Personality trait

The idea of personality *trait* is different from that of personality *type*. While a personality may be *of* a particular type, it *has* a trait. Whereas types are distinct categories, traits occur in continuously variable dimensions.

In a very influential study in the early 1960s, David McClelland identified a 'need for achievement' (along with various other characteristics) as the fundamental driving trait in the personality of successful entrepreneurs. Other factors which have also been viewed as important include the need for autonomy, the need to be in control of a situation, a desire to face risk, creativity, a need for independence and the desire to show leadership qualities.

While conceptually very powerful, the trait approach to the entrepreneurial personality raises a number of questions. To what extent are traits innate? Are they fixed features of personality or might they actually be learnt? How does a trait as measured in a personality test relate to behaviour in the real world? Does possession of certain traits lead to entrepreneurship or does pursuing an entrepreneurial career merely provide an opportunity to develop them? Do entrepreneurs simply act out the traits they feel are expected of them?

The idea of traits in the personality of entrepreneurs provides a very important paradigm for the study of entrepreneurial motivation. However, the available evidence suggests it is unwise to advocate, or to advise against, an entrepreneurial path for a particular manager based on the perception of traits they might, or might not, possess.

Social development

Both personality type and trait are seen as innate. They are determined by a person's genetic complement (nature) or by early life experiences (nurture) or by some combination of both. (The relative importance of these two things and how they might interact is a highly controversial issue in social theory.) Personality type or trait are also seen as being 'locked into' a person's mental apparatus, and therefore relatively fixed. They can change only slowly, or under special conditions.

The social development view regards personality as a more complex issue. In this view entrepreneurship is an output which results from the interaction of internal psychological and external social factors. The view is that personality develops continuously as a result of social interaction and is *expressed* in a social setting rather than being innate to the individual. The way people behave is not predetermined, but is contingent on their experiences and the possibilities open to them.

In this view, entrepreneurs are not born, they are *made*. While their predisposition may be important it does not have any meaning in isolation from their experiences. A person is not, once and for all, entrepreneurial. He or she may, for example, decide to become an entrepreneur only at one particular stage in his or her life. Equally, he or she may decide to give up being an entrepreneur at another.

A number of factors are seen as significant to the social development of entrepreneurs. In general, they fall into one of three broad categories:

1 *Innate* – factors such as intelligence, creativity, personality, motivation, personal ambition, etc.;
2 *Acquired* – learning, training, experience in 'incubator' organisations, mentoring, existence of motivating role models, etc.;
3 *Social* – birth order, experiences in family life, socio-economic group and parental occupation, society and culture, economic conditions, etc.

The social development model provides a more plausible picture of entrepreneurial behaviour than those that assume entrepreneurial inclination is somehow innate. Entrepreneurship is a social phenomenon. It is not inherent within a person, rather it exists in the interactions *between* people. While entrepreneurs may actively grasp opportunities, they do so within a cultural framework. The social development approach is sophisticated in that it recognises that entrepreneurial behaviour is the result of a large number of factors, some internal to the entrepreneur, and others which are features of the environment within which entrepreneurs express themselves. However, this is also a weakness. While it identifies the factors which might influence entrepreneurship, it usually cannot say *why* they influence it. While social development models are good at indicating what factors might be involved in entrepreneurial behaviour, they often suggest so many factors might be involved that their predictive power is very limited.

The limitations of personality models

Personality is a concept of central importance in psychology. It plays a crucial role in aiding our understanding of the social interaction between people and it has both illuminated our understanding of, and enriched our appreciation of, the entrepreneur. However, it is important that we do not let an inappropriate idea of personality distort our view. There is no real evidence to suggest that there is a single 'entrepreneurial personality'. People of all personality types, attitudes and dispositions, not only become entrepreneurs but become *successful* entrepreneurs. A consequence of this is that personality testing does not provide a good indicator of who will, or will not, be a successful entrepreneur.

To be a successful entrepreneur takes many things: ambition, drive, hard work, effort in learning to understand a business and practice as a manger. But it does not demand a particular personality. Experience shows that a reserved introvert who carefully calculates their next move can look forward to as much entrepreneurial success as their more 'theatrical', and instinctive, counterpart. No one with entrepreneurial ambitions should ever dismiss the option of an entrepreneurial career because they do not feel they are the 'right type' of person. To do so reveals more about their misconceptions of entrepreneurship than it does about their potential.

1.5 Cognitive aspects of entrepreneurship

KEY LEARNING OUTCOME
An appreciation of the importance of individual cognitive style and strategy in entrepreneurial decision-making.

Cognitive psychology is that branch of the psychological sciences that is concerned with how human beings acquire, store and process information about the world. It attempts to understand how we make decisions, act and react in different situations. Interest has grown in the cognitive aspects of management in general and entrepreneurship is particular.

Cognitive psychology has made great strides in enhancing our understanding of human thinking. It is now recognised that we all have our own cognitive styles that we use to process information and that we adopt particular cognitive strategies when called upon to use that information in order to solve problems. Many of these strategies and styles resonate with our experiences of how other people approach challenges. We may, for example, note that some people are 'big-picture', that is, they only like to take the essential, important facts into account when they first meet a new problem. Others are 'small-picture'. They like detailed and extensive information before attempting a solution. At other times we may recognise that some people prefer tried and trusted solutions; others are willing, eager even, to find new ways of doing things. At a deeper level, some people compartmentalise new information into a pre-existing set of categories and see new things in established terms. We may regard such people as fixed in their thinking. Other people prefer to set up new categories and so see things in new ways. We may regard these as more open in their thinking. These general observations about how people work, however useful as rules of thumb, cannot be accepted at face value, though. Cognitive psychology is a science. It is concerned with establishing the well-defined and experimentally reproducible processes that are revealed through the actions taken in response to specific cognitive challenges. Cognitive processes are sometimes split into three types.

- *Perception processes* – These are concerned with how we see the world and gather information about it. Examples are *complexity–simplicity*, the number of dimensions that are used to categorise the world, *levelling–sharpening*, the use of existing or the creation of new categories to incorporate new information and *verbalising–visualising*, the use of verbal or, alternatively visual, imagery to develop understanding.
- *Problem solving processes* – These govern how information is used when an individual is called upon to make a decision. Examples include *scanning–focusing*, how much information is called in order to solve a problem, *serialism–holism*, referring to whether problems are approached in a linear, reducing way, or are dealt with as an integrated whole and *adaptation–innovation*, the preference for established solutions or new solutions.
- *Task processes* – These are concerned with determining the way in which we approach particular jobs. Themes here include *constricted–flexible*, the preference for new types of task over established ones, *impulsive–reflective*, the tendency to act in a decisive or considered way and *uncertainty accepting–cautious*, the willingness to take on tasks with an element of risk in them.

John Hayes and Christopher Allinson (1994) give a full review of cognitive styles and their relevance to management.

Cognitive styles and strategies may be linked to, and provide a basis for, what we consider to be personality. They are, however, distinct from it. Individuals may rely on well-honed cognitive approaches, but they are not necessarily fixed. Our cognitive approaches are subject to learning and may be modified, either intentionally or unintentionally, in the light of experience.

The cognitive aspect of entrepreneurial behaviour is a new and rapidly developing area of research. It is probably premature to suggest that entrepreneurs, as a group, share any particular set of cognitive approach. The 'best' cognitive approach in any situation is dependent on that situation. Entrepreneurial situations are as varied as any other type of situation. However, it is true that entrepreneurs do tend to be innovative, are receptive to new ideas and do set out to find new ways of doing things. How this general observation can be rationalised in terms of specific, well-defined cognitive strategies is a subject of much interest in cognitive research.

1.6 Classifying entrepreneurs

KEY LEARNING OUTCOME
An understanding of how different types of entrepreneur might be distinguished.

As we have seen, there is no universally accepted definition of an entrepreneur. However, it has been found useful to classify entrepreneurs into different types. Such classification provides a starting point for gaining an insight into how entrepreneurial ventures work and the factors underlying their success. There are a number of potential classification schemes. This section aims to give a flavour of the approaches taken rather than an extensive review of all the schemes. There are two main approaches: either to classify the entrepreneurs *themselves* or to classify their *ventures*.

An early move was to differentiate between *opportunist* entrepreneurs who were interested in maximising their returns from short-term deals, and *craftsmen* who attempted to make a living by privately selling their trade or the products they produced. Craftsmen were less interested in profits as such, but in being able to earn a stable living from their specialist skills. The idea of the 'opportunist' entrepreneur is quite vague, and a later development was to replace it with two more definite types: the *growth-orientated* entrepreneur who pursued opportunities to maximise the potential of their ventures and the *independence-orientated* entrepreneur whose main ambition was to work for themselves. These latter kind of entrepreneurs preferred stability to growth and so were willing to limit the scope of their ventures. A further distinction can be made between craftsmen entrepreneurs whose expertise is based on *traditional skills* and those whose expertise is scientific or *high-technology*.

The American entrepreneurship academic Frederick Webster (1977) considers classification schemes for both the individual entrepreneur and for their ventures. Four types of individual entrepreneur are recognised within his scheme. The *Cantillon* entrepreneur (named after the 18th century French economist Richard Cantillon) brings people, money and materials together to create an entirely new organisation. This is the 'classic' type of entrepreneur who identifies an unexploited opportunity and then innovates in order to pursue it. The *industry maker* goes beyond merely creating a new firm. Their innovation is of such importance that a whole industry is created on the back of it. They develop not only new products, but also a whole technology to produce them. Examples include Henry Ford and the mass production of motor vehicles, Thomas Edison and domestic electrical products, and Bill Gates with software-operating systems. The *administrative entrepreneur* is a manager who operates within an established firm but does so in an entrepreneurial fashion. Usually occupying the chief executive or a senior managerial role they are called upon to be innovative and to provide dynamism and leadership to the organisation, particularly when it is facing a period of change. An example here is Lee Iacocca's rejuvenation of the Chrysler Motor Company or Jan Carlzon's turnaround of the Scandinavian Airlines System (SAS). Nowadays administrative entrepreneurs are often referred to as *intrapreneurs*. The *small business owner* is an entrepreneur who takes responsibility for owning and running their own venture. The business may be small because it is in an early stage of growth or they may actually wish to limit the size of their business, because they are satisfied that it gives them a reasonably secure income and control over their lives.

Webster further classifies entrepreneurial ventures by the ratio of the amount that is expected to be received as a result of the venture's success (the *perceived payoff*) and the number of investors involved (the *principals*). Three types of venture are identified:

1 *Large payoff: many participants* (i.e. a major venture with the risk spread widely over a large number of investors);
2 *small payoff: few participants* (i.e. a limited venture with the risk taken on by a few key investors only);
3 *large payoff: few participants* (i.e a major venture with the risk taken on by a few key investors).

The remaining possibility, that is, a small expected payoff with a large number of investors, is not considered to be a likely scenario.

Landau (1982) has proposed that the characteristics of innovation and risk taking discussed earlier might provide a basis for classifying entrepreneurs. He suggests that both factors are independent of each other and may be defined as high or low. This gives the quadrant illustrated in Fig. 1.1.

The *gambler* is the entrepreneur (or better, his or her venture) that is characterised by a low degree of innovation and a high level of risk. The gamble, of course, arises from the fact that without a significant innovation, the entrepreneur is taking a big chance in being more able to deliver value better than existing players in the market. The *consolidator* is the entrepreneur that develops a venture based on low levels of both

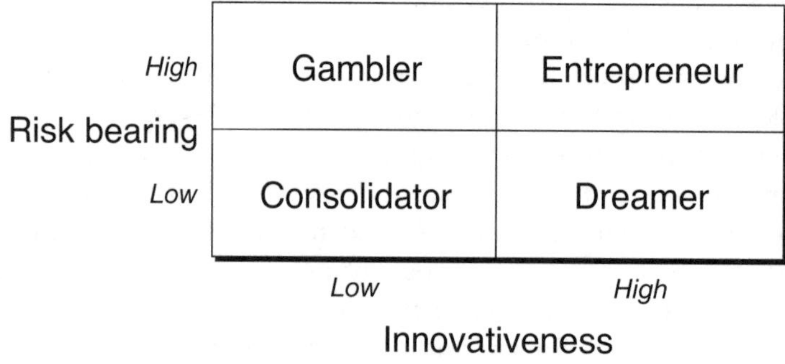

Fig. 1.1 Landau's classification of entrepreneurial types

innovation and risk. This consolidates in that it is really, at best, a marginal improvement on what existing players are doing. Though risks are low, so too must be expected returns. The *dreamer* is the entrepreneur who attempts to combine a high level of innovativeness with low risk. All entrepreneurs would, of course, love to operate here. Many attempt, quite properly, to do so. However, Landau suggests the 'dream' cannot be realised. All innovation by its nature introduces risk. The more significant (and hence potentially valuable) the innovation, the greater the risk of the unknown. The final quadrant combines high innovativeness with high risk. This is where true entrepreneurs operate. They (or their investors) must accept risk, but by understanding their innovation and why it appeals to the market they minimise and manage the risks.

Technology-based entrepreneurs are especially important in modern business as it is they who are taking advantage of new scientific developments especially in the areas of information technology, biotechnology and engineering science and offering their benefits to the wider world. Investors are attracted by the high growth potential of their ventures. Jones-Evans (1995) offers a fourfold categorisation of such technology-based entrepreneurs based on their technical and commercial experience prior to making the move to entrepreneurship:

- The 'research' technical entrepreneur: Research technical entrepreneurs are those whose incubation has been in a research environment. Two sub-types are suggested: *'Pure research'* entrepreneurs who have been based in academic research environments and who have not had significant commercial experience and *'research-producer'* entrepreneurs who while working in an academic or industrial research environment have had exposure to commercial decision making.
- The 'producer' technical entrepreneur: Producer technical entrepreneurs are those whose incubation has included an exposure to decision-making in a commercial setting along with experience in technological development.
- The 'user' technical entrepreneur: The user technical entrepreneur is an individual whose main experience has been commercially based but has involved contact with, and the development of knowledge about, a technical development. This may be because they have been employed in its marketing or sales, or perhaps in procuring that technology for a business.
- The 'opportunist' technical entrepreneur: The opportunist technical entrepreneur is one who has no previous exposure to a technology but has seen a commercial opportunity in relation to it and has pursued that with a new venture. Opportunist technical entrepreneurs may call upon a general technical knowledge base and are keen to develop an understanding of the new technology and what it offers.

This approach to classifying technical entrepreneurs is useful for two key reasons. First, it indicates the type of support the entrepreneur will need in order to drive his or her venture forward successfully. The research and producer technical entrepreneur, while in command of the technical aspects of what they are doing, may need support with the commercial management of their ventures. User and opportunist entrepreneurs may call upon dedicated technical experts to underpin their commercial moves. Second, it enables investors to judge the managerial balance of the ventures to which they are called upon to commit themselves. An investor seeks not only a good idea, but also one that has a clear market potential and is backed by a managerial team that can not only invent but also deliver that invention to the customer profitably.

Wai-Sum Siu (1996) has examined the types of new entrepreneur who operate in China and he gives a fascinating snapshot of the people behind this fast-growing economy. Basing his assessment on *employment, managerial, financial, technical* and *strategic* criteria he identifies five types of entrepreneur. The *senior citizen* undertakes a venture to keep occupied during his or her retirement. The business is small and based on personal expertise. It is privately funded and has no long-term strategic ambitions. *Workaholics* are also retired but show more ambition for their ventures than do senior citizens. They often possess administrative experience and their businesses are bigger, drawing on a wider range of technical skills. Strategic goals may be explicit and employees may be invited to make a personal investment in the future of the venture. *Swingers* are younger entrepreneurs who aim to make a living from making deals. They may have only limited industrial and technical experience and rely on networks of personal contacts. Their ventures may be moderately large, but they tend not to have long-term strategic goals. The main aim is to maximise short-term profits. Funding is provided through retained earnings, family contributions and personal loans. *Idealists* are also younger entrepreneurs who run moderate-sized ventures. However, their motivation is based less on short-term profit than the sense of achievement and independence that running their own venture gives them. They serve a variety of end-markets and their ventures may be based on high-technology products. Financing is through retained profits, family contributions and private investment. *High-flyers* are motivated in much the same way as idealists. However, their ventures are much larger reflecting success in the marketplace. Again, a variety of products are offered. Corporate goals and strategy tend to be much more explicit than in the idealist's venture, and investment is drawn from a wider variety of sources, including institutional and international agencies.

1.7 Serial entrepreneurship

KEY LEARNING OUTCOME
An understanding of the types of serial entrepreneur and the motivation of the entrepreneur to lead a series of ventures.

The motivations of entrepreneurs are many and varied. As will be discussed in more detail later, entrepreneurs are driven by a desire for autonomy, prestige and a sense of achievement as much, if not more than, the desire to make money. This is most evident in that group of entrepreneurs who, having led one business success, move on to start another. Such entrepreneurs, called *serial entrepreneurs*, clearly gain their rewards from the establishment and building of businesses, not their long-term management. It is notable that some commentators, for example William Gartner (1985), argue that once the building stage of the venture ends, then so does true entrepreneurship.

Serial entrepreneurs, as well as being particularly interested in the start-up and early growth phase of the venture, may also have particular decision-making expertise, and therefore gain their personal competitive advantage in relation to this stage. Such skills might be reflected in an ability to spot new opportunities, to evaluate markets and in dealing with financial backers. An entrepreneur who can point to a record of success will also be a more attractive proposition to an investor than one who cannot. Further, the capital generated from an initial venture (retained profits or money made through its sale) may provide a source of funds to start up a further venture. The establishment of additional ventures may also reflect the strategic concerns of the entrepreneur. It may be that the competitive advantage gained in the initial business can be successfully transferred to a subsequent one. Further, several businesses may be a way of diluting risk. These strategic advantages must, of course, be measured against the risk inherent in the entrepreneur spreading his or her attention over a broader area. Management buy-outs and buy-ins are a fruitful area for serial entrepreneurs. According to Wright *et al.* (1997a) as many as a quarter of managers involved in buy-ins have previously held a significant equity holding as well as managerial responsibility in another venture.

Serial entrepreneurs may be sub-divided into two types: those who start new businesses in sequence, only running one at any time, and those who run several businesses simultaneously. The former are referred to as *sequential entrepreneurs*; the latter as *portfolio entrepreneurs*. James Dyson who started the ball-wheelbarrow business before moving on to the cyclone vacuum cleaner business is a good example of a sequential entrepreneur. Richard Branson, who has diversified his Virgin group into a number of different areas, is a portfolio entrepreneur. Wright *et al.* (1997b) have suggested that serial entrepreneurs might be classified in the following way:

- *Defensive serial entrepreneurs* are those who undertake subsequent ventures because of a forced exit from an earlier one. This need not be because it failed. It could be because the venture was sold, or floated on the stock market to pay off venture capital investment.
- *Opportunist serial entrepreneurs* are those who undertake subsequent ventures because they perceive the opportunity for financial gain, perhaps on a short-term entry–exit basis.
- *Group-creating serial entrepreneurs* are those who undertake serial entrepreneurship because creating a number of businesses is fundamental to the strategy they are pursuing. Two sub-types of group-creating serial entrepreneurs are suggested. *Deal-making serials* use acquisition as a major part of gaining the new businesses. *Organic serials* start new businesses from scratch and grow them.

Whatever the approach of the serial entrepreneurs, their desire to succeed with more than one business demonstrates the excitement the entrepreneurial career offers.

1.8 Entrepreneurship and small business management: a distinction

KEY LEARNING OUTCOME
An appreciation of why the entrepreneurial venture is distinct from the small business.

Both small business management and entrepreneurship are of critical importance to the performance of the economy. However, it is useful to draw a distinction between them since small businesses and entrepreneurial ventures serve different economic functions. They pursue and create new opportunities differently, they fulfil the ambitions of their founders and managers in different ways. Supporting them presents different challenges to economic policy makers. Drawing this distinction is an issue of classification. There are two possible approaches, namely to make a distinction between the characteristics of *entrepreneurs* and *small business managers* or between *entrepreneurial ventures* and *small businesses*.

The former is problematic. As discussed in section 1.4, the entrepreneur is not distinguished by a distinct personality type and there is no independent test that can be performed to identify an entrepreneur. The question is consequently a matter of personal opinion. Some people may regard themselves as true entrepreneurs while others may judge themselves to be 'just' small business managers. This can be an emotive issue and it is not clear what benefits are to be gained by placing people into different conceptual bags in this way. Rather than trying to draw a distinction between managers, it is more valuable to differentiate what they manage, that is, between the small business and the entrepreneurial venture.

There are three characteristics which distinguish the entrepreneurial venture from the small business.

1 Innovation

The successful entrepreneurial venture is usually based on a significant *innovation*. This might be a technological innovation, for example a new product or a new way of producing it; it might be an innovation in offering a new service; an innovation in the way something is marketed or distributed; or possibly an innovation in the way the organisation is structured and managed; or in the way relationships are maintained between organisations. The small business, on the other hand, is usually involved in delivering an established product or service. This does not mean that a small business is not doing something new. They may be delivering an innovation to people who would not otherwise have access to it, perhaps at a lower cost or with a higher level of service. However, the small firm's output is likely to be established and produced in an established way. So while a small business may be new to a locality, it is not doing anything essentially new in a *global* sense, whereas an entrepreneurial venture is usually based on a *significantly new* way of doing something.

2 Potential for growth

The size of a business is a poor guide as to whether it is entrepreneurial or not. The actual definition of what constitutes a small business is a matter of judgement depending on the industry sector, for example a firm with one hundred employees would be a very small shipbuilder, but a very large firm of solicitors. However, an entrepreneurial venture usually has a great deal more *potential* for growth than does a small business. This results from the fact that it is usually based on a significant innovation. The market potential for that innovation will be more than enough to support a small firm. It may even be more than enough to support a large firm and signal the start of an entire new industry. The small business, on the other hand, operates within an established industry and is unique only in terms of its locality. Therefore, it is limited in its growth potential by competitors in adjacent localities. A small business operates *within* a given market; the entrepreneurial venture is in a position to *create* its own market.

A word of caution is necessary here, since having the potential to grow is not the same as having a *right* to grow! If it is to enjoy growth, it is still necessary that the entrepreneurial venture be managed proficiently and that it compete effectively, even if it is creating an entirely new market rather than competing within an existing one.

3 Strategic objectives

Objectives are a common feature of managerial life. They take a variety of forms, for example they may be formal or informal, and they may be directed towards individuals or apply to the venture as a whole. Most businesses have at least some objectives. Even the smallest firm should have sales targets if not more detailed financial objectives. Objectives may be set for the benefit of external investors as well as for consumption by the internal management.

The entrepreneurial venture will usually go beyond the small business in the objectives it sets itself in that it will have *strategic* objectives. Strategic objectives relate to such things as:

- *Growth targets* – year-on-year increases in sales, profits and other financial targets;
- *Market development* – activities actually to create and stimulate the growth and shaping of the firm's market (for example, through advertising and promotion);
- *Market share* – the proportion of that market the business serves; and
- *Market position* – maintaining the firm's position in its market relative to competitors.

These strategic objectives may be quantified in a variety of ways. They may also be supplemented by a formal mission statement for the venture. This is an idea that will be discussed more fully in Chapter 10.

The distinction between a small business and an entrepreneurial venture is not clearcut. Generally we can say that the entrepreneurial venture is distinguished from the small business by its *innovation, growth potential* and *strategic objectives*. However, not all entrepreneurial ventures will necessarily show an obvious innovation, clear growth potential or formally articulated strategic objectives and some small businesses may demonstrate one or two of these characteristics. However, in combination they do add up to distinguish the key character of an entrepreneurial venture, that is, a business that makes significant changes to the world (see Fig. 1.2).

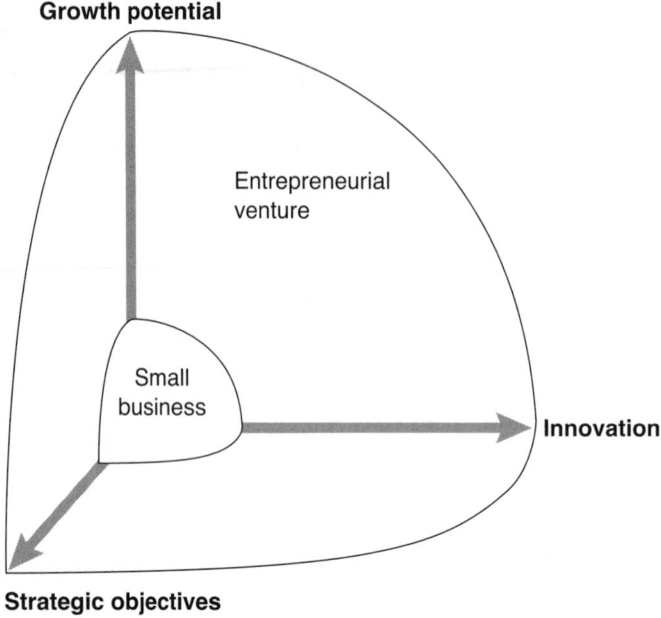

Fig. 1.2 The difference between a small business and an entrepreneurial venture

1.9 Entrepreneurship: a style of management

KEY LEARNING OUTCOME
A recognition that entrepreneurship is management aimed at pursuing opportunity and creating change.

The discussion so far has emphasised what the entrepreneur is *not*, as much as what they *are* because it is important to dispel certain myths about the entrepreneur. In particular, it is important to discount the theories that the entrepreneur is someone with a particular type of personality or that certain people are somehow born to be entrepreneurs. We must also recognise that the entrepreneur does not have a clearcut economic role. However, we must now consider what the entrepreneur actually *is* by developing a *perspective* that will illuminate the way entrepreneurs actually go about their tasks *as* entrepreneurs rather than providing a potentially restrictive *definition* of the entrepreneur.

What we can say with confidence is that an entrepreneur is a *manager*. Specifically, he or she is someone who manages in an *entrepreneurial way*. More often than not they will be managing a specific *entrepreneurial venture*, either a new organisation or an attempt to rejuvenate an existing one. The entrepreneurial venture represents a particular management challenge. The nature of the entrepreneurial venture characterises and defines the management that is needed to drive it forward successfully. Drawing together the themes that have been explored in this chapter it is evident that entrepreneurial management is characterised by three features.

1 A focus on change

Entrepreneurs are managers of *change*. An entrepreneur does not leave the world in the same state as they found it. They bring people, money, ideas and resources together to build new organisations and to change existing ones. Entrepreneurs are not important as much for the *results* of their activities as for the *difference* they make.

Entrepreneurs are different from managers whose main interest is in maintaining the status quo by sustaining the established organisation, protecting it and maintaining its market positions. This is not to deprecate a desire for equilibrium as an objective, it can be very important and is an essential ingredient in the effective running of a wide variety of organisations, but it is not about driving change.

2 A focus on opportunity

Entrepreneurs are attuned to opportunity. They constantly seek the possibility of doing something differently and better. They innovate in order to create new value. Entrepreneurs are more interested in pursing opportunity than they are in *conserving resources*.

This is not to suggest that entrepreneurs are not interested in resources. They are often acutely aware that the resources available to them are limited. Nor does it mean that they are cavalier with them. They may be using their own money and, if not, they will have investors looking over their shoulders to check that they are not wasting funds. What it *does* mean is that entrepreneurs see resources as a means to an end, not as an end in themselves.

Entrepreneurs expose resources to risk but they also make them work by stretching them to their limit in order to offer a good return. This makes them distinct from managers in established businesses who all too often can find themselves more responsible for protecting 'scarce' resources than for using them to pursue the opportunities that are presented to their organisations.

3 Organisation-wide management

The entrepreneur manages with an eye to the *entire* organisation, not just some aspect of it. They benchmark themselves against organisational objectives, not just the objectives for some particular department. This is not to say that functional disciplines such as marketing, finance, operations management, etc. are unimportant. However, the entrepreneur sees these as functions which play a part in the overall business, rather than as isolated activities.

4 Entrepreneurial managers as venturers

In short, the entrepreneur is a manager who is willing to *venture*: to create change and to pursue opportunity rather than to just maintain the status quo and conserve resources. Of course, the effective entrepreneur does *all* these things when appropriate. There are times when the status quo is worth sustaining, and times when it is unwise to expose resources. Part of the skill of the effective entrepreneur is knowing when *not* to venture. However, when the time is right, the entrepreneurial manager *is* willing to step forward.

This is a 'soft' definition. There is no hard and fast distinction between the entrepreneur and other types of manager. This does not make the entrepreneur any less special, nor does it make what entrepreneurs do any less important. What it does do is open up the possibility of entrepreneurship. In being 'just' a style of management it is something that can be learnt. Managers can chose to be entrepreneurial.

A very illuminating characterisation of entrepreneurship is offered by Czarniawska-Joerges and Wolff (1991) who use the language of theatrical performance rather than economics to distinguish between *management* which is:

> **the activity of introducing order by coordinating flows of things and people towards collective action,**

leadership which is:

> **symbolic performance, expressing the hope of control over destiny,**

and *entrepreneurship* which is, quite simply:

> **the making of entire new worlds.**

In conclusion, we can say that entrepreneurial management is characterised by its *whole organisation* scope, its objective of creating *change* and a focus on *exploiting opportunity.* These characteristics are shown in Fig. 1.3.

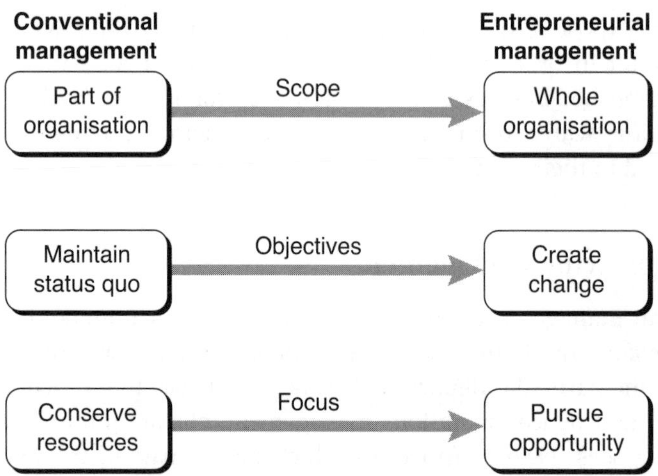

Fig. 1.3 Conventional management and entrepreneurial management: a comparison

Summary of key ideas

- There is no universally agreed definition of entrepreneurship. The wide variety of definitions in the literature emphasise three aspects:
  - the entrepreneur as an *economic agent* generating particular *economic effects;*
  - the entrepreneur as an *individual* of a particular *personality;* and:
  - the entrepreneur as a *manager* undertaking particular *tasks.*
- It is far from clear that there is a particular 'entrepreneurial' personality which predisposes people to business success.
- An entrepreneur is best regarded as a manager who *pursues* opportunity and *drives change* to create *new value.*
- The entrepreneurial venture is distinguished from the small business by virtue of being based on a significant *innovation,* having the potential for *growth,* and having clear *strategic* objectives.

Suggestions for further reading

Baumol, W.J. (1968) 'The entrepreneur: introductory remarks', *American Economic Review,* Vol. 58, pp. 60–3.

Barton-Cunningham, J. and **Lischeron, J** (1991) 'Defining entrepreneurship', *Journal of Small Business Management,* Jan, pp. 45–61.

Boyett, I. (1977) 'The public sector entrepreneur – a definition', *International Journal of Entrepreneurial Behaviour and Research,* Vol. 3, No. 2, pp. 77–92.

Brockhaus, R.H. (1987) 'Entrepreneurial folklore', *Journal of Small Business Management,* July, pp. 1–6.

Bygrave, W.D. and **Hofer, C.W.** (1991) 'Theorising about entrepreneurship', *Entrepreneurship Theory and Practice,* Vol. 16, No. 2, pp. 13–22.

Carland, J.W., Hoy, F., Boulton, W.R. and **Carland, J.C.** (1984) 'Differentiating entrepreneurs from small business owners: a conceptualisation', *Academy of Management Review,* Vol. 9, No. 2, pp. 345–59.

Chell, E. (1985) 'The entrepreneurial personality: a few ghosts laid to rest', *International Small Business Journal,* Vol 3, No. 3, pp. 43–54.

Cole, A.H. (1968) 'Entrepreneurship in economic theory', *American Economic Review,* Vol. 58, pp. 64–71.

Cromie, S. and **O'Donaghue, J.** (1992) 'Assessing entrepreneurial inclination', *International Small Business Journal,* Vol. 10, No. 2, pp. 66–73.

Czarniawska-Joerges, B. and **Wolff, R.** (1991) 'Leaders, managers and entrepreneurs on and off the organisational stage', *Organisation Studies,* Vol. 12, No. 4, pp. 529–46.

Drucker, P.F. (1985) *Innovation and Entrepreneurship,* London: Heinemann.

Dunkelberg, W.C. and **Cooper, A.C.** (1982) 'Entrepreneurial typologies: an empirical study', in Vesper, K.H. (ed.), *Frontiers of Entrepreneurial Research,* Wellesley, MA: Babson College Centre for Entrepreneurial Studies, pp. 1–15.

Gartner, W. (1985) 'A conceptual framework for describing the phenomenon of new venture creation', *Academy of Management Review,* Vol. 10, No. 4, pp. 696–706.

Gartner, W.B. (1988) '"Who is an entrepreneur" is the wrong question', *American Journal of Small Business*, Spring, pp. 11–32.

Gartner, W.B. (1990) 'What are we talking about when we talk about entrepreneurship?' *Journal of Business Venturing*, Vol. 5, pp. 15–28.

Ginsberg, A. and **Buchholtz, A.** (1989) 'Are entrepreneurs a breed apart? A look at the evidence', *Journal of General Management*, Vol. 15, No. 2, pp. 32–40.

Green, R., David, J., Dent, M. and **Tyshkovsky, A.** (1996) 'The Russian entrepreneur: A study of psychological characteristics', *International Journal of Entrepreneurial Behaviour and Research*, Vol. 2, No. 1, pp. 49–58.

Guzmán Cuevas, J. (1994) 'Towards a taxonomy of entrepreneurial theories', *International Small Business Journal*, Vol. 12, No. 4, pp. 77–88.

Hayes, J. and **Allinson, C.W.** (1994) 'Cognitive style and its relevance to management', *British Journal of Management*, Vol. 5, pp. 53–71.

Hornaday, R.W. (1992) 'Thinking about entrepreneurship: a fuzzy set approach', *Journal of Small Business Management*, Oct, pp. 12–23.

Jones-Evans, D. (1995) 'A typology of technology-based entrepreneurs', *International Journal of Entrepreneurial Research and Behaviour*, Vol. 1, No. 1, pp. 26–47.

Julien, P.A. (1989) 'The entrepreneur and economic theory', *International Small Business Journal*, Vol. 7, No. 3, pp. 29–38.

Kilby, P. (1971) 'Hunting the Heffalump', in Kilby, P. (ed.), *Entrepreneurship and Economic Development*, New York: The Free Press.

Kuznetsov, A., McDonald, F. and **Kuznetsov, O.** (2000) 'Entrepreneurial qualities: A case from Russia', *Journal of Small Business Management*, Vol. 38, No. 1, pp. 101–7.

Landau, R. (1982) 'The innovative milieu', in Lundstedt, S.B. and Colglazier, E.W., Jr (eds), *Managing Innovation: The Social Dimensions of Creativity, Invention and Technology*, New York: Pergamon Press.

Leibenstein, H. (1968) 'Entrepreneurship and development', *American Economic Review*, Vol. 58, pp. 72–83.

McClelland, D. (1961) *The Achieving Society*, Princeton, NJ: Van Nostrand.

Mill, J.S. (1848) *Principles of Political Economy with Some of their Applications to Social Philosophy*, London: J.W. Parker.

Olson, P.D. (1986) 'Entrepreneurs: opportunistic decision makers', *Journal of Small Business Management*, July, pp. 29–35.

Olson, P.D. (1987) 'Entrepreneurship and management', *Journal of Small Business Management*, July, pp. 7–13.

Peterson, R.A., Albaum, G. and **Kozmetsky, G.** (1986) 'The public's definition of small business', *Journal of Small Business Management*, July, pp. 63–8.

Petrof, J.V. (1980) 'Entrepreneurial profile: a discriminant analysis', *Journal of Small Business Management*, Vol 18, No. 4, pp. 13–17.

Say, J.B. (1964) *A Treatise on Political Economy: Or, the Production, Distribution and Consumption of Wealth*, New York: A.M. Kelly (reprint of original 1803 edition).

Scherer, R.F., Adams, J.S. and **Wiebe, F.A.** (1989) 'Developing entrepreneurial behaviours: a social learning perspective', *Journal of Organisational Change Management*, Vol. 2, No. 3, pp. 16–27.

Schumpeter, J.A. (1928) 'The instability of capitalism', *Economic Journal*, pp. 361–86.

Schumpeter, J.A. (1934) *The Theory of Economic Development* (1961 translation by Redvers Opie), Cambridge, MA: Harvard University Press.

Sharma, R.A. (1980) *Entrepreneurial Change in Indian Industry*, New Delhi: Sterling Publishers.

Siu, Wai-Sum (1996) 'Entrepreneurial typology: the case of owner managers in China', *International Small Business Journal*, Vol. 14, No. 1, pp. 53–64.

Soltow, J.H. (1968) 'The entrepreneur in economic history', *American Economic Review*, Vol. 58, pp. 84–92.

Stanworth, J., Stanworth, C., Grainger, B. and **Blythe, S.** (1989) 'Who becomes an entrepreneur?' *International Small Business Journal*, Vol. 8, No. 1, pp.11–22.

Watson, T.J. (1995) 'Entrepreneurship and professional management: a fatal distinction', *International Small Business Journal*, Vol. 13, No. 2, pp. 34–46.

Webster, F.A. (1977) 'Entrepreneurs and ventures: an attempt at classification and clarification', *Academy of Management Review*, Vol. 2, No. 1, pp. 54–61.

Wright, M., Robbie, K. and **Ennew, C.** (1997a) 'Venture capitalists and serial entrepreneurs', *Journal of Business Venturing*, Vol. 12, pp. 227–49.

Wright, M., Robbie, K. and **Ennew, C.** (1997b) 'Serial entrepreneurs', *British Journal of Management*, Vol. 8, pp. 251–68.

Selected case material

Innovation and risk taking that break free of bureaucracy

28 April 1998

The public sector has started to embrace ambitious visionaries. But teachers, doctors and police officers need encouragement, says **Charles Leadbeater**

Norma Redfearn's working life seems to be the managerial equivalent of Dr Dolittle's famous pushmi-pullyu, the animal that faced in two directions at once: she is a public sector entrepreneur.

At first sight the idea of public sector entrepreneurship seems a contradiction. The public sector is made up of large, often slow-moving bureaucracies. Managers are often seen as no more than administrators, implementing policies decided by politicians. They operate within tight rules, designed to protect public money against fraud, which inhibit risk taking and innovation.

Yet there is much more entrepreneurship in the public sector than many people realise and if the public sector is to deliver the ambitious social goals set by the government, we will need a great deal more of it. Take Mrs Redfearn as an example.

When she became head teacher at West Walker primary school in Newcastle in 1986, she took over a school in a state of near collapse. About three-quarters of the children had free school meals. Most of the parents were unemployed single mothers. Only a few of the school's 18 classrooms were occupied.

In a decade Mrs Redfearn and the parents have transformed the school. She realised that to educate her pupils, she had to educate their families. To involve the parents, the school had to become more than classrooms – and was turned into a catalyst for community renewal.

The school's attendance record is now in the 90 per cent range. Scores in national tests are improving. And it is home to a thriving adult education centre with a lively cafe providing breakfast for 60 children and lunch for parents doing courses. Parents who met while building a nature garden formed a housing association, which has built 70 homes opposite the school.

Mrs Redfearn realised that to revive her school she had to be more than a head teacher; she had to be a civic entrepreneur. Civic entrepreneurship is vital to meet demands from clients for better services, politicians for greater effectiveness and taxpayers for more value for money.

We do not need to further restructure or rationalise the public sector, but must revive and revitalise it. A spirit of entrepreneurship, creating social capital in pursuit of social value, is vital. We need not only more output from the public sector, but better outcomes. Not more arrest warrants issued and hospital beds filled, but less crime and better health. The question is not only how big or small the state should be, but what skills it needs.

Civic entrepreneurship is vital. At the grass roots of the public sector, a generation is emerging frustrated by bureaucracy and prepared to take risks to create new ways of delivering services.

Like entrepreneurs in other walks of life, they are ambitious, visionary, rule breakers and risk takers. Often great story-tellers and lateral thinkers, they are quick to seize on opportunities. Yet entrepreneurship in the public sector takes a different form.

Civic entrepreneurship is about political renewal as well as managerial change. Public organisations cannot be revitalised unless they renew their sense of purpose. Entrepreneurship requires risk taking.

In the public sector managing those risks requires political skill and leadership. That is why straight business entrepreneurship will not work in the public sector: business entrepreneurs are not good at managing political risks or winning public legitimacy for change.

In the private sector there is a myth of entrepreneur as hero. Civic entrepreneurship is collaborative, because creating more effective services usually means working across boundaries between professions and organisations. Mrs Redfearn realised that her school would only be revived if she was interested in what her pupils were eating, the quality of the homes they came from and the environment they played in.

The good news is that there is a lot more entrepreneurship in the public sector than people think. The bad news is that there is nowhere near enough.

What would it take to create a more entrepreneurial public sector? First, the government needs to finance more risk taking and innovation, for instance by creating an innovation fund. The public sector needs its own venture capitalists.

Second, the government needs to reward and recognise innovation, for instance by allowing innovative organisations to keep a share of savings they generate or by creating a new Queen's Award for Excellence.

Third, the public sector needs a better system to disseminate innovation. Each Whitehall department could have a Lesson's Learned Unit, dedicated to promulgating good ideas, modelled on the highly effective unit run by the US Army.

Fourth, entrepreneurship in the public sector is virtually impossible without political leadership. Reform to local government, for instance through directly elected mayors, should be aimed, in part, at promoting innovation.

Fifth, the public sector needs to develop a cadre of public sector managers, trained, motivated and rewarded to act as civic entrepreneurs.

The public sector remains central to British society. It can become a source of energy, creating social value and social capital rather than consuming it, but only if more of our head teachers, police officers and doctors are encouraged to become civic entrepreneurs.

Tunisia puts faith in micro-credit to dull the appeal of Islamist movement

24 November 1999

Empowering women by providing loans for starting up small businesses may weaken the lure of militants among poor communities, writes **Mark Huband**

Souad Ghazouani laughs at the suggestion that the second-hand clothes business she started four years ago has brought a revolution both in her family, and in the poor district of Tunis where she lives.

"I never believed I would ever end up like this, running a business. Before this started, I would go out of the house perhaps once a year, other than to the public baths.

"But the business has brought me into contact with people. They ask me for advice, and I have joined the ruling party," said Mrs Ghazouani, proudly displaying the party badge she keeps in a drawer beneath her shop counter.

Four years ago Mrs Ghazouani and five neighbours took up the offer of micro credit from Enda Inter-Arabe, a non-governmental organisation.

With loans of TD900 ($818) she set up her clothes business and a small grocery shop. Her neighbour, Keraidi Zohra, opened another shop. The six grouped together to provide mutual guarantees that the loans would be repaid. Two later fell into arrears, but the other four do not appear to resent paying their share.

Their effort has transformed the atmosphere of their dusty street in the poor M'nihla district, inhabited mainly by unemployed immigrants from rural areas. The shops are modest, but they mark a shift towards the economic empowerment of the poor and the encouragement of women in particular to take on the main economic role once jealously guarded by men.

"At first my husband refused to allow me to go the market to buy the clothes I would repair and sell. Now he comes to the market with me," Mrs Ghazouani said. "If he wasn't happy with all this, then I would do it on my own."

Since 1995, Enda has disbursed TD1.43m ($1.2m) of loans of between TD200 to TD500, to 1,266 clients. Just over half the recipients are women. In four years, 98 per cent of the loans have been repaid. The government has subsequently established the Banque Tunisienne de Solidarite, to provide micro-credit to individuals lacking the collateral to secure bank credit.

The need to satisfy the hopes of the poor has intensified pressure on government and NGOs to find ways to remedy the dire social conditions regarded by political analysts as having created support for Tunisia's Islamist movement in the 1980s.

"This area was the fief of the Islamists," said Essma Ben Hamida, founder of Enda, speaking of the Hay Ettadhamen district in which the NGO started with aid from the European Union and other foreign sources as well as Tunisia's Ministry for Women's and Family Affairs.

"The Islamists bought people, and the Islamist movement came from the economic problems," said Ms Ben Hamida.

However, the principles behind Tunisia's tradition of secular politics and the defence of women's rights have been severely tested by the state's draconian measures to crush Islamist and other political opposition. The security measures have been accompanied by the creation of a centralised police state, which has until now prevented the emergence of effective NGOs and other aspects of civil society.

"The problem in Tunisia is that the state is too strong. It is omnipresent. It does everything, at least until recently," said a political analyst.

Despite 5 per cent economic growth in recent years, Tunisia's economy is fragile. Unemployment stands at 16 per cent, but is much higher among the young. A free health service and free education up to university level have not ended the poverty regarded as the breeding ground of political extremism.

Confessions of a serial entrepreneur

11 February 1999

David Love tells his tale and says the intricacies of entrepreneurship are likely to defeat any Budget pledges

The government wants Britain's entrepreneurs to behave more like Americans. Start a company or two and, if one fails, pick yourself up and start over. Next month's Budget, we are told, will contain help for so-called serial entrepreneurs.

Who are they kidding? Entrepreneurial types carry on regardless of such nonsense because they know of no government that shares their vision, and of no bank inclined to share their risk. So, if you've made your pile and decide to have another go – I chose information technology – be sure to keep the return ticket handy.

In 1974 I started a logistics business. By the heady mid-1980s, I employed about 200 people and annual profits were heading towards £500,000. But I could never shake off the fear that one day it might crash and burn. So when a Plc hungry to diversify came along I happily sold out. I spent the next two years, less happily, working for my new owners. But at least I had crystallised my investment – I'd spread my risk.

At 43, heading for the beach was never an option, so I started an IT consultancy, hired four programmers and trawled for business from old contacts. The next few years were challenging, profitable and fun.

About three years ago, dazzled by Microsoft, spurred on by the belief that nirvana was owning intellectual property, needing to find an exciting new project for my techies, we decided to publish our own software. Our home market was limited, so we looked for a bigger one. We targeted the recruitment market where we saw size, growth, and no dominant competitor.

We cut a deal with a firm of headhunters to develop a program to manage the process of matching people with jobs. The problem was that each side had different expectations: we needed funding, ideas and credibility; the customer wanted a program that worked just like the old one but looked prettier.

Emboldened by the resulting prototype, we convinced ourselves that critical mass, the point where regular support fees fund future development, would surely follow if only we made enough noise. So we commissioned an expensive brochure, hired a PR company and attended myriad exhibitions. We won deals, but because of the high cost of sales we lost money on each one. Yet the feedback was warm, friendly and rose-tinted. That was when I made a critical mistake.

I'd met two people who had written a similar program to ours, but for barristers. Their niche was crusty, but had some serious movers and shakers whose support promised rapid change. And we were both using similar technologies. The synergy! We bought the rights to their half-finished program and set about bringing it to market. A second office, more staff, advertisements, brochures, PR, exhibitions. We had long since spent the year's profit from the consultancy and I was now drip feeding from my own resources – £30,000 here, £50,000 there. But the consultancy side was doing well, the staff looked busy, and I felt confident.

It was when customers started using our programs for real that the cool features failed to perform. The users got fractious and the people who should have been developing the program became firefighters. Many of the hitches were not of our making, but we figured that if we were nice to the little people, they would be nice back and tell their friends. The trouble was, their friends were little people too, so we lost even more money.

By now I was becoming nervous about my accumulated loans, so I asked the bank to double our overdraft. They sensed trouble and demanded that our borrowings, already secured by my own cash, should be subject to a charge over the company's assets "to protect the bank's position". Sharp words ensued and the bank relented. But it had shown scant interest and little faith. I was on my own.

It was time to take stock of the barristers' software venture. Over one weekend my instinct – to protect my investment – urged me to cut my losses. Within a fortnight I'd sold the rights and customer list to a competitor. But the process of exiting that market was traumatic and became a portent of worse to come.

Back on the recruitment front, the sales people fed me morsels of jam tomorrow while the clamour for resources grew louder ("If only we'd had feature X we'd have won that deal"). A Big Fish played us along. But, to maintain their confidence, we had to keep the profile high.

By spring, I knew that critical mass was a mirage. But could we net Big Fish before the staff walked? The choice was clear: find a partner or close the business.

I'd ruled out venture capitalists because I didn't have the stomach for beauty parades, business plans and spreadsheets. No, my partner would be a customer, a competitor or another software house. So I hit the phone. At each meeting that followed, a question hung in the air: "If your prospects are as good as you say, why do you need us?". And I was amused that our competitors thought we were bigger and stronger than we were. The advertising had worked.

Meanwhile, Big Fish swam closer. But when should I pop the question that could never be retracted? Time was running out: the techies were bombarded by better offers and had started to walk. I met Big Fish at four hours' notice and blurted out my proposal. Buy the rights to the software, take on the techies (quick, before they reach the door), develop our program for your own use. No licence fees, big competitive edge. Bingo! I would get my money back (earlier, sensing danger, and to protect my investment, I'd taken out a debenture), but it left the problem of the little customers. So I cut a deal with a competitor, who would help them while moving them over to their own system. They would pay twice and they were angry. So would I have been. Threats of litigation flared, then subsided.

So we signed the deals and I slinked back to my roots – database consultancy, vanilla flavour. What a relief! After years of working for everybody but myself, I felt lucky, safe. I was making money again. And I'd protected my investment.

Could politicians have influenced the outcome? Not unless they had taught me how to blend technical and commercial acumen, or told me the importance of learning my customers' business from the inside out.

I thought we could make it by combining star quality with hype. The fact that Bill Gates became the US's richest man by brilliantly exploiting those two devices means nothing. He's not a serial entrepreneur.
dlove@btinternet.com

Review questions

Consider 'civil' entrepreneurship in relation to 'ordinary' entrepreneurship. In particular:

1 How can an entrepreneurial approach help deliver projects in a non-profit environment?

2 What might be the challenges to being entrepreneurial in such an environment?

3 Can 'civil' entrepreneurship offer the same rewards as 'ordinary' entrepreneurship?

4 What are the roles for entrepreneurs in the development of Tunisia's economy?

5 What type of serial entrepreneur is David Love? What do you feel are David Love's motivations to being a serial entrepreneur?

2 The entrepreneurial process

Chapter overview

This chapter is concerned with developing a model of the process by which entrepreneurs create new wealth. It suggests that entrepreneurship, in the first instance, is driven by a desire for creating ***change*** *on the part of the entrepreneur. This desire for change leads the entrepreneur to bring together three contingencies,* ***opportunity****,* ***resources*** *and* ***organisation****, in an innovative and dynamic way.*

The chapter also considers the limits of entrepreneurship and whether it extends beyond the profit-making domain to the management of artistic, social and cultural endeavours.

2.1 Making a difference: entrepreneurship and the drive for change

KEY LEARNING OUTCOME
An understanding of the changes that entrepreneurship makes.

Entrepreneurship is about bringing about change and making a *difference*. The world is not the same after the entrepreneur has finished with it. In a narrower sense, entrepreneurship is about exploiting innovation in order to create value which cannot always be measured in purely financial terms.

The entrepreneur is concerned with identifying the potential for change. He or she exists in a state of tension between the *actual* and the *possible,* that is, between what *is* and what *might be* (see Fig. 2.1). This tension is manifest in three dimensions: the *financial*, the *personal* and the *social*.

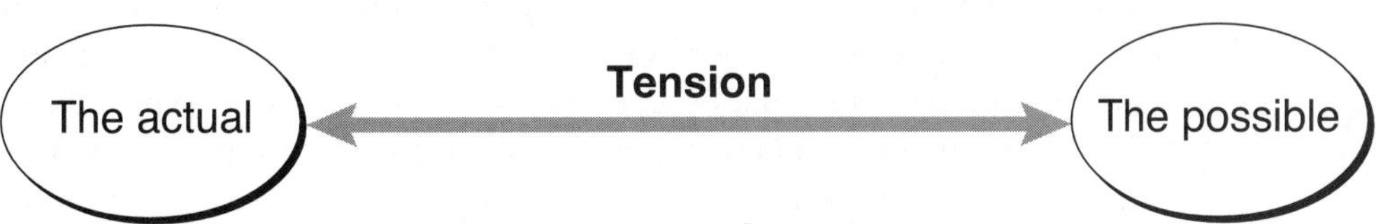

Fig. 2.1 Tension in the entrepreneurial process

The financial dimension: the potential to create new value

Entrepreneurship is an economic activity. It is concerned, first and foremost, with building stable, profitable businesses which must survive in a competitive environment. If they are to thrive and prosper they must add value more effectively than their competitors. The new world created by the entrepreneur must be a more valuable one than that which existed previously. The opportunity exploited and the innovation present must create additional value if the venture is to be successful in the long term since entrepreneurs compete to attract the resources with which they reward their stakeholders.

A point worth noting here is that in creating *new* value, entrepreneurship is not a 'zero sum game'. Even though business is competitive, it is not inevitable that if an entrepreneur wins then someone somewhere else must lose. Entrepreneurship often presents win–win scenarios. The new value the entrepreneur creates can be shared in a variety of ways.

The personal dimension: the potential to achieve personal goals

Entrepreneurs are motivated by a number of factors and although making money may motivate some, it is not the only factor, nor necessarily the most important. A sense of achievement, of having created something, or of 'making an entire new world' is often a much more significant driving factor. The entrepreneurial venture can be an entrepreneur's way of leaving his or her mark on the world, reminding it of his or her presence.

Entrepreneurs may also be motivated by the challenge that the competitive environment presents, namely a chance for them to pit their wits against the wider world. Driving their own ventures also gives entrepreneurs a chance to design their own working environment and instils a sense of control. In order to understand entrepreneurial motivation it is essential to recognise that for many entrepreneurs what matters is not the *destination* of the business they finally build up, but the *journey* – the process of creating the business.

The social dimension: the potential for structural change

Entrepreneurs operate within a wider society. In making an 'entire new world' they must, of course, have an impact on that society. They provide the society with new products and access to new services. They provide fellow citizens with jobs. They help make the economic system competitive. This may be good for the economic system as a whole, but not for the less dynamic and efficient competitors they will drive to the wall.

All of this gives the entrepreneur power to drive changes in the structure of a society. The kind of world that an entrepreneur envisages, perhaps the possibility of a better world, can be an important factor in motivating the entrepreneur. It also means that the entrepreneur must operate with a degree of social responsibility. The kind of world that the entrepreneur would like to see is often a part of their *vision* for their firm and for the future. This vision may be enshrined in the mission that the organisation sets itself.

2.2 The entrepreneurial process: opportunity, organisation and resources

KEY LEARNING OUTCOME
An understanding of the factors in the process of entrepreneurial value creation.

Every entrepreneurial venture is different with its own history. Its successes are the result of it having faced and addressed specific issues in its own way. Nonetheless, it is useful to consider the process of entrepreneurship in a generalised way since this gives us a framework for understanding how entrepreneurship creates new wealth in several terms and for making sense of the detail in particular ventures. It also provides us with a guide for decision making when planning new ventures.

The approach to the entrepreneurial process that will be described here is based on four interacting *contingencies*. The entrepreneur is responsible for bringing these together to create new value. A contingency is simply something which *must* be present in the process but can make an appearance in an endless variety of ways. The four contingencies in the entrepreneurial process are the *entrepreneur*, a market *opportunity*, a business *organisation* and *resources* to be invested (see Fig. 2.2). Each of these will now be explored in some depth.

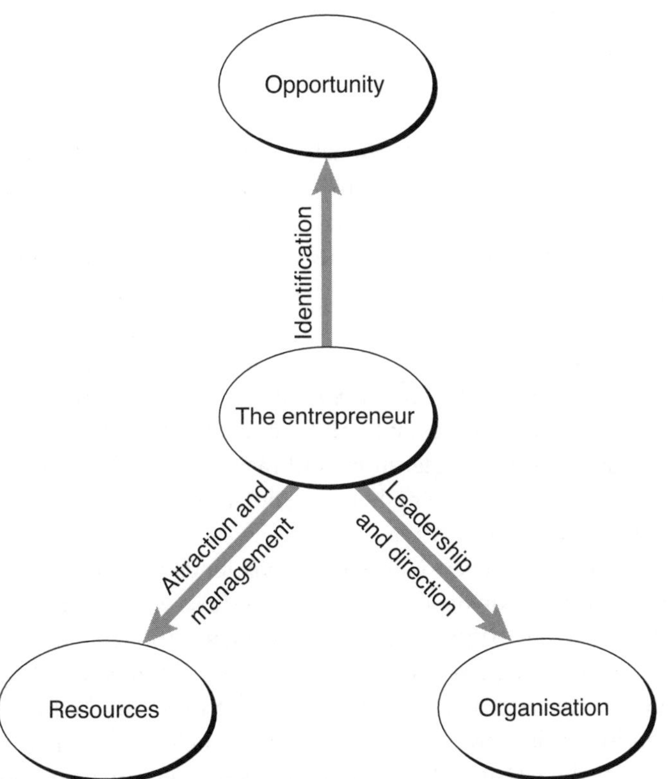

Fig. 2.2 The entrepreneurial process: opportunity, resources and organisation

The entrepreneur

The entrepreneur is the individual who lies at the heart of the entrepreneurial process, that is, the manager who drives the whole process forward. Entrepreneurs often act singly but in many instances *entrepreneurial teams* are important. Different members of the team may take on different roles and share responsibilities. They may be from the same family, for example the Benetton siblings from Northern Italy who revolutionised the manufacture of textiles, or alternatively, they be from an existing management team who have joined together to initiate their own venture, perhaps through a management buy-out.

Opportunity

An opportunity is the gap left in a market by those who currently serve it. It represents the potential to serve customers better than they are being served at present. The entrepreneur is responsible for scanning the business landscape for unexploited opportunities or possibilities that something important might be done both *differently* from the way it is done at the moment and, critically, done *better* than it is at the moment. The improved way of doing it is the innovation that the entrepreneur presents to the market. If customers agree with the entrepreneur that it is an improvement on what exists already and if the entrepreneur can supply the innovation effectively and profitably then new value can be created.

Organisation

In order to supply the innovation to the market, the activities of a number of different people must be co-ordinated. This is the function of the organisation that the entrepreneur creates. Organisations can take on a variety of forms depending on a number of factors such as their size, their rate of growth, the industry they operate in, the types of product or service they deliver, the age of the organisation and the culture that it adopts.

Entrepreneurial organisations are characterised by strong, often charismatic, leadership from the entrepreneur. They may have less formal structures and systems than their more bureaucratic, established counterparts. In many respects the entrepreneurial organisation is still learning, but rather than judge this to be a handicap the business turns it into a strength by being receptive to new ideas and responsive to the need for change.

Current thinking on entrepreneurial organisations tends not to draw a hard and fast distinction between those inside the organisation and those who are on the outside. It has been found more productive to think in terms of the organisation in a wider sense as being a *network* of relationships between individuals with the entrepreneur sitting at the centre. This network stretches beyond just the individuals who make up the formal company to include people and organisations outside the venture such as customers, suppliers and investors. The relationships that make up the network are very diverse. Some are defined by contracts, whereas others are defined by open markets; some are formal and some informal; some are based on self-interest, while others are maintained by altruism; some are driven by short-term considerations, and others by long-term interests.

In the network view, the organisation is a fluid thing defined by a *nexus of relationships*. Its boundaries are permeable. The idea of a network provides a powerful insight into how entrepreneurial ventures establish themselves, how they locate themselves competitively, and how they sustain their positions in their markets by adding value to people's lives.

Resources

The final contingency in the entrepreneurial process is resources. This includes the money which is invested in the venture, the people who contribute their efforts, knowledge and skills to it, and *physical assets* such as productive equipment and machinery, buildings and vehicles. Resources also include *intangible assets* such as brand names, company reputation and customer goodwill. All these features can be subject to *investment*. One of the key functions of the entrepreneur is to attract investment to the venture and to use it to build up a set of assets which allow the venture to supply its innovation competitively and profitably.

The entrepreneur plays a critical role in identifying opportunity, building and leading the organisation, and attracting and managing resources. The three external contingencies quickly develop a momentum of their own and become independent of the entrepreneur at the centre. As the organisation grows, it develops processes and systems and the people within it adopt distinct roles. The entrepreneur must delegate responsibility within the organisation and specialist functions may take over some aspects of the entrepreneur's role. For example, the marketing department may identify opportunities and innovate the firm's offerings to take advantage of them; the finance department may take on the responsibility for attracting investment. In this way, entrepreneurial ventures quickly take on a life of their own. They become quite distinct from the entrepreneur who established them. Consequently, the entrepreneur must constantly address the question of his or her role within the organisation.

2.3 The entrepreneurial process: action and the dynamics of success

KEY LEARNING OUTCOME
A recognition that entrepreneurship is a dynamic process in which success fuels success.

The entrepreneurial process results from the *actions* of the entrepreneur. It can only occur if the entrepreneur acts to develop an innovation and promote it to customers. The entrepreneurial process is *dynamic*. Success comes from the contingencies of the entrepreneur, the opportunity, the organisation and resources coming together and supporting each other over time. The entrepreneur must constantly focus the organisation onto the opportunity that has been identified. He or she must mould the resources to hand to give the organisation its shape and to ensure that those resources are appropriate for pursuing the particular opportunity. These interactions are the fundamental elements of the entrepreneurial process and together they constitute the foundations of the *strategy* adopted by the venture.

Opportunity–organisation fit

The nature of the opportunity that is being pursued defines the shape that the organisation must adopt. Every organisation built by an entrepreneur is different. Organisations are complex affairs and there are a variety of ways in which they might be described and understood. The essential features are the *assets* of the organisation, that is, the things which it possesses; its *structure*, namely how it arranges communication links (both formal and informal) within itself; its *processes*: how it *adds value* to its inputs to create its *outputs*; and its *culture*, that is, the attitudes, beliefs and outlooks that influence the way people behave within the organisation (see Table 2.1).

Assets, structure, process and culture are not separate parts of an organisation. They are merely different perspectives we may adopt in describing it. These four perspectives on the organisation form a unified whole which must be appropriate for the opportunity that the organisation is pursuing. The organisation must be shaped to *fit* the market gap that defines the opportunity.

Resource–organisation configuration

Resources are the things that are used to pursue opportunity. They include *people*, *money* and *productive assets*. In a sense, an organisation is 'just' a collection of resources.

Table 2.1 An outline of organisational *assets, structure, process* and *culture* for three global entrepreneurial businesses

Organisation	*McDonald's*	*The Body Shop*	*Microsoft*
Opportunity pursued	Desire for fast, convenient, consistent meals	Desire for toiletries produced with a concern for the environment	Desire to process information
Assets	Brand name, outlets, locations, people	Brand name, outlets, locations, people	People, knowledge, patents, brand name
Structure	Series of production/ retail outlets	Series of retail outlets	Project teams based at one location
Process	Production and distribution standardised at outlets. Central financial and marketing	Production centralised. Distribution through outlets. Promotion largely by store presence	Product development, production, distribution and marketing centralised
Culture	Positive attitude, concern for quality, customer focus	Attitude of concern. Emphasis on wider social responsibility for organisation	Innovative and creative 'technophilia'. Emphasis on managerial informality

The *configuration* of the resources is the way in which a particular mix of resources is brought together and blended to form the organisation's assets, structure, process and (through the attitude of the people who make it up) its culture.

Resource–opportunity focus

The entrepreneur must decide what resources will make up the organisation; for example, its mix of capital, how this will be converted into productive assets and the nature and skills of the people who will make it up are all matters to be decided by the entrepreneur in the first instance. If the organisation is to develop the assets, structure, process and culture that will enable it to fit with its opportunity then the resource mix must be correctly balanced.

Entrepreneurs must be active in attracting resources to their venture such as suitably qualified employees, financial backing in the form of investor's money, the support of customers and suppliers. Even so, they usually find that they do not have access to the same level of resources as established players in a market and because their risks may be higher, they will find the resources to be more expensive. If they are to compete successfully then entrepreneurs must make the resources they can get hold of work much harder perhaps than many established players do. The entrepreneur must be single-minded and *focus* those resources definitely and unambiguously onto the opportunity that has been identified since the performance of the entrepreneurial organisation depends on how well the contingencies of opportunity, organisation and resources are linked together (see Fig. 2.3).

Learning organisations

These three aspects of the entrepreneurial process – making the organisation *fit* the opportunity it aims to exploit, *configuring* the resources to shape the organisation and

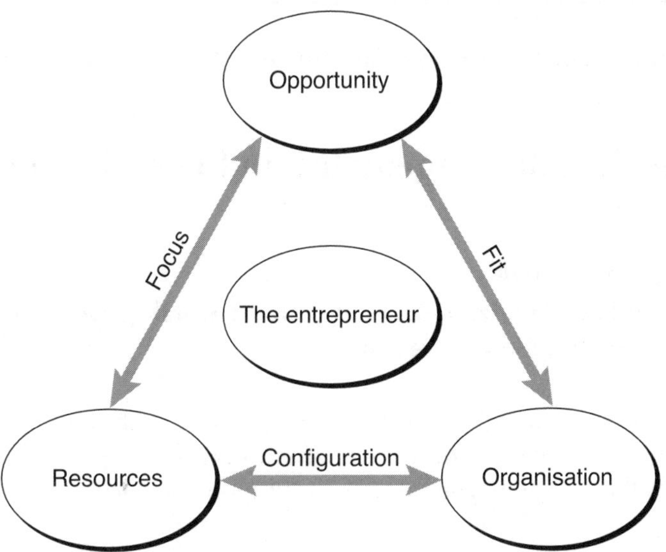

Fig. 2.3 The entrepreneurial process: focus, fit and configuration

focusing the resources in pursuit of the opportunity – are not reflected in separate spheres of activity. They merely provide different perspectives on the same underlying management process. However, they do illuminate the essence of the entrepreneur's task and the direction their leadership must take. That leadership must be applied *constantly* since organisations are fluid things and left to themselves they can lose their shape and sense of direction. Furthermore, the entrepreneurial organisation must be a *learning* organisation. That is, it must not only *respond* to opportunities and challenges but must also *reflect* on the outcomes that result from that response and *modify* future responses in the light of experience. The venture cannot afford to acquire assets and set up structures and systems which are incapable of evolving as the organisation develops. Assets and structures must be modified as the organisation grows and changes and, critically, learns from its successes and failures. The entrepreneur must take responsibility for stimulating the firm to change in the light of experience. This learning process is shown in Fig. 2.4.

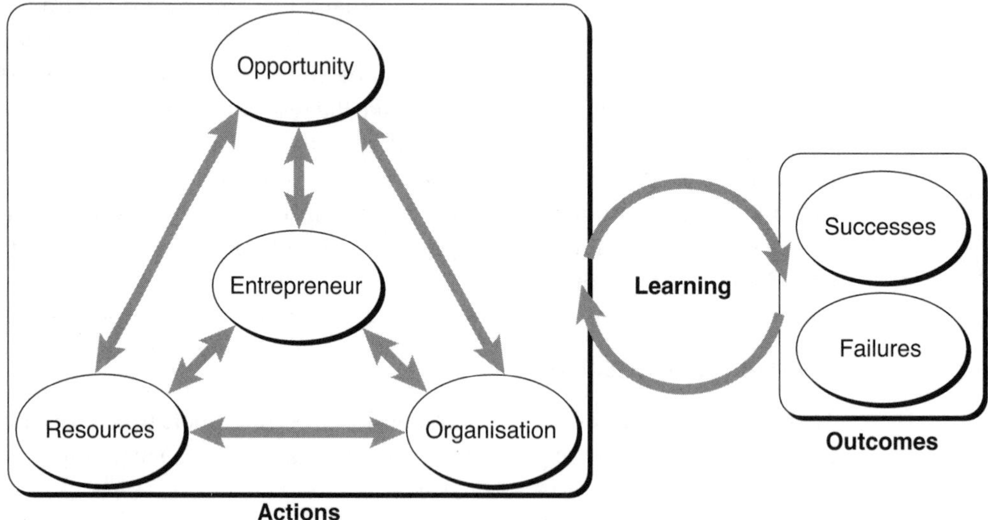

Fig. 2.4 The entrepreneurial organisation constantly learns from its successes and failures

2.4 Beyond profit: entrepreneurship in the social and public domains

KEY LEARNING OUTCOME
An appreciation that an understanding of entrepreneurship can help make non-profit making activities more successful.

Entrepreneurship, as an activity, is intimately associated with the world of business and making profits. However, the picture of entrepreneurship we have developed here has insights that can go beyond purely profit-motivated activity. In particular, we have seen that:

- Entrepreneurship is a style of management;

- Entrepreneurs are managers who are very effective at pursuing opportunity and creating change;
- Entrepreneurship is a social as well as an economic activity; and
- The motivations of the entrepreneur are varied and go beyond a desire to make money; they also involve a desire to create a new and better world.

From this it is clear that we might take a much wider view of 'entrepreneurship' and consider many activities outside the world of business as 'entrepreneurial'. For example, a great cultural, artistic or political endeavour could be entrepreneurial. It is not uncommon to hear talk of 'entrepreneurial' artists or politicians. This is not meant to imply that such people are simply interested in making money out of being artists or politicians (though, of course, many do!), rather it is to imply that such people approach their careers with drive, ambition and a clear vision of what they want to achieve. In order to fulfil their ambitions they are willing to develop and use entrepreneurial skills such as effective communication and leadership.

A hierarchy of entrepreneurial activities functioning in different social areas can be constructed as shown in Fig. 2.5. At the core is what we conventionally understand to be entrepreneurship, namely managing the profit-making venture. At the next level is management of non-profit-making organisations such as charities. Above this we might place endeavours in the social and cultural arena such as sporting and artistic ventures. At the top of the hierarchy there are activities aimed at creating wholesale social change such as political activity. These levels are not completely separate, of course, and there will be some overlap.

Even though we can recognise entrepreneurship in these wider social arenas it is wise to keep management of the profit-making venture as the central concern for entrepreneurship. If we fail to do so the subject could become so wide as to be in danger of losing its coherence as a field of study. Therefore, this book will concentrate on profit-motivated activities. However, this does mean that insights gained from the management of the profit venture cannot be used to help achieve success in non-profit-making ventures, or, conversely, that an understanding of success outside the business sphere cannot be used to illuminate the ways in which entrepreneurship might be improved within that sector.

In a narrow sense, many non-profit activities may still demand a managerial approach. They often involve managing money. Thus the charity still has to attract financial resources to distribute to its clients; sport may involve financial sponsorship; artists must still sell their creations; political parties must attract money from

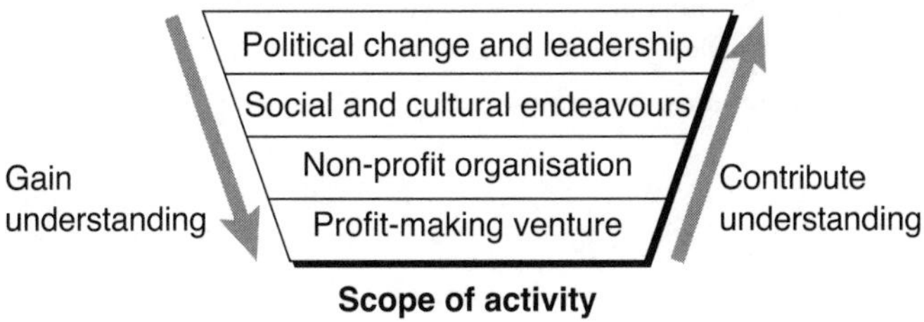

Fig. 2.5 The hierarchy of entrepreneurship in its wider social context

supporters if they are to function. All these activities can call upon insights from other business areas such as marketing and human resource management. In a broader sense though, entrepreneurship, perhaps more than many other management disciplines, goes beyond the mere management of money. Money is just a means to an end for the entrepreneur, and the end is the creation of a better world. We may offer a description of entrepreneurship at a fundamental level by claiming that it is about:

> **creating and managing vision and of communicating that vision to other people. It is about demonstrating leadership, motivating people and being effective in getting people to accept change.**

This description reflects entrepreneurship as a management skill practised and perfected in a human setting. As such it can play a crucial part in driving any venture forward whether that venture be in the business, social, cultural or political domain.

Summary of key ideas

- The entrepreneurial process is the creation of *new value* through the entrepreneur identifying new *opportunities*, attracting the *resources* needed to pursue those opportunities and building an *organisation* to manage those resources.
- The process is *dynamic* with the entrepreneur and the entrepreneurial organisation learning through *success* and *failure*.
- As a style of management, entrepreneurship has much to offer to, and also much to learn from, the management of projects in the not-for-profit, artistic and political arenas.

Suggestions for further reading

Batstone, S. and **Pheby, J.** (1996) 'Entrepreneurship and decision-making: The contribution of G.L.S. Shackle', *International Journal of Entrepreneurial Behaviour and Research*, Vol. 2, No. 2, pp. 34–51.

Bhave, M.P. (1994) 'A process model of entrepreneurial venture creation', *Journal of Business Venturing*, Vol. 9, No. 3, pp. 223–42.

Bouchiki, H. (1993) 'A constructivist framework for understanding entrepreneurial performance', *Organisation Studies*, Vol. 14, No. 4, pp. 549–70.

Gartner, W.B. (1985) 'A conceptual framework for describing the phenomenon of new venture creation', *Academy of Management Review*, Vol. 10, No. 4, pp. 696–706.

Lessem, R. (1978) 'Towards the interstices of management: developing the social entrepreneur', *Management Education and Development*, Vol. 9, pp. 178–88.

Hill, R. (1982) 'The entrepreneur: an artist masquerading as a businessman?' *International Management*, Vol. 37, No. 2, pp. 21–6.

Selected case material

Childcare grows up from small beginnings

13 January 2000

Toy-strewn day nurseries are becoming big business, says **Jenny Benjamin**

With its tricycle-strewn garden and cut-out covered windows, the average day nursery seems very distant from the world of big business.

And yet in the past 10 years social and economic trends have transformed childcare provision into a boom industry attracting substantial City funding. Encouraged by government measures such as the Child Care Tax Credit, women with small children are returning to work in ever greater numbers and are increasingly opting for day nurseries rather than childminders or more informal playgroups.

According to the Local Government Management Board, the number of all independent nursery places in England rose by 457 per cent between 1987 and 1997. Since then the rate of expansion has accelerated, and still demand outstrips supply.

With the rapid growth of the day nursery sector has come the rise of the nursery chain. Parents accustomed to the more home-like environment of the small, single nursery used to regard chains as bland and impersonal. Now many working parents prefer chain nurseries because they are more likely to offer convenient hours, good facilities and smart, purpose-built premises.

The entrepreneurs behind these growing childcare empires fall roughly into two groups: those who have built up their businesses gradually from small beginnings, acquiring management skills and funding on the way, and a newer breed of City-backed business people whose access to money and management know-how has enabled them to start big and grow rapidly.

Yvonne Birrell falls squarely into the first category with her Glasgow group the Birrell Collection. A former primary school teacher with definite ideas about education, Birrell used £3,000 of her savings to set up her first nursery in one room of her rented flat. She opened in 1988 with just one child, but had 20 within three months.

After two years she set up a second nursery in a disused drama unit rented from a local college, and six months later she entered into a similar arrangement with a Glasgow hospital.

In 1992 Ms Birrell bought her first property, a Victorian tenement. She installed herself in the attic and her fourth nursery on the lower floors. Seven years later, at the age of 38, she is married with a separate home and has opened her fifth nursery, a brand new facility that she built last year with a £350,000 overdraft from her bank. Her business is worth about £750,000.

Before launching her first venture Ms Birrell attended a management course organised by Lothian and Edinburgh Enterprise (LEAL). The experience was invaluable. "I have constantly referred to it and relied on it ever since," she says.

It is clear, however, that much of her success resulted from total commitment to the project. "The job was very time-intensive," she says. "It did rule my life for a number of years. But then, I enjoyed it – there was nothing that would please me more than poring over my accounts of an evening."

Her family background was also important. "I have a very entrepreneurial father, and when you are steeped in that culture it gives you courage to take steps that are quite risky," she says.

Meanwhile, Leapfrog Day Nurseries had big ideas from day one. Founded in April 1998, the chain has 13 purpose-built nurseries as far apart as Evesham and Edinburgh, and 43 more in the pipeline.

Initial funding came through chief executive Derek Mapp, who joined Leapfrog from the unlikely world of brewing. He met MD Sue Husbands and her team when they were looking at a potential site next to one of his Tom Cobbley chain of pubs, later sold profitably to Rank.

"He liked our ideas and we got on well," says Ms Husbands. "We needed someone with a knowledge of funding to captain our ship and he seemed like a good choice because he was also chairman of a Regional Development Agency."

Mr Mapp's main backers on the pub venture, EAC (European Acquisitions Cap ital), invested £7m in his new business. A further £11m came from other venture capitalists and £1m from senior management.

Ms Husbands, who has 15 years' experience in education, cites her team's "good chemistry", passion for the job and lack of complacency as the main reasons for Leapfrog's success.

Their approach clearly works with their employees, many of whom are trained in-house: staff turnover is only 5 per cent a year, compared to an industry average of about 40 per cent.

Ms Husbands compares the nursery sector to the market for care homes 10 years ago, with "lots of investment still available" for competent newcomers. In fact, a number of backers and managers have made the move from care homes.

Richard Padgett, chief executive of the seven-strong Bright Horizons nursery chain, was a nurse who moved into, and did well out of, homes for the elderly. He then set up Bright Horizons in 1997 as principal shareholder. His active involvement began in April 1999.

In common with everyone else in the industry, Mr Padgett is at pains to stress that, for him, nursery ownership is more than just a business opportunity. He has a five-year-old son, and says that he sees his work "from a parent's point of view".

For those who feel uneasy about the juxtaposition of small children and big profits, this reassures more than any high-sounding sentiments about responsibilities and educative roles. The new nursery moguls can talk about mergers and share options as much as they like, as long as they remember that every one of their small clients is somebody's baby.

A Nasdaq for intellectual property

FT

17 December 1999

Marcus Gibson meets a man whose website acts as go-between among sellers and buyers of technologies

Those jokes about the scarcity of famous Belgians are beginning to wear thin – at least on the internet where some are playing an important, albeit low profile, role in many strategic developments.

The co-founder of the internet was a Belgian – Robert Caillou, working at Cern, the European nuclear physics research laboratory; more recently BelSign has become one of Europe's leading digital certification authorities, or "net passport" providers.

Now Chris de Bleser, Belgian chief executive of Massachusetts-based website firm Yet2.com, is hoping to make his mark on the web into the bargain.

Yet2.com is devoted to the sale of technologies – or scientific intellectual property – held by a 25-strong group of some of the largest companies in the US, Europe and Asia, which undertake 10 per cent of all commercial research. Due to start in January, Yet2.com will act as a go-between among sellers and would-be buyers of technologies.

In the US, companies such as Monsanto, Procter & Gamble, Polaroid, 3M, Boeing, Dow Chemical, DuPont, Ford Motor – and, in Europe, Philips – have joined what Mr de Bleser claims is the first comprehensive forum for technology exchange on the internet. "Our goal is to become the Nasdaq for intellectual property," he says.

Mr de Bleser spent much of his career frustrated by the fact that large research organisations utilise and market only a fraction of the technologies they create. "Global corporations have been fortresses of IP (intellectual property) – so most technologies never see the light of day," he says.

Born in the Congo, educated at Antwerp's RUCA state university, and employed in the UK and Australia with Black & Decker and Unilever, Mr de Bleser worked most recently for Polaroid where he revived its technical and digital imaging division through the re-application of Polaroid technologies into a whole raft of new products.

The experience, and his background, prompted Mr de Bleser to start an ambitious global business of his own.

Yet2.com will list thousands of technologies – without naming owners. Registering and searching on Yet2.com for a brief description of a technology will be free. For more detailed data, the site will charge $25 (£40) per person, or $500 for a full year's unlimited access to all technologies for 10 people.

An introduction to a technology owner, plus an initial meeting to discuss licensing terms, will cost a minimum of $1,000, with 50 per cent going to the seller. "If a deal is reached and there is revenue from that deal," says Mr de Bleser, "we ask for 10 per cent, capped at $50,000." There will be no advertisements.

An initial problem was how to describe the true technical potential of the technologies. "Simply putting a patent description on the site would have been meaningless. Patent language is designed to hide and protect an innovation – not highlight all of its commercial applications."

A similar problem arose when the Japanese Patent Office tried to create a 'Technomart' of available IP. As a result, contributing companies to Yet2.com will provide write-ups and benefit statements. Often, however, there is no common vernacular to describe a technology outside its original sector.

A second difficulty has been that companies in one sector will not use the technology of a company in the same, or even adjacent, sector. "An engineer's intellectual property companion often lies outside his area of activity," says Mr de Bleser. Similarly, an inventor may see dozens of applications for an innovation – but his employer only one.

But Mr de Bleser firmly believes that the site's best opportunity is in breaking down these barriers – by demonstrating the potential of its technologies. "Companies can now acquire them at a fraction of the cost of creating it themselves," he says.

He gives an example. The chemistry that produced Tide detergent includes 12 different technologies – including one that has since been adopted in cleaning fluid for contact lenses. Ben du Pont, the site's co-founder, offers another. New uses for Lycra have been found outside fashion, he says, such as in surgical gloves.

At present, the technology licensing market is worth about $100m (£62m). "But it should be worth far more if everyone could find the right technology easily and economically," says Mr de Bleser. "There is a whole new class of IP deals between $5,000-$200,000 to be created."

And that is why the website name was chosen. "Yet2.com gets across the idea that an engineer's next solution is out there," he says. The company has raised $10m to take it through to early 2000 – before revenues begin to arrive. With a staff of 50 by next year, the site will need to prove itself short-term. "We need to prove the concept quickly, and find any basic flaws," says Mr de Bleser candidly. Such sentiments have their sceptics.

Earlier IP websites have not achieved their promise. One snag is that synergies across industries have been fiendishly difficult to identify. There are already a dozen websites devoted to IP, admits de Bleser, including TechEx and IPTex. "The world doesn't need another IP licensing site," he admits. "What we'll provide is a technology service – and thousands of proven technologies from big players."

With his top 25 companies in place, he believes Yet2.com will create the network effect that will push it past the rest.

There is no shortage of partner plaudits. Jackie Michel, Monsanto's director of intellectual assets, says: "We believe Yet2.com provides a cost-effective market for creating revenues from these assets." Bruce Gerding, vice-president at aerospace group TRW, says the site would become a "dynamic forum to showcase our IP . . . beyond our traditional range of customers."

Mr de Bleser remains upbeat. The average product engineer solves between four and six problems a year, he says, and licenses technology only once between five to 10 years. "They are constantly on the lookout for new technologies. Our solution has been to capture that quest . . . in our name."

Review questions

Use the model of the entrepreneurial process to evaluate the contingencies in the development of:

1 The Birrell Collection

2 Yet2.com.

3 The individual entrepreneur

Chapter overview

*This chapter is concerned with developing a picture of the entrepreneur as an **individual**. It considers the **type** of people who choose an entrepreneurial path, the **characteristics** successful entrepreneurs bring to the job and the **skills** they use. The chapter concludes by emphasising the importance of understanding the entrepreneur in a social setting and the influences exerted by the culture in which they operate.*

3.1 Who becomes an entrepreneur?

KEY LEARNING OUTCOME
A recognition of the kind of people who take up an entrepreneurial career.

The discussion in Chapter 1 should make it clear that we should be very wary of trying to answer the question 'who becomes an entrepreneur?' by looking for a certain type of personality or trying to identify innate characteristics. In these terms, *anyone* can become an entrepreneur. A more fruitful approach is to look at the broader life experience and events which encourage a person to make a move into entrepreneurship. A number of general life stories or 'biographies' can be identified.

The inventor

The *inventor* is someone who has developed an innovation and who has decided to make a career out of presenting that innovation to the market. It may be a new product or it may be an idea for a new service. It may be high-tech, or it may be based on a traditional technology.

The inventor often draws on technical experience of a particular industry in order to make his or her invention. However, it may be derived from a technology quite unrelated to the industry in which they work. It may be based on technical expertise they have gained as the result of a hobby. Alternatively, the invention may result from a 'grey' research programme carried out unofficially within the inventor's employer organisation or it may be the product of a private 'garden shed' development programme.

It is an unfortunate fact of life that, in general, many such 'inventors' have a poor track record in building successful businesses. This is not because their ideas are not good: their innovations are often quite valuable. More often, it is due to the fact that no new product, regardless of how many benefits it might potentially bring to the customer, will manufacture and promote itself. Successful entrepreneurship calls upon a wide range of management skills, not just an ability to innovate. The entrepreneur must establish a market potential for their innovation and lead an organisation which can deliver it profitably. They must sell the product to customers and sell the venture to investors. Inventors can often be so impressed with the technical side of their innovation (often justifiably) that they neglect the other tasks that must be undertaken. An example of an inventor who combined technical insight with consummate business skills is James Dyson who built up not one but two highly successful businesses to market innovative products.

The unfulfilled manager

Life as a professional manager in an established organisation brings many rewards. It offers a stable income, intellectual stimulation, status and a degree of security. For many people, though, this is still not enough. The organisation may not offer them a vehicle for all their ambitions: for example, the desire to make a mark on the world, to leave a lasting achievement, to stretch their existing managerial talents to their limit and to develop new ones. It may simply not let them do things *their* way. Such a manager, confident in their abilities and unsatisfied in their ambitions, may decide to embark on an entrepreneurial career.

The question they often face is 'doing what?' The desire and the ability to perform entrepreneurially means nothing if a suitable opportunity has not been spotted and an innovation to take advantage of it developed. In a sense, the unsatisfied manager faces the opposite problem to the inventor: entrepreneurial ability but nothing to apply it to. If they are to be successful they must put effort into identifying and clarifying a business idea and developing an understanding of its market potential. This can often be resolved by working as part of an entrepreneurial team with an inventor who dreams up the initial idea.

The displaced manager

The increasing pace of technological and economic change means that managers are likely to make an increasing number of career changes during their professional lives. Restructuring trends such as 'downsizing' and 'delayering' means that unemployment among professional groups is increasing in many parts of the world. This increases the pressure on managers to work for themselves and one possibility is to undertake an entrepreneurial route. The severance package which may be offered by their organisations (often supplemented with training and support) can sometimes facilitate this possibility.

Many managers approach redundancy positively, seeing it as an opportunity to achieve things they could not within the organisation. In effect, they recognise themselves as unfulfilled managers and feel grateful for the push they have been given. Others, however, may not adopt such a positive approach. They may see the uncertainties looming larger than the possibilities. Making entrepreneurship successful is very difficult, if not impossible, unless it is approached with enthusiasm. If a person does not find the prospect of an entrepreneurial career attractive then it is plainly wrong for them. However, one should not underestimate the power of a few early successes to change attitudes and to alter a manager's perception of possibilities.

The young professional

Increasingly, young, highly educated people, often with formal management qualifications, are skipping the experience of working for an established organisation and moving directly to work on establishing their own ventures. Despite some very high-profile success stories, not least with Internet ventures, such entrepreneurs are often met with suspicion. There may be a concern that whatever their 'theoretical' knowledge, they lack experience in the realities of business life. While youthful enthusiasm *may* hide a lack of real acumen, the young entrepreneur should not be dismissed out of hand.

In the mature economies of the Western world, young entrepreneurs have been disproportionally important in leading *new* industries, particularly in high-tech areas such as computing, information technology and business services. The fast-growing emergent economies of the Pacific Rim and the developing world have populations which are generally much younger in profile than those of the West. Entrepreneurs may *have* to be younger if sufficient entrepreneurial talent is to be available to drive the economy's growth. The post-Communist world of eastern and central Europe is currently undergoing a radical economic and social restructuring. To a great extent it is young people who are taking the lead and making the adaptations necessary to take advantage of the new possibilities these changes are offering.

The excluded

Some people turn to an entrepreneurial career because nothing else is open to them. The dynamism and entrepreneurial vigour of displaced communities and ethnic and religious minorities is well documented. This is not because such people are 'inherently' entrepreneurial, rather it is because, for a variety of social, cultural, political and historical reasons, they have not been invited to join the wider economic community. They do not form part of the established network of individuals and organisations. As a result they may form their own internal networks, trading among themselves and, perhaps, with their ancestral countries.

Ethnic entrepreneurship can be very important within a national economy. Small communities often make a contribution to the overall entrepreneurial vigour of a country in a way which is quite disproportionate to their number. Nevertheless, one of the main challenges faced by ethnic entrepreneurs is making the move from running a small business to starting a full-blown entrepreneurial venture. This is because to achieve its growth potential the entrepreneurial venture must spread its network of relationships quite widely in order to achieve its growth potential, and this often involves going beyond the confines of the relatively small community in which it starts. In a sense, this goes against the reason for the business coming into existence in the first place. In making the move, the ethnic entrepreneur may face risks that the non-ethnic entrepreneur does not.

There is growing evidence that after a time, say three or four generations, small business managers from ethnic minorities are increasingly willing to make the move to entrepreneurism. In doing so they add another spur to the wider economy.

In a new and far-reaching study David Blanchflower and Andrew Oswald (1998) have investigated the factors that lie behind the drive to become an entrepreneur. The basis of their research was information on the *National Child Development Study* (NCDS), a database recording biographical information, psychometric and personality test data on all individuals born in Great Britain between 3 and 9 March 1958. Taking a broad view of entrepreneurship, that is, starting one's own business, the researchers attempted to identify the factors that predisposed individuals to take this career option. They found no correlation between personality factors, important life events and entrepreneurial inclination. This is a finding that reinforces this book's proposition that successful entrepreneurship is personality dependent. The one thing they did find to be important was receiving a lump sum of money, say, in the form of a legacy, that allowed individuals to make the initial investment in a start-up. The authors then develop an econometric model of entrepreneurial labour economics. This finding confirms the importance of access to initial capital as a key event in the entrepreneurial process.

This is not to say that one cannot become an entrepreneur if one does not receive a legacy. But it does emphasise the importance of building a good relationship with investors. This is an issue that will be explored further in Chapter 19.

3.2 Characteristics of the successful entrepreneur

KEY LEARNING OUTCOME
A recognition of the characteristics exhibited by successful entrepreneurs.

Although there does not seem to be a single 'entrepreneurial type' there is a great deal of consistency in the way in which entrepreneurs approach their task. Some of the characteristics which are exhibited by the successful entrepreneur are discussed below. However, we should be careful to draw a distinction between personality 'characteristics' and the character somebody displays when working. The former are regarded as innate, a permanent part of the make-up of their personality. The latter is just the way they approach a particular set of tasks. This is just as much a product of their commitment, interest and motivation to the tasks in hand, as it is a predisposition.

Hard work

Entrepreneurs put a lot of physical and mental effort into developing their ventures. They often work long and anti-social hours. After all, an entrepreneur is their own most valuable asset. That said, balancing the needs of the venture with other life commitments such as family and friends is one of the great challenges which faces the entrepreneur.

Self-starting

Entrepreneurs do not need to be told what to do. They identify tasks for themselves and then follow them through without looking for encouragement or direction from others.

Setting of personal goals

Entrepreneurs tend to set themselves clear, and demanding, goals. They benchmark their achievements against these personal goals. As a result, entrepreneurs tend to work to internal standards rather than look to others for assessment of their performance.

Resilience

Not everything goes right all the time. In fact, failure may be experienced more often than success. Entrepreneurs must not only pick themselves up after things have gone wrong but must learn positively from the experience and use that learning to increase the chances of success the next time around.

Confidence

The entrepreneur must demonstrate that they not only believe in themselves but also in the venture they are pursuing. After all, if they don't, who will?

Receptiveness to new ideas

However, the entrepreneur must not be *overly* confident. They must recognise their own limitations and the possibilities that they have to improve their skills. They must be willing to revise their ideas in the light of new experience. One of the main reasons that banks and venture capitalists give for *not* supporting a business proposal is that the entrepreneur was *too* sure of themselves to be receptive to good advice when it was offered.

Assertiveness

Entrepreneurs are usually clear as to what they want to gain from a situation and are not frightened to express their wishes. Being assertive does not mean being aggressive! Nor does it mean adopting a position and refusing to budge. Assertiveness means a commitment to *outcomes*, not *means*. True assertiveness relies on mutual understanding and is founded on good communication skills.

Information seeking

Entrepreneurs are not, on average, any more intelligent than any other group. They are, however, characterised by *inquisitiveness*. They are never satisfied by the information they have at any one time and constantly seek more. Good entrepreneurs tend to question rather more than they make statements when communicating.

Eager to learn

Good entrepreneurs are always aware that they could do things better. They are aware of both the skills they have and their limitations, and are always receptive to a chance to improve their skills and to develop new ones.

Attuned to opportunity

The good entrepreneur is constantly searching for new opportunities. In effect, this means that he or she is never really satisfied with the way things are any moment in time. The entrepreneur uses this sense of dissatisfaction to make sure he or she never becomes complacent.

Receptive to change

The entrepreneur is always willing to embrace change in a positive fashion, that is, to actively embrace the possibilities presented by change rather than resist them.

Commitment to others

Good entrepreneurs are not selfish. They cannot afford to be! They recognise the value that other people bring to their ventures and the importance of motivating those people to make the best effort they can on its behalf. This means showing a commitment to them. Motivation demands an investment in understanding how people think. Leadership is not just about giving people jobs to do; it is also about offering them the support they need in order to do those jobs.

Comfort with power

Entrepreneurs can become very powerful figures. They can have a great impact on the life of other people. Power can be one of the great motivators for the entrepreneur. Effective entrepreneurs are *aware* of the power they possess and recognise it as an asset. They are not afraid to use it and never let themselves be intimidated by it. However, the *true* entrepreneur uses power responsibly, as a means to an end and not as an end in itself.

These are essential characteristics. How they become manifest is, of course, subject to political and economic conditions. They are recognised and judged in a social setting subject to social norms and expectations. How these characteristics are developing in social systems that have undergone major changes (such as the post-Communist bloc of central and eastern Europe) is of particular interest. Green *et al.* (1996) and Kuznetsov *et al.* (2000) offer studies of the emergence of entrepreneurial characteristics in Russia.

3.3 Entrepreneurial skills

KEY LEARNING OUTCOME
A recognition of the skills which enhance entrepreneurial performance.

A skill is simply knowledge which is demonstrated by action. It is an ability to perform in a certain way. An entrepreneur is someone who has a good business idea and can turn that idea into reality. To be successful, an entrepreneur must not only identify an opportunity but also understand it in great depth. He or she must be able to spot a gap in the market and recognise what new product or service will fill that gap. He or she must know what features it will have and why they will appeal to the customer. The entrepreneur must also know how to inform the customer about it and how to deliver the new offering. All this calls for an intimate knowledge of a particular sector of industry. Turning an idea into reality calls upon two sorts of skill. General management skills are required to organise the physical and financial resources needed to run the venture and people management skills are needed to obtain the necessary support from others for the venture to succeed.

Some important general management business skills include:

- *Strategy skills* – An ability to consider the business as a whole, to understand how it fits within its marketplace, how it can organise itself to deliver value to its customers, and the ways in which it does this better than its competitors.
- *Planning skills* – An ability to consider what the future might offer, how it will impact on the business and what needs to be done to prepare for it now.
- *Marketing skills* – An ability to see past the firm's offerings and their features, to be able to see *how* they satisfy the customer's needs and *why* the customer finds them attractive.
- *Financial skills* – An ability to manage money; to be able to keep track of expenditure and to monitor cash-flow, but also an ability to assess investments in terms of their potential and their risks.
- *Project management skills* – An ability to organise projects, to set specific objectives, to set schedules and to ensure that the necessary resources are in the right place at the right time.
- *Time management skills* – An ability to use time productively, to be able to prioritise important jobs and to get things done to schedule.

Businesses are made by people. A business can only be successful if the people who make it up are properly directed and are committed to make an effort on its behalf. An entrepreneurial venture also needs the support of people from outside the organisation such as customers, suppliers and investors. To be effective, an entrepreneur needs to demonstrate a wide variety of skills in the way he or she deals with other people. Some of the more important skills we might include under this heading are:

- *Leadership skills* – An ability to inspire people to work in a specific way and to undertake the tasks that are necessary for the success of the venture. Leadership is about more than merely directing people; it is also about supporting them and helping them to achieve the goals they have been set.

- *Motivation skills* – An ability to enthuse people and get them to give their full commitment to the tasks in hand. Being able to motivate demands an understanding of what drives people and what they expect from their jobs. It should not be forgotten that, for the entrepreneur, an ability to motivate oneself is as important as an ability to motivate others.
- *Delegation skills* – An ability to allocate tasks to different people. Effective delegation involves more than instructing. It demands a full understanding of the skills that people possess, how they use them and how they might be developed to fulfil future needs.
- *Communication skills* – An ability to use spoken and written language to express ideas and inform others. Good communication is about more than just passing information. It is about using language to influence people's actions.
- *Negotiation skills* – An ability to understand what is wanted from a situation, what is motivating others in that situation and recognise the possibilities of maximising the outcomes for all parties. Being a good negotiator is more about being able to identify win–win scenarios and communicate them, than it is about being able to 'bargain hard'.

All these different people skills are interrelated. Good leadership demands being able to motivate. Effective delegation requires an ability to communicate. The skills needed to deal with people are not innate, they must be learnt. Leadership is as much an acquired skill as is an ability to plan effectively. The ability to motivate and to negotiate can be learnt in the same way as project management techniques.

Entrepreneurial performance results from a combination of *industry knowledge, general management skills, people skills* and *personal motivation* (see Fig. 3.1). The successful entrepreneur must not only use these skills but learn to use them and to learn from using them. Entrepreneurs should constantly audit their abilities in these areas, recognise their strengths and shortcomings, and plan how to develop these skills in the future.

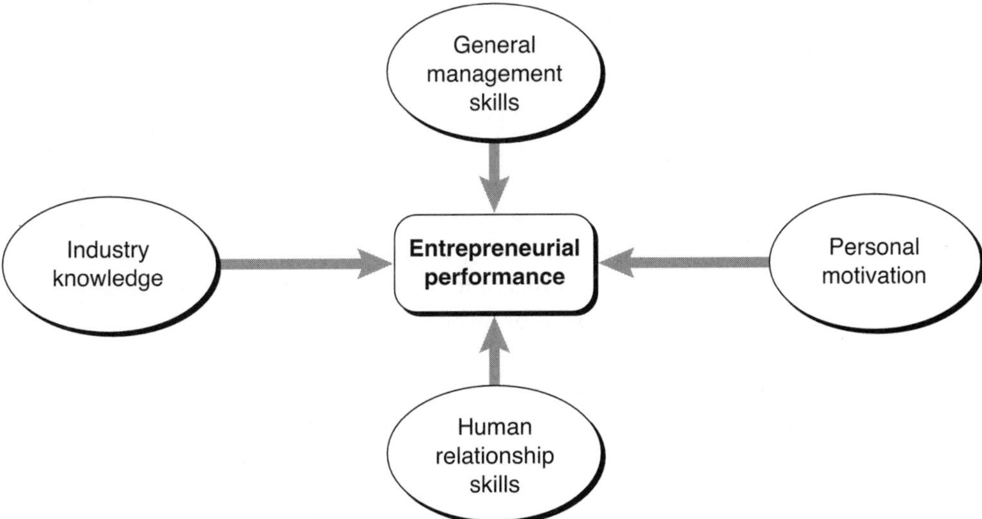

Fig. 3.1 Factors influencing entrepreneurial performance

3.4 Entrepreneurship and culture

KEY LEARNING OUTCOME
A recognition that the behaviour of entrepreneurs is influenced by a wide range of cultural and social factors.

Entrepreneurs are not robots blindly fulfilling an economic function. They cannot pursue opportunities, or strive for economic efficiency without exhibiting some concern for wider issues. Entrepreneurs are human beings operating within societies which define, and are defined by, cultures. Clearly, an American entrepreneur tends to act differently from a Japanese one who, in turn, behaves differently from a Peruvian one. There are not only great differences *between* these cultures which influence the way entrepreneurs work, there is also a wide variety of ways in which *individual* entrepreneurs work *within* these cultures. Culture is expressed in both the value *judgements* an individual makes and the value *system* of their wider community.

The analysis of culture falls properly within the domain of anthropology. The insights gained by anthropologists are of increasing interest to those who study business behaviour and performance. One of the driving forces behind this growth in interest has been the impressive economic growth achieved by countries in various parts of the world. Of particular interest at present are the 'tiger' economies of the Pacific Rim. The contribution that a range of structural, social and cultural factors have made to their success is widely debated.

This debate has been rekindled by the recent meltdown in many economies in this region. If cultural factors are called upon to explain long-term success, how might they be called upon to explain short-term collapse? How do 'cultural' and 'economic fundamentals' act together? Many are now suggesting that culture means little in the face of primary economic realities.

An analysis of culture is not a straightforward matter since a culture is not something that can be placed under a microscope. It is something we construct in order to explain the world rather than something we experience directly. There is a gulf between those who think that a culture can be examined as an objective reality and those who think it must be interpreted as something that impresses on our experience at a personal level. There is not scope within this book to consider all these issues. We must be content to note that entrepreneurs are necessarily the product of their cultures and that their cultures mould and influence their actions. What follows is meant to give a flavour of the *factors* which are significant to understanding entrepreneurship in a cultural setting and how they might be approached.

Religious beliefs

Religious belief is a very important factor in shaping a culture. It leads to a view of the world which will influence the individual's approach to entrepreneurship. The sociologist Max Weber famously associated the Industrial Revolution in Western Europe and the USA with the attitudes engendered by Protestant religious beliefs known as the 'Protestant work ethic'. Modern commentators speculate on the influence of Confucian 'discipline' to the success of Asian economies.

Personal relationships

The type and scope of personal relationships that a culture encourages will be a critical factor in the way entrepreneurial behaviour is expressed. A very important study by the Dutch sociologist of business, Geert Hofstede, analysed human relationships along four dimensions:

1. *Power distance*: the degree of authority people expect between managers and subordinates, and their willingness to accept that power is not distributed equally.
2. *Uncertainty avoidance*: in essence, this is the desire to be in a situation where uncertainty is minimised. Its opposite is a willingness to take risks.
3. *Collectivity*: the need to feel that one is part of a group and that one's actions are sanctioned by that wider group. Its opposite is a desire to exhibit individualistic behaviour.
4. *Masculinity*: the degree to which the culture emphasises 'masculine' values such as the acquisition of money, prioritising the material over the spiritual, a lack of concern versus a caring attitude, etc.

These four factors give a good account of how attitudes towards personal relationships give rise to different styles of entrepreneurial behaviour over a wide range of national cultures.

Attitude towards innovation

Innovation lies at the heart of entrepreneurship, yet to believe in innovation we have to see the world in a certain sort of way. We have to believe in a future that will be *different* from the present. We have to believe that we can act so as to *influence* the world and change it by our actions. Further, if we are to be encouraged to innovate, we must believe that it is appropriate that we are *rewarded* for our efforts in developing innovation.

Many West Europeans will regard these things as 'obvious'. However, they are beliefs which are sensitive to culture. While a West European sees the future as something which brings uncertainties 'towards' them, many cultures, for example, some in west Africa, have a different perspective. They draw a distinction between a 'potential time' which is full of things that *must* happen and a 'no-time' of things which might or might not happen. The potential time is *here and now*, a part of the present whereas no-time is not really a part of time at all. From this perspective, there really is no such thing as the 'future'.

Even if we believe in a future we may not believe that we can influence it. Physical science has often emphasised that the future is *determined*. Marxism is founded on a belief that the world evolves along a pre-destined path. If an innovation occurs, it occurs because it was meant to occur. Hence, it is not the result of personal inventiveness which might *not* have occurred, and if this is so, why then should we reward the innovator? The entrepreneurship scholar Mark Casson (1994) has suggested that such a cultural perspective might be significant to the development of entrepreneurship in the post-Communist world.

Networks

A network is the framework of individual and organisational relationships which form the stage upon which entrepreneurial performance is played. It is composed of personal and social contacts as well as economic relationships. A network is shaped by the culture in which it is formed.

The network does not just provide a route for people to sell things to each other. It is a conduit for information. A well-developed network is crucial if entrepreneurial behaviour is to express itself. It defines the terrain in which new business opportunities might be identified and assessed, and it provides a means by which contracts are agreed and risk might be evaluated and shared. It offers an escape route for people who do not think their investments are safe. This occurs not only through formal structures such as stock markets but also through informal confidences and relationships. The structure and functioning of such networks is sensitive to a wide range of cultural factors.

It is neither possible nor particularly useful to draw hard and fast rules about managing within a particular culture. However, the idea that a culture provides a perspective within which individuals work might suggest an approach. The entrepreneur must recognise that an individual's response to a particular situation will, to some extent, be shaped by cultural influences. This will affect the way they can be led and motivated. However, the entrepreneur must not forget that individuals are individuals with their own characteristics, and do not necessarily behave with a collective consciousness. Entrepreneurs will also recognise that their own decision making is the product of their cultural experiences. Recognition of these things is becoming increasingly important as the opportunities for entrepreneurial ventures become ever more international. In the global arena, the effective entrepreneur learns to use cultural differences to advantage rather than to be impeded by them.

Entrepreneurs who have built global concerns such as Rupert Murdoch (News International) and the late Rowland 'Tiny' Rowland (Lonhro) are renowned for their ability not just to manage people within one culture but to manage across cultures.

Summary of key ideas

- A wide variety of people can become entrepreneurs. Common backgrounds include inventors with new business ideas; managers unfulfilled by working in established organisations; displaced managers; and people excluded from the established economy.

- Whatever their background, successful entrepreneurs are characterised by being hard working and self-starting; setting high personal goals; having resilience and confidence in their abilities; being receptive to new ideas and being assertive in presenting them; being attuned to new opportunities, receptive to change and eager to learn; and being confident with power and demonstrating a commitment to others.

- Effective entrepreneurs use a variety of formal management skills combined with industry knowledge and personal motivation.
- The way entrepreneurs actually manage their ventures is dependent on the culture in which they operate. Good entrepreneurs are sensitive to cultural values.

Suggestions for further reading

Blanchflower, D.G. and **Oswald, A.J.** (1998) 'What makes an entrepreneur?', *Journal of Labour Economics*, Vol. 16, No.1, pp. 26–60.

Casson, M. (1994) 'Enterprise culture and institutional change in eastern Europe', in Buckley, P.J. and Ghauri, P.N. (eds), *The Economics of Change in East and Central Europe*, London: Academic Press.

Drucker, P.F. (1985) 'The discipline of innovation', *Harvard Business Review*, May-June, pp. 67–72.

Green, R., David, J., Dent, M. and **Tyshkovsky, A.** (1996) 'The Russian entrepreneur: A study of psychological characteristics', *International Journal of Entrepreneurial Behaviour and Research*, Vol. 2, No. 1, pp. 49–58.

Hisrich, R.D. and **Brush, C.** (1986) 'Characteristics of the minority entrepreneur', *Journal of Small Business Management*, Oct, pp. 1–8.

Hofstede, G. (1980a) *Culture's Consequences: International Differences in Work-Related Values*, London: Sage Publications.

Hofstede, G. (1980b) 'Motivation, leadership and organisation: do American theories apply abroad?' *Organisational Dynamics*, Summer, pp. 42–63.

Jones-Evans, D. (1996) 'Technical entrepreneurship, strategy and experience', *International Small Business Journal*, Vol. 14, No. 3, pp. 15–39.

Kuznetsov, A., McDonald, F. and **Kuznetsov, O.** (2000) 'Entrepreneurial qualities: A case from Russia', *Journal of Small Business Management*, Vol. 38, No. 1, pp. 101–7.

McClelland, D.C. (1987) 'Characteristics of successful entrepreneurs', *The Journal of Creative Behaviour*, Vol. 21, No. 3, pp. 219–33.

McClelland, D.C. and **Burnham, D.H.** (1976) 'Power is the great motivator', *Harvard Business Review*, Mar-Apr, pp. 100–10.

Morden, T. (1995) 'International culture and management', *Management Decision*, Vol. 33, No. 2, pp. 16–21.

Olson, S.F. and **Currie, H.M.** (1992) 'Female entrepreneurs: Personal value systems and business strategies in a male dominated industry', *Journal of Small Business Management*, January, pp. 49–57.

Phizacklea, A. and **Ram, M.** (1995) 'Ethnic entrepreneurship in comparative perspective', *International Journal of Entrepreneurial Behaviour and Research*, Vol. 1, No. 1, pp. 48–58.

Sui, Wai-Sum and **Martin, R.G.** (1992) 'Successful entrepreneurship in Hong Kong', *Long Range Planning*, Vol. 25, No. 6, pp. 87–93.

Williams, A. (1985) 'Stress and the entrepreneurial role', *International Small Business Journal*, Vol. 3, No. 4, pp. 11–25.

Selected case material

Wall Street goes Dutch on software

13 May 1988

Geoff Nairn on the Baan success story and its founders' unusual attitude towards money

It is the dream on which Silicon Valley is based: a good idea and a successful initial public offering turn a company's founders into billionaires overnight. But for Jan and Paul Baan, the two Dutch brothers who have built enterprise software company Baan into one of the hottest stocks on Wall Street, immense wealth holds little attraction.

Both are devout Calvinists and prior to Baan's IPO in 1995, the brothers transferred their majority stake in the company to a foundation they created to finance charitable work around the world. In the past two years, it has disbursed more than $150m (£90m). "We were afraid that if the business continued to grow we could be worth more than $100m (each) and we asked ourselves if we could handle that," says Jan Baan, the chief executive. Had the brothers not transferred their shares, both would be billionaires as the stake the foundation holds in Baan is worth about $4bn. "If I had to give my stake away today it would be very difficult," admits Mr Baan. "It is a thousand times easier to give away money before rather than after you get it."

Baan is one of the few big software companies that specialise in complex business software called enterprise resource planning (ERP) systems. The ERP market is booming and analysts predict it could treble in size from $10bn to more than $30bn in three years. "It is maybe the most attractive market in the IT industry," says Mr Baan.

The company likes to see itself as the "enfant terrible" of the ERP industry, driving innovation and challenging bigger players, in particular Germany's SAP. "Sometimes it seems like there is only SAP, but we have grown from being 10 times smaller (than SAP) a few years ago to just four times smaller today," he says.

Mr Baan started the company in 1978 and for 15 years it prospered quietly as a supplier of off-the-shelf manufacturing software based in the small Dutch town of Putten. In 1993, the company's fortunes were transformed when a US venture capital firm realised the enormous potential for Baan's software in the US and invested in the Dutch company. A successful IPO soon followed.

"People in the US are born with dollar signs in their eyes, but when we started we did not even know what 'IPO' meant," Mr Baan says. Baan revenues have grown at a compound annual rate of 75 per cent from $227m in 1995 to $685m in 1997. Wall Street believes there is plenty of room for growth as more organisations turn to Baan's ERP software to automate their business processes.

"The company has good products, a solid senior management team and plays in a rapidly expanding market," says US investment bank Salomon Smith Barney.

Put simply, what an ERP system does is to keep track of business transactions in the areas of finance, customer order management and manufacturing. To do this well requires a mass of "business rules" to be drawn up to describe the business processes and an army of consultants to help implement the rules. Consultancy fees can easily double the cost of an ERP project. Mr Baan says the average order for Baan software is around $400,000, but for larger ERP customers the cost can run to many millions of dollars and implementation may take several years.

Baan's largest customer is Boeing, the aircraft manufacturer, which in 1994 chose the Dutch company, then hardly known in the US, over established ERP suppliers SAP and Oracle. "Boeing is doing probably the biggest business process re-engineering implementation in the industry with 25,000 users," says Mr Baan.

The company is using Baan's software to reduce the lead times needed for aircraft from 16 months to just six and so hopefully leap-frog its European arch-rival Airbus Industrie.

"Baan is the cockpit of Boeing," says Mr Baan, referring to the software's ability to control myriad planning, distribution, manufacturing, logistics and accounting functions.

One of the traditional criticisms of ERP is the need to install or upgrade a complete system in one go, which creates big upheavals in organisations. Baan recently un-veiled a new component-based product suite that aims to do away with this approach by allowing customers to upgrade just parts of the system and at their own pace.

This practice is being copied by other ERP vendors and is particularly important in reaching smaller companies that baulk at the high costs of a traditional monolithic ERP system.

"The next gold mine is in this mid-market," says Mr Baan, who says smaller companies could account for half of Baan's revenue in two years. The company last month formed a division focused on such customers.

For all its rapid growth of recent years, Baan is still a small player in the business software industry, and so alliances and acquisitions are essential to extend its reach. It has invested in 10 companies in the past year alone. Baan's biggest partner is Microsoft and chairman Bill Gates last month announced the two companies' "common vision for the integrated enterprise". The agreement means Baan will use Microsoft technology in its component-based software and the two companies will collaborate on future Microsoft technology.

ERP has been described as the best software business Mr Gates does not own, and Mr Baan hopes to keep it that way by treating him as an ally rather than potential competitor. "Mr Gates will not go into this business – it's just too complex," he says.

Review questions

What are the characteristics and skills that Jan Baan has brought to his venture? How consistent do you feel his attitude towards money is with the drive for entrepreneurial success?

4 Making the move to entrepreneurship

Chapter overview

This chapter is concerned with an exploration of the economic, social and personal factors which encourage an individual to pursue an entrepreneurial career.

4.1 The supply of entrepreneurs

KEY LEARNING OUTCOME
An understanding of the forces which encourage and inhibit entrepreneurship.

If we look at any of the world's economies we will see a certain number of entrepreneurs operating within them. The exact number will depend on how we define entrepreneurship, but their importance to the economy within which they operate will be evident. They will be responsible for providing economic efficiency and bringing new innovations to the market. In mature economies, such as Western Europe and North America they are responsible for most new job creation. In the former Communist world, the emergence of an entrepreneurial class is a necessary prelude to establishing a market-driven economic order. The question is, what governs the number of entrepreneurs who will emerge at any given time?

If we assume that entrepreneurs are born, or that entrepreneurship is the result of inherent personality characteristics, then the supply of entrepreneurs must be fixed. The number will depend on the number of people who are impelled to pursue an entrepreneurial career. This might reflect deep-rooted cultural factors but it will be largely independent of external influences. On the other hand, if we assume that entrepreneurs are managers who have freely decided to become entrepreneurs, then the number of entrepreneurs at any one time will be sensitive to a variety of external factors.

A simple approach to explaining this uses a model in which there are two pools of labour: a *conventional* labour pool in which people take up paid employment, and an *entrepreneurial* pool in which people are pursuing an entrepreneurial career. Such a model assumes that there is a clear definition of what constitutes entrepreneurship and that it is distinct from 'ordinary' labour. These assumptions, while clearly artificial, do serve to make the model simpler. However, they can be relaxed and more complex models developed to reflect reality more closely. These more complex models still work on the same basic premise. Managers are assumed to make a choice between the two options: a 'conventional' career versus an 'entrepreneurial' one (see Fig. 4.1). The process of moving from the conventional labour pool to the entrepreneurial pool is known as *start-up*. The reverse process of moving from the entrepreneurial pool back to the conventional labour pool is *fall-out*. The choice will depend on the relative attractiveness of the two options as perceived by the individual manager.

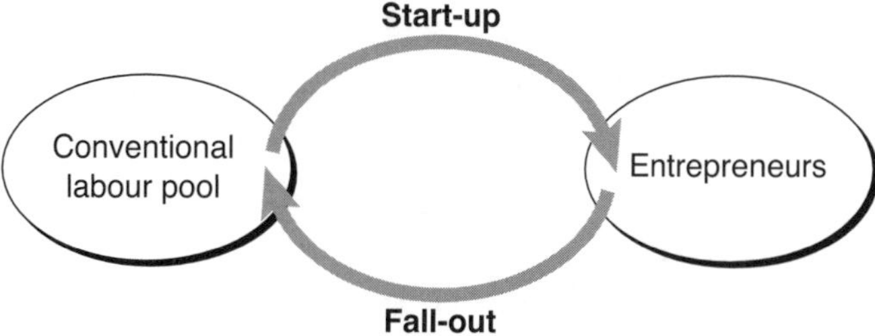

Fig. 4.1 The dynamics of entrepreneurial supply

Two forces are said to work driving the manager from the conventional labour pool to the entrepreneurial: pull factors and push factors. *Pull factors* are those which encourage managers to become entrepreneurs by virtue of the *attractiveness* of the entrepreneurial option. Some important pull factors include:

- the financial rewards of entrepreneurship;
- the freedom to work for oneself;
- the sense of achievement to be gained from running one's own venture;
- the freedom to pursue a personal innovation;
- a desire to gain the social standing achieved by entrepreneurs.

Push factors, on the other hand, are those which encourage entrepreneurship by making the conventional option *less attractive*. Push factors include:

- the limitations of financial rewards from conventional jobs;
- being unemployed in the established economy;
- job insecurity;
- career limitations and setbacks in a conventional job;
- the inability to pursue a personal innovation in a conventional job;
- being a 'misfit' in an established organisation.

The number of entrepreneurs operating at any one time will depend on the strength of the pull and push forces. If they are strong, then a large number of entrepreneurs will emerge. However, the supply of entrepreneurs will still be limited if *inhibitors* are operating. Inhibitors are things which prevent the potential entrepreneur from following an entrepreneurial route, no matter how attractive an option it might appear. Some important inhibitors include an inability to get hold of start-up capital; the high cost of start-up capital; the business environment presents high risks; legal restrictions on business activity; a lack of training for entrepreneurs; a feeling that the role of entrepreneur has a poor image; a lack of suitable human resources and personal inertia. Politicians and economic policy makers increasingly put the elimination of inhibitors to entrepreneurism at the top of their agenda. This is because they recognise the importance of increasing the number of entrepreneurs within the economy to stimulate growth. Figure 4.2 indicates the type of factors operating on managers considering a move to entrepreneurship.

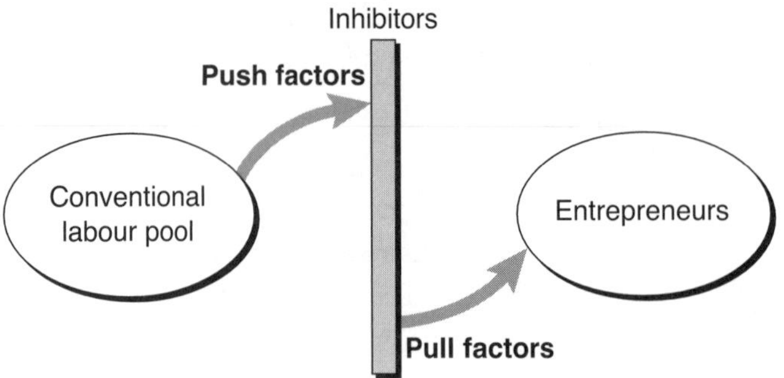

Fig. 4.2 Factors in entrepreneurial supply

It will be appreciated that life experiences and situations will have an impact on the decision to make the move into entrepreneurship. A study of business start-ups in Western Australia by Mazzarol *et al.* (1999) revealed that gender, employment by government and redundancy had an impact on an individual's desire to start a small business. A host of other factors including age, marital and family status and history of family business were less important.

Labour economists and psychologists studying the factors that are influential in encouraging entrepreneurship often use models based on sophisticated econometric and statistical methodologies. A full discussion of these is not possible in this book. The student who has an interest in these approaches though is referred to the Mazzarol study above, the Blanchflower and Oswald study discussed in section 3.1 and also a study on business start-up in the UK by Galt and Moenning (1996). Full bibliographic details are given in the suggestions for further reading at the end of this chapter.

4.2 Influences in the move to entrepreneurship

KEY LEARNING OUTCOME
An understanding of the factors involved in making the decision to become an entrepreneur.

Whatever the forces acting on the labour market to encourage entrepreneurship the decision to become an entrepreneur is an individual and personal one. We need to understand the factors involved in driving and shaping that decision in order to understand entrepreneurs. We are all active in an economy because we seek the rewards it brings. However, an economy is part of a wider pattern of social life and, although money is important, we seek more than purely financial rewards from the world in which we live. The decision to pursue an entrepreneurial career reflects a choice about the possibility of achieving satisfaction for a variety of economic and social needs.

We might classify the needs of individuals under three broad headings.

(i) *Economic needs*. These include the requirement to earn a particular amount of money and the need for that income to be stable and predictable. The amount desired will reflect the need for economic survival, existing commitments such as the home and family, and the pursuit of personal interests.

(ii) *Social needs*. These represent the desire a person has to be a part of, and to fit into, a wider group and their desire to be recognised and respected within that group. The satisfaction of social needs is reflected in the creation and maintenance of friendships and other social relationships.

(iii) *Developmental needs*. These relate to the desire a person has to achieve personal goals and to grow intellectually or spiritually.

A manager seeking to satisfy these needs is faced with a number of possibilities. There may be a choice between two or more conventional career options as well as the possibility of pursuing an entrepreneurial career. The entrepreneurial career itself may present itself in a number of ways. The manager's decision on which path to take will be based on the potential each option has to satisfy the needs they perceive for themselves (see Table 4.1). If the entrepreneurial route is seen to offer the best means of satisfying them then this will be chosen. However, making the move between different options will be sensitive to four factors: *knowledge* of entrepreneurial options open, the *possibility* for achieving them, the *risks* they present and *valence* – the way in which the potential entrepreneur is willing to play off different needs against each other. Figure 4.3 represents a model of the factors involved in making the move to entrepreneurship.

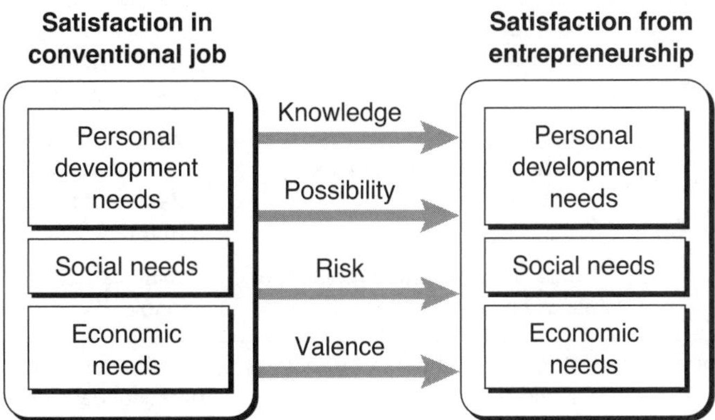

Fig. 4.3 A model of the move to entrepreneurship

Knowledge

The individual must *know* that the entrepreneurial option exists and they must be *aware* of its *potential*. In the case of establishing an entrepreneurial venture, the manager must be aware of a particular business opportunity and have an idea how it might be exploited profitably. After all, the desire to be entrepreneurial must be expressed through the actuality of running a *specific* business venture. It cannot exist in a vacuum.

Possibility

The individual must have the *possibility* of pursuing that option. This means that there must be no legal restrictions on them undertaking the venture (as there was in the former Communist bloc, for example). They must also have access to the necessary resources: start-up funding, human resources and access to the established network. Finally, they must have (or at least feel that they have) the necessary experience and skills in order to make a success of the venture.

Risk

The entrepreneur may have a detailed knowledge of a business opportunity and access to the resources necessary to initiate it. However, the entrepreneur will only make the move if the *risks* are seen as being acceptable. The entrepreneur must be comfortable with the level of risk the venture will entail, and he or she must be sure that the

Table 4.1 A comparison between the potential of entrepreneurial and conventional careers for satisfying economic, social and personal development needs

	Entrepreneurial career	Conventional career
Economic needs	Can offer the possibility of high financial rewards in the long term.	Financial rewards typically lower, but secure and predictable.
	However, income may be low in early stages and risks are high.	Risks are relatively low.
Social needs	Entrepreneur creates organisational change.	Established organisation usually provides good stage for making social relationships.
	A great deal of freedom to create and control network of social relationships.	However, manager may have only limited scope to control potential of social relationships formed.
	Social status of the entrepreneur usually high.	Social status of manager variable.
Personal development needs	Entrepreneur in control of own destiny.	Good potential to pursue personal development.
	Possibility of creating an 'entire new world'.	However, the direction of personal development may need to be compromised to overall organisational objectives and values.
	Venture may be powerful vehicle for personal development and expression of personal values. However, this is dependent on success of venture.	Career options limited and subject to internal competition.

potential rewards are such that it is worth taking the risk. It is useful to distinguish between the *actual* level of risk in the venture, and the level of risk that is *perceived* by the entrepreneur. These may be quite different. Entrepreneurs can often be over-confident and under assess risk. In addition to convincing themselves, entrepreneurs must convince any investors asked to back the venture that the risks are of an acceptable level.

Valence

The conventional career option and the option to start an entrepreneurial venture do not offer separate opportunities to satisfy economic, social and developmental needs, rather they offer a different *mix* of opportunities. The final factor which will influence the option selected is *valence*, that is, the way we are attracted to different options.

Different people are willing to play off different needs against one other in different ways. While many people 'play safe' and give priority to economic needs, by no means everyone does so. Some people prioritise social needs. Thus they may continue to work in an organisation they enjoy, with people they like, even though the option to move to a higher-paid job elsewhere is available to them. The artist starving in a garret or the religious aesthete are pursuing the need for personal development even though it is causing them economic hardship. Similarly, the entrepreneur may be so drawn to the possibilities of personal development offered by the entrepreneurial option, that they will pursue it even though it carries greater economic risks and perhaps, for the foreseeable future, a lower income than a conventional managerial career that is available to them.

An interesting example of valence in action is revealed by Khandwalla in a series of studies of Indian managers and entrepreneurs. Khandwalla (1984, 1985) defines a pioneering-innovative motive which leads individuals to 'make path-breaking achievements through the accomplishment of unique tasks'. This pioneering-innovative drive encourages individuals to pursue an entrepreneurial carreer even if the financial and personal risks are perceived to be very high.

Summary of key ideas

- The supply of entrepreneurs is determined by three sets of factors, namely *pull factors* which promote entrepreneurship as a positive option; *push factors* which drive people out of the established economy; and *inhibitors* which prevent the entrepreneurial option being taken up.
- Managers make the move to entrepreneurship after considering the way the option for an entrepreneurial career can satisfy *economic*, *social* and *self-development* needs.

Suggestions for further reading

Dandridge, T.C. and **Dziedziczak, I.** (1992) 'New private enterprise in the new Poland: Heritage of the past and challenges for the future', *Journal of Small Business Management*, Apr, pp. 104–9.

El-Namaki, M.S.S. (1988) 'Encouraging entrepreneurs in developing countries', *Long Range Planning*, Vol. 21, No. 4, pp. 98–106.

Gallagher, C. and **Miller, P.** (1991) 'New fast-growing companies create jobs', *Long Range Planning*, Vol. 24, No. 1, pp. 96–101.

Galt, V. and **Moenning, C.** (1996) 'An analysis of self-employment using UK census of population data', *International Journal of Entrepreneurial Behaviour and Research*, Vol. 2, No. 3, pp. 82–8.

Gilad, B. and **Levine, P.** (1986) 'A behavioural model of entrepreneurial supply', *Journal of Small Business Management*, Oct, pp. 45–53.

Khandwalla, P.N. (1984) 'Pioneering-Innovative (PI) management', *International Studies of Management and Organisation*, Vol. XIV, Nos 2–3, pp. 99–132.

Khandwalla, P.N. (1985) 'Pioneering-Innovative management: A basis for excellence', *Organization Studies*, Vol. 6, No. 2, pp. 161–83.

Kiselev, D. (1990) 'New forms of entrepreneurship in the USSR', *Journal of Small Business Management*, July, pp. 76–80.

Mazzarol, T., Volery, T., Doss, N. and **Thien, V.** (1999) 'Factors influencing small business start-ups', *International Journal of Entrepreneurial Behaviour and Research*, Vol. 5, No. 2, pp. 48–63.

Selected case material

The generation game

16 December 1999

Specialist companies nurturing dot-com start-ups offer a bewildering range of support to these entrepreneurs, says **Katharine Campbell**

In the wacky, weird world of internet start-ups, the latest fad is the incubator. Six months ago, the UK had virtually none. Today there are perhaps 100 outfits broadly peddling a service that nurtures embryo dot-coms.

It is bewildering for the aspiring entrepreneur. Many are still in the formative stages – businesses as untried as their prospective customers.

At the web address of one of the best-funded, antfactory, the large red ant is still only "Marching Soon" – despite the $40m (£25m) of backing already assembled.

Christopher Spray, partner at venture capitalist Atlas Venture, says: "Everything is still very much at the stage of the cheque being in the mail."

People are almost making it up as they go along. Take Azeem Azhar, behind esouk.com. "We are not 'incubating'. We were accelerating', but then McKinsey [which has set up an operation called Accelerator@McKinsey] did that. Now we think we may be 'generating'."

So what exactly are incubators (or accelerators or generators)? Why are there so many of them? And which start-ups need them?

The UK Business Incubation Centre, sponsored by the Department of Trade and Industry, defines business incubation as broadly involving workspace, and an "instructive and supportive environment". It, however, has yet to catch up with the internet, making reference to just one dot-com incubator on its web site.

The proliferation in services is one aspect of the feeding frenzy surrounding the web. The success of the first wave of internet entrepreneurs has unleashed a rush of me-too companies who are candidates for incubation, and a slew of investors desperate for a piece of the action.

The argument for incubating dot-com start-ups is particularly strong, according to Nick Greenspan at bainlab, an incubator set up at Bain, the global consultancy. "The internet is a race to market. Anything you can do to speed up the process creates value."

The system is developing rather differently from the US.

There, a few well-established internet incubators – such as IdeaLab, founded by Bill Gross – have made their mark. This year there has also been a spate of new ones, according to Rick Summer at vcapital.com, a specialist information provider, partly spawned by the scramble to get into deals ever earlier because of sky-high valuations.

Yet there are already proportionately far more internet incubators in the UK – partly because a genuine gap exists. The business angel community is far less developed; there are fewer really experienced early stage venture capitalists, and the extensive web of specialist lawyers and other advisers is lacking.

So, as Andrew Hawkins, a partner at Palamon Capital Partners, says: "All these UK outfits appear to make sense. But some are actually hopeless."

Michael Elias, chief executive of venture capitalist Kennet, adds: "The least successful model in my mind is someone offering shared office space, and access to a photocopier. That's not very different from Regus [the serviced office provider]. That's not what is blocking development of hot companies in Europe; What is needed is access to really good strategy and networks."

Others provide money, but not much else – and money, in the current frenzy, is the easy part. New Media Spark, which listed on Aim, the alternative investment market, in October, and has seen its shares soar, muddied its incubator credentials by making its first investment in an already quoted company.

In the absence of any track record for incubator businesses, prospective applicants need to scrutinise the backgrounds of the individuals involved – not least because "what you do depends a lot on where you come from", as Mr Greenspan puts it. "My bias is that I think strategy is the most important issue".

Rob Bier, chief executive of antfactory and a former consultant, adds: "We are very focused on transferring best practice from the hard world of industrial economics to the dot-coms.

The in-house management consultant incubators such as bainlab and Accelerator@McKinsey have attracted some scepticism, because, reluctant as they are to admit it, much of their motivation lies in the need to try to halt the haemorrhaging of their best people to dot-com start-ups.

Two of the three current bainlab projects are by former Bain staff, although Mr Greenspan insists bainlab was started primarily because it was "a great business opportunity".

Former investment bankers such as Stewart Dodd and his team at Brainspark have a different slant, illustrated by his role in helping his first company Petspark.com forge a "global partnership" with – and receive a significant investment from – Pets.com of the US. He, like others, will pursue the Bill Gross model, generating ideas and finding people to execute them.

Meanwhile, the Hammond brothers at Ideas Hub say their strength is knowing first hand that the process is "like an SAS assault course". In fact it was a course they themselves did not quite stay.

Taxi Interactive, their online shopping company, is now managed in-house by Chrysalis, which owns a 43 per cent stake. "It was a great idea but management needed to be strengthened," says one observer.

Further confusion lies in the blurring between incubators and venture capitalists. The well-funded incubators look rather like venture capitalists in disguise, while venture capitalists are backing people at ever earlier stages. Mr Spray thinks that "the strongest ideas and teams probably don't need the services of an incubator".

Robert Norton at Atlas-funded clickmango.com had been at America Online for two years, and his partner at Disney for five. "We felt we had enough experience, although we have banking and consultant friends who are slightly bewildered about where to start."

Incubators can be expensive in terms of equity, too. One participant complains the business is "getting a lousy name with people taking 10 per cent of a company just for physical space".

Many cheerfully admit to taking 35 to 40 per cent. "That is a huge structural problem for a venture capitalist if someone has given up that much of the equity and not raised enough money to move the ball significantly down the field," according to Mr Spray.

In other words, picking the right incubating deal, particularly at the height of this fad, is itself something of a challenge.

California dreams cross over

6 April 2000

All three of the US internet operations regarded as role models by European counterparts have now crossed the Atlantic, writes **Katharine Campbell**

When one UK venture capitalist recently learnt of plans by Idealab, one of America's best known internet incubators, to expand into Europe, he was slightly sceptical: "They will first have to work out how to clone Bill Gross."

Mr Gross, who set up Idealab in Pasadena, California, in 1996, has made his name by hatching ideas – distinguishing him from most venture capitalists who back someone else's company at business-plan stage at the very earliest.

The outfit's bestknown investments – which are nurtured with a series of operational and financial support from cradle to initial public offering and beyond – include eToys, GoTo.com, and Tickets.com.

Cloning is not one of the services on offer in Pasadena, but this week Larry Gross, Bill's younger brother, was appointed head of Idealab Europe.

The London office, which marks Idealab's first steps outside the US, aims to spawn European start-ups with a particular focus on the mobile internet area, as well as to provide international support for companies in the US portfolio.

There has been an explosion of activity in Europe in the past nine months of vehicles loosely termed incubators. The more savvy among them say they want to emulate what they see as their US counterparts – with Idealab, CMGI and Internet Capital Group the most frequently cited role models.

No wonder, for although success in Europe may be far from assured, they have certainly been achieving some eye-watering valuations in the US – before taking a distinct battering in the turbulence of the past few days.

Floated in 1994, CMGI still has a market capitalisation of about $24bn (£15bn) – after hitting a high of more than $40bn at the beginning of the year. Internet Capital Group, which went public last summer, was up at $50.6bn at one point, although it is now at a more modest $18bn.

Idealab, meanwhile, recently raised $1bn in private equity from investors including Dell Computer and Japanese internet group Hikari Tsushin. While executives refused to comment, it was thought – at least before the latest correction – to be preparing a multibillion-dollar initial public offering.

Valuations aside, however, would-be imitators are wrong to think the three are all that similar.

While Idealab's trademark lies in the genesis of its own ideas, CMGI – whose executives are faintly irritated by the mass of UK incubators claiming to resemble it – is a very different animal. With its origins in an outfit called College Marketing Group founded in 1968, it was the subject of a buy-out in 1986, led by David Wetherell, CMGI's current chief executive, who began to transform a niche direct marketing company into today's network of more than 65 internet businesses.

A recent Goldman Sachs research report calls it an "opervesting" company, denoting the fact that it behaves both as an operating company and a venture capitalist.

Under the former guise, it takes majority stakes in companies ranging from Engage Technologies, a marketing solutions company, to AltaVista, the internet search engine, which is scheduled to float this month. It also has a venture capital affiliate, @Ventures, which takes minority positions in internet start-ups. Its pitch is the power of the synergies it says it can bring across its network.

While it is sometimes perceived as being focused on the currently unfashionable business-to-consumer arena, its five areas of concentration also include internet enabling tools and technology, and business-to-business vertical exchanges.

CMGI has had a presence in Europe for more than two years – even if it has so far kept pretty quiet about it. Marcus Bicknell, European president, says that recruitment has been tough, but he hopes to gear up significantly in the next few months.

He recently made the first acquisition in Germany – a majority interest in Adtech, an advertising service provider, which is to be integrated with Adforce, an existing portfolio company.

Internet Capital Group is different again, with its tight focus on developing business-to-business e-commerce companies across traditional industries. It set up in Europe last November – a market it believes is even more promising than the US on account of the fragmented nature of many of the region's supply chains.

Investing across most stages of a company's development, it likes to compare itself to an embryonic General Electric, distinguished by the "depth" of its in-house resources. For instance, it has built what Stephen Duckett, joint European managing director, claims is the largest headhunting firm in the business-to-business arena: 30 executives handling about 120 simultaneous searches worldwide.

It also stresses the operational experience it can offer its partner companies. Mary Coleman, former chief executive of Baan, the troubled Dutch software group, has for example popped up working for ICG in San Francisco.

Local competitors will be watching to see which model proves most amenable to international cloning – always assuming that the stock markets do not act as a brake on expansive ambitions.

Capitalising on women entrepreneurs

11 November 1999

Ministers hope loans aimed at aspiring businesswomen will encourage more start-ups, writes **Rosemary Bennett**

Ministers are nearing completion of a deal with the Financial Services Authority and a number of leading banks to offer commercial loans and other financial packages specifically designed for women.

Baroness Jay, minister for women, has highlighted access to capital as one of the main stumbling blocks preventing women from starting their own businesses in greater numbers.

She hopes improved access to commercial loans through the scheme, combined with other projects outlined in Tuesday's pre-Budget report such as grants bridging the gap between benefits and business start ups, will help boost the number of women setting up on their own.

These and other policy developments are due to be discussed at a two-day seminar by the Smith Institute, the Labour think tank, starting today at 11 Downing Street.

Hosted by Gordon Brown, the chancellor, and under the patronage of Cherie Booth, the prime minister's wife, the seminar will look at the example of the US which has led the way in women's enterprise.

Hillary Clinton hosted a similar event in the WhiteHouse earlier this year. Half of all new businesses in the US are led by women. Government research indicates that, by next year, more than half employees in small businesses will work for women-owned companies.

That compares with only 30 per cent of new businesses being set up by women in Britain and 25 per cent of all existing businesses run by women.

In the US, commercial loan packages for female entrepreneurs are flourishing. Wells Fargo launched a $1bn (£600m) loan fund in 1996 and had such success the loan pool has increased to $10bn.

Baroness Jay thinks this sort of scheme would give female entrepreneurship a boost here.

"We are working very hard with the FSA and some of the private sector banks to try to create a financial package which would enable women, both in their commercial life and their private life, to have access to money on amuch more gender-friendly basis," she said. The scheme should be in place before Christmas.

Some of the other policy initiatives Baroness Jay has been pushing popped up in Tuesday's pre-Budget report, including a £30m package to promote enterprise in deprived areas in "incubator" business centres, which house a number of small firms with advisory services on hand. That cash will also fund a network of business mentors.

However, Baroness Jay is pleased that the chancellor has agreed to consider a system of grants to bridge the gap between unemployment benefits and business start ups, another idea borrowed from the US. The scheme should help attract more venture capitalists.

"If somebody is good enough to get a public sector grant for their business, that should be seen by venture capitalists as a form of underwriting," she said.

Among US ideas that may be examined at this week's seminar, is a proposed tax credit giving companies 25 per cent rebate on what they spend building and running creches and nurseries.

In her address, Baroness Jay will highlight the problem of women's failure fully to use their skills in the labour market.

"Women may be in the labour force but they are certainly not achieving their full potential," she will say.

"High shares of educated women are found in marginal part-time jobs. Indeed a recent survey showed that 18 per cent of British mothers with a tertiary education work under 20 hours a week."

"There is a widespread general mismatch between women's skills and what they are actually doing, which means that, for the government, there is a very serious issue about skilled, highly educated women dropping out of the labour force completely or working in jobs where they talents cannot be used to the full."

Review questions

1 Discuss the role of incubator organisations in encouraging entrepreneurial start-up.

2 How might push, pull and inhibitor factors account for the under-representation of women entrepreneurs?

3 How might the changing relationship between entrepreneurs and venture capitalists affect the profile of pull and push factors?

5 The nature of business opportunity

Chapter overview

This chapter presents an examination of the starting point for the entrepreneurial process, that is, the ***business opportunity****. Entrepreneurs are* ***motivated*** *by the pursuit of opportunity. A analogy is developed through which a business opportunity can be pictured as a gap in the landscape created by existing business activities. The different types of* ***innovation*** *that can fill that gap and so offer a means of* ***exploiting*** *opportunity are considered. It is recognised that exploiting opportunities creates new* ***wealth*** *which can be* ***distributed*** *to the venture's stakeholders.*

5.1 The landscape of business opportunity

KEY LEARNING OUTCOME
An understanding of what comprises a business opportunity.

All living systems have *needs*. At a minimum, animals need food and oxygen, plants need sunlight and water. Human beings are different from many living organisms in that we are not content simply to survive using the things nature places to hand. We build highly structured societies and within these societies we join together to create *organisations*. Human organisations take on a variety of forms. However, they all exist to co-ordinate *tasks*. This co-ordination allows people to specialise their activities and to collaborate in the production of a wide variety of *goods* (a word taken to mean both physical products and services). Goods have *utility* because they can satisfy human needs. The products produced in the modern world can be used to satisfy a much more sophisticated range of human wants and needs, and to satisfy them more proficiently than can the raw materials to be found in nature.

An organisation is an arrangement of *relationships* in that it exists in the spaces between people. Organisations exist to address human needs. Their effectiveness in doing this is a function of the form adopted by the organisation and the way it works. As the number of people involved increases, so too do the ways of organising them. In fact, the possibilities quickly become astronomical. This leads to a simple conclusion: whatever the organisational arrangement is at the moment, there is probably a *better* way of doing things! Even if, by chance, we did find the optimum arrangement, it would not stay so for long. The world is not static. Technological progress would quickly change the rules.

Ideas from classical economics suggest that the optimal (that is, the most productive) organisation is one in which individuals work to maximise their own satisfaction from the goods available and freely exchange those goods between themselves. Such behaviour is said to be *economically rational*. While this provides a very powerful framework for thinking about economic relations it is clearly only an approximation. People gain satisfaction from a variety of things, not all are exchanged through markets (how much does a beautiful sunset, or a personal sense of achievement 'cost'?). Nor is it obviously the case that individuals will maximise their own utility without any consideration towards their fellows. We can, and often do, act from altruistic motives.

Even if we *wanted* to act rationally, we probably could not. We simply do not have access to the information we would need to make decisions on purely rational lines. If all the information *were* available, individuals would still be limited in their ability to process and analyse it. In response to this, some economists talk of *satisficing* behaviour. That is, individuals aim to make the best decision available given a desire to address a wider sphere of concerns than purely economic self-satisfaction and taking into account limitations in knowledge.

An opportunity, then, is the possibility to do things both *differently* from and *better* than how they are being done at the moment. In economic terms, *differently* means an innovation has been made. This might take the form of offering a new product or of organising the company in a different way. *Better* means the product offers a *utility* in terms of an ability to satisfy human needs, that existing products do not. The new organisational form must be more *productive*, i.e. more efficient at using resources than existing organisational forms. Yet the decisions as to what is different and whether it is better are not made by economic robots. Both entrepreneurs and the consumers who buy what they offer are social beings who engage in satisficing behaviour. They must also base their decisions on the knowledge they have to hand, and their ability to use it. Furthermore, they make their decisions while following the rules they have laid down for themselves and the rules of the culture that shapes their lives.

We may think of business opportunity as being rather like a *landscape* representing the possibilities open to us. As we look across the landscape we will see open ground, untouched and full of new potential. We may see areas which are built up, leaving few new opportunities to be exploited. We will see other areas which are built up but where the buildings are old and decrepit, waiting to be pulled down, and something new built in their places. Effective entrepreneurs know the landscape in which they are operating. They know where the spaces are and how they fit between the built-up areas. They know which buildings can be pulled down and which are best left standing. Critically, they know where to move in and build themselves.

5.2 Innovation and the exploitation of opportunity

KEY LEARNING OUTCOME
An appreciation that innovation is the key to exploiting opportunity.

A business opportunity, therefore, is the *chance* to do something differently and better. An innovation is a *way* of doing something differently and better. Thus an innovation is a *means* of exploiting a business opportunity. Innovation has a definite meaning in economics. All goods (whether physical products or services) are regarded as being made up of three factors: *natural raw materials, physical and mental labour* and *capital* (money). An innovation is a new combination of these three things. Entrepreneurs, as innovators, are people who create new combinations of these factors and then present them to the market for assessment by consumers. This is a technical conceptualisation of what innovation is about. It does not give the practising entrepreneur much of a guide to what innovation to make, or how to make it, but it should warn that innovation is a much broader concept than just *inventing* new products. It also involves bringing them to market. Some important areas in which valuable innovations might be made will be discussed below.

New products

One of the most common forms of innovation is the creation of a new product. This may exploit an established technology or it may be the outcome of a whole new technology. The new product may offer a radically new way of doing something or it may simply be an improvement on an existing theme. David Packard built a scientific instrumentation and information processing business empire, Hewlett-Packard, based on advanced scientific developments. Frank Purdue (founder of the major US food business Purdue Chickens), on the other hand, built his business by innovating in an industry whose basic product was centuries, if not millennia, old: the farmed chicken. Whatever the basis of innovation, the new product must offer the customer an *advantage* if it is to be successful: a better way of performing a task, or of solving a problem, or a better quality product.

Products are not simply a physical tool for achieving particular ends. They can also have a role to play in satisfying *emotional* needs. *Branding* is an important aspect of this. A brand name reassures the consumer, draws ready-made associations for them and provides a means of making a personal statement. The possibility of innovations being made through branding should not be overlooked. The English entrepreneur, Richard Branson, for example, has been active in using the Virgin brand name on a wide variety of product areas following its initial success in the airline business. To date, it has been used to create a point of difference on, among other things, record labels, soft drinks and personal finance products.

New services

A service is an *act* which is offered to undertake a particular task or solve a particular problem. Services are open to the possibility of new ideas and innovation just as much as physical products. For example, the American entrepreneur, Frederick Smith, created the multi-million dollar international business, Federal Express, by realising a better way of moving parcels between people.

Like physical products, services can be supported by the effective use of branding. In fact, it is beneficial to stop thinking about 'products' and 'services' as distinct types of business and to recognise that *all* offerings have product and service aspects. This is important because it is possible to innovate by adding a 'customer service' component to a physical product to make it more attractive to the user. Similarly, developments in product technology allow new service concepts to be innovated.

New production techniques

Innovation can be made in the way in which a product is manufactured. Again, this might be by developing an existing technology or by adopting a new technological approach. A new production technique provides a sound basis for success if it can be made to offer the end-user new benefits. It must either allow them to obtain the product at lower cost, or to be offered a product of higher or more consistent quality, or to be given a better service in the supply of the product. An important example here is Rupert Murdoch's drive for change in the way newspapers were produced in the 1980s. Production is not just about technology. Increasingly new production 'philosophies' such as just-in-time (JIT) supply and total quality management (TQM) are providing platforms for profitable innovation.

New operating practices

Services are delivered by operating practices which are, to some extent, routinised. These routines provide a great deal of potential for entrepreneurial innovation. Ray Kroc, the founder of McDonald's, for example, noted the advantages to be gained in standardising fast-food preparation. As with innovations in the production of physical products, innovation in service delivery must address customer needs and offer them improved benefits, for example easier access to the service, a higher quality service, a more consistent service, a faster or less time-consuming service, a less disruptive service.

New ways of delivering the product or service to the customer

Customers can only use products and services they can access. Consequently, getting distribution right is an essential element in business success. It is also something which offers a great deal of potential for innovation. This may involve the *route* taken (the path the product takes from the producer to the user), or the *means* of managing its journey.

A common innovation is to take a more direct route by cutting out distributors or middle-men. A number of successful entrepreneurial ventures have been established on the basis of getting goods directly to the customer. This may be an indirect way into high street retailing, for example Richard Thalheimer in the USA with The Sharper Image catalogue or the Littlewoods chain in the UK. Another approach is to focus on the distribution chain and specialise in a particular range of goods. This type of 'category busting' focus has allowed Charles Lazarus to build the toy retail outlet Toys "Я" Us into a worldwide concern.

New means of informing the customer about the product

People will only use a product or service if they *know* about it. Demand will not exist if the offering is not properly promoted to them. Promotion consists of two parts: a *message*, what is said, and a *means*, the route by which that message is delivered. Both the message and the means present latitude for inventiveness in the way they are approached. Communicating with customers can be expensive and entrepreneurs, especially when their ventures are in an early stage, rarely have the resources to invest in high-profile advertising and public relations campaigns. Therefore, they are encouraged to develop new means of promoting their products.

Many entrepreneurs have proved to be particularly skilful at getting 'free' publicity. Anita and Gordon Roddick, for example, have used very little formal advertising for their toiletries retailer The Body Shop. However, the approach adopted by the organisation, and its stated corporate values, have made sure that The Body Shop has featured prominently in the widespread commentary on corporate responsibility that has regularly appeared in the media. As a result, awareness of their organisation is high and consumer attitudes towards it are positive.

New ways of managing relationships within the organisation

Any organisation has a wide variety of communication channels running through it. The performance of the organisation will depend to a great extent on the effectiveness of its internal communication channels. These communication channels are guided (formally at least) by the organisation's *structure*. The structure of the organisation offers considerable scope for value creating innovations. Of particular note here is the development of the *franchise* as an organisational form. This structure, which combines the advantages of small business ownership with the power of integrated global organisation, has been a major factor in the growth of many entrepreneurial ventures, including The Body Shop retail chain, the Holiday Inn hotel group and the McDonald's fast food chain.

New ways of managing relationships between organisations

Organisations sit in a complex web of relationships to each other. The way they communicate and relate to each other is very important. Many entrepreneurial organisations have made innovation in the way in which they work with other organisations (particularly customers) into a key part of their strategy. The business services sector has been particularly active in this respect.

The advertising agency Saatchi and Saatchi, founded by the brothers Charles and Maurice in 1970, did not build its success solely on the back of making good advertisements. The brothers also realised that managing the relationship with the client was important. An advertising agency is, in a sense, a supplier of a service like any other, but its 'product' is highly complex, expensive and its potential to generate business for the client is unpredictable. Thus advertising is a high-risk activity. The brothers realised that if advertising were to be managed properly, the agency had to become an integral part of the management team within the client organisation and not just to create advertisements but to work with them at resolving the issues generated by advertising, as well as helping them to exploit its potential. In effect, they broke down the barrier between their organisation and their customers.

Multiple innovation

An entrepreneurial venture does not have to restrict itself to just one innovation or even one type of innovation. Success can be built on a *combination* of innovations: for example, a new product delivered in a new way with a new message.

5.3 High- and low-innovation entrepreneurship

KEY LEARNING OUTCOME
An understanding of the distinction between high and low innovation approaches to exploiting business opportunities.

Even though innovation has been defined as a key characteristic of the entrepreneurship and has been used as one of the factors that distinguishes the entrepreneurial venture from the small business, particular entrepreneurial ventures differ in terms of the degree of innovation they adopt. Manimala (1999) in a major study of entrepreneurship in India has drawn a distinction between what he refers to as *high* and *low pioneering–innovativeness* (PI) entrepreneurship. These two types can be distinguished on the basis of a variety of strategic characteristics, the selection of which reflect the innovation discovered, the business opportunity and resources available and the personal preferences of the entrepreneur. These characteristics are summarised (with modification) in Table 5.1.

5.4 Opportunity and entrepreneurial motivation

KEY LEARNING OUTCOME
An understanding of how the effective entrepreneur is motivated by business opportunity.

Thus an opportunity is a gap in a market or the possibility of doing something both differently and better; and an innovation presents a means of filling that market gap, that is, a way of pursuing the opportunity. Such definitions, while they capture the *nature* of opportunity and innovation from both an economic and a managerial perspective, do little to relate the *way* in which opportunity figures in the working life of the entrepreneur. Opportunity *motivates* entrepreneurs. Therefore, it is the thing that attracts their attention and draws their actions. But good entrepreneurs are not blindly subject to opportunities; they take control of them. It is important to understand how entrepreneurs should relate to business opportunities and allow themselves to be motivated by them.

Table 5.1 High and low pioneering–innovativeness entrepreneurial strategies

Strategic characteristics	Low PI entrepreneurship	High PI entrepreneurship
Idea management	Tend to rely on local contacts and ideas from existing products.	Tend to be more inventive and obtain ideas from a wider source, perhaps internationally.
	Strategic vision starts limited but may evolve over time.	Strategic vision ambitious from the start.
	Stick to and repeat earlier successes.	Eager for new ideas.
Management of autonomy	Prefer to manage autonomy by working with close-knit team.	Will appoint individuals with relevant expertise even if personal knowledge of them is limited.
	Develop own expertise through experience.	Will develop expertise through employment opportunities and formal training.
Management of competition	Tend to stick to what is tried and trusted. Avoid competing when experience is limited.	Will undertake, new, higher-risk competitive moves.
	Tend to build good working relationship with limited number of key customers (say, as sub-contractor).	Greater drive to bring new customers on board. Emphasis on product, quality and service.
Growth strategy	Desire for growth but rely on clear and unhindered market opportunity to achieve growth.	Desire for growth but more willing to actively compete for market space.
	Unlikely to make risky diversification moves.	More likely to make risky diversification moves.
Human resource management	Tend to rely on known, experienced workers.	Experts brought on board as and when needed.
	More likely to rely on directions and routines as a means of control.	More likely to rely on strategy, culture to exert control.
Risk management	Limit risk taking. Tried and trusted route.	More likely to manage risk through information, e.g. market researching.
	Seeking of institutional and governmental support for expansion moves	Also keen for institutional and governmental support, but more willing to make unsupported risky moves.
Network development	Mainly local. Keen to use informal as much as formal networks.	Broader base and range of networking. Use local base for further expansion. Also use informal networks, but more adept at managing formal networks.

Entrepreneurs are attuned to opportunity

Entrepreneurs are always on the look-out for opportunities. They scan the business landscape looking for new ways of creating value. As we have seen, this value can take the form of new wealth, a chance to pursue an agenda of personal development or to create social change. Opportunities are the 'raw material' out of which the entrepreneur creates an 'entire new world'. To be motivated by opportunity entails the recognition that the current situation does not represent the best way of doing things; that the status quo does not exhaust possibilities. While this may be a spur to move forward, it could also create motivational problems. If we are too conscious of *what might be*, do we not become disillusioned with *what is*? Can the entrepreneur ever get where he or she is going?

There is no simple answer to this question. There are certainly some entrepreneurs who are driven forward because they are not satisfied with the present. However, many, while not losing their motivation for what might be, are still able to enjoy what is. Some gain satisfaction, not from reaching the end-points of their activity, but in the *journey* itself. Others make sure they create space for themselves to take pride in what they have achieved, as well as looking forward to what they might achieve. Entrepreneurs must be aware of their motivation. As well as knowing *what* they want to achieve they must be aware of *why* they want to achieve it and why they will enjoy the *process* of achieving it.

Opportunity must take priority over innovation

It is easy to get excited over a new idea. However, an innovation, no matter how good it is, should be secondary to the market opportunity that it aims to exploit. The best ideas are those which are inspired by a clear need in the marketplace rather than those that result from uninformed invention. Many innovations which have been 'pushed' by new product or service possibilities rather than 'pulled' by unsatisfied customer needs have gone on to be successful. However, without a clear understanding of why customers buy and what they are looking for, this can be a very hit-or-miss process. Mistakes are punished quickly and they can be expensive. Failure is certainly demotivating, but this is not to suggest that new product ideas should necessarily be rejected. It does mean that they provide the inspiration to assess their market potential, not to rush the idea straight into the market.

Identifying real opportunities demands knowledge

One of the misconceptions that many people entertain about entrepreneurs is that they are the 'wanderers' of the business world. The notion that they drift between industries, opportunistically picking off the best ideas missed by less astute and responsive 'residents', is widely held. This idea can be traced back to the view that the entrepreneur is a 'special' type of person. If they are entrepreneurial by character, then they will be entrepreneurs wherever they find themselves. So, they can move at will between different areas of business taking their ability with them. Such an idea is not only wrong, it is dangerous because it fails to recognise the knowledge and experience that entrepreneurs must have if they are to be successful in the industries within which they operate.

Some important elements of this knowledge include knowledge of:

- the technology behind the product or service supplied;
- how the product or service is produced;
- customers' needs and the buying behaviour they adopt;
- distributors and distribution channels;
- the human skills utilised within the industry;
- how the product or service might be promoted to the customer;
- competitors: who they are, the way they act and react.

This knowledge is necessary if good business opportunities are to be identified and properly assessed. Acquisition of this knowledge requires exposure to the relevant industry, an active learning attitude and time. Most entrepreneurs are actually very experienced in a particular industry sector and confine their activities within that sector. Many have acquired this experience by working as a manager in an existing organisation. This 'incubation' period can be very important to the development of entrepreneurial talent.

However, industry-specific knowledge does not produce entrepreneurs on its own. It must be supplemented with general business skills and people skills. If an entrepreneur with these skills were to be transplanted between industries, these skills would still be valuable but they would be unlikely to come into their own until the entrepreneur had learnt enough about the new business area to be confident in making good decisions. It is interesting to note that entrepreneurs who do move between industries demonstrate a skill in drawing out and using the expertise that exists within those different industries. Richard Branson, for example, is renowned for his ability to work effectively with industry specialists.

5.5 The opportunity to create wealth

KEY LEARNING OUTCOME
An appreciation of the role of wealth creation in the entrepreneurial process.

Entrepreneurs can often become well-known public figures. They are of public interest because they have been *successful*, and this success has often made them quite wealthy. Their success is of interest in its own right, but their wealth may give them a good deal of social (and perhaps political) power. So while entrepreneurship, and the desire to be an entrepreneur, cannot usually be reduced to a simple desire to make money, it must not be forgotten that making money *is* an important element in the entrepreneurial process.

Business success, and the accumulation of wealth this brings, creates a number of possibilities for the entrepreneur and their ventures to dispose of that wealth.

Reinvestment

If the entrepreneur wishes to grow the business they have initiated then it will demand continued investment. Some of this may be provided by external investors but it will also be expected, and may well be financially advantageous, that the business reinvest some of the profits it has generated.

Rewarding stakeholders

The entrepreneurial venture is made up of more than just the entrepreneur. Entrepreneurs exist in a tight network of relationships with a number of other internal and external stakeholders who are asked to give their support to the venture. They may be asked to take risks on its behalf. In return, they will expect to be properly rewarded. Financial success offers the potential for the entrepreneur to reward them, not just financially, but in other ways as well.

Investment in other ventures

If reinvestment within the venture has taken place, and the stakeholders have been rewarded for their contributions, and there are still funds left over then alternative investments might be considered. The entrepreneur may start an entirely new venture (an option which can be particularly tempting to the serial entrepreneur when his or her business has matured and they feel that its initial excitement has gone). Another option is that of providing investment support to another entrepreneur. Successful, established entrepreneurs will often act as 'business angels' and offer their knowledge and experience, as well as spare capital, to young ventures.

Personal reward

Some of the value created by the entrepreneur and their venture (though by no means *all* of it) can be taken and used for personal consumption. Funding a comfortable lifestyle is part of this. It may be regarded by the entrepreneur as a just reward for taking risks and putting in the effort the success has demanded. Some entrepreneurs may also be quite keen to put their money into altruistic projects, for example they may sponsor the arts or support social programmes. This may reflect their desire to make a mark on the world outside the business sphere which is part of their desire to leave the world different from the way in which they found it.

Keeping the score

For many entrepreneurs, money is not so important in itself. It is just a way of quantifying what they have achieved; a way of keeping the score on their performance, as it were. The money value of their venture is a measure of how good their insight was, how effective their decision-making was, and how well they put their ideas into practice.

As far as the entrepreneur is concerned, money is more usually a *means* rather than an *end* in itself. That we notice the entrepreneurs who are highly rewarded for their efforts should not blind us to the fact that this reward is more often than not the result of a great deal of hard work and it is a reward that is far from inevitable.

5.6 The opportunity to distribute wealth

KEY LEARNING OUTCOME
A recognition of who expects to be rewarded from the entrepreneurial venture.

No entrepreneur works in a vacuum. The venture they create touches the lives of many other people. To drive their venture forward, the entrepreneur calls upon the support of a number of different groups. In return for their support, these groups expect to be rewarded from the success of the venture. People who have a part to play in the entrepreneurial venture generally are called *stakeholders*. The key stakeholder groups are: *employees, investors, suppliers, customers*, the local *community* and *government*.

Employees

Employees are the individuals who contribute physical and mental labour to the business. Its success depends on their efforts on its behalf and therefore upon their motivation. Employees usually have some kind of formal contract and are rewarded by being paid a salary. This is usually agreed in advance and is independent of the performance of the venture, although an element may be performance related. Employees may also be offered the possibility of owning a part of the firm through share schemes.

People do not work just for money. The firm they work for provides them with a stage on which to develop social relationships. It also offers them the possibility of personal development. When someone joins an organisation they are making a personal investment in its future and the organisation is investing in their future. Changing jobs is time-consuming and can be expensive. Someone who decides to work for an entrepreneurial venture is exposing themselves to the risk of that venture, even if they are being paid a fixed salary.

Investors

Investors are the people who provide the entrepreneur with the necessary money to start the venture and keep it running. There are two main sorts of investor. *Stockholders* are people who buy a part of the firm, its *stock*, and so are entitled to a share of any profits it makes. Stockholders are the true owners of the firm. The entrepreneur managing the venture may, or may not, be a major shareholder in it. *Lenders* are people who offer money to the venture on the basis of it being a *loan*. They do not actually own a part of the firm. All investors expect a return from their investment. The actual amount of expected return will depend on the risk the venture is facing and the other investments that are available at the time. The actual return the stockholder receives will vary depending on how the business performs. Lenders, on the other hand, expect a rate of return which is agreed independently of how the business performs before the investment is made. Lenders usually take priority for payment over stockholders whose returns are only paid once the business has met its other financial commitments.

Lenders consequently face a lower level of risk. However, there is still the possibility that the venture might become insolvent and not be able to pay back its loans.

Suppliers

Suppliers are the individuals and organisations who provide the business with the materials, productive assets and information it needs to produce its outputs. Suppliers are paid for providing these *inputs*. The business may only make contact with a supplier through spot purchases made in an open market or contact may be more direct and defined by a formal contract, perhaps a long-term supply contract.

Suppliers are in business to sell what they produce and so they have an interest in the performance of their customers. Supplying them may involve an investment in developing a new product or providing back-up support. A new venture may call upon the support of its suppliers, perhaps by asking for special payment terms to ease its cash flow in the early days. Information and advice about end-user markets may be provided. The chance to build a partnership with suppliers should never be overlooked.

Customers

As with suppliers, customers may need to make an investment in using a particular supplier. Changing suppliers may involve *switching costs*. These include the cost of finding a new supplier, taking a risk with goods of unknown quality, and the expenses incurred in changing over to new inputs. If a customer decides to use the products offered by a new venture rather than one with an established track record they may be exposing themselves to some risk. (This is something the entrepreneur needs to take into account when devising a selling strategy.) The entrepreneur's business may sell to its customers on an open market but, as with suppliers, the possibility of building a longer-term partnership should always be considered.

The local community

Businesses have physical locations. The way that they operate may affect the people who live and other businesses which operate nearby. A business has a number of responsibilities to this local community, for example in not polluting their shared environment. Some of these responsibilities are defined in national or local laws, others are not defined in a legal or formal sense, but are expected on the basis that the firm will act in an *ethical* way.

Corporate responsibility is a political and cultural as well as an economic issue. If the firm is international and operates across borders then the way it behaves in one region may influence the way it is perceived in another. For example, a number of well-known sports shoes manufacturers were criticised recently for paying Indian workers less than half a US dollar for manufacturing shoes that retailed for over $200 in the USA. Whatever the fair 'market' price of labour in India, the firm's managers had to react to the damage this criticism did to the brand names they were trying to market in the West.

Government

A major part of a government's responsibility is to ensure that businesses can operate in an environment which has political and economic stability, and in which the rule of law operates so contracts can be both made and enforced. The government may also provide central services such as education and health-care which the workforce draws upon. These services cost money to provide and so the government taxes individuals and businesses. In general governments aim to support entrepreneurial businesses because they have an interest in their success. Entrepreneurs bring economic prosperity, provide social stability and generate tax revenue.

Distribution of rewards

All the stakeholders shown in Fig. 5.1 expect some reward from the entrepreneurial venture. By working together they can maximise its success. Even so, the new wealth created by the entrepreneur is finite. It can only be shared so far. The entrepreneur must decide how to distribute the wealth among the various stakeholders. To some extent the entrepreneur's hands are tied since the sharing of the profits is, in part, determined by external markets. Legal requirements and binding contracts also play a part in deciding what goes where.

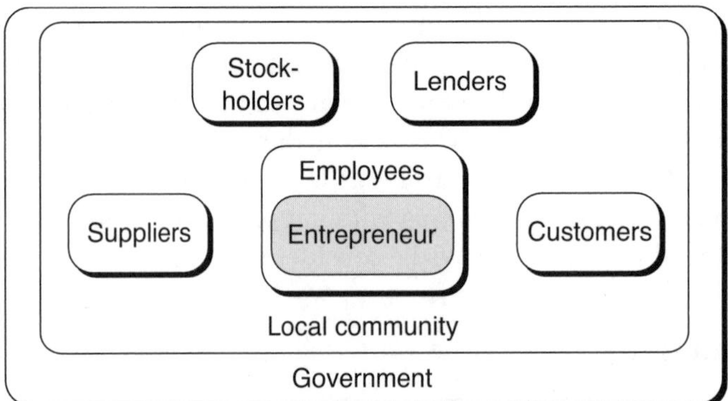

Fig. 5.1 Stakeholders in the entrepreneurial venture

However, the entrepreneur has *some* freedom to decide who gets what. Customers can be rewarded for their loyalty. Higher payments may be used to motivate employees. Profits can be used to support projects in the local community. Distributing the rewards created by the venture is a great responsibility. Using this latitude for rewarding stakeholders creatively is very important to the future success of the venture. If rewards are distributed in a way which is seen as fair and proper they can motivate all involved in the venture. However, a distribution which is seen as illegitimate is a sure way to cause ill feeling.

Summary of key ideas

- A business opportunity is a *gap* in the market which presents the possibility of *new value* being created.
- Opportunities are pursued with *innovations* – a better way of doing something for a customer.
- Entrepreneurs are attuned to new opportunities and are motivated to pursue them.
- Entrepreneurs decide not only how to create new wealth but also how to distribute it to the venture's *stakeholders*.

Suggestions for further reading

Drucker, P.F. (1985) 'The discipline of innovation', *Harvard Business Review*, May-June, pp. 67–72.

Donaldson, T. and **Preston, L.E.** (1995) 'The stakeholder theory of the corporation: Concepts, evidence and implications', *Academy of Management Review*, Vol. 20, No. 1, pp. 65–91.

Gray, H.L. (1978) 'The entrepreneurial innovator', *Management Education and Development*, Vol. 9, pp. 85–92.

Katz, J. (1990) 'The creative touch', *Nation's Business*, March, p. 43.

Manimala, M.J. (1999) *Entrepreneurial Policies and Strategies*, New Delhi: Sage.

Selected case material

Entrepreneurs eager to put sport firmly in the net

5 January 2000

The web seems the ideal place to cater for sports fans, and there is a will to win, say **Patrick Harverson** and **Matthew Garrahan**

Sport and the internet look like a marriage made in heaven, and there is no shortage of companies trying to make money out of the union.

Sport works so well, both as online content and as a vehicle for e-commerce, because of the unmatched enthusiasm and loyalty it generates among consumers. Sport thrives on results, statistics and news, all of which can be provided easily and swiftly on the internet.

Also, sports fans love the internet because it is convenient and accessible 24 hours a day. As Andrew Croker of Sportal, the sports website operator, puts it: "It does not matter how much sport there is on TV, the broadcasters are giving it to you when they want to. With the net, it is entirely consumer-driven. You can get it when you want, and the content can be customised to your interests."

Sportal is one of the four main specialist sports internet companies in the UK, along with Sports.com, Sports Internet and 365 Corporation. Investors have already latched on to the potential of sports on the net: the last two are both quoted on the London stock market, Sports.com is owned by the US quoted Sportsline. Sportal is due to float this year.

All have plenty of money, ambition and big plans for 2000, yet their strategies are not identical. Sportal is a web-site operator focusing on UK and non-US markets, running sites for well-known franchises, such as European soccer clubs and national associations like the South African Rugby Union.

Sports.com is developing sport-specific sites for the European market and building a network of editorial offices throughout the continent, whereas Sports Internet's strategy is to integrate sports and statistical content with an online betting operation.

Finally, 365 runs football, cricket and rugby sites, but its reliance on its telecommunications business – it runs premium-rate phone lines – suggests sport is perhaps not going to be its core business.

However, because of its sports content, 365 attracted a lot of attention at its flotation in November. Currently valued at £327m, it is the biggest of the two London-quoted companies, with Sports Internet worth £238m.

Based on a recent $50m (£31m) fund raising, Sportal's worth is put at about $170m, while Sports.com recently announced £49m worth of investment from funds including IMG Chase Sports Capital Partners and Soros Private Equity Partners that valued the company at $210m.

Sportal and Sports Internet have both recently signed content-sharing deals: Yahoo!, the most popular web site on the internet, is to use Sports Internet's soccer statistics on its fantasy soccer game, while Cable and Wireless agreed to use Sportal's rugby and soccer sites on its digital television platform.

These sorts of deals make sense, say internet analysts. "Horizontal portals,like Yahoo! are looking for content, whereas vertical portals, like Sports Internet, are looking for reach (access to a wider audience)," says Brian Condon, director of Close Brothers Corporate Finance.

Rather than spending heavily on advertising and marketing, "we're looking to do clever deals with partners that will deliver consumers to us," says Jeremy Fenn, chief executive of Sports Internet.

As for Sportal's link-up with C&W, deals between television companies and sports internet companies are likely to become more common, says Mr Condon. But that will not last long.

"It gives the sports portals the ability to play around with broadcasting. If sensible bandwidth were available, they wouldn't need to do it. When bandwidth improves, sports internet companies will be able to compete with broadcasters."

It is the ability to broadcast quality live and recorded pictures of sports events that is the sector's Holy Grail: when it comes, web sites will be able to charge users to access video. The difficult, and costly, part will be acquiring the internet rights to sport, and the owners of those rights are are only now waking up to their value.

For the moment, however, the sports web companies will focus on building strategic partnerships.

Sports.com aims to build loyal and local audiences across Europe, but is focusing more on generic sports rather than specific groups of supporters."To win in this sector we have to be on the ground more than another company which could exist in cyber space," says Anthony Khan, UK managing director.

Needless to say, this is expensive, which is why the sports web companies have been raising and spending so much money.

Nick Jones, an analyst with Jupiter Communications, the internet research company, agrees that a closer relationship between internet businesses and users is crucial to success: "It's not just content publishers who have to learn this, it's all retailers."

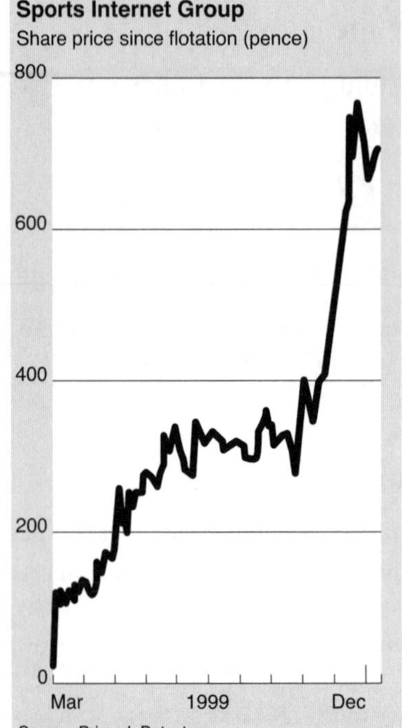

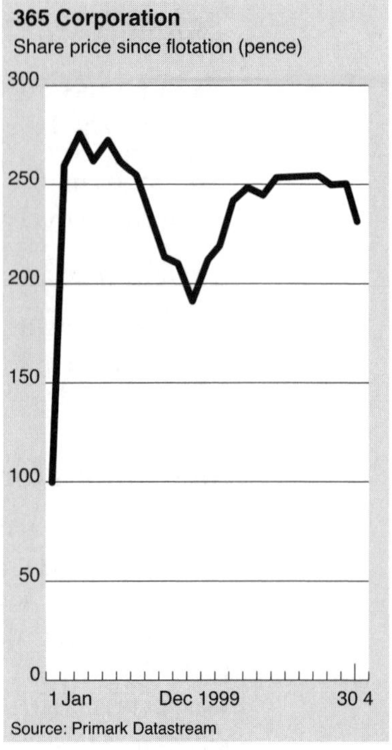

The shovel-sellers who offer end-to-end internet fulfilment for e-tailers

9 December 1999

Share in N Brown have risen 95 per cent while GUS has slipped to near seven-year lows; **Susanna Voyle** investigates the gap

When there is a gold rush, the smartest people flock to the area to sell shovels. With the internet seen as the modern equivalent of the Wild West dash for wealth, clever operators are positioning themselves as shovel-suppliers to online retailers.

Catalogue retailers, with their advanced back office systems and long-established home delivery networks, are seen as naturals to provide these so-called "internet fulfilment" services for electronic commerce.

Those that have jumped on the fulfilment bandwagon have flourished – but not all have managed the jump.

Share in N Brown, the direct mail order group, have risen by more than 95 per cent since it announced plans to offer internet back-up services to other retailers less than three months ago.

Over the same period, shares in Great Universal Stores, the catalogue retailer which owns high street chain Argos, have fallen by more than 25 per cent. That adds up to a 20 per cent underperformance of its generally depressed peers, and many observers blame the group's failure to articulate an online vision for the severity of its fall.

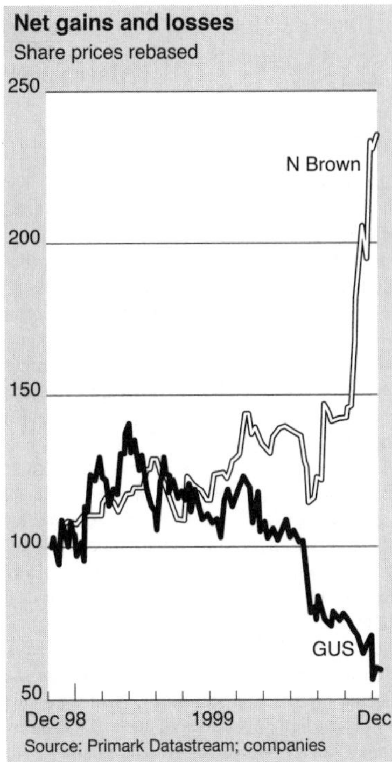

Source: Primark Datastream; companies

At N Brown, Jim Martin, chief executive, launched his Zendor.com service at the start of October – and said setting up a similar infrastructure from scratch would cost about £100m.

N Brown boasts that Zendor offers "end-to-end fulfilment " – providing assistance with product sourcing, warehousing, call centres, customer care, accounts, web site preparation, home delivery, and collection and processing of returns.

GUS, meanwhile, saw its shares fall 20 per cent on the announcement of its interim results last week. This was largely because of a sales drop in its core home shopping division – but the group's failure to offer a coherent explanation of its strategy to capitalise on its home delivery infrastructure did not help.

The group, which owns the White Arrow delivery business, already carries out fulfilment work for third parties, and has appointed an e-commerce strategy director. But at results presentations the group's thinking appeared muddled.

"GUS hasn't really grasped the need for a strategy for the new economy," said one analyst. "But for N Brown, Zendor represents an attempt to move quickly to use the existing skill sets...to establish a recurring revenue stream from e-tailers."

Of course there are other issues that differentiate the two businesses. At its most basic level, N Brown's core business is still growing, with first-half pre-tax profits up 13 per cent at £21.4m.

GUS last week reported interim trading profit in its home shopping division of £14.5m – a fall of more than 70 per cent – and admitted that it did not yet know if that was a one-off step change, or the start of a precipitous drop.

The structure of the two businesses is key to understanding N Brown's outperformance. It deals directly with its customers, with a niche offering of clothing in larger sizes through a series of smaller catalogues. GUS operates mainly through an agency structure with a far wider offering under a "big book" approach. For GUS, this means forgoing relationships with individuals who carry out sales on a neighbourhood basis, and the size of the catalogue means the group can look lumbering when it comes to pricing.

With many retailers capitalising on the value inherent in their customer relationships and leveraging off their databases, GUS is at an immediate disadvantage. N Brown, on the other hand, uses its database to carry out more direct marketing to its existing customers and to be able to change prices.

There are also comparisons to be drawn with the high street – where hide-bound middle-market retailers have lost out to more nimble operators at both the top and bottom of the price chain. The catalogue retailers that have been doing well are canny operators in niche areas: if GUS is Marks and Spencer, N Brown is The Gap.

GUS has also been hit by the transfer of many of its traditionally credit-constrained customers to the credit card market, freeing them to shop in the high street. The niche catalogue retailers, meanwhile, have thrived by selling goods not on offer elsewhere.

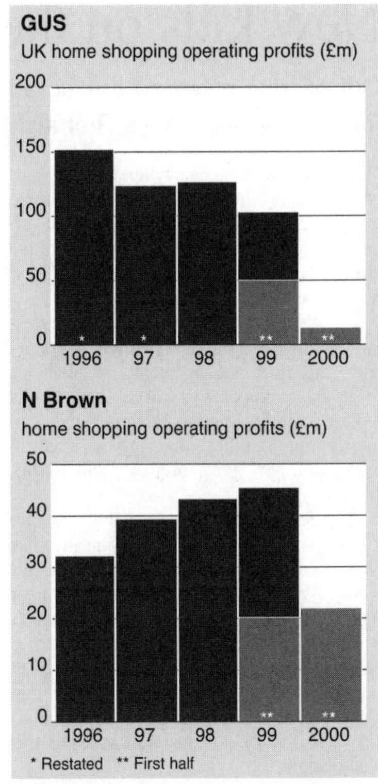

These weaknesses, together with the lack of a fulfilment offering, have combined to push GUS shares to near seven-year lows.

There is a third way for catalogue retailers to take advantage of the fulfilment market. Littlewoods, the UK's biggest privately-owned retailer, is pursuing a strategy that uses its expertise in home delivery – but only where the group can take an equity stake in the venture. Barry Gibson, chief executive, is keen to stay away from what he fears could quickly become a commoditised market.

While few industry observers reach the same conclusions when forecasting what effect e-commerce will have on retailing, they all agree on one thing: there will be change, and we can expect plenty more shovel-sellers to start coming over the horizon.

New kids on the digital block

1 March 2000

Outsiders are seizing the lucrative business of fitting out companies for e-commerce, says **Richard Poynder**

There is a new race in cyberspace. As corporate enthusiasm for e-commerce grows, technology companies and consultancies are jostling for a slice of the lucrative business of re-engineering corporate IT systems for e-business.

The identities of the early leaders are raising eyebrows. The large systems integrators and "big five" management consultancies might have expected to win the bulk of this work. To their chagrin, however, they are increasingly finding themselves elbowed aside by a new generation of smaller companies.

A recent report published by ITEuropa.com, the research company, has christened these upstarts "interactive architects". According to Max Hotopf, editor of the report, their unique competitive edge is based on their ability to provide expertise not just in the specialist IT skills needed to integrate corporate back-office systems into e-commerce applications, but also in marketing and strategic consultancy, as well as web design.

"Until recently people tended to specialise in just one of these areas," says Mr Hotopf. "There was no one capable of offering all three."

Many interactive architects, like US Web/CKS, Agency.com and Razorfish, are US corporations that have expanded overseas. Others, such as Berlin- based PixelPark, the French Le Studio Grolier and UK-based Blueberry New Media, are local companies serving national, or regional, markets.

In addition, there are a handful of European companies – mainly Scandinavian – that also harbour global ambitions. "Sweden's Icon Medialab and Framfab are the two largest interactive architects operating in Europe today," says Mr Hotopf. "They have grown on the strength of the Nordic market, and now see a huge opportunity to go international."

Most started out as small creative agencies specialising in the design of corporate "brochure ware" sites. But as their clients have embraced e-commerce, so they have acquired new competencies. "We began as a web design company in 1991," says Christoph Geier, executive vice-president for systems and technology at PixelPark. "But we soon realised that our customers were going to need to integrate the internet into the overall strategy of the whole company, and that this would require us to expand into strategic consulting and IT as well."

With their broader skill-set, interactive architects now frequently out-pitch their larger competitors. "We often find ourselves up against large consultancies like McKinsey; and we often win contracts against them," says Dr Geier. "This is because they have to team up with a systems house like IBM, whereas we can offer a one-stop shop, and a more integrated approach."

According to Mark Curtis, European vice-president for skills and vision at Razorfish, interactive architects also bring a more modern strategic perspective. "The vital component that we offer is a digital vision," he says, "whereas many traditional companies still use an industrial-age model of consulting: they have yet to grasp the full implications of the digital economy."

The new generation also better understands the need to mould technology to the user experience, says Ian Black, head of communications at BAe Systems, who recruited Razorfish to help develop BAe's web activities. "We found Razorfish to be more focused on what we are very passionate about, which is that it doesn't really matter how good the technology is, what matters is how you interface that technology with a human. Systems integrators are generally hopeless when it comes to graphical interfaces, or general purpose public access on the internet."

Conscious that they are being left behind on the digital high road, however, systems integrators and management consultants are determined to catch up. "These larger companies have been caught napping, which is going to hurt them," says Mr Hotopf. "But they now recognise that they have to develop these new skills themselves, or acquire them."

Last December, Cap Gemini announced that it was launching a new 1,000-person e-business unit designed, said Pierre Hessler, Cap Gemini board member, to "beat the pure players at their own game".

In the same month PwC, the consultants, bought a 50 per cent stake in Evisor, a Belgian web designer, and in January International Business Machines announced plans to build a portfolio of global "Centres for IBM e-business Inno-vation".

The aim, says Lee Morgan, director of e-business services for the distribution sector, IBM Global Services, is to create small, self-contained environments in which the full range of competencies needed for develop ing e-business applications can be effectively brought together, and become "as fast and as nimble as the new interactive architects".

He adds: "I wouldn't disagree that some of these new niche players have made some significant inroads, and won some significant business, but IBM defined e-business a few years ago: we built this space, and quite frankly we are going to claim it back."

However, not everyone is convinced that, in the long run, the wide spread of skills espoused by interactive architects can be efficiently delivered by one company alone.

"Certainly e-commerce applications demand a very wide skill set, and today there are companies trying to provide all of those in a one-stop-shop environment," says Heather Stark, principal consultant at Ovum, the research company. "But there are highly skilled specialists in each of the component areas competing for the business, so they will need to demonstrate best-of-breed capabilities in each area."

John Lythall, managing director of IS Solutions, a UK-based systems integrator, believes that interactive architects are a short-term phenomenon, engendered by the state of flux introduced by the web.

"While things seem to be coming together now, the market will split again," he says. "There will be at least two types of business: one for the technology, and another more marketing and media-oriented. The IT component of e-commerce will pass back to the systems integrators."

Whatever the future holds, these new companies are growing at breakneck speed today, with the leading companies experiencing year-on-year sales growth of 60 per cent, and more. "The problem we face is that of handling all the business coming in," says Bjorn Westerberg, managing director of Icon Medialab, Sweden. "We are experiencing huge demand from so many different customers, and the projects are getting bigger all the time."

This explosive demand has triggered consolidation, with new deals being announced practically every week.

"I expect to see a lot of acquisitions in the near future because all the players in the market are going to have to grow very rapidly, and given the speed of development it won't be possible to do this through organic growth," says Dr Geier, "So 2000 will be a very important year for the development of the industry."

Ironically, with large interactive architects such as Razorfish and Icon Medialab already employing more than 1,000 staff, and traditional players acquiring the skills they lack, there could soon be little to choose between old-style systems integrators and consultancies, and the new interactive architects.

In the short-term, however, rising demand, coupled with a finite pool of skilled personnel, suggests that the battle will be fought as much over staff as over contracts. "The most important thing for our management team is to nurture an attractive culture in order to ensure that people want to work at Icon Medialab," says Mr Westerberg. "We have a lot of large companies in Sweden, and the war for talent is becoming extremely fierce."

In fact, staff retention could well prove the key to survival, says Mr Hotopf. "The winners will be those companies who have the culture to attract and retain staff."

Corporate odd-job men get some big ideas of their own

18 September 1998

Outsourcing started with cleaning and catering but the fashion has spread to white collar sectors, says **Susanna Voyle**

They may be the corporate odd-job men – doing the work companies no longer wish to do for themselves – but support services businesses have become big in their own right, driven by the fashion for outsourcing.

The trend started in the unglamorous blue-collar worlds of cleaning, catering and security. But it has moved on. A new wave of contracts has emerged as companies outsource white-collar operations such as payrolls, pensions administration and call centres. Hays, Capita and Serco, leading outsourcing specialists, this month announced big jumps in pre-tax profits. Last month's interim figures from Rentokil Initial may have robbed Sir Clive Thompson, chief executive, of his "Mr 20 per cent" title but the 18.4 per cent it did achieve is nothing to sniff at.

"The market is growing because businesses are focusing more and more on their core business competence," said Ross Jobber, analyst with Deutsche Morgan Grenfell.

The markets are relatively mature in areas such as cleaning, security and catering, he says, but it is in "whole business process" that real growth is yet to come. The key here is often having capabilities in information technology and service. "Those truly in the new wave are those who have contact with their customers' customers," says Mr Jobber.

ITNet, the computer services company, highlights the changes. The group – the former information technology services division of Cadbury Schweppes, the soft drinks and confectionery group – was spun off and floated in June. It is now expanding its business process outsourcing arm and one of its biggest customers is Cadbury Schweppes.

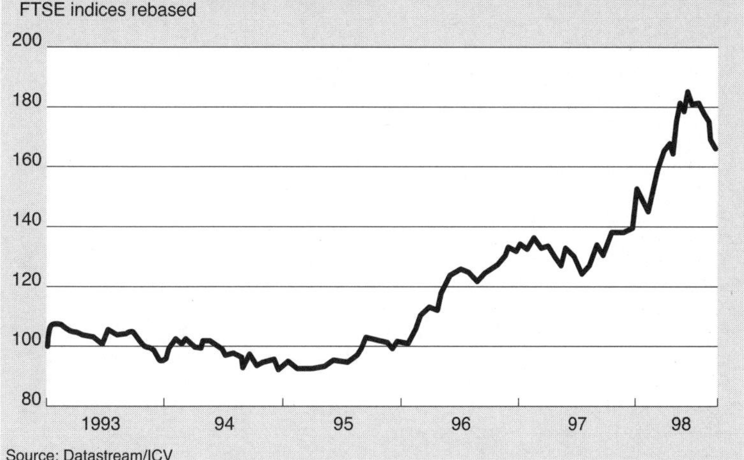

Outsourcing: a growing business

Turnover of leading companies
£m

	1993	1994	1995	1996	1997
Rentokil	**588.1**	**719.6**	**856.7**	**2,269.6**	**2,812.1**
Hays	**477.1**	**631.9**	**808.4**	**966.0**	**1,129.8**
Serco Group	**187.0**	**260.2**	**323.3**	**397.0**	**489.0**
Capita Group	**50.2**	**73.8**	**87.0**	**111.9**	**172.9**

The companies in the sector say there is plenty more growth to come. Rod Aldridge, chairman and chief executive of Capita, says the scope in the UK market is immense, with some estimates putting turnover at £10bn a year. In the first half of this year Capita won three times as many contracts as in the first half of 1997.

Ronnie Frost, chief executive at Hays, says he does not spend his time trying to steal business from rivals. He concentrates on identifying new opportunities. Sometimes it can take up to two years to persuade a corporation to contract out. But they are unlikely to go back once they have switched.

But what about signs of an economic slowdown? Mr Frost this week said he saw no signs of recession but he added that he would welcome one because tough times make companies reassess their cost structures.

Support services companies with a heavy focus on volume-related delivery and personnel business could suffer but the rest are hoping for an increase in business.

Robert Morton, an analyst with Charterhouse Tilney, says the main driver for outsourcing is the need to reduce costs. "When we come into recession people are more concerned about their costs than they are when times are good, so we get a pick up in demand," he said.

On Wednesday Goode Durrant, the van leasing group, said it had increased its vehicle fleet by more than 8 per cent since May because of increased demand. The "less confident economic news" was persuading customers to switch from buying vans to renting them, the group said.

Rentokil Initial, Hays and Serco have expanded internationally.

The market in the UK is much more mature than in the rest of Europe – spurred by the government's own outsourcing initiatives. It is one of the few areas in which the government is often a more sophisticated customer than public companies. Many outsourcing specialists say it is easier to make money out of public companies than out of government.

But big government contracts often bring kudos. At Serco, Richard White, chief executive, says he often meets a wall of mistrust when he is looking for new business. But doubts about handing over work usually disappear when he explains that Serco's first contract was looking after Britain's four-minute warning against nuclear attack.

Review questions

Discuss the nature of the business opportunities provided by:

1 The Internet – Business to consumer links

2 The Internet – Business to business links

3 Outsourcing by large firms.

What sort of questions should be asked about innovations that might capitalise on them?

6 Resources in the entrepreneurial venture

Chapter overview

People, money and operational assets are essential ingredients of the entrepreneurial venture. This chapter explores each of these resource types and the management issues they raise for the entrepreneur. The chapter concludes with a discussion of why investment in such resources leads to risk for the backers of the venture.

6.1 Resources available to the entrepreneur

KEY LEARNING OUTCOME
An understanding of the nature and type of resources that the entrepreneur uses to build the venture.

Resources are the things that a business uses to pursue its ends. They are the inputs that the business converts to create the outputs it delivers to its customers. They are the substance out of which the business is made. In broad terms, there are three sorts of resource that entrepreneurs can call upon to build their ventures. These are:

1 *Financial resources* – Resources which take the form of, or can be readily converted to, cash.
2 *Human resources* – People and the efforts, knowledge, skill and insights they contribute to the success of the venture.
3 *Operating resources* – The facilities which allow people to do their jobs: such as buildings, vehicles, office equipment, machinery and raw materials, etc.

The entrepreneurial venture is built from an innovative combination of financial, operating and human resources (see Fig. 6.1). Thus when Frederick Smith founded the US parcel air carrier Federal Express he needed to bring together people: a board of directors, pilots, operational staff, etc., together with a fully operational airline which was able to give national coverage. This demanded an investment in the order of $100 million.

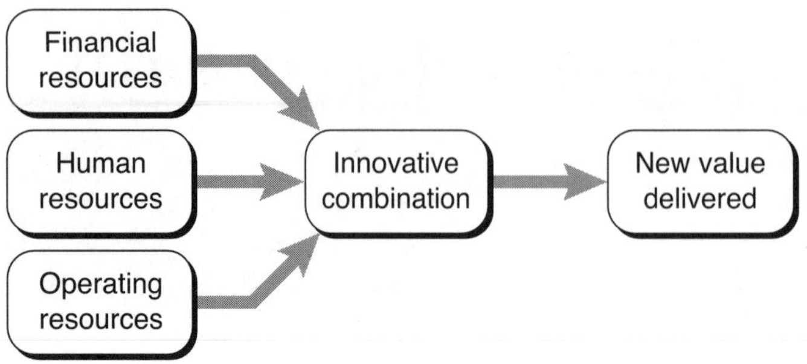

Fig. 6.1 Entrepreneurship and the combination of resources

Regardless of the form they take, all resources have a number of characteristics in common. Resources are *consumed*; they are converted to the products which customers buy and there is competition to get hold of resources. A number of businesses, entrepreneurial and otherwise, will be trying to acquire a particular resource; consequently, managers are willing to pay for resources. Third, resources have a cost.

The cost of a resource is an indication of how it might be used by a business to create new value. Resources are bought and sold by businesses and their cost is determined by the market created for that resource. Resources with the potential to create a lot of new value will be expensive. This cost is not the same as the *value* of the resource to a *particular* business since the value of a resource lies in the way a business will use it, how innovative they will be with it and how hard they will make it work for them.

One type of resource can be converted into another. This process normally involves selling a resource thereby converting it into cash, and then using this cash to buy something new. However, in some cases resources may be exchanged directly through 'asset swaps'. In places where financial markets are not well developed, such as in parts of the developing world and the former Communist bloc, 'bartering' may be important. Not all markets for resources are equally accessible. Some markets are more developed than others. The ease with which a particular resource can be converted back into ready cash is called its liquidity: *liquid* resources are easily converted back, *illiquid* resources are converted back only with difficulty.

Entrepreneurs must be active in acquiring resources for their ventures. The path through which resources are obtained and exchanged make up the network in which the business is located. In the long run, the entrepreneur only has access to the same resources as any other business. Competitiveness in the marketplace cannot normally be sustained on the basis of having access to unique resource inputs. If an input is valuable, other businesses will eventually find a way to get hold of it or of something like it. What entrepreneurs must do to be competitive is they must *combine* the resources they have access to in a unique and valuable way. That is, to *innovate* with them and then they must make those resources work harder than their competitors do. It is this which ultimately enables the entrepreneur to deliver new value to the customer.

6.2 Financial resources

KEY LEARNING OUTCOME
An appreciation of the financial resources available for use by the entrepreneur.

Financial resources are those which take a monetary form. Cash is the most liquid form of resource because it can be used readily to buy other resources. The following are all financial resources which have a role to play in the entrepreneurial venture:

- *Cash in hand* – This is money to which the business has immediate access. It may be spent at very short notice. Cash in hand may be held either as money, i.e. petty cash, or it may be stored in a bank's current account or other direct access account.
- *Overdraft facilities* – Such facilities represent an agreement with a bank to withdraw more than is actually held in the venture's current account. It is a short-term loan which the business can call upon although overdrafts are normally quite expensive and so tend to be saved for emergencies.
- *Loans* – Loans represent money provided by backers, either institutional or private, which the business arranges to pay back in an agreed way over a fixed period of time at an agreed rate of interest. The payback expected is usually independent of the performance of the business. Loans may be secured against physical assets of the business which can be sold off to secure repayment. This reduces the risk of the loan to the backer.
- *Outstanding debtors* – This represents cash owed to the business by individuals and firms which have received goods and services from it. Many debtors will expect a period of grace before paying and it may not be easy to call in outstanding debt quickly. Outstanding debtors are one of the main reasons why cash-flow may be negative in the early stages of the venture's life.
- *Investment capital* – This is money provided to the business by investors in return for a part-ownership or share in it. Investors are the true owners of the business. They are rewarded from the profits the business generates. The return they receive will be dependent on the performance of the business.
- *Investment in other businesses* – Many businesses hold investments in other businesses. These investments may be in unrelated businesses but they are more often in suppliers or customers. If more than half a firm is owned, then it becomes a *subsidiary* of the holding firm. Investments can be made through personal or institutional agreements, or via publicly traded shares. A firm does not normally exist solely to make investments in other firms. Individual and institutional investors are quite capable of doing this for themselves. However, strategic investments in customers and suppliers may be an important part of the dynamics of the network in which the business is located. For this reason such investments tend to represent long-term commitments and although they can be sold to generate cash, doing so is not routine.

All financial resources have a cost. This cost takes one of two forms. The *cost of capital* is the cost encountered when obtaining the money: it is the direct charge faced for having an overdraft; the interest on loans; the return expected by investors, etc.

In addition to this direct cost, there is an *opportunity cost*. Opportunity cost is the potential return that is lost by not putting the money to some alternative use. For example, cash in hand and outstanding debts lose the interest that might be gained by putting the money into an interest-yielding account.

Financial resources are the most liquid, and thus the most flexible, resources to which the venture has access. However, they are also the least productive. Cash, of itself, does not create new value. Money is only valuable if it is put to work. This means it must be converted to other, less liquid, resources. The entrepreneur must strike a balance. A decision must be made between how liquid the business is to be, how much flexibility it must have to meet short-term and unexpected financial commitments, and the extent to which the firm's financial resources are to be tied up in productive assets.

Such decisions are critical to the success of the venture. If insufficient investment is made then the business will not be in a position to achieve its full potential. If it becomes too illiquid, it may be knocked off-course by short-term financial problems which, in the long run, the business would be more than able to solve. Managing the *cash-flow* of the business is central to maintaining this liquidity balance. The financial resources to which an entrepreneur can gain access will depend on how well developed the economy they are working in is and the type of capital markets available. In the mature economies of Western Europe and the USA, capital is usually provided by explicit and open institutional systems such as banks, venture capital businesses and stock markets. In other parts of the world, provision of financial resources may be through less formal networks. Displaced communities often create financial support networks around the extended family. One of the main challenges to developing entrepreneurism in the former Communist bloc is the setting up of supportive financial institutions.

6.3 Operating resources

KEY LEARNING OUTCOME
An appreciation of the operational resources available for use by the entrepreneur.

Operating resources are those which are actually used by the business to deliver its outputs to the marketplace. Key categories of operating resources include:

- *Premises* – The buildings in which the business operates. This includes offices, production facilities and the outlets through which services are provided.
- *Motor vehicles* – Any vehicles which are used by the organisation to undertake its business such as cars for sales representatives and vans and lorries used to transport goods, make deliveries and provide services.
- *Production machinery* – Machinery which is used to manufacture the products which the business sells.
- *Raw materials* – The inputs that are converted into the products that the business sells.
- *Storage facilities* – Premises and equipment used to store finished goods until they are sold.

- *Office equipment* – Items used in the administration of the business such as office furniture, word processors, information processing and communication equipment.

Operating resources represent the capacity of the business to offer its innovation to the marketplace. They may be owned by the business, or they may be rented as they are needed. Either way, they represent a commitment. Liquid financial resources are readily converted into operating resources, but operating resources are not easily converted back into money. The markets for second-hand business assets are not always well developed. Even if they are, operating resources depreciate quickly and a loss may be made on selling.

In order to use operating resources effectively it is important that entrepreneurs make themselves fully conversant with any technical aspects relating to the resources; legal issues and implications relating to their use (including health and safety regulations); suppliers and the supply situation; and the applicable costs (both for outright purchase and for leasing). It is in this area that partnerships with suppliers can be rewarding, especially if the operating resources are technical or require ongoing support in their use.

The commitment to investment in operating resource capacity must be made in the light of expected demand for the business's offerings. If capacity is insufficient, then business that might otherwise have been obtained will be lost. If it is in excess of demand, then unnecessary, and unprofitable, expenditure will be undertaken. It is often difficult to alter operating capacity in the light of short-term fluctuations in demand. This results in *fixed costs*, that is, costs which are independent of the amount of outputs the firm offers. Critically, fixed costs must be faced *whatever* the business's sales. Fixed costs can have a debilitating effect on cash-flow. The entrepreneur must make the decision about commitment to operating capacity in the light of an assessment of the sales and operating profits that will be generated by the business's offering, that is, on the basis of an accurate *forecast* of demand. Even good demand forecasting cannot remove all uncertainty and therefore the entrepreneur must be active in offsetting as much fixed cost as possible, especially in the early stages of the venture. This may mean renting rather than buying operating resources. It can also mean that some work is delegated to other established firms. In the early stages of the venture, managing cash-flow and controlling fixed costs may be more important than short-term profitability. It may be better to subcontract work to other firms rather than to make an irreversible commitment to extra capacity even if this means short-term profits are lost.

6.4 Human resources

KEY LEARNING OUTCOME
An appreciation of the human resources available for use by the entrepreneur.

People are the critical element in the success of a new venture. Financial and operating resources are not unique and they cannot, in themselves, confer an advantage to the business. To do so they must be *used* in a unique and innovative way by the people who make up the venture. The people who take part in the venture offer their labour towards it. This can take a variety of forms:

- *Productive labour* – A direct contribution towards generating the outputs of the business, its physical products or the service it offers.
- *Technical expertise* – A contribution of knowledge specific to the product or service offered by the business. This may be in support of existing products, or associated with the development of new ones.
- *Provision of business services* – A contribution of expertise in general business services, for example in legal affairs or accounting.
- *Functional organisational skills* – The provision of decision-making insights and organising skills in functional areas such as production, operations planning, marketing research and sales management.
- *Communication skills* – Offering skills in communicating with, and gaining the commitment of, external organisations and individuals. This includes marketing and sales directed towards customers, and financial management directed towards investors.
- *Strategic and leadership skills* – The contribution of insight and direction for the business as a whole. This involves generating a vision for the business, converting this into an effective strategy and plan for action, communicating this to the organisation and then leading the business in pursuit of the vision.

The entrepreneur represents the starting point of the entrepreneurial venture. He or she is the business's first, and most valuable, human resource. Entrepreneurs, if they are to be successful, must learn to use themselves as a resource, and use themselves effectively. This means analysing what they are good at, and what they are not so good at, and identifying skill gaps. The extent to which the entrepreneur can afford to specialise their contribution to their venture will depend on the size of the venture and the number of people who are working for it. If it is moderately large and has a specialist workforce then the entrepreneur will be able to concentrate on developing vision and a strategy for the venture and providing leadership to it. If it is quite small then the entrepreneur will have to take on functional and administrative tasks as well. Even so, the entrepreneur must be conscious of how the human resource requirements of the business will develop in the future by deciding what skill profile is right for their business and what type of people will be needed to contribute those skills. But employing people with the right skills is not enough, they must be directed to use those skills. They must also be motivated if they are to make a dedicated and effective contribution to the business. This calls for vision and leadership on the part of the entrepreneur.

Human resources represent a source of fixed costs for the business. The possibility of taking on, and letting go of, people in response to short-term demand fluctuations is limited by contractual obligations, social responsibility and the need to invest in training. Further, motivation can only be built on the back of some sense of security. Hence, making a commitment to human resources involves the same type of decisions as making a commitment to operating resources, namely: what will be needed, to what capacity, over what period, must the resource be in-house or can it be hired when needed? However, people are still people even if they are also resources and such decisions must be made with sensitivity.

6.5 Resources, investment and risk

KEY LEARNING OUTCOME
An understanding of how and why investing in resources creates risk for the entrepreneurial venture.

In one sense, a business is 'just' the financial, operating and human resources that comprise it. Only when these things are combined can the business generate new value and deliver it to customers. Resources have a value and there is competition to get hold of them. A business is *not* being competitive when it converts input resources into outputs of higher value. It is only being competitive if it is creating more value than its *competitors* can do. Thus resources are used to pursue opportunities and exploiting those opportunities creates new value. The profit created by an entrepreneurial venture is the difference between the cost of the resources that make it up and the value it creates. This is the *return* obtained from investing the resources. Though profits are important for survival and growth, the performance of an entrepreneurial venture cannot be reduced to a simple consideration of the profits it generates. Profits must be considered in relation to two other factors: *opportunity cost* and *risk*.

Resources are bought and sold in markets and so they have a price. This price is not the same as the cost of *using* a resource. The true cost incurred when a resource is used is the value of the opportunity *missed* because the resource is consumed and so cannot be used in an alternative way. This is the *opportunity cost*. If the entrepreneur uses the resources he or she obtains in the most productive way possible then the value created will be higher than that which might have been generated by an alternative investment and so the opportunity cost will be less than the value created. If, on the other hand, the resources are not used in the most productive way possible then some alternative investment could, potentially, give a better return, elsewhere. The opportunity cost will be greater than the value created. Opportunity cost is a fundamental factor in measuring performance. This is because investors are not concerned in the first instance with the *profit* made by a venture but with the *return* they might get if they put their money to an alternative use.

The second factor in considering how well an entrepreneur is using resources is *risk*. We cannot predict the future with absolute accuracy so there is always a degree of uncertainty about what will actually happen. This uncertainty creates risk. No matter what return is anticipated, there is always the possibility that some unforeseen event will lead to that return being lower. Customers may not find the offering as attractive as was expected. Marketing and distribution may prove to be more expensive than was budgeted for. Competitors may be more responsive than was assumed to be the case. Investors make an assessment of the risk that a venture will face. If the risk is high then they will expect to be compensated by a higher rate of return. If they perceive that it is low then they will be happy with a lower return. Consequently there is a pay-off between risk and return. The exact way in which expected return is related to risk is quite complex and is a function of the dynamics of the market for capital. The risk–return relationship for investment in an entrepreneurial venture is shown in Fig. 6.2. In practice, institutional investors will aim to hold a *portfolio*, that is, a collection of investments with different levels of risk and return. The objective here is to reduce the overall level of risk for the portfolio.

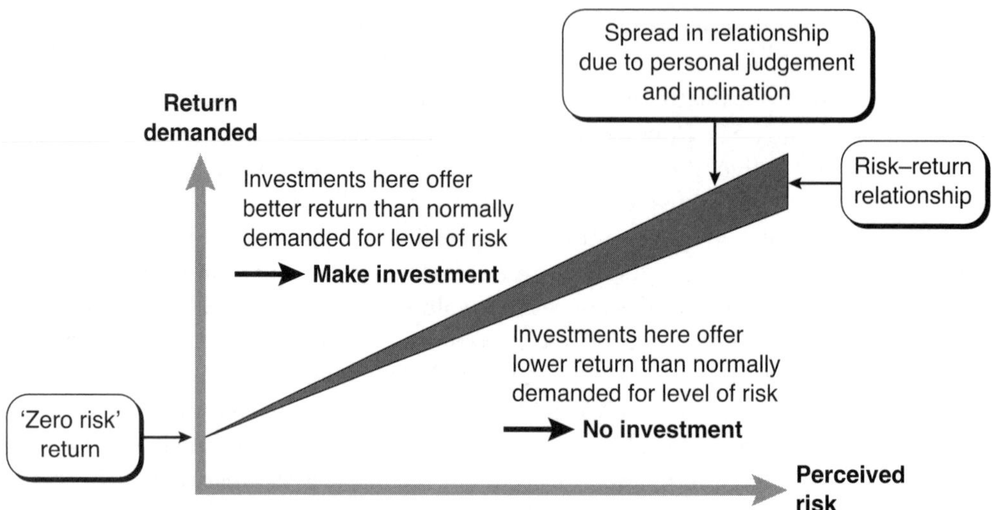

Fig. 6.2 The risk–return relationship for investment in an entrepreneurial venture

Risk occurs because resources must be *committed* to a venture. Once money is converted into operating and human resources it is either too difficult or too expensive, or both, to convert it back. Therefore, once resources have been brought together and shaped to pursue a particular opportunity there is no going back if a better opportunity demanding a different shaping of the resources is identified later. In this way, entrepreneurial innovation demands an irreversible commitment of resources (see Fig. 6.3). The opportunity cost must be faced and it is the investor in the venture who must absorb this cost, not the entrepreneur (although obviously the entrepreneur may be an investor as well).

In summary, if an entrepreneur identifies an opportunity that might be exploited through an innovative way of using resources and then asks investors to back a venture pursuing that opportunity, two fundamental questions will come to the investor's mind. These are: how do the returns anticipated compare to the alternative investments available and what will be the risks? The decision to support the venture or not will depend on the answers to these questions. It should not be forgotten that although investors are people who put *financial* resources into a venture, individuals who work for a business are also making a *personal* investment in it. They expect to be rewarded for their efforts and to be given an opportunity to develop. They also face opportunity costs in not being able to offer their efforts elsewhere, and face the risk of the venture not being successful. Similarly, non-financial commitments may also be made by customers and suppliers who build a relationship with the venture. In this way risk is spread out through the network in which the venture is located.

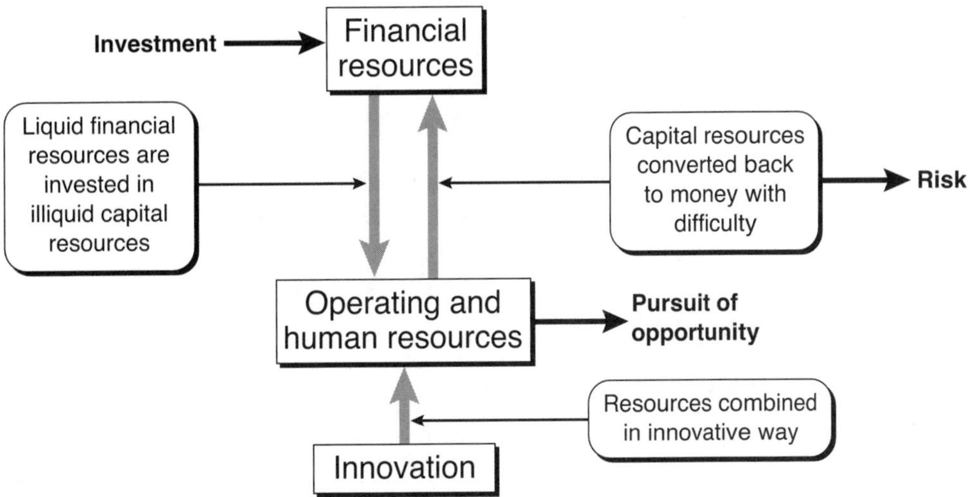

Fig. 6.3 Resource commitment in the entrepreneurial venture

Summary of key ideas

- Entrepreneurs must attract resources to their ventures in order to pursue business opportunities.
- The main categories of resources are *financial, human* and *operating*.
- Resources are *valuable* and are traded in *markets*.
- The entrepreneur must *compete* with other businesses to get hold of resources by offering a good return from using them.
- Dedicating resources to a particular venture exposes investors to *risk,* namely the possibility that the return gained will be less than expected.

Suggestions for further reading

Amit, R. and **Schoemaker, P.J.H.** (1993) 'Strategic assets and organisational rent', *Strategic Management Journal,* Vol. 14, pp. 33–46.

Collis, D.J. (1994) 'How valuable are organisational capabilities?', *Strategic Management Journal,* Vol. 15, pp. 143–52.

Hall, R. (1992) 'The strategic analysis of intangible resources', *Strategic Management Journal,* Vol. 13, pp. 135–44.

Peteraf, M.A. (1993) 'The cornerstones of competitive advantage: A resource based view', *Strategic Management Journal,* Vol. 14, pp. 179–91.

Wernerfelt, B. (1984) 'A resource based view of the firm', *Strategic Management Journal,* Vol. 5, pp. 171–80.

Wernerfelt, B. (1995) 'The resource based view of the firm: Ten years after', *Strategic Management Journal,* Vol. 16, pp. 171–4.

Selected case material

Germany embraces venture capitalism

7 January 2000

The industry has mushroomed in the last few years with the help of the government but there are risks, writes **Bertrand Benoit**

Once a distinctly Anglo-Saxon pursuit, venture capitalism is growing roots across Europe and few countries are embracing the change with more enthusiasm than Germany.

Long reliant on banks for financing, the country has seen an explosion in the number of funds providing increasingly aggressive entrepreneurs with a pool of capital hard to imagine only five years ago.

According to the Berlin-based German venture capital association, private equity investment has trebled over the last five years to reach DM3.3bn (€1.68bn, $1.69bn) last year, a quarter of it going into early-stage finance.

Compared with neighbouring countries and particularly the UK, Germany remains a lightweight. Total funds available for investment account for a mere 0.07 per cent of its GDP, putting the country neck-and-neck with Portugal. Yet these funds are expected to grow nearly 80 per cent this year.

The key factor behind this increase has been the simultaneous rise in demand for, and supply of capital. "Low interest rates, expensive stock markets, and dismal real estate returns mean people are looking for alternative investments," says Falk Strascheg, co-founder of Technologieholding, Germany's largest venture capital fund based in Munich. "At the same time, there is renewed confidence in entrepreneurs, who are no longer seen as evil blood-suckers but as nice job-creators."

The German government has played a central role in kick-starting the industry. The state-sponsored EXIST programme, launched in 1997, has encouraged university-based networks to come up with high-technology ventures. Once concentrated around Munich – the "laptop and Lederhosen" capital of Germany – high-tech companies are mushrooming all over the country, whether linked to universities, in the case of Freiburg, or on the rubble of older industries in the Ruhr and North-Rhine Westphalia regions.

Meanwhile, the state has also provided venture capitalists with the sort of financial support their British and US counterparts could only dream of. Federal agencies such as KFW, the development bank, and regional ones, such as Bayern Kapital in Bavaria, can provide up to two-thirds of venture capital investments in the form of loans, in addition to various guarantees protecting funds against losses.

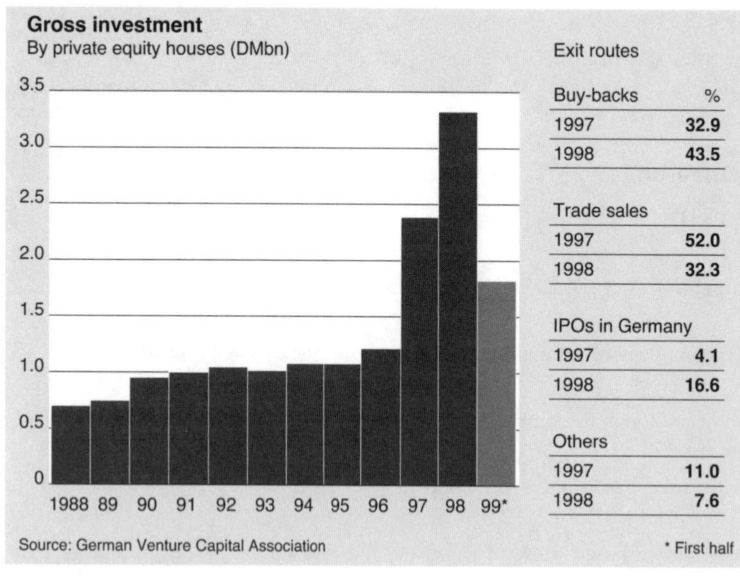

Source: German Venture Capital Association

* First half

"There is a snow-balling effect that increases the capital available to funds while considerably minimising their risks," says Alexander Wessendorff, editor of Deutsche, a private equity newsletter. The most radical transformation, however, has been the emergence of a viable exit route for funds, avoiding the disasters of the 1970s when banks bought into high-tech companies that later proved impossible to sell.

The creation in 1997 of the Neuer Markt, the Frankfurt-based high-growth/high-risk market, and its strong performance, have allowed funds to realise their investments through IPOs. These constituted 17 per cent of exits for private equity houses last year, against a mere 4 per cent in 1997. Trade sales, once the preferred exit route, now make up less than a third of the total. For venture capital funds, this has translated into handsome returns.

Technologieholding claims that its two funds generated net returns to investors of 52.9 and 130.1 per cent respectively in 1998. In recent months, however, competition for deals between venture capitalists has become so rife that some are turning sceptical about the future of the industry.

Germany's corporate giants have added to the pressure by setting up their own funds. These incubators give the companies access to products and innovations at a fraction of the cost of in-house research and development programmes, not to mention the recent entrance in the start-up market of large Anglo-Saxon equity houses with capital available for investment often in excess of DM2bn.

Meanwhile, investors in the Neuer Markt are growing selective in their support for IPOs and the market is screening new entrants more cautiously, which could limit exit opportunities.

"Visibility and reputation are increasingly important in building a solid flow of deals and keeping transaction prices low," says Jurgen Leschke, managing partner at TFG Venture Capital KGAA. Mr Leschke says the fund's flotation has been instrumental in maintaining a high level of enquiries from entrepreneurs. But he warns that the industry could face a setback within two to three years, when some funds reap the consequences of overpriced, low quality transactions.

Ideas that blossom in company

19 January 1999

Vanessa Houlder on a scheme that provides inventors with something more than just financial backing

When AEA Technology, the technology services company, launched its Innovation Plus scheme in 1997, it was billed as a perfect marriage of ideas and resources.

The scheme – which invited inventors to share their ideas with the company – promised to give AEA access to new thinking and possible new commercial partnerships. Inventors, for their part, would improve their chances of seeing their ideas brought to the market.

Sceptics pointed out that this sort of corporate venturing has often proved a disappointment. Although the idea of companies supporting small, entrepreneurial businesses is relatively well-established in the US, it has struggled to take root in the UK. Poor returns and pressure on companies to focus on core activities meant that corporate venturing fell out of fashion in the UK in the late 1980s.

But 18 months after its launch, AEA believes Innovation Plus is starting to bear fruit. "I am convinced it will work," says Peter Watson, chief executive. "I am convinced it will add value to the business."

After the launch, ideas flooded in. About 350 proposals were put forward from individuals, small companies and universities. A few were dismissed as "wacky", but more than 20 were good enough to go through a preliminary evaluation. About eight of those have gone through a detailed investigation.

Among the most promising projects is one that could lead to new hormone treatments for disorders such as enlarged hearts or prostates. This idea, which was put forward by John Hart, a former marketing manager for Amersham, stems from an insight into the way the body regulates the size of organs which he developed when he was writing up his PhD work for a scientific paper in the late 1980s.

Dr Hart is enthusiastic about the Innovation Plus scheme, which has given him the part-time help of half a dozen AEA staff working on his project. There is an excellent fit between AEA's expertise, laboratory facilities and commercial contacts, he says. It feels like moving "from a treadmill to an escalator".

Dr Hart is hoping to complete the scientific work over the next 18 months, before deciding whether to continue to develop the product within AEA or whether to license it.

Dr Hart, who originally secured help from business angels to develop his idea, has also won backing from 3i, the venture capitalists. In his view, corporate venturers can be a useful adjunct to venture capitalists. "I think we needed mentoring on the business side and help on the scientific side. We wouldn't have got that with venture capital alone," he says.

The idea that inventors need help on business is entirely accurate, says Terry Collinson, head of AEA's Innovation Plus. "For every product that gets to the market, there are hundreds that don't because the person doesn't have the resources. Marketing skills, technical skills and commitment are important as well as money," he says.

But despite these advantages, entrepreneurs are often wary about approaching a company with their ideas. As Dr Hart says: "When lone inventors come to AEA, they are in a vulnerable position."

They fear that if they lose control of their project or, worse, if the company steals their idea, there is little they can do.

AEA Technology recognises the need for safeguards. If the inventor has not yet patented the idea, AEA will not ask any detailed questions until it has signed a confidentiality agreement. "We have a reputation to maintain. We would not want to put ourselves in a position where we would take advantage of them," says Mr Collinson.

But the risks in corporate venturing also apply to the companies backing the inventors. It can distract managers' attention from their main businesses and lead them into new markets where they lack expertise. Mr Watson, AEA's chief executive, is aware of the pitfalls. He championed an experiment similar to Innovation Plus when he worked at GKN, the engineering company, in the 1980s. The scheme was eventually dropped when GKN decided to sharpen its focus on its core activities.

But AEA Technology argues that its core business is sufficiently broad to absorb most ideas that are thrown up by the Innovation Plus scheme. Something that clearly fell outside its expertise would be rejected or, possibly, passed on to another organisation.

According to Mr Watson, AEA Technology is a "much more natural home" for this sort of scheme than GKN. "We are smaller but broader. It just seems to fit our kind of business."

In his view, the scheme goes right to the heart of the challenge facing AEA. "Without good ideas we will never grow and some of those ideas have to come from outside."

Investment in training proves to be a profitable process

19 October 1998

A specialist engineering company believes training has played a big part in keeping it successful in hard times, **writes Peter Marsh**

Training record in the engineering sector

Industry sector	Apprentice in-take (%)*	Graduate in-take (%)*	Training (% of sales)
Basic metals	0.9	0.2	0.3
Machinery and equipment	0.9	0.5	0.5
Telecom equipment	0.4	1.0	0.9
Instrumentation	0	0.3	1.0
Motor vehicles	0.5	0.3	0.4
Other transport equipment	1.1	0.5	0.6
Average	0.7	0.4	0.5

Source: Engineering and Marine Training Authority

* As a proportion of employees/year

Sue Hunter, managing director of Process Scientific Innovations, a specialist engineering company, has been having a difficult time in the past two years.

The company, of which she is majority owner and which she runs with her four sons, exports 86 per cent of its production and has seen its profits under pressure due to the strong pound.

Nonetheless Mrs Hunter expects that Process Scientific Innovations' profit margins will stay constant this year, on sales up about 10 per cent compared with last year to £3.4m, due largely to the resources her company has devoted to training during the 1990s.

"I'm very proud of what we have achieved," she says.

Mrs Hunter's company is one of 178 to have been put under the microscope in a pioneering study being published today showing the investment the engineering industry is making in training.

It also takes a stab at indicating how this affects commercial performance.

The report, organised by the Engineering and Marine Training Authority and the Engineering Employers' Federation, has received the support of ministers who say it could form a model for how other industrial sectors attempt the tricky task of measuring the costs and benefits of training initiatives.

In the past, this has been difficult partly because of varying definitions on how to measure training costs. There have also been problems persuading individual businesses to part with the data, which some regard as being useful to competitors.

The two engineering bodies tackled these issues by agreeing that the research would examine only "off-the-job" training – done away from the workplace, either "off-site" or "on-site". Training at the workplace – "learning from Nellie" – was deemed too hard to mea-sure.

Investment on off-the-job training was defined as wages paid to workers for the time they are being trained (and therefore not productive), the costs of external trainers plus other expenses such as travel costs.

The organisers got round the problem of confidentiality by persuading the companies taking part – all of which agreed to be named and have their data published – that the exercise would benefit the whole of industry through establishing "benchmarks" from which everyone could learn.

Even so, only a small proportion of the 22,000 companies in the engineering industry have taken part in the study.

Michael Sanderson, chief executive of the Engineering and Marine Training Authority, a private-sector body that receives some government funding, says the report is a "useful first step" in looking at the complete picture.

One of the star performers from the study is Process Scientific Innovations, based near Durham, which makes air filters for compressors and vacuum pumps.

Last year the company spent £230,000 on off-the-job training, equivalent to 8 per cent of sales, or £2,600 for each employee.

The figures are far higher than the comparable numbers of 0.5 per cent and £700 for all the 178 companies in the survey.

Mrs Hunter says the high figures for the filter maker are due to her policy of bringing in consultants and other outsiders to teach new quality and "teamworking" techniques to the company's 87 employees. She estimates workers and managers spend up to 30 per cent of their time on such training exercises.

They have also benefited from paying visits to bigger companies with plants in north-east England such as Nissan and Black & Decker that have developed new quality and efficiency initiatives.

"Some of the new ideas have been nerver-acking but we have become quicker and smarter as a result," says Mrs Hunter.

While Process Scientific Innovations is among the mainly small companies whose training data appear in the report, among the large companies to have participated is the Rover car group, which spends just 0.4 per cent of its sales on training, equivalent to £700 for each employee.

The report looks at sales growth of the individual companies and concludes – tentatively, as a result of the small sample – that "devoting greater attention to training improves business performance".

Review questions

How do you see the opportunity for entrepreneurs to get access to critical resources being enhanced by:

1 Growth in venture capital provision

2 Corporate venture schemes like that of AEA Technology

3 In-employment training?

7 The entrepreneurial venture and the entrepreneurial organisation

Chapter overview

The fundamental task of the entrepreneur is to create or to change an organisation. This chapter explores what is meant by 'organisation'. The first section explores the way in which entrepreneurs (and other managers) use metaphors (either consciously or unconsciously) to create a picture of the organisations they manage. The second section looks at how entrepreneurs use organisations to control the resources that make up the venture. The third and fourth sections develop a broader view of organisation and consider the entrepreneur operating within a network of resources. The final section considers how this can provide an insight into developing a practical entrepreneurial strategy.

7.1 The concept of organisation

KEY LEARNING OUTCOME
An appreciation of how different ideas of 'organisation' aids understanding of the entrepreneurial approach to management.

The notion of 'organisation' is fundamental to management thinking. An organisation is what a manager works for and organising it is what they do. The entrepreneur may create a new organisation or develop an existing one. Whichever of these options they choose, they create a new organisational world. Organising resources is the means to the end of creating new value. If entrepreneurship is to be understood then the nature of organisation needs to be appreciated.

There are a number of ways in which we can approach the concept of organisation. We cannot see any organisation directly, all we can actually observe is individuals taking actions. We call upon the idea of organisation to explain why those actions are co-ordinated and directed towards some common goal. If we wish to understand how an organisation actually co-ordinates those actions we must create a picture of it using *metaphors*. Thus, we can think of the organisation both as an *entity*, an object in its own right, and as a *process*, a way of doing things. The type of metaphor which is used is important because it influences the way in which management challenges are perceived and approached. They underlie the entrepreneur's management style.

Gareth Morgan (1986) provides an extensive and critical study of how we understand organisation through metaphor in his book *Images of Organisation*.

Some conceptualisations of organisation which are important to understanding entrepreneurship are as follows.

The organisation as a co-ordinator of actions

People do not work in isolation in an organisation. They get together to co-ordinate and share tasks. Differentiating tasks allows a group of people to achieve complex ends that individuals working on their own could not hope to achieve. An organisation is a framework for co-ordinating tasks. It provides direction, routines and regularities for disparate activities. An organisation has goals which are what the people working together in the organisation aim to achieve as a group. The organisation acts to align and direct the actions of individuals towards the achievement of those goals.

Entrepreneurs are powerful figures within their own organisations. Indeed the organisation is the vehicle through which they achieve their ambitions, it extends their scope and allows them to do things that they could not do as an individual. The organisation is the tool entrepreneurs use to create their entire new world. They use their influence and leadership to shape the organisation and direct it towards where they wish to go.

The organisation as an independent agent

An agent is simply something that acts in its own right. Regarding the organisation as an agent means that we give it a character quite separate from that of the people who make it up. The organisation takes actions on its own behalf and has its own distinguishing properties. Thus we can talk about the organisation 'having' a strategy which it uses to pursue 'its' goals. We can talk about the assets 'it' owns and the culture 'it' adopts. This conceptualisation is important from a social and legal perspective. The business organisation is regarded as a legal entity in its own right, quite separate from the identities of its owners and managers. The firm has rights and responsibilities which are distinct from those of its managers. Recognising the organisation as an independent agent is important because it reminds us that the organisations created by entrepreneurs have an existence independent of their creators.

The organisation as a network of contracts

Organisations are made up of people who contribute their labour to the organisation on the basis that they will receive something in return. The organisation is the means people use to pursue their own individual ends. The idea that the organisation is a network of contracts is based on the notion that people work together within a framework of agreements defining the contribution that each individual will make to the organisation as a whole, and what they can expect from the organisation in return. These agreements are referred to as *contracts*.

Organisational contracts take a variety of forms. They may be quite formal and be legally recognised, for example a contract of employment. Frequently, however, a major part of the contract will not be formalised. Many of the commitments and responsibilities that people feel toward their organisation and those they feel it has towards them are unwritten. They are based on ill-defined expectations as to how people should work together and act towards one other. These aspects of the contract may not even be recognised until they are broken by one party. Organisations are built on *trust* and the nature of the contracts that hold the organisation together are a major factor in defining its culture.

The idea of the organisation as a network of contracts is important because it reminds us that individuals do not completely subsume their own interests to those of the organisation, rather the organisation is the means by which they pursue their own goals. They will pursue the organisation's interests only if they align with their own. This concept of the organisation also highlights the fact that the individual's relationship with his or her organisation goes beyond the written legal contract. It is also defined by trust and unspoken expectations. Individuals will only be motivated to contribute to the organisation if those expectations are met, and their trust is not broken.

The organisation as a collection of resources

Organisations are created from resources including capital (money), people and productive assets such as buildings and machinery. The resource-based view of the firm sees it in terms of the collection of resources that make it up. The organisation is built from resources that can be bought and sold through open markets. What makes a particular firm unique is the *combination* of resources that comprise it. Innovation is simply finding *new* combinations of resources.

Having access to appropriate resources and using them both creatively and efficiently is central to entrepreneurial success. It should not be forgotten that people are the key resource since only they can make capital and productive resources work in new and different ways. The idea of the firm as a collection of resources reminds us that the entrepreneur must be an effective manager of resources which means being a manager of people as much as a manager of assets and processes.

The organisation as a system

A system is a co-ordinated body of things, or elements, arranged in a pattern of permanent, or semi-permanent relationships. The notion that the business organisation is a system develops from the idea that a firm takes resource inputs and attempts to convert them into outputs of higher value. The greater the value that is added, the more productive the system. The elements of the organisational system are the people who make it up and the manner in which they are grouped. The actions people take are defined by the pattern of relationships that exist between them. Permanent relationships and consistent actions lead to regular routines and programmes. The systems view of organisation explains the way organisations develop and evolve by drawing on ideas such as feedback loops and control mechanisms.

The idea that the organisation is a system is valuable because it emphasises the dynamic nature of the organisation. It is what the organisation *does* that matters. It also draws attention to the fact that routines take on a life of their own as the system develops its own momentum. Control mechanisms freeze the organisation's way of doing things. This is valuable. They lock in the organisation's source of competitive advantage. However, in order to remain innovative, the entrepreneurial organisation must avoid inertia which requires a continual assessment of the way it does things and a willingness to challenge existing routines if necessary. Entrepreneurial businesses achieve success by being more flexible and responsive to environmental signals than established firms. New contributions to systems thinking from areas such as chaos theory and non-equilibrium dynamics are providing a valuable new perspective on the way entrepreneurial businesses function and how they succeed.

The organisation as a processor of information

Information is a critical part of business success since information, properly used, leads to knowledge and knowledge can lead to competitive success. The organisation can be thought of as a device for processing information, for example information on what needs the customer has, what products will satisfy those needs, how they can be prepared and delivered efficiently, how their benefits can be communicated to customers and so on. In this view, the performance of the firm is determined by the quality of the information it has and how well it uses it. Further, by co-ordinating the intelligence of the people who constitute it, the organisation as a whole can exhibit intelligence. It not only uses information, but can constantly learn how to use information better.

Innovation is at the heart of entrepreneurship and innovation must be based on knowledge. The idea of the organisation as an information processor highlights the fact that the success of the entrepreneurial organisation does not just lie in its innovation but in the way it *uses* that innovation and learns to go on using it. The entrepreneurial organisation achieves flexibility and responsiveness through its willingness to learn about its customers and itself.

Overview

These different perspectives on the organisation are not mutually exclusive, indeed to some extent they are complementary. None of the perspectives gives a complete picture of what the entrepreneurial firm is about, rather each gives a different set of insights into what the firm is, how it performs its tasks, the relation it has to the people who make it up and what the basis of its success might be. If entrepreneurs are to fully understand their business then they must learn to use all these perspectives to gain a complete view.

7.2 Organisation and the control of resources

KEY LEARNING OUTCOME
An understanding of the way the entrepreneur controls resources in their organisation.

Entrepreneurs use resources to achieve their aims in that they combine resources in a way which is innovative and offers new value to customers. This *is* the pursuit of opportunity. Resources are brought together under the control of an organisation. The power of entrepreneurs to control resources directly is limited because there is only so much that they can do as individuals. Therefore, entrepreneurs must shape the organisation they build and use it to configure the resources to which they have access. As the organisation grows and increases in complexity, tasks must be delegated down the organisational hierarchy. Controlling the resources in the organisation means controlling the actions of the people in the organisation who use them. If entrepreneurs are to be effective in leading and directing their organisation then they must understand how the resources that make it up can be controlled.

Entrepreneurs must make a decision as to what they will control themselves and what control they will pass on to others. The balance of this decision will depend on the size and complexity of the organisation, the type and expertise of the people who make it up, the type of resources with which the organisation is working and the strategy it adopts. This decision must be subject to constant revision as the organisation grows, develops and changes. Even if an entrepreneur has delegated the management of resources to other people within the organisation this does not mean that he or she has given up *all* control over them. A number of control mechanisms are retained (see Fig. 7.1).

Directed action

The entrepreneur may retain control by directing that specific tasks are undertaken. The course to be followed will be instructed in detail. The actions are likely to be short-term, or repetitive, with well-defined outcomes. By directing specific actions the entrepreneur is using others to undertake tasks he or she would perform themselves but lack the time to do so.

Routines and procedures

Routines and procedures are used to establish patterns of action to be repeated. No direct control is exercised, but people are expected to follow the course of actions set down. The actions defined by the routine may be specified either in outline or in great detail. The possibility of deviating from the pattern or modifying it will vary depending on the degree of control desired and the need to constrain the outcomes of the actions. When the organisation is too complex to be controlled by directed action, the entrepreneur may concentrate on controlling through procedures.

Organisational strategy

A strategy is a framework for thinking about, and guiding the actions of, individuals within the organisation. The organisation's strategy will be directed towards the achievement of specific goals. It will define the major areas of resource deployment (usually through *budgeting*) and outline the main programmes of activity. The strategy may be imposed by the entrepreneur, or it may be developed through discussion and consensus. People within the organisation might be given a great deal of latitude to develop their own projects of action within the strategy. They will, however, be expected to be guided by the strategy, work towards its goals and operate within its resource constraints. A strategy, even if well defined, offers a greater scope for interpretation than does a routine.

Organisational culture

The concept of organisational culture is a very important one. A culture is the pattern of beliefs, perspectives and attitudes which shape the actions of the people within the organisation. An organisation's culture is largely unwritten. Its existence may not even be recognised until someone acts outside its norms. Culture is very important in creating motivation and setting attitudes. It can be a critical aspect of competitiveness. For example, a positive attitude towards customer service, constantly seeking innovation or greeting change positively are all determined by culture. Things such as these cannot be enforced through rules and procedures so culture is difficult to manage. It is a state of mind, rather than a resource to be manipulated. However, the entrepreneur can help establish a culture in their organisation by leading by example and being clear and consistent about what is expected from people, what behaviour is acceptable to the organisation and what is not. Tom Peters and Robert Waterman (1982), in their highly influential study of US business, *In Search of Excellence,* identified culture as a critical factor in the success of an organisation.

Communicated vision

A vision is a picture of the better world the entrepreneur wishes to create. The vision is the thing that draws the entrepreneur forward and gives them direction. The entrepreneur can, by sharing that vision, communicate the direction in which the organisation must go. If the people who make up the organisation see the vision and accept what it can offer, then the organisation as a whole will gain a sense of direction. However, a vision only specifies an end, not a means. It indicates where the organisation can go, not the path it must take. A vision leaves open the potential for a wide range of possibilities and courses of action. Different courses must be judged in terms of how effective they will be in leading the organisation towards the vision.

The hierarchy of resource control devices

These means of controlling resources form a hierarchy as shown in Fig. 7.1. As it is ascended the entrepreneur becomes less specific in their direction. Their control becomes less direct and immediate. On the other hand, they give the people who work

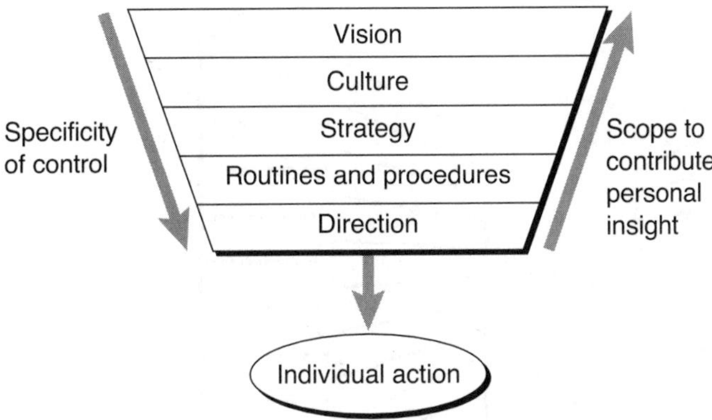

Fig. 7.1 Factors influencing individual action in the entrepreneurial venture

with them more latitude to use their own talent and insights and so make a more substantial contribution to the business. The exact mix of controls used will depend on the size of the organisation, the people who make it up, the tasks in hand and the entrepreneur's personal style. The controls adopted, and the way they are used, will form the basis of the entrepreneur's leadership strategy.

7.3 Markets and hierarchies

KEY LEARNING OUTCOME
An appreciation of the distinction between the market and the hierarchy as forms of organisation.

The business world is full of organisations which offer goods and services to each other and to individual consumers. These goods and services are traded in *markets*. Organisations and markets represent different ways in which individuals can arrange exchanges between themselves.

A market consists of a range of sellers offering their goods to a number of buyers. It is characterised by short-term contracts centred on exchanged products, as shown in Fig. 7.2. Buyers are free to select the seller they wish to buy from. The seller must offer goods at a price dictated by the market. Classical economics assumes that the goods of one supplier are much the same as the goods of any other, although in practice, sellers may be able to differentiate their products from those of competitors. If this differentiation offers advantages to the buyer, then the seller may be able to sustain a price higher than the market norm. In a market, the relationship between the buyer and seller is centred on the product exchanged between them. The seller has no obligation other than to supply the product specified and the buyer has no obligation other than to pay for it. The relationship is short-term with the buyer being free to go to another supplier in the future.

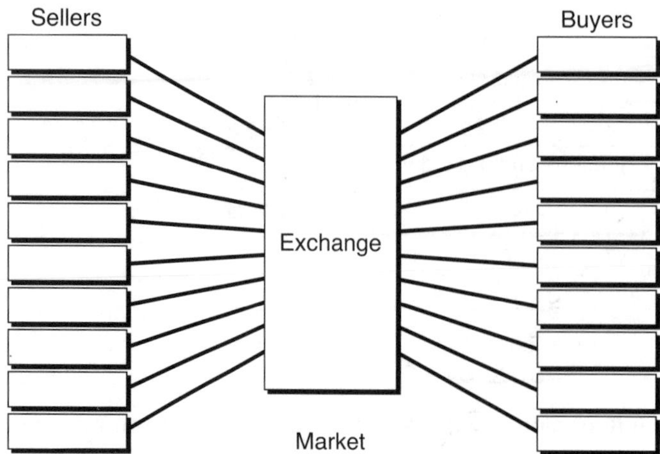

Fig. 7.2 The market as a form of organising exchange

People do not just use markets as a means of organising exchange, they also form organisations such as business firms. Organisations are sometimes referred to as non-market *hierarchies* indicating the way in which the individuals who make them assign responsibilities. In a hierarchy individuals still supply a product, their *labour*, to the organisation. Different parts of the hierarchy will supply products and services to other parts and to the organisation as a whole. The factory may pass on its products to the marketing department for example, or the accounts department may supply financial services. In a hierarchy the relationship between individuals goes beyond the mere product or service they agree to supply. It has a long-term character based on both formal and informal criteria. A hierarchical organisation is based on long-term commitments as depicted in Fig. 7.3.

A hierarchy represents a loss of economic freedom. Within an organisation individuals must use each other's services. They cannot shop around in the market for a better deal. Why then do organisations form? The answer is that markets do not come for free. There is a cost associated with assessing what is available. Gathering information may be expensive. If individuals set up long-term contracts then this cost is reduced. Further, if the product is complex and the relationship short-term, the seller may be tempted to cheat and supply less than expected. The buyer may face a cost associated with *monitoring* what the seller supplies. The monitoring cost is reduced if the buyer and seller *trust* one other. Trust is best built in a long-term relationship, and most easily built if the buyer and seller are part of the same organisation.

The 'market' and the 'hierarchy' are pure types lying at the opposite ends of a spectrum of organisational types. Organisations in the real world lie somewhere in between. They have some of the characteristics of a hierarchy with relationships based on long-term agreements and formal contracts, and some of the characteristics of markets in which individuals come and go, offering their labour and services on a competitive basis. This is true not only within organisations, but also between them. Organisations do not just rely on markets, they set up contracts and make long-term

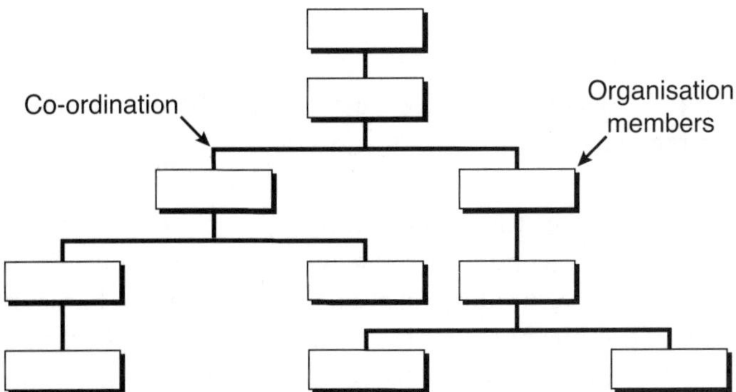

Fig. 7.3 Hierarchical organisation

commitments to each other. The network provides a more realistic model of how entrepreneurial ventures actually operate than either of the pure types of the market and the hierarchy.

This observation has led to the development of a powerful economic approach to understanding why organisations form and the shape they take. This approach is known as *transaction cost economics*. The fundamental idea behind transaction cost economics is that some market exchanges have costs associated with them. These costs arise because with some transactions one party may believe that there is a chance that the other party will renege on the deal at some point in the future. This means that they must invest in setting up binding contracts and then policing them. If these contract costs become too high, then it may be better for the parties to work together within an organisational setting, so locking their interests together. There is a cost associated with this move in that the efficiency the market might have provided is lost. However, if this loss is lower than the expected transaction cost, setting up the organisational structure will still be the most efficient option. Oliver Williamson has been at the forefront of the development of the transaction cost perspective and a full exploration of the insights of this approach can be found in his 1985 book *The Economic Institutions of Capitalism* and his 1991 article listed in the suggestions for further reading at the end of the chapter.

It is often the case that entrepreneurs prefer to work within an organisational setting rather than 'expose' themselves to market uncertainties. One area of resistance that is often encountered is in entrepreneurs sharing the secrets of their innovation with outsiders, who they feel might 'steal' it. Another is they might doubt the commitment of external investors (particularly banks and venture capitalists) to the broader aims of the venture, asserting that they are 'only out for themselves'. As a result of these concerns, they try to bring as many transactions within their organisation as possible. However real such concerns are, the entrepreneur must be aware of the costs, both direct and in terms of loss of flexibility, in adopting organisation-based rather than market-based solutions.

7.4 Networks

KEY LEARNING OUTCOME
An understanding of the concept of the network and its role in the entrepreneurial process.

Individuals use both organisations and markets to facilitate exchanges between themselves. Markets offer a freedom to chose whereas permanent hierarchies emerge when trust is important. Real-life organisations possess some characteristics of both markets and hierarchies. A business organisation has a definite character. It is an agent with legal rights and responsibilities, it has a name. People will know whether they work for it or not. It will have some sort of internal structure.

A business organisation does not exist in isolation. It will be in contact with a whole range of other organisations. Some of these relationships will be established through the market but others may have a longer-term, contractual nature. Businesses set up contracts with suppliers. They may agree to work with a distributor to develop a new market together. An organisation providing investment capital to the venture may be invited to offer advice and support. An entrepreneur may call upon an expert friend to offer advice on marketing. An old business associate may provide an introduction to a new customer. Rather than think about an organisation as closed and sitting in a market, it is better to think of it as being located within a *network* of relationships with other organisations and individuals. In this view the firm does not have a definite boundary. The individuals who make it, and the organisations it comes into contact with, merge into one another. The network is built from relationships which possess both hierarchical and market characteristics. These relationships will be established on the basis of market-led decisions, formal contracts, expectations and trust.

When a new venture is established it must locate itself in a network. This means that it must work to establish a new set of relationships with suppliers, customers, investors and any others who might offer support. The new venture will need to compete with established players. This means that it must break into and modify the network of relationships that *they* have established. A tight network is one in which relationships are established and the parties to them are largely satisfied with these relationships. A loose network is one in which relationships are distant and easily modified. A tight network will be hard to break into, a loose one will be easier. Once a firm is located in a tight network it will find it easier to protect its business from new challengers.

Understanding the nature of the network is important to the success of the entrepreneurial venture. Managing the network will be a crucial part of the strategy for the venture. In particular, the entrepreneur must make decisions in relation to the following questions:

- What is the existing network of relationships into which the new venture must break?
- What is the nature of the relationships that make up the network? Is the network tight or loose? Are the relationships based on formal contracts or on trust?
- How can the new venture actually break into this network of relationships? (Who must be contacted? In what way? What must they be offered?)

- How can the network be used to provide support to the venture?
- What resources (capital, people, productive assets) will the network provide?
- How can risk be shared through the network?
- How can relationships in the network provide a basis for sustaining competitive advantage?

The process of developing answers to these questions will be explored in Part 3 of this book.

In short, a network is a kind of glue which holds a business community together. An entrepreneur initiating a new venture must be active in breaking into a network. Once this has been achieved, the network can be called upon to support them (see Fig. 7.4).

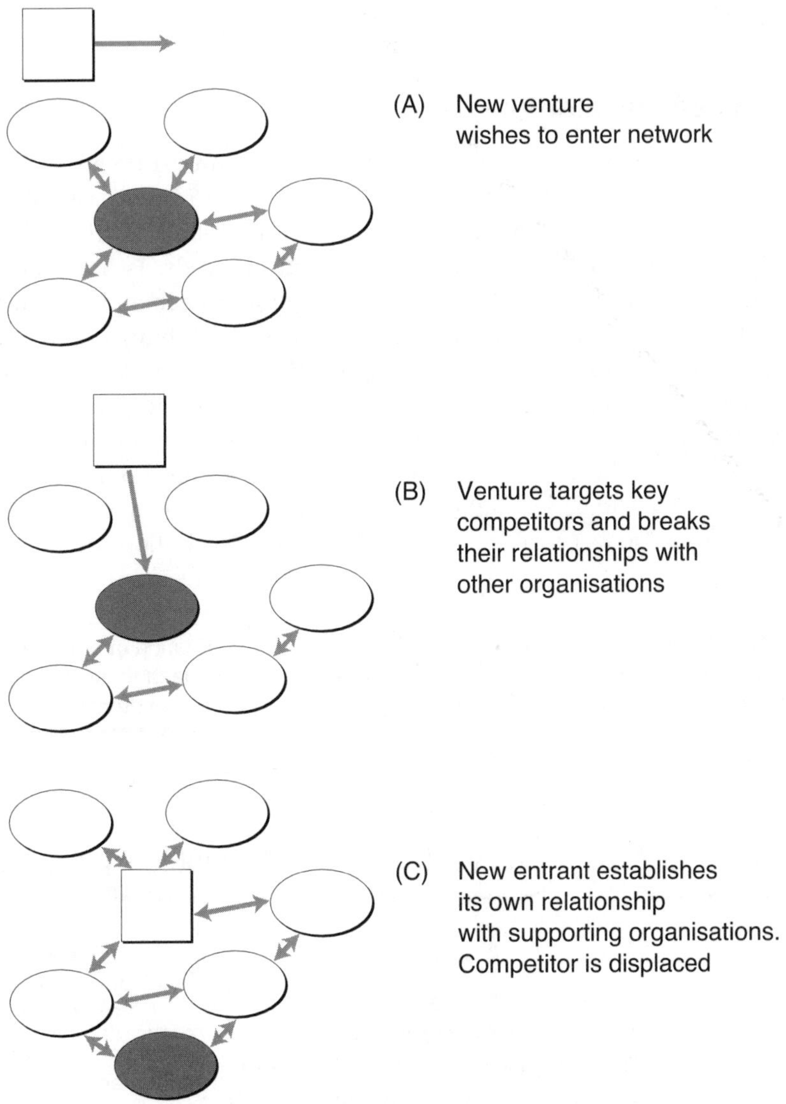

Fig. 7.4 Network formation and the entrepreneurial start-up

7.5 The hollow organisation and the extended organisation

KEY LEARNING OUTCOME
An understanding of how the network may be used to increase the power of the entrepreneurial organisation.

The idea that an organisation is wider than that part of it which is legally defined as the firm provides the entrepreneur with an opportunity. The network offers entrepreneurs the possibility of moving beyond the limits of their own organisation and achieving a great deal more than it would allow them to achieve in isolation. Two types of organisation in particular use the potential of the network.

1 Extended organisations

The extended organisation is one which uses the resources of other organisations in its network to achieve its goals (see Fig. 7.5). Access to these resources is gained by building long-term, supportive and mutually beneficial relationships. Particularly important are suppliers who provide the venture with the inputs it needs, associated organisations in the same business who can help manage fluctuations in demand, and distributors who can get the firm's goods or services to its customers. Distributors need not be limited to the functions of storing and transporting goods. They can also be active partners in developing a new market and add their support to achieving and sustaining a strong competitive position. The business may also develop a productive relationship with other businesses who supply the same customers with non-competing products. Here information on customers and their needs can be exchanged and market research costs shared. It may also be possible to share selling and distribution costs.

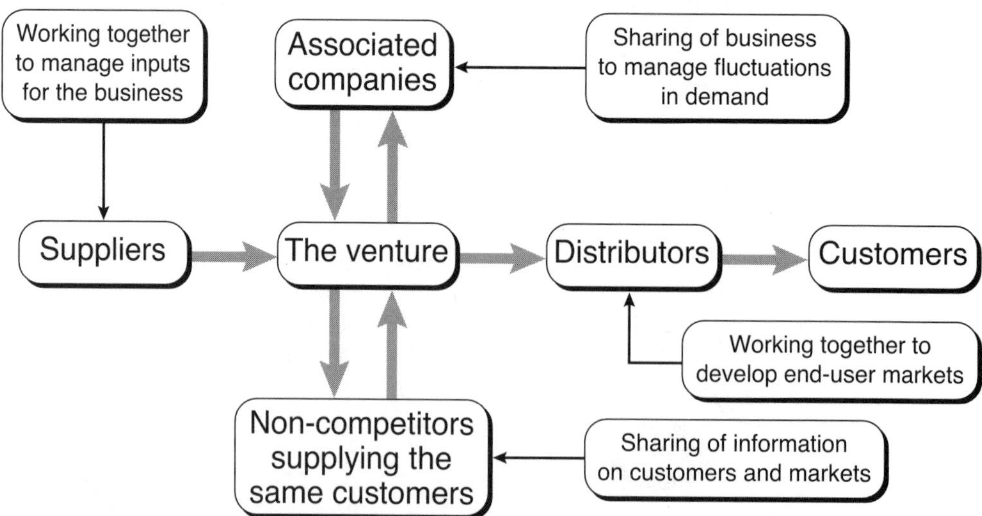

Fig. 7.5 Co-operative relationships in the entrepreneurial network

2 Hollow organisations

The hollow organisation is one which exists not so much to do things itself but to bring other organisations together. In effect it creates value by building a new network or making an existing one more efficient (see Fig. 7.6). The formal organisation is kept as small as possible, it may only be a single office, and it sticks to its essential or *core* activities. A common example of a hollow organisation is one which simply 'markets' products. It will buy these products from the company which manufactures them. It will use independent distributors to get the product to customers. It may call upon the services of separate market research and advertising agencies. It may even contract-in its sales team. The hollow organisation does not manufacture, distribute or advertise goods or services. It simply exists to bring together the organisations that perform these functions. It is rewarded from the value it creates by co-ordinating their activities.

An excellent example of what can be achieved by adopting a hollow organisation strategy is that of Naxos Records, a venture founded by the Hong Kong-based, German entrepreneur, Klaus Heymann. This is a business which has established a market-leading position in the low-cost classical CD market. Yet the core organisation does little itself except co-ordinate the production and marketing of the product. Musicians and orchestras (often from eastern Europe) are commissioned as they are needed. Recording facilities are hired in. Production of the CD and packaging of it are out-sourced (usually in the Far East). Distribution is via independent retailers.

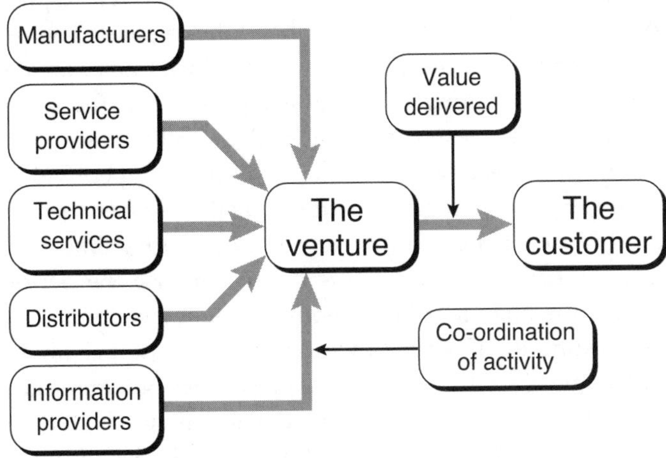

Fig. 7.6 The hollow organisation

Factors affecting choice of organisation

Both the extended organisation and the hollow organisation are attractive options for the entrepreneur. There are a number of reasons for this:

- they are easy to set up;
- the initial investment needed is small and entry costs are low;
- they allow the entrepreneur to concentrate on their core skills;

- they are flexible and can be easily modified;
- fixed costs are minimised;
- they allow the entrepreneur access to the resources of other organisations;
- growth is relatively easy to manage.

Competition to set up hollow and extended organisations can be quite intense because they are both such attractive options for starting new ventures. If they are to be successful entrepreneurs must be quite sure of the strategy they are adopting. In particular they must be confident about:

- where the business will be located in the value-addition chain;
- the value they are adding, i.e. why customers will benefit from what the business has to offer;
- why the product they are offering is different from what is already on offer;
- how they will manage the relationships on which the business will depend;
- how they will sustain those relationships in the face of competitors trying to break the relationships it has established.

These are important ideas which will be developed further in Part 3 of this book.

The Internet has made a great impact on the world of business. New Internet ventures like the book retailer Amazon and the computer supplier Dell have been very high-profile stock market successes. The merger of the media company Time Warner with the on-line service provider *America On-Line* (AOL) has created great interest and a considerable mark-up on the stock-market value of the separate companies.

The Internet is primarily a communication system, albeit one of great sophistication and reach. The reason it is creating such high expectations is the way it is enabling information to be stored and accessed by organisations and the facility it offers to pass information between them. Advocates of the potential competitive advantages the Internet are offering to business are keen to draw a distinction between what is referred to as *E-commerce*, the use of the Internet as an adjunct to selling and promotional activities, and *E-business*, the use of the Internet to enhance the performance of the organisation's entire operational stance. E-business goes beyond just selling. It is concerned with managing the business's whole value-addition chain and creating an active, two-way dialogue with the customer, not just sending a message to them.

Strategically, the Internet is encouraging the development of hollow organisations. This is because it is so powerful in co-ordinating the activities of otherwise separate organisations in an efficient and relatively low-cost way. Many new Internet start-ups are concerned not so much with manufacturing or even direct service delivery. They are providing a facility that brings traditional suppliers and potential consumers together. Customers appreciate the power of the Internet in terms not only of making purchase easy but also of its ability to provide information, making the purchase decision more informed. Suppliers recognise the potential to create new business through a relatively low-cost route. However, many also appreciate the tendency of the Internet to make buyer price comparison easier, and so competition, keener.

The key question for the Internet-based hollow organisation is not so much gaining entry, which is quite straightforward: it is gaining long-term competitive advantage that presents the challenge. Low entry costs are attractive for entrepreneurs, and investors, because they reduce risk. However, this also means competitors find it easy to follow. Achieving competitive advantage is more difficult. Internet distributors, like any other distributor, cannot significantly alter the final product or service the consumer uses. Internet distributors have lower costs than traditional distributors, but costs can only be reduced so far. In any case, offering the buyer a lower price reduces the venture's profits. Ultimately, successful Internet ventures will be those who build a relationship with customers based on range of offerings, quality of service and reputation supported by a trusted brand. The Internet may be changing the business world, but it is not changing its fundamental rules.

Summary of key ideas

- The entrepreneur must bring the resources they use together in the form of an *organisation*.
- Organisations are best understood through the use of *metaphors*: the things they are 'like'.
- The *open market* and the *closed hierarchy* are pure forms of organisation.
- The entrepreneurial organisation is best thought of as a *network* of relationships defined through markets and formal hierarchies. The network lies somewhere between the two pure forms.
- Entrepreneurs can create new value by building *hollow* or *extended* organisations which co-ordinate the activities of other organisations.

Suggestions for further reading

Anderson, J.C., **Håkansson, H.** and **Johanson, J.** (1994) 'Dyadic business relationships within a business network context', *Journal of Marketing*, Vol. 58, pp. 1–15.

Anderson, P. (1992) 'Analysing distribution channel dynamics: Loose and tight couplings in distribution networks', *European Journal of Marketing*, Vol. 26, No. 2, pp. 47–68.

Birley, S. (1985) 'The role of networks in the entrepreneurial process', *Journal of Business Venturing*, Vol 1, pp. 107–17.

Birley, S., **Cromie, S.** and **Myers, A.** (1991) 'Entrepreneurial networks: Their emergence in Ireland and overseas', *International Small Business Journal*, Vol. 9, No. 4, pp. 56–74.

Boisot, M.H. (1986) 'Markets and hierarchies in a cultural perspective', *Organisation Studies*, Vol. 7, No. 2, pp. 135–58.

Cheung, S.N.S. (1998) 'The transaction cost paradigm', *Economic Inquiry*, Vol. 36, No. 4, pp. 514–21.

Falemo, B. (1989) 'The firm's external persons: Entrepreneurs or network actors?' *Entrepreneurship and Regional Development*, Vol. 1, No. 2, pp. 167–77.

Jarillo, J.C. (1988) 'On strategic networks', *Strategic Management Journal*, Vol. 9, pp. 31–41.

Jones, G.R. and **Hill, C.W.L.** (1988) 'Transaction cost analysis of strategy–structure choice', *Strategic Management Journal*, Vol. 9, pp. 159–72.

Larson, A. (1992) 'Network dyads in entrepreneurial settings: A study of the governance of exchange relationships', *Administrative Science Quarterly*, Vol. 37, pp. 76–104.

Larson, A. (1993) 'A network model of organisation formation', *Entrepreneurship Theory and Practice*, Vol. 12, No. 2, pp. 5–15.

Morgan, G. (1986) *Images of Organisation*, London: Sage Publications.

Perry, M. (1996) 'Network intermediaries and their effectiveness', *International Small Business Journal*, Vol. 14, No. 4, pp. 72–9.

Peters, T. and **Waterman Jr, R.H.**, (1982) *In Search of Excellence*, New York: Harper & Row.

Szarka, J. (1990) 'Networking and small firms', *International Small Business Journal*, Vol. 8, No. 2, pp. 10–22.

Tyosvold, D. and **Weicker, D.** (1993) 'Co-operative and competitive networking by entrepreneurs: A critical indent study', *Journal of Small Business Management*, Jan, pp. 11–21.

Williamson, O. (1985) *The Economic Institutions of Capitalism*, New York: Free Press.

Williamson, O. (1991) 'Comparative economic organization: The analysis of discrete structural alternatives', *Administrative Science Quarterly*, Vol. 36, pp. 269–96.

Selected case material

Silicon subcontinent

15 March 1999

India's software industry is thriving thanks to the millennium bug. **Krishna Guha** and **Paul Taylor** ask whether it can make it to the big-time league

Forget Silicon Valley. Investors looking for the next Bill Gates should set their sights on India's software entrepreneurs.

Infosys Technologies, an 18-year-old company based in Bangalore, India's capital of high tech, last week became the first Indian company to list on Nasdaq alongside some of the world's leading technology stocks. In India, the event was greeted as the coming of age for its software industry.

With other Indian companies planning Nasdaq listings, Nandan Nilekani, managing director of Infosys, says the industry is moving on to a new plane: Indian software companies will enjoy a higher international profile, their access to capital will be enhanced, and companies will have lucrative share-option schemes (in dollars, of course) with which to attract talented software engineers.

The Infosys listing is a testament to the extraordinary progress made by India's software industry – the nation's only outright success story of the 1990s.

For the past eight years, the sector has expanded at annual rates of more than 50 per cent. The growth forecast for this year is 70 per cent. The value of the Bombay market software index has risen 15-fold since the start of 1997.

The industry, whose star performers include Infosys, Wipro, NIIT, Satyam, Tata Infotech and Pentafour, now commands a market capitalisation of $15bn. And this does not include Tata Consultancy Services, the largest Indian software company, which is still in private hands.

Export earnings, estimated at $2.6bn this year, are still modest but are growing rapidly. The government is predictably upbeat. A National Task Force on Information Technology recently set a target of $50bn exports by 2008, by which time it predicts software will be India's biggest export. Many industry insiders believe that target is too conservative.

And yet the industry is not 20 years old. The first software companies were established in the mid-1980s, when the government removed tariff barriers and began to encourage inward investment from US technology groups.

It was not just low wages that attracted companies such as Texas Instruments, Motorola and Oracle; the educational standards of young Indian programmers and their command of English were seen as important advantages over competing locations elsewhere in Asia or in Eastern Europe. Foreign investment spurred local imitators and the creation of wealth on an unprecedented scale.

Nevertheless, a small number of sceptics suggest that the phenomenal growth of India's software industry this decade was at least partly due to an accident of timing.

The Year 2000 computer date problem triggered a wave of demand for services which could not be met by the available pool of programmers in Europe and the US. So problem solvers began outsourcing some of the work to India.

"God's gift to India was Y2K," says Srinivasan Raju, executive director of Satyam.

But will the country's software entrepreneurs have a future once current Y2K projects are completed?

Dewang Mehta, head of the National Association of Software and Services Companies (Nasscom), which represents most Indian software companies, says the industry has developed enough to flourish beyond 2000. Already, big companies earn less than a quarter of revenues from Y2K recoding work; some less than 10 per cent.

Mr Raju, of Satyam, says Y2K work gave Indian companies the resources, international credibility and project management skills to progress to more complex and higher value contracts.

This is not to ignore some big obstacles in the path of the industry's future development.

First, an industry that took off because of its low-cost base is now beginning to suffer from the impact of skills shortages and wage inflation. The salaries of Indian software programmers are still only one-third of their

US counterparts, but they are rising at a rate of 25 to 30 per cent a year, according to Mr Nilekani of Infosys. "Unless we are able to get commensurate increases in prices we will be squeezed on margins," he says.

The high cost and poor quality of India's state-owned telecommunications is another barrier to growth, and the industry is lobbying for faster telecoms reform, with some success. In January the government announced an end to the public sector monopoly in internet service provision, and last week the telecoms regulator ordered big cuts in fees for leased lines.

But if India is to reach its target of $50bn software exports by 2008, it needs to educate 1.5m programmers, and provide all the infrastructure demanded by high tech companies. Just air-conditioning the offices of the high-tech sector will require 2,250 MW of power in a country where power black-outs are endemic and force most software companies to rely on back-up generators.

Nirmal Jain, managing director of Tata Infotech, believes companies will only succeed in higher value services if they have expertise in business sectors as well as programming. "We have to build vertical industry capabilities which will help us go up the value chain," he says.

Some companies are planning to develop niche products which do not compete directly with existing market leaders. Others want to develop products that can be sold on to US software giants.

Most are under no illusions about the fierce competition they will face from existing software companies and established global consultancy firms. But they believe they will benefit from two fundamental changes in the IT landscape: the growth of the internet and the development of e-commerce.

"This is a new market where there is no clear leader, says N. Krishna Kumar, chief executive of Wipro Infotech. He says Indian companies are poised to develop e-commerce systems, content, interfaces, network management, encryption, and business support systems such as on-line billing.

Moreover, the internet has given the Indian entrepreneur a bridge with which to reach customers, regardless of marketing budgets or geographical distance.

"On the internet I am just another John," says one of India's top software executives. "No-one can tell I am a brown John."

Many in India believe the software industry is the most powerful modernising force in their country today. It competes with other forces – organised labour, religious fundamentalists, oppressed castes – some centuries old. How the software industry fares in this contest will shape not only its own success, but the kind of country India will be in the new millennium.

High-risk strategy begins to pay off for Indian high-tech pioneer

18 March 1999

Ramco software group is becoming a world-class enterprise, writes **Mark Nicholson**

India's old "licence raj" can not be thanked for inspir ing much world-class enterprise. But the discredited and largely dismantled system of centralised industrial licensing can take some credit for inspiring India's first serious entrant into the global market for enterprise resource planning software.

When the Raja family of industrialists in Madras scouted for opportunities to diversify from cement and textiles in the 1980s, the trick was to find a sector that did not need a licence or any attendant political lobbying.

"At that time licensing was intense," says PR Venketrama Raja, founder of Ramco Systems. "We were not interested in going into the politics to get projects, so we decided the answer was new technology and computing, for which you didn't need a licence."

The Rajas also wanted to widen their horizons, having established profitable, but modest-sized cement, yarns and roofing businesses based in Madras, with total turnover of around $250m. "We thought, we're a good national player, how do we become international?" says Mr Raja. "We have the cash, and people, maybe we should invest in computing."

It was similar thinking for similar reasons – the lack of any need for licensing – that fuelled a small explosion of software start-ups across India in the late 1980s and early 1990s, particularly in Bangalore. These, in turn, have matured to turn software into India's most vibrant export industry.

But unlike most of his peers, Mr Raja chose not to enter the sector on the bottom rung by offering basic software services to foreign clients, based largely on the simple advantage of cheap labour. Instead, he formed the nucleus of Ramco Systems 10 years ago, aiming to develop fully-fledged ERP products – among the most complex and commercially risky in the industry. He began with an initial team of 15 software engineers and start-up capital from the other family firms.

ERP products are a suite of programmes or integrated software modules that combine to offer companies a single view of a big enterprise. Generally, they include modules providing anything from stock control, sales analysis, payroll management and monitoring and control of complex manufacturing processes.

"Creating an ERP product is a bigger task than creating an operating system," says Mr Raja. "You need a massive mastery of various disciplines." It also takes faith, since by Mr Raja's reckoning it takes between seven and eight years of development, with a team of several hundred software engineers, to create the architecture for a fully developed ERP product. This period is one mostly of investment and rarely of reward – which means only companies with existing cash flow or resources can contemplate such things.

"You can't start up an ERP company just with a garage full of a few bright software engineers," says Mr Raja. "Then,

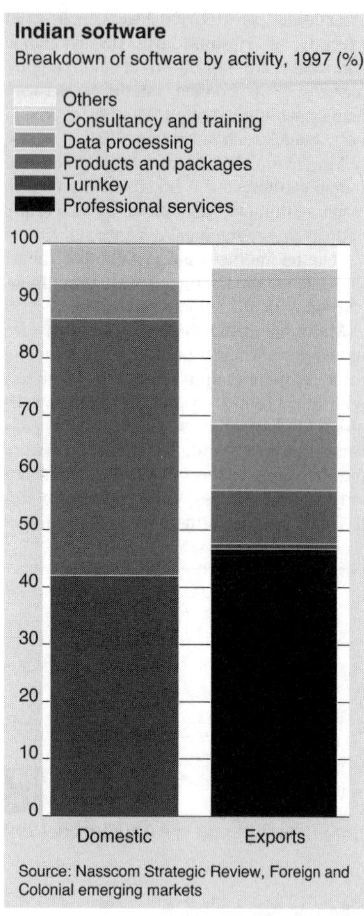

at the end of it, you still don't know if you have created a current, acceptable product. So you have to have great foresight, or luck, or a bit of both."

Early versions of Ramco's product entered the market in 1994. By this year, turnover from early sales had reached $30m, the workforce had grown to 1,200, and the company is now marketing a refined version of its ERP product, Ramco Marshal 3.0. "It was a massive enterprise," says Mr Raja, "that no-one thought a company from India could manage."

Altogether, he says the project has cost $40m to develop, drawn chiefly from some debt and internal revenues from the parent Ramco businesses – around 12 per cent of the likely cost of such a project in developed countries. The Microsoft-based product offers the panoply of ERP applications, including plant maintenance, inventory control, accounts, process planning and controls, sales forecasting and analysis and personnel management.

Ramco has adapted the product for use anywhere from open-cast mining to managing power stations. And, according to Mr Raja, the company is beginning to find itself shortlisted by clients alongside some of the big ERP suppliers.

The ERP market is worth tens of billions of dollars globally, dominated by SAP, the German software house, followed by Oracle and PeopleSoft of the US and BAAN of the Netherlands.

So far, among more than 80 clients for the product, Marshal has been adopted by Bemis, the biggest flexible packaging maker in the US, which is using the Ramco logistics system in 15 of its 40 US plants. Six months ago ETA, the Swiss watchmaker, also installed Marshal in 12 of its factories.

Ramco Systems' turnover this year was twice last year's. Mr Raja believes it can double again for 1999-2000 to $55m-$60m, sustaining similar growth until turnover hits around $200m.

By the time the company hits sales of around $80m, he suggests, it would look to demerge from its parent Ramco Industries, a Rs5bn ($118m) capitalised business making roofing sheets, and list separately, on the Indian market and in the US, through an ADR offering.

The US listing is partly motivated by the need to be able to offer its employees stock option income in hard currency – an increasingly fashionable perk in the Indian software sector to keep staff loyal.

Having developed its product, Ramco Systems is now focused on marketing it, and is looking to raise between $15m and $25m from venture capital funds and elsewhere, to expand its international presence.

"Everyone is watching us very closely to see whether all this investment can actually be turned to profit," says Mr Raja. The Indian stock market clearly believes so. The share price of Ramco Industries has been buoyed recently by speculation over an eventual demerger.

Diverse routes to the region's riches

10 November 1999

ENTREPRENEURS by **Stefan Wagstyl:** Businesses have been built on everything from determination and chance to connections gained through ties to the old regime

For Dinu Patriciu, one of the wealthiest men in Romania, doing business in the 1990s has been about getting in first.

After the fall of Nicolae Ceausescu, the Romanian dictator, Mr Patriciu was the first person to register a private company in the country – called Alpha, it was given the registration number 00000001. An architect by profession, Mr Patriciu was also among the first to grasp the value of property. Just before Bucharest land prices took off amid the high inflation of the early 1990s, he sold a car and a video recorder and put the money into property. Simultaneously, he received a string of architectural contracts from others wanting to develop sites.

The boom later fizzled out and some of Mr Patriciu's projects were never built. But the fees were paid, and Mr Patriciu was on his way to financial success. Today, aged 49, he runs a business group that includes property development, asset management and Rompetrol, one of Romania's largest oil companies with its own refinery.

He has his problems, notably with a loss-making shipping company he founded. However, the group as whole, which employs about 2,000 people, makes profits of 5-10 per cent of turnover which Mr Patriciu says will this year reach $120m-$130m and $200m next year.

Mr Patriciu says that determination and chance played an equal part in his success. "I was stubborn and I was lucky," he says. He was also fortunate. As one of Romania's top architects he taught at Bucharest University, which had extensive national and international contacts. In the 1980s, he won an international scholarship which led to work overseas and, as he says, "contact with the market economy".

Mr Patriciu's story highlights one of the most important economic and social trends of post-communist eastern Europe – the rise of the entrepreneur. Once the chains of totalitarianism were broken, business people grasped opportunities to make money – as free market theorists said they would – even in the toughest macro-economic conditions such as those in Romania.

The scale and importance of newly-created private business varies greatly between countries. The biggest number of active entrepreneurs is probably in Poland, where business has been stimulated by traditional independence of mind, by frequent contact with relatives and others in the west, and by favourable macroeconomic policies.

Hungary, too, has generated many businesses, notably in high-technology, where some companies have been so successful that they have moved lock, stock and barrel to the US. Czech companies, stifled by red tape and economic stagnation, have done less well. In the former Soviet Union, the most successful have been those who have won control of oil, gas and other natural resources businesses, quickly turning themselves into some of Europe's wealthiest people.

Entrepreneurs also often differ in their origins. Some, like Mr Patriciu, made use of their existing skills and contacts. Others had businesses before 1989, especially in Poland and Hungary, where small-scale private enterprise was tolerated.

For example, Wojciech Kruk, president of Kruk, Poland's best-known jeweller, runs a business started by his family in 1840. It never closed, operating in basement workshops during the height of Stalinist oppression. Today, Mr Kruk has a turnover of $10m a year, employs 300 and is considering a stock market flotation.

Many business people are former members of the communist political elite. Directors of state-run factories often, through privatisation, won personal control of all or part of their old operations. This element is strongest in Russia and Ukraine, where a new phrase has been invented to describe the process – "nomenklatura capitalism".

Rem Vyakhirev, chief executive of Gazprom, the gas group, is one of the more successful of thousands of former officials. Anti-communist politicians often condemn nomenklatura capitalism as unfair, but, at least within the former Soviet Union, the Communist party had such a grip on talent that there are few alternative sources of well-educated people with business experience.

Outside the former Soviet Union, ties to the old regime are less important. in terms of numbers, the most important school of entrepreneurship is small-scale trade.

Taking goods from one place to another, often across borders, allowed tens of thousands to accumulate a little capital in the 1980s and early 1990s and later to establish a shop, a bar, a workshop or a software company. Among them is one of Poland's richest business people, Zbigniew Niemczycki, who began in the 1980s by trading goods including fruit juice and now employs about 1,000 people at his group called Curtis International.

For a younger generation, such possibilities still exist but offer a long hard road to success. Some try to short-circuit the process by working as employees for a while to accumulate cash and experience.

For example, in Hungary, 31-year-old Erno Duda – who first made a name for himself managing Copy General, a US-owned chain of copy shops – left the company to set up a student restaurant in Szeged, his home town. He impressed some local lawyers who asked him to join them in establishing LP Invest, a venture capital group.

Recently, he was so struck by one high-technology company which approached LP Invest that he decided to help finance it and work for it full time. The company, Solvo, makes sophisticated blood-testing kits for use in chemotherapy. "Business is creative," says Mr Duda. "I love a challenge."

He also likes the freedom to make his own decisions and the perks of being in charge. LP Invest's office, from where he runs Solvo, has its own swimming pool. "Where else could I have that?" he asks.

Terra Networks joins the stars

19 November 1999

Christopher Price, **Paul Betts** and **Tom Burns** examine whether the Spanish internet company can sustain its spectacular market debut

Madrid brokers are calling it the terramoto – a play on terremoto, Spanish for earthquake. The success of this week's market debut of Terra Networks has made the Spanish internet company by far the most valuable internet stock in Europe.

Listed on Madrid's Bolsa and New York's Nasdaq on Wednesday, Terra's market capitalisation soared to €10bn ($10.3bn) on Wednesday – three times its pre-flotation valuation.

In part, its strong debut reflects the internet's rapid expansion in Europe, as evidenced by the equally successful public offerings in two other big internet service providers: Tiscali of Italy and Freeserve of the UK. It also demonstrates that Europe is not immune to the internet fever gripping the US.

But the debuts of all three internet service providers also reveals a great deal about the particular nature of the European internet market – and consequently how valuations in Europe are likely to differ from those in the US.

Investor enthusiasm in Europe has been underpinned by factors common to all three leading stocks. First, Tiscali, Freeserve and Terra Networks, although only recently established, have quickly grown to be substantial businesses.

All three occupy the leading position in their respective markets. Thus, Tiscali has a 15 per cent share of the Italian internet market, Freeserve has a 20 per cent share in the UK, while Terra Networks holds 30 per cent of the Spanish market. In terms of subscribers, this translates into 630,000, 1.5m and 860,000 respectively.

Third, establishing national brands and business strategies within smaller markets defined by country, language and culture has enabled them to expand their services more quickly than in a huge continent like the US. Freeserve and Tiscali, for example, are just over one year old, Terra a little less than that.

In the cases of Tiscali and Freeserve, they have revolutionised their respective national markets by introducing free internet access. This has been a crucial factor in Europe where, unlike the US, telecommunications users pay for their local calls on a metered basis.

Seen in this light, their investor appeal is obvious. "To make the internet service provider business model succeed, particularly those with free access, you have to have a mass market," says Sarah Skinner, an internet analyst with Durlacher, the London-based research group. "And that is what these three companies have got."

But questions remain about whether their premium ratings – Terra's in particular – are justified. At yesterday's close, the market capitalisation of Terra, Freeserve and Tiscali stood at €6.7bn, €3.9bn and €2.3bn, respectively.

All three companies are lossmaking and have similar business models based on becoming "portals". They want their subscribers to spend more time on their own web sites – to shop, read, chat – instead of jumping off into the wider web. "They have to convert their eyeballs into e-commerce revenues and other revenue streams – and that's a big challenge," says Ms Skinner.

In terms of the value the market places on each of their subscribers, all three European stocks are on big premiums to their US peers, such as Mindspring and Earthlink. At yesterday's market close, Terra has a per subscriber valuation of €7,821, Freeserve €1,993 and Tiscali €3,538.

That said, there are particular features of the Spanish, Italian and UK markets that must be taken into account in each case. For example, Jaime Bergel, managing director in Spain of Goldman Sachs, the US bank that was joint co-ordinator of the Terra issue, says: "Terra has the leadership in the Spanish and Portuguese-speaking worlds and Freeserve cannot claim the same in the English-speaking world."

A key attraction of Terra is that it leads the field in Spain, Portugal and Latin America, which have a combined population of 520m. It also aims to tap the 30m strong Spanish-speaking market in the US.

Indeed, in recent months Terra has been aggressively buying up local internet service providers and portals from Mexico to Chile. Following its listing, the company's purchasing power is greatly enhanced.

In addition, internet penetration is low in the areas where Terra has set up for business and it is set to grow fast. Another strength is that its parent, Spain's Telefonica group, operates the biggest telecoms franchise in Latin America. Juan Perea, Terra's chairman, forecasts that it will have 18m subscribers in seven years' time.

Both Tiscali and Freeserve have had similar effects on their respective markets. Both were the first to introduce mass-market free internet access, and both have forced domestic rivals to follow suit.

By being the first to market, the two companies have built up enviable leads over the competition. The challenge for both is to maintain that lead, and it is this that has led to their lower valuations in comparison with Terra. Freeserve shares in particular have been volatile, falling below their issue price at one stage, on fears over increased competition from larger rivals such as America Online.

Further, the UK internet market is growing at a slower rate than Italy or Spain. In Italy, for example, only 4 per cent of the country's population were using internet in the first quarter of this year compared with 17 per cent in the UK, 10 per cent in Germany and 6 per cent in France, according to the Fletcher research group.

On the other hand, Freeserve does have the part-ownership and backing of Dixons, the UK's biggest electrical retailer. Tiscali, which was founded by a Sardinian entrepreneur, lacks the deep pockets of a substantial owner.

These considerations make comparisons for the pan-European investor all the more difficult than for investors in a more homogenous region like the US. But judging by the pent-up demand for the big three European internet issues so far, it seems that they are concerns many investors are choosing to worry about later rather than sooner.

Review questions

1 How do you think India, Romania and Spain might compare in terms of the balance between 'market' and 'hierarchical' organisational forms for co-ordinating economic activity?

2 How might the Internet be changing this?

3 What new opportunities and challenges will this present to the entrepreneur?

4 Who might be players in the extended network for the Indian, Romanian and Spanish ventures described?

8 The meaning of success

Chapter overview

Entrepreneurship is about success. This chapter is concerned with defining what success really means and the ways in which it can be measured. Business success is considered not only in financial terms but also in a broader social context. The chapter concludes with an exploration of the converse of success: failure. Failure is not seen as completely negative but rather an experience which is occasionally necessary and which presents an opportunity for the organisation and the entrepreneur to learn.

8.1 Defining success

KEY LEARNING OUTCOME
An understanding of what entrepreneurial success actually means.

Entrepreneurs aim to be successful. It is the possibility of success that drives them on and success is the measure of their achievement. Success is, however, quite a difficult concept to define because it is multi-faceted. Both individuals and organisations enjoy success. It may be measured by hard and fast 'numbers' but also by 'softer', qualitative criteria. Success is something which is both visible in public but is also experienced at a personal level.

Success can be best understood in terms of four interacting aspects:

1 the performance of the venture;
2 the people who have expectations from the venture;
3 the nature of those expectations; and:
4 actual outcomes relative to expectations.

The performance of the venture is indicated by a variety of quantitative measures. These relate to its financial performance and the presence it creates for itself in the marketplace. The indicators can be absolute and compared to the performance of competitors. Such performance measures relate to the organisation as a whole. However, an organisation is made up of individual people and success, if it is to be meaningful, must be experienced by those individuals as well as by the organisation.

Organisational success is a means to the end of *personal* success. The organisation creates the resources which interested individuals can use to improve their lives. The individuals who have an interest in the performance of the venture are its *stakeholders*. Thus the success of a venture must be considered in relation to the expectations its stakeholders have for it (see Fig. 8.1).

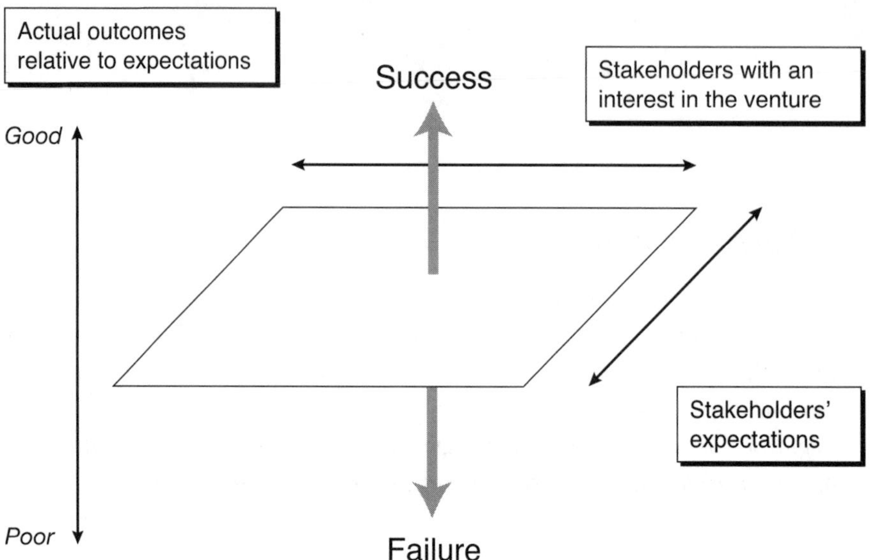

Fig. 8.1 A model of entrepreneurial success

The entrepreneurial venture has six groups of stakeholder, each of which has its own interest and expectations from the venture. The *entrepreneur* (and their dependents) expects the venture to be a vehicle for personal ambitions; *employees* expect reward for their efforts and personal development; *suppliers* expect the venture to be a good customer; *customers* expect the venture to be a good supplier; *investors* expect the venture to generate a return on the investment they have made; and the *local community* expects the venture to make a positive contribution to the quality of local life.

The performance of the venture as an organisation provides the means by which individual stakeholders can use fulfil their own goals. Personal goals are manifest at three levels:

- the *economic* – monetary rewards;
- the *social* – fulfilling relationships with other people; and
- the *self-developmental* – the achievement of personal intellectual and spiritual satisfaction and growth.

Success experienced at a personal level is not absolute. Success is recognised by comparing actual outcomes to prior *expectations*. At a minimum, success is achieved if outcomes meet expectations and success is ensured if expectations are exceeded. If expectations are not met, however, then a sense of failure will ensue.

Different stakeholders will hold different expectations. They will look to the organisation to fulfil different types of goals. The investor may only be interested in the venture offering financial returns whereas the customers and suppliers will want financial rewards, but they may also hope to build rewarding social relationships with people in the organisation. Employees will expect a salary but this will only be their minimum expectation. They will also expect the venture to provide a route for self-development. The venture will be central to the personal development of the entrepreneur.

Success, then, is not a simple thing. The organisation's financial and strategic performance is only part of the picture. Success is achieved if the organisation uses its performance to meet, or better to *exceed*, the financial, social and personal growth expectations of the people who have an interest in it. The success of a venture depends on how its performance helps stakeholders to achieve their individual goals, and the way different people judge the success of the venture will depend on how well these expectations are met (see Fig. 8.2).

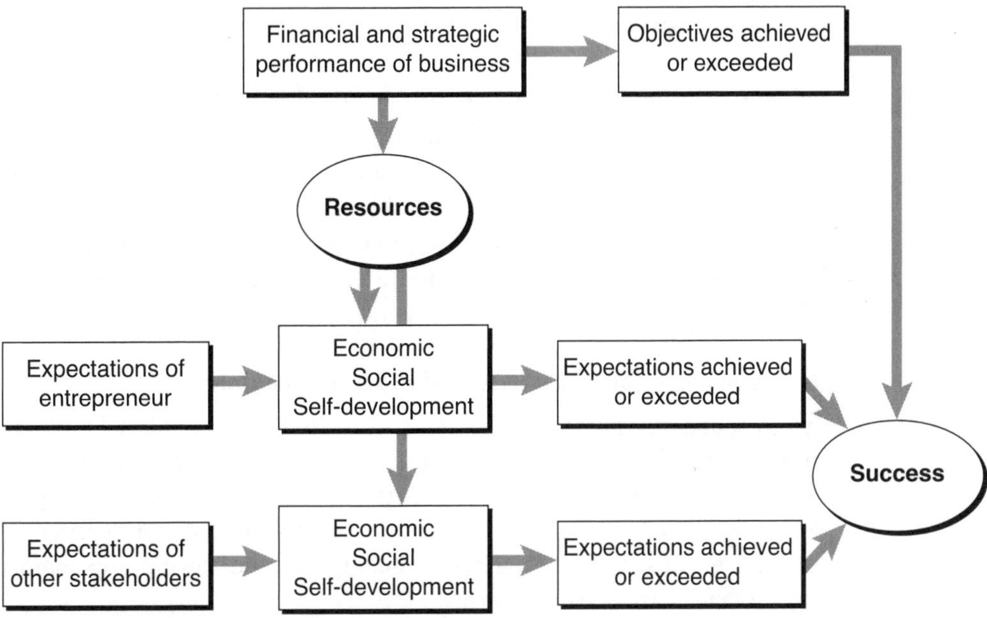

Fig. 8.2 The dynamics of entrepreneurial success

8.2 Success factors for the new venture

KEY LEARNING OUTCOME

An appreciation of some of the main factors involved in the success of a new venture.

A venture is successful if it meets the aspirations of its stakeholders. In order to do this it must survive and prosper in the marketplace. It must attract resources, reward its stakeholders for their contributions and be financially secure. Every venture is different, but a common set of factors lies behind every successful business.

The venture exploits a significant opportunity

The opportunity spotted by the entrepreneur is real and significant. The venture is faced with the possibility of delivering sufficient value to a large enough number of customers to make the business viable in terms of income and profits.

The opportunity the venture aims to exploit is well defined

The venture must be clear as to why it exists. It must understand the nature of the opportunity it aims to exploit. This may be codified in the form of a *mission statement* (discussed further in Chapter 10). The danger is not just that the business may fail to find a sufficiently large opportunity for its innovation but also that in pursuing too many opportunities, and opportunities that are not right for the business, the venture will dilute its resources across too many fronts and fail to focus its efforts on creating a sustainable competitive advantage in the areas where it has real potential to be competitive.

The innovation on which the venture is based is valuable

The innovation behind the venture, that is, its new way of doing things, must be effective and different from the way existing businesses operate. It must be appropriate to exploit the opportunity identified. Recognising an opportunity, and innovating to exploit it, can only occur if the entrepreneur thoroughly understands the market and the customers who make it up. All new ideas, no matter how good, must be scrutinised in the light of what the market *really* wants.

The entrepreneur brings the right skills to the venture

The entrepreneur possesses the right knowledge and skills to build the venture to exploit the opportunity. These include knowledge of the industry sector they are working in, familiarity with its products and markets, general management skills and people skills such as communication and leadership. The entrepreneur must not only have these skills, but also be active in refining and developing them. The effective entrepreneur learns how to learn.

The business has the right people

Entrepreneurs rarely work alone. They draw other people into their ventures to work with them. The business as a whole must have the right people working for it. Entrepreneurs do not need to employ copies of themselves, rather they need people with skills and knowledge to complement their own. The business will need specialists and technical experts as well as people to actually make the product or deliver the service the business offers. It will need general managers and people able to build relationships outside the firm. The people who make up the organisation will be linked in a suitable framework of communication links and responsibilities, both formal and informal. As the business grows, identifying and recruiting the right people to support its growth is a task of primary importance for the entrepreneur.

The organisation has a learning culture and its people a positive attitude

The new venture is in a weak position compared to established players in the marketplace. It is young and relatively inexperienced. It has not had a chance to build up the expertise or relationships that its established counterparts have. It will not have access to their resource levels. The entrepreneurial organisation must turn this on its head and make the disadvantage into an advantage. The entrepreneurial venture must use the fact that it is new to do things in a fresh and innovative way. It must recognise its inexperience as an opportunity to learn a better way of doing things. This can only be achieved if the organisation has a positive culture which seeks ways of developing and which regards change as an opportunity. Adversity must be met as a learning experience. Culture comes down to the attitudes of the people who make up the organisation. They must be motivated to perform on behalf of the venture. The entrepreneur is responsible for establishing a culture in their organisation through leadership and example.

Effective use of the network

Successful entrepreneurs, and the people who work with them, use the network in which the organisation finds itself to good effect. They look towards suppliers and customers, not as competitors for resources, but as partners. They recognise that entrepreneurship is not a zero sum game. If all parties in the network recognise that they can benefit from the success of the venture – and it is down to the entrepreneur to convince them that they can – then the network will make resources and information available to the venture and will be prepared to share some of its risks.

Financial resources are available

The venture can only pursue its opportunity if it has access to the right resources. Financial resources are critical because the business must make essential investments in productive assets, pay its staff and reimburse suppliers. In the early stages, expenditure will be higher than income. The business is very likely to have a negative *cash-flow*. The business must have the resources at hand to cover expenditure in this period. Once the business starts to grow it will need to attract new resources to support that growth. Again, cash-flow may be negative while this is occurring. The entrepreneur must be an effective resource manager. He or she must attract financial resources from investors and then make them work as hard as possible to progress the venture.

The venture has clear goals and its expectations are understood

A venture can only be successful if it is *seen* to be successful. This means that it must set clear and unambiguous objectives to provide a benchmark against which performance can be measured. Success can only be understood in relation to the expectations that stakeholders have for the venture. These expectations must be explicit. This will be critical in the case of investors, who will be very definite about the return they expect. The business must be sure of exactly what its customers want if it expects them to buy its offerings. Understanding expectations is also important in dealing with employees since it is the starting point for motivating them. The entrepreneur must learn to recognise and manage the expectations of all the venture's stakeholders.

8.3 Measuring success and setting objectives

KEY LEARNING OUTCOME
An understanding of the criteria used to set objectives for the entrepreneurial venture and to monitor its performance.

Ultimately, success is personal. The entrepreneurial venture is a vehicle for individual success as much as organisational success. If it is to be an effective vehicle, the venture must be successful as a business. The performance of the venture is subject to a variety of measures including:

- *absolute financial performance* – e.g. sales, profits;
- *financial performance ratios* – e.g. profit margin, return on capital employed;
- *financial liquidity ratios* – e.g. debt cover, interest cover;
- *absolute stock market performance* – e.g. share price, market capitalisation;
- *stock market ratios* – e.g. earnings per share, dividend yield;
- *market presence* – e.g. market share, market position;
- *growth* – e.g. increase in sales, increase in profits;
- *innovation* – e.g. rate of new product introduction; and
- *customer assessment* – e.g. customer service level, customer rating.

These performance indicators are quantitative and are relatively easy to measure. They provide definite goals for the venture to attain. They are *strategic* goals in that they relate to the business as a whole and refer to the position it develops in its external market as well as to purely internal criteria. An entrepreneurial venture is distinguished from a small business by the ambition of its strategic goals.

The specifics of the objectives set for the venture will depend on the type of business it is, the market in which it is operating and the stage of its development. They will be used by management to define objectives, evaluate strategic options and to benchmark performance. Different businesses will set objectives in different ways: they will vary in specificity; they may be for the organisation as a whole or they may define the responsibilities of particular individuals; they may be based on agreement and consensus or they may be 'imposed' on the organisation by the entrepreneur. The way the entrepreneur defines and sets goals, and uses them to motivate and monitor performance is an important aspect of leadership strategy.

The objectives of the firm may not be an entirely internal concern. Financial and market performance measures may form part of the agreement made with investors. They provide manageable and explicit proxies for the success of business and indicate the returns it can hope to generate. They provide a sound and unambiguous basis for monitoring its development. They may also be used in communication with suppliers and customers to indicate the potential of the business and to elicit their support.

8.4 Success and social responsibility

KEY LEARNING OUTCOME
An appreciation of how entrepreneurial success impacts on social responsibility.

An entrepreneurial venture touches the lives of many people. All its stakeholders have an interest in its success since this success provides the means by which they can fulfil their personal goals. People have expectations about what an entrepreneurial business can achieve and how it should undertake its business. Some of these expectations are formal, others are informal. Some are explicit, others implicit. Some result from binding contracts, others from trust that has been accumulated. Entrepreneurs perform on a social stage and in creating an entire new world they must take responsibility for its ethical content as well as its new value. The moral dimension of their activity cannot be ignored. There are rarely clear-cut answers to moral issues and there are rarely definite methods by which moral issues can be resolved, only frameworks and perspectives for understanding them. The social responsibility ascribed to an organisation, and the people who comprise it, must be determined by precedents, cultural norms and personal judgement. The entrepreneur must be conscious of the nature, and scope of the social responsibility they accept for the organisations they create. Archie Carroll (1979) suggests a multi-dimensional approach to understanding corporate social responsibility. In particular, four dimensions can be identified, as shown in Fig. 8.3.

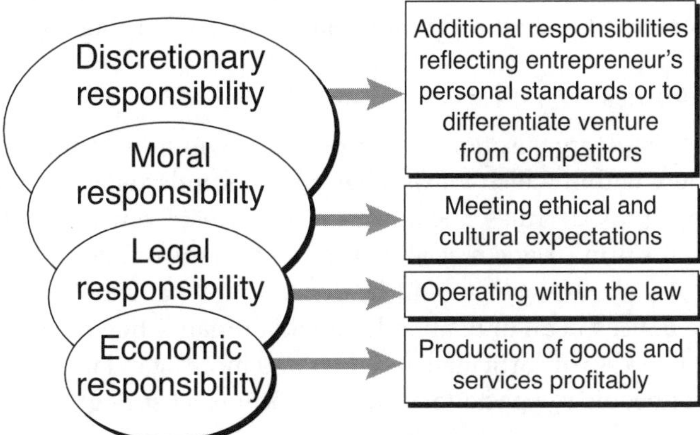

Fig. 8.3 Levels of entrepreneurial responsibility

The first dimension: the *people* to whom the venture has a social responsibility

Potentially, the entrepreneurial venture has a social responsibility towards all those who are affected by its activities, that is, its *stakeholder groups*. Stakeholders may be members of distinct groups but they are also individuals. The venture has responsibilities towards both individuals and organisations or groups.

The second dimension: the *levels* of social responsibility accepted

The business may accept a variety of different types of social responsibility. These may be described as *economic, legal, moral* and *discretionary*.

Economic responsibility

Economic responsibility refers to the basic function of the firm and demands that it produce goods or services and sell them at a profit. This is a minimum level of responsibility. The firm must do this merely to survive within its market. Beyond this basic responsibility, however, the business will recognise a number of other responsibilities.

Legal responsibility

The firm's *legal responsibility* constrains it to operate within the law. The law under which a business operates is defined by the state. Different laws will dictate the way the business operates financially and the way it sets up contracts with other organisations and with individuals. Important examples of laws affecting business are tax and accounting laws and the rules of employment law. A business will be subject to both *criminal* and *civil* law. If the criminal law is broken, the state will act as prosecutor. If a civil law is breached, then it is up to the injured party to bring an action.

Moral responsibilities

A business is a social organisation which operates within a framework of cultural norms. The society within which it exists has ethical standards which it believes must be upheld. These provide rules and norms which create constraints for behaviour. These constitute the firm's *moral responsibilities* and they are difficult to define. They are the unwritten rules about 'what should be done' and 'what should not be done' and they may not be noticed at all until an individual or organisation breaks them. Though a society will not necessarily articulate its ethics and moral standards, they still form an important part of people's expectations and they will react strongly if they are broken.

Discretionary responsibilities

Economic, legal and moral responsibilities comprise the standard constraints operating on the actions of the business. In addition, the entrepreneur may decide to accept *discretionary responsibilities*. Discretionary responsibilities are ones the entrepreneur accepts for their venture even though it is not generally expected that businesses need accept them. They are responsibilities that go above and beyond the norm. Discretionary responsibilities may relate to the way the business will treat its employees, the standards it sets for its products or the way it manages the impact of its activities on the environment. They may reflect beliefs and standards which are held dear by the entrepreneur. They may be used to give the business a point of difference from competitors.

The third dimension: the *issues* which form part of the venture's social responsibility

There are a variety of issues which the entrepreneur can accept as part of the venture's social responsibility. Minimum standards in the treatment of employees, occupational health and safety and product liability will usually be subject to legal regulation. Entrepreneurs frequently take a positive attitude towards wider social issues such as the treatment of the environment, relationships with developing nations and ethnic and sexual discrimination. Occasionally, they may also take a stand on much broader issues relating to social trends such as the growth in 'consumerism'.

The fourth dimension: the venture's *approach* to its social responsibility

The business faces a choice in the way in which it approaches its social responsibilities. It may be *defensive*. This means that the business decides that its social responsibilities are a liability and that they hinder its performance. It may then try to avoid them and to minimise their impact. This may boost short-term profits but it can easily lead to a reaction by stakeholders, especially, but not exclusively, its employees and customers. The business must then put its efforts into defending its actions which can lead to a vicious, and expensive, circle. The more the firm seeks to avoid its responsibilities the stronger can be the reaction by stakeholders so more effort must be put into the defence. This can easily result in a debilitating 'bunker' mentality within the business whereby it feels that its stakeholders are an enemy, rather than partners. Alternatively the business may decide not to go looking for social responsibilities, but will accept them when confronted by them. In this it is *reactive*. The business does not see social responsibilities either as a source of advantage or as a problem, they are just something else that has to be managed. Accepting social responsibility is probably less expensive than defending against it in the long run, but in being reactive the business is allowing itself to be confronted by uncertainties it would otherwise be able to control. Another option is for the business to be *positive* towards its social responsibilities. It can choose to regard them not as liabilities but as opportunities and use them as a source of competitive advantage. Adopting a positive attitude towards social responsibilities brings them under control. They can be made part of the venture's strategy. They can be used to motivate employees and to build a strong relationship with customers and suppliers or they can be used to address the wider concerns of investors and so gain their support. A positive approach to its social responsibilities can be made into a success factor for the entrepreneurial business.

Social responsibilities constrain the actions of a business. They often define what it *cannot* do, rather than what it can. This does not mean they are bad for business. They provide a sound, and shared, set of rules within which the business community can operate. They ensure that the benefits of business activity are distributed in a way which is seen to be fair and equitable. This sustains the motivation of all stakeholders in the venture. Businesses are rarely penalised for meeting their social responsibilities positively. On the other hand, they will be punished if they are seen to evade their responsibilities. This ensures that ventures which set high standards are not penalised by being undercut by those that have lower standards.

Taking on discretionary responsibilities and being proactive with them may be a strategic move. If this meets with the approval of customers and other stakeholders, it can provide a means by which the business can make itself different from competitors and gain an advantage in the marketplace. In recognition of this fact, the entrepreneur may specify the business's social responsibilities in its mission statement. Using discretionary responsibilities to give the business an edge need not conflict with the personal values of the entrepreneur. The entrepreneur can only improve the world with those values if the business is successful. The social responsibilities the venture accepts, and how it defines them, are not merely 'add-ons' to the entrepreneur's vision, they lie at its core. They are the character of the new world the entrepreneur seeks to build.

8.5 Understanding failure

KEY LEARNING OUTCOME
An understanding of what business 'failure' actually means.

Entrepreneurs are always faced with the possibility of failure. No matter how much they believe that their innovation offers new value to customers and regardless of how confident they are that they can build a business to deliver it, they will ultimately be tested by the market. However many success factors they think are present, they may be found wanting in some respects. Uncertainty and risk are always present. Statistics of business failure are widely reported and they are usually quite frightening. Yet 'failure' is not a simple notion. It implies the absence of success and, like success, it can only be understood in relation to people's goals and expectations. Failure happens when expectations are not met. It is a question of degree and means different things to different stakeholders.

From the perspective of the entrepreneur at least eight degrees of 'failure' can be identified based on the performance of the business and way the entrepreneur retains control of it. These are listed in an increasing order of severity below.

1 The business continues to exist as a legal entity under the control of the entrepreneur

(a) The business performs well financially but does not meet the social and self-development needs of the entrepreneur

To most outsiders the business may appear to be a success. It may be performing well financially and making an impact on its market. It may be providing for the economic needs of the entrepreneur and his or her dependants but this does not necessarily mean it is meeting higher needs. The work necessary to keep the business running may be disrupting the entrepreneur's social life. The entrepreneur may have had unrealistic expectations about how the venture would satisfy his or her self-development needs. If the entrepreneur feels that he or she has failed in this respect it will be demotivating and can have an impact on their personal performance. The entrepreneur may feel that he or she has failed personally despite the financial success of their venture.

(b) The business fails to achieve set strategic objectives

The business may meet the financial targets that have been set for it by the entrepreneur and its investors but even so may fail to meet the strategic targets, such as market share, growth and innovation rate set for it. This may not be of immediate concern if profits are being generated. However, it may warn of challenges ahead and potential problems with the long-term performance of the business. Much will depend on how sensitive to the strategy adopted the performance of the business is and how flexible that strategy is.

(c) The business fails to perform as well as was planned but is financially secure

The venture may not meet the financial objectives set for it by the entrepreneur and investors but still remain financially secure. The objectives may have been quite ambitious setting income targets which were very comfortable in relation to necessary expenditure. Though the business may not be in immediate danger investors may feel disappointed in the returns they will receive. Planned investments may have to be forgone. The entrepreneur may be called upon to address the business's strategy and revise its plans to improve performance in the future.

(d) The business fails to perform as well as was planned, and needs additional financial support

The financial performance of the business may be so weak that income cannot cover necessary expenditure. Cash-flow problems will be encountered and it is likely that the business will not survive without a further injection of cash. This is likely to come from investors but additional support may also be gleaned by agreeing special terms with customers and suppliers. In this instance the entrepreneur is likely to be called upon to address the direction of the business and the way it is being run.

If financial performance falls below a certain level, and the commitments of the business exceed its ability to meet them, then investors and creditors may lose confidence altogether. A change in management may be called for. A number of scenarios are possible.

2 The business continues to exist as an independent entity but the entrepreneur loses control

(a) The business is taken over as a going concern by new management

The business an entrepreneur creates is separate to them in that it has its own legal and organisational identity. It is possible that the business can continue and prosper even if the entrepreneur is no longer involved in its running. The entrepreneur may leave the business for a variety of reasons. Though successful, the entrepreneur may feel that it doesn't offer them sufficient challenges or they may feel that managing it does not fulfil them (as in 1(a) above). They may sell their interest to a new manager or management team and move on to do something else. If this is what the entrepreneur wants to do then it must be counted as a success. The entrepreneur may, however, be called upon to leave the business against their wishes.

If the business is not performing, its backers may decide that their best interests are served by bringing in new management with different ideas and different ways of doing things. Their ability to oust the resident entrepreneur will depend on how much of the business they own, the ability of the investors to liquidate their investment and the contracts they have with the entrepreneur.

(b) The business is taken over with restructuring

As in scenario 2(a), the entrepreneur is called upon to leave. However, rather than run the business much as it was the new management team may feel that performance can only be improved if the business undergoes a fundamental restructuring. This can involve changing its employees and making major acquisitions and divestments of assets.

3 The business does not continue to exist as an independent entity

(a) The business is taken over as a going concern and absorbed into another company

One business may be acquired by another through a takeover. It may retain some of its original character, and a modified legal status, by becoming a subsidiary of the parent. It loses its separate identity and all legal character if it is merged with the parent. In this case its employees move to work for the parent and its assets are combined with the parent's assets. A takeover, or merger, may take place at the behest of the entrepreneur who wishes to sell their interest and move on to something else. It may also be instigated by investors who have lost confidence in the entrepreneur and the venture and wish to cut their loses by liquidating their investment. The entrepreneur may, or may not, retain an involvement by becoming a manager for the new parent.

(b) The business is broken up and its assets disposed of

Takeover and mergers take place if there is a belief that the venture has some potential, even if a completely new management approach is called for. If there is no confidence even in this, then the business may be broken up and its assets sold off as separate items. The proceeds are used to reimburse stakeholders. Creditors and outstanding loans take priority. The investors, i.e. the actual owners of the venture, are only entitled to anything left after all creditors have been paid (see Fig. 8.4).

Managing failure

Failure is a fact of business life. It is the possibility of failing that makes success meaningful. Failure is not always a disaster and it does not inevitably mean the end of the venture. Failure is part of the learning process. Minor failures can be positive indicators of how things might be done better. Such failures should not be ignored. They must be addressed before they become the seeds of larger failures. Success and failure exist relative to *expectations*. Failure occurs when expectations are not met. Managing success, and managing failure, have a lot to do with managing people's expectations for the venture, keeping them positive, but at the same time keeping them realistic.

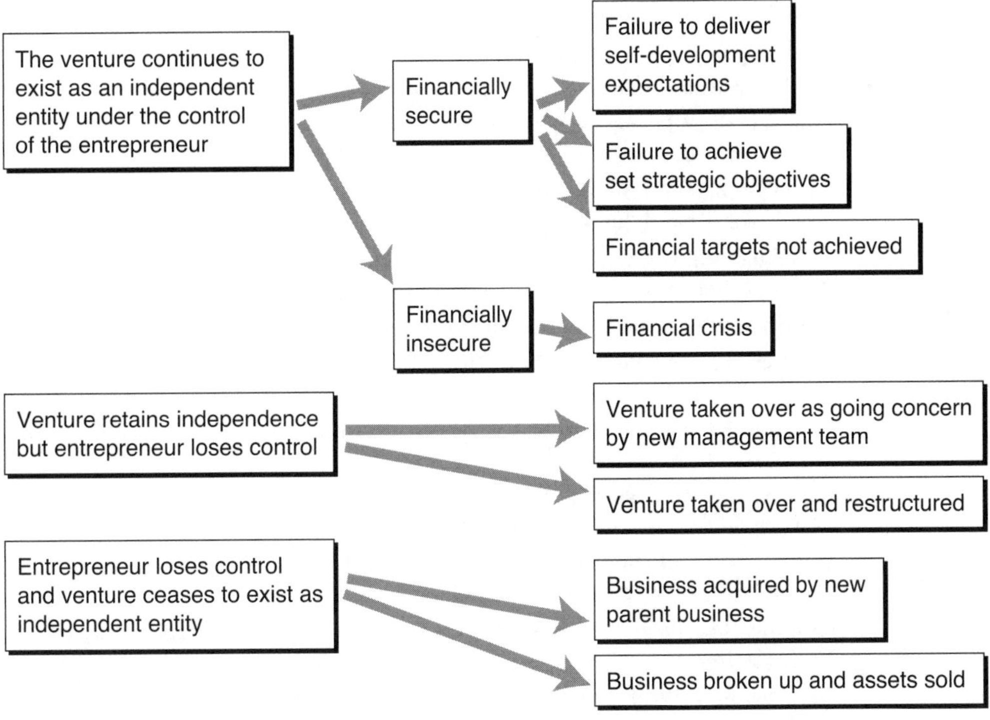

Fig. 8.4 Levels of entrepreneurial failure

Summary of key ideas

- The success of the entrepreneurial venture must be understood through three dimensions – the *stakeholders* who have an interest in the venture; their *expectations* of the venture; and actual *outcomes* relative to those expectations.
- The most effective entrepreneurs define objectives for success in relation to *all* the venture's stakeholders (not just its investors) and operate with a keen sense of social responsibility.
- Many successful entrepreneurs have demanded that their businesses operate with a higher level of social responsibility than other businesses operating in their sectors.
- 'Failure' has many degrees and is an integral part of venturing. Good entrepreneurs learn from failure.

Suggestions for further reading

Atkinson, A.A., **Waterhouse, J.H.** and **Wells, R.B.** (1997) 'A stakeholder approach to strategic performance measurement', *Sloan Management Review*, Spring, pp. 25–37.

Brown, D.M. and **Laverick, S.** (1994) 'Measuring corporate performance', *Long Range Planning*, Vol. 27, No. 4, pp. 89–98.

Carroll, A.B. (1979) 'A three-dimensional model of corporate performance', *Academy of Management Review*, Vol. 4, No. 4, pp. 497–505.

Dollinger, M.J. (1984) 'Measuring effectiveness in entrepreneurial organisations', *International Small Business Journal*, Vol. 3, No. 1, pp. 10–20.

Douma, S. (1991) 'Success and failure in new ventures', *Long Range Planning*, Vol. 24, No. 2, pp. 54–60.

Harrison, E.F. and **Pelletier, M.A.** (1995) 'A paradigm for strategic decision success', *Management Decision*, Vol. 33, No. 7, pp. 53–9.

Harrison, E.F. and **Pelletier, M.A.** (2000) 'Levels of strategic decision success', *Management Decision*, Vol. 38, No. 2, pp. 107–17.

Kaplan, R.S. and **Norton, D.P.** (1996), 'Linking the balanced scorecard to strategy', *California Management Review*, Vol. 39, No. 1, pp. 53–79.

Longenecker, C.O., **Simonetti, J.L.** and **Sharkey, T.W.** (1999) 'Why organizations fail: The view from the front line', *Management Decision*, Vol. 37, No. 6, pp. 503–13.

Osborne, R.L. (1993) 'Why entrepreneurs fail: How to avoid the traps', *Management Decision*, Vol. 31, No. 1, pp. 18-21.

Osborne, R.L. (1995) 'The essence of entrepreneurial success', *Management Decision*, Vol. 33, No. 7, pp. 4–9.

Routamaa, V. and **Vesalainen, J.** (1987) 'Types of entrepreneur and strategic level goal setting', *International Small Business Journal*, Vol. 5, No. 3, pp. 19–29.

Seglod, E. (1995) 'New ventures: The Swedish experience', *Long Range Planning*, Vol. 28, No. 4, pp. 45–53.

Smallbone, D. (1990) 'Success and failure in new business start-ups', *International Small Business Journal*, Vol. 8, No. 2, pp. 34–47

Watson, J. and **Everett, J.** (1993) 'Defining small business failure', *International Small Business Journal*, Vol. 11, No. 3, pp. 35–48.

Watson, K., **Hogarth-Scott, S.** and **Wilson, N.** (1998) 'Small business start-ups: Success factors and support implications', *International Journal of Entrepreneurial Behaviour and Research*, Vol. 4, No. 3, pp. 217–38.

Selected case material

Lara Croft turns respectable and wins City friends

16 December 1999

Eidos, her creator, is close to matching her popularity, says **Christopher Price**

Not even Lara Croft, the improbably endowed heroine of Tomb Raider, has seen as much action this year as the shares of Eidos, the computer game's developer.

This week they hit a new high, as the company unveiled a deal with the Disney entertainment group to develop three new computer games.

It left the shares celebrating an 11-fold gain over the past 12 months, and outperforming the FT All-Share index five-fold on the way. Indeed, not even last month's increased half-year losses and lower revenues could stem investor appetite.

The rise is all the more remarkable because of both the nature of Eidos's business and its previously poor relations with the City.

The group has become used to the perception that it is too dependent on Tomb Raider. The game's massive success – it has sold some 5m copies in its various versions – has meant that Eidos's fortunes have ridden on how each sequel has been received by critics and public alike.

Against the odds, however, Eidos has sustained the success of Tomb Raider in a crowded games market. It is being made into a Hollywood film, which suggests that its longevity will be guaranteed for some time yet.

At the same time, Eidos's success in nourishing other best-sellers has also been recognised.

Championship Manager and Formula One, for example, are two of half a dozen titles that have achieved sales of more than 1m.

This has resulted in the Tomb Raider franchise accounting for an increasingly smaller proportion of group revenues. In the past three years, it has shrunk from 90 to 57 per cent.

Next year, analysts are forecasting, it could fall to as low as 30 per cent of group sales.

Another crucial factor in Eidos's growing popularity with investors is its improved relations with the City.

Two years ago, erratic movements in the share price added to market concerns over the quality of the business and fortitude of the management. In addition, Charles Cornwall, chief executive, had a low profile, as did other senior executives.

However, much has changed in the past 18 months. The directors and company advisers have undertaken a charm offensive with large institutional investors, leading to Eidos's share register now including many of the big names in fund management.

The management's reputation has also been helped by corporate activity in the past year, which has seen investments in a range of smaller games studios, in Europe and the US, underlining the group's determination to widen its portfolio. Deals, such as that struck with Disney this week, have underpinned this trend.

The result of all this has been the significant re-rating of the stock.

Helen Snell at ABN Amro says that Eidos's perception a year ago had led to the stock trading on a p/e below nine.

"It was grossly underrated," she says. Now, however, with the surge in the past year, the stock is trading on a forward multiple of 30.

"Even that is not expensive, when compared with competitors such as Electronic Arts in the US, which trades on 40-plus," says Ms Snell. "And Eidos has a better earnings record and a diversified portfolio of titles."

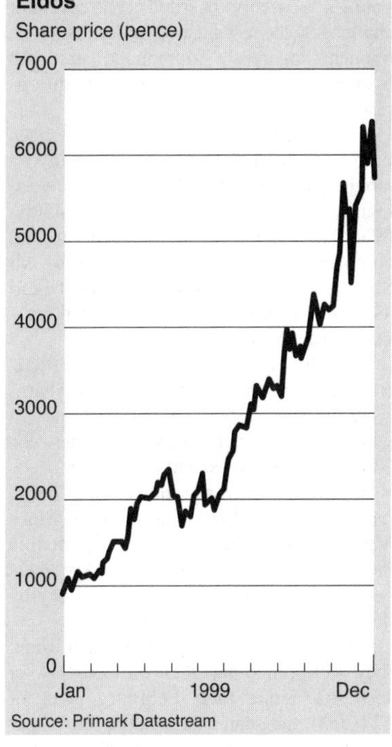

Notwithstanding this, Eidos has also made no secret of its intention to have a significant web presence. It plans to make its web site a games portal, building a community of games fans throughout the online world.

This strategy was underlined recently with the $55m (£33.9m) purchase of a 20 per cent stake in Maximum Holdings, a US internet group. Based in Los Angeles, Maximum has already built an entertainment internet portal that brings together interactive computer games, music, and entertainment services.

It intends to distribute and market Eidos's games through its network of other web sites, including GameCave.com, an e-commerce site focused on video games. This attracts some 3.5m visitors a month, whereas Eidos's web site pulls in about 380,000 users.

Analysts are forecasting pre-tax profits in the year to March 31 of about £50m, against £42m in 1998-99.

Hikari Tsushin's rollercoaster keeps investors holding tight

7 April 2000

After a dizzy ride to the top, the internet investment group is plunging back to ground level, writes **Paul Abrahams**

The rise and fall of Hikari Tsushin and its 34-year-old president Yasumitsu Shigeta resembles a Shakespearean tragedy. A young, "scarcely bearded" entrepreneur challenges the established order; is for a moment apparently triumphant; and then over-reaches himself with calamitous results.

Certainly, Hikari Tsushin's fall has been dramatic. In February the company, a mobile phone distributor and internet investment vehicle, was worth ¥7,450bn ($70.5bn) making it one of Japan's top 10 companies by market capitalisation. Mr Shigeta's own personal stake in Hikari Tsushin – which only listed in September – was worth ¥5,110bn.

But his aspirations did not end there. Bankers say that as the group's shares reached ever greater heights in February, it was preparing a rights issue, worth between $3bn and $5bn, to expand still further.

Yesterday, such ambitions were but a memory. Hikari Tsushin is unloved. Since March 30, the shares have been untraded; in the past five trading sessions there have been no buyers, as they slump each day by the maximum permitted.

Today, if they fall again by their limit, they will plunge past their previous low of ¥51,500. Since their February peak of ¥241,000, the shares have collapsed 77 per cent taking the market capitalisation to just ¥1,662bn.

The clouds only appeared to begin gathering last month. The most significant indication of the gravity of the impending crisis was an extraordinary personal attack on Mr Shigeta by Yoshitaka Kitao, finance director of Softbank, Japan's leading internet investment group. Mr Kitao called for Mr Shigeta to resign from his post as non-executive director at Softbank.

The unprecedented attack by an executive director against a non-executive director followed the publication of a salacious extended article about Hikari Tsushin and Mr Shigeta in a weekly tabloid magazine, Bungei Shunjyu. The magazine made personal allegations against Mr Shigeta that were libellous, but the story also questioned the validity of Hikari Tsushin's business model.

Foreign fund managers were at this stage perplexed and worried, but still believed the company was fundamentally sound. Hikari Tsushin had two types of business. Like Softbank it was an internet investment fund. But unlike Softbank it was also an operating company, generating genuine cash flow.

Its chain of 2,200 Hit Shops appeared hugely profitable, selling mobile phones and satellite subscriptions for Sky Perfect TV.

In the past week both parts of Hikari Tsushin – the investment fund and the operating business – appear to have run into trouble.

Last Thursday the company admitted it had been over-optimistic in its forecasts for mobile handset sales. It had missed targets that would have triggered bonuses from the service operators. These commissions would undershoot by ¥17bn, and the company report an operating loss of ¥13bn in the half year to February 29.

But Mr Shigeta insisted the group would make a net profit by selling some of its internet holdings.

"One moment Hikari was saying 'look at us we have real cash flow'," says Thomas Rodes, internet analyst at Nikko Salomon Smith Barney in Tokyo. "The next they fall into an operating loss and say 'don't worry, we're an investment fund really, so we'll sell some of our internet holdings to post a

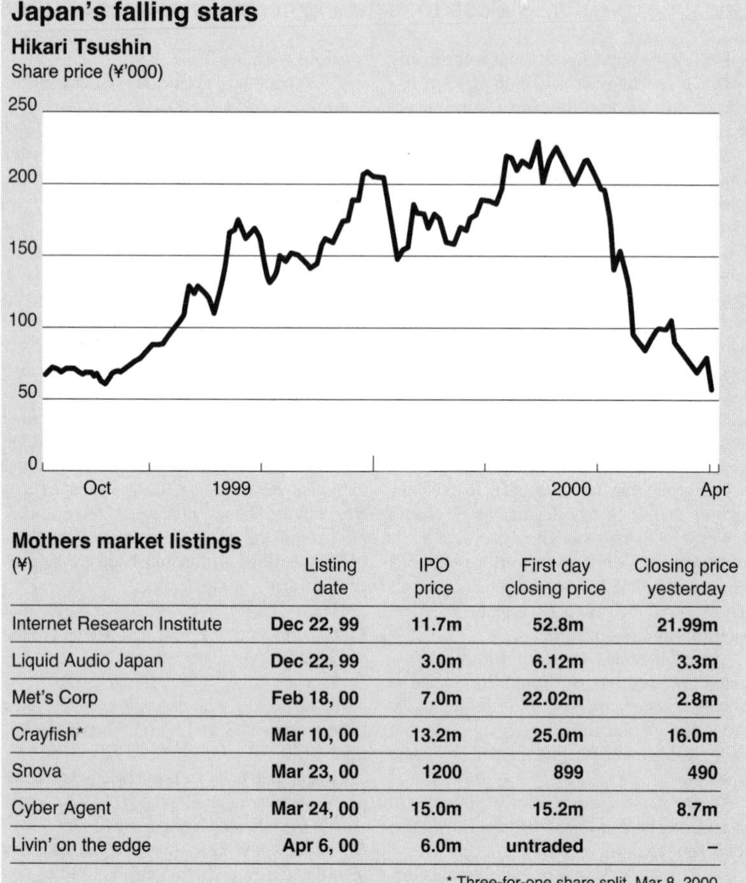

Mothers market listings

(¥)	Listing date	IPO price	First day closing price	Closing price yesterday
Internet Research Institute	**Dec 22, 99**	**11.7m**	**52.8m**	**21.99m**
Liquid Audio Japan	**Dec 22, 99**	**3.0m**	**6.12m**	**3.3m**
Met's Corp	**Feb 18, 00**	**7.0m**	**22.02m**	**2.8m**
Crayfish*	**Mar 10, 00**	**13.2m**	**25.0m**	**16.0m**
Snova	**Mar 23, 00**	**1200**	**899**	**490**
Cyber Agent	**Mar 24, 00**	**15.0m**	**15.2m**	**8.7m**
Livin' on the edge	**Apr 6, 00**	**6.0m**	**untraded**	**–**

* Three-for-one share split, Mar 8, 2000

Source: Primark Datastream; Reuters

net profit'. That was really damaging to the group's credibility. Mr Shigeta moved the goal posts."

But Mr Shigeta's switch in strategy to an investment fund holds its own dangers. Yesterday one of Hikari Tsushin's subsidiaries listed on Mothers, the Tokyo Stock Exchange's recently started market for small companies. Daiwa Securities lead managed the issue for the appropriately named Livin' on the Edge. The issue for the web site management company turned to disaster: the shares tumbled 25 per cent and still found no buyers.

Many large funds recognised the stock was risky, but its market capitalisation had become so large that they could not afford not to own it. If Hikari Tsushin continued to rise and they did not own the stock they would underperform their rivals badly. Instead, many funds will be nursing huge losses on their investments. Their only consolation is that most of their rivals also hold losses.

For retail investors, the danger is much greater. Many did not have the cash to buy stock and instead acquired it on margin. As the shares collapse, they are being asked by their brokers on a daily basis to put more money into their accounts. They cannot sell Hikari Tsushin because there are no buyers. The risk is that they will have to sell shares in other companies to cover their losses, dragging the market down overall. "The question is when do you catch the falling knife?" asks Mr Rodes.

Tokyo Mitsubishi Securities believes it has the answer. It forecasts Hikari Tsushin's shares could hit ¥10,000. That would value the company at ¥309bn – just $2.9bn.

From internet giant to speculative stock in just one month: the risks of holding Hikari Tsushin have become clear. For the moment there seem no rewards.

Review questions

1 In what ways might Eidos see 'success' as a challenge (albeit a positive one!) to be managed?

2 Given its recent problems, what are the key learnings for Hikari Tsushin and its chief executive Yasumitsu Shigeta?

3 To what extent do you see the success of the entrepreneurial venture as the responsibility of government and its policies?

PART 2

Choosing a direction

9 Entrepreneurial vision

Chapter overview

The presence of a powerful, motivating personal ***vision*** *is one of the defining characteristics of entrepreneurial management. This chapter is concerned with exploring the concept of vision and understanding how it can be used by the entrepreneur to give the venture a sense of direction and purpose. It also addresses how vision can be refined, articulated and communicated to make it into an effective managerial tool.*

9.1 What is entrepreneurial vision?

KEY LEARNING OUTCOME
An appreciation of the power of entrepreneurial vision and of the value it offers for the venture.

Entrepreneurs are managers. They manage more than just an organisation, they manage the creation of a 'new world'. This new world offers the possibility of value being generated and made available to the venture's stakeholders. This value can only be created through change – change in the way things are *done*, change in *organisations* and change in *relationships*. Entrepreneurs rarely stumble on success. It is more usually a reward for directing their actions in an appropriate way towards some opportunity. Effective entrepreneurs know where they are going, and why. They are focused on the achievement of specific goals.

The entrepreneur's vision is a picture of the new world he or she wishes to create. It is a picture into which the entrepreneur fits an understanding of why people will be better off, the source of the new value that will be created, and the relationships that will exist. This picture is a very positive one and the entrepreneur is drawn towards it. He or she is motivated to make their vision into reality. Vision exists in the tension between what *is* and what *might* be. A vision includes an understanding of the rewards that are to be earned by creating the new world and why people will be attracted to them. Vision specifies a *destination* rather than a route to get there. It is created out of possibilities, not certainties.

Entrepreneurial visions have detail. This detail may be extensive, as if the picture were painted with fine brush strokes. Alternatively the detail may be limited and the picture drawn from broad strokes. The details may be in sharp focus and thoroughly defined, or they may be quite vague, calling for further clarification. Whatever the shape of the details, the different parts of the vision will fit together to form a coherent whole. To the entrepreneur the vision pulling the venture forward will have an existence of its own, a unity quite separate from its component parts.

A vision is a 'mental' image in that it is something the entrepreneur carries around in their head. This does not mean it is insubstantial, indeed far from it. It is a very powerful tool for the management of the venture. In particular:

- it provides a sense of direction by being the 'light at the end of the tunnel';
- it helps the entrepreneur to define his or her goals;
- it provides the entrepreneur with a sense of 'warmth' and encouragement when the going gets tough;
- it guides the generation of strategy for the venture;
- it gives the venture a moral content and helps define social responsibilities;
- it can be used to communicate what the entrepreneur wishes to achieve to other people;
- it can be used to attract people to the venture and motivate them to support it; and
- it plays a crucial role in supporting the entrepreneur's communication and leadership strategy.

Vision is an important tool for the entrepreneur. It defines where the entrepreneur wants to go, illuminates why he or she wants to be there and provides signposts for how they might get there. If it is to be an effective tool, vision must be used actively. However, vision must be properly shaped and nurtured. It must be refined and tested. A vision which is unachievable, or which is based on wrong assumptions, or which points in the wrong direction, will easily lead the venture astray. The entrepreneur must learn to challenge vision. It must be defined and shaped so that it is appropriate, viable and achievable, before it can be put to use.

9.2 Developing and shaping vision

KEY LEARNING OUTCOME

An understanding of how entrepreneurial vision can be developed and shaped by the entrepreneur to make it into an effective tool for the management of the venture.

Vision is the starting point for giving shape and direction to the venture. Some sense of vision must exist before strategy development and planning can start. If it is to lead the business in the right direction, vision must be properly examined, refined and evaluated.

Vision develops from the idea that things might be different from, and better than, they are currently. A vision might 'present' itself to the entrepreneur quite suddenly, or alternatively it may emerge slowly, taking shape as the entrepreneur explores an opportunity and recognises its possibilities. No matter how it comes about, vision is something which is constructed personally. It is, first and foremost, a communication with oneself. Communicating with oneself follows similar rules to communicating with anyone else. The objectives behind making the communication should be understood and it must be thought through and properly articulated. If vision is to be used effectively as a force for self-motivation and as a guide to setting goals, developing strategy and attracting support, then the entrepreneur must become aware of his or her vision, isolate it, communicate it to themselves, and refine it.

The vision will be a picture of the new world the entrepreneur seeks to create. It is constructed personally and will vary from entrepreneur to entrepreneur. Whatever form it takes, the entrepreneur must learn to question the vision. At first, the entrepreneur's vision will be ill-defined, with its details out of focus. Questioning it helps bring it into focus. Some important questions to ask are:

- What will be the *source* of the value to be created in the new world?
- Who will be *involved* in this new world (i.e. who are the stakeholders)?
- Why will those involved be *better off* in the new world than they are at present?
- In what way will they *gain* (financially, socially, through personal development)?
- What financial reward will be received *personally* for creating the new world?
- What new *relationships* will need to be developed?
- What is the *nature* of the relationships that will be built in the new world?
- Why will this new world fulfil, or offer the potential to fulfil, personal *self-development* goals?

In short, entrepreneurs must understand *why* their vision offers a picture of a more valuable world and how it will reward them and the other stakeholders involved in the venture. To do this they must understand their personal motivation and the motivations of the stakeholders involved. This questioning must be a *continual* process. Vision must be constantly refined and kept in focus. While it should provide a consistent and constant sense of direction it should be kept flexible. Its shape may change as the entrepreneur's understanding of their personal motivations and the motivations of others evolves. To keep it fresh, entrepreneurs should constantly renegotiate their vision with themselves. Vision should always pull entrepreneurs forward. It should never hold them back (see Fig. 9.1).

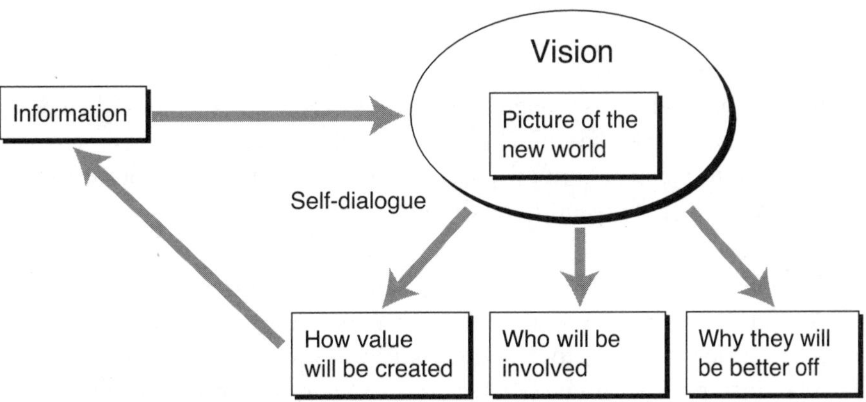

Fig. 9.1 Shaping entrepreneurial vision

9.3 Communicating and sharing vision

KEY LEARNING OUTCOME
An appreciation of how entrepreneurial vision can be used to motivate and attract support for the venture.

The entrepreneur's vision gives their venture direction, and motivates them to progress it. Vision is, in the first instance, a personal picture of the new world the entrepreneur seeks to create. If it is to be used to attract other people to the venture this new world must be communicated to them. They must be invited to share in what it can offer. Communication is not just about relating information. It is about eliciting *action* on the part of the receiver. It is not so much about getting people to know things, as about getting them to *do* things. Effective entrepreneurs understand how their vision can be used motivate others as much as it can be used to motivate themselves.

The first stage must be to understand why other people will find the vision attractive. The entrepreneur must identify what the new world will offer stakeholders, both as individuals and as groups. The questions the entrepreneur must ask in relation to the stakeholders are:

- What benefits will they gain if the new world comes into being?
- How will they be able to address their economic, social and self-development needs better in the new world than they can in the existing one?
- Will they be attracted by the moral and discretionary social responsibility entailed in the vision and the specific issues that it addresses?
- What risks will the new world present to them?
- How credible will they find the possibility of achieving the new world?
- How will they view the journey they must take to get to the new world?

Finding the answers to these questions is part of the process the entrepreneur must go through in shaping and refining their vision. The answers will influence the way they communicate it to others. Some important approaches to communicating vision are as follows.

'I have a dream . . .'

In this approach entrepreneurs are explicit about their vision. They describe the better world just as they see it. The vision is presented as a coherent whole. Its parts fit together to create a unified picture. Entrepreneurs expect other people to find it as attractive as they do and to be drawn towards it.

Talking specific goals

Alternatively, entrepreneurs can break down their vision into a series of specific goals, relating, for example, to economic outcomes, to the value that will be gained, to the relationships that will be created, and to the moral content of the new world. Each of these is communicated separately or in particular combinations. The choice of what is communicated will depend on to whom the vision is being communicated, when it is being communicated in what situation and with what intention.

Talking strategy

Here entrepreneurs do not talk so much about *ends* as about *means*. Strategy relates to the approach that the business will take to achieving its goals and the tasks that must be undertaken in order to create the new world. In this entrepreneurs are reliant on the fact that people will be attracted to the journey as well as the destination.

Story-telling

In using this approach entrepreneurs think of their vision as a 'stage' on which the venture is played out. The stakeholders are actors who play parts on that stage. Entrepreneurs give their vision a dynamic form by describing scenarios and telling stories about what might happen. The communication takes shape by relating future events and the roles that people can play in them. Entrepreneurs aim to motivate people by attracting them to their roles within the story.

Why things can be better

The entrepreneur emphasises what is wrong with the world as it *is* rather than what will be better in the new world. The aim is to push people forward using their sense of dissatisfaction, rather than to pull them forward by using the attractions of new possibilities. While it may shake people out of their complacencies, too much emphasis on this approach runs the risk of simply sounding negative and being demotivating, especially if no positive alternative appears to be offered.

What's in it for you

In this approach entrepreneurs focus on the particular benefits that will be gained by the recipient of the communication. The vision is broken down and 'packaged' for the individual. Tailoring the vision in this way is a good way of ensuring the commitment of a particular person. If over-used, however, the recipient may feel that their commitment is being bought. This approach to communication runs the danger of giving the impression that the entrepreneur regards the recipient as being 'mercenary' and purely motivated by personal gain.

Selecting a communication strategy

These approaches to communicating vision are not mutually exclusive. They are individual strands that can be brought together to make up an overall communication strategy for the entrepreneur's vision. By using a diverse approach to communicating this vision the entrepreneur keeps it relevant, avoids being repetitive and keeps the message fresh to recipients. The particular strategy adopted will depend on a number of factors. Some of the more important include:

- the nature of the vision being shared (how complex is it? How much detail does it have?);
- the entrepreneur's leadership style (is it collaborative, democratic, authoritarian?);
- the stakeholders to whom the vision is being communicated (who are they? How many?);

- the nature of the commitment desired from them;
- the stakeholders' particular needs and motivations (economic, social, self-development);
- the stakeholders' relationship to the entrepreneur;
- the situation of the communication (formal or informal, one-to-one, one to many, etc.); and
- the medium through which the communication is transmitted (face-to-face, verbal, written, etc.).

An ability to articulate the vision and communicate it effectively to different stakeholders in a way that is appropriate to them and in a way that is right for the situation is the basis on which the entrepreneur builds his or her leadership and power.

Summary of key ideas

- Entrepreneurs are managers with a *vision*.
- A vision is a picture of the *new and better world* that the entrepreneur wishes to create.
- Vision can be refined and articulated as a *management tool*.
- Vision can be used as the basis of a powerful *leadership strategy*.
- Visionary leadership demands *communication* of the vision in a way which draws stakeholders towards the venture and *motivates* them to work for its success.

Suggestions for further reading

Campbell, A. and **Yeung, S.** (1991) 'Vision, mission and strategic intent', *Long Range Planning*, Vol. 24, No. 4, pp. 145–7.

Filion, L.J. (1991) 'Vision and relations: Elements for an entrepreneurial meta-model', *International Small Business Journal*, Vol. 9, No. 1, pp. 15–31.

Gratton, L. (1996) 'Implementing a strategic vision – Key factors for success', *Long Range Planning*, Vol. 29, No. 3, pp. 290–303.

Lipton, M. (1996) 'Demystifying the development of organisational vision', *Sloan Management Review*, Summer, pp. 83–92.

Shirley, S. (1989) 'Corporate strategy and entrepreneurial vision', *Long Range Planning*, Vol. 22, No. 6, pp. 107–10.

Stewart, J.M. (1993) 'Future state visioning – A powerful leadership process', *Long Range Planning*, Vol. 26, No. 6, pp. 89–98.

Westley, F. and **Mintzberg, H.** (1989) 'Visionary leadership and strategic management', *Strategic Management Journal*, Vol. 10, pp. 17–32.

Selected case material

Incubator for a nation of net titans

8 December 1999

Graham Bowley meets a Canadian aiming to foster a new breed of online entrepreneurs

Canadians have warmed quickly to Paul Alofs since his return home to Canada in a blaze of publicity at the end of October. To them, the former Disney, Bertelsmann and MP3.com executive is the tanned, hip music boss, who went to California, fell in love with the internet and has come back to preach the online gospel and drag Canada into the internet age.

The excitement surrounding his homecoming has been overwhelming. In the first two weeks, he was bombarded by 5,000 business plans from aspiring entrepreneurs eager to be part of his big idea, to create Canada's most high-profile internet "incubator", feeding and cultivating young companies with money and management expertise.

His home telephone has been "swamped". He now leaves his two mobile phones switched off in his briefcase and gives his e-mail address to nobody. "This idea is right for Canada," he says. "It is two years behind the US in internet development." Yet – and this is where his hope for Canada and his own business future lies – "you can't go into a coffee shop in Silicon Valley, or a meeting, and not run into a Canadian."

Mr Alofs' return comes as Canadians – like many nations – are engulfed in an emotional debate about how they can compete in the internet revolution that is setting its big neighbour to the south alight. While the Canadian economy is currently doing well, it is mainly in traditional, old-fashioned industries such as manufacturing, and large swathes of the economy are still dominated by commodities such as agriculture and mining.

It may have several world-beating high-tech companies such as Nortel Networks, one of the world's leading telecoms equipment manufacturers, but it still lacks the vibrant array of small, innovative internet start-ups found in the US and which many predict will be the business titans, creators of wealth, and big employers, of the not-so-distant future.

The debate is taken more seriously in Canada than elsewhere because of the proximity of the US and the powerful attraction it has always exerted on Canada's brightest talents and best companies – now intensifying because of the growth of Silicon Valley. Canadians see it as ironic that Canadians occupy senior positions at several established US technology giants (Jeff Mallett at Yahoo!, Robert Young at Red Hat, Paul Gauthier at Inktomi), whereas Canada has no Yahoo!s, Red Hats or Inktomis of its own.

Canada has one of the highest levels of internet "connectedness" (between 25 and 40 per cent of households have access) and yet Canadians spend most of their time and their money on US internet sites. "We are a very wired country, no doubt, but a lot of money is flowing south and being spent there," says Rick Broadhead, a Toronto-based internet analyst and writer.

It is a problem Canada's government has recognised. Officials are especially troubled by the growing exodus of bright scientists and programmers who move their start-ups south after only a few years. John Manley, industry minister, calculates that "Canada right now is getting about 1 per cent, compared to the US, of internet initial public offerings. It should be getting about 15 per cent." He adds: "The technology is here, the infrastructure is here, but there is a huge market south of the border. That is very compelling."

Good examples of US companies with strong Canadian roots include PhotoPoint.com, a digital photograph archive, Bamboo.com, an online real estate business, and Sycamore Networks, which recently went public and has a market capitalisation of more than US$15bn.

"The business case for moving to the US is drop-dead simple," says David Rowley, chief executive of PhotoPoint.com. "Some of the venture capitalists we were talking to in Toronto were very uncomfortable with the internet model."

According to Mr Alofs, Canada's dire lack of venture capital – essential for financing a nascent internet industry – is its biggest problem. This is a shortcoming shared by other countries, such as Germany, which similarly recognise a pressing need to stimulate high-tech companies but where traditional-minded investors have until now been unwilling to back young, risky businesses in sectors with little or no track record of making money. The contrast with the US, where venture capital has poured into areas such as biotechnology and the internet is stark. "Canadians are typically more financially conservative than in the US," says Mr Alofs, pointing out that investment in oil and gas, infrastructure and manufacture is done very well, but not in the internet.

His solution, an internet incubator, is meant to fill this gap. It will supply early-stage seed capital (investors will provide a pool of C$20m, with up to C$500,000 earmarked for each start-up), as well as office space and management and engineering support. It is an idea borrowed "shamelessly," he concedes, from Idealab!, the successful US incubator that has sponsored companies such as eToys.

Alofs's incubator will try to give entrepreneurs financial help earlier in their corporate lifetime than would normally be the case with regular venture capitalists. It will also take a smaller stake in each company in return. This strategy, says Mr Alofs, will give his young pioneers a greater incentive to succeed.

He lists what each company must deliver: first, it must generate online traffic and possess "stickiness", or an ability to entice users back to the internet site; second, it must create revenues; and only then will he expect it to begin to make money.

Eventually, successful companies would float their shares publicly, a process he went through recently with MP3.com, when the online music retailer launched its big IPO in the US.

Ultimately, the secret of internet success, Mr Alofs says, will be brand and marketing because the technology behind the internet is relatively easy. "It does not cost much money to set up a web site," he says. Canadians hope his flair for publicity means Toronto's coffee shops will soon be buzzing with internet excitement just like Silicon Valley.

The Law of office dynamics

5 February 1999

It's trendy, it's hip and some see it as the company of the future. **Lucy Kellaway** talks to its chairman who firmly believes in turning the workplace upside down

Shepherd's pie. John Lennon. Films of Stanley Kubrick. A carol called The Three Kings. James Joyce's *Ulysses*. These are a few of Andy Law's favourite things.

You may be wondering why you should care about the favourite things of the chairman of a small advertising agency. The answer is that St Luke's is not any old agency, but the trendiest, hippest agency in London.

And at St Luke's, favourite things are part of the cool culture. At monthly meetings individuals are called on to name five favourite things to prove that each of them is a uniquely fascinating human being.

There was, as it happened, no shepherd's pie on the menu at Bank, the smart new place where Mr Law and I had lunch. But he seemed not to mind. He sat, wearing a worn grey jumper, looking around as if this were a glamorous world with which he was quite unfamiliar.

"I don't go out to restaurants very often," he said. "I'm more likely to have lunch with Rose the cleaner in the office."

Rose the cleaner, like all the 100 employees at St Luke's, owns the business. Every year she gets the same number of shares as Mr Law himself, depending on how well the agency is doing. And in its four-year life it done well, very well.

So well, in fact, that St Luke's is held up by some as an example of a company of the future, and Mr Law has become a darling of the alternative business scene.

Indeed, the day before our lunch he had been in Vienna sharing a platform with Mikhail Gorbachev and telling a large audience of British Telecommunications employees all about revolution.

According to Mr Law, both he and the former president of the Soviet Union know a bit about deconstruction. Only Mr Law's story – which began with the buy-out of Chiat/Day in London – ended rather more happily than that of his co-speaker. According to him, St Luke's has become *the* place for young things to work in advertising and it is being offered so much new business it is turning some away.

"If you deconstruct everything, a lot of things don't make sense," says Mr Law. One thing that apparently doesn't make sense is wearing a suit. "I think people are fascinating," he says fixing his eyes at a point over my shoulder. "Suits are at odds with a world of work that is increasingly based on ideas."

I suggest that work clothes are a handy uniform: they prepare you for a more polite and more orderly world.

Only St Luke's is not orderly and it is certainly not polite. Everyone is encouraged to say what they think as they cruise the building – no one has their own desks or offices.

"You ask people how they are and they might say: 'Fuck off – actually I've had a shit day'." He tells me this as if it were something to be proud of. He is also proud that no one takes the slightest bit of notice of him as chairman. "I can't bullshit the company," he boasts.

Yet he does not pretend that all the owners of St Luke's are equal. There might not be a formal hierarchy, but there is nevertheless a "hierarchy of opinion". Some people are listened to more than others.

Much of what goes on at St Luke's is absurdly faddy: the swearing and the T-shirts and the favourite things. But Mr Law does not seem in the least offended when I point this out. "Some of the things we do are ludicrous. At Monday morning meetings – falling backwards into other people's arms to see if they will hold you. We should try to be *more* absurd."

What St Luke's is really about is making people do their very best, to make them as happy and creative as possible. Or, as Mr Law puts it, "recognising the genius that is in everyone".

I wonder if Rose the cleaner is a genius. If so, why is she a cleaner? Gently I suggest that all this stuff about being brilliant and fascinating sounds a touch smug.

"Yeah," he says nodding his head thoughtfully. "I think we've got very complacent recently." He tells me there is a special group in the company that has the specific function of destabilising the status quo.

Listening to him talk, it sounds as if his staff spend so much time playing trust exercises, swearing and trying to destabilise each other that it is hard to see how they have any time to work.

He admits that some recruits are equally confused: it had not occurred to them that work was part of the deal. "Perhaps we are creating false expectations. Anyone who comes in thinking they've found a safe haven from the horribleness of life is in for a rude awakening."

Mr Law himself has stopped doing anything that normal people would recognise as work. The reason, according to him, is that he is too experienced. "Experience dulls intuition. Intuition is so important. I would be a disaster running anything now. I'm a resource."

What he does instead is sort out squabbles (of which there are many) and champion the corporate model inside and outside the company. He is head of "the movement", as he sometimes calls it.

But is St Luke's, a small creative business, really a business model for the 21st century, as he claims in his book, *Open Minds*?

"What we are trying to communicate is not that we have *the* answer. What I am proud of is that we have reorganised the business around the aspirations of everybody. It is about re-arranging your forces to release energy."

There could be no doubt as to his sincerity: the adopted son of a priest, he really believes.

"All change takes sacrifice. Unless you are prepared to give up something that will make your heart ache you'll never move forward." Mr Law has lost out financially – he earns £150,000 (which is a lot until you look at what other top people in advertising are getting). Like everyone else at St Luke's, he has a hand in setting his own pay and has not asked for more money in years so as to instil the principle of fairness. He has no corner office and not much say over the direction of the business.

Despite his distance from the day-to-day running of the business, one wonders what it would be without him. Would it be like Body Shop without Anita Roddick, which is sliding awkwardly towards an ordinary company?

"For the company to have a validity, I and David Abraham [another founder] should leave. But I don't understand that. It's a paradox."

The St Luke's model seems to work well for now. But what would happen if business turned down? Would everyone stop being crazily creative and become angry and demoralised?

"That's another paradox! I would like to force a real crisis. To put our philosophy to the test. It would be brilliant! It would make us stronger!"

Over the course of our lunch Andy Law has said a good many questionable things. About how he believes in love and hate at work. About his terror of mediocrity. About how he wanted everyone's salary stuck up on the office fridge. About how he believes in an afterlife; and that is what stops him from killing the people he doesn't like.

But he would be the first to admit that he should not be taken too seriously. We stood on the pavement and he shook my hand and issued a warning: "Half of what I say is shit."

Review questions

Compare and contrast the entrepreneurial visions of:

1 Paul Alofs

2 Andy Law.

(*Hint*: Consider how the entrepreneurs are articulating their visions. How much detail do they have? Who will be involved? What might stakeholders gain if the vision is fulfilled?)

10 The entrepreneurial mission

Chapter overview

This chapter is concerned with the development of a ***mission*** *for the entrepreneurial venture. A mission is a formal statement defining the purpose of the venture and what it aims to achieve. It is a powerful communication tool which can both guide internal decision making and relate the venture to external supporters. After establishing how a formal mission can actually help the venture, a prescriptive framework for generating, articulating and communicating the venture's mission is developed.*

10.1 Why a well-defined mission can help the venture

KEY LEARNING OUTCOME
An appreciation of the value of a formal mission for the venture.

A mission is a formal statement as to the purpose of the venture. It defines the *nature* of the venture, *what* it aims to achieve and *how* it aims to achieve it. It provides entrepreneurs with a way to codify their vision, to be clear about the difference they will make. Recent surveys indicate that some eighty per cent of all major businesses have a mission or value statement of some kind. Developing a formalised mission can be valuable to the entrepreneurial venture for a number of reasons.

It articulates the entrepreneur's vision

Developing a mission offers entrepreneurs a chance to articulate and give form to their vision. This helps them to refine and shape their vision, and it facilitates communication of the vision to the venture's stakeholders.

It encourages analysis of the venture

The process of developing a mission demands that entrepreneurs and those that work with them stand back and think about their venture in some detail. If the mission is to be meaningful, then that analysis must made in a detached way. Entrepreneurs must be able to subject their own vision to impartial scrutiny and consider how realistic and achievable it is. It will challenge them to consider what they wish to achieve, to audit the resources they have to hand, to identify what additional resources they will need, and to evaluate their own strengths and weaknesses. Developing a mission is a piece of communication with oneself. This process is iterative. Entrepreneurs must negotiate the possibilities of creating new worlds with their ambitions and the actuality of what they can achieve.

It defines the scope of the business

An entrepreneurial venture exists to exploit some opportunity. Opportunities are most successfully exploited if resources are dedicated to them and brought to bear in a focused way. This demands that the opportunity be defined precisely. The business must know which opportunities lie within its grasp and which it must ignore. Often, success depends not only on the venture taking advantage of a big enough opportunity but also on it not being tempted to spread its efforts too wide. The mission helps to distinguish between those opportunities which 'belong' to the venture and those which do not.

It provides a guide for setting objectives

A mission is usually *qualitative*. It does not dictate specific quantitative outcomes. This is the role of *objectives*. The mission provides a starting point for defining specific objectives, for testing their suitability for the venture and for ordering of their priorities.

It clarifies strategic options

A mission defines what the venture aims to achieve. In this it offers guidance on what paths might be taken. The mission provides a starting point for developing *strategic options*, for evaluating their consistency in delivering objectives and for judging their resource demands.

It facilitates communication about the venture to potential investors

Attracting the support of investors is crucial to the success of the new venture. This is not simply a matter of presenting a series of facts to them, rather it demands that the facts be communicated in a way which makes the possibilities of the venture look convincing. One of their first questions will be *'what is the business about?'* The mission provides the entrepreneur with a clear, succinct and unambiguous answer to this question. Answering in this way efficiently locates the venture positively in the investors' minds. This facilitates commitment and encourages further inquiry about the opportunity the venture aims to exploit and the rewards it may offer. It also suggests that the entrepreneur has thought about the business in a professional way, that is, it has defined its scope and is focused in its goals.

It draws together disparate internal stakeholder groups

The different stakeholders who make up the business may not agree what the business is about. They may disagree on the goals it should have, how it should go about achieving them and how they will benefit if they are achieved. Organisations are frequently *political* and the mission can be used to provide a common point of reference around which to draw internal stakeholders together. It can guide arbitration when conflicts occur. A broad qualitative mission may be more useful than specific objectives in this respect. Often the very detail of objectives reduces flexibility and can provide a focus for discontent and disagreement.

It provides a constant point of reference during periods of change

The organisation driving the entrepreneurial venture will have the potential to achieve growth. Growth is good because it reflects the success of the business and increases its ability to reward stakeholders. It does, however, present the challenge of managing *change*. As the organisation grows and develops, it will be in a state of flux. It will acquire new assets and develop new relationships. Individuals will come and go. New customers will be found, old ones lost. In these turbulent circumstances, the mission can provide the organisation with a fixed point or a recognisable landmark connecting the organisation's past to its future.

It acts as an aide-mémoire for customers and suppliers

The mission statement can be communicated to the other key stakeholders in the venture, namely its customers and suppliers. It locates the business in the minds of customers and reminds them of what it offers and the commitment being made to them. It also gives the venture a presence in the minds of suppliers, reminding them of the opportunity it presents and of the need for their commitment to that opportunity. This encourages them to give the venture priority and service.

Key features of the mission

The mission provides the entrepreneur with a powerful management tool. However, if it is to be effective and to contribute positively to the performance of the venture, it must be right for the business, it should encapsulate useful information and it must be properly developed and articulated.

10.2 What a mission statement should include

KEY LEARNING OUTCOME
An understanding of what information should be included in the mission statement for an entrepreneurial venture.

A mission statement may define both *what* the business aims to achieve and the *values* it will uphold while going about its business. It relates both what the business does and why its members are proud of what it does. These two parts are often referred to as the *strategic* and the *philosophical* components of the mission statement respectively. For example, The Body Shop emphasises corporate values in its mission. It claims to:

> **Make compassion, care, harmony and trust the foundation stones of business. Fall in love with new ideas.**

The fast-growing Scandinavian furniture retailer, *Ikea*, on the other hand, is much more strategic in its approach to defining products, markets and benefits. The company states its 'business idea' in the following terms:

We shall offer a wide range of home furnishing, items of good design and function, at prices so low that the majority of people can afford them.

The strategic component of a mission statement can, potentially, include the following elements:

1 *Product/service scope* – This element specifies exactly what the firm will offer to the world. It stipulates the type or range of products or services that the firm will engage in producing and delivering.

2 *Customer groups served* – This element stipulates which customers and distinct customer groups that will be addressed by the firm.

Both product/service scope and customer groups need to be specified with three things in mind. First is the *total market* in which the business operates. This is the 'universe' in which the business's offerings are located. Second are the markets that the business *currently* serves since these are the base onto which the business must build its growth. Third are the market sectors, or *niches*, that the business *aspires* to serve. These are where the growth will come from since these niches lie between the current business and the total market. These sectors must stretch the business and make its aspirations demanding, yet they must be realistic given the resources to which the business has access and its capabilities. The sectors must also represent distinct segments of the total market within which the firm's innovation can provide a sustainable competitive advantage.

3 *Benefits offered and customer needs served* – This element specifies the particular needs that the customer groups have and the benefits that the firm's products or services offer to satisfy these needs. Needs (and the benefits that satisfy them) can be defined at a number of levels. Spiritual, social and developmental needs are as important, and often more important than, economic or functional ones.

4 *The innovation on which the business is based and the sources of sustainable competitive advantage* – This element defines the way in which the firm has innovated, how it is using this to exploit the opportunity it faces and how this provides it with a competitive advantage in the marketplace that can be sustained in the face of pressure from competitors.

5 *The aspirations of the business* – This element defines what the business aims to achieve. It indicates how its success will be measured. It may refer to financial performance, for example to be 'profitable' or to 'offer shareholders an attractive return', or it may refer to market position, for example to be a 'market leader' or to be 'a significant player'. Care should be taken that the aspirations are *realistic*, specify an achievement which is *meaningful* and provide a real *benchmark* for measuring achievements.

In addition to the strategic elements, reference may be made to the discretionary responsibilities taken on by the venture, that is, to the *company values* upheld by the business. The philosophical component of the mission statement illuminates the values and moral standards that the organisation will uphold while pursuing its business. This may refer to the way in which the company aims to treat its employees or customers. It may also specify the discretionary social responsibilities that the business will accept (see section 8.4 above). Values may be included in the mission because they reflect the personal principles of the entrepreneur or because the business believes its higher standards will appeal to customers and perhaps investors. These two reasons are not incompatible, indeed positive values are best upheld by a successful business.

Figure 10.1 shows a schematic representation of the elements in a mission statement for the entrepreneurial venture.

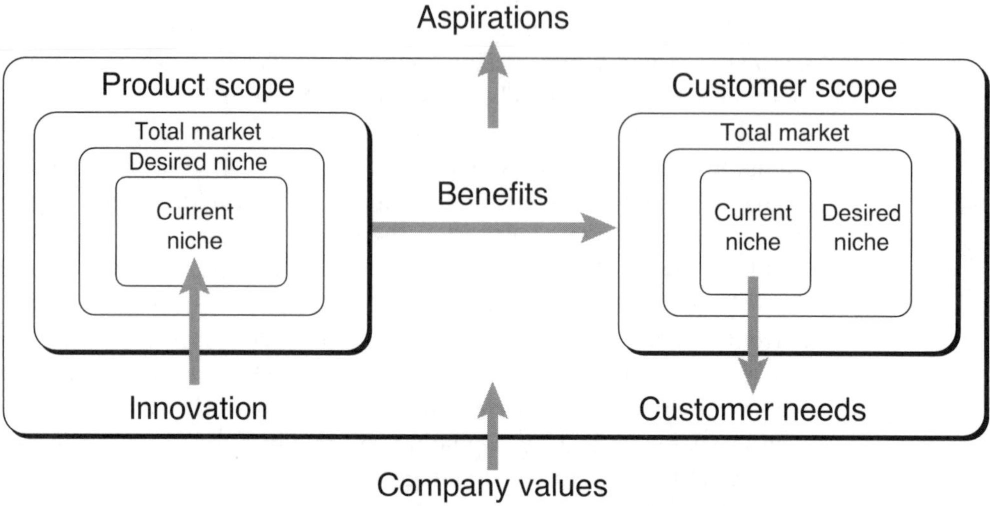

Fig. 10.1 Components of the entrepreneurial mission statement

10.3 Developing the mission statement

KEY LEARNING OUTCOME
An appreciation of the practical ways in which a mission can be developed for the venture.

If it is to help the venture, the mission must be right for it and it must be appropriate given the opportunity it aims to exploit and the innovation it intends to utilise. Further, if it is to be more than just so many words, then it must inform and influence people's decision making. A mission must be relevant to those who make up the venture and they must take ownership of it. These conditions will only be met if the mission is developed in the right way. The mission should stretch the business but be consistent with its ambitions, be realistic in terms of the opportunity it faces, and be compatible with its capability to exploit that opportunity. The mission must be developed alongside, and be judged in the light of, a strategic audit for the business. An audit of this nature includes:

- consideration of what the entrepreneur wishes to achieve;
- consideration of what other stakeholders aim to achieve and how the venture might help them;

- an assessment of the opportunity the venture aims to exploit;
- an assessment of market conditions;
- an assessment of the challenges and risks that will be encountered in exploiting that opportunity;
- an assessment of the business's capabilities and its competitive advantages;
- an evaluation of the resources the business has access to, future resource requirements and the resource gap this implies; and
- an assessment of the structure of, and conditions in, the firm's network.

The entrepreneur must also consider how the mission will be generated. Broadly, there are two approaches.

Through consensus

This approach involves getting the whole, or as many parts as possible, of the organisation to contribute towards the development of the mission. The aim is to gather information, create ideas and gain as many insights as possible for generating and evaluating the mission. Allowing people to be involved in creating the mission also gives them a feeling of ownership and so a commitment towards to it. The entrepreneur may go as far as inviting people from outside the formal organisation such as investors, and possibly important suppliers and customers, to make a contribution too. This can be a powerful way of attracting the commitment of these groups and strengthening the network.

Developing the mission in this way may present a logistical challenge, especially if a large number of people are involved. It may be necessary to set up a special forum for the exercise. There is also the question of how the ideas generated will be evaluated and judged and then fed into the final mission. This must be seen to be a rational and fair process, otherwise there is a danger that people may feel their contribution has been ignored or rejected.

By imposition

Alternatively, the entrepreneur may feel that consensus is not the best way to generate the mission. He or she may decide that it is better for them to develop the mission him- or herself, or in consultation with a small group, and then to impose it on the organisation as a whole. There may be a number of good reasons for this approach. The entrepreneur may see the mission as an articulation of his or her personal vision which may not be negotiable in the way that a consensus-building approach would demand. The entrepreneur may be the only person who has sufficient knowledge about the business and its situation to develop a meaningful mission. If the organisation is growing rapidly, it may be difficult to keep reassessing the mission as new people come in. It might also be inappropriate; after all, the mission is meant to be a constant in a time of flux. New people as they come on board will be asked to accept the mission as it stands (they may, of course, have been attracted by it in the first place!). The entrepreneur may also feel that it suits his or her leadership strategy to impose the mission on the organisation, that is to be seen to give direction and to 'lead from the front'.

Choice of approach

Both these routes for developing a mission have things to offer. The decision as to which is best will depend on the venture, how complex its business is, the way in which it is developing and the leadership style adopted by the entrepreneur. Developing a mission may in fact be one of the key exercises through which the entrepreneur establishes and demonstrates his or her leadership approach to the venture as a whole.

10.4 Articulating the mission statement

KEY LEARNING OUTCOME
An understanding of how the mission for the venture might be phrased.

Once the mission of the venture has been rationalised in terms of the elements in its strategic component and the values the venture wishes to uphold, then it needs to be *articulated* in the form of a definite statement. This statement then *becomes* the mission for the venture. If it is to be a valuable and an effective tool for the management of the venture it must fulfil several conditions. In particular, it must emphasise what is distinct about the venture; it must be informative; it must be clear and unambiguous; it must have impact; and it must be memorable. A balance between each of these requirements must be achieved. One generic format which includes all the elements described in the previous section is as follows:

> **The {*company*} aims to use its {*competitive advantage*} to achieve/maintain {*aspirations*} in providing {*product scope*} which offers {*benefits*} to satisfy the {*needs*} of {*customer scope*}. In doing this the company will at all times strive to uphold {*values*}.**

The starting point for articulating the mission in this way is to find phrases describing each italicised element. These must be quite short or the mission statement will become too long, therefore it will be difficult to remember and so will lose impact. Single words are best! Not every element need be included, thus if a particular element is obvious, does not really inform or does not distinguish the business from its sector in general then it may be safely dropped. If in doubt, it is probably better to make the mission statement more, rather than less, succinct.

The business will be faced with numerous opportunities to communicate its mission. It may be posted prominently within the organisation. It may form a starting point for setting objectives. It can be included on promotional material sent to customers. It will feature in the business plan presented to investors. However, not all communication need be so formal. The mission need not always be presented as a formal 'statement', it can easily be slipped informally into conversations. It is, after all, only the answer to the question: 'well, what does your business aim to do?'

Summary of key ideas

- A *mission* is a positive statement which defines what a particular venture is about and what it aims to achieve.
- A well-defined mission helps the venture by encouraging analysis of its situation and capabilities; drawing together its internal stakeholders; and facilitating communication of the venture to external stakeholders.
- The mission statement can include a definition of the venture's market scope, what it aims to do for its stakeholders, its ambitions and its values.
- Entrepreneurs can use development of the venture's mission as part of their leadership strategy.

Suggestions for further reading

Baetz, M.C. and **Bart, C.K.** (1996) 'Developing mission statements which work', *Long Range Planning,* Vol. 29, No. 4, pp. 526–33.

Campbell, A. (1989) 'Does your organisation need a mission statement?' *Leadership and Organisational Development Journal,* Vol. 10, No. 3, pp. 3–9.

Campbell, A. and **Yeung, S.** (1991) 'Creating a sense of mission', *Long Range Planning,* Vol. 24, No. 4, pp. 10–20.

David, F.R. (1989) 'How companies define their mission', *Long Range Planning,* Vol. 22, No. 3, pp. 90–7.

Germain, R. and **Bixby Cooper, M.** (1990) 'How a customer mission statement affects company performance', *Industrial Marketing Management,* Vol. 19, pp.47–54.

Klemm, M., Sanderson, S. and **Luffman, G.** (1991) 'Mission statements: Selling corporate values to employees', *Long Range Planning,* Vol. 24, No. 3, pp. 73–8.

Wickham, P.A. (1997) 'Developing a mission for an entrepreneurial venture', *Management Decision,* Vol. 35, No. 5, pp. 373–81.

Selected case material

Six ball bearings and a piece of bedroom carpet

23 October 1998

Christopher Swann profiles Renishaw, a maverick maker of measuring devices

During the recession of the early 1990s, Reni-shaw seemed to take a daredevil pride in its rapid fall in profits.

As earnings spiralled southwards with gathering speed, the maker of high-technology measuring devices continued to spend a towering 13 per cent of turnover on research and development and refused to cull a single engineering job or cut the prices of its market-leading probes.

It is this kind of idiosyncrasy – or long-termism – which has led some otherwise admiring analysts to suggest that the company should join the growing rank of small-capitalisation stocks going private.

In spite of its success, both in winning an impressive market share and garnering an array of design and export awards, it is a maverick that bears many of the hallmarks of a family-run concern.

From its base in Wotton-under-Edge, Gloucestershire, a combination of university campus and factory, the company maintains a distance from the City which is more than geographic. And it is hard to see how the largely-nominal linkage provided by a Stock Exchange listing serves its interests.

Renishaw emerged after a weekend of inspiration in the early 1970s. David McMurtry, then a designer at Rolls-Royce, the aero-engine group, invented the touch trigger probe using, among other things, six ball bearings and a section of his bedroom carpet.

The device, the first three-dimensional sensor, revolutionised the inspection of manufactured components, and formed the basis of a generation of Renishaw probes.

The company now produces a broad range of measuring probes and lasers, most precise to within several millionths of a metre and ranging in price from £2,500 and £250,000.

Mr McMurtry, chairman, and John Deer, deputy chairman, still own 53 per cent of the company, a holding which keeps Renishaw in a no-mans land between public and private.

Vertically integrated and secretive, the group flouts many of the dictums of shareholder value.

It retains a £34m cash pile for comfort – behaviour more typical of a family concern.

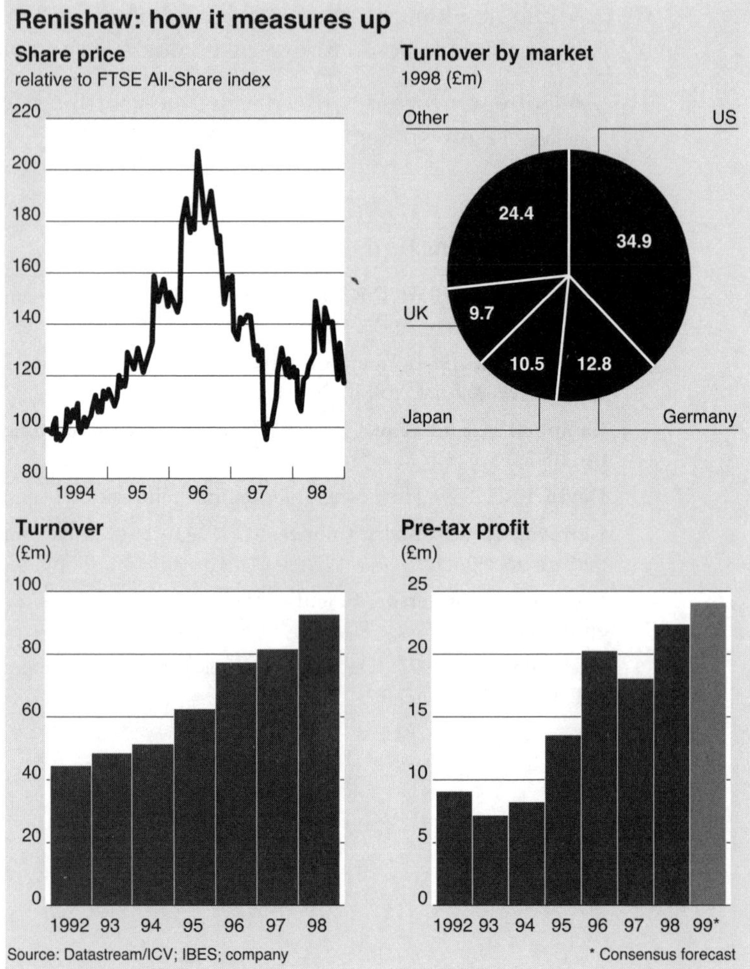

Mr McMurtry says it "helps him to sleep better", but shareholder orthodoxy would dictate that the cash be paid out or spent.

The company's demand for high levels of accuracy has led it to manufacture as well as design its probes. It has developed its own continuous unmanned manufacturing system, Ramtic. This enables the manufacture of short runs and keep stocks down.

Analysts say it is so advanced that Renishaw could almost certainly earn fees advising other engineers on efficient manufacturing.

Yet, this reluctance to trust others to do things that Renishaw can do well itself contravenes one of the key commandments of modern management theory: Thou shalt specialise.

Further evidence of the DIY approach is that the group owns its own travel agent. With 90 per cent of output going abroad and a strong tradition of customer care, Renishaw has a £2m annual travel budget. "It's a very odd thing to do," one analyst said. "But who is going to tell them not to?"

But Renishaw's success and management's control of the equity preserve it from the pressure to conform. Having woven a thicket of about 370 patents around its probes, Renishaw commands the lion's share of its chosen markets. Marpos, an Italian group with which Renishaw has locked horns in patent litigation, is one of its few substantial specialist competitors.

Fear of encouraging entrants to the market seems to be behind the unwillingness to disclose market share and profit margin breakdowns.

"We assume that the market is expanding and that margins are high," said one analyst. "But because the market does not fully understand the company and finds its results hard to predict it applies a discount."

A 1998 operating margin of 22.6 per cent indicates the group may be making handsome margins, even on older, off-patent products.

But its guarded approach to figures, while strategically shrewd, runs contrary to the stock market ethos of ever increasing openness.

Renishaw has not even used the market to raise capital. In its 15 years as a listed company it has made only one acquisition – which was small and funded from cash reserves.

The principal benefit appears to be the opportunity to incentivise employees through share schemes.

Yet for all its idiosyncrasies, the company's shares have outperformed the market, albeit by a small margin, while the its capitalisation has grown almost six-fold since flotation to £492m.

The 'silver surfers' may be solid gold for net enterprise

18 August 1999

Launch of web site aimed at the over-45 'can do' generation has commercial and social potential. **Caroline Daniel** reports

For a country more familiar with the concept of silver service than "silver surfers" the notion of elderly people heading for their internet terminals may seem a little futuristic.

But that is exactly the perception that Richard Spinks, 32, wants to dispel when tomorrow he launches a new lifestyle web site, called Vavo.com, aimed at the over-45s.

"This is the first service of its type in Europe set up to meet the needs of this age group, aged 45 to 105," says Mr Spinks. A trial version has been piloted for a month and developed in consultation with 100 "community leaders" between 50 and 80 years old. "This is an empowerment thing," says Mr Spinks.

Even the name was checked with users. "They rejected names such as 50plus.com because they didn't want age involved. There were no preconceptions about the word Vavo. It means what people want it to mean". There was one small scare, however. "One person thought it meant grandmother in colloquial Portuguese," says Mr Spinks.

The service, which may use a larger than average typeface for its screen display, offers content on health, travel, finance, community, games, pressure groups and shopping. It also offers simple e-mailing.

Vavo hopes to be able to get enough critical mass from its users – it has a target of 500,000 in its first year – to force discounts out of online retailers. Already about 1,600 products are on offer on the site, as well as two cruises.

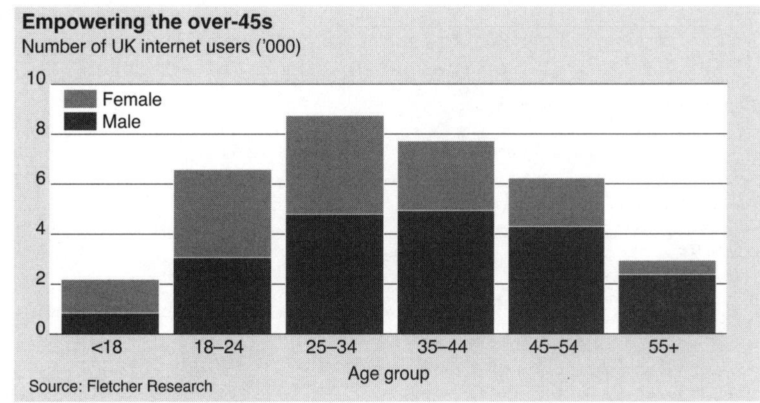

Over the next three months, Vavo wants to attract a further 900 community leaders whose mission will be to cajole friends into having a go, provide feedback and police internet content.

Asked if the Queen Mother, 99, had been approached, Mr Spinks says: "We would want to sign her up."

Mr Spinks, who has been involved in internet businesses for several years, says Len Dight, 75, his father-in-law, who became a widower this year after 46 years of marriage, was the "major inspiration" behind the service.

Although Mr Dight had never used a computer before, Mr Spinks taught him how to use the internet. "I can honestly say it kept me from depression, because it is interactive. TV wasn't the same because it's too trivial," says Mr Dight. He now plays chess and bridge online – sometimes all night – and has become involved as a community leader.

Tony Carpenter, 70, who lives in Norfolk, is also active in Vavo. "I came out of a very busy life to retirement and was absolutely lost, with little communication out in the country. Then, through my son's insistence, I found the internet about two years ago."

He has used it for genealogical research, and has traced his family back to 920 "when we were crusaders". The crusade he has now embarked on is to cajole others into overcoming their internet fears. "I can go out to the over-60 clubs and show them they can do it."

But both he and his wife Gill are averse to the idea of obvious age-related content, such as a concentration on ill-health – an attitude which mirrors that in the US, where the most popular web sites for the mature market are those with a can-do attitude, rather than those reminding users of the aches and pains of ageing.

ThirdAge.com, founded in the US in 1996, sets a precedent for the potential success of Vavo. That portal, aimed at the 45-65 age group, is targeted at "vital and energetic baby boomers". This group "represents both the fastest growing segment of the US population and of online users", it says.

The commercial attraction of tapping a more mature market, was underlined in June, when ThirdAge Media, which operates Third-Age.com, revealed that investors – including CBS and Merrill Lynch – had put $89m (€55.6m) into the group. According to Fletcher Research, a UK internet consultancy, 8 per cent, or 800,000 internet users, in the UK are over 55. This is growing fast. Statistics show they are as willing to buy online as younger counterparts.

According to Vavo's research, the UK's over-45s control 80 per cent of the nation's wealth and 40 per cent of consumer spending, worth €145bn a year. No wonder a US venture capitalist has committed $2m towards developing Vavo in the UK. They must feel that silver surfers could be gold for business.

Review questions

Using the elements of a mission discussed in the chapter, propose outline missions for:

1 Renishaw

2 Vavo

3 In what ways might such mission statements be used to help the business?

11 The strategy for the venture

Chapter overview

***Strategy** is a central concept in modern management practice. This chapter looks at business strategy from the entrepreneurial perspective. The value of a well-considered and well-defined strategy to the venture is advocated, and the way in which entrepreneurs can control strategy development is considered. The chapter concludes by exploring the strategies entrepreneurs can use to initiate their ventures.*

11.1 What is a business strategy?

KEY LEARNING OUTCOME
An understanding of the key elements of the business strategy for the entrepreneurial venture.

The idea that an organisation has a 'strategy' lies at the centre of much management thinking. A strategy can be defined as the actions an organisation takes to pursue its business objectives. Strategy drives *performance* and an effective strategy results in a good performance. An organisation's strategy is multi-faceted. It can be viewed from a number of directions depending on which aspects of its actions are of interest. A basic distinction exists between the *content* of a business's strategy, the strategy *process* that the business adopts to maintain that strategy and the environmental *context* within which the strategy must be made to work. The strategy content relates to what the business actually *does* while the strategy process relates to the way the business *decides* what it is going to do. The strategy content has three distinct decision areas: the *products* to be offered, the *markets* to be targeted and the approach taken to *competing*.

Strategy content

Strategy content relates to three things: the final product range, the customers it serves and the advantage it seeks in the marketplace.

The product range

This covers the type and range of products that the firm supplies to its markets (note that the word product here is used in a general sense to include both physical products and services). The decisions the entrepreneur faces here are:

- What type of products should the business offer?
- What should their features be?
- How will they address customer needs? What benefits will they offer?
- What mix of physical and service elements should be offered with the product?
- If the product is are to be successful, in what way(s) must the customer find it more attractive then those of competitors?
- What unit cost is acceptable? (How does this relate to price?)
- How wide should be the product range offered? How many product variants will be necessary?

Market scope

The market scope defines the customer groups and market segments that will be addressed by the firm. Key decisions here include:

- How is the total market to be defined?
- What features (e.g. customer types; customer needs; buying behaviour; location) are important for characterising the market and defining its sectors?
- On what group(s) of customers should the business concentrate?
- In what sectors will these customers be?
- Should the firm concentrate its efforts on a narrow group, or spread its efforts more widely?
- Why will the group(s) selected find the firm's offerings more attractive than those of competitors?
- What will be the geographic location and spread of the customers (e.g. local, regional, national, international)?

Clearly, decisions on product range and market scope are interlinked. The decisions made with respect to one influence the decisions that must be made for the others. Therefore, it may be better for the entrepreneur to regard themselves as facing a *single* set of decisions about the combined *product–market domain* of the firm.

Competitive approach

Competitive approach refers to the way in which the firm competes within its product–market domain to sustain and develop its business in the face of competitive pressures. This aspect of strategy content reflects the way in which the firm tries to influence the customer to favour their offerings. Important decisions to be made in relation to this approach include:

- How should the product be priced relative to competitors? (Should a discount or premium be offered?)

- What distribution route will be used to get the product to the customer?
- What financial rewards and incentives will be offered to intermediaries and distributors?
- What support (e.g. exclusivity; preferential selling; display) will be expected from distributors?
- How will the customer's buying decision be influenced?
- What message will be sent to consumers about the product?
- How will the message be delivered? (For example, by advertising; by personal selling, or through distributors?)
- Will customers be encouraged to compare the product to the offerings of competitors? (If so, on what basis: price, quality, features, performance?)
- Or will customers be told that the innovation is so great that there is nothing else like it?

The strategy content which the business aspires to achieve must be consistent with the entrepreneur's vision and the mission they have defined for the venture. Decisions about strategy content must be made in the light of an understanding of 'external' conditions such as characteristics of the market, the competitive situation and the way in which different sectors can be served, and in the light of 'internal' concerns such as the mission and goals of the organisation, the resources it has to hand and its capabilities. The strategy content for the venture is the way in which it competes to sustain and develop its product–market domain (see Fig. 11.1).

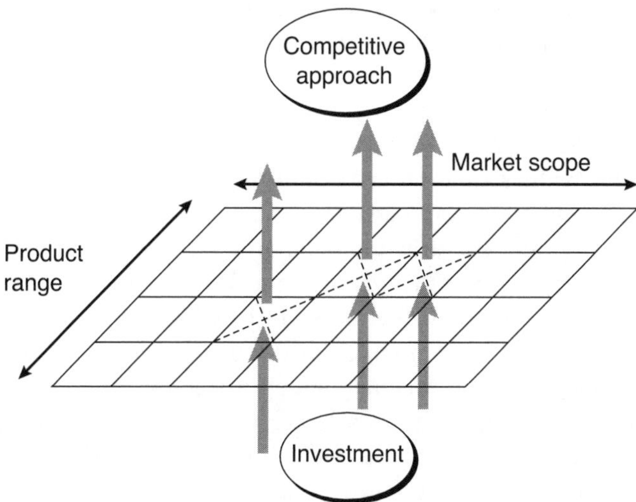

Fig. 11.1 Strategy content and product–market domain

The venture will achieve success if it directs its resources in an appropriate way towards delivering a rewarding and sustainable strategy content. The strategy content dictates the investment of resources that the business must undertake. Investments in financial, operating and human resources will all play a part in supporting the strategy content. Consequently, strategy content decisions must be evaluated in terms of the investments that they entail, the rewards that are likely and the risks involved.

11.2 Strategy process in the entrepreneurial business

KEY LEARNING OUTCOME
An understanding of the ways in which an entrepreneurial business decides on the strategies it will adopt.

The firm's strategy process is the way in which the business makes decisions about the strategy content it wishes to achieve (see Fig. 11.2). It is reflected in the way the organisation considers its future, how it selects its goals and the way it decides on how to allocate resources in order to achieve them. Strategy process is embedded in the structures, systems and processes that the organisation adopts, as well as its culture and the leadership style of the entrepreneur running it.

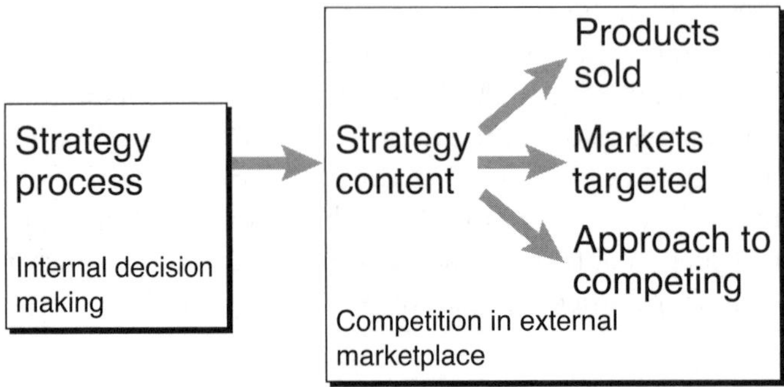

Fig. 11.2 Strategy content and strategy process

One of the most important themes in modern strategic management is the distinction between and relative values of *deliberate* (or *planned*) and *emergent* approaches to strategy creation. A deliberate approach to strategy creation is one in which the entrepreneur sets out to define a strategic policy for the venture in which the future goals and competitive approach of the business are clearly defined and translated into specific objectives. The entrepreneur then sets out to achieve this strategy through an explicit process of implementation in which instructions as to objectives and budgets are passed down the organisation. An emergent approach to strategy creation is one in which future goals and strategic approach are left more ambiguous. Rather, the entrepreneur concentrates on managing the venture's short-term capabilities and exploiting the opportunities that present themselves as the business moves forward. Here, the entrepreneur is not so concerned with where the business is going; he or she just makes sure it goes somewhere interesting.

The traditional approach to strategic management emphasised the deliberate approach. Planning for the future was not just an important responsibility for senior managers; it was their *primary* responsibility. Managers who did not plan were failing in a critical respect. Entrepreneurs who often rejected the strictures of formal planning and advocated action over producing plans were regarded to be particularly at fault.

Of late though there has been a reaction against this belief. This is exemplified in Henry Mintzberg's seminal 1994 book *The Rise and Fall of Strategic Planning*. The critique of the planning approach is based on two arguments. First is that empirical observation of business performance does not show a strong correlation with formal planning activity. Many businesses that do not carry out a lot of planning are as successful as those who invest heavily in it. The second argument is that the planning approach is theoretically flawed. Planning only works if the future can be predicted with some certainty. This is rarely the case, especially for the fast-growing entrepreneurial venture in a dynamic, unpredictable environment. It also assumes that managers can control everything the extended organisation does. Experience of organisations suggests that managers (even entrepreneurs with strong leadership skills) cannot control every detail. As a result, emergent approaches to strategy creation should not be dismissed as wrong. They reflect a perfectly good managerial approach to developing at least some businesses given their capabilities and the opportunities the environment offers them.

As with many debates in which opinions are polarised, the resolution of the planning–emergent debate has, to a great extent, resulted in a broader perspective in which both positions are integrated. Drawing a hard and fast distinction between the stages of creating – *formulating* – and putting into practice – *implementing* – a particular strategy is seen as artificial. 'Implementers' who have played no part in the development of a strategy are unlikely to take ownership of it from the 'formulators' who have. A strategy must be modified between the drawing board and taking to the air.

Entrepreneurs make good strategies happen through leadership, not just planning, and leadership demands listening to people, learning from them and taking their ideas on board. Leadership also means giving people the latitude to make their own decisions and put their own insight into practice. This is the only way an organisation can learn and be flexible. However, leaving room for an organisation to grow and develop does not mean the entrepreneur has no view on where it should go. As we discussed in Chapter 9, even if an entrepreneur does not have a definite, highly detailed plan in mind, he or she should certainly have a vision as to where the venture should be heading. Such a vision may offer a space into which the business might go, rather than a definite destination, but nonetheless it will control its destiny. A cognitive study comparing entrepreneurial intentions with actual outcomes by Jenkis and Johnson (1997) suggests that many entrepreneurs adopt an emergent approach to strategy creation and are adept at using it.

Colin Eden and Fran Ackerman have suggested an integrated and participative approach to strategy creation in their 1998 book *Making Strategy*. They suggest that good strategies emerge from an interactive process that they refer to as the 'Journey' of strategy where the word Journey is an acronym for 'Jointly, Understanding, Reflecting and Negotiating'. In this process individuals still have a responsibility for identifying and evaluating strategic options. However, these options are flexible 'opening positions' and can evolve as they are implemented through the 'journey' the strategy takes through the organisation. Making the strategy happen is as important as making it in the first place. In the context of the entrepreneurial venture, this process resonates with the entrepreneur defining, articulating and communicating his or her vision.

The entrepreneurial approach to management is distinct at the level of strategy process, not content. Its not what an entrepreneur *does* (the business they are in) that matters. What makes a manager entrepreneurial is the *way* he or she organises the venture and uses it innovate and to deliver value to the customer in a way that existing players cannot.

At any point in time the venture will have a strategy content, that is, a product range being sold to a distinct group of customers with a particular approach taken to attracting those customers and competing within the marketplace. The strategy content will evolve as the business grows and develops. New products will be introduced, old ones dropped. The competitive approach may alter as the organisation learns and market conditions change. At any moment in time the entrepreneur and other managers in the organisation will have views and expectations about what the business's strategy content should be in the future. This interest may also extend to other stakeholders such as important customers looking for specific new products and influential investors who offer advice on how the business might develop.

The strategy process adopted by the organisation is defined by the way in which decisions about strategy content are taken. As shown in Fig. 11.3, it is reflected in the relationship that exists between the *existing* strategy content, the strategy content *desired* by the business for the future and the strategy content that is actually *achieved*. The results of these decisions influence the investments made by the venture.

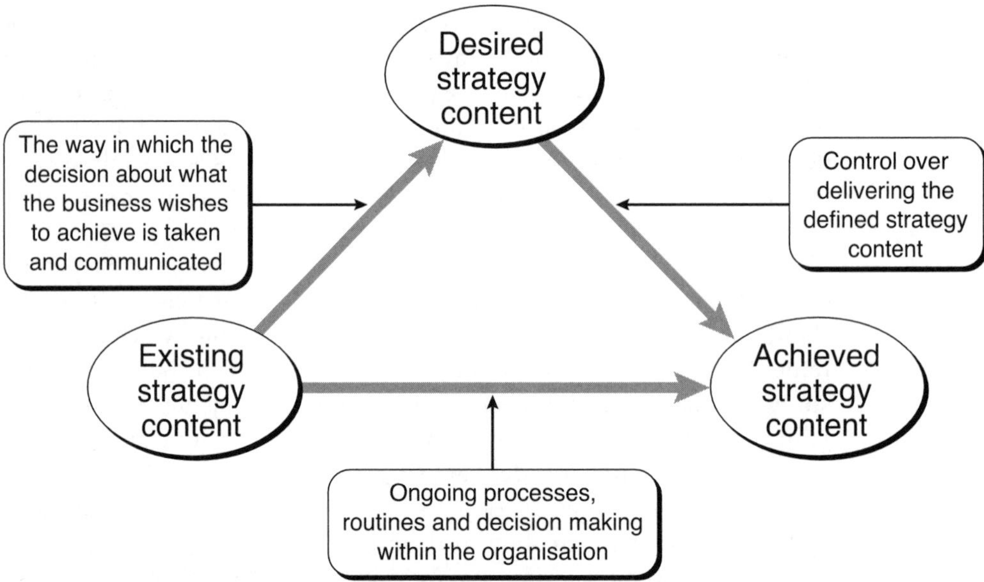

Fig. 11.3 A model of strategy process

The link between existing strategy content and the strategy content achieved in the future

The strategy content of the business will evolve over time. The way in which the business modifies its range of products, changes its customer base and develops its competitive approach will be the result of a series of ongoing decisions and actions taken by the people who make up the organisation. These decisions will occur even if the organisation does not have an explicit strategy to guide them. They may be incremental and the result of short-term pragmatic considerations or they may be made in response to immediate market opportunities. However, this does not mean that these decisions are not controlled. They will be shaped by a wide variety of organisational and environmental factors including:

- the reporting relationships that define the organisation's structure;
- the mechanisms the organisation adopts to control the allocation of resources;
- the organisation's systems for motivating and rewarding performance;
- the way the organisation manages information and identifies opportunities;
- the organisation's technological competence and any technical developments;
- the organisation's historical performance;
- resource availability within the organisation;
- the organisational culture;
- internal disputes and political infighting within the organisation; and
- the expectations and influence of external stakeholders such as customers and investors.

If these features are allowed to control decision making about the evolution of a business's strategy content without reference to an overriding strategic context then the firm's strategy process may, using the terminology of Henry Mintzberg and James Waters (1985), be said to be *emergent*.

The link between existing strategy content and desired strategy content

An emergent strategy may establish itself for a number of reasons. However, an entrepreneur is unlikely to be satisfied unless the organisation operates with at least some sense of what it might achieve in the future. After all, the entrepreneur is motivated by the difference between what *is* and what *might be*. The future state desired by the entrepreneur can take a variety of forms. It will vary in several particulars, including:

- the types of detail it contains;
- how specific those details are;
- the latitude the entrepreneur will accept in its achievement;
- the time period over which it is to be achieved;
- the way in which it is communicated to other stakeholders; and
- the extent to which it is negotiable with other stakeholders.

There are a number of ways in which the organisation can become aware of the desired strategy content.

The entrepreneur's communication of their vision

The entrepreneur can articulate and communicate their vision to the rest of the organisation. This may be sufficiently powerful and attractive to motivate the whole organisation. A vision may (deliberately) lack detail but it should highlight the desirability of achieving certain strategy contents in preference to others.

The definition of a mission

The organisation's mission will specify the key elements of a strategy content. The amount of detail it provides will depend on how the strategic component in the mission is specified. The mission will, at a minimum, be able to provide a test as to what strategy contents are desirable and acceptable. The mission may be developed by a process of consensus or it may be imposed on the organisation by the entrepreneur.

The setting of objectives

The desired strategy content may be defined explicitly by the setting of specific objectives. These may be financial or strategic in nature. They may refer to the organisation as a whole, or they may relate to a particular project or they may fall within the responsibility of an individual. Objectives may be subject to negotiation and agreed through consensus, or alternatively, they may be imposed by the entrepreneur without opportunity for debate. The approach taken depends upon the entrepreneur's personal style and leadership strategy. Quantified objectives provide a means of benchmarking the achievement of a desired strategy content.

Through informal discussion

The identification of a desired strategy content may not occur by a formal process. It may become evident through ongoing discussions about the business and the opportunities offered by the market. These discussions may involve a variety of people both within, and perhaps from outside, the organisation and they may take place over a period of time.

The link between desired strategy content and achieved strategy content

This link is manifest in the ability of the entrepreneur to actually deliver the strategy content they desire for their organisation. Two things may limit this, and first is the potential to achieve that strategy content in the marketplace. If the strategy content is to be delivered it must be both *achievable* given the market conditions and the competitive forces present, and *feasible* in terms of the resources available to make the necessary investments. The second possible limitation is the control the entrepreneur has over the organisation.

Even though it might be 'their' organisation entrepreneurs are limited in the extent to which they can control the actions of the people who make up their organisation. They cannot enforce their will over it completely. Some of the organisation's strategy will always be 'emergent'. The way in which entrepreneurs control the organisation and ensure that it delivers the strategy content they desire is dependent on a large number of factors. Some of the more critical include:

- their personal leadership style;
- the consensus they build for the desired strategy;
- their ownership of resources;

- the way in which they control resources;
- he control mechanisms and procedures they have established;
- their technical expertise;
- their access to information and their ability to control that information within the organisation;
- the way they set objectives;
- the way in which they reward achievement of objectives;
- their creation of, and the way they are legitimatised by, symbolic devices within the organisation;
- their influence over, and control of, organisational politics;
- the relationship they build with external stakeholders; and
- the way they manage *attributions*, that is, the way they associate themselves with success and dissociate themselves from failure within the organisation.

The entrepreneur will be motivated by a distinct picture of how the world should be. That is what their vision *is*. Yet they must always match their desire to achieve particular outcomes with their ability to control what the organisation can actually do both internally and in its marketplace. They must also balance their need to control the organisation with giving the people who make up the organisation latitude to make their own decisions and use their insights and intuitions to further its ends.

11.3 Controlling strategy process in the venture

KEY LEARNING OUTCOME
A recognition of the decisions the entrepreneur must make to control the strategy process in their venture.

If the entrepreneur is to maintain control of the organisation and focus it on the opportunities that it seeks to exploit then he or she must control its strategy. This demands control of its strategy *process* as well as its strategy *content*. This means controlling the way the organisation identifies options for its future, the way in which these are communicated and shared, the way in which control is maintained over resource investments aimed at achieving the desired outcomes and the way in which rewards are offered for delivering the outcomes.

The essential decisions that the entrepreneur must make in relation to developing and controlling the strategy process include:

1 Decisions relating to the development of the mission

- By what process will the business mission be developed (through consensus, or by imposition)?
- How will it be articulated?
- To whom will it be communicated?

2 Decisions relating to the development of strategy

- Who in the organisation will be invited to contribute to the development of the desired strategy content?
- How will their ideas be evaluated and judged?
- Where will the information needed to develop the strategy content come from?
- Who in the organisation will collect, store and control that information?
- How will the desired strategy content be communicated to the rest of the organisation?
- How will the strategy content be communicated to external stakeholders?

3 Decisions relating to the control of resources

- What procedure will control how investment decisions are made?
- Who will have responsibility for what level of investment?
- How will new investments be distinguished from routine payments?
- How will budgets be allocated?
- What budgetary control systems will be put in place?
- How will information on budgetary control be stored, manipulated and shared?
- By whom will information on budgetary control be stored, manipulated and shared?

4 Decisions relating to the way objectives will be set, monitored and rewarded

- How will objectives be set?
- Who will be responsible for setting them?
- For whom will objectives be set (the organisation, functions, teams, individuals)?
- What will be the nature of the objectives (financial or strategic?)
- Will objectives be negotiable? If so, in what way and by whom?
- What information will be needed to monitor objectives?
- How will this information be collected and stored? Who will have access to it?
- What will be the rewards for achieving set objectives? What will be the response if they are not achieved?

These decisions will be very influential in giving the organisation its form, structure and systems because they will influence the culture it develops. Consequently they must be subject to constant revision and review as the business grows and develops.

11.4 Why a well-defined strategy can help the venture

KEY LEARNING OUTCOME
An appreciation of the value in generating an explicit strategy for the venture.

Working under an emergent strategy is a far more common feature of managerial life than many textbooks on business planning would have us believe. Developing, assessing and communicating a strategy content represents an *investment*. It takes time, effort and money to achieve a well-defined strategy. Like any investment it must be assessed in terms of the returns it will bring in the way it will improve organisational performance. If this return is not forthcoming then the organisation may well benefit from allowing its strategy to be emergent

There are a variety of conditions under which an organisation's strategy tends to become emergent, for example:

- when its expectations are limited, i.e. when the desired strategic content is not very different from the existing one;
- when it is experienced in pursuing its business, i.e. when knowledge of how to achieve a particular strategic content is well established and not subject to extensive discussion;
- when the competitive environment is stable, i.e. when environmental shocks do not occur;
- when the competitive structure is stable, i.e. when competitors do not tend to infringe on each other's business;
- when the rules of competition are established, i.e. when competitor's reactions are predictable;
- when the industry technology is established, i.e. innovations are few and of limited scope;
- when patterns of investment are routinised, i.e. managers do not seek guidance at a strategic level when making investment decisions;
- when the organisation's leadership is weak, i.e. when power to impose a particular strategy content is limited; and
- when the organisation is political, i.e. when agreement on a particular strategy content could not be gained.

These conditions tend to be found in mature, established organisations whose decision making has become routinised and even bureaucratised. They are not the typical conditions to be found in a new, fast-growing venture which is innovating and changing the rules of competition within its marketplace. Thus the entrepreneurial venture would be expected to gain in the following ways from investing in developing a strategy and communicating it to stakeholders.

A strategy encourages the entrepreneur to assess and articulate their vision

A strategy represents the way in which the entrepreneur will achieve their vision. The potential to make a vision into reality will be dependent on the possibility of creating a strategy to deliver it. This possibility will be a function of the *achievability* of the strategy in the competitive marketplace and of the *feasibility* of the strategy in terms of the resources available.

A strategy ensures auditing of the organisation and its environment

A strategy is a call to action. If it is to be successful then it must be based on a sound knowledge of the environment in which the organisation finds itself; the conditions within its marketplace, particularly in terms of the competitive pressures it faces; and of its own internal capabilities and competencies. Developing a strategy demands that the organisation's capabilities and competencies are audited.

A strategy illuminates new possibilities and latitudes

A strategy is developed in response to the dictates of the entrepreneur's vision. However, the process is iterative. Strategy development feeds back to vision. It reinforces the vision's strong parts and asks the entrepreneur to readdress its weaknesses. It clarifies the possibilities the venture faces and the latitude the entrepreneur will accept for the achievement of them.

A strategy provides organisational focus

A strategy provides a central theme around which the members of the organisation can focus their activities. It relates the tasks of the individual to the tasks of the organisation as a whole. A strategy is the stream of actions that make up the organisation. As such it is a unifying principle which gives organisational actions meaning and significance in relation to each other.

A strategy guides the structuring of the organisation

A strategy highlights the tasks necessary for the entrepreneur to achieve his or her goals. Some of these tasks will be short-term, others long-term; some will be of a 'general' management nature, others will be specialist; some will be concerned with generating and sustaining external relationships, while others will be concerned with internal technical issues. The nature of the tasks that must be undertaken defines the roles that must be filled within the organisation. This in turn guides the entrepreneur in developing a structure for the organisation.

A strategy acts as a guide to decision making

A strategy provides a framework for making decisions. A decision is a response to proffered possibilities. The strategy helps to highlight and evaluate these possibilities. It indicates how significant a particular decision will be, and the impact its outcomes will have. It illuminates the information that will be needed if the decision is to be made confidently. The strategy then enables the various options to be evaluated and the right course of action to be rationalised.

A strategy provides a starting point for the setting of objectives

By specifying the tasks that need to be undertaken in order to achieve desired outcomes, a strategy provides a starting point for defining quantified measurable objectives for both the organisation as a whole, and for the individuals who comprise it.

A strategy acts as a common language for stakeholders

An organisation is characterised by its strategy. The strategy provides the context in which the organisation acts. It is the perspective which enables individuals to make sense of the organisation's actions and their own part in those actions. The organisation's strategy provides a way for its stakeholders to relate to each other: they *interact* through its strategy. Strategy is a common language they can use to talk to each other about the organisation and their relationship to it.

Vision, mission and strategy in the entrepreneurial process

Vision, mission and *strategy* are intertwined aspects of a single entrepreneurial perspective (see Fig. 11.4). Each of these components represents both a different aspect of the world the entrepreneur seeks to create and the means by which they will create it. Together, they turn the entrepreneur's desire to make a difference in the world into an effective management tool for delivering change. This tool works by reconciling the entrepreneur's vision with actual possibilities and capabilities, by articulating that vision so that it may be communicated to others and by defining the actions necessary to progress the venture.

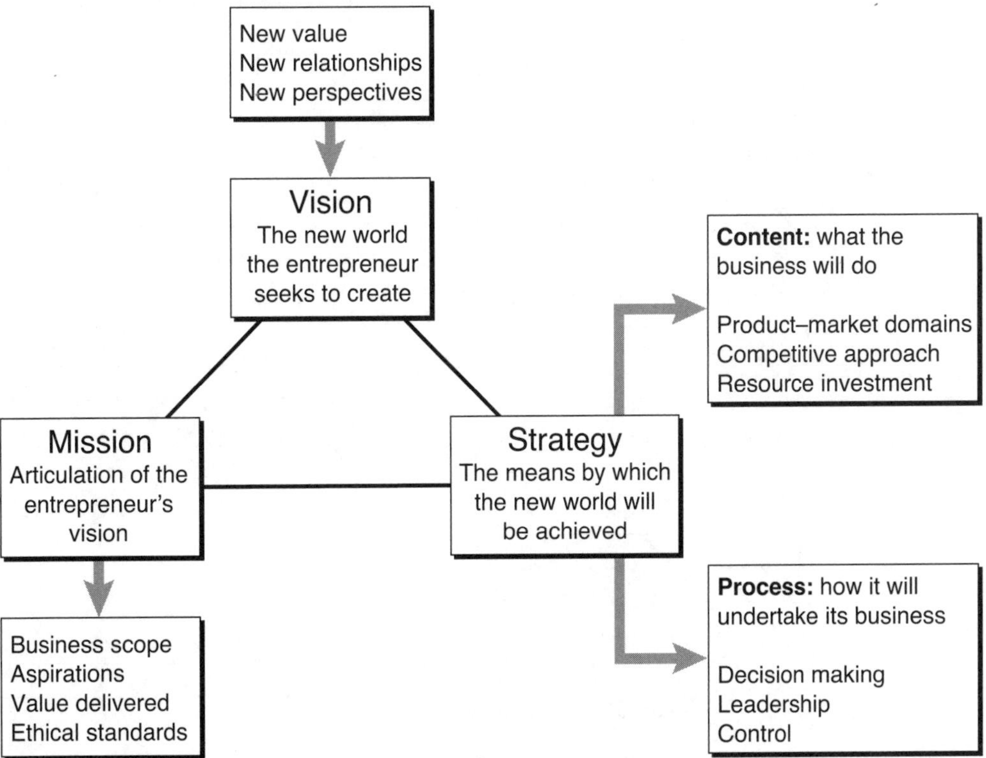

Fig. 11.4 Vision, mission and strategy in the entrepreneurial process

11.5 An overview of entrepreneurial entry strategies

KEY LEARNING OUTCOME
A recognition of the strategies adopted by entrepreneurs to establish their ventures.

A strategy is the pattern of actions that define an organisation. Every entrepreneurial venture is different, and each has its own strategy. However, there are common and recognisable patterns in the way in which businesses compete with one other. These are called *generic strategies*. Entrepreneurial ventures adopt a number of generic strategies in order to establish themselves in the marketplace. These strategies differ in the way in which the venture offers new value to the marketplace and the market they wish to serve (see Fig. 11.5).

Product–market domain

The entrepreneur must select the product market domain in which to establish their venture. This defines the scope of the product they wish to offer to what market segments. The product scope is the range of product categories the firm will provide. Product scope must be understood in terms of the way customers distinguish between different products in the market. Important factors are product features, product quality, patterns of product usage in terms of place, time and quantity, market

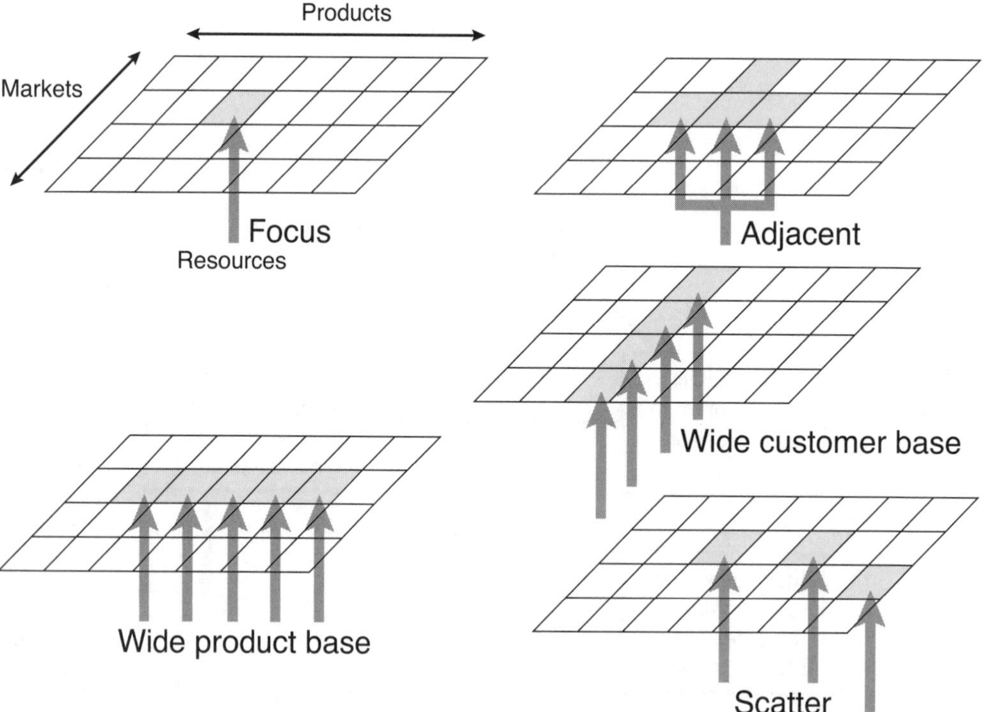

Fig. 11.5 Entrepreneurial entry strategies

positioning, and branding and imagery. The market sectors served are the distinct customer groups addressed by the firm.

Customer groups must be classified in terms of the way their needs both coincide and differ. Important factors for consideration here are demographic and sociographic characteristics, psychographic profile, customer location, buying behaviour and usage patterns. Such analysis is a well-established part of marketing thinking. The entrepreneur has five generic entry strategies in relation to product–market domain. These are:

1 *Focused entry* – addressing a single well-defined product–market domain.
2 *Product spread* – offering a wide range of products to a single well-defined market.
3 *Customer spread* – delivering a single or narrow range of products to a wide base of customers.
4 *Adjacency* – offering a wide range of products to a broad customer base. All product–market segments are adjacent in that the characterising features of each segment are continuous or can be related to each other.
5 *Scatter* – a variety of different products are offered to a variety of different customers. The segments are not adjacent.

Competitive approach

Competitive approach refers to the way the venture attracts customers by offering them value that existing competitors do not. Generic strategies in relation to this approach include the following.

Offering a new product or service

Delivering the customer an innovative product or service. This must perform a task for the customer, or solve a problem for them, in a way which is both different from, and better than, existing products.

Offering greater value

Offering the customer a product or service which is comparable to those already in existence but at a lower price, so offering them greater value for money.

Creating new relationships

The entrepreneur exists in a network of relationships built on trust. Trust both reduces costs and adds value. The entrepreneur can be competitive by creating new relationships between providers and users, and by managing existing relationships better.

Being more flexible

Customers' needs are not fixed. Even if they are in the same market segment, different customers will present a slightly different set of needs. Further, a particular customer's needs are subject to constant change. However, at any one point in time a group of customers must satisfy their needs with the limited range of products and services on offer. The entrepreneur can create new value for the customer by being flexible in terms of what they offer. This may involve modifying the products and services they provide to make them specific to the requirements of the customer or developing a means by which the product can be continually modified in response to customers' requirements.

Being more responsive

As customer needs change and evolve, existing products serve those needs less effectively. As a result new opportunities emerge and take shape. The entrepreneur can add value in the marketplace by being attuned to those changes, in terms of recognising the new opportunities as they develop and responding quickly to them by modifying their existing offerings and innovating new ones.

Choice of entry strategy

These two aspects of generic entry strategy, namely product–market domain and the competitive approach, exist in an iterative relationship to each other. The choice of competitive approach will depend on the particular characteristics of a product-market segment. How that presents itself as an opportunity to the business will depend on the resources it has to hand and its capabilities. Exploiting that opportunity will reward the business with further resources to maintain and expand its presence in its product–market domain. The choice of generic entry strategy depends on the resources and capabilities of the organisation (see Fig. 11.6).

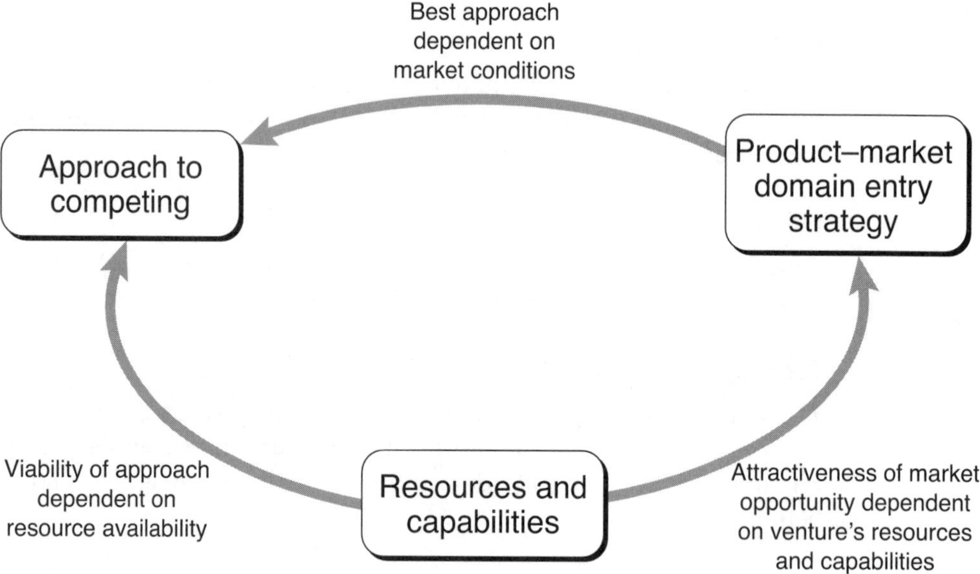

Fig. 11.6 The relationship between strategy, resources and capability

11.6 Talking strategy: entrepreneurial strategic heuristics

KEY LEARNING OUTCOME
A recognition of heuristics as guides to, and indicators of, entrepreneurial decision-making

The discussion of entrepreneurial strategy so far has adopted a formal approach. Entrepreneurial strategy has been described from the 'top-down' perspective, that of an outsider looking in, as much as that of an entrepreneur looking out. This is a legitimate approach. Just as a doctor brings along knowledge and expertise and can diagnose a disease, so the expert in entrepreneurship can recognise strategic approaches individual entrepreneurs may not themselves recognise. Entrepreneurs do not necessarily, or even usually, have formal learning in business strategy. An expert in strategy may be able to identify the strategic posturing of the venture even if the venture's managers cannot, or do not see any point in, articulating it in formal terms. This is not to say that they may be implementing the strategy very effectively!

This distance between the 'professional strategic expert' and the practising entrepreneur must, however, be closed. The expert must be able to resonate with the way in which the entrepreneur actually makes decisions if he or she is to both understand the entrepreneur's venture and be able to effectively articulate support and encouragement. Ronald Mitchell (1997) has advocated attention to entrepreneurs' own 'oral histories' as an approach to understanding entrepreneurship. A very meaningful way of closing the gap has come from recognising the *heuristics* that entrepreneurs use.

A heuristic is a *decision rule* based on insight and experience. It is called into play when an entrepreneur is required to analyse a situation and make a decision in relation to it. Entrepreneurs are often able to articulate, quite succinctly, the heuristics they use. These often take the form of punchy aphorisms. They are rarely specific. Rather they are general statements, 'rules of thumb', that reveal the entrepreneur's attitudes and approaches. These not only provide a practical insight into the approach that the entrepreneur is taking. They can also be used as analytical devices to describe and analyse entrepreneurs and their ventures (a good example of their use is provided by Manimala, 1999).

Table 11.1 describes a series of entrepreneurial strategic heuristics and their opposites that might be described as counter heuristics. As will be appreciated, the terms heuristic and counter-heuristic are interchangeable. A heuristic and its counter both have resonance and reflect an equally valid 'common sense' approach to business. Neither is right or wrong. They must be judged in terms of the entrepreneur's characteristics, the nature of the venture they are pursuing and the success they bring. This list is not exhaustive. It is intended to illustrate the heuristic themes entrepreneurs develop and use.

Table 11.1 Examples of entrepreneurial strategic heuristics

Strategic theme	Heuristic	Counter-heuristic
Innovation	Avoid run-of-the mill products	Stick to what is tried and trusted
	Search out new ideas from many sources	Keep an eye on one or two key areas
Flexibility	Keep an open mind to new approaches	Once you have found a good way of doing things – stick to it
	Success only comes from continual improvement	Keep on using a successful formula
Vision	Develop a vision and never compromise it	Let your vision evolve
	Share a vision – but don't negotiate it	Let others contribute to your vision
Start-up strategy	Start small and build	Go for it big time before someone else does
Using external support	All businesses benefit from professional help	Professionals are a poor investment. If they know so much, why aren't they rich?
	Build a partnership with investors	Avoid bringing in investors. They are only interested in what's in it for them
Sharing information	(With non-competitors at least) a good way of reducing costs	Never give anything away. Everyone is a competitor!
	Information is power	It's not what we know that matters – it's what we do
Delegation	Leadership is about empowering people to make their own decisions well	It's my job to make all the important decisions
	The only way the business can grow	I don't pass decisions down. Whose business is it anyway!
	We need to push decision making down	I don't delegate. The buck stops here!
Expertise	Developing employee expertise is a priority	The business needs the entrepreneur at the helm
	The most important expert is the entrepreneur	Everyone is an expert in his or her own way
Entry strategy	Limited, confident start followed expansion	Make yourself known in the market from day one
Expansion	Grow in sure-footed stages	Build quickly on the innovation
	Establish our presence in as many markets as possible, as early as possible	Exploit our established markets before moving on
Competition	Avoid head-to-head conflicts	An entrepreneur must compete. Hit them where it hurts!

Table 11.1 Examples of entrepreneurial strategic heuristics *continued*

Strategic theme	Heuristic	Counter-heuristic
Investment	Less risk using own money	Borrow to grow. Use other people's money
Risk	Avoid risk wherever possible	Risk should be managed, but at the end of the day risk is what it is all about
	Entrepreneurs and investors must work together to manage risk and return	Let investors take the risk – I'll have the return!

Summary of key ideas

- A strategy is the means by which the venture will achieve its aims.
- Strategy *content* defines the products the venture will offer, the customer groups to be targeted and the way in which the venture will compete within its markets.
- Strategy *process* defines the way in which the venture will make *decisions* about the strategy content to adopt.
- A well-defined strategy aids the venture by defining the means by which it will achieve its goals in the marketplace.
- A strategy acts as a guide for decision making and provides a common language for the venture's stakeholders.
- Entrepreneurs often express their venture's strategy in the form of *heuristics*.

Suggestions for further reading

Atkins, M. and **Lowe, J.** (1994) 'Stakeholders and the strategy formation process in small and medium enterprises', *International Small Business Journal*, Vol. 12, No. 3, pp. 12–24.

Bowman, C. and **Ambrosini, V.** (1996) 'Tracking patterns of realised strategy', *Journal of General Management*, Vol. 21, No. 3, pp. 59–73.

Calori, R. (1985) 'Effective strategies in emerging industries', *Long Range Planning*, Vol. 18, No. 3, pp. 55–61.

Eden, C. and **Ackermann, F.** (1998) *Making Strategy: The Journey of Strategic Management*, London: Sage.

Gallen, T. (1997) 'The cognitive style and strategic decisions of managers', *Management Decision*, Vol. 35, No. 7, pp. 541–51.

Grieve Smith, J. and **Fleck, V.** (1987) 'Business strategies in small high-technology companies', *Long Range Planning*, Vol. 20, No. 2, pp. 61–8.

Idenburg, P.J. (1993) 'Four styles of strategy development', *Long Range Planning*, Vol. 26, No. 6, pp. 132–7.

Jenkis, M. and **Johnson, G.** (1997) 'Entrepreneurial intentions and outcomes: A comparative causal mapping study', *Journal of Management Studies*, Vol. 34, No. 6, pp. 895–920.

Manimala, M.J. (1999) *Entrepreneurial Policies and Strategies: The Innovator's Choice*, New Delhi: Sage.

McDougall, P. and **Robinson, R.B.** (1990) 'New venture strategies: An empirical identification of eight "archetypes" of competitive strategies for entry', *Strategic Management Journal*, Vol. 11, pp. 447–67.

Miller, D. (1992) 'The generic strategy trap', *The Journal of Business Strategy*, Jan/Feb, pp. 37–41.

Mintzberg, H. (1973) 'Strategy making in three modes', *California Management Review*, Vol. XVI, No. 2, pp. 44–53.

Mintzberg, H. (1978) 'Patterns in strategy formation', *Management Science*, Vol. 24, No. 9, pp. 934–48.

Mintzberg, H. (1988) 'Generic strategies: Towards a comprehensive framework', *Advances in Strategic Management*, Vol. 5, pp. 1–76.

Mintzberg, H. (1994) *The Rise and Fall of Strategic Planning*, London: Prentice Hall.

Mintzberg, H. and **Waters, J.A.** (1985) 'Of strategies deliberate and emergent', *Strategic Management Journal*, Vol. 6, pp. 257–72.

Mitchell, R.K. (1997) 'Oral history and expert scripts: Demystifying the entrepreneurial experience', *International Journal of Entrepreneurial Behaviour and Research*, Vol. 3, No. 2, pp. 122–39.

Quinn, J.B. (1978) 'Strategic change: Logical incrementalism', *Sloan Management Review*, Autumn.

Selected case material

Media titans in $327bn merger

11 January 2000

By **Andrew Hill** and **Richard Waters** in New York

America Online, the internet service provider, yesterday unveiled a $160bn (€97.7bn) all-stock takeover of Time Warner, the US media conglomerate, aimed at revolutionising the way news, entertainment and the internet are delivered to the home.

The agreed deal, the largest ever, is the logical result of the spectacular rise in the valuation of internet companies.

The merger amounts to a huge bet that content providers such as Time Warner and online distributors such as AOL will converge to dominate the home entertainment market.

The possibility that other internet and media companies might pursue the same "convergence" strategy energised stock prices in Europe and in the US yesterday, pushing the Goldman Sachs internet index up nearly 6 per cent. The technology-heavy Nasdaq index rose 167 points or 4.3 per cent to 4,049.66.

AOL and Time Warner said the deal was a "strategic merger of equals", but it would give shareholders in AOL, new media's flagship, 55 per cent of the combined company and effective control of Time Warner. The new company will be worth $327bn at yesterday's share prices, and have revenues of $30bn.

At a press conference in Manhattan, Steve Case, AOL's chairman and chief executive, vied with Gerald Levin, his counterpart at Time Warner, to lay out the grandest vision for the new company.

Mr Case, who will chair AOL Time Warner, proposed the merger in a phone call to Mr Levin in October. He suggested Mr Levin take the chief executive's role, overseeing management of the merged company, while he would take responsibility for technological developments and policy initiatives.

"It's a very big idea," said Mr Levin. "But most important to me is the ability to work with a group of people who are bright, aggressive, hip, and new-media-oriented."

The merger will bring together some of the biggest names from the new and old US media sectors, including Ted Turner, vice-chairman of Time Warner and founder of CNN. Mr Turner, 61, said he had promised

Selected world internet stocks
By market capitalisation * ($bn)

Company	$bn
America Online	**163.2**
Yahoo!	**107.2**
CMGI	**33.8**
Amazon	**23.7**
Yahoo! Japan	**23.1**
EBAY	**17.4**
Verisign	**17.2**
Terra Networks	**16.1**
Exodus Comms.	**14.9**
@Home Corp.	**13.5**

Selected media companies
By market capitalisation * ($bn)

Company	$bn
Time Warner	**76.4**
Walt Disney	**65.2**
MediaOne Group	**46.2**
CBS	**44.2**
Viacom	**37.2**
Comcast	**33.3**
Clear Channel Comms	**29.9**
Cox Communications	**25.5**
British Sky Broadcasting	**25.5**
Gannett	**20.9**

* As at Jan 7 2000

his 9 per cent stake in Time Warner to the deal "with as much or more excitement than on that night when I first made love, some 42 years ago".

Mr Case said the new company would have headquarters in both New York, where Time Warner is based, and Dulles, Virginia, where AOL was founded 15 years ago. He conceded that there were "a lot of cooks" involved in the deal, but added: "There's a big meal to serve here."

Warner Brothers' stores will promote AOL online services; Time Warner and AOL's Moviefone service will begin cross-promotion of Time Warner movies and other events; and CNN.com programming will feature prominently on AOL.

Shareholders in AOL, which was advised by Salomon Smith Barney, will receive 1.5 shares in the new company for each AOL share. Investors in Time Warner, advised by Morgan Stanley Dean Witter, will receive one AOL Time Warner share for each of their shares.

Time Warner's share price leapt $25 5/16 to $90 1/16 yesterday. AOL shares started higher, but eased to close $1 7/8 lower at $71, valuing each Time Warner share at $106 1/2.

A new media world

11 January 2000

AOL's takeover of Time Warner marks a dramatic shift in the balance of power between traditional and online companies. But it will be hard to unite their cultures, says **Richard Waters**

The new media have risen up and swallowed the old. From now on, the landscape for entertainment and communications companies around the world will be very different.

That is the message from yesterday's ground-breaking purchase of Time Warner by America Online, a combination that will match some of the best-known names in the entertainment industry with a company that has risen from obscurity on the back of the internet.

If it works – and the union faces big challenges – the deal will also herald the second phase of the youthful online industry. The new AOL Time Warner mixes very different brands, management teams and share valuations. It is the first significant test of whether an internet company can prosper in the "real" world of traditional business.

Some analysts were yesterday betting that sheer size alone should carry AOL Time Warner through. "This will leave everyone else in the dust," said Peter Kreisky, head of the media practice at Mercer Management Consulting. He said it was "impossible" to find two companies with similar strengths in their respective businesses. Such comments show the similarity of yesterday's deal to last year's merger of Citicorp and Travelers Group, a deal that threatened to change the rules of the game in financial services. Like the new Citigroup, AOL Time Warner will start out with a wide array of brands and distribution systems. It will try to use its new clout to sign more customers for each of its services.

Many of those customers are subscribers, making up a combined base of 100m paying customers. Time Warner has subscribers to its cable television systems, the second-biggest in the US with 13m customers; its HBO premium cable television channel, which has 35m; and its publishing division, which has 28m. AOL has 22m subscribers to its flagship online service.

But while the combination is strong, the most striking aspect of the deal is which partner has emerged as the more powerful of the two. Gerald Levin, chairman of Time Warner, has agreed to hand over control of one of the world's great media empires to a company that only three years ago was widely derided for its poor service. AOL was dismissed even by many in its own industry as an interim company that would fade in strength once people no longer needed its hand-holding approach to the internet.

Now Mr Levin has yielded to a company with only a quarter of his company's cashflow and revenues. It amounts to one of the biggest votes of confidence yet demonstrated in the power of the new medium by the old. The union "is a statement by me that the value creation in the internet is real. The cashflow streams are real, can be calculated and can be realised – especially by this company", said Mr Levin.

The history of the internet as a mass-market phenomenon may be measured only in months, but the process that has led Mr Levin to this point has taken years to unfold. His company has already tried and failed to find its own way into the interactive world through two experiments in interactive television. First came Warner Amex in the 1980s, and then an expensive experiment in Orlando, Florida, in the early 1990s. "AOL is the company Time Warner has been trying to create for years," says Mr Kreisky.

Of course, Mr Levin's willingness to cede control has been made easier by the price AOL has paid – equivalent to a 69 per cent premium to Time Warner's share price before the deal was announced. Given that it is an all stock deal, the premium is based entirely on AOL's share price and – by extension – Wall Street's confidence that AOL will continue to lead the internet media revolution.

The huge volatility in AOL's share price, mirroring that of the internet at large, helps explain the scale of the premium it has had to offer. AOL's shares fell by more than half after the first big wave of internet enthusiasm last April, before recovering to reach a new peak a month ago. Since then, they have lost a quarter of their value.

Other attempts to mix internet and traditional media assets in this way have conspicuously failed. The most notable attempt was last year's proposed merger of the internet portal company Lycos with USA Networks, controlled by Barry Diller. To succeed, Steve Case, AOL's founder and chairman, must do better in convincing the stock market that internet valuations can survive within a traditional media conglomerate.

It would be an achievement to rival that of Bernie Ebbers, chief executive of MCI WorldCom, the telecommunications group. Mr Ebbers has used his company's highly valued stock to buy bigger, traditional telephone companies. But the hybrid has been given the benefit of the doubt by the stock market, allowing it to continue its buying spree.

To judge by yesterday's initial stock market reaction, AOL stands a decent chance of pulling it off. "Investors want to make a bet on the entertainment industry that combines new and old," says Michael Wolf, head of the media practice at Booz Allen & Hamilton.

"This is the next step in a world where all the media platforms are combined."

In practice, combining these different media platforms will create significant management challenges – not least because of Wall Street's love affair with internet stocks. Time Warner employees may have their morale tested by having to rub shoulders with a cadre of internet multimillionaires. Equally, AOL employees could end up resenting the fact that their stock options are weighed down by their company's array of traditional assets.

AOL executives have already been frustrated by the stock market's unwillingness to look beyond their main subscription service to the company's other internet brands. These include ICQ, a free instant communications service with 50m users. Within a conglomerate, the risk will increase of the whole being valued at less than the sum of the various parts.

Provided it can overcome the formidable cultural and issues, the new AOL Time Warner will pose a formidable challenge to other media groups. AOL's success at selling dial-up internet service to a mass market – it has nearly 10 times the number of customers as its nearest competitor – had already marked it out as a competitor to companies as diverse as AT&T and Microsoft.

By merging with Time Warner, it will now have access to cable systems, and some of the best entertainment "content" around. AOL already has deals to deliver high-speed internet access over telephone wires and through DirecTV, a satellite television service. Yesterday's deal will instantly give it much greater access to broadband distribution.

The scale of the revolution that could be sparked off by yesterday's news is best illustrated by the question mark it leaves over the strategies of a wide range of media and communications companies. These include Yahoo!, the biggest internet portal, and NBC, the only US television network to remain outside a broader media group. Ted Turner, the volatile Time Warner vice chairman, has long cherished a television network, and was said recently to have tried to persuade the company's board to buy NBC from its owner, General Electric.

When he was asked last month whether AOL would itself buy a traditional television network, Mr Case was dismissive. "Television will get reinvented over the next 10 years, and it will look more like the internet," he said. By buying Time Warner, he has thrown down the gauntlet to traditional media companies everywhere. Either they must reinvent themselves in ways that the stock market will value as highly as AOL, or they must risk getting reinvented.

Time Warner wins premium in marriage with new media

11 January 2000

By **Peter Thal Larsen** in London and **Andrew EdgecliffeJohnson** and **Gary Silverman** in New York

Perhaps the most striking feature of the merger between AOL-Time Warner is the premium the media group has extracted in return for accepting payment in internet shares.

Before the deal was announced, AOL was capitalised at around $160bn – roughly twice the size of Time Warner. Yet, according to the terms of the merger, AOL shareholders will receive 55 per cent of the enlarged group while Time Warner shareholders will take the remaining 45 per cent.

On one interpretation, the deal is a victory for Gerard Levin, Time Warner's chief executive, who has managed to extract a premium of nearly 70 per cent for his shareholders, while also ending up as chief executive of the combined group.

But the transaction also points to the difficulties of reconciling the different valuations attached to internet and traditional groups.

The AOL-Time Warner deal is believed to be the first large transaction where a traditional company with mainly non-internet interests has agreed an all-share takeover from an internet company. The two had operated in separate spheres, with internet companies using shares only to buy other internet firms.

The two companies also had to reconcile the fact that the market assumes different growth rates for internet and traditional media businesses and came up with a hybrid valuation model.

Added to the concerns about the stock market's willingness to accept such a marriage of old and new media was the fact that the structure of the deal means AOL will have to absorb more than $100bn of goodwill.

In addition, while negotiating the final exchange ratio, advisers had to overcome the fact that investors place far lower valuations on the internet assets of traditional media companies than they do on standalone internet companies.

This was solved by stripping out Time Warner's own internet businesses and attempting to value them as if they were separately listed. The move is likely to have acted in Time Warner's favour, because its pre- merger share price did not attach a similar value to its internet operations.

Bankers said the structure would act as a model for other transactions. "What is interesting is not the premium but the fact that a hard-copy media company is prepared to accept this basis of valuation in the first place," said one banker. "It must have been a hard pill to swallow."

The deal is scattered with superlatives. It is the largest takeover ever, beating last year's purchase of Sprint, the US telecoms group, by its rival MCI Worldcom. Based on a market value of around $327bn, the combined company, to be called AOL Time Warner, will be one of the world's five largest companies, along with Microsoft, General Electric, Cisco and Wal-Mart.

The company will have combined revenues of more than $40bn and earnings before interest, tax, depreciation and amortisation of $10bn. It will have more than 100m regular subscribers to its internet service, magazines and cable network.

Steve Case, AOL chief executive, will be chairman of the combined group, responsible for strategy and policy. Mr Levin will run the day-to-day operations, assisted by Richard Parsons and Bob Pitman, who will be co-chief operating officers.

Ted Turner, the media mogul who has been Time Warner's vice-chairman since agreeing to a takeover of his own company, will be vice-chairman of AOL Time Warner. He has agreed to accept the deal on behalf of his 9 per cent shareholding in Time Warner.

The deal is structured as a tax-free merger, with Time Warner shareholders receiving 1.5 shares in the new entity for each share they own. AOL shares will be converted on a one-for-one basis.

However, AOL must account for the deal as a purchase, requiring it to absorb and amortise the huge amounts of goodwill involved. The goodwill is likely to be amortised over a period of 20 years.

The deal, which requires the approval of shareholders and anti-trust authorities, is expected to be completed before the end of the year.

Satisfaction at the top as the old and the new meet

11 January 2000

By **Christopher Parkes** in Los Angeles

It took Wall Street most of the 1990s to accept that the merger of Time's "old" media businesses with the "new" represented by Warner Communications made sense. Yesterday it took only seconds for news of the combination of Time Warner and America Online to send shares in the prospective partners rocketing (although AOL later fell back).

The enthusiastic welcome from the combination of the world's biggest entertainment and media group and the top internet service provider was a moment to relish for Gerald Levin, Time Warner chairman and chief executive.

Even as investors warmed to his strategy in the past three years, murmurings circulated that the group was in danger of missing the internet boat.

While rivals were staking out each unfamiliar landscape of cyberspace, buying portals, web sites, and forging alliances with dozens of dot-com hopefuls, all Mr Levin had to show was Entertaindom.com, an entertainment site, and a plan for five "hubs" to mirror the structure of the "old" Time Warner.

There would be business, news, women's interest, sports and entertainment. Solid enough, but nothing much there to excite investors looking for the "Next Big Thing".

Mr Levin seemed barely to give a thought to the fashionable idea of bundling his internet assets into a separate business to be spun off and provide the company with what Michael Eisner, Wall Disney chairman, recently called "Mickey Mouse" currency to buy more internet assets.

He did not feel any "compulsion" to follow the crowd, he said last spring. Even so, he added; "I believe if you want to play the internet, you ought to be buying Time Warner stock."

Yesterday, the prospective chief executive of AOL Time Warner proclaimed the "digital transformation" of his company, but in characteristic style refused to let himself be carried away.

He lent more importance to the old-fashioned virtues of the link, such as the "natural fit" between two blue-chip companies with strong subscriber bases – spanning print, cable television, the internet, music and news – and a commitment to building and protecting their brands. By the brash standards of internet personalities, AOL's Steve Case, who will be chairman of the new group, seems almost dull.

Dedicated from the earliest days to developing a reliable brand for internet access, he held to dissipate the aura of mystique enveloping the new technology.

Even now, subscribers receive a regular e-mail letter from Mr Case, and if that is not enough he uses his own web site as a conduit to the market.

At yesterday's press conference, when all involved praised the merits of the power-sharing arrangements that left none affronted, there was naturally no suggestion that cultural clashes might mar the marriage.

America Online
Share price relative to S&P Composite

2500
2000
1500
1000
500
0
1997 98 99 2000

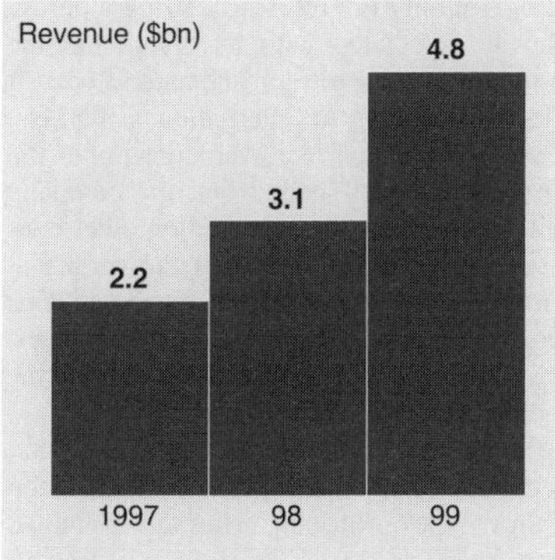

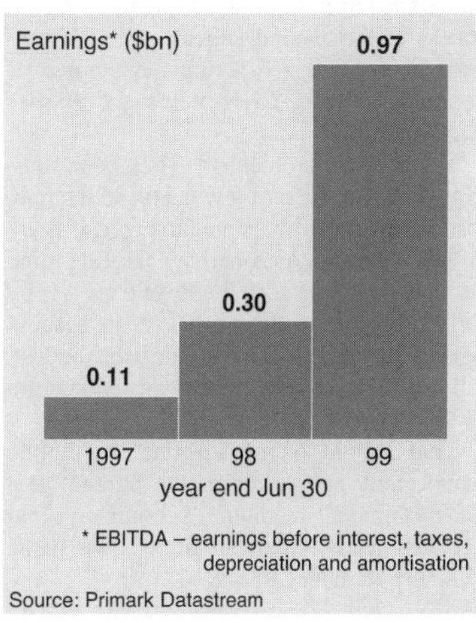

* EBITDA – earnings before interest, taxes, depreciation and amortisation

Source: Primark Datastream

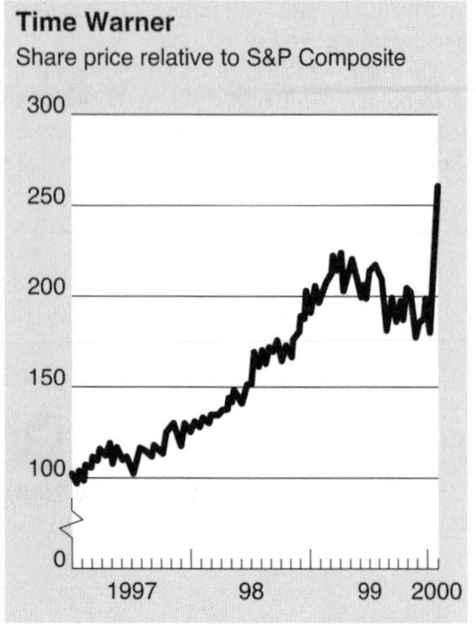

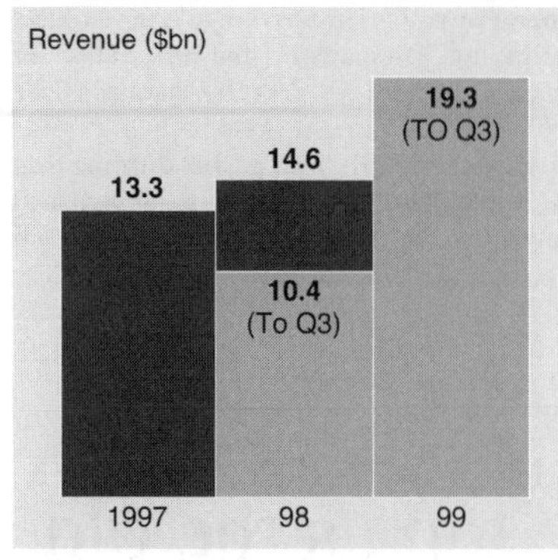

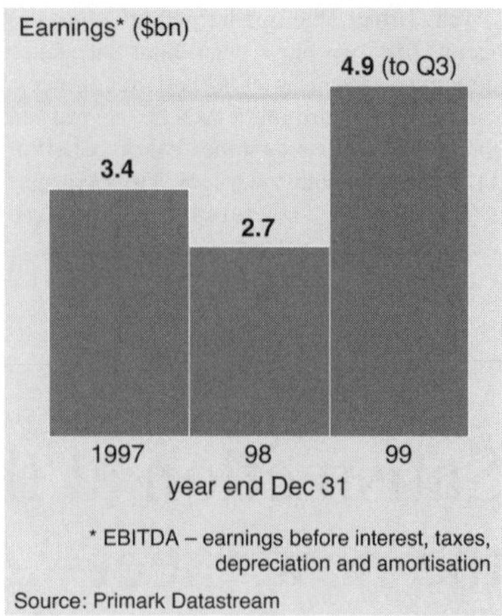

And there are some grounds for confidence. One of Mr Levin's less noted achievements has been to meld the disparate personalities of print, film, cable technology and music into what is now recognised as the most successful media and entertainment group in the business.

Even Ted Turner, vice-chairman, who owns about 9 per cent of Time Warner by virtue of the 1996 assimilation of the Turner Broadcasting Services, has stayed on board, confounding those who believe the irascible entrepreneur would not last six months among the Time Warner suits.

An incorrigible tease, Mr Turner has lately taken to entertaining anyone who will listen with his notion that Time Warner should by General Electric's NBC broadcast network. It is a personal ambition that dates to the 1980s when he courted at CBS, when broadcast television was still king.

But as yesterday's events show, Mr Levin was looking in the other direction.

The only way for Mr Turner to fulfil his dream will be to press on alone or in some alliance other than with his more forward-looking colleagues.

As the owner of "more or less 100m" Time Warner shares, he can afford a handsome down-payment.

AOL solves an identity crisis

12 January 2000

The megamerger may allow the company to be readily accepted on more than just one continent. By **Louise Kehoe**

America Online has just solved one of its biggest problems. The online giant's plan to acquire Time Warner provides it with access to the second largest cable TV network in the US and a rich new source of "content", from CNN news to Warner Brothers movies.

Yet another problem that has been dogging AOL for the past few years, which may also be resolved by its megamerger, is quite simply its name. As America's largest online service, AOL – headed by Steve Case – is by far the biggest in the world, yet its success outside its homeland has so far been modest. All but 3.2m of AOL's 20m subscribers are in North America.

That should be no surprise. At a time when many people regard the internet as a US-dominated medium, a company that declares itself American in its own name was sure to meet resistance.

It is not as if AOL has not tried to adapt. In the UK, colleagues tell me, AOL has replaced its signature greeting: "You've got mail", with the odd sounding: "You've got post".

This goof says a lot. Nobody calls e-mail "e-post", neither in the UK nor anywhere else. Not only is AOL squandering a phrase closely associated with its brand, but the company has clearly misunderstood what it means to adapt to international markets. Perhaps as AOL Time Warner, without the "American" part spelled out, the company will be more readily accepted on other continents. It might also help if the people at Time Warner, whose magazines and movies have long found big international audiences, teach their new online owners that in the media business, words matter.

Sometimes reaching out across the pond can be a confusing experience for Silicon Valley types. Recently Hummer Winblad Venture Partners, a highly successful San Francisco venture capital group, tried to draw entries to its "February Madness" student business plan competition from universities in the UK.

The first reaction was not at all what the venture capitalists had expected. "How do I know that this is not an internet scam?" asked a professor at a well known UK institute of learning.

In reality, the California venture capitalists were trying to demonstrate that they were open to new business ideas worldwide. Stanford and Harvard did not have a monopoly on good ideas, they reasoned.

The competition, which has a February 4 deadline, promises an opportunity for finalists to present their business plans to Hummer Winblad partners, who will offer funding to the winning team as well as establishing an equity stake for the university (details at *http://winbig.humwin.com*).

Are there risks in submitting your business plan to a competition of this sort? Of course. But risk is the name of the game in the internet economy and anybody – whether he or she is a university student or a more experienced professional – must recognise that new business plans are worthless unless you have the ability to execute them.

After all, anyone who would hesitate to submit an entry is probably not suited to the role of internet entrepreneur.

The venture capital business is changing rapidly. When Garage.com (*www.garage.com*) was established a year ago, the Silicon Valley group planned to link entrepreneurs to so-called "angel" investors, or wealthy individuals willing to risk money on high-tech start-ups.

Instead, Garage.com has found itself playing the middle man to established VC firms and corporate venture funds that struggle to identify potential winners.

The group, opening offices in London this week, has vetted some 10,000 business plans during its first year of operations, and picked out about 30 it believes will be winners. Garage.com aims to "democratise" venture capital, says founder Guy Kawasaki, by eliminating the "old or new boys networks".

Whom you know, where you went to college, or any other distinguishing characteristics are irrelevant when it comes to evaluating business plans, Mr Kawasaki insists. He eliminates any favour or prejudice by accepting start-up business plans only via the group's web site.

This pure meritocracy approach harks back to Mr Kawasaki's role as Apple Computer's original Macintosh "evangelist". At Garage.com he is creating "venture capital for the rest of us".

But Garage.com does not have its head in the clouds. The group's web site features a section called "stories from hell", tales of failed ventures and disillusioned entrepreneurs. It should be required reading for anyone thinking of forming or joining a new "dot-com".

For several weeks leading up to Christmas the airwaves were full of advertisements for "dot-coms". On television and radio online retailers fell over one another attempting to draw consumers to their services. Now you are more likely to see or hear an advert for a traditional business.

Advertising data for the fourth quarter are not yet available, but it looks as if the windfall of dot-com spending that traditional media enjoyed during the past few months has come to an abrupt halt.

What does this tell us about e-commerce and advertising? For a start, it suggests that many dot-coms blew their marketing budgets on an all-out push to increase holiday sales. It also raises questions about how many will see another Christmas. If a company is in it long term, surely now is the time to reinforce online buying habits adopted during the pre-Christmas gift-buying season. They should be trying to turn consumers who enjoyed the convenience of ordering gifts online before Christmas into regular customers.

The sudden drop in traditional advertising may also signal a new cycle of offline/online marketing.

Savvy online retailers are now using the customer data they gathered from pre-Christmas orders to target consumers with e-mail marketing.

The lesson for traditional media may be that the benefits of the "new economy" may be short-lived, or at best cyclical, as online merchants build their customer bases and then mine that data to increase sales during the "off season".

Giants' embrace threatens network of online alliances

FT

12 January 2000

By Our Financial Staff

"We don't believe one company can own it all. We don't believe we can do it to all." So said Bob Pittman, President of America Online, in an interview less than a month ago. Yet by buying Time Warner, AOL has put itself in position to own more of the media content and distribution business than anyone else.

In the process, it risks upsetting a global network of alliances with other traditional media companies. Stitched together through a mixture of exclusive and non-exclusive deals, those arrangements were meant to ensure AOL uses the pick of the best media and entertainment content.

The planned union with Time Warner could conflict with some of these alliances. And that has thrown back into the spotlight an issue that has come to dominate the strategic thinking of media and communications businesses everywhere: whether vertical integration is creating a dominant group of conglomerates that will give pride of place to their own content – and leave non-aligned media companies out in the cold.

The expected departure of Thomas Middlehof, chairman of Bertelsmann, from the AOL board is the first indication of potential conflict. A direct competitor of Time Warner, Mr Middlehof is expected to leave AOL before the merger is completed. Marjorie Scardino, chief executive of Pearson, the UK media group that owns the Financial Times, is also an AOL board member.

Until now, AOL executives have carved out a role for their company as a collector, rather than a producer, of media and entertainment brands.

"What makes AOL work is the aggregation of a lot of content in a programme environment," Jonathan Sacks, the head of the flagship AOL service, said last month. "We're into aggregating brands."

Alliances have been the preferred way of doing business on the internet since AOL signed up Time magazine in 1994 as its first big name content provider. Now, no week goes by without news of another "strategic partnership" between the information providers of the old media and content-hungry internet distribution channels such as AOL.

The skill of a company like AOL has been in collecting a mass online audience, and in the programming skills that convince users to stay on the AOL network rather than wander off to the wider internet.

"Like Disneyworld, it's a predictable environment," said Mr Sacks. "Eighty-five per cent of the time, people stay in the programmed environment" of AOL rather than go to the internet.

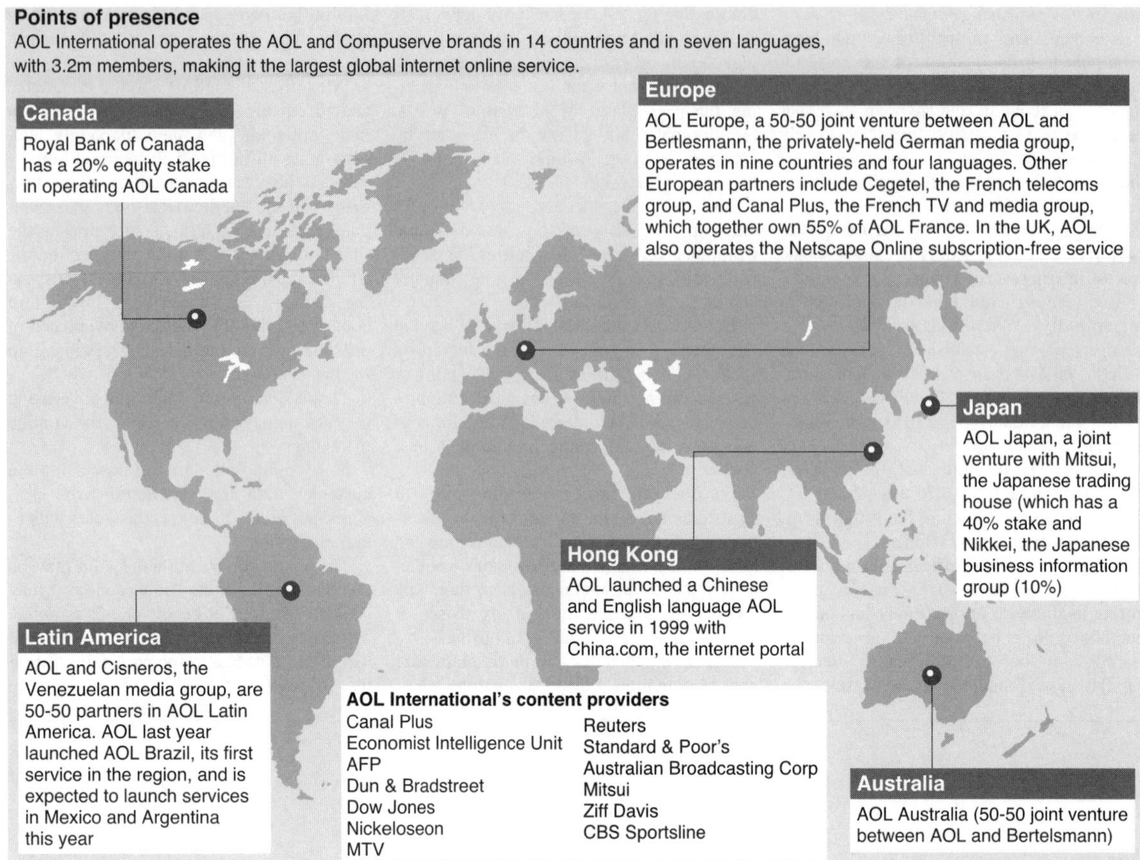

That, however, has led to a host of content deals that could conflict directly with Time Warner. Besides exclusive deals to carry news from CBS, as well as content from CBS Sportsline and CBS Marketwatch, AOL has forged alliances with two of Viacom's most popular businesses: Nickelodeon and MTV. Many of these compete directly with Time Warner businesses, from the Cartoon Network, a rival of Nickelodeon, to Sports Illustrated, a competitor of Sportsline.

For now, at least, many of AOL's distribution deals looks solid, given that they are generally covered by long-term contracts – a fact noted with obvious satisfaction by CBS, among others.

There is also ample reason for companies like CBS to maintain their ties with AOL. Laura Martin of Credit Suisse First Boston said AOL's existing partners were unlikely to jump ship purely because of the Time Warner deal: "if it made sense for these companies to have access to AOL's eyeballs, that didn't change yesterday."

Review questions

1 Compare and contrast the strategy contents of AOL and Time Warner.

2 How do these complement each other and justify the merger?

3 Compare and contrast the strategy processes operating in AOL and Time Warner.

4 What issues will the differences in strategy for the two businesses present to Steve Case and Bob Pitman in integrating the two businesses?

12 The business plan: an entrepreneurial tool

Chapter overview

A business plan is an essential tool for the entrepreneur. This chapter explores the role of the business plan and the kind of information it should include. It considers the way a business plan can help the venture by guiding analysis, creating a synthesis of new insights, communicating the potential of the venture to interested parties, and promoting management action. The chapter concludes by looking at the ways in which business planning can increase the flexibility and responsiveness of the venture.

12.1 Planning and performance

KEY LEARNING OUTCOME
A recognition of the influence of formal planning activity on the performance of the entrepreneurial venture.

Entrepreneurs, like many other managers, are often called upon to prepare formal, written plans. They may do this of their own accord or it may be at the instigation of external investors such as venture capitalists or banks. The picture of the entrepreneur 'locked away' writing a formal business plan sits ill at ease with the image of them as dynamic individuals actively pursuing their business interests. Many entrepreneurs object to preparing plans because they feel their time would be better spent pushing the venture forward. They claim that they already know what is in the plan and that no-one else will read it!

This objection highlights an important point in that developing a plan demands time, energy and (often) hard cash. It ties up both the entrepreneur and the business's staff. A business plan represents an *investment* in the venture. It must be justified as an investment, that is, in terms of the return it offers the business. The relationship between formal planning and business performance has been the subject of numerous statistical studies; however, no clear picture has emerged. The correlation between *formal* planning and performance is weak so it is not possible to say with certainty that formal planning will improve the performance of a particular business. As a result, there has been something of a reaction against formal planning in recent years, especially in relation to smaller businesses. As noted in the previous chapter, Henry

Mintzberg has offered a profound criticism of at least a narrow approach to planning in his book *The Rise and Fall of Strategic Planning*.

However, the poor statistical correlation should not be taken to mean that performance is unaffected by planning. Statistical studies usually compare 'planning activity' (the definition of this varies between studies) against performance measured in financial or growth terms. Inevitably, these studies must reduce a complex organisational phenomenon to simple variables. Planning is not an easily defined, isolated activity, rather it is an activity embedded in both the wider strategy process of the organisation and the control strategy of the entrepreneur. Financial performance is important but it is not the only measure of achievement which motivates the entrepreneur. The entrepreneur may compromise financial gains in order to achieve less tangible benefits. They may even *plan* to make this compromise. Common sense suggests both that a good plan will lead to an improved performance and equally, that a bad one will lead the business astray. There is also the problem of distinguishing between the existence of a plan and whether that plan is actually *implemented*.

Statistical studies of planning and performance also face the issue of causation; that is, when two things seem to correlate, how can we be sure which is the cause and which the effect? It may be that the variation in performance observed is not so much due to the mere existence of planning but rather to the *quality* of the planning that takes place. It has even been suggested that planning does not lead to performance, but rather that a good performance allows managers the time and money to indulge in planning!

The planning/performance debate reflects the problems to be encountered in teasing out cause-and-effect relationships in a system as complex and subject to as many variables as an entrepreneurial venture. In short then, it is impossible to give a straight 'yes' or 'no' answer to questions like: 'Should entrepreneurs produce a formal plan?' or 'Should entrepreneurs formalise the way their organisation plans?' Over-generalisation is unwise. The decision to engage in formal planning, like most other decisions the entrepreneur faces, must be made in the light of what is best for the individual venture, the way it operates and the specific opportunities it faces. Planning, if it is approached in a way which is right for the venture and is aimed at addressing the right issues, would seem to offer a number of benefits. The remainder of this chapter will examine the decision to create a formal plan and explore the ways in which it might benefit the business.

12.2 The role of the business plan

KEY LEARNING OUTCOME
An understanding of how the business plan works as a management tool.

The activity of creating a formal business plan consumes both time and resources. If it is to be undertaken, and undertaken well, there must be an appreciation of the way in which the business plan can actually be made to work as a tool for the business. In principle, there are four mechanisms by which a business plan might aid the performance of the venture.

By working as a tool for analysis

A business plan contains information. Some of this information will be that used as the basis for articulating and refining the entrepreneur's vision, for generating the mission statement and for developing a strategy content and strategy process for the venture. The structure of the business plan provides the entrepreneur with an effective checklist of the information they must gather in order be sure the direction for their venture is both achievable and rewarding. Creating the plan guides and disciplines the entrepreneur in gathering this information.

By working as a tool for synthesis

Once data have been gathered and analysed in a formal way then the information generated must be used to provide a direction for the venture. The information must be integrated with, and used to refine, the entrepreneur's vision and used to support the development of a suitable mission and strategy. The planning exercise acts to *synthesise* the entrepreneur's vision with a definite plan of action in a unified way. This synthesis converts the vision into a strategy for the venture, and then into the actions appropriate to pursuing that strategy.

By working as a tool for communication

The business plan provides a vehicle for communicating the potential of the venture, the opportunities it faces and the way it intends to exploit them in a way which is concise, efficient and effective. This may be of value in communicating with both internal and external stakeholders. The plan may draw internal people together and give them a focus for their activities. The business plan is particularly important as a tool for communicating with potential investors, gaining their interest and attracting them to the venture.

By working as a call to action

The business plan is a call to action. It provides a detailed list of the activities that must be undertaken, the tasks that must be performed and the outcomes that must be achieved if the entrepreneur is to convert his or her vision into a new world. The plan may also call upon formal project management techniques such as critical path analysis in order to organise, prioritise and arrange tasks in a way which makes the best use of scarce resources.

The four ways in which the planning exercise contributes to the success drive of the venture do not operate in isolation. They underpin and support each other and the performance of the venture (see Fig. 12.1). Together they define not only the plan that should be developed for the venture, but also the way the venture should engage in planning.

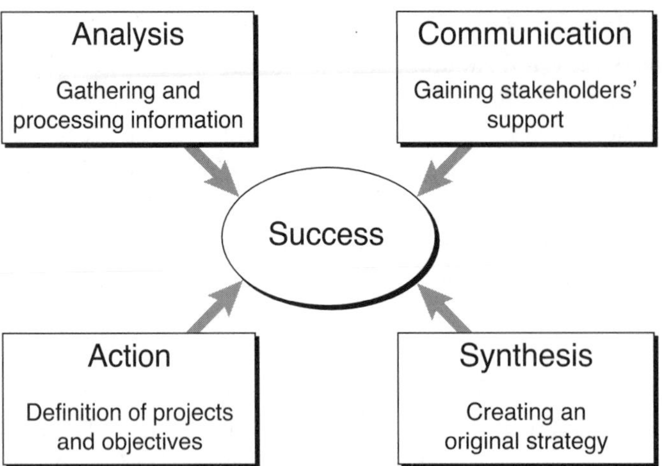

Fig. 12.1 Planning: analysis, communication, synthesis and action

12.3 What a business plan should include

KEY LEARNING OUTCOME
An appreciation of the type of information to be included in a business plan.

There are no hard and fast rules about what a business plan should include since a business plan must be shaped to reflect the needs and requirements of the venture it represents. The entrepreneur and the management team will have their own preferences. The information included will depend on what stage the venture is at: the plan for a new venture may be more exhaustive than the ongoing yearly plan for one which is quite well established. Very importantly, the plan will reflect the information required by the audience at whom the plan is directed and the action the entrepreneur desires from them. Financial backers may dictate both the format the business plan must take and the information it should include.

The following list indicates the type and scope of information and themes that might be included in a fairly exhaustive business plan.

- ***Mission***
  - *The mission for the venture:* the formal mission statement that defines the business.
- ***Overview of key objectives***
  - *Financial objectives:* the turnover and profit targets for the period of the plan; the growth desired over the previous period.
  - *Strategic objectives:* achievements in the market and gains to be made in market position.
- ***The market environment***
  - *Background to the market:* i.e. how the market is defined; the size of the market; major market sectors and niches; overall growth rate; key trends and developments in consumer behaviour and buying habits; and technological developments in the product, service delivery and operations.

- *Competitors:* key competitors, their strengths and weaknesses; competitors' strategy and likely reaction to the venture's activity.
- *Competitive conditions:* the basis of competition in the market; the importance of price, product differentiation and branding; the benefits to be gained from positioning.
- *Competitive advantage of the venture:* the important strengths of the venture relative to competitors; sources of competitive advantage.
- *Definition of product offerings:* the products/services that the business will offer to the market.
- *Definition of target markets:* the way in which the market is split up into different sectors; the dimensions of the market important for characterising the sectors; and the market sectors that will be prioritised for targeting by the business.

- ***Strategy***
  - *Product strategy:* the way in which the product/service will be differentiated from competitors (e.g. features/quality/price); why this will be attractive to customers.
  - *Pricing strategy:* how the product/service will be priced relative to competitors (e.g. offer of a premium, discounting); means of establishing price; promotional pricing and price cutting; pricing policy and margins to be offered to intermediaries.
  - *Distribution strategy:* the route by which the product/service will be delivered to the customer; intermediaries (wholesalers, distributors, retailers) who will be partners in distribution; strategy for working with distributors; policy for exporting and international marketing if appropriate.
  - *Promotional strategy:* approaches to informing the customer (and intermediaries) about the product/service; advertising message, means and medium; sales activity and approach to selling; sales promotions (including price promotions); public relations activity.
  - *Networking:* relationship between the organisation and other organisations in the network; use of the network to create and support competitive advantage.
- ***Financial forecasts***
  - *Income:* revenues from trading activity; structure of the capital provided by investors.
  - *Routine expenditure:* expenditure on salaries, raw materials and consumables; payment of interest on debt.
  - *Capital expenditure:* major investment in new assets; how these assets will enhance performance.
  - *Cash flow:* difference between revenues and expenditure by period; cash flow reflects the liquidity of the business and its ability to fund its activities. If income is more than expenditure then cash flow is positive. If expenditure is more than income then cash flow is negative.
- ***Activity***
  - *Major projects:* the key projects that will drive the venture forward and deliver the objectives, for example: new product developments, sales drives, launches with distributors and advertising campaigns.
- ***People***
  - *Key players in the venture:* the individuals behind the venture; the skills and experience they will contribute to the business; evidence of their achievements; personal profiles and CVs.

The information included in the business plan will depend on how it is intended to use the plan and to whom it will be communicated. The business need not be restricted to a single version of the plan and it may prove advantageous to use different formats for different audiences. A detailed and exhaustive 'master' plan may act as a source for the rapid, and informed, production of such specific plans.

12.4 Business planning: analysis and synthesis

KEY LEARNING OUTCOME

An appreciation of how business planning facilitates analysis of the venture's potential and a synthesis of its strategy.

Effective planning requires information. Information is all around us but it rarely comes for free. Information has a cost: this may be relatively low, a trip to the local library perhaps, or it may be very expensive, commissioning a major piece of market research, for example. Even if it has no direct cost, gathering and analysing information takes time. Hence information must be gathered with an eye to how it will be used. The benefits to be gained from having the information must justify its cost.

Information is used to manage uncertainty. Having information means that uncertainty is reduced which in turn reduces the risk of the venture and improves the prospects of its success. Essentially, the entrepreneur is interested in answering the following questions:

- **What are the customer's fundamental needs in relation to the product category? (What benefits does the product offer? What problems do customers solve with the product?).**
- **How does the market currently serve those needs? (What products are offered? What features do they have?)**
- **In what way(s) does the market fail to serve those needs? (Why are customers left dissatisfied? How often are they left dissatisfied?)**
- **How might customer needs be served better? (How might the product on offer be improved?)**

Marketing, as a discipline, offers a number of techniques to develop these answers. In addition, the entrepreneur must know:

- **How does the better way being advocated add up as a real business opportunity?**
- **What risks are likely to be present in pursuing such an opportunity?**

These final two points are of course critical. Developing an answer to these questions and understanding the decisions they involve, will be explored fully through the development of the *Strategic Window* in Part 3 of this book.

Planning certainly supports strategy development but it is not *equivalent* to it. Henry Mintzberg, observes that planning is about *analysis*; it is about breaking down information to spot opportunities and possibilities. Strategy, on the other hand, is about *synthesis*; it is about bringing the capabilities of the business to bear on the opportunity in a way which is creative and original. Developing answers to the questions listed above is the analysis part of the equation. Reconciling them into a workable, rewarding strategy is the synthesis part. This synthesis must include both the strategy *content* and the *process* to deliver it.

In order to synthesise an original strategy the entrepreneur must decide:

- How will the venture address the needs of the customer (i.e. what is the nature of the opportunity that has been identified)?
- Why will the venture's offerings serve those needs better than those of competitors? (What is the *innovation*? Why is it valuable?)
- How will demand be stimulated? (This involves issues of communication, promotion, distribution.)
- Why can the entrepreneur's business deliver this in a way that competitors cannot? (What will be the *competitive advantage* that the business enjoys? What will it be able to do that its competitors cannot do that is valuable for its customers?)
- What is it about the business that enables them to do this? (What are the *competencies* and *capabilities* of the business?)
- Why will competitors be unable to imitate them? (In what way(s) is the competitive advantage *sustainable*?)

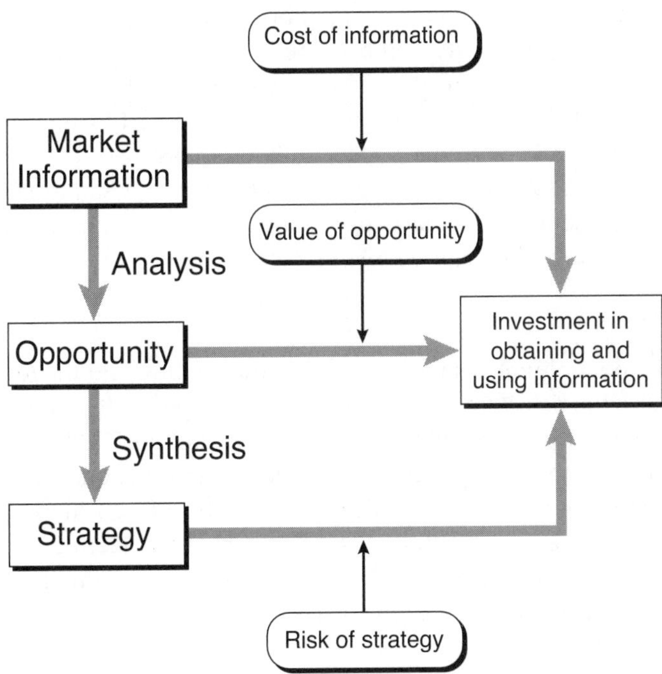

Fig. 12.2 Factors governing investment in market information

Planning helps the business by first demanding an analysis of information about the market, customers and competitors. This information provides a sure basis for decision making. Planning goes on to help the business by synthesis, that is, by integrating the information into a strategy. This strategy gives the venture a shape and a direction. It forms the basis for plans and projects which offer definite actions for the people who make up the venture and those who support it to follow. Thus information is valuable because it links the analysis of opportunity with the synthesis of strategy in a planning framework (see Fig. 12.2).

12.5 Business planning: action and communication

KEY LEARNING OUTCOME
An appreciation of how the business plan may be used as a communication tool and as a call to action.

Communication is not just about passing on information. It is an attempt to elicit a particular *response* from someone. In business it is not just what we want people to *know* that matters; it is also what we want them to *do*. The ways the business plan functions both as a piece of communication and as a recipe for action are intimately interrelated.

The business plan is a communication that relates in a succinct way a precise and unambiguous account of the venture *and* what it aims to achieve. It defines the decisions the entrepreneur has made in relation to: the opportunity that has been identified; the way the opportunity will be exploited; the value the entrepreneur aims to create as a result of exploiting it; the resources that will be needed in order to progress the venture; the risks those resources will be exposed to; and the projects the entrepreneur will undertake with the resources they receive.

These decisions are communicated with the intention of gaining support for the venture. The entrepreneur will be particularly interested in communicating with and influencing the following groups of people.

Investors

The business plan not only relates the potential of the venture and the rewards it offers to investors but also the risks that it entails. It is also an opportunity for the entrepreneur to convince the investor of the skills they have and make them feel confident that the goods can be delivered. Numerous studies have found that the quality of the business plan and the effectiveness of its communication is a critical factor in gaining investors' interest and support. See, for example, the studies by Macmillan *et al.* (1985, 1987), Knight (1994) and Mason and Harrison (1996) in the further reading at the end of this chapter. This is an issue we will revisit in Chapter 19.

Employees

Employees make their own investment in the business by committing themselves to it. The business plan can give them confidence in the future of the venture. It will also specify the key projects that need to be undertaken, so defining individual objectives and the way in which the role the individual plays fits with the goals of the organisation as a whole. Jan Carlzon, the entrepreneur who turned around the failing Scandinavian Airline Systems (SAS) in the early 1980s, issued each of the organisation's 20 000 or so employees with a plan which outlined the vision and strategy he had devised. This plan became known as the 'little red book'.

Employee commitment does not just come from letting people in on the plan. Letting them get involved in *creating* it in the first place is also a sure way to gain their support.

Important customers

A customer may face a cost in taking on a new supplier. Moving between suppliers demands the time and attention of managers. In some cases there may need to be a direct investment in new equipment so that the products can be used. If the product is new, the customer may have to learn to use it, for example staff may need additional training. The customer may be willing to face these costs if the benefits offered by the new product are high enough. They will resist, however, if they have doubts about the long-term viability of the supplier. Sharing the business plan with them is an effective way of giving them confidence in the entrepreneurial venture and encouraging them to make the necessary commitment. Customers are usually flattered to be asked to become involved with the venture in this way. Therefore, for a new venture, communicating the business plan as well as the product offering, can be an important part of the selling strategy.

Major suppliers

Suppliers may also need to make an investment if they wish to supply the venture. This may take the form of dedicated selling and support activity and may even involve developing bespoke products. Although the venture offers the prospect of new business they will, like the venture's customers, resist making the investment if they harbour doubts about the long-term viability of the venture. Again, the business plan may be used to give them the confidence to make an investment of time and resources on behalf of the venture.

In short, the business plan is a communication tool which can be used by the venture to help build the network of relationships which will be critical to its long-term success.

12.6 Strategy, planning and flexibility

KEY LEARNING OUTCOME
An understanding of how planning may be used to make the business responsive, rather than rigid, in the face of opportunity and uncertainty.

Many entrepreneurs are suspicious of formal planning. They may see the written plan as restrictive, and feel that it reduces their room for manoeuvre. They may be concerned that by defining future actions it limits their options. However, these suspicions are ill-founded. If approached in the right way, planning increases, rather than restricts, flexibility. The right sort of strategy can make the business more, not less, responsive.

Focus on ends rather than means

Goals should be given priority over plans. It's what the business aims to achieve that matters. It may be that there is more than one way in which the business can reach its objectives. If so, all the possibilities should be explored. Not all are likely to be equally attractive and one route may be given priority. However, a knowledge of the alternatives allows for contingency plans to be made and an alternative course can be followed if some routes become blocked.

Challenge assumptions

What are the assumptions on which the plan is based? For example, what assumptions have been made in measuring the size of markets and the venture's rate of growth, in determining how attractive the innovation is to customers and in gauging the strengths of competitors? How sensitive is the plan to these assumptions? What will happen if they are wrong? How can the plan be 'immunised' against poor assumptions by building in contingencies for when they are wrong?

Model scenarios

What are the likely outcomes if the plan is implemented? How certain are these outcomes? In the face of uncertainty what is likely to be the *best* of all possible worlds and what is likely to be the *worst*? What is the *most likely* outcome? Determine what scenarios will result if an *optimistic*, a *pessimistic* and a *realistic* attitude is taken to the outcomes that are expected (particularly in relation to income and expenditure). How will the business fare in the face of each eventuality? How exposed is the business if the pessimistic scenario comes about? Has it (or can it get) the resources to manage the optimistic? Furthermore, have investors been made party to all scenarios, not just the best?

Create strategic flexibility

At the end of the day, a strategy is just a way of doing things. Strategic flexibility is a way of doing things well when faced with uncertainty. It involves actively responding to outcomes and adjusting activity, not just blindly following set plans. Strategic flexibility comes from questioning moves. For example, can the product or service be modified in the light of consumer responses to it (*positive* as well as negative)? If one target market is proving hard to break into, can an alternative one be approached? Can costs be managed in response to demand (for example, how exposed is the business to fixed costs?)? If some relationships in the network prove to be less valuable than expected can new relationships be built quickly?

Leave space to learn

The way in which entrepreneurs and their businesses meet opportunities and respond to challenges is dependent on how they see the world, the knowledge that they have and their range of skills. All these factors must evolve through learning. The entrepreneur must constantly question the business. Are the underlying assumptions still valid? Is this still the best way to do things? Success does not speak for itself and it is important to question why is a particular outcome a success? What was done right? In what way might they have been even *more* successful? What where the failings?

How might they be avoided next time? Learning is an active process. The good business plan identifies and highlights those areas where learning can take place. In short, a good strategy should be about flexibility, about enabling the business to take advantage of opportunities as they take shape and to manage the unexpected. It is not about setting a rigid course of action.

Summary of key ideas

- There is no simple correlation between investment in planning and business performance.
- However, a business plan can help the entrepreneurial venture by:
  - ensuring that a full analysis of the situation and the environment has been undertaken;
  - encouraging the synthesis of insights to generate a vision and a strategy;
  - acting as a call to action; and
  - being a medium for communication with both internal and external stakeholders.
- A well-defined business plan will actually increase the venture's flexibility, not impair it.

Suggestions for further reading

Ackelsburg, R. (1985) 'Small businesses do plan and it pays off', *Long Range Planning,* Vol. 18, No. 5, pp. 61–7.

Allaire, Y. and **Firsirotu, M.** (1990) 'Strategic plans as contracts', *Long Range Planning,* Vol. 23, No. 1, pp. 102–15.

Ames, M.D. (1994) 'Rethinking the business plan paradigm: Bridging the gap between plan and plan execution', *Journal of Small Business Strategy,* Vol.5, No. 1, pp. 69–76.

Bhide, A. (1994) 'How entrepreneurs craft strategy', *Harvard Business Review,* Mar-Apr, pp. 150–61.

Bracker, J.S., Keats, B.W. and **Person, J.N.** (1988) 'Planning and financial performance among small firms in a growth industry', *Strategic Management Journal,* Vol. 9, pp. 591–603.

Chakravarthy, B.S. and **Lorange, P.** (1991) 'Adapting strategic planning to the changing needs of a business', *Journal of Organisational Change Management,* Vol. 4, No. 2, pp. 6–18.

Cooper, A.C. (1981) 'Strategic management: New ventures and small business', *Long Range Planning,* Vol. 14, No. 5, pp. 39–45.

Grieve Smith, J. and **Fleck, V.** (1988) 'Strategies of new biotechnology firms', *Long Range Planning,* Vol. 21, No. 3, pp. 51–8.

Hamel, G. and **Prahalad, C.K.** (1993) 'Strategy as stretch and leverage', *Harvard Business Review,* Mar-Apr, pp. 75–84.

Higgins, J.M. (1996) 'Innovate or evaporate: Creative techniques for strategists', *Long Range Planning,* Vol. 29, No. 3, pp. 370–80.

Knight, R.M. (1994) 'Criteria used by venture capitalists: A cross cultural analysis', *International Small Business Journal,* Vol. 13, No. 1, pp. 26–37.

Macmillan, I.C., Siegel, R. and **Subba Narashima, P.N.** (1985) 'Criteria used by venture capitalists to evaluate new venture proposals', *Journal of Business Venturing,* Vol. 1, pp. 119–28.

Macmillan, I.C., Zeeman, L. and **Subba Narashima, P.N.** (1987) 'Effectiveness of criteria used by venture capitalists in the venture screening process', *Journal of Business Venturing*, Vol. 2, pp. 123–38.

McKiernan, P. and **Morris, C.** (1994) 'Strategic planning and financial performance in UK SMEs: Does formality matter?' *British Journal of Management*, Vol. 5, Special Issue, pp. S31–41.

Mason, C. and **Harrison, R.** (1996) 'Why "business angels" say no: A case study of opportunities rejected by an informal investor syndicate', *International Small Business Journal*, Vol. 14, No. 2, pp. 35–51.

Mintzberg, H. (1994) *The Rise and Fall of Strategic Planning*, London: Prentice Hall.

Schwenk, C.R. and **Shrader, C.B.** (1993) 'Effects of formal planning on financial performance in small firms: A meta-analysis', *Entrepreneurial Theory and Practice*, Vol. 17, No. 3, pp. 53–64.

Shuman, J.C., Shaw, J.J. and **Sussman, G.** (1985) 'Strategic planning in smaller rapid growth companies', *Long Range Planning*, Vol. 18, No. 6, pp. 48–53.

Thurston, P.H. (1983) 'Should smaller companies make formal plans?' *Harvard Business Review*, Sept-Oct, pp. 162–88.

Waalewijn, P. and **Segaar, P.** (1993) 'Strategic management: The key to profitability in small companies', *Long Range Planning*, Vol. 26, No. 2, pp. 24–30.

Selected case material

Finishing touch for starters

16 March 2000

Good ideas and a sound business plan may be funded by the Shell Livewire scheme, writes **Sally Watts**

"I have sometimes sat on the stairs at 2am wondering how I was going to avoid being skint," Andy Mead recalls of the early days in 1987 when, aged 24, he started his own business.

Today, with more than 200 full-time employees and a £2m turnover, Mr Mead's print finishing and magazine distribution business, The Finishing Line, is one of hundreds to have benefited from Shell Livewire, which encourages people under 30 to regard start-up as a viable career choice.

Livewire provides an information pack tailored to a particular business idea, with the opportunity of free, local-based, one-to-one help from a business adviser, perhaps through a Training and Enterprise Council (Tec), a Local Enterprise Agency (Scotland), The Prince's Trust or a Shell co ordinator.

An added incentive to take part in the Livewire scheme is the annual cash awards. Each year contests are held at local, regional and national levels, with judges such as Shell employees and people with banking and sales/marketing experience.

The national finalist judged Young Entrepreneur of the Year – largely on their business plan and evidence of the skills to fulfil it – receives £10,000. There are two runner-up awards of £2,000. Livewire has awarded prizes totalling £2.4m since 1982.

Susan Saloom, manager of Shell UK's Enterprise Unit, says the company supports Livewire because the small business sector holds many of Shell's customers, suppliers and contractors. "So it is in our interest to make a contribution to a small-business sector that boosts Britain's economy and creates employment opportunities for young people."

An e-commerce online information exchange and a hotline have been added to the service and this year the Shell Livewire awards will add a new e-commerce category.

The original maximum age of 25 has been raised to 30 but the minimum age is still 16.

When Mr Mead won the eastern region award in 1988, he put his £1,000 prize money towards working capital for The Finishing Line, at Basildon, Essex.

"It was nice to be recognised when I was busy firefighting every day," he says of the award and the publicity that followed. Clients today include leading publishing houses seeking sophisticated finishing processes, and there is a separate mailing division.

Mr Mead says: "The key to success is training. It's no good government giving grants if business heads and staff are untrained." He learned business skills at Essex Tec, of which he is now a director. His company has a training culture and budget and is working towards an Investors in People award.

Shell UK introduced Livewire in Scotland in 1982, when unemployment was high. The first winner, Stewart Graham, then 19, was judged Scotland's most promising young entrepreneur. That has been fulfilled: this year his turnover will be £8m.

He began with lobster pots. As an engineering diploma student, he was working part-time in a pub in Stornoway, in Scotland's Western Isles, when some fisherman customers asked him first to mend their creels, and then to make some. This inspired his business idea; £5,000 in grants and loans from a bank and the then Highlands and Islands Development Board (now Highlands and Islands Enterprise) and £1,000 of his own money launched his manufacturing and supply enterprise, Gael Force Marine Equipment.

With 100 employees, he says Gael Force is the only UK company operating in the five marine sectors: commercial fishing, aqua culture, commercial, offshore and leisure marine. To counter the reduced home fishing industry, Mr Graham has established overseas markets.

Livewire, too, is "exporting" by setting up similar schemes abroad. Livewire in the UK is run by Shell UK; overseas it is operated by Shell International.

When Sarah Fenton won the London and South-east Livewire award of £1,500 for Scarlett Jewellery in Battersea, south London, she spent it on producing a mail order brochure.

Ms Fenton, a 28-year-old anthropology graduate, completed a two-year jewellery course and a year in a jeweller's shop. She began with £10,000 from her parents, £3,000 of her own money, and £200 from The Prince's Trust for market research.

Her designs are made mostly in Thailand, where stones and production cost less. After 20 months, her turnover approached £90,000. At Christmas she had her first week off for two years – and used it to write her next business plan.

A small name but huge aspirations

26 January 2000

The displays group is keen to expand abroad, writes **Sathnam Sanghera**

Its name may sound diminutive but Mice Group, which designs and installs exhibition and museum displays, has big aspirations.

The company aims to become a global presence in its field and has grown rapidly over the past two years through a succession of acquisitions around Europe.

In December, Mice – whose name is derived from its four divisions: museums, interiors, conferences and exhibitions – had one of its busiest months.

As well as delivering on its $3m (£1.8m) contract from the government of Macau to conduct the hand-over ceremony of the colony from Portugal back to China, the group also saw the unveiling of the Millennium Dome, where it carried out £4.9m of work in the Retail, Time, Body and Rest zones.

Last September, the Coventry-based company reported a 23 per cent rise in pre-tax profits to £1.4m on turnover of £24.7m (£16.3m) for the six months to June 30.

Antony Legge, at Beeson Gregory, the company's broker, is predicting pre-tax profits of £4m on turnover of £60m for the full year. With 1998's pre-tax profits at £2.56m, that represents growth of some 60 per cent. "We completed about £9.2m of orders in December," reflects Mike Curley, group chairman and chief executive. "When we went public 5 years ago that was our annual turnover."

Strengths

Consolidating the shares on a 1-for-4 basis last March helped the group cast off its penny share status and Mice is now gaining critical mass and a wider institutional appeal.

In 1998, the group made eight acquisitions.

Last year, it made eight more, spending £3m on Marler Haley at St Neots, and £400,000 on Huntingdon-based Hartingdon, both of which specialise in the manufacture and installation of modular exhibition systems.

Brian Patient, a small companies analyst at JM Finn, says that such acquisitions are promoting the company's profile.

It is becoming a one-stop shop for significant spenders in exhibition and events markets, such as IBM, BMW and NEC, which are all seeking to concentrate their spending through fewer suppliers.

Weaknesses

Although Mice has become experienced in acquiring relatively small companies, it has less experience in the challenge of acquiring and turning round larger entities.

Despite the company's global ambitions – 60 per cent of sales are outside the UK – Mr Curley also admits that employees have a shortage of language skills.

"We are still a predominantly British company," he says. "It can be rude to do business in English in Japan and Germany, for example."

Some analysts think the group is overly dependent on the charismatic Mr Curley for marketing, although other senior managers have increased their prominence in recent years.

Threats

Whereas the museum and conference divisions are growing at about 40 per cent a year, the interiors and shopfitting division, which represents some 15 per cent of turnover, is being hampered by slowing orders. Retailers are reining in spending on product displays and it is managing growth of about 7 per cent.

Mice

CEO Mike Curley

History Silver Knight Exhibitions was formed by Mr Curley in Sheffield in 1969. Ten years later Reflections was established in Rugby to make displays for Wedgewood, Royal Brierley and Edinburgh Crystal and in 1990 Mice was created to provide design and project management. Unigate's Giltspur UK exhibition stand division was purchased a year later; companies amalgamated into Mice Group, floated in 1994. Employs 1,000 people in 22 companies around the world.

Finance In March Mice raised £9.1m through a 3-for-11 rights issue at 80p.

Shareholding Directors and management 28 per cent; institutional 28 per cent; private 44 per cent.

Mr Curley says the threat posed to the business by the growth of e-commerce is not serious. "The hands-on experience will still be there," he argues. "Motor shows are getting better attendances."

"In areas such as pharmaceuticals and telecommunications, manufacturers cannot isolate the product, they still have to talk about it – conferences and exhibitions are growing quickly in these industries." Mr Legge comments that "companies will be ordering bigger and better exhibition and display stands, which means that quality and fees go up although quantity falls."

Opportunities

Looking ahead, the introduction of digital television is expected to reduce prime-time TV advertising opportunities, as viewers watch a wider variety of channels.

This should mean that international companies will want to promote their brands through more direct marketing such as roadshows and exhibitions, benefiting Mice.

Elsewhere, the contract completed in Macau to mark the ending of 422 years of Portugese rule was crucial for Mice because it underlined the international aspirations of the group and was won against competition from a large US conference organiser.

Although the group has been the leading operator in the UK market, analysts and Mice management believe the company's future lies in international expansion, first into Europe and ultimately into the US.

The group already has six offices in Germany, Belgium and the Netherlands, with agents in Austria and Switzerland. There is also an office in Dubai and agents in Cairo.

In September, the company said that its overseas investment had been beneficial in winning big contracts and in ensuring costs were incurred in the location and currency of the projects, thus partially overcoming the continued problem of sterling fluctuations.

The recent C$4m (£1.6m) cash acquisition of Kadoke, a Canadian group that operates in the US and Germany, marked Mice's intention to enter the world's biggest and most competitive mark-ets.

"Our industry in the UK is very small," says Mr Curley. "The British Contractors Association has 600 members turning over £300m a year. It's a cottage industry here, but the demand for our product is not just local, regional or even national, but global."

Review questions

Compare and contrast the analysis, synthesis, communication and planning functions of an entrepreneurial business plan for:

1 A new venture start-up by a young entrepreneur

2 A rapidly expanding small business

3 A professional interested in developing an entrepreneurial venture based on his or her knowledge and experience.

PART 3

Initiating the new venture

13 The strategic window: identifying and analysing the gap for the new business

Chapter overview

Entrepreneurs identify and exploit new opportunities. This chapter considers why there will always be gaps in a market that the entrepreneur can exploit, despite the presence of established businesses. The chapter goes on to develop a picture of opportunity as a strategic 'window' through which the new venture must pass.

13.1 Why existing businesses leave gaps in the market

KEY LEARNING OUTCOME
An understanding of why an established business environment will always leave opportunities for the entrepreneur.

In principle, established businesses are in a strong position relative to entrepreneurial entrants. This is because they have gained experience in their markets through serving customers; they have experience in operating their businesses; they have established themselves in a secure network of relationships with customers and suppliers; they face lower risks and so their cost of capital is usually lower; they may enjoy lower costs by having developed experience curve economies; and they have an established output volume which gives them an economy of scale cost advantage. Despite these advantages, entrepreneurs do compete effectively against established, even entrenched, players. They identify and exploit new opportunities despite the presence of experienced competitors. There is always, it seems, a better way of doing things. There are a variety of reasons why existing businesses leave gaps in the market that the innovative, entrepreneurial venture can exploit.

Established businesses fail to see new opportunities

Opportunities do not present themselves, they have to be actively sought out. A business organisation has not merely a way of *doing* things; it also has a way of *seeing* things. The way in which a business scans the business environment for new opportunities is linked to the systems and processes that make up that organisation. *Organisational inertia*, that is, resistance to change in response to changing circumstances, is a well-documented phenomenon. An established organisation can become complacent. It can look back on its early success and take its market for granted. Its opportunity-scanning systems can become rigid and bureaucratised or caught up in political infighting. It might adopt a particular perspective or 'dominant logic' which leads it to see the world in a certain way. That perspective may not change as the world changes. As a result it may be less attuned to identifying new opportunities in the market than a hungry new entrant. For example, IBM missed the opportunity for software-operating systems that would enable Bill Gates's Microsoft to become one of the world's largest companies.

New opportunities are thought to be too small

The value of a new opportunity must be seen as relative to the size of the business which might pursue it. The chance to gain an extra £100 000 of business will mean far more to a business with a turnover of £1 million than for one with a turnover of £100 million. As a result 'small' opportunities may be ignored, or at least not pursued vigorously, by large, established players. The smaller new entrant will, however, find them attractive. They may prove to be just the foot in the door they need!

Technological inertia

Opportunities are pursued by innovation. An innovation is founded on some technological approach. However, a technology is simply a way of doing things. It is a means to address a need. An established organisation may regard its business as based on a particular technology rather than the serving of customer needs. It might prefer to rely on the technological approach 'it's good at'. However, new technological approaches to satisfying needs can develop rapidly. Such technological inertia leaves the field open for new entrants to make technological innovation the basis of their business.

For example, the last mechanical typewriter manufacturer closed recently. The typewriter industry had a great deal of expertise in designing, manufacturing and marketing machines which produced documents. The manufacturers were very good at their business. However, they defined themselves in terms of the mechanical technology used by typewriters. They did not think of themselves as providing customers with a document management service. As a result, they were easy prey for a whole generation of entrepreneurs who moved in with electronic word processing products which provided a much better way to manage documents.

Cultural inertia

Along with its technology, an established business has its own 'way of doing things'. This way of doing things – its culture – influences the way in which it delivers value to its customers. The best way to deliver value to customers will change as the competitive climate evolves. If the business does not change its way of doing things to meet new challenges then it may not be in a position to exploit new opportunities. Newer entrants may take advantage of this by adopting a culture more appropriate to the altered climate.

Thus the Swedish entrepreneur Jan Carlzon turned Scandinavian Airline Systems

(SAS) into a great aviation success story by changing its culture from one where the needs of aircraft and airports were managed to one where the needs of customers were given priority.

Internal politics

Managers in established organisations often engage in political infighting. This occurs when individuals and groups do not feel their interests and goals are aligned with each other or with the organisation as a whole. Organisations pursue new opportunities in order to achieve their objectives. Being focused on a new opportunity demands a commitment to objectives. If this is not present then, at best, there will be disagreement on the value particular opportunities present. At worst, different factions will work against one other. As a result, opportunities will slip by. This will leave the more focused and less political new entrant free to exploit them.

Anti-trust actions by government

Governments are concerned to ensure that monopolies do not distort the workings of an economy. If a firm is felt to be gaining too much dominance in a market, then the government may be tempted to act against its growth. By definition, this action will work against the dominating players and so will favour the new entrant. An example of this is topical. At the time of writing, a number of entrepreneurs in the information technology sector are eagerly awaiting implementation of the US Supreme Court ruling that the giant Microsoft be split into two. The court's ruling is based on the belief that Microsoft's monolithic market power is restricting entrepreneurial entry into the sector and hindering the development of smaller players who are already present.

Government intervention to support the new entrant

In general, governments are acutely aware of the importance, both economic and political, of small and fast-growing new firms in an economy. They are responsible for providing economic efficiency, for bringing innovations to market and for creating new jobs. As a result governments are tempted to provide support for both the smaller business and the new entrant. This can take the form of tax incentives and more liberal employment laws or it can be more direct and involve cheap loans and credit. Support may also be offered for technical development, education and consulting. Again, this support tips the balance in favour of the new entrant.

An economic perspective on entrepreneurial gaps

The points made above relate to how businesses function. They are *institutional* effects. In these terms, established businesses leave gaps largely because they lack adeptness in exploiting some opportunities, leaving a space into which entrepreneurs can move. The classical economic perspective suggests that such institutional effects represent a failure of economic efficiency and that the managers of established businesses are not acting fully rationally. If managers of established firms were more effective, then they could devise strategies that would keep out entrepreneurial upstarts.

However, a recent analysis by Richard Arend (1999) suggests this may not always be the case. In this study, Arend explores economic interactions more subtly. The study suggests that under some circumstances established businesses may still leave gaps for new entrepreneurial entrants (who will become competitors) even if they are aware of the entrepreneurial opportunity that is available and act rationally to exploit it. Arend's argument is developed using a game-theoretical perspective. Game theory is a branch of mathematics that is concerned with the way in which a set of agents will act to achieve the outcomes they desire given that the actions of one agent will affect the outcomes of all others. Individual agents must judge the actions (the *strategy*) they adopt, given the likely actions of other agents, knowing that other agents will modify their strategies in response to the actions they take. Game theory has proved to be very important to economics, particularly in describing competitive behaviour.

Reflecting the mathematical rigour of game theory, Arend's article is somewhat technical. However, the basic argument can be stated qualitatively. Classical economics suggests that competing firms have only one optimal strategy if they wish to maximise profits. This conclusion is based on two assumptions, though: first, that all competitors have equal access to the technology that is used to create and deliver the industry's products; second, that this technology is fixed and does not change over time. In general terms, we can regard 'technology' as being the chance to exploit a new opportunity.

If we make the (more realistic) assumption that technology is changing in a way that promises to make firms more efficient (new opportunities are coming along) and that all firms have equal access to this technology (a condition economists refer to as *exogenous*) then something interesting happens. Under these circumstances firms have not one but two optimal strategies. Even though the technology (opportunity) is offered to the firm by the 'outside' world (firms do not have any research and development costs) they still face a cost in integrating that technology into their operations (that is, investing in exploiting the opportunity). The first strategy a firm can adopt is to ignore the technological advance, not face the cost of integrating it, and so maintain short-term profitability. This is referred to as a *static efficiency strategy*. The second option is to integrate the technology. This increases short-term costs but it offers the promise (with some risks of course) in increasing long-term profitability. This is referred to as the *dynamic efficiency strategy*. There is no (efficient) middle ground between these strategies. A firm must choose one or the other and both are equally valid attempts to maximise profits.

Using a game-theoretical argument, Arend demonstrates a remarkable result. Under such conditions incumbent players will, in certain circumstances, ignore technological advances and will allow new entrants to take advantage of them, *even if the new entrant eventually displaces them*. In doing so they are still acting rationally. This is because, once locked together in a competitive battle, at no point can the incumbent increase its profitability by switching to the new technology. Further, no such move can increase the total profitability of the two firms. Hence, even if managers were willing to make the move, investors with an interest in both firms would not support it.

While this argument may sound arcane, Arend uses it to make predictions about entrepreneurial entry under different situations of competition and technological change. His empirical evidence bears out the model. The conclusion is that the institutional 'inefficiency' of established players in exploiting new opportunities might not be inefficiency at all. Leaving gaps for entrepreneurs may just be an inevitable (and for the wider world a welcome) feature of competitive life.

A word of warning

The large, established business, despite its inherent advantages, leaves gaps into which the ambitious new entrant can move because they often undervalue new opportunities, are complacent about them and are unresponsive due to internal inertias. While exploiting this, entrepreneurs should never forget that this is a fate that can also await them as their businesses grow!

13.2 The strategic window: a visual metaphor

KEY LEARNING OUTCOME
An appreciation of how the metaphor of the 'strategic window' can be used to give form to the process of identifying and exploiting opportunity.

Metaphors are ever present in our communication. They represent an attempt to illuminate an idea by drawing attention to something it is like. Understanding is created because we can draw parallels between the two ideas and see how the interconnectedness of themes in one idea might be reflected in the other. Metaphors may be *active*. We can use one deliberately to create effect. For example, we can say that an entrepreneur is like the 'captain of a ship' and the idea of the entrepreneur taking charge and leading a group who share an interest and taking them somewhere new is created. At other times they may be *dormant*. A dormant metaphor is one that is used frequently and we may not recognise it as a metaphor unless we think about it. As considered in Chapter 7, the word 'organisation' shares its roots with the words 'organism' and 'organic'. An *extinct* metaphor is one that we use so often that we may never recognise that it is a metaphor. Note the visual metaphor implied in the use of the words 'see', 'draw', 'parallel' and 'reflected' in the sentences above. An active metaphor that can be used to help us picture, and remember the details of, the process of identifying, evaluating and exploiting a new business opportunity is that of the *strategic window*.

The first stage in this metaphor is to picture a solid wall. This represents the competitive environment into which the entrepreneur seeks to enter. The wall is solid because of competition from established businesses. They are active in delivering products and services to customers in an effective way. The entrepreneur can do nothing new or better and so new value cannot be created. However, as we discussed in the previous section, established businesses leave gaps. There are areas where entrepreneurs can do something new and better. These gaps represent windows of opportunity through which the entrepreneur can move. It is through the window that the entrepreneur can see the 'whole new world' he or she wishes to create. The first task of the entrepreneur is to scan the business environment and find out where the gaps, the windows, are.

Having spotted a window the entrepreneur must measure it. The entrepreneur must be sure that the window – the opportunity – is big enough to justify the investment needed to open it. Opening the window represents the start-up stage of the venture. Moving thorough the window means developing the business and delivering new value to customers. The final stage is closing the window. The window must be closed because if it is not, competitors will be able to move through after the entrepreneur and exploit the opportunity themselves. Closing the window refers to building in competitive advantage, in short, ensuring that the venture's customers keep coming back, so that competitors are locked out.

This metaphor – opportunity as a window, exploiting that opportunity as moving through the window – is a powerful *aide-mémoire* for analysing, and planning, the process of opportunity identification and exploitation. We will now explore each stage in more detail.

Seeing the window: scanning for new opportunities

This involves scanning the solid wall presented by existing players to find the windows and spot the gaps in what they offer to the market. This process demands an active approach to identifying new opportunities and to innovating in response to them.

Locating the window: positioning the new venture

This involves developing an understanding of where the window is *located*. It demands an understanding both of the *positioning* of the new offering in the marketplace relative to existing products and services and of how the venture can position itself in the marketplace relative to existing players to take best advantage of the opportunity presented.

Measuring the window

This involves evaluating the opportunity and recognising the potential it offers to create new value. In short, it means finding out how much the opportunity might be worth. This demands getting to grips with the market for the innovation, measuring its size, understanding its dynamics and trends, evaluating the impact the innovation might make in it and ascertaining how much customers might be willing to spend on it. Measuring the window also demands that the entrepreneur develop an understanding of the risks the venture might face.

Opening the window: gaining commitment

Having identified, located and measured the window the next stage is to *open* it. Opening the window means turning vision into reality, i.e. actually starting the new business. Critical to this stage is the need to get stakeholders to make a commitment to the venture, to attract investors and employees, to develop a new set of relationships and to establish the venture within its network. Once the window is opened, then the entrepreneur can then move through it, metaphorically speaking, by actually starting up the business.

Closing the window: sustaining competitiveness

Once the window has been opened and the entrepreneur has passed through it then the window must be closed again. If it is not, then competitors will follow the entrepreneur through and exploit the opportunity as well. This will reduce the potential of the entrepreneur's business. Closing the window to stop competitors following through means creating a long-term *sustainable competitive advantage* for the business. This provides the basis on which the entrepreneur can build the security and stability of the business and use it to earn long-term rewards.

Each of these stages presents itself to the entrepreneur as a series of *decisions*. Developing the business means addressing those decisions. The following five chapters will explore these decisions in detail.

Summary of key ideas

- A business environment is full of opportunities because existing businesses always leave gaps. There is always the potential to create new value.
- The *strategic window* is a visual metaphor which allows entrepreneurs to make sense of the opportunities they pursue.
- The five stages of the strategic window are: *spotting, locating, measuring, opening,* and *closing.*

Suggestions for further reading

Abel, D.F. (1978) 'Strategic windows', *Journal of Marketing*, July, pp. 21–6.

Arend, R.J. (1999) 'Emergence of entrepreneurs following exogenous technological change', *Strategic Management Journal*, Vol. 20, pp. 31–47.

Bettis, R.A. and **Prahalad, C.K.** (1995) 'The dominant logic: Retrospective and extension', *Strategic Management Journal*, Vol. 16, pp. 5–14.

Cyert, R.M., Kumar, P. and **Williams, J.R.** (1993) 'Information, market imperfections and strategy', *Strategic Management Journal*, Vol. 14, pp. 47–58.

Hannan, M.T. and **Freeman, J.** (1984) 'Structural inertia and organisational change', *American Sociological Review*, Vol. 49, pp. 149–64.

Prahalad, C.K. and **Bettis, R.A.** (1986) 'The dominant logic: A new linkage between diversity and performance', *Strategic Management Journal*, Vol. 7, pp. 485–501.

Yao, D.A. (1988) 'Beyond the reach of the invisible hand: Impediments to economic activity, market failures and profitability', *Strategic Management Journal*, Vol. 9, pp. 59–70.

Selected case material

From pain to financial gain

9 December 1999

Gillian Cribbs on a philosophy graduate who turned an amusing idea into a business proposition

For Gary Lancet, the path to becoming an entrepreneur began four years ago, quite literally with a pain in the neck.

Mr Lancet, who was a fundraiser for the charity Action Aid, found that long hours studying for an Open University course had left him with severe neck pain. His physiotherapist advised him to use a bookstand, but the only one he could find was an expensive reproduction from Harrods. So he decided to invent his own.

He hit on the idea of a miniature deckchair. "It had to be sturdy but adjustable, for reading at different angles. The deckchair is a classic piece of furniture – simple and practical, but more than that, the idea made me laugh," he says.

But Mr Lancet took the idea seriously. He spent £1,000 commissioning a furniture designer to draw plans for the basic model and offered a £250 prize to art students at Middlesex University to design its packaging. He also took a course in basic management at the OU. By March 1997 he had the prototype for Bookchair, a sturdy pine and canvas bookstand that can be adjusted for reading at three angles.

Since then, he has sold about 5,000 Bookchairs, mainly through deals with bookstore chains such as Waterstone's, Dillons and Methven's, although it is also on sale in the Back Shop and Purves and Purves furniture store, both in London. Turnover is £50,000-£60,000 a year and rising.

Mr Lancet is an unlikely entrepreneur. A philosophy graduate, he runs the business from his home in north London, which acts as office and store for up to 5,000 Bookchairs. He has a partner who helps with packaging and plans to employ extra staff in the new year. "Early on, I held back because I did not want to expand too quickly. I had to learn as I went, so I kept things as simple as possible."

He was guided by two principles: that the product should be made from sustainable resources and that it should be manufactured in the developing world. Bookchair is made in the Philippines using pine from managed forests in New Zealand. Mr Lancet is about to place an order with another factory in Bangladesh. He says he became interested in environmental issues and sustainable development after a voluntary service posting to Tanzania in 1993.

He is also very serious about how his product can help people. As well as being recommended by ergonomists and physiotherapists, Bookchair has been adopted by a number of NHS hospitals to help bed-ridden patients read, and the National Federation of Access Centres, which offers advice to disabled students.

"Bookchair is also helpful for teaching youngsters to adopt a better posture early on so they can avoid neck and back pain in future. I could tell them about that," Mr Lancet adds.

Riding high on a growing appetite for specialist entertainment

13 December 1999

The phenomenal growth of lads' mags is being eclipsed by fishing, camcorders and mobile phones, writes **Gautam Malkani**

Highbury House Communications is riding high on the magazine market's growing appetite for specialist titles.

The once phenomenal growth rates of so-called 'lad's mags', have been eclipsed by those of home entertainment titles, while the spread of new technology has led to growth in publications on camcorders and mobile telephones.

The shift in the market is good news for Ian Fletcher, Highbury's chief executive. The small publisher is the UK market leader in home entertainment magazines – such as What Satellite TV and Total DVD.

The company's shares have jumped from 7 3/4p to 60p over the past year.

Strengths:

The consumer titles – the bedrock of the publishing business, accounting for 37 per cent of last year's £25.6m turnover – also include broader subjects such as health. As with business-to-business, sports and commemorative titles, they are less dependent on the advertising cycle because they contain few recruitment and property ads.

Robert Corden, an analyst with Charles Stanley, is positive on the low-cost, low-risk way Highbury has built its portfolio of more than 90 titles. Instead of investing in big launches, it has tended to upgrade supplements to quarterlies and bi-monthlies before taking the plunge with a separate monthly.

The market is mostly enthralled by Highbury's handful of internet activities. But Mr Fletcher's approach to the internet is that of a traditional publisher. Highbury's first fully-fledged online magazine – www.fishing – will be grown on the back of its profits. "We're just applying the commercial disciplines to this that most people apply to other activities, but which don't seem to apply to the internet world," he said. The site has attracted an approach from WH Smith about an e-commerce deal for selling fishing books.

Weaknesses:

The home entertainment market could turn down.

But the main weak spot is the contract magazine division – a remnant of Highbury's past and where it does not own the titles. Before Mr Fletcher took over at what was then called Harrington Kilbride in 1995, the publisher was making losses of more than £5m.

It returned to the black in 1997 and paid its first dividend in 1998, with pre-tax profits of £1.67m (£280,000).

The contract magazine division is still the least promising performer. However, its contribution has been reduced from 80 per cent of the publishing business to about 30 per cent.

It is likely to shrink further. Mr Fletcher has ruled out any acquisitions in the division so it will increasingly be a smaller part of the total business.

Threats:

The company owns other potentially lucrative domain names: www.shooting and www.gardening. It has decided to learn from www.fishing before launching the others. "People who go fishing don't spend a lot of money online, but people spend a lot of money gardening," said Mr Corden. A cautious approach to developing each site in turn may mean it misses out on the benefits of having an online version of its magazines.

Highbury's confident entry into the market for telephone revenues from internet services earlier this year is likely to fall short of initial expectations because of competition. Highbury bought 50 per cent of UK Access, giving it software that cuts out the need to locate a web page via an internet service provider.

UK Access shares the telephone revenues even when the user jumps to other sites. The software is promising because it allows the site to serve as a home page and UK Access as an ISP. But since the flotation of Freeserve, the market has become crowded and Highbury has lost its original edge. "The amount of revenue you can get has gone down but it has not cost them any money because it's a virtual company," says Mr Corden.

Opportunities:

"We are not trying to make this company into an internet stock," quips Mr Fletcher. Analysts have not yet included a profits contribution from its new media activities.

Last month Highbury spent £4m buying RVC, an internet software developer which can transfer publications on to the internet straight from QuarkXpress software, the standard design package.

The acquisition bolsters a position it already holds in creating and managing others' web sites. Its Easypress software system already enables magazines to be published on the web without their publishers having any programming knowledge or internet skills.

It will probably squeeze even more out of its internet activities through Wyvern Crest, a database marketer bought in July for £3.3m.

Even more promising would be the prospect of floating its internet activities to crystallise its value. James Middleweek, at Collins Stewart, the company's broker, has flagged this potential.

"It's a possibility but it's not part of our current thinking," Mr Fletcher said.

Highbury House

Trade and consumer magazine publisher

Sector Media

Market Capitalisation £67m

The Boss Ian Fletcher

Headquarters Highbury Station Road, Islington, North London

Yahoo! goes native in local markets

29 March 2000

Portal plays to regional strengths, write **Alexandra Nusbaum** and **Rahul Jacob**

Think global, act local may be the oldest maxim in the international textbook, but it is the foundation upon which Yahoo!, the US internet portal, has successfully built its overseas business.

Yahoo!'s sites throughout Asia, a far-from-homogeneous continent, have taken the lesson to heart; each is tailored to suit local tastes and preferences.

"The interests are different so the sites are different," says Savio Chow, who heads Yahoo! in the Greater China region. He uses the analogy of Coca-Cola and McDonald's which, he says, rely on their global brands to make an impact overseas but subtly alter the product to suit local tastes.

The Taiwanese, for example, are more interested in culture than people in Hong Kong who enjoy film gossip and are obsessed with financial information.

In Japan, online shoppers are concerned about the quality and reliability of internet purchases, so Yahoo!Japan adapted the company's US e-commerce site to address these issues. "In the US, a merchant willing to pay $100 per month can open an internet storefront on Yahoo!. We decided not to take this approach," says Masahiro Inoue, chairman of Yahoo!Japan. "If anybody can open a store, we can't control the quality of the merchant."

Listings on Yahoo!Japan's e-commerce site are by invitation only. So far, the company has selected only 28 Japanese merchants to offer their wares online.

Unlike the US site, Yahoo!Japan uses this selectivity to force merchants to pay up: the fee is nearly $500 per month, plus roughly 4 per cent of each transaction.

In Greater China, where Yahoo!'s popularity lags that of mainland companies such as Sina.com and Sohu.com, local flavour is accentuated using domestic news feeds which are unedited.

This can be a virtue when dealing with countries such as China where censorship would create problems. Beijing demands that internet companies be responsible for policing the content on their sites which Yahoo! adheres to by using content mostly from state media.

Yahoo! is also tackling the buoyant internet market in Korea, where it recently announced plans to invest $60m in a joint venture to acquire Korean internet companies.

Yahoo!Japan, a joint venture between Yahoo! and Softbank, Japan's leading internet investment company, captures more eyeballs than any other site in Japan. Earlier this month, the number of page views in a single day climbed to a new high of 60m.

Thomas Rodes, internet analyst at Nikko Salomon Smith Barney, says it is becoming increasingly difficult for other companies to compete with Yahoo!Japan. "They are approaching the untouchable," he says.

Softbank, Japan's leading investment company, has been primarily responsible for Yahoo!'s move into Asia. Masayoshi Son, the Korean-born chairman of Softbank, invested in Yahoo! in 1995, after a single meeting with Jerry Yang, the company's Taiwanese-born founder.

In early 1996, Mr Son exported Yahoo! to Japan and launched the local portal under his Japanese colleague, Mr Inoue.

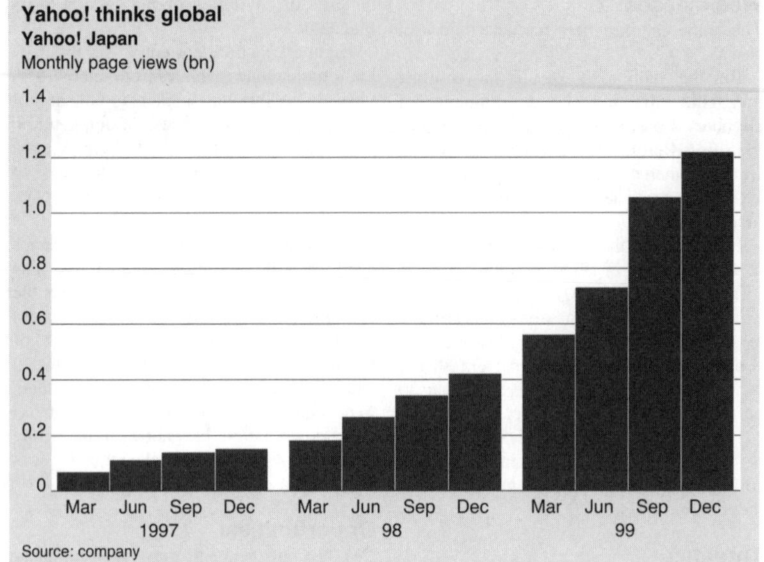

Review questions

Discuss the creative processes that:

1 Gary Lancet (Bookchairs)

2 Ian Fletcher (Highbury House Communications) and

3 Jerry Yang (Yahoo!)

might have engaged in to identify their respective business opportunities.

14 Seeing the window: scanning for opportunity

Chapter overview

*The first stage in using the strategic window is **identifying** it. This chapter looks at how new opportunities may be spotted, screened and selected.*

14.1 Types of opportunities available

KEY LEARNING OUTCOME
An understanding of the types of opportunity that present themselves to the entrepreneur.

An opportunity is the chance to do something in a way which is both different from, and better than, the way it is done at the moment. It offers the possibility of delivering new value to the customer. In its details, every opportunity is different, but there are some common patterns in the way in which opportunities take shape.

The new product

The new product offers the customer a physical device which provides a new means to satisfy a need or to solve a problem. A new product may be based on existing technology or it might exploit new technological possibilities. It might also represent a chance to add value to an existing product by using an appropriate branding strategy.

The new service

The new service offers the customer an act, or a series of acts, which satisfy a particular need or solve a particular problem. Many new offerings have both 'product' and 'service' dimensions. Robert Worcester, for example, built the enormously successful market research business, MORI, founded not so much on the basis that business and politicians wanted a *product* (market information) as on the recognition that they wanted a *service* that would help them make decisions.

New means of production

A new means of producing an existing product is not an opportunity in itself. It will offer an opportunity if it can be used to deliver *additional* value to the customer. This means the product must be produced at lower cost or in a way which allows greater flexibility in the way it is delivered to the customer. For example, Takami Takahashi, the founder of the diversified Japanese multi-national Minebea, grew the business from being a small niche player in the ball-bearing market by exploiting its experience in small component manufacturing to offer low-cost products to the electronics, engineering and precision instruments markets.

New distribution route

A new way of getting the product to the customer means that the customer finds it easier, more convenient, or less time consuming to obtain the product or service. This may involve the venture developing an innovative way of getting the product to the end-user or a new way of working with intermediaries.

Improved service

This is an opportunity to enhance the value of a product to the customer by offering an additional service element with it. This service often involves maintaining the product in some way but it can also be based on supporting the customer in using the product or offering them training in its use. Frederick Smith's inspiration for the US parcel service, Federal Express, was a recognition of the gap in the market for a business that would be dedicated to providing a high-quality parcel delivery service. This gap was left by existing suppliers, chiefly passenger airlines, who offered a parcel service as a side-line to use up excess weight capacity on aircraft but did not consider it to be an important part of their business, and so did not consider the service element to be important to their customers.

Relationship building

Relationships are built on trust, and trust adds value by reducing the cost needed to monitor contracts. Trust can provide a source of competitive advantage. It can be used to build networks which competitors find it hard to enter. A new opportunity presents itself if relationships which will be mutually beneficial to the entrepreneur and the customer can be built. Rowland 'Tiny' Rowland's ability to develop close and trusting relationships with African leaders was an important factor in the success of the Lonhro empire. The Saatchi brothers did not merely provide an advertising service, they also concentrated on building relationships with their clients.

Opportunities do not have to be 'pure'. It is often the case that a particular opportunity comprises a mixture of the above elements. A new product may demand an additional support service if customers are to find it attractive. Getting the product to them may demand that relationships are formed. The entrepreneur must take an open mind and a creative approach to the way in which opportunities may be exploited.

14.2 Methods of spotting opportunities

KEY LEARNING OUTCOME
An appreciation of the methods which might be used to identify new opportunities.

It is often assumed that entrepreneurs are graced with some special kind of insight that enables them to see opportunities and the way in which they might be exploited. While creativity is certainly important, the view that entrepreneurs work purely by inspiration undervalues the extent to which they are rewarded for the hard work involved in actively seeking out and evaluating new opportunities. There are a variety of techniques that can be of help in this search. Some are rather rough and ready while others are more formal. Some are so straightforward the entrepreneur may not even realise that he or she is using them. They may be articulated in the form of a heuristic or rule of thumb. Others are complex and may demand the support of market research experts if they are to be used properly. It is useful to be aware of the ways in which a market may be scanned for new opportunities, and of the techniques available to assist in this process.

Heuristics

Entrepreneurial heuristics have been considered earlier in section 11.6. Heuristics are an integral part of creativity. The heuristics entrepreneurs call upon to generate business ideas can be seen to involve two types. The first are *analysis* heuristics. These are the cognitive strategies entrepreneurs adopt in order to gain and integrate new information about the world, to understand the patterns in this information and to spot market gaps. The second are *synthesis* heuristics. Synthesis involves using a cognitive

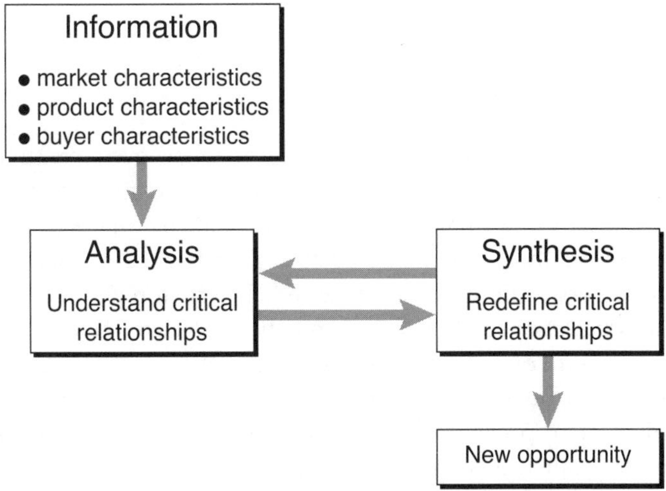

Fig. 14.1 Heuristic discovery: information, analysis and synthesis

strategy to bring the ideas developed from analysis back together again in a new and creative way generating a new perspective on customer needs and how they might be addressed. Analysis is about spotting opportunities; synthesis is about creating innovations that might exploit those opportunities. These two sets of heuristics lie at the centre of a process with information as an input and new business opportunities as an output. This process is *iterative*. Each cycle refines the insight into the opportunity and makes it clearer. This process may be made explicit but more often it is simply the way in which the entrepreneur has learnt (perhaps even *actively* taught him- or herself) to develop a decision when faced with opportunities and challenges.

Problem analysis

This approach starts by identifying the needs individuals or organisations have and the problems that they face. These needs and problems may be either explicit or implicit. They may or may not be recognised by the subject. The approach begins by asking the question 'what could be better?' Having identified a problem the next question is to ask 'how might this be solved?' An effective, rewarding solution represents the basis of a new opportunity for the entrepreneur. This approach demands a full understanding of customer needs and the technology that might be used to satisfy them.

Customer proposals

A new opportunity may be identified by a customer on the basis of a recognition of their own needs. The customer then offers the opportunity to the entrepreneur. Customer proposals take a variety of forms. At their simplest they are informal suggestions of the 'Wouldn't it be great if...' type. Alternatively, they can take the form of a very detailed and formal brief, for example, if the customer is an organisation and a large expenditure is involved. Some organisations are active in 'reverse marketing' their needs to potential suppliers. Whatever the means used, an effective entrepreneur is *always* keen to solicit ideas from customers.

Creative groups

An entrepreneur does not have to rely on his or her own creativity. The best entrepreneurs are active in facilitating and harnessing the creativity of other people too. A creative group consists of a small number of potential customers or product experts who are encouraged to think about their needs in a particular market area and to consider how those needs might be better served. The customers may be the ultimate consumers of the product or service or they may be industrial buyers.

Creative groups need control and leadership and their comments to be properly analysed if they are to be really informative. Getting people together in the right environment may also present a logistical challenge. Many market research companies offer specialist services in setting up, running and interpreting such creative group sessions.

Market mapping

Market mapping is a formal technique which involves identifying the dimensions defining a product category. These dimensions are based on the features of the product category. The features will differ depending on the type of product, but indicators like price, quality and performance are quite common. The characteristics of *buyers* may also be used to provide a more detailed mapping. A map is created of the market by using the feature-buyer dimensions as *co-ordinates*. Products separate out into distinct groups depending on their location on the map. The map defines the *positioning* of the product. The map may be used to identify gaps in the market and to specify the type of product that might be used to fill them.

A variety of statistical techniques are available for sorting out the information and presenting it in a two-dimensional form. Often, though, just an imaginative sketch will do. The map then provides a powerful visual representation of what is in the market, how different offerings are related to each other and, critically, the gaps that are present in it.

Features stretching

Innovation involves offering something new. This means looking for ways in which changes might be made. Features stretching involves identifying the principal features which define a particular product or service and then seeing what happens if they are changed in some way. The trick is to test each feature with a range of suitable adjectives such as: 'bigger', 'stronger', 'faster', 'more often', 'more fun' and so on and see what results from such testing.

Anita Roddick's Body Shop provides a good example. Her initial inspiration was to provide good quality toiletries in packs much *smaller* than those offered by other high street retailers. (Environmentalism came later!)

Product blending

As with features stretching, this technique involves identifying the features which define particular products. Instead of just changing individual features, however, new products are created by blending together features from different products or services. This technique is often used in conjunction with features stretching. Both features stretching and features blending make good team exercises and can prove to be quite good fun. A good example here is Alan Sugar's success with the Amstrad stack hi-fi system which combined the features of CD player, tuner and amplifier into a single unit.

The combined approach

Effective entrepreneurs do not rely on inspiration alone. They actively encourage creativity by thinking methodically about the market areas in which they have expertise. They also encourage other people such as employees, independent technical experts and customers to be creative on their behalf. The techniques listed are not exclusive of each other. They may be used together. Using them in a new way offers the potential to identify new and unexploited opportunities. For example, Richard Branson, the chief executive of the highly diverse Virgin Group, is renowned for his ability to bring out the creative talents in those around him.

14.3 Screening and selecting opportunities

KEY LEARNING OUTCOME
An understanding of the decisions to be taken in selecting opportunities.

Not all opportunities are equally valuable. A business with limited resources cannot pursue every opportunity with which it is faced. It must select those opportunities which are going to be the most rewarding. The key decisions in screening and selecting opportunities relate to the size of the opportunity, the investment necessary to exploit it, the rewards that will be gained and the risks likely to be encountered. Specifically, the entrepreneur's decision should be based on the answers to the following questions.

1 How large is the opportunity?

- How large is the market into which the innovation is to be placed? (What products will it compete with? What is the total value of their sales?)
- What share of the market is likely to be gained? (How competitive will it be against existing products? What percentage of customers can be reached? What fraction will convert to the innovation?)
- What gross margin (revenue minus costs) is likely? (What price can be obtained? What is the unit cost likely to be?)
- Over what period can the opportunity be exploited? (How long will customers be interested? How long before competitors move in?)

2 What investment will be necessary if it is to be exploited properly?

- What are the immediate capital requirements? (What investments in people, operating assets and communication will be required to start the business?)
- What will be the long-term and ongoing capital requirements? (What future investments will be necessary to continue exploiting the opportunity?)
- Does the business have access to the capital required?
- If the opportunity is as large as expected will the business have sufficient capacity?

- If not, can it be expanded or be (profitably) offset to other organisations?
- What human resources will be needed? Are they available?

3 What is the likely return?

- What profits will be generated? (What will be the rates? What will costs be like?)
- Over what period?
- Is this attractive given the investment necessary? (How does return on investment compare to other investment options? What is the opportunity cost?)

4 What are the risks?

- How sound are the assumptions about the size of the opportunity? (How accurate were the data on markets? Have *all* competitor products been considered?)
- What if customers do not find the offering as attractive as expected?
- What if competitors are more responsive than expected? (Have all competitors been considered? How could they react in principle? How might they react in practice?)
- To what extent is success dependent on the support and goodwill of intermediaries and other third parties? (How will this goodwill be gained and maintained?)
- How sensitive will the exploitation be to the marketing strategy (particularly in relation to: pricing, selling points against competitors, customers targeted) that has been adopted?
- Can adjustments be made to the strategy in the light of experience? How expensive will this be?
- Can additional resources be made available if necessary? (Will these be from internal sources or from investors?)
- What will be the effect on cash flow if revenues are lower than expected?
- What will be the effect on cash flow if costs are higher than expected?
- How should investors be prepared for these eventualities?
- How should future revenues be discounted?
- Under what circumstances might investors wish to make an exit? (Will this be planned or in response to a crisis?)
- If so, how will they do it? (By being paid from profit stream or by selling their holding?)

Opportunities only have meaning in relation to each other. The entrepreneur must select opportunities not in absolute terms but after comparing them with each other. A business (like an investor) will find an opportunity attractive only if it represents the *best* option in which they have to invest for the future. Opportunities must be prioritised. They must compete with each other for the business's valuable resources. What matters is not so much cost but *opportunity* cost, that is, not the cost of actually using resources, but the potential returns lost because they were not used elsewhere.

14.4 Entrepreneurial innovation

KEY LEARNING OUTCOME
An appreciation of market, technological and capability knowledge as the basis for entrepreneurial innovation.

Innovation lies at the heart of the entrepreneurial process and is a means to the exploitation of opportunity. Economically, innovation is the combining of resources in a new and original way. Entrepreneurially, it is the discovery of a new and better way of doing things. Innovation goes beyond invention. The new way does not stand on its own merits. It will only create new value if it offers customers an improved way to approach tasks and to solve problems. Innovation is not something that happens at some point in time. It is a process. This process of innovation can be described in terms of Fig. 14.2.

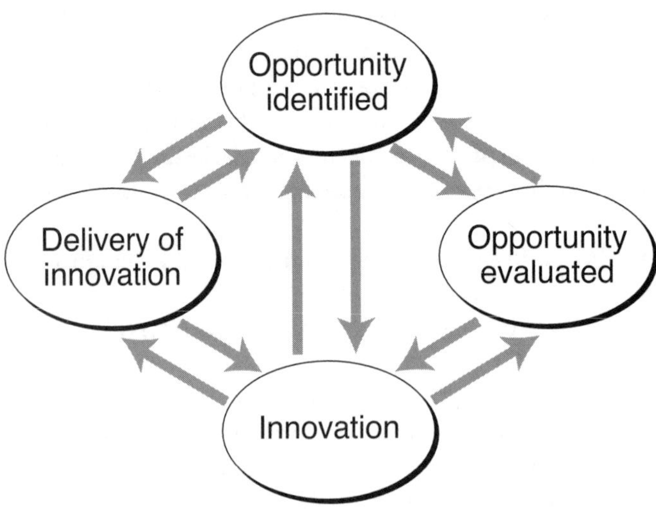

Fig. 14.2 The process of entrepreneurial innovation

The first stage is the identification of a new opportunity, a gap in the market competitors are leaving unfilled in their way of doing things. This opportunity must be evaluated. This evaluation consists of both a *qualitative* aspect (Who are the potential customers? What needs do they have? Why are existing products not meeting these?) and a *quantitative* aspect (How much would exploiting the opportunity be worth? What level of investment is appropriate?). The next stage is designing an innovation that will fulfil customer needs. This may involve invention, the creation of a new product or service, but it goes beyond this. Innovation also includes an understanding of how a new product can be delivered to customers and how it might be promoted to them. The final stage is the actual delivery of the innovation to customers. Each stage is iterative.

Understanding of the opportunity develops as potential innovations are considered. Means of delivery and promotion will be explored as the innovation takes shape. The opportunity and the innovation may be reconsidered in terms of promotional and distribution constraints.

Of course, innovation has many degrees. Any new way of doing things is an innovation. The magnitude may be of any order. One way of understanding the type of innovation an entrepreneurial venture is exploiting is to consider the technological base of the innovation, whether it is established or new, and the venture's ambitions in terms of market impact. Figure 14.3 illustrates the four quadrants these alternatives define.

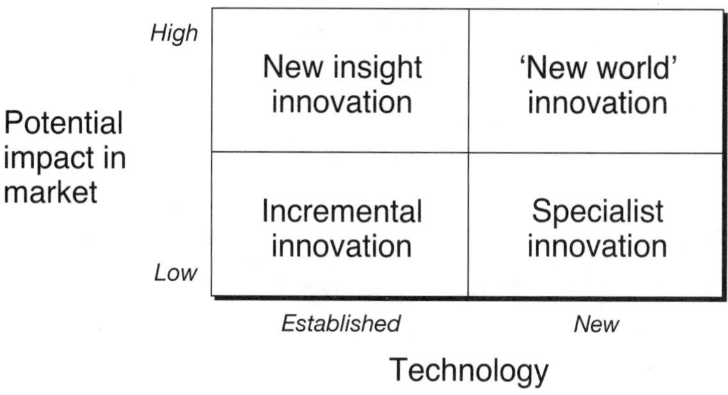

Fig. 14.3 Types of entrepreneurial innovation

Incremental innovation is concerned with minor improvements to an existing technology with limited market ambitions. If market ambitions are higher, but still based on modifications to existing technology, and competition will be dependent on a new way of using the technology then the innovation can be described as *new insight innovation*. If the innovation is based on a new technology, but with limited market ambitions and competition will be based on an appeal to a narrow group of customers then the innovation can be described as *specialist innovation*. An innovation founded on a new technology with high market impact ambitions can be called a *'new world' innovation*.

Innovation is a knowledge-based process. A new way of doing things must be based on a new way of seeing things. Successful innovation is founded on knowledge in three areas. *Market knowledge* is concerned with customers, their needs, demands, likely demand growth and what competitors are supplying. *Technological knowledge* relates to the effective development and production of the product or service aimed at the customers. These two areas of knowledge must be brought together with a third knowledge area. This is *capability knowledge*, the venture's understanding of what it does and why it does it well. This includes knowledge of the informational, cost, flexibility and human advantages the venture can call upon to compete effectively. If these three knowledge areas are brought together in a new, inventive and valuable way to drive the innovation process then the venture has the potential to break out of the trap that the industry's 'what we do and how we do it' thinking sets and so create new value (Fig. 14.4).

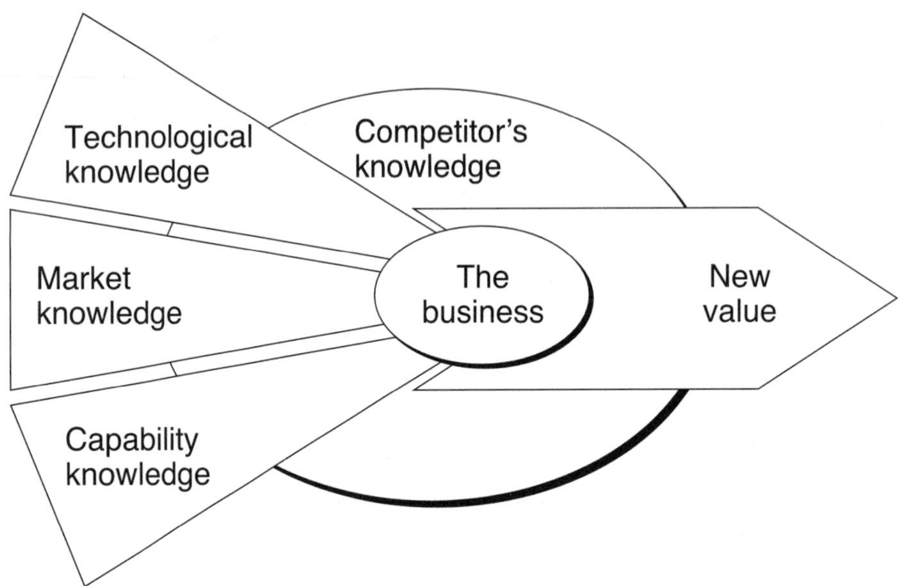

Fig. 14.4 Innovation breakout

Innovation is not, of course, something that is unique to the entrepreneurial venture. All businesses, no matter how mature, must be active innovators if they hope to maintain their position in the market. There are differences between the way entrepreneurs manage innovation and the way it is progressed in the large, mature firm. Entrepreneurial innovation is driven by vision, the desire to create a new world. Corporate innovation tends to be strategy driven. Though managerial vision may be important, the main driver is the recognition by the business that it must move forward if it is not to be left behind. Entrepreneurial innovation is, as far as the venture is concerned, radical. Its success or otherwise will have a major impact on performance. Corporate innovation is more likely to be marginal. Success will add to the business's performance rather than be fundamental to it. Entrepreneurial innovation usually involves the whole business. The venture's structure and processes will be defined around the need for innovation. A large business is more likely to compartmentalise the management of innovation within a particular function or teams. These different approaches are not hard and fast alternatives. They are ends of a spectrum. Entrepreneurs are particularly good at managing the innovation process. This is one of the main reasons why intrapreneurship (entrepreneurship within an established business) is of such interest. This is an issue to be considered in section 25.5.

Summary of key ideas

- The first stage in the strategic window is *spotting* it.
- Spotting the window means identifying a new opportunity in terms of the possibility of creating new value.
- There are a variety of methods, both formal and informal, by which entrepreneurs can spot new opportunities.
- Entrepreneurs keep themselves attuned to new opportunities.

Suggestions for further reading

Assael, H. and **Roscoe Jr, M.** (1976) 'Approaches to market segmentation analysis', *Journal of Marketing*, Oct, pp. 67–76.

Hague, P. (1985) 'The significance of market size', *Industrial Marketing Digest*, Vol. 10, No. 2, pp. 139–46.

Haley, R.I. (1968) 'Benefit segmentation: A decision-orientated research tool', *Journal of Marketing*, July, pp. 30–5.

Johnson, R.M. (1971) 'Market segmentation: A strategic management tool', *Journal of Marketing Research*, Feb, pp. 13–18.

Mattson, B.E. (1985) 'Spotting a market gap for a new product', *Long Range Planning*, Vol. 18, No. 1, pp. 87–93.

Selected case material

Engineering alchemist

10 May 1999

Peter Marsh meets the Kenya-born head of an innovative fuel cell company which is the force behind electric-powered cars

On the outskirts of Vancouver in a laboratory-cum-factory, latter-day alchemists are conjuring electricity from the seemingly magical combination of hydrogen and oxygen, two of the most abundant materials on earth. The scientists at Ballard Power Systems are working on fuel cells, a pollution-free battery which is expected to run the cars and power stations of the future.

Overseeing the work is a Kenya-born industrial engineer with the manner of a kindly schoolmaster. Firoz Rasul, who joined Ballard as chief executive in 1988, has stewarded the company from its origins as an obscure battery business to one of the world's hottest investment stocks alongside the internet and biotechnology start-ups.

Dozens of companies and research institutes are developing fuel cells. But Ballard is considered the furthest advanced in a technology that brings together physics, chemistry, electronics and materials engineering.

The company became interested in fuel cells in 1984, having worked until then on new batteries for the Canadian military.

Ballard has attracted attention mainly because fuel cells could replace the internal combustion engine early next century. For this to happen, cars would need to carry their own store of hydrogen in a liquid form, or some other substance (such as methanol) from which hydrogen can be obtained. The oxygen needed for the reaction would come from air.

A second use for fuel cells could be the supply of low-cost electricity for homes, factories and offices. In this case, fuel cells would feed off natural gas (a convenient source of hydrogen) supplied from pipelines. This would be converted into electricity at the point of use, without the greenhouse gases associated with burning fossil fuels in power stations.

The ideas behind fuel cells have been around for 150 years, and they have been used since the 1960s to provide electricity for manned spacecraft. But their prohibitive cost has deterred wider commercial applications. Only in the past decade have technological advances reduced the cost of the cells to a point where they start to become economically feasible.

The promise of "green machines" powered by fuel cells is so appealing, that DaimlerChrysler and Ford have each

Essential Guide: Firoz Rasul

Born in Kenya in 1952. Went to school there, then did degree in industrial engineering at Hatfield Polytechnic (now University of Hertfordshire) in the UK.

Early career: spent two years as an engineer in the St Helens, Lancashire, headquarters of Pilkington, Britain's biggest glass company. Took an MBA at McGill University, Canada, then worked in marketing in the UK for Black & Decker and General Foods, two US companies. Emigrated to Canada in 1981 (now a Canadian citizen) to work as vice-president for marketing at MDI, a data communications company. Joined Ballard in 1988 as chief executive, where he has presided over a 25-fold expansion in staff, plus the company's flotation in 1993.

Management philosophy: a shared approach to developing technology. "Our [Ballard's] commercialisation track is intrinsically linked to developments by other people," says Rasul. Has joint ventures on power plant development with companies including Ebara, the Japanese engineering group, and GPU, a US electricity company.

Company he most admires: Intel, the world's biggest microprocessor maker, because of the way it adds value by exploiting science and technology, and for its creation of an exciting environment for research.

Vision: likes the idea of developing a company whose "green" credentials make it a highly popular place to work.

Approach to reliability: background as an industrial engineer is displayed when he says: "Demonstrating that fuel cells will work for 50 hours in a laboratory is not enough. For then to be useful for the vehicle industry they have to work 5,000 hours without attention or maintenance."

acquired a stake in Ballard of 20 per cent and 15 per cent respectively. Power equipment makers including Alstom, the Franco-British consortium, have also entered into joint-ventures with the Canadian company.

Because of Ballard's technological lead, its stock market value is about $3bn (£1.9bn) – not bad for a business which last year made an underlying Canadian $62m (£27m) loss on sales of Canadian $25m.

Complex engineering means the electricity produced by fuel cells costs $500 per kilowatt. A car would typically require between 50 and 200 kilowatts of power, putting the price of a fuel-cell engine at between $25,000 and $100,000.

As befits a man who started his industrial career in the downbeat surroundings of a northern England glassworks, Mr Rasul is keen not to add to the large amounts of hype that fuel cells have attracted. He says cautiously that it is "not inconceivable" that in the next few years the cost of fuel cells can be further reduced by a factor of about 10 on today's devices.

DaimlerChrysler certainly seems confident: it recently demonstrated an electric vehicle powered by Ballard's cells that it says could be in mass production by 2004. The car maker is investing $1.4bn in the technology. As for home and office energy systems, commercial applications could come sooner – Ballard is testing products that could be on the market in the next two years. Also interested in the technology is General Electric, the US power plant giant, which aims by 2003 to gain annual sales of up to $300m from fuel cell-based domestic energy systems, using technology from one of Ballard's competitors.

Ballard's employees are mainly scientists and engineers: they account for 450 of the total staff of 550. Mr Rasul says one of his main jobs is knitting together different disciplines in the company. "The aim is to produce an environment in which people can do highly creative work. Some of the things we are doing here have never been achieved before," he says.

One example of Ballard's pioneering work is the development of a microscopic membrane whose pores are wide enough to allow electrons through, but small enough to prevent the passage of molecules. This, Mr Rasul says, was a vital breakthrough in the technology required for the chemical reactions in a fuel cell.

Mr Rasul says he brought a healthy scepticism when he joined the company 11 years ago, when Ballard had fewer than 20 employees. His background was in industrial engineering and marketing, and he had not worked in the energy products business. Even so, he says he demanded from his scientists "evidence that ideas developed in the laboratory would work in practice".

This down-to-earth approach to technological research led to a crucial aspect of the company's development: a "corporate networking" strategy in which Ballard sought to learn about the experience of other companies which agreed to use its early fuel cells. Mr Rasul says: "We leased our products to businesses around the world so they could be subjected to other people's experiments. It was a good way of getting feedback and increasing Ballard's credibility."

Organisations as diverse as General Motors, Matsushita, Vickers, the UK engineering company, and the Los Alamos nuclear research laboratory in the US tried out Ballard's cells. The company also organised informal links with suppliers of key technologies. Among them were the UK metals company Johnson Matthey, which came up with the new catalysts required in the hydrogen-oxygen reaction, and Dow Chemical and Du Pont, the US's two biggest chemicals makers, which worked on special membranes needed in the cells.

Mr Rasul says no new technical breakthroughs are needed to push fuel cells into full-scale use: just solid engineering work to reduce costs and increase reliability, and developments by other companies to incorporate fuel cells into their products. Assuming all goes to plan, Ballard should be ready for large-scale production around 2003. It might also consider licensing its technology to other fuel cell users.

How much will this cost? Ballard has so far required about $700m in development funds, and will need perhaps another $300m in the next five years. Billions more dollars will have to be spent by companies using the technology – not to mention the expense of converting petrol stations to supply either hydrogen or methanol.

But if fuel cells can fulfil their promise, and provide low-cost, low-polluting power, Mr Rasul believes the outlay will have been well-spent.

Getting it all together

1 May 1998

Jack Bock saves relationships by assembling furniture, says **Grania Langdon-Down**

Faced with a flatpack of furniture, even the most hardened do it yourself enthusiast sometimes quails at the sight of badly translated instructions and poorly drawn diagrams.

As tempers start to fray, Jack Bock can offer a soothing antidote – within 48 hours he will send a handyman or woman who will assemble the pile of apparently unrelated bits and pieces. In the process, he claims, he often saves relationships. If there are any of those irritating jobs that need to be done – the roller blind still in its pack, the unhung picture, the broken hinge – they will be fixed as well as part of the new Handyman Service Bock is developing alongside the assembly business.

Bock says: "The majority of people who call us for help are women. The men tend to stay mumbling in the background, conscious they may seem inept. There can be a lot of conflict involved in assembling furniture, whether it is a wardrobe, a children's climbing frame or a table tennis table – and we restore domestic harmony."

He started the Screwdriver business in his west London home in November 1995 but it took seven months to put together a network of more than 100 individual Screwdrivers – mainly retired professionals – around the country to offer a viable assembly service. To find his assemblers, who work for him on a freelance basis, Bock advertised in the national and local press, receiving 2,000 replies. By the end of 1999, he plans to have 300 to 400 assemblers on his books. The service is already truly national with some coverage in Scotland.

"I look for mad DIY fanatics who view flatpack furniture as a doddle. Most of those I have taken on are 55-plus and retired – former bank managers, civil servants, company executives, architects, policemen, firemen. I also have five female Screwdrivers.

"We are totally reliant on having responsible people so I have gone for this age group as they are of the old school where responsibility, pride in your work, is paramount. We ring back after a job has been done to check the customer is satisfied. One mistake, one complaint and that assembler is out."

Despite his own antipathy to DIY, Bock knows how long it takes to assemble each item. He goes out on jobs – "just to make sure no one can pull a fast one about how long it takes to put something together".

Bock, 57, says Screwdriver is proving great fun. He had spent 30 years in the clothing trade – learning some hard lessons when one of his companies, which manufactured leather clothes, went bust in 1970 – before taking a 13-year "sabbatical" with his wife Lena in West Cork in Ireland.

"It was a glorious time. My son was born there. I sold Irish peat to the Scandinavians, designed garden furniture and created a new brine for ham. But I didn't make any money and we came back to London in January 1994."

He spent that year researching ideas for a new business which would not involve a large capital outlay or extended credit terms and which provided a service rather than a product.

By then separated from his wife, he bought a small terraced house near Kew Bridge in west London and set up an office in a back bedroom. "I hate DIY. So when I got the flatpacks of shelves and tables home I called in someone to as-semble them for me. And I realised there must be so many people like me who cannot get it together, who aren't looking to start a new hobby but just to get that piece of furniture up and finished with."

He spent three months researching the market in self-assembly. In the autumn of 1995, he approached the John Lewis Partnership with his idea of offering an assembly service. But he only had 30 people organised around the country as assemblers, mostly in the south-east. "I spoke to one of the store's furniture buyers who said it was a grand idea but questioned whether I had enough people to provide a quick response."

But by June 1996, his network of Screwdrivers had grown to more than 100 and he started building up his contacts with the big retail stores. John Lewis, Habitat, House of Fraser, Ikea, Courts, Furniture Village, the Co-op's Living and Homeworld stores and Selfridges now recommend his service to customers.

"We do between 75 and 100 jobs a week at an average price of £60, including VAT, with a minimum charge of £28," explains Bock, who operates as a sole trader. "When a customer rings up, we can give an immediate price for the job as we have the time it takes to assemble every piece of furniture retailed in this country – 4,000 in all – on our database. We have an insurance policy for all our assemblers so the customer can be confident any damage will be covered."

The three-strong administrative team then matches the jobs with the nearest available Screwdriver. "We are bursting out of here – I am looking at taking on an office somewhere along the river," he said.

Turnover has risen steadily. He achieved £80,588 sales from June 1996 to March 1997, with a trading profit of £20,000. The biggest overhead is the cost of the assemblers, who receive about £10 an hour, representing about 42 per cent of turnover.

In the last financial year, turnover reached nearly £140,000. The target for April to March 1999 is £192,000. Net profit is running at between 15 and 20 per cent and Bock pays himself a salary of £20,000 a year.

The business is proving just what he wanted. "It is cash-rich. We get paid on completion of the job so there is no credit and we pay the assembler the following week." But he is impatient. "It is frustrating. I know this business could be growing 10-fold. But it is all about credibility; about the general public feeling confident they can trust us. At the moment, the returns from advertising don't warrant the expense. The best recommendation for us is from stores to their customers."

His aim is to develop the business to a point where it has a turnover of more than £1m so that he could then sell it in about five years.

In the meantime, he is looking over his shoulder to see if any competition springs up – "we need a bit to keep us sharp". There are similar businesses on mainland Europe and he is going to France, Germany and Scandinavia to see if he can learn from their experiences.

His key to success, he maintains, is: "Make sure you are fulfilling a need – don't try to create one."

Review questions

Consider the opportunity scanning systems used by:

1 Ballard Power Systems

2 Screwdriver

3 Why have existing businesses left gaps through which these entrants have moved?

15 Locating the window: positioning the new venture

Chapter overview

The second stage in using the strategic window is to ***locate*** *it. This means relating the opportunity to the business activity of established firms and understanding it as a gap in what they offer to the market. The idea of* ***positioning*** *provides a powerful conceptual framework for doing this.*

15.1 The idea of positioning

KEY LEARNING OUTCOME
An appreciation of how the concept of positioning may be used as a guide to entrepreneurial decision making.

The idea of positioning provides a very powerful tool to aid entrepreneurial decision making. Positioning provides a framework for *locating* the venture in relation to its competitors. Existing suppliers to a market do not serve its customers as completely as they might. They leave gaps in the market which a new venture can attempt to fill so gaining a foothold in that market. Identifying the window of opportunity means spotting where these gaps are. A new venture is, at face value, in a weak position relative to established competitors. Even if the established players had not previously spotted the window of opportunity, a new start-up will signal its presence to them. Their greater resources, established network of relationships and lower costs may put them in a much stronger position to exploit the window.

Positioning the venture means locating it in relation to a market gap such that it can exploit that gap in a profitable way. This involves structuring the business so that it can serve the requirements of a particular market niche *better* than existing competitors. An effective positioning means that the business will be able to develop a *competitive advantage* in serving this niche. This makes the niche *defendable* against competitors. It also enables the new venture to move into the market in a way which avoids direct head-on competition with established players. Head-on competition is usually a difficult game for the new venture to play since the playing field is tipped in favour of the established player. At best, head-on competition will prove to be expensive, and at worst, it will result in failure for the new venture.

Positioning relates to a *location*, and location means occupying a *space*. Understanding positioning and using it as a decision-making tool demands an appreciation of the characterisation of the competitive space in which the venture operates. In general, a competitive space is characterised by the ways in which competitors seek to distinguish themselves from each other. Two distinct approaches to positioning provide different and complementary insights. *Strategic positioning* looks at the way in which the business's approach to delivering value to its customers is distinct from that of its competitors. Strategic positioning is concerned with the way in which the business *as a whole* distinguishes itself in a valuable way from competitor businesses. *Market positioning*, on the other hand, looks at the way in which the business's *offerings* to the market are differentiated from those of its competitors. Market positioning is concerned only with the business's products and services. Strategic positioning and market positioning can be used as decision-support tools for the entrepreneurial business.

15.2 Strategic positioning

KEY LEARNING OUTCOME
An understanding of the decisions which define the venture's strategic positioning.

Identifying a strategic position is a fundamental element of the strategic planning process. A strategic position is the way the business as a whole is located relative to competitors in the playing field of the market, that, is the *competitive space*. Derek Abell (1980), in his book *Defining the Business*, suggests that this competitive space can be defined along four dimensions.

1 Stage in value addition

The goods that are bought by consumers, or which are used by those who provide services to them, are usually highly refined. Yet, ultimately, they are all made from raw materials obtained from the earth. However, there may be a lot of businesses who play a role in the process between the extraction of a raw material and the delivery of the final product.

Consider, for example, a home computer that has been purchased from a distributor. That distributor will have purchased the computer from a hardware manufacturer. The manufacturer will have bought a variety of components such as silicon chips, plastic parts and glass screens from component suppliers. Those component suppliers will have made them from refined raw materials obtained from suppliers of pure silicon, plastics and glass. These suppliers will have refined their products from raw commodities obtained from the businesses who collect sand and extract oil from the earth. This process whereby the outputs of one business provide the inputs for the next business along is called the *value addition chain* (see Fig. 15.1).

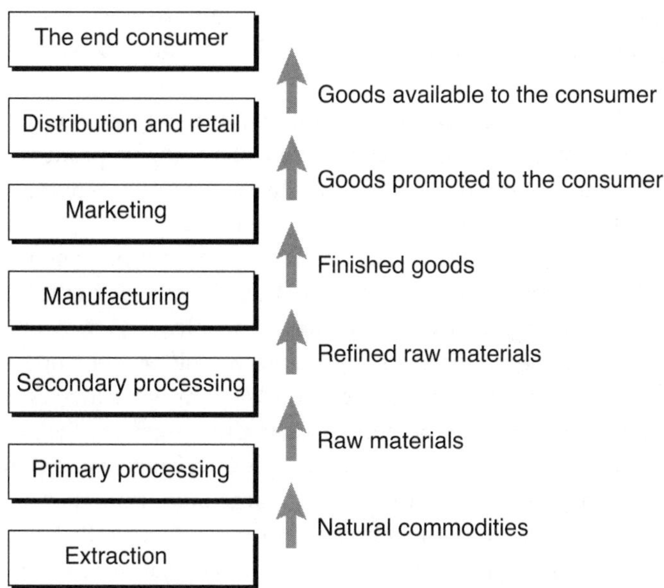

Fig. 15.1 Value addition in an industry chain

An entrepreneur must decide what stage, or stages, in the value addition process they expect their venture to occupy. This resolves itself into questions about the inputs and the outputs of the business. These questions are:

- **Will the business make a particular input (which might be a physical product or a service) for itself or will it buy it in?**
- **Will the business sell on a particular output to another business for further processing or will it try to add that value itself?**

The decisions made in response to these questions must be based on an appreciation of the competencies of the business, its resources and its competitive advantage relative to both competitors and the businesses adjacent to it in the value addition chain.

2 Customer segments addressed

It is rare that a business can serve the needs of an *entire* market. The strengths of a particular business lie in the way it can appeal to certain groups of customers. When Richard Branson started the Virgin Airline he concentrated on business passengers who wanted to cross the Atlantic. Alan Sugar, when founding his consumer electronics business Amstrad, was explicit about the fact that he was targeting the 'lorry driver and his family' rather than the hi-fi aficionado. Selecting a well-defined customer segment enables the business to focus limited resources, to concentrate its efforts and to defend itself against competitors.

There are a variety of ways in which a customer segment can be defined. Some of the more important include:

- *Geographic location*: where the customer is. Many entrepreneurial ventures start out serving a small local community. As they grow they expand to achieve national and even international scope.
- *Industry*: the industrial sector of organisational buyers. In its early stages an entrepreneurial venture may decide to concentrate on selling its product to a particular industry segment. This option may be attractive because the needs and buying habits of that sector are thoroughly understood by the entrepreneur.
- *Demographics of buyer*: e.g. social class, age, personal attitudes or stage in life cycle. For example, Gerald Ratner revitalised the high street jewellery trade in the UK by targeting his business towards young, relatively low-income people.
- *Buying process*: the way the product is bought and the role of influencers and decision makers. Entrepreneurs may concentrate their efforts towards businesses which buy in a certain sort of way. For example, business service firms such as the market research company MORI are adept at negotiating the complex decision-making process that lies behind the buying and use of market research in large organisations.
- *Psychographics*: buyers' attitudes toward the product category. Richard Branson, for example, has moved his Virgin brand into personal financial services on the basis that it offers trust in an area where many buyers have suspicions about the existing products on offer.

3 Customer needs addressed

Consumers and businesses have many, and complex, needs and wants. No single business could hope to serve them all. An entrepreneur must decide exactly which of the customer's needs his or her venture will exist to serve. Success depends on gaining customer commitment and the best way to do that is to genuinely serve the needs and to solve the problems they have.

Customers may be aware of their needs or they may not have articulated them to themselves yet these needs can be explicit or implicit. Different needs are not independent of each other, they often interact and must be prioritised. Satisfying one need may mean that others go unsatisfied. The entrepreneur must learn to understand the needs of their customers, to rationalise them and to distinguish them from each other. The entrepreneur must often articulate the needs of customers on their behalf.

4 Means of addressing needs

Satisfying a need represents an end and there are a number of means by which that end can be achieved. The need to communicate with someone, for example, can be served by a postage stamp, a telephone, the Internet or by going to visit them. Having decided which particular customer needs they will satisfy, the entrepreneur must decide the means, or *technology*, that they will adopt in order to do so. Alan Sugar recognised people's desire to be entertained by listening to music. He provided them with electronic equipment to replay recorded music. He might, conceivably, have served that desire by building concert halls or by providing a service whereby musicians would come and play to people in their homes. For whatever reasons, these were technological alternatives he avoided.

The industry building entrepreneur is often the one who has recognised a whole new technological approach for addressing a basic need. Henry Ford recognised that a low-cost motor car was a better way of moving from one place to another than horse and cart. Bill Gates recognised that a computer with the right software could transform the way in which a variety of domestic and office information-processing tasks would performed. Innovation is not just about creating new technology. It is about understanding how a particular technology can be used to address a need in a new and fruitful way.

These four dimensions as shown in Fig. 15.2 describe the strategic positioning of a venture or its location in competitive space (see also Day, 1984, p.21). This is the niche where the new venture sits. It defines who its competitors are and the way in which they are competitors. Of course, merely occupying the niche is not enough. The business must structure itself and adopt operating processes and a culture which allows it to serve that niche effectively.

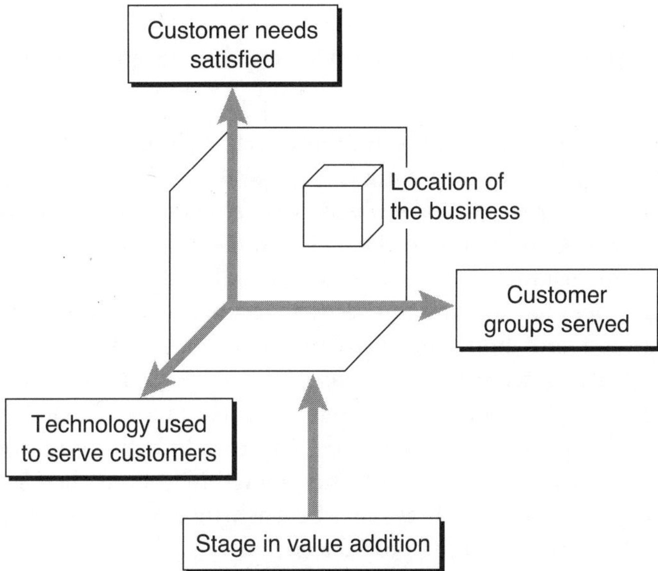

Fig. 15.2 The dimensions of strategic positioning

15.3 Market positioning

KEY LEARNING OUTCOME
An understanding of how the idea of market positioning can be used to differentiate the venture's offerings from those of its competitors.

Strategic positioning describes the way the venture is located in a competitive space. *Market positioning* describes the way its outputs, products and services are located in the marketplace relative to those of competitors. Success will only be achieved if the new venture offers customers something which is *different* from and more *attractive* than that offered by existing players. This means it must offer them greater value by being more suited to their needs or the same level of benefits at lower cost.

The first stage in market positioning is to develop an understanding of the criteria by which buyers distinguish between the different products on offer to them and the extent to which they consider them to be substitutable. Some general factors in market positioning are:

- *Price* – how the offering is priced relative to competitors
- *Perceived quality* – quality seen as high or low (what matters is perceived value for money, i.e. quality relative to price)
- *Demographic imagery* – up-market versus down-market, young versus old; dynamic versus conservative
- *Performance* – high performance or more limited performance
- *Number and type of features* – e.g. advanced versus basic; complex versus simple; hi-tech versus low-tech
- *Branding imagery* – the associations that the branding elicits
- *Service and support* – additional assistance offered in understanding, using and maintaining the product
- *Attitude towards supplier* – positive or negative associations gained from ethical stance of supplier.

Different buyers will prioritise and weight these factors differently.

One way of thinking about positioning is to consider three aspects of the product or service being offered. A product can be positioned using one or more of the three ways in which its consumer relates to it – see Fig. 15.3. At the centre is the *functional core*; that is, the features of the product or service which actually deliver its functional benefits. Surrounding this functional core are the aesthetic attractions of the product or service. These include design and branding elements which make the product or service attractive to use. At the outer level are the *emotional benefits*. These are those aspects of the product or service which appeal directly to the consumer's emotional and spiritual needs rather than their purely functional ones. This may be achieved through branding which allows the consumer the chance to say something about themselves by being seen to consume the product. It may also be enshrined in the way the product is sourced, or the values adapted in its production.

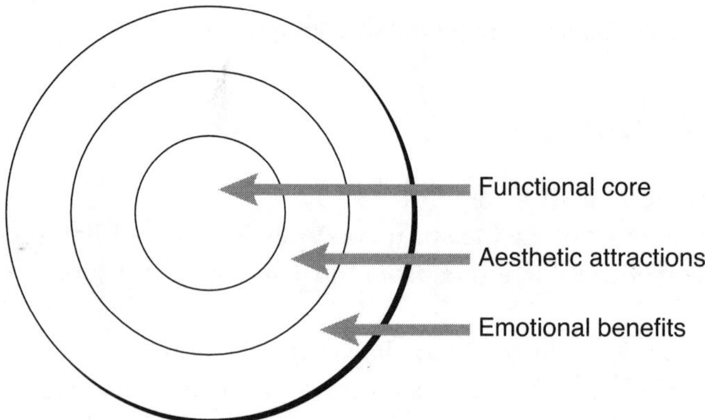

Fig. 15.3 Positioning of the venture's product

The aim of positioning is to reduce the extent to which the customer feels that the product or service is *substitutable* by those of competitors. In effect, this means focusing the offering on the needs of the customer in a unique and effective way. The positioning need not be solely in its functional core. Differentiation can often be achieved very effectively by giving the product or service a unique aspect in its aesthetic attractions and emotional benefits. For example, a £3.99 digital watch may be as good as a Cartier watch for telling the time, but the owner of the Cartier would not think it a good swap! The buyer may see their purchase set into a wider social and moral context. The actual 'physical' products offered by The Body Shop are easily imitated by other high street retailers, but its customers still feel that The Body Shop offers them something more valuable because of its ethical stance. The eponymous chain of jewellers set up by Gerald Ratner revolutionised the UK jewellery retailing sector in the 1980s but did not pretend to be offering products of the highest quality. Nonetheless it was felt to be fun, accessible and unstuffy by its young customers. Charles and Maurice Saatchi of Saatchi and Saatchi reinvented advertising in the 1960s and 1970s by positioning themselves as partners in the management process rather than by just supplying advertisements for clients. The McDonald's chain of fast-food outlets as established by Ray Kroc are not just places to eat; they are an invitation to share the American Dream.

Positioning is a valuable entrepreneurial tool. It guides the entrepreneur in offering the customer something new and valuable and it avoids the need for head-on competition with established (and more powerful) players. Effective positioning is a critical success factor for the new venture.

Summary of key ideas

- The second stage in the strategic window is *locating it*.
- Locating the window means developing a *position* for the new venture and its offerings to the marketplace.
- *Strategic positioning* relates to the way the venture fits in the marketplace in relation to its stage in the value addition chain; the customer groups it serves; the customer needs it addresses; and the technology it adopts to serve its customers.
- *Market positioning* relates to the way the venture's offerings fit in the marketplace in relation to the offerings of competitors.

Suggestions for further reading

Aaker, D.A. and **Shansby, J.G.** (1982) 'Positioning your product', *Business Horizons*, May-June, pp. 56–62.

Abell, D.F. (1980) *Defining the Business: The Starting Point of Strategic Planning*, Englewood Cliffs, NJ: Prentice Hall.

Datta, Y. (1996) 'Market segmentation: An integrated framework', *Long Range Planning*, Vol. 29, No. 6, pp. 797–811.

Day, G.S. (1984) *Strategic Market Planning*, St Paul's, MN: West Publishing, p. 21.

Day, G.S., Shocker, A.D. and **Srivastava, R.K.** (1978) 'Customer-orientated approaches to identifying product-markets', *Journal of Marketing*, Vol. 43, pp. 8–19.

Garda, R.A. (1981) 'Strategic segmentation: How to carve niches for growth in industrial markets', *Management Review*, August, reproduced in Weitz, B.A. and Weley, R. (eds) (1988) *Readings in Strategic Marketing: Analysis, Planning and Implementation*, New York: Dryden Press.

Selected case material

Wraps come off chocolate's best-kept secret

5 June 1998

Barry Callebaut flotation will raise its profile to the level of rivals Cadbury and Suchard, says **William Hall**

Ask most chocolate lovers to name Europe's biggest chocolate manufacturer and Barry Callebaut will not spring immediately to mind.

But while Mars, Nestlé, Suchard and Cadbury each have around 10 per cent of the market and some well known chocolate brands, they are still overshadowed by Barry Callebaut. The Swiss company, with strong French and Belgian roots, is well known to professionals in a fast-consolidating global industry where it competes with US agribusiness giants such as Cargill and Archer Daniels Midland.

It buys more than 10 per cent of the world's cocoa beans and produces a third of so-called industrial chocolate. It supplies the chocolate for everything from Unilever's Magnum ice-cream bars, to Danone's biscuits and the classy chocolates produced by Thorntons of the UK.

Barry Callebaut is about to emerge from the shadows. This week Klaus Jacobs, 61, the Swiss owner, announced plans to reduce his stake in in the company to around 70 per cent and raise around SFr200m ($135m) of new equity. The stock market flotation will probably value the company at more than SFr1.5bn, or around 19 times estimated current earnings.

Barry Callebaut was formed in August 1996, when Callebaut, Mr Jacobs' Belgian chocolate company, acquired Cocoa Barry, a French company specialising in sourcing cocoa, the main raw material for chocolate. The deal more than doubled the size of Mr Jacobs' group but also left it highly geared with equity of SFr363m supporting net debt of SFr791m.

With shares of companies such as Danone, Nestlé and Cadbury rising by around 50 per cent this year, Mr Jacobs is in a hurry to tap the stock market's new-found love of chocolate-coated equities to strengthen the balance sheet. After flotation, the gearing should drop to around 80 per cent and the interest cover increase from 5 times to 6.7 times.

In spite of the company's limited record, Pierre Vermaut, Barry Callebaut 50-year-old chairman, believes his company can grow considerably faster than the 3 per cent a year industry average. Thirty years ago the majority of chocolate companies were vertically integrated, doing everything from processing cocoa beans to marketing the final consumer product.

However, it is a capital intensive business, and "companies are increasingly focusing their investment on marketing and supporting their brands, rather than investing in something they can buy from companies like us", says Mr Vermaut, who joined Callebaut in 1981. It is not a commodity business, but "a high-tech food ingredient business", and Barry Callebaut's 17 plants pump out 1,500 types of chocolate and compute up to 10,000 different prices a day.

A second reason why Barry Callebaut is confident that it can grow its business faster than average, is its strategy of following its multinational clients into emerging markets, where annual chocolate consumption is a fraction of the average in Europe, where Barry Callebaut has a 50 per cent market share. By contrast, it is hardly represented in Latin America and only 3 per cent of its sales go to the Asia-Pacific region.

It wants to exploit demand for higher-margin gourmet chocolate and the increasing use of cheaper compound coatings. It is investing SFr15m a year on research in a bid to replicate its success in premium ice cream bars, where production moved from nothing to 10 per cent of the total in six years.

James Amoroso of Bank Julius Baer believes the company has the right financial ingredients to boost its earnings from SFr80.9m in the year to August 1998 to SFr117.5m by 2000. It has an experienced management team, with all but two of the top executives from the Callebaut side. It also has a reliable source of quality cocoa, a critical ingredient to success in the industry.

It appears to have insulated itself from potential supply and quality control problems resulting from the forthcoming liberalisation of the cocoa trade of the Cote d'Ivoire.

The small west African country is the world's biggest cocoa producer and supplies 70 per cent of Barry Callebaut's needs. In April, it bought the bulk of the cocoa stocks of Phibro Commodities, which controlled a quarter of the world's cocoa stocks. It has also established its own bean collecting system in the Ivory Coast.

At the same time, the company is selling control of Saco, the Côte d'Ivoire supplier of a third of its cocoa bean needs, back to Mr Jacobs. This strengthens its balance sheet and limits its exposure to disruptions in the country. The deal is a reminder that the company will still be controlled by Mr Jacobs, who also owns another large consumer chocolate company.

Not only does this limit the liquidity in Barry Callebaut shares, but it also raises questions about future conflicts of interest.

However, given the recent stock market success of Mr Jacobs' Adecco, the world's leading employment agency, investors may well be prepared to forget the past controversy over his treatment of minority shareholders when he sold his family's Jacobs Suchard to Philip Morris for SFr3.1bn in 1990.

If can-do won't do

14 January 1999

An outstanding but loss-making niche operator is determined to 'build a business that could not lose money', says **Peter Marsh**

Meltog, a world leader in a niche area of the machine tool industry, had always wanted to be bigger, according to Crowther Laycock, its managing director. Since it was acquired by its management a year ago, however, the loss-making operation has set out specifically "to build a business that could not lose money," Mr Laycock says.

The switch – which has involved becoming more ruthless in new machinery development – underlines the kind of decisions many growing businesses face when honing strategies in a specialised area of manufacturing.

Since it was set up nearly 50 years ago, West Yorkshire-based Meltog has concentrated on a particularly narrow niche. It is one of only five companies in the world making equipment to turn out decorative cans – used as up-market packaging for products such as biscuits, pencils and whisky.

Unlike most packaging, this goes beyond the strictly utilitarian, and the care that goes into designing the cans is reflected in the machinery required to make them. They work at much lower speeds than standard can-making machinery and invariably have to be customised for a specific application. While Meltog's machines turn out cans at about 60 a minute, high-speed systems for making Coca-Cola cans work at up to 1,200 a minute.

In the past, Meltog was not nearly selective enough about the new machinery projects it took on. In its keenness to expand volumes, costs would balloon when it was asked by a customer to produce, say, a set of machines to make heart-shaped chocolate tins.

"We had to become more determined to say 'no' if the project is too much of a one-off and the design costs seem prohibitive," says Nigel Pulling, Meltog's finance director and one of four of its managers who bought the company from Ropner, a conglomerate.

The £2.8m transaction in September 1997 was backed by 3i, the venture capital group that put up £1m for a 35 per cent stake. Barclays Bank lent £2m to cover a working capital facility and to help finance the costs of the purchase.

The change in Meltog's business philosophy has precipitated a radical turnaround in the company's finances. Two years ago it had 140 employees, with annual sales of £7m, and made a loss. Today, it has 85 people, with annual sales of about £5.5m, and pre-tax profits of roughly £500,000.

The improvement in profits is all the more impressive given that Meltog exports 80 per cent of its output. The company's overseas competitors are mainly in the US and Italy. They have therefore had the advantage in the past 18 months of having their costs based in more competitive currencies than sterling, which has appreciated significantly in this time.

Closer attention to assessing the potential of new machinery projects has not stopped developments at the company. The reverse is true, says Mr Laycock, who before the buy-out had worked elsewhere in Ropner.

While the company has reduced overall staff numbers during the past two years, the numbers employed mainly in design and development has roughly doubled to 11.

Mr Laycock says the accent on producing new designs is tied to Meltog's ambition of ensuring that within a year or two, four-fifths of its sales will be from products that are less than five years old. In the mid-1990s the comparable figure for the company was only 20 per cent, underlining Meltog's reliance on relatively mature products.

Since the buy-out, the company has also significantly increased its new factory investment, spending £350,000 on in-house machine tools required to make components more efficiently and accurately. The spending has increased productivity and helps to explain why the company has managed to cut its number of workers without a big drop in output.

The Meltog managers are now casting around for other underperforming engineering companies that they think they can also reinvigorate. In recent weeks, they have purchased two UK companies: Sutton, a toolmaker, and Billoway, which makes packaging systems. Other acquisitions are planned during 1999.

An eye-catching educational enterprise

26 March 1998

Simon Targett looks at Nord Anglia, the rapidly-expanding £46m company which is the UK's first quoted schools operator

Hull Grammar School, the alma mater of William Wilberforce, the anti-slave trade campaigner, would seem to have little in common with a nursery school in Rotherham, a language academy in Moscow, an art and design college in New Zealand, and the careers service for Ministry of Defence schools in Germany, Cyprus and Gibraltar.

But it does: all are run by Nord Anglia, the fast-growing £46m company based in Cheadle in Cheshire, which shot to prominence last year when it became the UK's first quoted schools operator. Since then, it has made some eye-catching progress, and the share price stands at 385p – more than double the 140p placing price. The architect of Nord Anglia's fortunes is Kevin McNeany, a diminutive Ulsterman who started providing English language vacation courses for students from continental Europe in 1972.

A former teacher who had earlier "dabbled" in the music business, Mr McNeany gradually expanded his education work, and formed the company in 1987 with plans for buying a series of UK-based independent schools. "This gave us the credibility to expand into the wider education market," he says.

In 1990, Nord Anglia secured £3m of venture capital funding from Charterhouse and opened new language schools as well as a series of British international schools for expatriates, beginning with Warsaw in 1992.

Since then, the company has set up a division to provide educational support services – especially school inspections and careers services – to the state-funded sector.

This promises to be the fastest growing part of a business which has seen pre-tax profits grow from £800,000 in 1993 to £2.4m in 1997. Last year, education services achieved operating profits of £662,000 – up from £181,000. By contrast, the independent

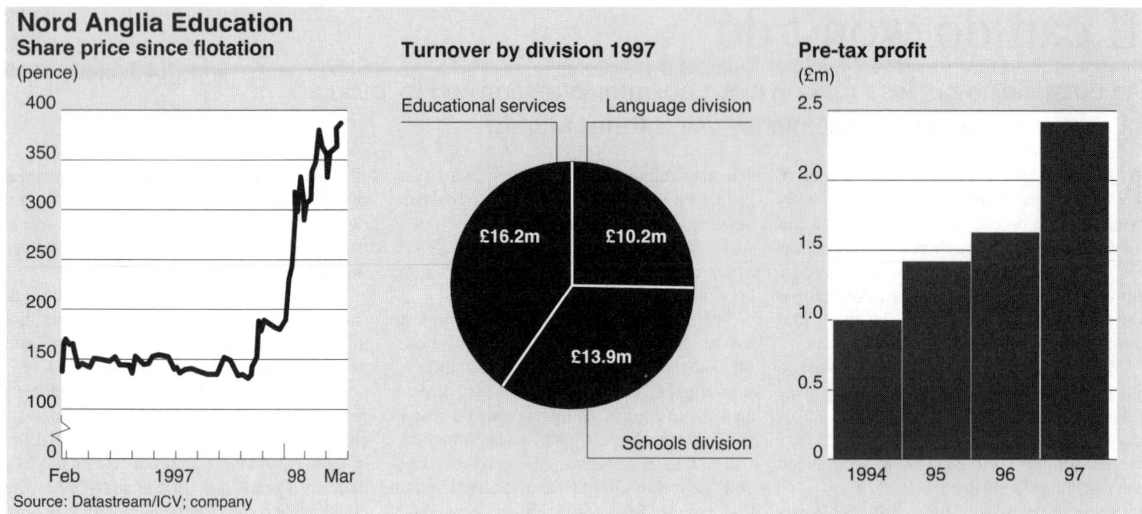

schools business rose from £1.15m to £1.52m and the language schools business, affected by the strength of sterling, rose even more modestly, from £536,000 to £554,000.

Paul Kavanagh, a partner at Killik & Co, the broker, is convinced this trend can continue, not least because of the Labour government's readiness to let private companies run failing state-funded schools in "education action zones".

"Nord Anglia is powerfully positioned to pick up one of the education action zones," he said.

"It has 25 years of experience, and no one else has that level of practical knowledge."

Mr McNeany, who confirmed he submitted "some bids" to run EAZs before last Friday's deadline, is more circumspect. He thinks it unlikely that private companies will be given free rein to run EAZs. But the prospect of taking over services controlled by local education authorities remains a real possibility.

Ministers have said LEAs have "no God-given right to run everything".

Henry Cooke Lumsden – Nord Anglia's broker – forecasts pre-tax profits to rise to £2.7m this year, producing earnings of 12.2p, compared with 11.53p last year and 10.87p in 1996.

"This makes the current share price look expensive," says Mark Sheppard, analyst at Hoare Govett. He points to the bearish view "that growth may never come through, and even if it does, it won't be for another two years". But Mr Sheppard is optimistic nonetheless. One reason is the government's emphasis on "education, education, education" and the wider shift towards an economy which places a high priority on knowledge and skills.

Another reason is Mr McNeany's entrepreneurial record. "You can't argue with a man who's made £20m," he says. On this, Sir David Trippier, a former Tory government minister for small business who joined Nord Anglia as a non-executive director just before flotation, agrees. "He is an original entrepreneur, someone who identified a niche in the market."

But the main reason is the American experience. "Three years ago, the sector wasn't very popular in the US," Mr Sheppard notes. "Now there are several companies worth well over $1bn (£600m)."

Mr McNeany also points to the US, citing the performance of the Apollo Group, which runs the University of Phoenix and is worth $2.4bn.

But his own expectations for Nord Anglia are altogether more modest. He sees turnover rising steadily to £300m through sustained organic growth. A new international school opens in Berlin in September, a clutch of purpose-built nurseries is planned for this year, and there are proposals to venture into the higher education market in the UK.

If this sounds like rapid expansion, Mr McNeany is careful not to get carried away.

As he says: "Education doesn't move swiftly, and although I would maintain that it is a very good long-term bet, I'm not contemplating a revolution." This is the latest in the Challengers series about small companies seeking to make a big impact.

Review questions

Discuss and distinguish between the strategic and market positioning for:

1 Barry Callebaut

2 Meltog

3 Nord Anglia.

How are these positionings helping the ventures to achieve success?

16 Measuring the window: analysing the opportunity

Chapter overview

The third stage in using the strategic window is to ***measure*** *it, that is, to* ***quantify*** *the opportunity and develop an understanding of how much new value might be created. Obtaining information on the opportunity is seen to be an investment in the business, and must be considered as such. Key issues relating to the analysis of opportunity are considered. Methods of market analysis are considered in overview.*

16.1 The need for information

KEY LEARNING OUTCOME
An appreciation of the importance of managing and using market information effectively.

Relevant market information is extremely useful to the entrepreneur. Entrepreneurs are decision makers. They are different from other types of manager because they make the decision to *venture*. Venturing means stepping out into the unknown and information provides a map of how to move forward into this unknown. Information eliminates uncertainty and so reduces *risk*. However, information on its own is not enough: if it is to be valuable, it must be analysed, understood and acted upon.

Information does not come for free, it has a cost. While the entrepreneur will know many things simply as a result of his or her experience within an industry, a lot of additional information may need to be gathered actively. Even if the information has no direct cost (for example, information gathered 'free' from a public library) valuable time is used in collecting it. Some information can have a high direct cost, for example information obtained through formal market research surveys can appear very expensive to the entrepreneur just starting out. However, information represents an *investment* in the business. It is used to increase the performance of the business. The pay-off for that investment needs to be appreciated before the information is gathered.

Information can guide action. However, lack of information should not be an excuse for *inaction*. While it may be sensible to hold back on a move until more information is available and that move can be made with more confidence, there are other times when the entrepreneur must rely on their instincts and 'go for it'. If they wait too long, someone else may make the move first. While information reduces risk, the entrepreneur cannot expect to eliminate *all* risk and sometimes they must make a step into the dark. The entrepreneur must walk a narrow path between making ill-informed and ill-judged decisions and an inertia caused by the venture becoming more interested in gathering and analysing information than in taking direct action. The founders of organisation systems thinking, F. E. Kast and J. E. Rosenzweig, called these two extremes 'extinction by instinct' and 'paralysis by analysis'.

Strategic management provides a wide variety of tools and conceptual frameworks to aid decision making. A variety of formal methods is available to guide resource allocation and make competitive moves. While the entrepreneur would be foolish to shun the insights that can be gained through such formal analysis of information they should not be solely dependent on it. Often it is the overall *pattern*, not the *detail* that matters. They must learn to develop their intuition and make judgements based on holistic thinking and their own heuristic approach. The successful entrepreneur learns to see the wood before the trees.

16.2 Analysing the market and identifying key issues

KEY LEARNING OUTCOME
An appreciation of the importance of analysing and understanding market conditions.

If they are to be successful, entrepreneurs must understand the market in which they are operating. This understanding is important because success depends on their ability to serve that market in a way which is better than that of their competitors.

There are a number of issues about which the entrepreneur must be informed if they are to make effective decisions in relation to their venture. These issues fall into four broad categories. These relate to the existing market conditions and the opportunity they present, the way in which the entrepreneur might innovate and offer something of value to the market, the way in which the entrepreneur can get the venture started and the way in which competitors are likely to respond to the venture. Some specific information requirements are:

- *General market conditions* (customers' needs and requirements; the size of potential markets; market growth rate and trends in its development; the structure of customer groups and segments; and customer and consumer buying behaviour).
- *The attractiveness of the innovation* (customers' satisfactions and dissatisfactions with current offerings; customers' reaction to the entrepreneur's new offering; competitor pricing and customers' pricing expectations; and likely volume of demand).
- *The way the new venture can be initiated and positioned in the marketplace* (resource requirements for start-up; resource requirements for the later development of the

venture; the structure of the network in which the venture will be located; sources of investment capital; customers and customer groups to be given priority; and means by which the customer might be informed about the new offering).

- *The way in which competitors might react to the new venture* (the nature, type, strengths and weaknesses of competitors; strategies adopted by competitors; and likely actions (strategic and tactical) by way of a response to the entrepreneur's start-up).

Information of this nature is available from a variety of sources. Some of it will be knowledge the entrepreneur already holds about his or her industry. Some may be obtained from existing published sources such as market reports and trade publications, and such sources are referred to as *secondary* sources. Alternatively, primary research involves a bespoke analysis of a market situation using market research techniques in answer to specific questions.

In many instances the entrepreneur may feel quite informed on these issues. In other instances it may be felt that information is lacking and greater certainty is needed. The entrepreneur must never be complacent. The rule must be always to challenge knowledge and assumptions. When deciding upon the degree of precision required for information, two questions must be asked. First, how sensitive will decision making be to the accuracy of the information used as the basis of those decisions? Second, with respect to this, is the cost of gaining the information worth the return it offers?

16.3 Analysing the opportunity: qualitative methods

KEY LEARNING OUTCOME

An appreciation of the methods by which the 'whys' of the opportunity may be understood.

There are two types of question that must be asked if a business opportunity is to be fully appreciated. Both may be answered by appropriate market research and analysis techniques. The first set of questions relate to the nature of the opportunity, its qualities and the approaches that might be taken to exploiting it. These are the 'who?', 'what?' and 'why?' questions. They are best answered using *qualitative* methods. The second set of questions relate to the value of the opportunity and the effort that should be put into exploiting it. These are the 'how much?' and 'how many?' questions. These are best answered using *quantitative* methods.

Qualitative methods might be used to answer questions of the following sort. Who are the customers? How are they defined as a group? How are they differentiated from non-customers? What needs do these customers have in relation to the product category (in terms of functional, social, emotional and developmental needs)? How do they articulate their needs (explicitly or implicitly)? How well do consumers find that current offerings satisfy those needs? In what ways are current offerings unsatisfactory? What are the customers' attitudes towards the product category in general (positive, negative or mixed)? Why do non-customers not use the product category? How might they be attracted to it? If the product is not available, how might other types of product be used as a substitute? How does this define a gap for an innovative offering? How do customers go about buying a product? How are they normally informed about the product category? What is their knowledge of the product category? Who influences their decision when making a purchase? Who influences the consumer when they use the product? How is such influence exercised? How do they greet innovations in the product category? (Positively or with suspicion?)

Many entrepreneurs will feel confident in their ability to answer these questions based purely on their experience in a particular industry sector working with customers and a particular product category. However, if the area is new to them, or they feel the innovation they are offering changes the rules, or they just wish to challenge assumptions then obtaining answers directly from customers and potential users will be a valuable exercise. There are a variety of methods for doing this.

Actively listening to customers

Customers must, ultimately, be the source of all information on a market and the opportunities it presents. After all, it is they who buy the product and reward the entrepreneur. Even an informal conversation with a customer can provide a good deal of information about their concerns, what they find satisfactory, what less so, what might be better, and so on. If this information is picked up on, it can be of enormous value to the acute entrepreneur. Acquiring this information demands *active* listening.

Listening is a communication skill. It does not come naturally. When in conversation, we often use the other person's speaking time as a chance to consider our reply rather than actually listen to what they are saying. It is easy to be distracted, but active listening demands that the conversation be kept on track. The right sort of questions must be asked. The listener should lock onto key phrases and comments and these should be explored if further information might be yielded. Non-verbal communication (facial gestures, body language) should also be noted. What does the conversation reveal about the customer's way of thinking about the product category? Is decision making rational and logical or is it influenced by emotional factors?

Selling situations provide a good opportunity to listen to customers. In fact, it is as important to listen to what they say as it is to present the product to them. Objections to making a purchase should be received positively. After all, if a customer is saying why they will not purchase this time, they are giving a clue as to how they could be persuaded to do so next time.

In-depth interviews

The in-depth interview is really a structured conversation. The objective of the conversation is to gather information and the specific information required is defined in advance. A series of questions to be asked are set out before the interview and these questions are used to prompt the interviewee. The interviewer can introduce additional questions if a particular avenue is opened up and is considered to be worth further exploration.

In-depth interviews are a very effective and flexible way of getting to know the customer and their way of thinking. They are, however, time consuming (for both interviewer and interviewee) and so can prove to be expensive if a large number need to be performed.

Focus groups

A focus group is a gathering of a small group of customers (usually about five to eight) who are questioned about their attitudes and opinions on a particular product category. This reveals not only their thinking as individuals, but also the way they interact with each other when considering the product.

Focus groups can be very revealing and can give substance to vague feelings about gaps in markets. However, they are difficult to run. Controlling them and keeping the discussion on track can be difficult. Interpreting what has been said is also a professional task. Focus groups work best when the right sort of venue is used. Video or sound recording facilities are needed. It can also be difficult to bring even a small group of buyers (especially industrial buyers) together. Consequently focus groups are often most productive when run by trained market researchers.

Usage and awareness studies

A usage and awareness study is based on a written questionnaire which is mailed to users of the product category. The questionnaire aims to explore the users' attitudes and feelings towards the product category, their knowledge of what is on offer, and the way they use products in the category. They provide written answers to the questions or tick prefigured questions and then send their answers back. Such studies can be used to confirm ideas on the types of gap that exist in a market. Usage and awareness studies are an efficient and (relatively) low-cost way of gathering the view of a large number of customers. However, return rates can be low. Care must be taken in the way in which they are designed and interpreted, and appropriate statistical methods must be adopted.

Product trials

A very effective way of obtaining customers' opinions on a new product, and how they view it in relation to alternatives, is to let them use it in the way they would be expected to under normal circumstances and then question them about their experience. Product trials work well when the offering is very innovative, when the customer has limited experience of the category and the customer needs exposure to the product before they can give an opinion on it. Product trials can be very informative. They can be used as part of the development process for a new product. They are particularly good at identifying what the customer finds attractive about the product and so can be used to refine the selling points of that product.

However, product trials do demand that the product is available to be tested. If the product is not in production then expensive working prototypes may be needed.

Many entrepreneurs also feel unsure about revealing their product too early, especially if competitors might imitate it quickly.

16.4 Analysing the opportunity: quantitative methods

KEY LEARNING OUTCOME
An appreciation of the methods which can be used to quantify a market opportunity.

Qualitative methods can be used to give shape to the nature of a market opportunity and the ways in which it might be exploited. However, they say little about how much that opportunity is worth and the entrepreneur needs to know whether an opportunity is worth pursuing and, if so, what amount of investment is sensible. To support this type of decision quantitative methods are needed. The kinds of questions answered by quantitative methods include the following. How large is the market (its volume)? How much is it worth (its value)? How fast is it growing? How large are the key segments in the market?

Market value and volume can be resolved into three subsidiary issues. How many customers are there in the market? How often do they buy? How much do they buy when they do so? These three factors together define the overall demand in the market and may be illustrated as in Fig. 16.1.

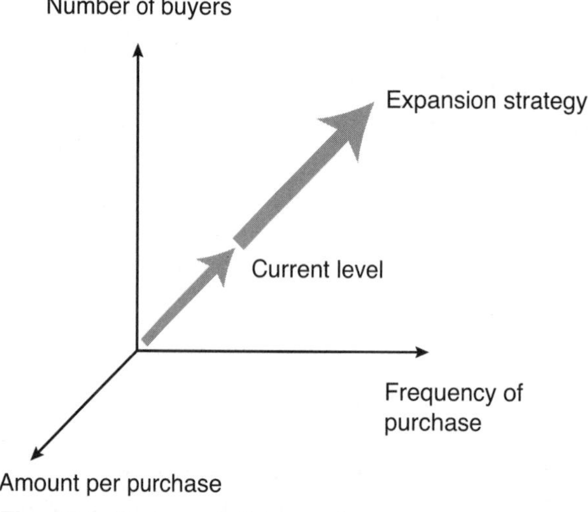

Fig. 16.1 Factors defining volume demand

As well as accepting this pattern of demand the entrepreneur may be seeking a strategy that expands overall demand by increasing the number of users, purchase amount or purchase frequency. Such expansion is likely to reduce overall competitive pressures as business can be increased without affecting competitors' sales. Also, distributors will be attracted by such a strategy. In addition, quantitative methods can be called upon to answer questions such as the market shares of competitors supplying the market and the level of investment they make to maintain and develop that share. In broad terms, three approaches can be used to obtain this information.

1 *User audits*

Questioning of a representative sample of users to learn how much and how often they make purchases in a particular product category and whose products they buy. This may be achieved by mailed questionnaire, telephone interview or face-to-face questioning. By classifying different types of customer, user audits can give information on the market segments that characterise the market and their relative sizes.

2 *Distributor audits*

Distributor audits involve monitoring how a particular product type moves through a distribution chain. A representative sample of distributors is asked to provide information on how much of a particular item they buy, how frequently they buy it, how much they keep in stock and how much they sell over a particular period.

3 *Manufacturer's output*

The market is assessed by adding together the outputs of all or a representative sample of the manufacturers who contribute products to the market.

All three types of audit can be carried out at regular intervals to give an indication of the extent to which and the ways in which a market is growing.

A reliable quantitative assessment of a market is time consuming and can prove to be expensive. The entrepreneur may undertake the exercise personally but is more likely to call upon the agencies of professional market researchers. Again, the entrepreneur must balance the need for reliable information with the investment he or she feels is proper for obtaining it.

A lot of information on various markets is routinely published by a variety of organisations. This information is quite easily accessed. Although such *secondary* information can be very informative, its value is limited. Only rarely will it examine a market from exactly the perspective that the entrepreneur would wish to see it. This is not least because the entrepreneur should be looking at the market in an innovative way and seeking new relationships between markets.

When examining markets, from either a qualitative or quantitative perspective, a little lateral thinking can be valuable. Insights may be gained not only by asking questions about the market itself, but also by asking questions about *related* markets (see Fig. 16.2). The effective entrepreneur also thinks about *end-use* markets (for example, when Lord Hanson bought the London Brick Company he wasn't thinking about the market for bricks but the growing market for new houses), about *supply* markets (for example, Alan Sugar of Amstrad was aware not only of the market for domestic hi-fi equipment but developments in the market for electronic components) and about the *co-use* market for products used in association with the product in question (thus Bill Gates of Microsoft did not so much concern himself with analysing the market for computer software but with the growth in ownership of computer *hardware* which would need software to operate it).

As always in entrepreneurship, a fresh and innovative approach to asking questions can pay dividends.

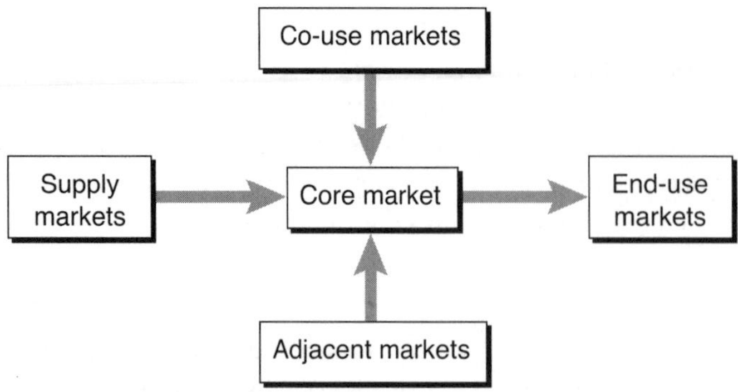

Fig. 16.2 Markets of interest to the entrepreneur

Summary of key ideas

- The third stage in the strategic window is *measuring* it.
- Measuring it means developing an understanding as to the size of the opportunity and what it might be worth.
- A business opportunity is analysed by *qualitative methods* which answer 'what' and 'why' questions and *quantitative methods* which answer 'how much' and 'how many' questions.
- Information can be expensive. Effective entrepreneurs weigh the value of information against the cost of obtaining it. Information is regarded as an *investment* in the business.

Suggestions for further reading

Eisenhardt, K. (1989) 'Making fast strategic decisions in high-velocity environments', *Academy of Management Journal*, Vol. 32, pp. 543–76.

Kast, F.E. and **Rosenzweig, J.E.** (1970) *Organization and Management: A Systems Approach*, New York: McGraw-Hill.

Langley, A. (1995) 'Between "paralysis by analysis" and "extinction by instinct"', *Sloan Management Review*, Spring, pp. 63–76.

Marlow, H. (1994) 'Intuition and forecasting – A holistic approach', *Long Range Planning*, Vol. 27, No. 6, pp. 58–68.

Selected case material

Caught in a tangled web of confusion

21 January 2000

The difficulty of measuring online audiences is a bar to growth in advertising, says **Richard Tomkins**

You are a big consumer goods company, and at last you have taken the plunge: you have placed your first advertisement on the internet.

Now just one question is bugging you. Did anybody actually see it?

For as long as advertising has existed, companies paying high prices for media space have worried about just how many eyeballs their billboards, newspaper advertisements or television commercials reach.

With the arrival of web advertising, it was thought, those anxieties would vanish. Because every click could be instantaneously tracked and recorded, advertisers would know down to the last digit how many people had seen their adverts.

It has not turned out that way. Instead, the difficulty of measuring online audiences has turned out to be one of the biggest barriers to growth in internet advertising, repeatedly cited by advertisers as a reason for staying away.

Top 20 US sites
Revenues from banner advertisements
4th quarter 1999

Site	Impressions* (m)	Revenue** $m
Yahoo!	6,300	125.0
MSN	1,600	48.0
Go	1,300	40.0
Geocities	1,700	35.0
AOL	1,600	33.0
Lycos	1,100	20.0
Netscape	830	18.0
AltaVista	730	15.0
ESPN	540	15.0
Cnet	350	10.0
CNN	350	10.0
FortuneCity	252	8.7
Xoom	560	8.4
Tripod	1,060	8.2
ZDNet	164	8.1
Excite	336	7.7
theglobe	250	7.4
HyperMart	310	6.2
HotBot	104	5.3
NBA	108	3.3

***Impressions** Is the number of advertisements downloaded.

****Revenue** Is an estimate based on the number of impressions and the charges quoted in the web publisher's rate card, and may overstate actual revenues.

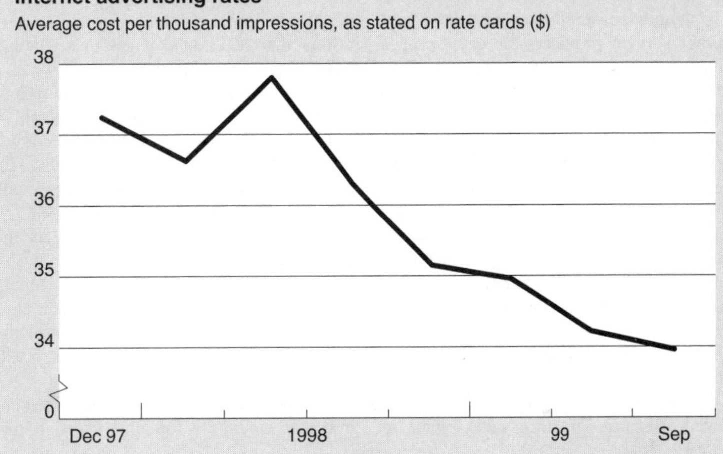

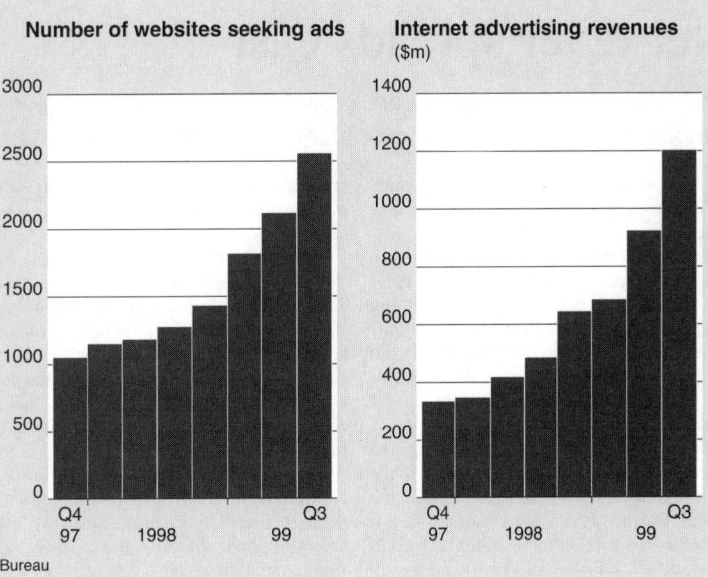

Source: AdRelevance; AdKnowiedge; Internet Advertising Bureau

The difficulties began when web publishers began to boast about how many hits their sites were getting. This was highly deceptive because a hit meant a text or image file loaded on to a browser, so a page made up of 10 text and image files would score 10 hits each time it was loaded.

With hits discredited, most web publishers have moved on to the more sensible method of counting page views, defined as one loading of one page on to one user's browser. If an advertiser has a banner advertisement on a page, the theory goes, then the number of page views should equal the number of times the advert is seen.

If only life were so simple. As it is, the method turns out to be fraught with inaccuracies.

One reason is the process known as caching. To avoid having to download the same page from the host web site each time it is requested, corporate networks and internet service providers store (or cache) copies of popular web pages in their memories and deliver the same page repeatedly to users. People who view pages from cache memories do not generate an impression on the host web site, so their page views go unreported.

Web publishers, whose advertising rates are typically based on a cost for each thousand times the advert is viewed, compensate for the undercounting by lifting their rates. But this makes the rates look uncompetitive, deterring would-be advertisers.

Undercounting is one problem – but overcounting is another. Just because a page is loaded, it does not mean an advert is viewed. Because graphics take longer to download than text, users often click on a link to another site before the advert has had time to download. And many adverts that appear below the bottom of the screen will never be seen unless the viewer scrolls down before moving on.

Also adding to the overcounting problem is the heavy activity of web crawlers, the inhuman agents of internet search engines that ratchet up vast numbers of page impressions as they scour the web even though no page has been seen.

Some advertisers and web publishers have been trying to build trust in online advertising by devising technological solutions to the audience measurement problems, such as cache-busters that order browsers to download a new version of the page each time it is requested.

But as fast as solutions are found, advancing technology threatens to interpose other problems, such as cache-buster-busters that still cache pages even though they are being told not to.

There is another issue, too. While it is in advertisers' and web publishers' interests to find a way of measuring cached page views, it is not in the web publishers' interests to fix the overcounting problems because this would lower their audience figures.

"A lot of people are working to fix the cached ads, but the web publishers aren't fixing the abort-ad measurement problem because it makes them look bad," says Robin Webster, senior vice-president of the Association of National Advertisers, a US industry body.

One solution to all the measurement problems would be for advertisers to pay only when users click on their adverts. But web publishers understandably complain that this is unfair, since adverts may influence consumers without necessarily prompting a direct response. And if people do not click on an advert, the web publishers point out, it may be because it is no good, not because few people see it.

With all these issues unresolved, many advertisers and web publishers seem to be muddling through with a compromise, adopting pricing models that combine traditional cost-per-thousand rates and payment by response.

According to a report this week from the Internet Advertising Bureau, an industry association, hybrid pricing models accounted for 55 per cent of internet advertising revenues in last year's third quarter, with the traditional cost-per-thousand model accounting for 37 per cent and payment by response 8 per cent.

Although the measurement problems have disappointed those who had expected more from the web, some media buyers point out that they are no worse than those afflicting traditional media.

"In fact, in terms of accountability, the internet is very unflawed by comparison," says Rob Norman, chief executive of Outrider, the interactive arm of the Tempus media buying group. "The difference is that there's less universal agreement about what the imprecisions are online than there is with traditional media.

"Once everybody's agreed on what the problems are, you can just get around them," Mr Norman says. "But if you can't agree, things get a little confused."

Net fever spreads east

FT

3 March 2000

Web access and e-business are growing throughout the region, despite many barriers to development, writes **Stefan Wagstyl**

A region where only one in three people has a telephone might seem an unlikely base for an internet boom.

But that is precisely what is happening in eastern Europe. The energy that local business people once put into trading everything from Coca-Cola to second-hand cars is now visible on the net. And the values being put on the region's internet potential are becoming big enough to interest even the largest inter-national investors.

In the most significant development so far, the Polish government is poised to make a profit of more than €1bn (£600m) from the global internet boom. Two months ago it cancelled an auction for a strategic stake in Telekomunikacja Polska (Tpsa), the partly privatised telecommunications utility, after months of marketing had produced just one offer.

This week it closed a new auction with four bidders, including France Telecom and Telecom Italia, despite a 60 per cent increase in Tpsa's market value. Fuelled by internet fever, Tpsa was this week worth €13.3bn, compared with €9bn in January. If the government now sells a 25-35 per cent stake, it could raise €1bn-€1.5bn more than in January.

The shift in the Polish treasury's fortunes is the most dramatic sign of the impact of internet fever in central Europe. Cesky Telecom and Matav, the Czech and Hungarian utilities, have also leapt ahead on the stock market, not least because they are among the few big local blue chip companies with internet businesses.

Smaller companies with internet links have performed even better – such as Agora, the Polish publishing group, Prokom and Optimus, the Polish software companies with investments in internet service providers (ISPs), and Uproar, the Hungary-based Easdaq-listed online gaming company that has most of its customers in the US.

Across the region there are hundreds of ISPs all hoping to attract clients and investors. Even Albania, Europe's poorest country, has about 12.

However most are small, with fewer than 5,000 subscribers apiece. The barriers to rapid development seem formidable. Even in the Czech Republic, Slovakia, Poland and Hungary, among the region's most developed countries, less than 10 per cent of the population has a personal computer, according to International Data Corporation (IDC), the market research group.

Inadequate competition in fixed-line telephony keeps local call charges high, notably in Hungary, where Matav's monopoly is set to endure until 2003. Consumers are not used to buying goods and services they cannot inspect or test. Face-to-face transactions dominate life, and protection against fraud is weak.

The region is not short of entrepreneurs, who spotted opportunities as early as their US counterparts but have so far been unable to reap the full rewards. Petr Ulrich, a 26-year-old Czech who started in e-commerce at the same time as Amazon.com, the US online book store, says: "If I'd had the same idea six years ago in the US, I'd be a multi-billionaire by now." Inet, Mr Ulrich's software company, operates a retail site called www.shop.cz, which generates a modest Kc1m (£17,000) a month in sales.

Yet the barriers are coming down. Telephone charges will be eroded in the next few years by deregulation. The fast growth of mobile telephony will help circumvent the under-developed terrestrial network and provide a high-tech basis for internet access.

CAIB, the Austrian investment bank belonging to Bank of Austria, forecasts that the percentage of the region's population with internet access could rise from 6 per cent now to 18 per cent in four years' time. By comparison, the estimated level in the US today is about 40 per cent, but in Italy it is only about 10 per cent.

The success of mobile telephones in the region suggests that east European internet companies – and their international competitors – will overcome their difficulties. In Poland, the Czech Republic, Slovakia, Hungary and Slovenia, the 15 per cent of the population who now use mobile phones are a prime market for internet services. This potential is particularly marked in Hungary, where schools and colleges are connected to the internet via a programme called shulinet.

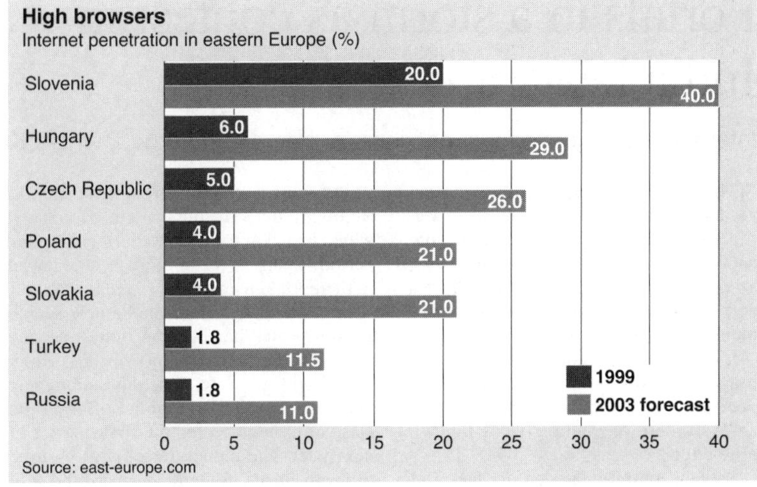

As elsewhere, the main use of the internet today is e-mail-based communication. Online transactions are still rare. But they are growing. Expandia Bank of the Czech Republic claims to be the first bank in the region to offer internet banking.

Even more than in the west, the prospects for business-to-business transactions are brighter than for business-to-consumer. The use of computers at work dwarfs home use. According to IDC, a survey last year of 959 companies in Poland, the Czech Republic, Hungary and Slovakia, revealed that over 53 per cent had web sites.

Salomon Smith Barney, the US investment bank, says the region's telephone utilities are well placed to capitalise from the internet. In Hungary, Matav's Alta Vizsla portal is the market leader. In the Czech Republic it is Cesky Telecom's Internet OnLine. However, in Poland the most popular portals are not Tpsa's but Onet, controlled by Optimus, and Wirtualna Polska, mostly owned by its founder, Centrum Nowych Technologii, a Gdansk high-tech company, and Prokom. Other Wirtualna Polska shareholders include Intel, the US chip maker, and the company is seeking a Nasdaq listing.

Foreign investors are already deeply entrenched in the market through local companies and, increasingly, directly. Tpsa hopes to secure its strategic partner this year. Cesky Telecom has long-term shareholders in KPN of the Netherlands and Swisscom.

Other western groups have invested in local ISPs, such as PSINet of the US, which last year paid (£19.3m) for Elender, Hungary's second- largest portal.

Meanwhile, international telecoms companies such as MCI of the US are attacking the market directly, notably in offering internet-based communication. Inter-national portals are also eyeing the region, including Yahoo! of the US.

As Salomon Smith Barney argues in a report, consolidation is inevitable. International groups will play a big role, as they have in other industries in eastern Europe. But investors are unlikely to ignore the better-established local companies. And as long as the global boom in internet companies lasts, the prices these investors are ready to pay could be attractive – as the Polish treasury has just discovered to its joy.

Additional reporting by Chris Bobinski in Warsaw, Kester Eddy in Budapest and Quentin Reed in Prague

Portals in a storm as contest in India heats up

10 December 1999

Internet groups jostle for subscribers at home and abroad, writes **Krishna Guha**

The race to dominate India's cyberspace has entered a decisive phase. At stake is a glittering prize: leadership of the internet economy in a nation of 1bn people and a booming technology industry. The winner, or winners, may emerge in a few months time.

Last week Satyam Infoway, India's biggest private sector internet service provider, pulled off a deal that many analysts believe could give it the winning edge.

Satyam Infoway agreed to buy India World, the No 2 internet portal company, for Rs5bn ($115m) in cash, using funds raised when it listed on Nasdaq earlier this year.

India World has a portfolio of high-profile web sites, including Khoj, the most popular search engine. These sites are particularly popular with Indians living in the US, because the content includes cricket, news and Indian recipes. In October, India World recorded 13m page views. Satyam Infoway's own portal site, Satyam Online.com, also had close to 13m views, mainly from India itself.

"It is a natural fit," says R. Ramaraj, managing director of Satyam Infoway. "Satyam Online.com focuses on the Indian audience in India. India World's properties focus on the Indian interest audience outside India. We now have a global audience. It gives us leadership in this business."

The merger poses a strong challenge to Rediff, India's leading portal company, which had 29m page views during the same period. Rediff is scrambling to stay ahead in the portal business.

In September, it launched a new search engine, which has become India's second most popular after India World's Khoj. Now Rediff plans to close the funding gap with its own initial public offering on Nasdaq, scheduled for the first quarter of next year. The money raised will be used to ramp up its content business and will give Rediff the option to buy other internet properties.

Rediff has the widest range of India-related content and services today, with a strong news service. But the content divide will narrow sharply when Satyam Infoway integrates its portal site with India World's sites. It is shaping up as a contest between an integrated internet business model and the content-only approach, and as a powerful example of the benefits of first-mover advantage.

Satyam Infoway aims to emulate the success of America Online. Rediff hopes to follow the example of Yahoo!. "We decided that we want to be active in all aspects of the internet: infrastructure, connectivity, content and commerce," says Mr Ramaraj. Satyam Infoway, the first private ISP, has more than 100,000 subscribers.

Mr Ramaraj says the extra content from buying India World would ensure these subscribers stick to Satyam Online.com as their portal site. This would allow the company to build revenues from advertising and e-commerce, even as competition whittles away its subscription fees.

Due to SEC regulations, Rediff is unable to comment on its strategy ahead of next year's listing. But the company is known to stand by its content-only approach, and has been in contact with Satyam Infoway's rival internet service providers.

"No private company will control more than 15 per cent of the internet service market," says an analyst who follows Rediff. "Rediff will provide content and services to the other 85 per cent. Those companies will not want to deal with Satyam Infoway."

Rediff was the first portal company to provide the range of features and services associated with the US "megaportals" and still benefits from early market leadership. But Satyam Infoway, with its stream of subscription revenues, beat both Rediff and its ISP rivals to Nasdaq.

It reaped a publicity bonanza and first choice of potential acquisitions. "It was very important to get to Nasdaq first," says Mr Ramaraj. Others argue that providing Rediff is able to list successfully in the US early next year, it will suffer no lasting disadvantage. "Lycos was the first to list in the US, Yahoo! was second or third," says the analyst who follows

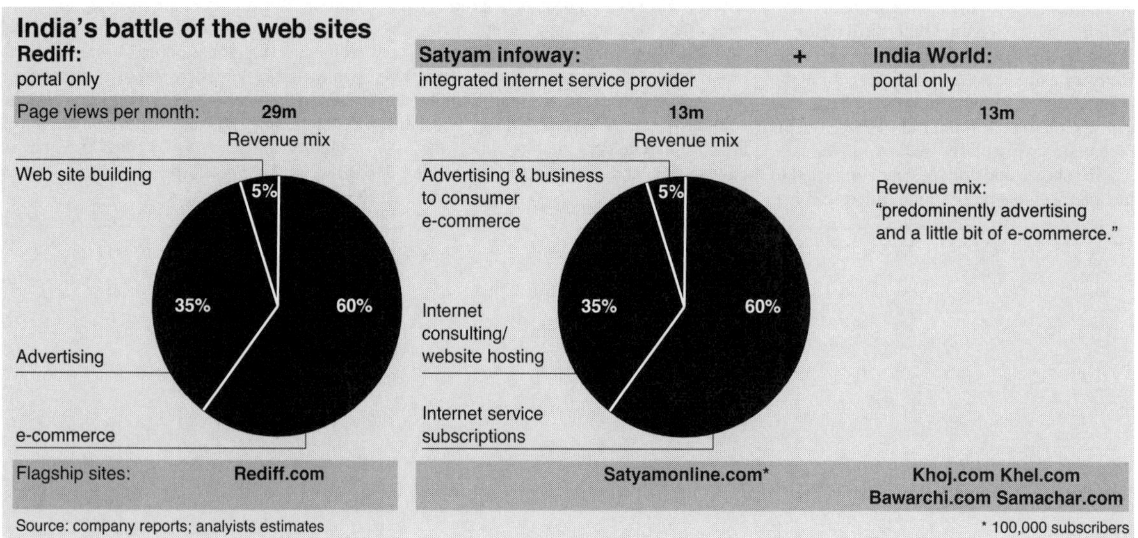

Rediff. "The important thing is to be in the first batch."

Other companies are also jockeying for position in India's cyberspace. These include Bennet Coleman, India's leading print media group; Zee Telefilms, the biggest multimedia company; Bharti, the number two private ISP; and VSNL, the former public sector monopoly that still has the biggest internet subscriber base.

But the betting is that Satyam Infoway or Rediff will emerge as India's dominant portal company. "This is not a market that can sustain 10 players," says Amit Chandra, co-head of investment banking at DSP Merrill Lynch. "India [which has less than 500,000 internet subscribers] will have maximum two megaportals, maybe only one."

Review questions

Develop a conceptual scheme for evaluating the size of the strategic window for a new venture aiming to become a significant (international) player in the Internet advertising market. The scheme should include:

1 Details of the information you require

2 Expected returns from and costs of the information

3 What investigative approaches you would use.

17 Opening the window: gaining commitment

Chapter overview

*The fourth stage in using the strategic window is to **open** it. This means initiating the business and drawing the commitment of stakeholders towards it. This chapter looks at how the venture can enter and establish itself in the business network. In particular the key issues relating to attracting financial and human support are considered.*

17.1 Entering the network

KEY LEARNING OUTCOME
An appreciation of the way in which a new venture redefines the network of relationships that exist within a business community.

Having spotted the window, that is, having identified a new opportunity, and having located and measured the window, that is, having defined and quantified the opportunity, the entrepreneur must then *open* that window. This means initiating the business. Initiation demands that a variety of stakeholders be drawn into the venture. The new venture and the entrepreneur driving it must create a new set of relationships with those stakeholders. Yet, in most instances, those stakeholders will already have relationships with a variety of other (possibly competing) organisations. In effect, starting a new venture means *redefining* the relationships that stakeholders have with third parties and with one another. The new venture must enter an existing network of relationships and, in doing so, modify that network of relationships. If the venture is to enjoy long-term success it must do this in a way which *increases* the overall value of the network to those who make it up.

The relationships in this network are both competitive and collaborative. The entrepreneur must decide on the way these two dynamics are to be complemented and balanced as the network is redefined. This balancing act must be considered in relation to each and every stakeholder and stakeholder group.

Relationship with investors

Investors seek out opportunities to invest. They look for the best returns on the capital they provide, consistent with a certain level of risk. Because capital, like any resource, is both valuable and limited, investors are selective in the investments they choose to support. Investors are less interested in the cost of an investment than its *opportunity cost*: the money that will be lost if an investment is not made *elsewhere*.

Entrepreneurs must compete for the attentions of investors. If an entrepreneur offers an investor an investment opportunity, then they are limiting the possibility for investment in other ventures by that investor. One entrepreneur's success in attracting investment capital will be another's, perhaps many others', failure. This is harsh. Yet, in the long run, this competition generates an overall increase in value for *all* entrepreneurs in two ways. First, by defining opportunity costs it provides a strong signal as to which opportunities are worth pursuing and which are not. Second, by offering investors a good return, it generates the capital that can be used to make further investments.

Relationship with suppliers

To a supplier, an entrepreneurial venture is a potential new customer. At face value this is good since a new customer offers the prospect of new business. However, the new venture may also complicate life for a supplier. The venture may be competing with an existing customer of the supplier. While the venture may be offering the potential for additional business it may also be simply threatening to replace one set of business arrangements with another. The supplier may not always see the entrepreneurial venture as new business. They can also see the costs of gaining one new (and untried) customer only to face the risks of losing an established one. Suppliers prefer entrepreneurs who intend to expand a market, rather than just to replace existing producers within it.

If the business is characterised by close and strong relationships between supplier and customer then that relationship may be strained if the supplier is called upon to provide for a customer's competitor. While in many economies a strong legal framework exists to ensure that trading is free and fair and that strong customers do not coerce weaker suppliers, and *vise-versa* this is not always the case. Even if a strong legal framework exists, informal agreements and expectations can still be influential.

In short, when approaching suppliers the entrepreneur must be conscious not only of the new business they are offering them but also of the way the relationship they are proposing to build will affect the existing relationships the supplier enjoys. New business may not always be as attractive as it first appears!

Relationship with employees

Entrepreneurial ventures can only be progressed if the right human skills are in place. They demand productive labour, technical knowledge, business insight and leadership.

Human inputs are traded in markets. Some categories of human skill may be in short supply. If this is the case the entrepreneur may have to compete to get hold of them. This competition takes the form of offering potential employees attractive remuneration packages and prospects for development.

If one entrepreneur employs an individual with a skill which is valuable and in short supply then another cannot employ that individual. More critically perhaps, it is likely that the entrepreneur will attract such a person from an existing business. Most would agree that individuals should have the right to offer their skills and insight to whomsoever they wish. Furthermore, the demand for people with rare talents, reflected by the rewards they are offered, provides an incentive for others to develop those skills.

In practice, however, individuals do not market themselves as commodities within a 'perfect' labour market. They build close relationships with the organisations for which they work. People are motivated by more than just the financial rewards of working. The 'contracts' individuals have with their organisations go beyond the simple terms of the formal written contract of employment. They involve unwritten, often unarticulated, expectations and loyalties on both sides.

As a consequence, while an entrepreneur seeking to attract an employee from a competitor is a proper functioning of the labour market, it can also be seen in negative terms as a kind of illegitimate 'poaching'. This can be traumatic and cause ill-feeling, particularly when the business community is close knit and the employee is felt to be offering not just their general experience, skills and insights but also insider knowledge to a competitor. Some employers use formal contractual devices to restrict the movement of employees in possession of sensitive knowledge to competitors.

While the entrepreneur should never feel ashamed at offering individuals a good reward for the skills and talents they have invested in creating for themselves, the effective entrepreneur must be sensitive to the human dimension of the business they are operating in and its rules when recruiting people. More often than not these rules about what is acceptable and unacceptable in recruitment practice are unwritten.

Relationship with customers

Customers are a key stakeholder group for the entrepreneur. It is their interest in what the venture offers and their willingness to pay for it, that ultimately provides the money which the entrepreneurial venture will use to reward all its stakeholder groups. The best way to attract the interest of customers is to provide them with goods and services which *genuinely* satisfy their needs, solve their problems and meet their aspirations.

A customer will not usually have a need which is both explicit and completely unsatisfied. Rarely will the entrepreneur be offering the customer something which they need in addition to everything else they consume. It is much more likely that they will be offering something that will *replace* something else they are using. In short, even an innovative entrepreneurial business will be competing with the potential customer's existing suppliers. Suppliers and their customers do not relate solely through the medium of a market. They also interact at a human level via the business network. In some instances this relationship may be trivial. In many, however, the relationship is far-reaching, deeply established and complex. The relationship may not be sustained by economic self-interest alone but also by friendship and trust.

When a new venture approaches a customer, it is asking not only that the customer buy the offering, but also that they stop buying, or replace the offering provided by a competitor. The success of the selling approach will depend on more than the way the entrepreneur's offering competes against the one they seek to oust. The wider relationship they seek to end and the new one they offer to replace it will also be important. If the entrepreneur is to be successful in marketing and selling his or her products and services to customers they must consider not just the product or service, but also the nature of the individual and organisational relationships that exist between customer and supplier in the marketplace. The entrepreneur must be prepared to create more rewarding relationships. This point will be developed further in section 18.1.

When starting their ventures entrepreneurs are not just offering their product or service into a melée of short-term market exchanges. They are breaking and then reforming a pattern of relationships. Those relationships are governed by rules, some formal, some informal, some based on self-interest, and others governed by altruistic motives. Some are articulated openly, while others are not even recognised – until they are lost. Effective entrepreneurs understand those relationships, and the rules that govern them, so that they can successfully manage their position within the network. This is not to say the entrepreneur should not occasionally break the rules, but they should be aware that they *are* breaking the rules and know *why* they are doing it.

17.2 Gaining financial investment: key issues

KEY LEARNING OUTCOME

A recognition of the main issues associated with attracting financial investment to the new venture.

An entrepreneur will be interested in obtaining a variety of different resources in order to progress his or her venture. However, it is money that is likely to take first place on the list of priorities. This is understandable. Money is the most liquid of resources. Once it has been obtained it can be used readily to obtain the other things the business needs.

Attracting investment capital is one of the primary functions of the entrepreneur. It is a process that raises a number of critical issues. The entrepreneur must consider these issues carefully and make some fundamental decisions in relation to them. This section will examine the issues in overview. They will be expanded upon in Chapter 19.

What level of investment is required?

Broadly, how much money will be needed to start the venture? This will of course depend on the nature of the venture, the opportunity it is pursuing, the stage in its development and the plans the entrepreneur has for the future. Initial investment levels are sensitive to the strategy the business is pursuing, in terms of the initial scope the business must have and the potential this leaves for growth. Some ventures can start on a small scale and build up over time. Anita Roddick started The Body Shop with a single outlet and a loan of £4000. The business grew as new outlets were added incrementally over time. On the other hand, when Frederick Smith started the US air freight business, Federal Express, he realised that if the business was to work he needed to offer customers a full service from the start. That meant acquiring a fleet of aircraft and a relatively large administrative and support structure. He sought $90 million of start-up financing.

Where is the investment to come from?

While there is an overall 'market for capital', there are a number of sources of investment capital. For example, the entrepreneur's own funds, bank loans, government loans, venture capital, share issues, business angels (experienced manager–investors who offer their expertise to new ventures along with capital), and so on. In other words, the market for capital is a fragmented one. Different capital providers occupy different niches in the market. They are characterised by the way they look for different types of investment opportunity, accept different levels of risk, expect different types of return and assume different levels of involvement in the running of the venture. To be effective in managing the project of attracting funds the entrepreneur must understand these different markets and the way in which they work.

What is the capital structure of the investment to be?

The *capital structure* of the venture is simply the mix of different investment sources that are used. In broad terms it refers to the ratio of 'equity' to 'debt' capital, that is, the mix of investors who expect a return that will be linked to the performance of the venture to those who expect a fixed return based on an agreed interest rate whatever the performance of the business. In addition, loan capital may be unsecured or secured against some assets of the business.

The capital structure of the venture reflects the way in which the entrepreneur is sharing risk with the investors. Clearly a secured loan exposes the investor to a lower level of risk than an equity share. At the same time, capital which exposes the investor to risk is more expensive than capital which does not. So by adjusting the capital structure entrepreneurs can, in effect, 'sell off' the risks inherent in their venture to different degrees.

How will the investors be approached?

Entrepreneurs and investors need to get in touch with each other before they can work together. Usually, the onus is on the entrepreneur to initiate the contact. That contact must be managed. While investors try to make rational decisions about investment opportunities they are not calculating machines. They are still human beings who are influenced by *how* things are said as well as *what* is said and first impressions are important. The way in which the entrepreneur first approaches the potential investor can have a bearing on the outcome of that contact. In essence, three things must be considered: the *who* of the contact, the *how* of the contact and the *what* of the contact.

First, the entrepreneur must identify suitable sources of investment. That is, *who* to contact. This involves identifying organisations that provide investment capital. However, organisations do not make decisions, *individuals* do and the entrepreneur may find it productive to find out which individual or individuals they should approach within the organisation. They may also consider the decision-making structure within the organisation, i.e. not only who actually takes the investment decisions but who influences them in that decision and the way in which their decisions are policed and judged within the organisation.

Second, the entrepreneur must consider the *how* of the contact. Should it be formal or informal? Does the investor lay down a procedure for making contact? (Most banks and venture capital companies, for example, do.) Does the investor expect a written proposal or a verbal one in the first instance? If it is verbal, do they expect a one-to-one chat or a full-blown presentation? If it is a written one, do they lay down a format for the proposal or do they give the entrepreneur latitude in the way they communicate? Many investors will simply reject a proposal out of hand if they are not approached in the right way.

Third, they must consider *what* to tell the investor. At the first contact stage, attracting the investor's attention and encouraging their interest is likely to be as important as giving them information. This will be particularly so if the investor is receiving a large number of approaches. Is it necessary to relate a detailed picture or will a broad outline be more effective? How much room for manoeuvre is there here if the communication has to comply with a set format?

What proposition is to be made to the investors?

The entrepreneur must consider what, exactly, they are offering the investor. Some of the critical dimensions here are:

- the amount of investment required;
- how that particular investment fits with the overall investment profile for the venture;
- the nature of the investment (e.g. loan or equity, secured or unsecured);
- the level of return anticipated;
- the nature (particularly the *liquidity*) of any security being offered;
- the degree of risk to which the capital will be exposed;
- the way 'in', i.e. how the investment will be made (what amount of money at what time); and
- the way 'out', i.e. how the investor will get their return (what amount of money at what time);
- the degree of *control* the investor will be given over (or be expected to contribute to) the way the venture is run.

These things constitute the 'package' that the entrepreneur is offering to the investor. It is on the basis of these factors that investors will make their judgement as to whether the investment opportunity is of the right sort for them. The entrepreneur must never forget that they are *selling* the venture to investors. The entrepreneur must put as much effort into this selling exercise as he or she would do in selling the business's products to customers.

17.3 Gaining human commitment

KEY LEARNING OUTCOME
An appreciation of how the commitment of key people to the venture may be gained.

On its own investment capital can achieve nothing. It must be used by *people* to progress the venture. The money obtained by one entrepreneur is exactly the same as the money obtained by another and, indeed, exactly like that held by established businesses. If an entrepreneurial venture is successful then it must be because its people do something *different* and *better* with the money to which they have access.

While it is conventional in management theory to talk of human beings as a 'resource' it should always be remembered that they are a *special* type of resource. There is more to gaining human commitment than simply bringing people into the business. They must certainly be attracted to the venture in the first instance. Once in, their motivation and dedication must be maintained and constantly developed. The entrepreneur does not just *recruit* to their venture, they must also *lead* it.

The entrepreneur faces a number of decisions in relation to developing the commitment other people have towards the venture.

What human skills are required?

Businesses need a variety of different types of human input. Technical skills, communication skills, functional skills and analytical skills are all critically important to the success of a venture. Different ventures need different mixes of these skills in order to progress. The entrepreneur must decide what profile of skills and experience is right for their venture as it stands now, and what profile will be needed as it grows and develops. In light of the fact that human resources are as likely to be scarce as any other, this may mean prioritising some requirements over others.

Where will those skills be obtained from?

Where are the people with those skills? Are they working for other organisations? If so are they working for competitors or for non-competitors? If they are working for competitors what issues will recruiting them raise?

What will be offered to attract those who have the skills?

In the first instance, this means pay and other aspects of the remuneration package. The entrepreneur must offer a package which is competitive in light of what other employers are offering. But pay is not the entirety of what an organisation offers an employee. Human needs go beyond purely financial concerns. It is critical to ask what the venture offers people as a stage on which to build social relationships. Is it a friendly environment? Will it be fun to work for? Further, what does the venture offer in the way of potential for self-development? How can people progress within it as it expands? What roles will they play? How does the venture represent a theatre for personal growth?

An entrepreneurial venture must compete for people not just with other entrepreneurial ventures but also with established organisations. The venture offers potential employees much the same thing that it presents to financial investors, that is, risk but with the promise of higher returns. The employee is exposed to the chance of the venture failing. However, there may also be the possibility of much higher rewards in the way of personal development, experience and achievement. Of course, financial investors and employees draw upon quite different mechanisms to manage risk and their exposure to it.

The entrepreneur must be aware of why the option of working for a dynamic, fast-changing, fast-growing organisation might be attractive (and why it might be unattractive) to potential employees.

How will potential employees be contacted?

People must be recruited. There are a variety of means for doing this. In the first instance personal contact and word of mouth can be very productive. If this is not possible then a more formal means of recruiting is called for. This may demand advertising (say, in a specialist press). It may even be felt expedient to delegate the task of attracting people to a specialist recruitment agency.

How will potential employees be evaluated?

Having contacted and attracted the interest of potential employees, then some evaluation and selection procedure must be invoked. Taking on a new employee represents a major commitment for both the business and the employee. Any effort expended in ensuring that the person is right for the organisation, and that the organisation is right for the person, at the recruitment stage, is likely to pay dividends. Mistakes can be expensive and painful for both parties. This is not just a process of ensuring that the person has the right technical skills but also that their attitudes and approach will fit with the organisation's approach, values and culture. However, the entrepreneur should be careful: there is strength in diversity!

If the entrepreneur knows a potential employee well, and has experience of the way in which they work, then the recruitment process may be quite informal (often little more than a job offer over a drink). If they are not acquainted with the person (and the contribution they might make) then at least some sort of interview is required. Some would go further and ask for some sort of *psychometric* or *attitudinal* testing. Of course, these tools exist to aid the entrepreneur is making recruitment decisions. They cannot make them on their own!

Should a skill be in-house or should it be hired when necessary?

Resources are scarce in the entrepreneurial venture. The entrepreneur must make the resources they have work hard. One question they should always ask when faced with the need for a particular human skill is whether it is best to bring that skill in-house, i.e. to recruit someone to perform the task or it is better to use an external agency to provide it. So should the business employ a financial expert or call on the assistance of a firm of accountants? Should it take on research and development staff or delegate a project to a university?

The 'employ or hire' decision is influenced by a variety of factors. How much of a particular skill input is required? Over what timescale will it be required? Will the business have a long-term need for it? How much control does the entrepreneur need over the person contributing that skill? How much will it cost to employ someone versus hiring them?

It may often appear that the hiring option is the more expensive. However, this expense needs to be considered in the light of the costs of recruitment. There are also risks associated with bringing someone new in to the business. What contribution will they *really* make? How will he or she fit? How will existing employees get along with them? Further, hiring someone tends to add to the business's marginal costs whereas employing them adds to fixed costs. Hiring may be more attractive from a cash-flow point of view especially when the venture's output may be variable and unpredictable. In light of this, in general, employment should only be considered when there is a clear, consistent, long-term need for a particular skill or a particular expertise within the business.

The way the business will gain from the additional level of control that comes from having the skill in-house should also be considered. If the business aims to develop a competitive advantage based on knowledge and an ability to use it to deliver value to the customer then it goes without saying that this knowledge should be held by people who are dedicated to the business.

Leadership and motivation strategy

Commitment is not just given, it must be maintained. In this the entrepreneur must be conscious of their own leadership and motivational strategy and the way they use it to bring out the best in their people. Developing and applying this strategy takes practice. The entrepreneur is the venture's key human resource. The skill they provide comes from being able to manage vision and to use it to lead the organisation.

Summary of key ideas

- The fourth stage in the strategic window is *opening it*.
- Opening the window means gaining the *commitment* of stakeholders and actually starting the venture.
- The key commitments are financial support from *investors*; productive support from *employees* and *network contacts*; agreements to provide inputs by *suppliers*; and agreement to purchase outputs by *customers*.

Suggestions for further reading

Cook, W.M. (1992) 'The buddy system', *Entrepreneur*, Nov, p. 52.

Gartner, W.B. (1984) *Problems in Business Start-up: The relationships among entrepreneurial skills and problem identification for different types of new venture,* Babson, Wellesley Park, MA: The Centre for Entrepreneurial Studies.

Hall, W.K. (1980) 'Survival strategies in a hostile environment', *Harvard Business Review,* July-Aug, pp. 75–85.

Schoch, S. (1984) 'Access to capital', *Venture,* June, p. 106.

Selected case material

Fading high-tech stars

6 June 1998

Some of the shine has gone from the sector that has driven US economic and stock market growth. But, say **Richard Waters** and **Louise Kehoe**, all is by no means lost

Even General Electric, the world's most valuable company, sometimes copies its best ideas from others. When it wanted to find a way to boost quality, GE turned to Motorola, a pioneer in driving quality problems from its manufacturing processes. It was a fanatical pursuit of perfection that helped make Motorola, a maker of portable telephones, pagers and semiconductors, one of the world's most admired companies.

But Motorola has fallen on hard times. The company has just announced one of the biggest retrenchments seen from a US company in recent years. One in 10 jobs are to go – 15,000 in all. These are the sort of headlines once associated with metal-benders like General Motors, rather than stars of the technology revolution. Motorola's problems have a lot to do with a high-flying company that has lost its way. But there have been signs elsewhere in the technology sector recently that all is not well.

Intel, the dominant supplier of microprocessor chips for personal computers, has been struggling to maintain its momentum in the face of tumbling prices. Its shares have gone nowhere over the past 12 months – after a decade in which they soared by an average 35 per cent a year. Even Microsoft (average increase: 45 per cent) has stuttered: its shares have dropped nearly 15 per cent from a record high in the weeks after the Department of Justice launched an antitrust case against the company.

Are these indications of broader problems in the technology industry? This is a question of general significance to the US stock market and economy. Increased spending on PCs and other technology equipment and services has accounted for the lion's share of US economic growth in the 1990s. Tech companies have been among the main engines behind the long rise in US share prices. If a slowdown in the technology sector is coming, will the bull market lose one of its most important supports?

The signs so far suggest that, while the pressure on some parts of the industry is acute, the overall damage may remain limited. Nevertheless, the tech sector's problems are likely to weigh on the stock market for some months, after having contributed to recent volatility on Wall Street. Some recent stars of the sector, such as Motorola, may find themselves sidelined as the baton of growth passes to other companies and other segments of the industry.

At the root of the tech industry's broader problems in recent months has been a collapse in the price of its most basic component: the semiconductor. This has been felt most acutely in the market for memory chips, known as D-Rams, but has also infected the microprocessors on which companies such as Intel rely. There is nothing new in falling chip prices. Indeed, the availability of ever-increasing computing power at ever-lower prices has been one of the driving forces behind the rise of the PC.

However, the semiconductor and PC makers have, since early this year, been going through one of those periodic phases when the virtuous circle of falling prices and rising demand is disrupted. The result can be seen in the gloomy outlook hanging over worldwide chip sales.

Until last autumn, the Semiconductor Industry Association was expecting the industry's revenues to grow by nearly 17 per cent this year. Progressive revisions have now left it predicting a decline in sales for the year of 1.8 per cent, compared with growth of 4 per cent last year.

There are several reasons. One lies in the economic collapse in Asia, where some US computer companies have already become more reliant than many longer-established multinationals. At the same time, some of the biggest manufacturers have been caught out by their own failure to spot the sudden popularity of lower-priced PCs in the US.

While demand has been shifting, supply has been soaring. Both chipmakers and the PC companies have been caught in this squeeze, with a glut of computers and components like semiconductors clogging the market since early this year.

For Intel, which has always thrived amid the tumbling prices that would destroy companies in other industries, this has come as an unpleasant shock. It failed to lead the move into lower-priced machines and has now been left in the unfamiliar position of trying to catch up. The company's gross profit margin, which peaked at 60 per cent last year, slipped to 54 per cent in the first quarter of this year and is likely to decline a further "few percentage points" in the current quarter, the company says.

These are the sort of profit margins companies in other industries would kill for. Not in the tech sector. And things could get worse. To boost its sales, Intel is expected to cut prices next week – a departure from its regular quar-

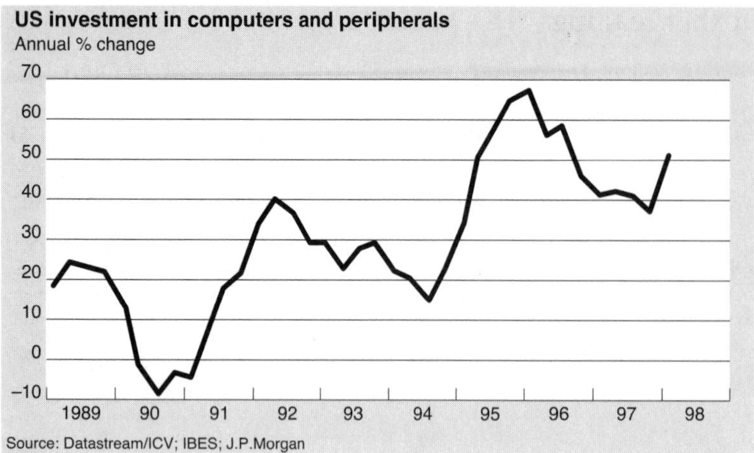

terly price adjustments.

Faced with these sorts of pressures, the computer industry is looking to an old standby to lift it: the one-two of a new operating system from Microsoft and a new generation of chips from Intel. Windows 98, due out later this month, may not represent the same sort of leap forward driven by Windows 95. However, most analysts on Wall Street still expect it to give a lift to PC sales in the second half of this year, just as the worst of the inventory glut recedes.

In the meantime, the PC industry will have to deal with the same issues faced by companies in other, more mature markets: a battle for market share and a consolidation among weaker companies in an effort to support profit margins. For the stock market, these forces should prove generally positive.

This is already evident among PC makers. According to Dataquest, the four largest producers – Compaq, IBM, Dell and Hewlett-Packard – increased their combined market share of PC sales from 28 per cent in the first quarter of 1997 to 34 per cent of this year.

The pressure to remain among the leaders is likely to get even more intense. Dell, which has pioneered a lean manufacturing and distribution approach that has cut its inventory levels to virtually zero and enabled it to undercut its rivals shows no signs of letting up. Last year's darling, Compaq, has fallen by the wayside as investors have stampeded over to Dell as a result.

While the computer and semiconductor companies struggle with these pressures, many other parts of the technology sector are thriving. If the desk-top PC drove the industry's growth in the 1990s, equipment and services that link PCs together will be one of the growth markets of the next decade.

That has given rise to a new generation of technology stars. Cisco Systems, which supplies much of the routing and switching equipment that holds the internet together, has seen its shares nearly double over the past year, making it one of the 20 biggest US companies in terms of stock market value. Lucent Technologies, a communications equipment company that was an arm of AT&T until two years ago, has ridden its success to a stock market value of nearly $100bn – considerably more than its former parent.

The growth in capacity of telephone networks is beginning to resemble the growth in processing power that has been seen in the desk-top computer. And, as with the PC, there is no obvious limit to the demand for more bandwidth, provided prices keep falling fast.

Software companies also stand to benefit from the plunging cost of desk-top computing power and the arrival of the internet. That has made start-ups like Yahoo! some of the hottest technology stocks on Wall Street: smaller software companies have seen their shares rise by an average of 50 per cent over the past year, according to analysts at J.P. Morgan.

Microsoft, the giant of the software industry, has also succeeded in hitching its fortunes to the internet bandwagon after a late start. Its prospects have been clouded in recent weeks by its head-on collision with the justice department. But for now, the message implied by the small pull-back in the company's share price is hardly alarming: the anti-trust suit may hang over the company for some time, but it will do little to break the company's position at the centre of the software industry.

All of this suggests that, short of a much sharper slowdown in PC sales, the outlook should remain generally positive for technology stocks – though not all companies, or parts of the industry, will benefit equally.

As Ed Yardeni, chief economist at Deutsche Securities in New York and one of the early proponents of the rise of technology stocks, says: "The secular trend is firmly in place: we're all very dependent on technology."

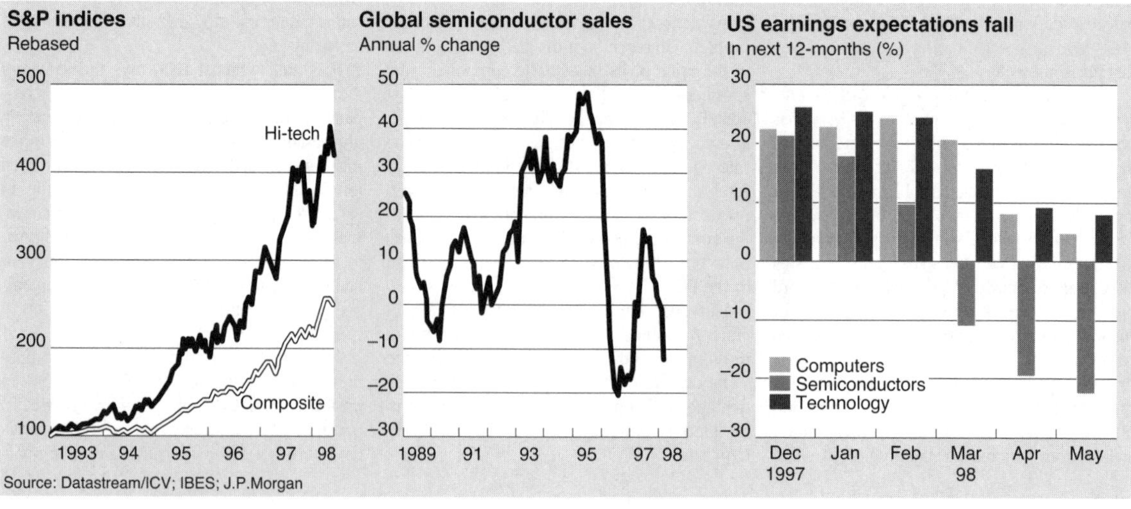

Charting a course to leadership

9 December 1999

21 Invest is raising £174m to purchase controlling stakes in mid-sized companies, says **Katharine Campbell**

As you enter 21 Invest's gracious London offices in Mayfair, you cannot help noticing the marine art – paintings of classic racing yachts line every wall.

Visiting Italian and Spanish clients want to think they are in an English merchant bank, explains managing director Andrea Bonomi, whose grandfather started the collection. "So it was a case of boats or horses".

21 Invest is no bank, but rather a private equity house proud of its multicultural adaptability.

Hitherto deploying the funds of the Benetton and Bonomi families, it is turning to outside investors for the first time as it raises €275m (£174m), of which €50m will come from 21 Invest, to buy majority stakes in mid-sized companies in southern Europe.

Fluent in Italian, Spanish, French and English, and surrounded by a more or less equally polyglot team, Mr Bonomi says the operation, started in 1992, has reached "cruising altitude" at the right moment.

Susan Lloyd of Susan Lloyd Associates, the fund's European placement agent, says that institutional investors are "full-up" with large pan-European buy-out funds.

Mr Bonomi adds that it is his good fortune that many of the established Anglo-Saxon firms are concentrating on large deals. "The leadership of the mid-market is up for grabs," he says.

That is something of an ambitious goal, and pits 21 Invest against established participants such as 3i, while newcomers including Palamon Capital Partners are very much alive to the possibilities of southern Europe.

Getting anywhere near that target will also require 21 Invest to establish its institutional credentials – shedding its reputation as a poorly understood grouping of family interests.

While built on money from the Benetton and Bonomi families, 21 Invest never in fact represented a strategic move into private equity by those groupings. Instead it came about because Alessandro Benetton, Luciano Benetton's son, and Mr Bonomi had both independently decided they wished to make their mark outside their powerful family groups.

Mr Benetton, who now chairs 21 Invest, established 21, Investimenti (21 denoting the new century) in 1992 – a private equity vehicle controlled by the Benetton family. Mr Bonomi, meanwhile, had set up Invest, also in private equity. The two outfits came together in 1994.

The track record to date is good – if relatively limited. Since 1992, the operation has backed 13 companies, involving total equity of €274m, more than half syndicated to other private equity firms. Over 90 per cent of the portfolio has been sold, and, unusually, there have been no losses or write-downs.

Two of the group's most successful investments are Grupo Picking Pack, a Spanish company built into a leader in the reprographic services sector and Basic Net, the Italian sportswear business behind the Kappa soccer brand, which has just floated in Milan.

Other transactions include Karrimor, the UK outdoor goods supplier, which was sold in February to Cullinan Holdings of the US. The group is in discussions about buying a stake in Formula One Administration.

Mr Bonomi says the investment philosophy has been refined over recent years. The group has learnt to shun small deals – "taking minority stakes in small companies in southern Europe is a no-go zone." It is the easiest market to enter – but the most difficult from which to extract a return.

21 Invest sets out to distinguish itself from other financial buyers by its industrial approach.

"We take an industrial view. The secret is to buy the right assets. We've done all the other mistakes – overpaying, getting the wrong management, calling the cycle slightly wrong. What you mustn't do is make an industrial mistake."

The "right assets" will often be what Mr Bonomi calls "mid-size pretender brands," of which Kappa is a typical example.

They have the makings of a European or a world class brand, but are "inherently fragile if you don't do something with them. What they want is cash." The Anglo-Saxon preoccupation with "succession issues" as the big opportunity for private equity investment is largely misguided, he thinks.

"These companies need help to make it across Europe. It is nothing to do with generational change."

The question is whether the young Bonomi and Benetton generation can build a firm that becomes a real player in helping spur those developments.

Plagued by frenzy and ignorance

20 March 2000

Victoria Griffith assesses the biotech sector's recent rollercoaster ride

On March 4, a visitor to a Labpuppy.com chat room posted the following message: "(Rumour has it that) none other than Tony Blair and William J Clinton are intending Celera to be the global genetic bank, storing ALL genetic data."

The frenzy around biotechnology stocks has caused their prices to soar. In what seems a reprise of the buzz surrounding internet shares, investors trade tips online and comb the news for relevant announcements.

Even after last week's correction, the Nasdaq index for the industry was up nearly 40 per cent for the year.

Valuations rival the dotcoms. Biotechnology groups, if they have any earnings at all, trade at astronomical price/earnings ratios. Genentech is valued at more than 200 times earnings, Immunex at 700 times earnings, and Millennium Pharmaceuticals at a whopping 17,175 times.

Share prices are – at least in part – being driven by daytraders and momentum investors who have nothing but the vaguest understanding of the companies they are buying. "There are certainly momentum investors in this market," says Kevin Starr, chief financial officer of Millennium. "That means we can't get too elated with rapid run-ups or too disappointed with falls."

A few facts. First, Mr Blair and Mr Clinton had no intention of making the genomics company Celera into a "global genetic bank". Data from the Human Genome Project, an international initiative funded by a number of governments, has always planned to make its information public; indeed, that is why it was created.

This certainly presents no threat to genomics companies, which have known for over a decade that this would be the case.

They plan to make money on other things: software to help scientists make sense of the genetic code, or expanded information about specific genes.

Celera has always said it would follow the same path. Yet in February, investors and competitors began to suspect the company had other plans. So when Mr Clinton and Mr Blair said the human genome would be public information, investors punished the stock. After driving the price of Celera up from $7 last June to $276 a few weeks ago, it was knocked back to a close of $129 on Friday.

The Clinton-Blair announcement was actually welcomed by the biotechnology sector. Yet sellers unloaded biotechnology stocks indiscriminately.

Yet biotechnology managers also find the shift confusing. "I can't be too critical of momentum investors, because they've given us so much money," says Joshua Boger, chief executive of Vertex Pharmaceuticals, which makes an important Aids drug. "But they clearly misunderstood the Clinton-Blair announcement last week. Because many biotech investors have little clue what they are investing in, observers speculate that a bubble has built up in the sector. Some of the interest has been in companies with strong products and pipelines: groups like Immunex, Biogen and Genentech. But money has also poured into start-ups with little more than an idea, and into genomics companies who may or may not find strong demand for their drug development programmes.

Analysts say the gap between pharmaceutical companies and biotechnology groups has become unsustainable. The share price differentials mimic those between bricks & mortar and online businesses.

Just a few weeks ago, for instance, the market capitalisation of Immunex was $35bn while that of the pharmaceutical group Pharmacia & Upjohn was less than $30bn. "That obviously doesn't make sense," says Sergio Traversa of research firm Mehta Partners.

Biotechnology has become one more example of the battle between the old and new economy companies. Last week, that gap closed, somewhat. Pharmaceutical groups swung up while biotech companies shifted down. Yet, like dotcoms, biotech remains red hot.

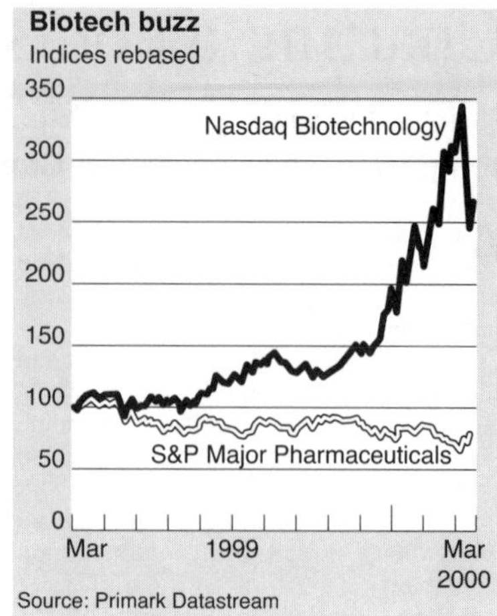

Where this will lead no one knows, but the events of last week show that biotech carries its own particular risks. Some groups may never come up with a viable product, and the science that determines the sector's success is too esoteric for lay people to understand.

Review questions

How might the entrepreneur take account of the fluctuations in market-assessed value for their sector when relating the venture to:

1 Venture capitalists

2 Small investors buying stock

3 Potential employees

4 Customers?

(*Hint*: Consider how the expectations of each stakeholder group and the outcomes of the venture might be influenced by market valuation for the venture.)

18 Closing the window: sustaining competitiveness

Chapter overview

The final stage in using the strategic window metaphor is to ***close*** *it. This means giving the venture some unique and valuable character so that competitors cannot follow through the window and exploit the opportunity it has identified as well. The concept of* ***competitive advantage*** *is introduced, what it is, how it can be established and how it can be maintained is considered.*

18.1 Long-term success and sustainable competitive advantage

KEY LEARNING OUTCOME
An appreciation of how business success is dependent on creating, developing and sustaining competitive advantage in the marketplace.

Having opened the strategic window by gaining financial and human commitment to the venture the entrepreneur must ensure that the long-term potential for success is not eroded by competitors moving in. Entrepreneurs must close the strategic windows to limit the possibility of competitors following them and exploiting the opportunity as well.

The notion of *sustainable competitive advantage* provides a powerful conceptual approach to recognising the ways in which the strategic window can be closed to help guarantee long-term success in the marketplace. It provides an insight into the decisions that must be made in order to keep the business in a position where it can compete effectively. Competitive advantage is a central pillar of strategic thinking which has been developed by Professor Michael Porter (1985) in particular.

It is important to distinguish between a *competitive advantage,* which must be understood in terms of what the business offers to the marketplace and the *source* of that competitive advantage which relates to how the business is set up to deliver that offering to the marketplace. Business life is, by definition, competitive. A particular competitive advantage may be imitated, in which case it loses its value. If a business is to enjoy a competitive advantage over the long term it must be one which competitors find difficult, and in business that means *expensive*, to copy. Consequently, a full delivery of competitive advantage demands decisions at three levels (see Fig. 18.1):

1 what will be offered to the marketplace that is unique and valuable – the *competitive advantage*;
2 how that offering will be maintained by the business – the *source* of the competitive advantage; and
3 how that competitive advantage will be protected from imitation by competitors – the way it will be *sustained*.

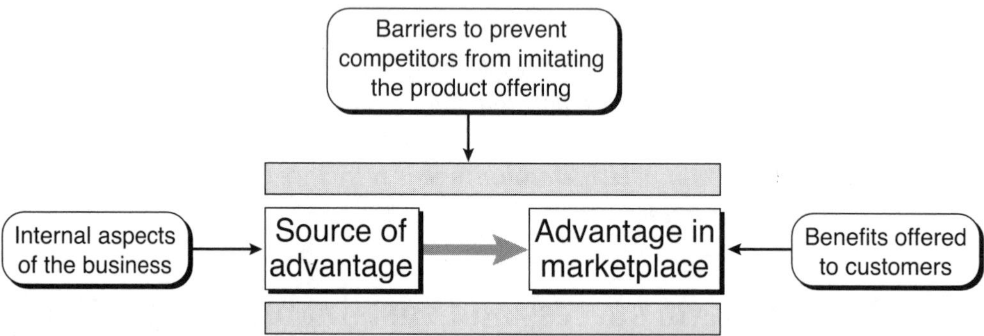

Fig. 18.1 The structure of competitive advantage

Competitive advantage

Competitive advantage is located in what is offered to the marketplace. A competitive advantage is present if the business consistently offers the customer something which is *different* from what competitors are offering, and that difference represents something *valuable* for the customer. In short, a competitive advantage is the reason why customers spend their money with one business rather than another.

The entrepreneur must decide what type of competitive advantage they aim to pursue. Some of the more critical include:

- offering the customer a *lower price*, that is, better value for money;
- differentiating the offering through its *features* or *performance*, that is, an offering which satisfies needs or solves problems for its customers better than a competitor's product does;
- differentiating the offering through *service*, that is, addressing needs or solving problems in a more effective way, or supporting the use of the product more effectively;
- differentiating the offering through *branding*, that is, through investment in communicating quality and the business's commitment to the offering;

- differentiating the offering through *brand imagery*, that is, by building in associations which address social and self-developmental needs as well as functional needs;
- differentiating through *access* and *distribution*, that is, by giving the customer easier, more convenient, less disruptive or less time-consuming access to the offering.

The source of competitive advantage

Being able to *consistently* offer something different and meaningful in the ways described above will only occur if the business is itself different from its competitors in some way. A competitive advantage in the marketplace must be delivered from within the business and be supported by it.

The English academic Professor John Kay has developed a perspective on competitive advantage which sees it as having its source in one of four distinct capabilities:

1 the *architecture* of the business, that is, its internal structure;
2 the *reputation* of the business, that is, the way key stakeholders view it;
3 the way the business *innovates*, that is, its ability to come up with new and valuable ideas; and
4 the business's *strategic assets*, that is, valuable assets to which it has access and its competitors do not.

These four distinctive capabilities are quite general and apply to all businesses. They can be related to four specific sources of competitive advantage for the entrepreneurial venture making its presence felt in the marketplace. These are: *costs, knowledge, relationships* and *structure.*

Cost sources

The business may enjoy an advantage due to lower costs. In economic terms this means that the business will be able to *add value* more efficiently. Cost advantages may be gained from four key areas:

- *Lower input costs* – The business may have access to input factors which are cheaper than those available to competitors. This can include raw materials, energy or labour. Lower input costs can be gained by a number of means. Particularly important are access to unique sources of inputs (say, through special contractual arrangements or from geographic location) and achieving buying power over suppliers.

- *Economies of scale* – A business must dilute its fixed costs (which are independent of output) over revenues (which are dependent on output). Hence, *unit* costs tend to fall as output increases. Fixed costs are those which must be borne regardless of the output achieved. These typically include 'head office' costs and often much of the marketing, sales and development activity. A larger output means that these costs are being used more productively. It may then give a business an overall cost advantage over competitors.

- *Experience curve economies* – Experience curve economies are a consequence of the business learning how to generate its outputs. As a business gains experience in adding value the cost of adding that value is reduced. In short, practice pays! A large number of studies over a variety of different industries has found that a strict mathematical relationship holds between unit cost and output experience. This relationship is exponential. That is, costs fall by a fixed amount every time output is doubled. This means that for a linear output, the cost reductions achieved in a particular time period are seen to fall off as time goes on. This exponential relationship is shown in Fig. 18.2.

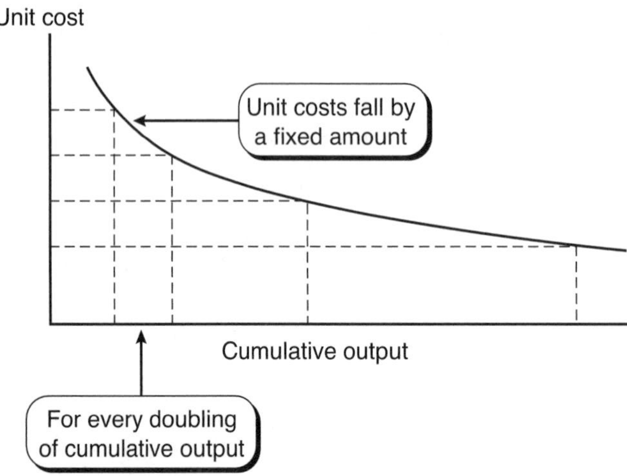

Fig. 18.2 The experience curve: costs fall exponentially as experience is gained

Like economies of scale, experience curve economies are related to output. However, the two should not be confused. Whereas economies of scale depend on output in a particular *period*, experience curve economies are a result of *cumulative* output. In general, the firm with the highest cumulative output in a market will be in a position to have developed the lowest unit cost. Most studies of experience curve economies have concentrated on production costs. However, the principle is a general one and applies to any cost of adding value. So experience curve economies may be sought in other parts of the firm's value addition process such as sales, marketing, procurement, etc.

- *Technological innovation* – A firm's costs are, technically, the cost of adding a particular amount of value to an input in order to create a saleable output. Costs are related to the technology used by the business to add value. A technological innovation can provide a cost advantage by enabling value to be added more efficiently. In practice a technological innovation can be used to 'reset' the experience curve at a lower level (see Fig. 18.3). Such innovation often relates to production technology but in principle it can apply to any value adding activity within the organisation.

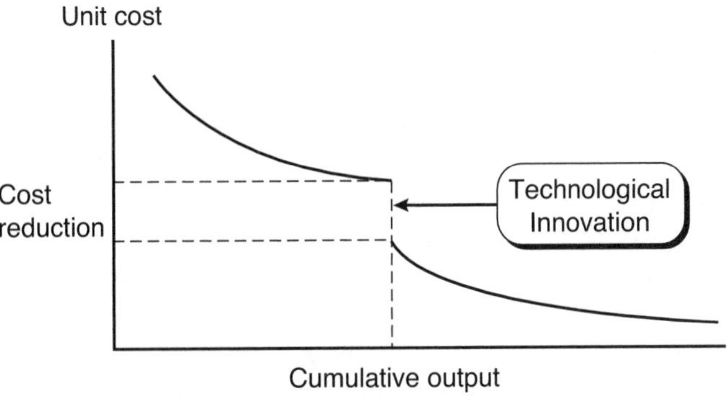

Fig. 18.3 The experience curve and technological innovation

Knowledge sources

Knowledge can be valuable. A firm may enjoy a competitive advantage if it knows things that its competitors do not. This knowledge might be in any one of a number of areas:

- *Product knowledge* – A special understanding of the products (or services) that make up the market. Critically, this knowledge must be used to create offerings which are more attractive to buyers. Product knowledge must be used in conjunction with knowledge of the *market*.
- *Market knowledge* – Special insights into the way the market functions. This includes areas such as the needs of the consumer, the way in which customers buy and what can be used to influence them. This knowledge can be used to create effective marketing and selling strategies.
- *Technical knowledge* – A special understanding and competence in making and delivering the offering to the marketplace. This knowledge is not valuable on its own. Rather it must be used to offer the customer something different: a better product, a lower cost product or a better service.

Knowledge does not come for free. It is the result of investment. Product and technical knowledge arise from research and development activities. Market knowledge comes from market research and market analysis. It should be remembered that knowledge is not in itself valuable. It only forms the basis of a competitive advantage if it is used to deliver new value to the customer.

Relationship sources

Relationships are not just a 'nice to have' add-on to business activity, they are fundamental to it. A relationship establishes trust and trust adds value by reducing the need for contracts and monitoring. A business may be able to build a competitive advantage on the basis of the special relationships it enjoys with its stakeholders. Building relationships is essential if the business is to locate itself in a secure, and supportive, network.

The idea of entrepreneurial networks has been considered earlier in section 7.4. The notion of building competitive advantage on the basis of relationships resonates with the idea of locking the venture into a set of secure and rewarding network links that competitors find it hard, or at least expensive, to break. Networks built on trust and confidence are valuable because they minimise transaction costs.

- *Relationship with customers* – A firm's relationship with its customers is, of course, a critical dimension of its success. The relationship can be built in a number of ways. Much depends on the nature of the products being sold to the customer and the number of customers the firm has to deal with. A business selling a small number of highly valuable products to a few customers is in a different situation from one selling a large number of relatively low-value items to a great number of customers.

  Relationships can be personal, that is, created through individual contact. Account management and sales activities are important in this respect. The sales-buyer interaction is both a one-to-one contact and a conduit through which value can flow from the business to its customers. If a large number of customers are involved, and personal contact is not possible, then contact may be sustained via the media through advertising and public relations.

  Critical to the relationship with customers is *reputation*. A reputation for delivering products which do what they say they will and for delivering them with a high degree of service and for undertaking business in a fair and equitable way is invaluable. Reputation can be hard to build up. It is, however, quite easy to lose.

- *Relationship with suppliers* – Suppliers are best regarded as partners in the development of an end-market. They are integral to the network the business needs to build up around itself. A business can put itself in a stronger position to deliver value to its customers if its suppliers themselves show flexibility and responsiveness. Further, suppliers can be encouraged to innovate on behalf of the business. All of this means that the relationship with suppliers has to go beyond just the concern with negotiating over prices. Though suppliers need to share value with their customers the game need not be zero sum. A customer working with its suppliers can address the end-market better and create more overall value to be shared than one working against its suppliers.

- *Relationship with investors* – Of all stakeholders it is, perhaps, investors who have the most transparent relationship with the entrepreneurial venture. In economic terms their concern is the most one-dimensional: they are concerned to maximise their returns. Investors are, however, still human beings. They engage in communication and relationship building with the entrepreneur. They respond not only to actual returns but also if they feel their interests are being properly addressed by the entrepreneur.

  The support of investors can be critical to success. Any venture will have its ups and downs, especially in its early stages. When things are not going too well, the support of investors is invaluable. If they insist on liquidating their investment then, at best, problems will be exacerbated; at worst, the business may not survive. The support of investors can be maintained by developing a strategy to communicate actively with them. This will involve managing the investors' expectations, building their confidence in the venture and avoiding 'surprises' which lead investors to make hasty judgements.

- *Relationship with employees* – Building a motivating and productive relationship with employees is one of the entrepreneur's most important activities. It is the employees who deliver the actions which convert the entrepreneur's vision into reality. The entrepreneurial venture may not enjoy many of the cost, technical and relationship advantages that established players can call upon. All they have is their people, their interest, motivation and drive on behalf of the business. The entrepreneur must draw this out by understanding their employees' motivations and adopting the right leadership strategies.

Structural sources

The final area in which the entrepreneurial business can aspire to develop a basis for competitive advantage is in its structure. Structural advantages arise as a consequence not so much of *what* the business does but the *way* it goes about doing things. This is a function not only of its formal structure, the pre-defined way in which individuals will relate to each other but also in its informal structure, the 'unofficial' web of relationships and communication links which actually define it and its *culture* which governs how those relationships will function and evolve. Since new entrants are unlikely to enjoy cost advantages in the early stages of the business at least, and because relationship advantages take time to build up and knowledge advantages require investment, the entrepreneurial business is likely to be highly dependent on structure-based advantages.

A business can gain a competitive advantage from its structure if that structure allows it to perform better in the marketplace. Such a structural advantage may arise from having the business co-ordinated by a strong leader who keeps the business on track and focuses it on the opportunities at hand. Such leadership ensures that resources are used effectively. The business may also be better at gaining information from the marketplace and using it to make decisions.

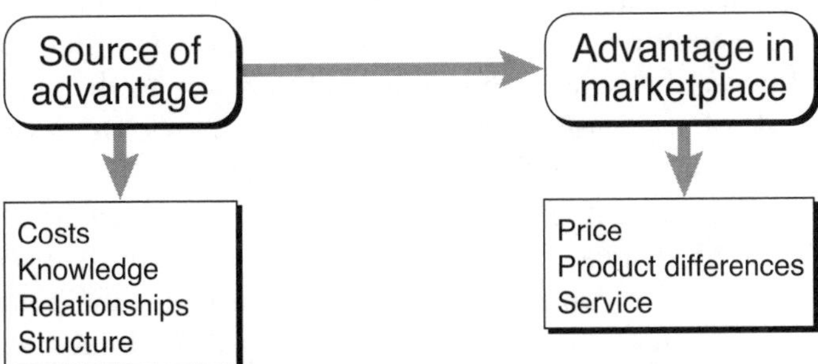

Fig. 18.4 Competitive advantage and its sources

This might allow it be more responsive to the needs of customers and so be quicker to offer them new products and services.

Another structural advantage can arise if the individuals who make it up emphasise *tasks* (what needs doing) rather than *roles* (what they feel their job descriptions say they should do). Such an attitude enables the business to be flexible, to focus on its customers and keep fixed costs to a minimum.

Competitive advantages in the marketplace can be built on a number of platforms within the organisation (see Fig. 18.4). Costs, knowledge, relationships and structures may all be used to offer the customer value in a way that competitors cannot. This makes them sources from which a competitive advantage may be developed in the marketplace. They have the potential to bring success to the venture. However, if this success is to be long-term, the competitive advantages must be maintained in the face of competitive activity. They must be *sustained*.

18.2 How competitive advantage is established

KEY LEARNING OUTCOME

An appreciation of the ways in which competitive advantages may be established but can be lost to competitors.

The business world does not stand still. Competitors are aware of each other to varying degrees. They become *acutely* aware if they lose business, or at least are prevented from gaining it, by the activities of a competitor. They may go on to develop an understanding of *why* that business is performing better than they are. A successful business cannot hide its competitive advantage for long. Competitors will then be tempted to imitate and recreate that competitive advantage for themselves. This may be easier said than done. If competitors find a competitive advantage hard to imitate, then the entrepreneurial firm may go on enjoying the rewards that advantage offers. If the advantage is hard to imitate it is said to be *sustainable*.

A reverse perspective is illuminating in this instance. To understand how competitive advantage may be sustained demands an appreciation of how it can be *lost*. Quite simply, a competitive advantage is lost if a competitor *gains* it. In order to offer something that gains an advantage in the marketplace means that a business must create for itself the *source* of that advantage. The framework developed in the previous section applies so competitive advantage is lost to competitors if they achieve lower *costs*; or gain *knowledge* that was exclusive to and valuable to the venture; or build a stronger network of *relationships* than the venture enjoys; or develop *structural* advantages (advantages in the way the business organises itself).

An entrepreneurial venture must constantly strive to prevent competitors gaining a relative advantage in these areas. While the venture actually meets its competitors in the marketplace the basis of competitive advantages provides the points of *strategic contact* between the venture and its competitors. It is these things which give the venture the *power* to compete (see Fig. 18.5).

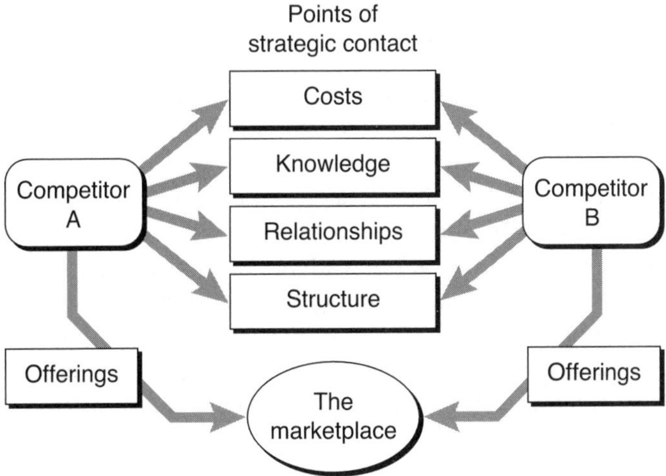

Fig. 18.5 Competitive advantage and competition

The entrepreneur must be on their guard as to the ways in which competitors might gain the upper hand in terms of competitive advantage. They must consider the possible ways in which competitors might gain the advantage, and be aware of these when they are developing their strategy. A sound strategy must be built on a competitive advantage which can be sustained. Knowing this is part of understanding the nature of the market, the players who make it up and competition within it. The decisions which relate to developing a competitive advantage must be made in relation to the considerations on how *costs, knowledge, relationships* and *structure* deliver advantages in the marketplace.

Some considerations in relation to cost advantages

Here the chief considerations relate to how cost advantages may be used in the marketplace to achieve volume gains (in other words, how price sensitive the customer is); how competitors can use factor prices to their advantage; and how volume gains are rewarded with further cost reductions (i.e. to what extent volume and cost are linked in a virtuous circle via economies of scale and experience effects). Also important is how established the cost structure of the industry is. In particular, is a technological innovation that changes the cost rules likely to occur, and if so, how quickly will it spread through the sector?

Some important specific questions are:

1 How important is price to the customer?
2 How important is price to intermediaries and distributors?
3 Can volume be gained if price is reduced (that is, is demand elastic)?

These questions may be answered by the use of appropriate market research techniques. Some key discoveries to be made through market research are:

- Have all the players in the market access to the same inputs?
- Do some players enjoy exclusive access to low-cost inputs?
- Are economies of scale important?
- If so, does one player have a significant *period* volume advantage?
- Are experience economies important?
- If so, has one player a *cumulative* volume advantage?
- Do any players have a *technological advantage* that influences costs?
- Is a technological innovation that will alter costs likely in the future?
- If so, how quickly would such a technological innovation spread through the industry?
- How expensive would it be to adopt any such cost-reducing technological innovations?

These questions may be answered by an analysis of the industry's structure and from knowledge of its technological base. The answers will illuminate the possibility of sustaining a cost-based advantage. In short, it will be sustainable if price is important to the customer and one player can gain a cost advantage from experience or technological sources.

Some considerations in relation to knowledge advantages

Here the considerations relate to how exclusive knowledge may be gained, used and protected by the players in a sector.

Some important specific questions are as follows.

- Is the knowledge the industry uses established or is it in a state of rapid development? (This involves consideration of whether the industry is a 'high-tech' one which spends heavily on product research and development or marketing research.)
- Do the businesses in the industry use a common pool of knowledge or do they rely on their own localised knowledge?
- Is knowledge developed 'in house' or are external organisations used (for example, business service firms such as market research agencies and consultancies and 'non-profit' organisations such as universities) important?
- How important to the industry are knowledge protection devices such as patents, copyrights and registered designs?

Again, these questions can be answered through an appropriate analysis of the industry, its environment and its technology. Clearly, knowledge which is important to delivering customer value is localised and is protectable offers a more sustainable basis for competitive advantage than knowledge which is accessible to all.

Some considerations in relation to relationship advantages

Relationships are the 'glue' that holds the business network together. If relationships are long-term and secure, then the network can be thought of as 'tight'. If relationships are transitory and easily broken, then the network is 'loose'. A new entrant will find a tight network hard to break into. It may be expensive to break old relationships and establish new ones. On the other hand, once a location in that network has been established the business will find it easy to defend its position. Conversely, a loose network, while being easy to enter, will offer little security from competitors. Some important specific questions are:

- What means are used to establish and maintain relationships with customers? (Personal contact (e.g. sales activity) or contact via the media (e.g. advertising).)
- Are relationships with customers long-term or short-term? (Consider whether purchases are one off or repeat. Is after-sales support important?)
- What *risks* does the buyer face in buying and using the product? (What sort of investment does it entail? What can go wrong when using it?)
- How can a sense of *trust* between the buyer and seller aid the management of those risks?
- How important is the seller's *reputation* to the buyer?
- On what basis can reputation be built? (Consider issues such as product quality, service, ethical standards, behaviour.)

A particularly effective entrepreneurial strategy is to identify a sector in which the network is loose and to create value through 'tightening it up' by offering a higher level of commitment and service. This also locks out competitors and makes the advantage gained sustainable.

Some considerations in relation to structural advantages

As noted in the previous section, structural advantages arise as a consequence not so much of *what* the business does, but the *way* it goes about doing things. A business can gain an advantage over its competitors by having a structure in which roles are more flexible (which can lead to lower costs), by being more focused on the market and so more responsive to signals from customers and competitors and then by using those signals to make faster and better decisions about how to serve the customer. Some important specific questions are:

- What kind of organisational *structures* do businesses in the sector adopt? (Consider, in particular, how important are functional departments, team working, *ad-hoc* structures.)
- How important are *formal* structures? (Consider how the way things *really* happen compares to the way businesses say they *should* happen.)
- What kind of *decision-making processes* are used? (Over what timescale are plans made? Who is involved in decision making? How are particular decisions justified within organisations?)
- How do firms in the sector identify, process and respond to market signals? (Consider whether the market research is formalised. How is pricing policy determined? How is new product development organised?)
- What *cultures* are adopted by businesses in the sector? (Consider customer focus versus internal concerns; entrepreneurial versus bureaucratic attitudes; the importance of tasks versus roles.)

- What leadership styles are adopted? (Consider whether they are authoritarian or consensus based. Is power exercised through the control of resources or the communication of vision? Is there a focus on tasks or a focus on people?)

Rigid structures provide the entrepreneur with a means of focusing and directing their organisation but they are ambivalent as a source of competitive advantage. It may be better to allow people to use their skills and insights by pushing decision making down the organisation – particularly when it is in a turbulent environment.

Understanding the answers to all of these questions gives the entrepreneur an insight into the way they can establish a competitive advantage in the marketplace in a way which has a secure and distinctive base within their business. Further, it indicates the potential which a particular competitive advantage has to be *sustainable* in the face of competitive pressure.

18.3 Maintaining competitive advantage

KEY LEARNING OUTCOME
An understanding of the ways in which competitive advantage may be sustained.

Identifying a competitive advantage, that is, something the customer finds both different and attractive, and securing that on the basis of some aspect of the business, be it *costs, knowledge, relationships* or *structure*, in a way which both provides a source for that advantage and differentiates the business from competitors is the *starting point* for long-term success. In order to *ensure* that it happens, the business must make sure that the competitive advantage cannot be imitated, and so the profits it promises cannot be eroded, by competitors. The entrepreneur must decide not only what the competitive advantage of the venture they establish will be but also how it will be *sustained*.

Sustaining cost advantages

The key decision here is how will the business keep its costs lower than competitors? There can only be *one* cost leader in a market. If it is to be based on scale and experience curve economies, cost leadership demands *output volume* leadership. This means gaining and maintaining the highest (or least highest volume) market share. This can prove to be expensive if the market is price sensitive. Competitors will be willing to compete by cutting their prices. The cost leader will have to use their cost advantage to establish a price below that of competitors' costs. This may mean a low, or even zero, profit margin. A cost leadership strategy may mean a long haul with poor profit levels until competitors have been 'seen off'.

The temptation to increase prices to gain short-term profits must be resisted since this will create a 'price umbrella' under which less efficient competitors can shelter. If the entrepreneur is a later entrant to the market and coming in from behind, then they may need to invest heavily in the short term to gain a rapid cumulative volume advantage over competitors. Again, this can prove to be expensive in the short run with substantial returns offered only in the long term. This, of course, introduces a number of risks.

Further, even though experience cost reductions are a function of output volume they do not occur by right. They have to be *managed*. For the cost leader, cost control has to take centre stage, i.e. driving costs down must take priority over all other considerations. This demands that powerful cost control systems be in place. This in turn will influence the leadership and motivation strategies adopted by the entrepreneur and the culture of the organisation they create. Such 'single-minded' organisations are not to everyone's taste, a factor which needs to be considered when recruiting and building the management team.

If the cost leadership is to be established on the basis of a technological innovation then the entrepreneur needs to be sure why they, and they alone, will have access to that technology. It is best to assume that competitors will eventually gain access to the innovation even if it is secured through patents and other intellectual property devices (see below). In respect to this it is best to use the innovation as the *starting point* to gain an initial cost advantage which can be built on and sustained using scale and experience effects.

Even if all this is achieved, the entrepreneur must be sensitive to the attentions of anti-trust regulators. A strategy which achieves a large market share on the basis of squeezing competitors out on price may be a just reward for doggedly pursuing efficiency. To outsiders, however, it may seem like an unfair monopoly.

In conclusion there can only be one cost leader in a market. A cost leadership strategy is one which is challenging and, in the short term at least, expensive, to sustain.

Sustaining knowledge advantages

Knowledge advantages are based on understanding of both the product and the market. These two things operate in tandem with one other. An understanding of what is offered must be tempered with an understanding of why the customer wants it. Generally in business, knowledge soon becomes public. Even if knowledge is 'secure' within the business, the process of launching products and promoting them to the customer sends clear signals to competitors.

Knowledge may be 'protected' by means of patents and other intellectual property devices such as copyrights and registered designs. In principle, these prevent competitors from using the knowledge. They grant the holder a monopoly over the innovation arising from the knowledge. In some industries intellectual property is very important, for example in the biotechnology industry. In others, such as engineering, it is less so. However, the use of intellectual property devices as a means of securing a competitive advantage should be approached cautiously. Patents and other devices are not granted for every new idea, rather they must reflect a *significant* technological innovation. Even if the new idea is significant, the registration process is time consuming, demands the aid of experts and can be expensive. Registration may also involve the public posting of the invention prior to any patent being granted. In effect this means presenting the patent to challenge by holders of other patents. This can tip off competitors. Often not just one but a number variations of the idea will have to be patented in order to ensure that competitors do not get round the patent by presenting minor variations to the market.

Furthermore, the patent registration will have to be obtained in a variety of regions if global cover is desired. If comprehensive cover is not obtained then competitors may get round the patent by producing the product in an area where the patent does not hold. Even if global cover is obtained, some countries are lax (because of weak legal structures or even, in some cases, as a matter of policy) in enforcing intellectual property law. If the law-enforcement mechanisms will act to protect the patent, it is still down to the patent holder to police their property and challenge infringements. Even if all this is done, there are strict time limits on the protection offered.

These drawbacks do not mean that patents are not valuable, just that they should not be relied upon to provide a source of competitive advantage on their own terms. Rather, they should be used *tactically* to provide an initial advantage which can then be used to develop other advantages based on cost and relationships.

Sustaining relationship advantages

Relationships are valuable because they establish *trust*, and trust brings down costs for a variety of reasons. First, it reduces the need for a buyer to be constantly scanning the market for offerings. They simply go to a supplier they know. Second, it eliminates the need to establish detailed contracts between buyer and seller. Third, it eliminates the need for a constant *policing* of those contracts. In this context, we may consider *all* stakeholders to be engaged in contract building with the venture, not just customers, though of course a trusting relationship with the customer is particularly important and has immediate pay-offs.

If trust is built up it can then form the basis for sustaining competitive advantage. Given that cost and knowledge advantages are most easily accrued by the large (and that usually means the established) business, trust can be a potent ingredient in entrepreneurial success, particularly in the early stages of the venture.

Trust can only be built by establishing and developing relationships which exist on a number of levels. At one level is the experience the parties have of each other through personal contact, say as a result of direct selling activities. The salesperson is not just informing the buyer of a firm's outputs; they are acting as an ambassador for the business as a whole. At the next level is communication through the media using advertising and public relations activity. Product branding and company image are important mediators. At another level is the general *reputation* that a business builds in the mind of the buyer through their wider experience of it. Reputation is established not through absolute outcomes but through outcomes in relation to *expectations*. Quite simply, if expectations are exceeded then a stakeholder will be very satisfied by the outcome; if they are not met then the stakeholder will be disappointed and feel let down.

Thus a strategy for building and maintaining trust must have three interlocking aspects:

1 *The management of expectations.* The entrepreneur must take charge of what the other party (be they a customer, an investor, a supplier or an employee) expects to come out of the relationship. While entrepreneurs are right to strive to deliver on behalf of the stakeholders in their venture they must avoid 'over-promising' as this can easily lead to disappointment, dissatisfaction and a feeling that trust has been broken if what has been promised is not delivered.

2 *The management of outcomes.* Entrepreneurs must take responsibility for what their venture delivers finally to its stakeholders. They must ensure that these outcomes at least meet, or are better than, what the stakeholder expected. If for any reason they are not (and no-one, not even the most effective entrepreneur, can control all contingencies) then the entrepreneur is faced with the challenge of addressing the stakeholder's disappointment and managing the process of rebuilding trust. The details of how this must be done will vary depending on the stakeholder, the circumstances and the extent of failure that has occurred. The golden rule, however, is that disappointment should *never* be ignored!

3 *The management of communication.* Expectations and the delivery of outcomes occur on a stage built by communication. Communications between the entrepreneur (and the venture's staff) and stakeholders can take a variety of forms. They can be formal or informal, personal or impersonal, directed to a specific stakeholder or widely broadcast. They may take place via a variety of media. The entrepreneur must be aware of the communication channels that connect, and draw the venture's stakeholders together, learning how to use them and how to reinvigorate them constantly. He or she must also take control of how those channels are used. In particular, the entrepreneur must take clear responsibility for the promises that are being made on behalf of the venture; not just the promises they make themselves, but also those being made by other people on behalf of the venture.

Sustaining structural advantages

Structural advantages arise when a business, by virtue of the way it organises itself, becomes more attuned to signals from the marketplace, more acute in its decision making and more flexible in responding to the needs of customers. Such responsiveness is a product of the organisation's structure, that is, the network of responsibilities and communication links which give the business its form.

As with relationship advantages, the entrepreneurial business is in a strong position to enjoy structural advantages over larger businesses. Established, older businesses may be hampered by internal structures. These structures may serve an important function but once started they tend to develop a momentum of their own. This can mean that they continue to exist after their usefulness has declined. In the entrepreneurial business, on the other hand, internal structures will be in a state of flux and will be forming in response to market demands.

Decision making within the established firm may also be less acute. Key decision makers may be insulated from the realities of the market, the signals it is sending and the opportunities it is presenting. Decision making may also be distorted by internal 'political' concerns which put internal factional interests ahead of those of the customer and the business as a whole. The entrepreneur, however, should be using the venture's organisation to facilitate and focus decision making, rather than to hinder it. In addition, they are in a position to use strong leadership to draw disparate groups together and co-ordinate their actions.

This demands that entrepreneurs keep themselves in touch with their market and that they do not allow themselves to be 'swamped' by their organisations. Communication systems should be designed with the primary objective of feeding information about the market to decision makers. While information on the internal state of the business is important, this should be used to support market-orientated decision making, not be used to compromise it.

Competitive advantage is *dynamic* not static. Once a venture gains a competitive advantage in the marketplace it must use the success this brings to constantly reinvent the advantage. Success offers rewards in excess of market norms. These rewards must be reinvested in the business. This investment should not be aimed at merely reinforcing the existing competitive advantage but at modifying it and, if need be, creating the basis for entirely new ones.

If the venture aims to become a *cost leader* then it must invest in volume leadership and cost control. If it aims to use *exclusive knowledge* then it must invest in developing its understanding of the products and services offered to the market, the way in which they meet the needs of customers and the way in which customers decide to buy. If *relationships* are to be used then investment must take place in developing existing relationships and creating new ones. This means managing expectations, outcomes and communication, and all of these in turn mean investment in the people who communicate to customers on behalf of the business. Maintaining a *structural advantage* demands investment in human and communication systems. The business cannot afford to become stale, that is, to let its structures gain a life and a *raison d'être* independent of their function in serving the market. It also demands investment in *change*. Change is not only a structural phenomenon, it also represents development in individual attitudes and organisational culture. The rewards gained from a competitive advantage must be reinvested to maintain, develop and renew the basis of that advantage within the business (see Fig. 18.6).

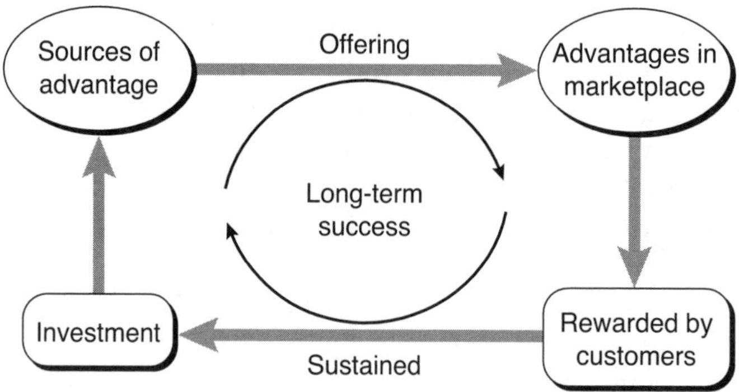

Fig. 18.6 Sustaining competitive advantage

Summary of key ideas

- The fifth, and final, stage of the strategic window is *closing it*.
- Closing the window means creating a *competitive advantage* so that the venture can go on exploiting the opportunity in the face of competitive pressures.
- A competitive advantage is something the business can do that is valuable for the customer which competitors find difficult to match.
- A competitive advantage has a source within the business. The key sources are lower *costs; knowledge* of the product and market; stronger *relationships* within the network; and a more flexible and responsive organisational *structure*.
- A competitive advantage must be actively maintained if it is to be *sustainable*.

Suggestions for further reading

Abernathy, W.J. and **Wayne, K.** (1974) 'Limits of the learning curve', *Harvard Business Review*, Sept–Oct, pp. 109–19.

Bamberger, I. (1989) 'Developing competitive advantage in small and medium-sized firms', *Long Range Planning*, Vol. 22, No. 5, pp. 80–8.

Barnett, W.P., Grieve, H.R. and **Park, D.Y.** (1994) 'An evolutionary model of organisational performance', *Strategic Management Journal*, Vol. 15, pp. 11–28.

Brock Smith, J. and **Barclay, D.W.** (1997) 'The effects of organisational differences and trust on the effectiveness of selling partnership relationships', *Journal of Marketing*, Vol. 61, pp. 3–21.

Doney, P.M. and **Cannon, J.P.** (1997) 'An examination of the nature of trust in buyer-seller relationships', *Journal of Marketing*, Vol. 61, pp. 35–51.

Ghemawat, P. (1985) 'Building strategy on the experience curve', *Harvard Business Review*, Mar-Apr, pp. 143–9.

Kay, J. (1993) *Foundations of Corporate Success*, Oxford: Oxford University Press.

Lieberman, M.B. and **Montgommery, D.B.** (1988) 'First mover advantages', *Strategic Management Journal*, Vol. 9, pp. 41–58.

Pitt, L.F. and **Jeantrout, B.** (1994) 'Management of customer expectations in service firms: A study and checklist', *The Service Industries Journal*, Vol. 14, No. 2, pp. 170–89.

Porter, M. (1980) *Competitive Strategy: Techniques for Analysing Industries and Competitors*, New York: Free Press.

Porter, M. (1985) *Competitive Advantage: Creating and Sustaining Superior Performance*, New York: Free Press.

Russell, M. (1984) 'Scales true economies', *Management Today*, May, pp. 82–4.

Snell, R. and **Lau, A.** (1994) 'Exploring local competencies salient for expanding small businesses', *Journal of Management Development*, Vol. 13, No. 4, pp. 4–15.

Stevens, H.H. (1976) 'Defining corporate strengths and weaknesses', *Sloan Management Review*, Spring, pp. 51–68.

Teas, R.K. (1993) 'Expectations, performance evaluation and consumer's perceptions of quality', *Journal of Marketing*, Vol. 57, pp. 18–34.

Tellis, G.J. and **Golder, P.N.** (1996) 'First to market, first to fail? Real causes of enduring market leadership', *Sloan Management Review*, Winter, pp. 65–75.

Voss, C. (1992) 'Successful innovation and implementation of new processes', *Business Strategy Review*, Spring, pp. 29–44.

Zahra, S.A., Nash, S. and **Bickford, D.J.** (1995) 'Transforming technological pioneering into competitive advantage', *Academy of Management Executive*, Vol. 9, No. 1, pp. 17–31.

Zeithaml, V., Berry, V. and **Parasuraman, A.** (1993) 'The nature and determinants of a customer's expectations of a service', *Journal of the Academy of Marketing Science*, Vol. 21, No. 1, pp. 1–12.

Selected case material

Coffee blended with emotion

20 May 1999

Companies such as Starbucks, The Body Shop and Swatch opened up new markets by changing the appeal of their products to consumers, say **W. Chan Kim** and **Renée Mauborgne**

In the late 1980s, Procter & Gamble, General Foods and Nestlé held 90 per cent of the US coffee market. All three companies viewed coffee as a commodity: generic beans bought from roughly equivalent Brazilian and Colombian producers, roasted and freeze-dried using similar equipment, sealed in standard containers, and sold at a price.

Apart from the name, colour of the jar and the advertising slogan, the coffee was remarkably similar. As in most commodity industries, there was heavy price-cutting and an unrelenting battle for market share to spread costs. The result was paper-thin profit margins and low growth.

Then came Starbucks. While the big three sold a commodity, Starbucks sold a retailing concept: the coffee bar, offering relaxation and conversation, and coffee drinks made with quality beans, frothy and flavoured milks, creams, syrups and ices.

While $3 (£1.85) for a cup of Starbucks' coffee is outrageous compared with the cost of a cup of instant coffee at home, consumers did not see it that way. They judged Starbucks as an indulgence, so the steep price appeared good value for money.

With almost no advertising, Starbucks became a national chain in less than 10 years. And it is growing, with profit margins roughly five times the industry average.

Competition in many industries converges on one of two bases of appeal. Some industries compete principally on price and functional performance; the appeal of these industries is rational. This was the case with coffee in the US before Starbucks.

Other industries compete largely on feelings, glamour and human relationships, where a product or service is bought for emotional reasons. Cosmetics is one example.

Rarely, however, are the products or services of an industry intrinsically and unalterably functional or emotional. Often companies have driven their industries in one of these directions based on competitive factors, and have unconsciously educated consumers about what to expect. A reinforcing cycle sets in between companies' behaviour and customers' demands. The result: functionally oriented industries are driven to become more so over time, as are emotionally oriented industries.

Companies can often create new markets and recreate existing ones by breaking out of this convergent behaviour and shifting the functional-emotional orientation of their industry.

The aim is to appeal to a completely different sense of self and purpose among buyers by transforming a product or service whose appeal is functional into one whose appeal is emotional, or vice versa.

The opportunities are often enormous. Typically, emotionally oriented industries provide lots of extras that add to the sale price but not to functional performance. It may be possible to remove these extras to reveal a simpler, lower-cost business model that is often a welcome reprieve after years of emotional binding.

Similarly, functional industries often have low creativity and have commoditised their products and services, leaving huge scope to stimulate demand by introducing emotion and pleasure of use.

Swatch did for watches what Starbucks did for coffee. In the early 1980s, budget watches were considered a functional item that people bought to keep track of time. Citizen and Seiko, the industry leaders, competed by using quartz technology to improve accuracy and digital displays to make reading the time easier.

Swatch set out to make fashion accessories. SMH, the Swiss parent company, created a design lab in Italy whose mission was to combine powerful technology with artwork, brilliant colours and flamboyant designs.

Before Swatch's debut, people usually owned only one watch, because one watch fulfilled the functional need of keeping time and all watches looked the same. Swatch encouraged repeat purchases because people viewed it as a fashion accessory.

In contrast to Starbucks and Swatch, The Body Shop created a new market in the cosmetics industry by shifting from an emotional appeal to a functional one. Contrary to industry orthodoxy, The Body Shop did not sell glamour, hope and fantasy: it sold health and well-being. While the cosmetics industry spent heavily on packaging, The Body Shop used plastic, refillable bottles.

While the cosmetics industry spent heavily on technology and secret beauty formulas, The Body Shop did away with the expense by focusing on simple methods and traditional formulas using natural ingredients.

While the cosmetic industry spent heavily on advertising and promises of eternal youth, The Body Shop drew attention to its natural formulas and their powers to polish, protect and maintain the skin and body.

The result: it was hard to recognise that The Body Shop was part of the cosmetics industry. Its products and approach were so simple, under-hyped, reasonably priced and honest, they appealed to consumers' commonsense and led to the creation of a new market space.

Many new markets are being created in service industries in much the same way. Sectors such as insurance, banking and investment have traditionally been emotionally oriented, selling human relationships and client bonding – "the relationship is the business".

New companies are stripping this away to create dramatic change in price and performance. Direct Line Insurance in the UK, US-based Vanguard in index funds and Schwab in the brokerage industry are creating new market spaces by transforming emotional, human-relationship oriented businesses into high-performance, low-cost functional businesses.

Where does your industry gravitate towards on the functional-emotional spectrum? Is it highly oriented toward one of these two bases of appeal? If so, your company may find new market space by shifting the appeal of your industry.

The relevant questions are: if emotional in appeal, what can you eliminate and reduce in your industry's offerings to reveal a fundamental breakthrough in price/ performance for customers? If functional, what can you create that your industry has never offered to build emotion, image and a powerful message into the products and services of your industry?

Next week, learn how Sony, Polo, Ralph Lauren, Accor and Champion Enterprises succeeded in breaking out of the strategic groups of their industry to create new market space.

W. Chan Kim is the Boston Consulting Group Bruce D. Henderson Chair Professor of International Management at Insead, France. Renée Mauborgne is the Insead Distinguished Fellow and Affiliate Professor of Strategy and Management. She is also president of ITM Research.

Previous articles in this series can be found at www.ft.com/hippocampus/dman.htm

---

Ananova the cyber newsreader leads DAG back to health

16 March 2000

Mark Nicholson on how the Scottish group refocused after share suspension

Digital personal assistants are generally as cold and prosaic as they sound – trim little gadgets though they may be. Imagine, however, having Ananova, the sultry cyberchick newsreader soon to go online on the PA web site, as your personal digitally animated assistant, or indeed a male version.

Digital Animations Group, the Aim-listed Scottish company behind the Ananova technology, believes it won't be long before you can call up an animated, personalised and interactive assistant on your internet-enabled mobile phone.

The company is already using its expertise in games and Full Motion Video to develop such micro-animation techniques and is also spawning virtual prototypes.

The promise of Ananova and her virtual siblings marks something of a reanimation for the company itself. DAG's shares were briefly suspended last year, but recently it joined the Crest settlement system to help meet rising private demand for its stock.

Intellectual assets, according to Mike Hambly, managing director, rest chiefly in the company's creative animators, rather than in proprietorial software or other technology. In fact, he argues, the company was too creative before the share suspension in September and not focused enough on either markets or strategy.

Mr Hambly was brought into the company largely by 3i, the venture capital group, following the suspension and just as the company received £700,000 in new funds from both 3i and NewMedia Spark, the internet and software investor.

Another DAG asset, however, is its ability to work in various animation formats, including video games, TV commercials and movie animation through to the internet-based Ananova.

DAG was founded 10 years ago by two architects to provide animations, or "walk throughs", for building designs. It branched out into computer game animation in the early 1990s and fast won a reputation that led to its Aim listing in July 1996.

It then further diversified and by last year was pitching to raise about £3m in a bid to secure rights to produce a fully animated TV series for a US company. This proved a stretch too far, and resulting cash flow difficulties led to the suspension and a re-evaluation by 3i, its primary investor.

Since the arrival of Mr Hambly and the recent investment, DAG has reshaped its strategy.

It will cease to be so reliant on the volatile games sector and instead seek shorter projects. This will enable it to respond flexibly to new schemes. It will also focus on developing Ananova-like animations and their possible applications.

These, Mr Hambly believes, include anything from the cellphone assistant to creating virtual tellers for internet banks and financial service organisations.

Ananova was a breakthrough for DAG in providing both a steady stream of income through royalties and an enhanced profile. Mr Hambly sees further potential in shifting characters into consumer devices or other uses.

"Everyone who's talking to us is talking about virtual characters," he says.

DAG is also in talks with a number of companies, which Mr Hambly declines to name, to create partners for the "delivery technology" for such products.

Alongside this, the company will continue to seek work in TV commercials and, increasingly, special effects for movies. It will also sustain its output of games animations.

"We're in discussions with a number of TV companies, advertising agencies and interactive entertainment organisations," says Mr Hambly.

DAG's last published results for the year to March 1999 are long out of date, given they preceded the September difficulties. They showed an 86 per cent rise in turnover to £1.15m and a pre-tax loss of £194,326. This year's figures are widely expected to prove rosier, as the 200 per cent rise in DAG's share price since January may indicate.

3i and NewMedia Spark effectively revived DAG's fortunes with their joint investment last November, which left them with stakes of 26 and 13 per cent respectively. The remaining shares are tightly held.

Ultimately, Mr Hambly recognises the company is going to make a further leap in scale to continue to compete globally. "This company's too small and there are only two ways to grow – by acquisition or by being acquired."

Review questions

Consider the ways in which:

1 The Body Shop

2 Starbucks and

3 Swatch

are using relationships with their customers to sustain their competitive advantages.

4 How might the refocusing of DAG help the business to regain and sustain its competitive advantage?

19 Gaining financial support: issues and approaches

Chapter overview

Attracting financial support for the venture is one of the entrepreneur's most important tasks. This chapter considers the supply of investment capital and how backers actually go about selecting investment opportunities. The chapter concludes by advocating that a major factor in successfully attracting investment is the entrepreneur having an understanding of the questions that investors need to ask and preparing answers to them.

19.1 Sources and types of financial investment

KEY LEARNING OUTCOME
A recognition of the different sources of capital available for investment in the entrepreneurial venture.

Investment capital is a valuable commodity. As with any other commodity, markets develop to ensure that supply meets demand. Though 'capital' is itself an undifferentiated commodity (one five-dollar bill is exactly like any five-dollar bill!) a number of different types of supplier emerge to offer investment capital. These different types of supplier differentiate themselves not in what they supply but in the *way* they supply the capital, the *price* they ask for that capital and the *supplementary services* they offer.

The interaction of supply and demand results in a *price* being set for the capital. This price is the *rate of return* the supplier (the lender or investor) expects from their investment. A number of factors influence the cost of the capital being offered. The critical factors are the *risk* of the investment (that is, the probability that the return will be less than that anticipated) and the *opportunity cost* (that is, the return that has to be forgone because alternative investments cannot be made). This *risk-rate of return line* provides one of the key dimensions along which investors differentiate themselves.

Key supplies of capital include the following.

Entrepreneur's own capital

This is money that the entrepreneur owns. It may derive from personal savings, or it may be a 'lump sum' resulting from a capital gain or a redundancy package in which case it might be quite a significant amount. The research by Blanchflower and Oswald quoted in Chapter 3 revealed the importance of inherited money in start-ups. Serial entrepreneurs liquidate their holdings in their ventures once they mature in order to pursue new business ideas. Clearly, the entrepreneur is free to use this capital as he or she wishes.

Informal investors

An entrepreneur may attract investment support on an informal basis from their family and friends. The expectations of what the returns will be, and when they might be gained, are usually set informally or, at most, semi-formally.

Internal capital networks

Many communities, especially those based around a group of people who are displaced and who are, or at least feel, excluded from the wider economic system, show strong entrepreneurial tendencies. This often enlivens and enriches the economy as a whole. Important examples include a variety of Asian groups in Britain, North Africans in France, Chinese expatriates in South-East Asia, and the Lebanese in West Africa. Such groups often encourage investment among themselves. These communities set up *internal capital networks* which direct capital towards new business opportunities within the community. These networks often have an international character. In emerging economies they provide very important conduits for inward investment.

Though often quite informal in a narrow legal sense these networks are guided by a rich set of cultural rules and expectations. Risk, return and the way in which returns are made are often embedded in complex patterns of ownership and control of ventures.

Retained capital

The profits that a venture generates are, potentially, available to be reinvested in its development. However, such profits belong neither to the venture nor to the entrepreneur; rather they are the property of the *investors* who are backing the venture (this group may, of course, include the entrepreneur). Reinvesting the profits might offer a good investment opportunity, but it is an opportunity which the investor will judge like any other on the basis of risk, return and the possibility of taking the profits and seeking alternative investment opportunities.

'Business angels'

Business angels are individuals, or small groups of individuals, who offer up their own capital to new ventures. They are usually people who have been successful in business (perhaps as entrepreneurs themselves) and as a result have some money 'to play with'. Investment structure and return expectations vary, but are usually equity-based and codified in formal agreements. Business angels differ from other types of organisational investor in one important respect. They like to get involved in the ventures they are backing, and in addition to capital backing, they offer their skills, insights and experiences. As a result they usually seek investment opportunities in ventures where their knowledge or business skills are appropriate.

Retail banking

Retail or 'high street' banks usually offer investment capital to new start-ups and expanding small firms. Support is almost inevitably in the form of loan capital and returns are subject to strict agreement. The bank will expect the entrepreneur to make a personal commitment and may seek collateral to reduce the risk of the deal.

Corporate banking

To an extent the corporate banking sector picks up where retail banking stops. Corporate banks are interested in bigger investment opportunities and may settle for longer-range returns. Loan capital dominates but some equity may also be offered. Deals may be quite complex and involve conversions between the two forms of investment. Again, a significant commitment by the entrepreneur and asset security may be sought.

Venture capital

Venture capital is a critical source of investment for fast-growing entrepreneurial ventures. Venture capital companies usually seek large investment opportunities which are characterised by the potential for a fast, high rate of return. As such, they tend to take on higher degrees of risk than banks. Venture capital companies will rarely involve themselves with investments of less than half a million dollars and typically seek annual returns in excess of 50 per cent to be harvested over five years or less. Usually the deals are equity-based and they may be complex. However, a clear *exit strategy* which enables the returns to the venture capital investment to be liquidated quickly must be in place.

Public flotation

A public flotation is a means of raising capital by offering shares in the venture to a pool of private investors. These shares can then be bought and sold in an open stock market or, on the continent, a *bourse*. There are a variety of stock markets through which capital may be raised. All mature economies have national stock markets of which London, New York and Tokyo are among the most important internationally. There are a number of *emerging* stock markets which trade stock from companies in the developing world and in the post-command economies of central and eastern Europe (that is, the economies that were under Communist control until the late 1980s).

In addition to the stock markets for established companies, there are special stock markets for smaller businesses and for fast-growing ventures. The most important European small-company stock market is the Alternative Investments Market (AIM) based in London. This market has some 265 companies listed and a capitalisation of nearly $10 billion. Other European small business markets include the Nouveau Marché in Paris, Easdaq based in Brussels and the Neuer Markt in Frankfurt. It is planned to link all these markets through a network dubbed EURO.NM. Small and fast-growing business investment in the USA is carried out through a market known as Nasdaq.

Government

Very few governments nowadays fail to see that they have an interest in encouraging enterprise. New businesses create jobs, bring innovation to the market and provide competitive efficiency. Across the world, however, governments differ in the extent to which and the way in which they engage in intervention to support the creation and survival of new and fast-growing businesses.

Support is usually given to new start-ups when capital for investment is hardest to obtain and when cash flow can be at its tightest. Generally direct government investment is in decline. However, there are a number of quasi-governmental agencies which can direct grants towards the entrepreneurial start-up. In addition to capital grants, government may offer support in the form of consulting services and training. Examples of this include the Training and Enterprise Councils (TECs) in the UK and the Small Business Administration (SBA) in the USA. In continental Europe (and increasingly also in central and eastern Europe) local chambers of commerce play an important role in this respect. In addition to overt support, governments often give smaller firms a head-start through tax breaks.

Commercial partnerships

An entrepreneurial venture may look towards existing businesses as a source of investment capital. This will usually occur when the established business has a strategic interest in the success of the venture, for example if it is a supplier of a particularly innovative and valuable input. The support demonstrated by IBM for Microsoft in its early days is a case in point. Commercial partnerships can also occur when the venture is developing a technology which will be important to the established firm. The wide range of investments by established pharmaceutical companies in biotechnology start-ups in the 1980s provides an example of this.

There is a range of arrangements by which the established firm can impose control over its investment in the entrepreneurial venture. At one extreme is complete ownership, and at the other is a simple agreement to use the venture as a favoured supplier. In between there are a variety of forms of *strategic alliance*.

Choice of capital supply

The types and range of investment capital providers operating in an economy depend on the stage of development of that economy and a variety of other political and cultural factors. The choice of capital supplier by the entrepreneur is a decision which must be made in the light of the nature of the venture, its capital requirements, the stage of its development and the risks it faces.

19.2 How backers select investment opportunities

KEY LEARNING OUTCOME
An appreciation of the process by which investors select investment opportunities.

Investment is a buying and selling process. The entrepreneur is trying to sell the venture as an investment opportunity, and the investor is looking to buy opportunities which offer a good return. As such, a consideration of the marketing-buying behaviour behind investment deals can provide an insight into how that process might be understood and so be managed to be more effective.

Tyebjee and Bruno (1984) have developed a model of the investment process. Though these workers used the model to understand venture capital investment, it is generic in form and so can be used to understand investment in general. The model is outlined in Fig. 19.1.

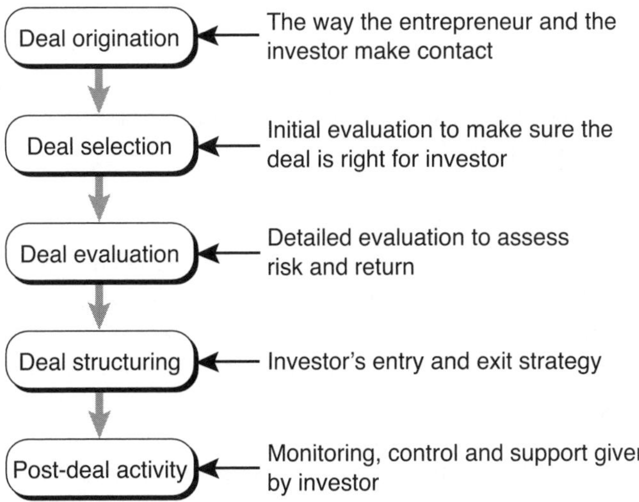

Fig. 19.1 A model of investment decision making
(Adapted from Tyebjee and Bruno, 1984)

The model identifies five key stages in the investment process and these are as follows.

Stage I: Deal origination

Deal origination is the process by which the entrepreneur and the investor first become aware of each other. This results from a mix of *searching* activity by the investor and *promotional* activity by the entrepreneur. Few venture capitalists actively search for new opportunities. They wait for the entrepreneur, or often a third party working on behalf of the entrepreneur, to approach them. Similarly, retail and corporate banks place the onus on the entrepreneur to make the first move.

If the business has shares which are available on a market then private and institutional investors will be active in seeking out stock which fits their portfolio and offers them an attractive return. Business angels are often informed about investment opportunities through informal networks of business contacts.

Stage II: Deal screening

Many investors specialise in certain types of investment. Deal screening reflects the initial evaluation of the proposal to see if it fits with the investor's profile of activities. Important criteria include the amount of investment being sought, the type of technology on which the venture is based, the industry sector of the venture and the venture's stage of growth.

Stage III: Deal evaluation

If the proposal fits with the investor's portfolio of activities, then a more detailed evaluation of the proposal may be carried out. The objective of this exercise is to compare the returns offered by the venture to the risk that it faces. The key factors to be considered in this evaluation will be the potential for the venture in terms of the innovation it is offering, the conditions in the market it aims to develop and the competitive pressures it will face. If this potential is good then consideration will also be made of the ability of the management team behind the venture to actually deliver it. The investor will also be interested in any security the entrepreneur can offer, say in the form of readily liquidisable assets.

Stage IV: Deal structuring

Deal structuring relates to the decisions that must be made in relation to how the initial investment will be made and how the investor will see that investment bear fruit. The critical issues in relation to the investment stage will be how much the entrepreneur is seeking and over what period that investment is to be made. Critical to the return stage will be the actual return offered, how long the investor must wait before that return is seen and the form it will take. For example, will it be cash or will it be a share in the company? If it is a stake in the company can it be liquidated readily?

Stage V: Post-investment activity

Investors, especially those with a significant interest in the venture, will usually retain a degree of involvement in it. There are two broad areas of post-investment activity: *monitoring* and *control*. Monitoring relates to the procedures which are put in place to enable the investor to evaluate the performance of the business so they can keep track of their investment. Financial reporting by way of a balance sheet and profit and loss account (see section 20.2) provides a legally defined means by which the investor can monitor the business. Important investors may demand more frequent and detailed information, perhaps going beyond purely financial data.

Control mechanisms give the investor an active role in the venture and power to influence the entrepreneur's and the venture's management decision making. One common control mechanism is for the investor to be represented on the firm's management team, perhaps as a director. Business angels often offer this not just as a control mechanism but, because of their experience and insights, as a positive contribution to the management of the venture.

This model highlights some of the key areas of information that are needed by the investor before they can make an effective investment decision. Providing that information and answering the investors' questions must form the basis of the entrepreneur's communication strategy towards the investor. This model can be seen in operation in a study by Mason and Harrison (1996) in which they describe the investment process of one particular group of business angels in great depth.

The group under study was formed by a retired UK businessman after seeing business angels operate in the USA. Its members, selected on the basis of experience, compatible personalities and commitment, were attracted by an advertisement in the business opportunities column of the *Financial Times* newspaper. Deals were initiated by a variety of means including newspaper advertisements and by independent business brokers. About half of all deals were initiated by the entrepreneur approaching the group. About one quarter were initiated by the group approaching an entrepreneur and the remaining quarter were the result of introduction by independent agents. All deals were initially offered in the form of a written proposal. Initial screening was undertaken by an individual member of the group. Some 80 per cent of the deals were eliminated at this stage because they did not look financially viable. The remaining 20 per cent were summarised in a standard format and offered to the whole group for comment. If the group felt the deal was worth exploring further (about 10 per cent of all initial proposals) then a project leader was appointed to evaluate the proposal in detail. This was done in conjunction with two other members of the group. This involved background research and a meeting with the investee company. After due consideration, the project team would make a formal presentation and recommendation to the whole group. If, and only if, all members of the group were in favour of the deal, then a formal offer would be made to the investee company. The project team would consider how to structure the deal for entry and exit and would probably offer support in the management of the venture.

19.3 The questions investors need answering

KEY LEARNING OUTCOME
A recognition of the kind of information investors need before they can make an investment decision.

In a narrow sense investors are *rational* in that they seek the best possible return from their capital for a given level of risk. However, such rational behaviour is dependent on investors having information from which to make decisions and on their being able to make those decisions efficiently. Neither of these conditions is ever met fully. There is always an *informational asymmetry* between entrepreneur and investor. Clearly, the entrepreneur knows more about his or her venture than does the investor.

That is why the investor employs the entrepreneur to run the business! Even if investors have all the information necessary to make an investment decision, they are still human beings who suffer the same cognitive limitations that all human beings face. Though they may be practised in making investment decisions, those decisions are not necessarily optimal in a precise economic sense. Rather, investors, like all human decision makers, exhibit *satisficing* behaviour; that is, they make the best decision given the information available, their abilities and the influence of cultural factors. Studies of business angels, for example, have revealed that they rarely use formal methods to determine the return on the investments they make mathematically, rather they seek investments that 'feel right'. A study by Shepherd (1999) draws a distinction between espoused and in-use decision making by venture capitalists. His findings indicate that the criteria venture capitalists *say* they are using may be different from what they *actually* use in decision-making practice.

Before an investor will make an investment they will need some information about the venture. Thus the entrepreneur will need to answer a series of questions about it. The key questions are as follows.

Is the venture of the right type?

Many, if not most, investors specialise in certain types of business. Private investors and business angels may confine themselves to industry sectors in which they have knowledge and experience. Some venture capitalists focus on investment opportunities in certain technological areas; for example: biotechnology or information technology. Another important dimension of specialisation is the *stage of development* of the business and the nature of the financing it requires. Of late, venture capitalists have shifted their attention away from new start-ups and have moved to investing in lower-risk management buy-outs (MBOs). Banks will support new start-ups through their retail arms, but will deal with expansion financing through their corporate operations.

The investor will need to be assured that the venture is in the right area and at the right stage for them.

How much investment is required?

Investors will be interested in the amount of financing required. This will be judged in relation to the business the investor is in, their expertise and the costs they face in monitoring and controlling their investments. Retail banks will offer loans from a few hundred to tens of thousands of pounds. Venture capitalists on the other hand, are not interested in investments of less than about £250 000, and are only really interested in investments of several million pounds sterling. A market flotation is usually concerned with raising at least 5 million pounds.

The key question is, is the investor really the right source given the level of investment needed?

What return is likely?

The return on investment is the likely financial outcome of making a specific investment. The investor will want to know on what basis this has been calculated.

Further, he or she will ask how reasonable it is given the potential for the venture and its management team. The decision to invest will be based on an assessment of the returns in relation to the risks and how the investment opportunity compares to others available. However, it should be noted that even for quite large investments, this comparison may be made on an intuitive rather than an explicit basis. Certain investors specialise in different levels of risk. Venture capitalists seek more risk than retail banks. Specialist high growth markets usually reflect higher risk investments than mainstream ones.

What is the growth stage of the venture?

Critically, this question relates to what the investment capital is required for. Is it to start a new business or is it to fund the expansion of an established business? Is the venture at an early stage in its growth requiring capital to fund an aggressive growth strategy or is the business at a mature stage with the capital to be used to fund incremental growth? How does this impact on the risk entailed and return offered? Is this stage of growth right for the investor?

What projects will the capital be used for?

This question relates to how the capital will be used within the venture. Is it to cover cash-flow shortfalls which result from strong growth or is it to be used for a more specific project, such as development of new products, funding a sales drive or marketing campaign or entering export markets? Again, the question is how does this impact on risk, return and specialism from the point of view of the investor?

What is the potential for the venture?

The investors will want to know what the venture can be expected to achieve in the future. This will depend on two sets of factors. First, on its *market potential*: that is, how innovative its offering is, how much value this offers the customer in relation to what is already available and the possibilities and limitations the venture faces in delivering this innovation to the customer. Second, it depends on the quality of the entrepreneur and the management team: that is, the skills and experience of the venture's key people and their ability to deliver the potential that the venture has. The critical question is will the investor find the venture's potential attractive and if not, why not?

What are the risks for the venture?

To an investor, the risk of the venture is the probability that it will not deliver the return anticipated. Critical to judging this is an understanding of the assumptions that have been made in estimating the likely return. Some critical areas are assumptions about customer demand, the ability of the business to manage its costs, the ability of the venture to get distributors and other key partners on board, and the reaction of competitors.

The investors' judgement of risk will also depend on their ability to exit the investment by liquidating their holding. An investor will ask exactly how liquid the business is and whether or not the investment can be secured against particular liquidisable assets. How do the risks match up with what the investor will expect?

How does the investor get in?

The investor will wish to know exactly how their investment is to be made. Is it to be a lump sum upfront or will it take the form of a regular series of cash injections? The entrepreneur must ask whether this is the way the investor normally operates.

How does the investor get out?

The investor will want to know how they will see their return. Will it take the form of cash? If so, will it be a single cash payment at some point in the future, or will it be a series of payments over time? Alternatively, will it take the form of a holding of stock in the firm? If so, how can such a holding be liquidated? Loans are usually paid back in cash form whereas an equity holding will mature as a holding in the firm. Venture capitalists with equity holdings will insist on a clear exit strategy which will enable them to convert their equity to cash, either by selling on a market or converting it with the venture.

What post-investment monitoring procedures will be in place?

An investor will want to know the means by which they will be able to keep track of their investment. A business plan will normally be required before an injection of capital is made. The business plan is an excellent way of communicating and of managing the investors' expectations. Regular financial reports will provide key information on the performance of the business and its liquidity (and hence its exposure to risk). The entrepreneur must consider whether the monitoring procedures on offer will be greeted as adequate by the investor.

What control mechanisms will be available?

Monitoring is of little use unless the investor can use the information gained to influence the behaviour of the venture's management. Investors who hold shares can signal their approval or otherwise by buying and selling their stock in the market. This buying and selling changes the value of the company. The ultimate sanction is for the value of the business to fall to a level where a takeover can happen and a new set of managers be brought in.

Large investors will usually take a more direct route to control. This may be by lobbying the venture's management or by having a representative permanently on the firm's board. The question that must be asked is how the control mechanisms on offer will influence the investor's decision.

Communication skills

Entrepreneurs and investors meet through a process of communication. Communication is a human process involving not only the passage of information but also an attempt to influence behaviour. Entrepreneurs communicate with investors not just because they wish to tell them about their ventures, but also because they want the investors to support them.

The process of communication between an entrepreneur and an investor is not just a matter of the *what* of the answers but also the *how*. The entrepreneur can exert a positive influence on investors by understanding the questions they are asking, by ensuring that the answers to those questions have been explored, and where appropriate, by having hard evidence to back up the answers given.

Venture capitalists reject the vast majority (over 95 per cent) of proposals made to them. Though banks may back a higher proportion of proposals, rejections still greatly outnumber acceptances. Even if the business idea is sound, an investment of time and energy in making sure that proposals and other communications to backers are sympathetic to their information needs, and are well constructed as pieces of communication, will help the investor make their decision and will reflect positively on the professionalism of the entrepreneur. This will ensure that the venture is in the forefront of the race to obtain capital.

Summary of key ideas

- Financial support is a critical factor in the success of the new venture.
- Suppliers of investment capital are differentiated by the *amount* of capital they will supply, the *risks* they will undertake and the way in which they will expect to see their investment *mature*.
- Investors select investment opportunities by *filtering* them for suitability. This filtering process has formal analysis and informal 'intuitive' aspects.
- The vast majority of investment proposals are rejected.
- Effective entrepreneurs approach investors with an understanding of the *questions* for which they will need answers before they decide to support the venture.

Suggestions for further reading

Boocock, G. and **Woods, M.** (1997) 'The evaluation criteria used by venture capitalists: Evidence from a UK venture fund', *International Small Business Journal*, Vol. 16, No. 1, pp. 36–57.

Camp, S.M. and **Sexton, D.L.** (1992) 'Trends in venture capital investment: Implications for high-technology firms', *Journal of Small Business Management*, July, pp. 11–19.

Fletcher, M. (1995) 'Decision-making by Scottish bank managers', *International Journal of Entrepreneurial Behaviour and Research*, Vol. 1, No. 2, pp. 37–53.

Haar, N.E., Starr, J. and **Macmillan, I.C.** (1988) 'Informal risk capital investors: Investment patterns on the east coast of the USA', *Journal of Business Venturing*, Vol. 3, pp. 11–29.

Hall, J. and **Hofer, C.W.** (1993) 'Venture capitalists' decision criteria in new venture evaluation', *Journal of Business Venturing*, Vol. 8, pp. 25–42.

Landström, H. (1993) 'Informal risk capital in Sweden and some international comparisons', *Journal of Business Venturing*, Vol. 8, pp. 525–40.

Knight, R.M. (1994) 'Criteria used by venture capitalists: A cross cultural analysis', *International Small Business Journal*, Vol. 13, No. 1, pp. 26–37.

Macmillan, I.C., Siegel, R. and **Subba Narashima, P.N.** (1985) 'Criteria used by venture capitalists to evaluate new venture proposals', *Journal of Business Venturing*, Vol. 1, pp. 119–28.

Macmillan, I.C., Zeeman, L. and **Subba Narashima, P.N.** (1987) 'Effectiveness of criteria used by venture capitalists in the venture screening process', *Journal of Business Venturing*, Vol. 2, pp. 123–38.

Maier, II, J.B. and **Walker, D.A.** (1987) 'The role of venture capital in financing small business', *Journal of Business Venturing*, Vol. 2, pp. 207–14.

Mason, C. and **Harrison, R.** (1996) 'Why "business angels" say no: A case study of opportunities rejected by an informal investor syndicate', *International Small Business Journal*, Vol. 14, No. 2, pp. 35–51.

Murray, G.C. (1992) 'A challenging marketplace for venture capital', *Long Range Planning*, Vol. 25, No. 6, pp. 79–86.

Norton, E. and **Tenenbaum, B.H.** (1992) 'Factors affecting the structure of US venture capital deals', *Journal of Small Business Management*, July, pp. 20–9.

Ray, D.M. and **Turpin, D.V.** (1993) 'Venture capital in Japan', *International Small Business Journal*, Vol. 11, No. 4, pp. 39–56.

Rea, R.H. (1989) 'Factors affecting success and failure of seed capital/start-up negotiations', *Journal of Business Venturing*, Vol. 4, pp. 149–58.

Roberts, E.B. (1991) 'High stakes for high-tech entrepreneurs: Understanding venture capital decision making', *Sloan Management Review*, Winter, pp. 9–20

Rock, A. (1987) 'Strategy *v* tactics from a venture capitalist', *Harvard Business Review*, Nov-Dec, pp. 63–7.

Shepherd, D.A. (1999) 'Venture capitalist's introspections: A comparison of "in use" and "espoused" decision policies', *Journal of Small Business Management*, Vol. 37, No. 2, pp. 76–87.

Sweeting, R.C. (1991) 'UK venture capital funds and the funding of new technology-based businesses: Process and relationships', *Journal of Management Studies*, Vol. 28, No. 6, pp. 601–22.

Tyebjee, T.T. and **Bruno, A.V.** (1984) 'A model of venture capital investment activity', *Management Science*, Vol. 30, No. 9, pp 1051–66.

Selected case material

When it pays not to keep the pedal flat on the floor

1 October 1998

The very fastest growing companies tend to be less successful in raising finance, a recent survey reveals. **James Smith** examines its findings

The whiff of recession is in the air, and the capital needs of small companies are bound to rise.

So they would be well advised not to keep the pedal flat on the floor, since the very fastest growing companies tend to be generally less successful in obtaining finance, according to a recent survey by the ESRC (Economic and Social Research Council) Centre for Business Research at Cambridge University.

The biennial survey, published this week, looked at 2,520 businesses with fewer than 500 employees. It found 40 per cent had sought a total of £432m of outside capital between 1995 and 1997 and obtained 80 per cent of their requirements.

Companies with more than 100 staff were significantly more successful than smaller companies, on average securing 95 per cent of what they asked for, compared with only 72 per cent at micro-companies (with under 10 staff).

Moreover, the longer the business had been established, the more likely it was to obtain the capital sought. Businesses with at least a 10-year history were granted 85 per cent of their requests, compared with 75 per cent for their younger brethren.

However, when classified according to employment growth, the highest achievers – growing at 40 per cent or more over three years – were noticeably less successful in obtaining finance. Capital providers tended to favour slower growth firms, awarding them 87 per cent of the amounts requested, compared with 82 per cent for fast-growth companies. "The very fastest growing companies are seen as more likely to trip up," says Alan Hughes, the centre's director.

Innovative businesses (defined as those that had introduced a product or process innovation during the period) sought on average twice as much outside capital as the rest. For both sorts of company, the bank was almost always the first port of call, and both stood an equally good chance of securing their needs.

But innovators were more likely to approach venture capital companies, and very significantly more likely to be successful when they did so. Banks rejected 17 per cent of applications for funds from innovators and the others. Venture capitalists rejected 55 per cent of the non-innovators but only 42 per cent of innovators.

Companies spending an above-average amount on research and development compared with sales tended to have problems with funding, according to the study. While they were neither more nor less likely to seek finance than other sorts of business, those that did sought half as much again as conventional companies, and were twice as likely to be turned down.

As with innovators, high-tech companies were more likely to knock on venture capitalists' doors than were conventional companies. Here though, the interest was not reciprocated; venture capitalists apparently preferred lower technology companies.

Overall, bank loans and overdrafts remained the main source of finance for small companies but their importance had diminished significantly in favour of hire purchase and leasing.

Venture capitalists provided only a tiny share of small businesses' capital needs and, of all the sources approached, they were by far the most likely to reject applications. Indeed, private individuals – typically business angels with experience and expertise to offer as well as money – financed more enterprises than venture capitalists.

Mr Hughes found small companies' relations with their banks had improved in recent years, while their financing needs had diminished since the early 1990s as profitability had improved markedly. "Just over half of the small companies in our 1993 survey had sought some kind of outside capital in the previous two years, compared with only 39 per cent during 1995-97."

In a recession however, smaller businesses become vulnerable, he continues, with their still relatively high dependence on trade credit and overdrafts.

A simpler route to buy-out success

1 October 1998

Why does a typical MBO take three months to complete?
3i is trying out a new fast-track system, writes **Juliette Jowit**

Maurice Wilson has just completed his first management buy-out. It took six weeks, the process was "simple" and on the day they signed champagne corks popped at 5pm.

It was a far cry from the image of traumatic waits of at least three months for completion, with long-winded paperwork and changing demands, he says. "I'd heard the horror stories, the duplicate forms, the costs behind it and financial people going through the same process, whether it's £5m or £500m, and all wanting to use their own documents. It just seemed to me such a simple process."

Mr Wilson led the first MBO completed under 3i's new fast track system, introduced in May this year for deals up to £5m.

The scheme was introduced to simplify the process, cutting time and therefore costs, says Paul Traynor, head of 3i in the west Midlands, one of two trial areas.

Introducing a focused question and answer application form, scaling down the due diligence process and using standard financial and legal documents can reduce the total deal time to as little as two to three weeks, he hopes.

"We are trying to drive costs out of the process both in a financial sense – we are trying to minimise the amount of money you give to your accountant and solicitor and everyone else – and in an opportunity cost sense – we should be clearer about decisions and more up front . . . so the experience of going through this process should be much better."

The new system breaks down into six phases, with time and cost savings made in each:

- Instead of a traditional business plan, companies fill out a standard application form targeting exactly the information required to make a decision. It is quicker and guarantees they provide the important details.
- 3i and an independent consultant consider the application and a decision is made in 48 hours. Previously it took 10-14 days.
- An offer is made using a new standard set of published criteria. For example the sale price is generally 8-12 times earnings.
- Accountants carry out a shortened due diligence process and make an oral presentation, taking one week instead of five.
- Bankers who have signed up to the system – so far NatWest and Bank of Scotland – use standard documents and waive the right to carry out separate due diligence.
- The legal documents are again standard. Variations are possible but not encouraged. "We are trying to convince the professional community they don't need to reinvent the wheel every time," says Mr Traynor.

It is impossible to coax any criticism out of Maurice Wilson, managing director of Nature's Store, the health foods business bought from Lloyds Chemists for £2.6m.

"I was totally impressed, one with the fast track system and, two, with the people. It really was a team effort and it was very impressive."

In the late 1980s 3i introduced a similar product, Core Capital, which fell by the wayside.

Mr Traynor believes there was not enough of a push behind the scheme, which concentrated on reducing internal paperwork. Eventually it was absorbed into the general system, including the new fast track.

The new system is not foolproof. The whim of the vendor is one of several factors beyond the control of 3i and the buyer and some professionals will continue to opt for their own paperwork.

Also there is the additional risk for the venture capitalists of cutting corners in the application, decision making and due diligence processes.

This is an acceptable risk for 3i due to its experience and the size of its market – about half of all sub-£5m deals – says Mr Traynor.

Long term the company hopes to increase its market dominance by winning more deals and by raising the percentage of inquiries which result in deals from about one in two to three in four.

"We think there's competitive advantage for us because it's making the portfolio bigger," he adds.

The scheme is being trialed in the east and west Midlands because of the high concentration of corporate activity – about 20 per cent of 3i's business – and a high proportion of MBOs.

A decision will be made in weeks about extending the fast track process nationwide. Long term the model could help simplify the process for bigger deals.

"We can't afford to take the short cuts with the big deals . . . but I think we have learned a lot about the way people can be attracted to the concept of MBOs," Mr Traynor says.

Businesses learn from past mistakes

19 November 1999

With banks reluctant to lend, many Italians have looked to family and friends for help providing start-up capital, writes **Ian Hamilton Fazey**

As the UK looks for new ways to encourage entrepreneurship, Italy might be thought a good place to look for lessons. It has a highly successful scheme to help young people start businesses; entrepreneurship seems part of the culture; working for yourself commonplace. There is an assumption that if people fail – and 46 per cent do so within five years – they will learn from their mistakes and start again.

Eighty per cent of the private sector comprises small and medium-sized owner-managed enterprises, while the Organisation for Economic Co-operation and Development has put the self-employed at more than 22 per cent of the workforce, a larger proportion than in other European economies.

Ironically, however, Italy until recently had no small business policy and looked to Britain to develop one. OECD figures show UK self-employment rose from 7 per cent of the workforce to 12.6 per cent between 1980 and 1994, while in the late 1980s the Italian government was impressed by British Steel (Industry), which helped create more than 108,000 jobs in steel closure areas.

BS(I)'s policy was based on three elements – advice, finance and premises – and national policy has echoed this ever since. Italy, with its short-lived governments, did not address these issues. Few Italians start a business with bank support. They save their start-up capital, sometimes for years, and borrow from parents, other family members and friends.

Italy has almost no merchant banks and the fragmented banking sector is tightly regulated because of past banking failures. Banks have therefore become risk-averse and reluctant to lend.

When Promozione e Sviluppo Imprenditoriale, or SPI, a government agency formed in the late 1980s to promote entrepreneurship, set up a loan guarantee scheme five years ago to encourage start-ups in the depressed Mezzogiorno regions of the south, Sicily and Sardinia, only one Italian bank, the Monte dei Paschi di Siena, joined up.

It capped its funds on the assumption that a quarter of businesses it backed would fail, even though the scheme operated only in nationallyfunded business incubators with a proven failure rate of just 5 per cent.

An OECD study of Italian business incubators concluded that culture, environment and social attitudes were probably more important than funding mechanisms in encouraging entrepreneurship, combined with positive public policies towards advice, premises and finance.

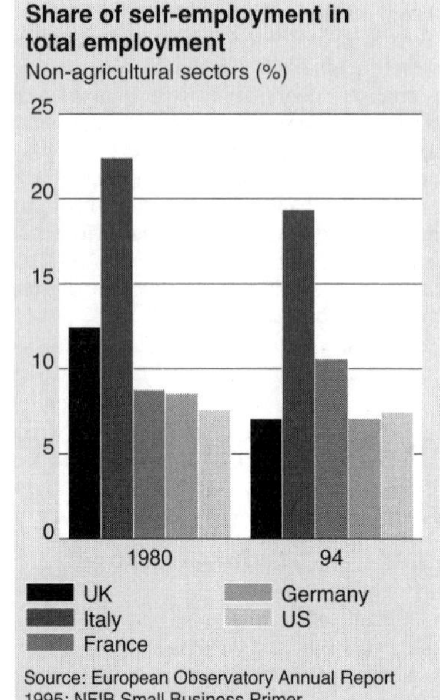

Source: European Observatory Annual Report 1995; NFIB Small Business Primer

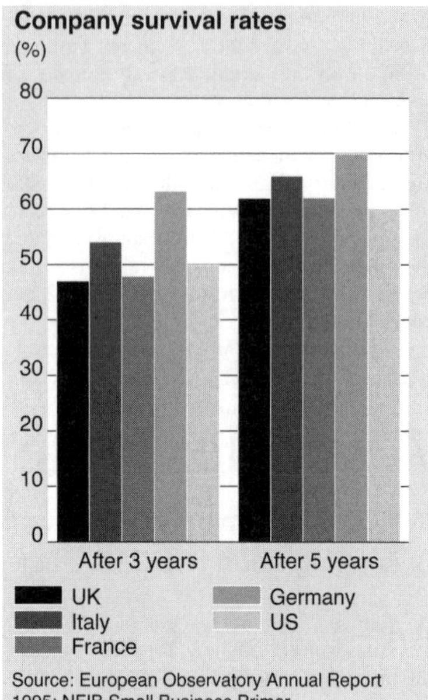

Source: European Observatory Annual Report 1995; NFIB Small Business Primer

Italy has a two-speed economy. It thrives from Rome northwards, but struggles in the south, where an endemic culture of dependency and, sometimes, a poor distribution of basic utilities such as power and water can make entrepreneurship difficult.

After rounds of European Union-enforced steel and shipbuilding closures in the 1980s, SPI was formed to attack the problem of unemployment. A network of incubators, each housing between 40 and 80 companies, was one answer.

The incubators' low failure rates are partly the result of tough selection policies. All run training courses for would-be applicants, but only one in 10 gets in.

Of scores of entrepreneurs interviewed for the OECD evaluation, only two had successfully borrowed money from the bank under the loan guarantee scheme, thus avoiding up to three years of saving to accumulate capital. The rest had started from their own or privately borrowed resources and then used growing turnover to expand. This was found to aid survival, nurturing financially conservative entrepreneurs, who did not over-extend and calculated risks carefully.

The entrepreneurs also tended to work with cash. The downside of this for the government is that it encourages the black economy and, in parts of Mezzogiorno, organised crime.

Parallel to this is an outstandingly successful government-funded scheme to encourage young entrepreneurs under 24. Highly selective, the Società per l'Imprenditorialità Giovanile – or Youth Entrepreneurship Agency – approved only 1,056 projects out of 4,603 applications in the first 10 years. Successful applicants are tutored and advised, and the survival rate is running at 82 per cent, with 20,662 jobs created at a cost of L149,000 (£49) each, compared with L60m a job in an incubator, and L350m a job via direct investment.

The agency is now allowed to take equity stakes in the most promising ventures. In addition, an unsecured "loan of honour" – voluntarily repayable from future profits – has been introduced in southern Italy to help get over the problems of financing businesses in poorer areas where the banks really could not care less.

In the gutter seeing stars

13 February 1999

Small companies have taken a bad beating over the past decade. But not everyone sees the sector as a basket case, writes **Philip Coggan**

In the 1960s, Richard Farina wrote a cult novel called Been Down So Long, It Looks Like Up to Me. Although not written about the smaller company sector, it could have been.

Smaller stocks have underperformed larger groups for seven of the past 10 years; indeed, almost ever since the "small company effect" was documented in 1987 by professors Elroy Dimson and Paul Marsh, at the London Business School. Enthusiasts keep hoping for a change in the trend but there was no sign of a reversal in 1998.

Smaller companies recorded their third-worst performance, relative to larger stocks, since 1955. The FTSE SmallCap index fell 10.5 per cent while the FTSE 100 gained 14.5 per cent.

This long period of poor performance has had its effect on market ratings. The price-earnings multiple of the SmallCap (ex-investment trusts) index has dropped to 14, but stocks in the blue-chip FTSE 100 are still able to command a multiple of 24. At one point, during the market correction of last autumn, small company stocks offered a higher yield than gilts.

Surely this should mean that there are profitable opportunities in the smaller company sector? Value investors know that the best profits are to be had when everyone else has finally given up on an asset class.

And, sure enough, there are some signs that sentiment is picking up. The SmallCap outperformed the FTSE 100 by 2.7 per cent last month, amid hopes that the UK economic slowdown might not be as severe as some had feared.

Moreover, corporate buyers seem willing to pay hefty bid premiums for smaller stocks – 100 per cent in the recent case of Adwest. This indicates that they feel the stock market might be underpricing smaller companies.

But hold on a moment. The revival of smaller company stocks in the 1990s has been heralded as often as the first cuckoo of spring. "Every year, a rally in January gets smaller company investors all excited again, only for them to be disappointed by the end of the year," says Scott Evans, a strategist at ABN Amro.

There have been two fundamental reasons why smaller stocks have been so disappointing. The first relates to economic conditions. The smaller company sector has a much higher weighting in manufacturing businesses – engineering, chemicals and the like – than the Footsie.

These businesses have been hurt badly by short-term factors – the early 1990s' recession, the recent strength of sterling – but they also face a longer-term problem. In an era of global competition, industrial over-capacity and slower economic growth, they have no pricing power and face a continuing squeeze on margins. Manufacturing is sinking remorselessly as a proportion of the UK economy.

Second, many investment institutions have lost patience with the sector which, in total, is worth far less than BP Amoco, the trans-Atlantic oil giant. With the market concentrated increasingly in the blue chips – 15 groups soon will account for 44 per cent of the entire UK market capitalisation – smaller stocks look irrelevant.

"There is value in the sector but it will not be realised unless there is someone to realise it for you," says Tim Steer, smaller companies analyst at Merrill Lynch.

"The big investors are not interested. They are not looking at the sub-£200m range – they are moving up the market cap range, particularly into Europe, where they can get liquidity."

Investors will show interest in smaller stocks if they can offer rapid growth prospects, as can be seen in the recent performance of the Neuer Markt in Germany which has a strong weighting in high technology companies. "I have talked to European investors and they have no interest in construction, engineering or chemical smallcap stocks," says Evans.

Of course, institutions are not the only ones that can buy smaller company shares. The sharp jumps last month in internet shares – OnLine rose twentyfold in a couple of weeks – were driven largely by private investors.

But institutional investors are the only ones able to exert the kind of pressure for change that has made several companies agree to bid approaches in recent weeks.

Phillips & Drew Fund Management, which holds substantial stakes in a number of smaller companies, has seen bid approaches for some of its holdings such as Avonside, BWI, Cornwell Parker, Mirror Group, Norcros, Primesight, Sears, Wace and Wembley.

Other big investors seem also to be encouraging the urge to merge. "One institution said to me that I had 120 companies in my portfolio last year and I have put into play 28 of those over the past 12 months," says Steer.

The larger corporate groupings created by these deals may find it easier to stand up to competition, while their shares should offer greater liquidity for big investors. Then, too, venture capital groups are fishing in the smaller company pond, taking advantage of low prices.

All this means that takeover activity in the sector has increased. According to BT Alex Brown, 6.8 per cent of the SmallCap index (by value) was subject to bids in 1997 and a further 6.7 per cent in 1998. That compares with a proportion of just 3.1 per cent in both 1995 and 1996.

So there is hope for the smallcap sector, in the long run at least. Individual small company plays offer the prospects for bid activity, as was illustrated again last week when Delphi, the IT staffing group, announced an approach that lifted the rest of the sector.

And while it might be quite some time before industrial stocks return to the kind of ratings they used to enjoy, the smaller company universe is evolving through sheer attrition – growth areas such as IT and support services are steadily becoming a larger proportion of the sector.

Small company investors may feel as if they are in the gutter, but some of them can still see the stars.

Review questions

Compare and contrast:

1 Venture capital to back up a new start

2 Venture capital to back up a management buy-out

3 Flotation, and

4 Family and network capital

in terms of their likely cost, the amount of risk they will accept and the entrepreneur's freedom to retain control of the venture.

PART 4

Managing the growth and development of the venture

20 The dimensions of business growth

Chapter overview

The potential for growth is a defining feature of the entrepreneurial venture. This chapter is concerned with an exploration of the process of business growth. A multi-faceted approach is developed and the growth of the entrepreneurial venture is considered from ***financial, strategic, structural*** *and* ***organisational*** *perspectives. The chapter concludes by considering how the growth of the venture creates opportunities for, and impacts on, the lives of its stakeholders.*

20.1 The process of growth

KEY LEARNING OUTCOME
An appreciation of the general dynamics of business growth.

Business growth is critical to entrepreneurial success. The potential for growth is one of the factors which distinguishes the entrepreneurial venture from the small business. Organisational growth, however, means more than just an increase in size. Growth is a dynamic process. It involves development and change within the organisation, and changes in the way in which the organisation interacts with its environment. Though an organisation grows as a coherent whole, organisational growth itself is best understood in a multi-faceted way. It has as many aspects as there are aspects of organisation itself. The case for a multi-perspective approach to understanding organisational growth and change was made very effectively by Henry Mintzberg in his book *The Structuring of Organisations* (1979).

Given the multi-faceted nature of organisation the entrepreneur must constantly view the growth and development of their venture from a number of different perspectives. Four perspectives in particular are important: the *financial*, the *strategic*, the *structural* and the *organisational*.

1 *Financial growth* relates to the development of the business as a commercial entity. It is concerned with increases in *turnover*, the *costs* and *investment* needed to achieve that turnover, and the resulting *profits*. It is also concerned with increases in what the business owns: its *assets*. Related to this is the increase in the *value* of the business, that

is, what a potential buyer might be willing to pay for it. Because financial growth measures the additional value that the organisation is creating which is available to be distributed to its stakeholders, it is an important measure of the *success* of the venture.

2 *Strategic growth* relates to the changes that take place in the way in which the organisation interacts with its environment as a coherent, *strategic*, whole. Primarily, this is concerned with the way the business develops its capabilities to exploit a presence in the marketplace. It is the profile of opportunities which the venture exploits and the assets, both tangible and intangible, it acquires to create *sustainable competitive advantages*.

3 *Structural growth* relates to the changes in the way the business organises its internal systems, in particular, managerial *roles* and *responsibilities*, reporting *relationships*, *communication* links and resource *control systems*.

4 *Organisational growth* relates to the changes in the organisation's *processes*, *culture* and *attitudes* as it grows and develops. It is also concerned with the changes that must take place in the entrepreneur's role and leadership style as the business moves from being a 'small' to a 'large' firm.

The four types of growth described are not independent of each other. They are just different facets of the same underlying process. At the heart of that process is the awarding of valuable resources to the venture by external markets because it has demonstrated that it can make better use of them, that is, create more value from them, than can the alternatives on offer. That better use of resources is a consequence of the entrepreneur's decision making.

The *strategic* perspective must take centre stage. It is this which relates the needs of customers to the ability of the business to serve them. *Financial* growth is a measure of the business's performance in serving the needs of its markets, thus it is a measure of the resources the market has allocated to the firm. The firm must convert those resources into assets. These assets are configured by the structure of the organisation. Additional resources means increasing the *assets* the business holds which in turn demands changes to the *structure* in which they are held.

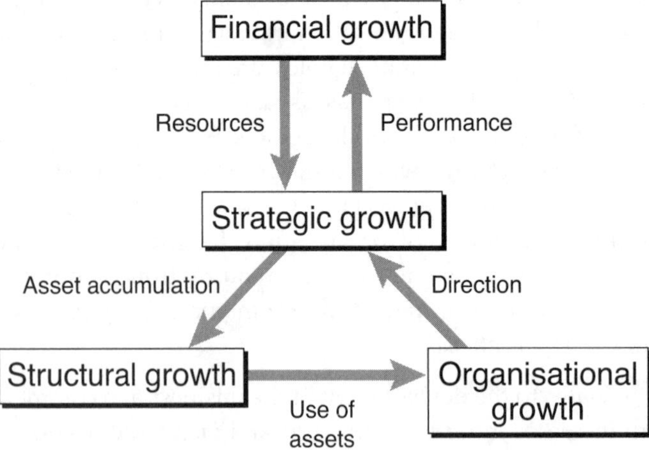

Fig. 20.1 The dynamics of growth for the entrepreneurial venture

This structure only provides a framework, however (see Fig. 20.1). The decisions which the individuals who make up the organisation make and the actions that they take in relation to the assets it owns are governed by wider dimensions of the organisation such as its culture and attitudes. Strategic growth has a *direction* and that direction results from the vision and leadership the entrepreneur offers.

It must also be added that although growth is a *defining* feature of the entrepreneurial venture, this does not mean that an entrepreneurial business has a *right* to grow. It merely means that, if managed in the right way, it has the *potential* to grow. Growth must be made an objective for the venture. It is an opportunity that must be managed effectively if it is to be capitalised upon. For the entrepreneur, growth is a reward for identifying the right opportunities, understanding how they might be exploited and competing effectively to take advantage of them.

20.2 Financial analysis

KEY LEARNING OUTCOME
An understanding of the way in which financial growth is recorded, reported and analysed.

The financial performance of a firm is important to all its stakeholders. A sound financial position brings security for employees, offers customers the prospect of good service and investment in future offerings, and promises suppliers a demand for their outputs. Investors, of course, have an interest in seeing a good return on their capital. They will take particular note of the financial performance of the businesses they have chosen to back.

Investors and businesses communicate in a number of ways. The degree of personal contact will depend on the type of investors, the amount of investment, and the stage of the business's development. The nature of the economic system in which the business is operating is also important. Investment systems in different parts of the world vary in both their formal and informal aspects. One key difference is in the way the investor seeks to influence the management of the business. If the business seeks investment in an open stock market then two main means are available to effect this. If the stock market is 'liquid' (as it tends to be in Britain and the USA) then investors can signal their assessment of the firm's performance by buying and selling shares. An increasing share price offers the business security for obtaining further investment. A falling share price can make a business susceptible to takeover. Other economies (typically those in continental Europe) tend towards a greater degree of intervention by investors. Institutional shareholders (such as pension funds and banks) may appoint directors to act on their behalf.

If the business has not yet reached the stage where it is ready to offer investment stock to the stock market and is reliant on private and institutional investment such as banks and venture capital instead, then a high degree of both investor scrutiny and involvement is likely.

Whatever the nature and means of the interaction between business and investor, financial reporting provides a common language by which they can communicate with each other. At the centre of this communication are two documents: the *balance sheet* and the *profit and loss account* (see Fig. 20.2). The balance sheet is a summary of *what the business owns*, that is, its *assets* and *liabilities*. It represents the state of the business at *a point in time*, specifically the date of the report. The profit and loss account is a report on *what the business has done* over the previous period, that is, its trading activity in terms of *sales* (or *turnover*), the *expenditure* involved in achieving those sales and the resulting *profits*. The reporting period is normally one year but can be a shorter interval if investors see the need for more detailed tracking.

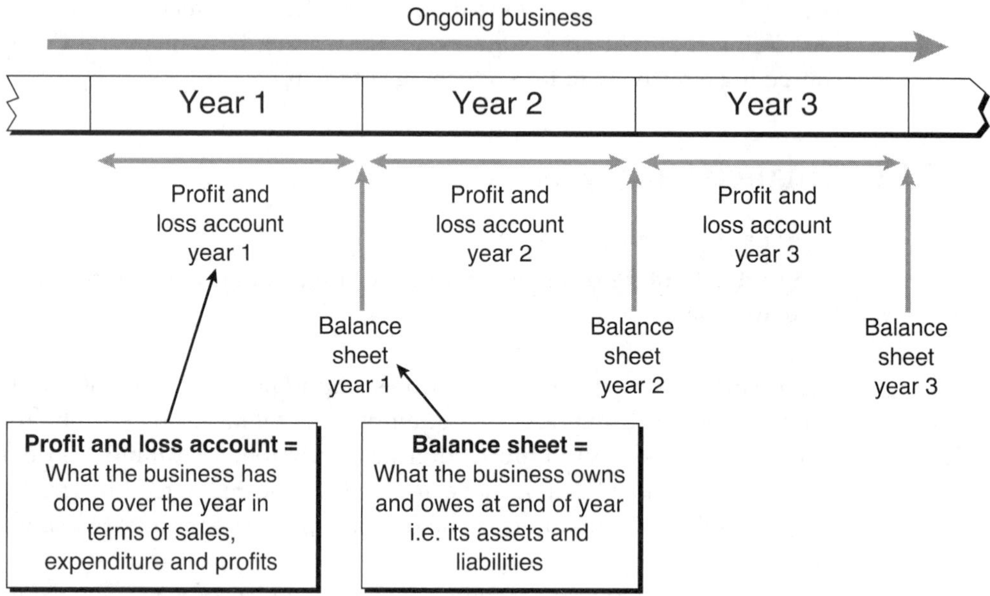

Fig. 20.2 The structure of financial reporting: the Balance Sheet and Profit and Loss Account

The balance sheet

The balance sheet is so called because it is usual to show the assets and liabilities of the firm as being equal (i.e. balancing). The details presented on the balance sheet vary between different countries, however, some of the key lines are as indicated in Table 20.1.

A number of important relationships can be derived from the balance sheet. Some of the more important are:

1 The fundamental balance sheet identity:

Total assets = Total liabilities

2 Net assets are the assets the business will actually have available over the coming year. Net assets represent the sum of assets and working capital. They can also be defined as:

Net assets = Total assets – Short-term liabilities to outsiders

Table 20.1 The Balance Sheet

Assets	Liabilities
Tangible assets The value of all buildings and machinery etc. owned by the firm.	Short-term creditors All creditors (people and organisations to whom the firm owes money) due for payment within one year.
+	+
Intangible assets The valuation of the things 'owned' by the firm, which have no physical form but can, potentially, be bought and sold, e.g. brand names and goodwill.	Long-term creditors All creditors due for payment after one year. Important elements include: • loan repayment due after one year; • dividends planned for investors (including the entrepreneur's remuneration); • long-term repayments agreed with suppliers; and • taxes owed to the government.
+	+
Current assets Cash in hand, stock (including finished goods, work in progress and raw materials), creditor and trade debts owed to the firm.	Called-up share capital The permanent capital of the firm in the form of the face value of issued shares.
+	+
Investments Investments held by the firm in other businesses, government stock and other financial instruments.	Capital reserves The profits held by the firm. Properly, these are the property of the investors in the firm. Some may be distributed to investors in the form of dividends; others may be retained for future investment.
=	=
Total assets	**Total liabilities**

Because of the balance sheet identity, net assets must be equal to the total of shareholders' funds.

3 Net current assets (also known as *working capital*) are those resources which are *liquid*, that is, they either already exist in the form of cash, or are expected to be turned into cash within twelve months of the report date. The definition is:

Net current assets = Current assets – Short-term liabilities

4 Capital employed is a measure of the total resources available for use by the firm's management. It is defined as:

Capital employed = (Long-term creditors + Called-up share capital + Capital reserves)

The profit and loss account

The profit and loss account provides a summary of the revenues obtained as a result of trading activity over the period in question. The key lines are shown in Table 20.2.

Table 20.2 The Profit and Loss Account

Income

Turnover from normal trading activities
The income generated as a result of the firm's normal business activities.

Extraordinary income
Additional income which is a result of activities which are not part of the firm's usual profile of business.

Income from investments
Income received as a result of investments owned by the firm in other businesses or other investment instruments.

Outgoing

Cost of sales
The expenditure that was necessary to deliver the sales that were achieved. Important cost elements are:

- raw materials and factors;
- salaries;
- purchase (or rental) of machinery and equipment;
- depreciation charges on machinery and equipment; and
- sales and marketing expenditure.

Interest on debt
Payments to cover interest charges on outstanding debts.

Extraordinary expenditure
Expenditure that has been made but which is not typical of the expenditure the business normally faces. It is a result of special circumstances or a one-off activity. Critically, it is expenditure the business does not expect to face again.

Taxation
Money owed to the government as a result of taxation.

Dividends
Money to be paid to investors as a return on their investment. (This may include some of the entrepreneur's remuneration insofar as the entrepreneur is an investor.)

Profits for a period represent the difference between income and outgoings. A number of different measures of profit level are important:

1 *Gross profits* – The basic profits generated by the business. This is sometimes referred to as profit before interest payable and tax (PBIT).

Gross profits = Sales – Cost of sales

2 *Profit before tax* – Profits left after interest on debts has been paid.

Profit before tax (PBT) = Gross profits – Interest

3 *Profit after tax* – Profits left after any tax owing to the government has been paid.

Profit after tax (PAT) = PBT – Tax

4 *Retained profits* – Any profit left after tax has been paid is properly the property of the firm's shareholders. Some of it may be distributed to them in the form of dividends. Some may, however, be retained by the firm for future investment. Such profits are called *retained profits*. The retained profit figure on the profit and loss account is equivalent to the *capital reserves* figure on the balance sheet.

Retained profits = PAT – Dividends

Ratio analysis

The performance of the entrepreneurial venture must be measured not only in terms of absolutes – the new value it generates – but also in relative terms, i.e. the new value created given the resources the entrepreneur has to hand. An investor in the venture is interested not so much in 'profits' as in the *returns* the venture will offer for a *given level of investment*.

Ratio analysis can be used to provide a valuable insight into the performance, condition and stability of the venture. As its name suggests, it is based on an evaluation of the ratios between different lines on the Balance Sheet and Profit and Loss Account.

Three types of ratio are important. *Performance ratios* indicate the way the business is performing, that is, the value it is creating from the resources to hand. *Financial status* ratios provide an indication of the financial security of the venture and how exposed a backer's investment is. If the venture has a stock market listing, then *stock market ratios* can be used to compare the performance of an investment in the venture with alternative investment opportunities. Some of these ratios will now be explored in more detail.

Performance ratios

Profit margin

The profit margin of a business is the ratio (expressed as a percentage) of profits to turnover. It is defined as:

$$\textbf{Profit margin} = \frac{\textbf{(Profits} \times \textbf{100\%)}}{\textbf{Turnover}}$$

The usual profit level for this ratio is profit before tax, but other profit measure levels may also be used.

Return on investment

Return on investment (ROI) is *the* fundamental measure of a venture's performance. Two different ROIs are used. Return on equity (ROE) is the ratio of profit after interest payments have been made but before tax (and normally before extraordinary items too) to shareholders' funds:

$$\textbf{Return on equity} = \frac{\textbf{(Profit before tax} \times \textbf{100\%)}}{\textbf{(Called up share capital + Capital reserves)}}$$

Return on net assets (RONA) is the ratio of gross profit to net assets:

$$\textbf{Return on net assets} = \frac{\textbf{(Gross profit} \times \textbf{100\%)}}{\textbf{Net assets}}$$

Although these two measures are related, they offer slightly different perspectives on the performance of the venture. ROE gives *investors* (especially ordinary shareholders) an indication of the profits which are (potentially) available to them in relation to the investment they have made in the venture. RONA gives the *venture's management* an indication of the profits they are generating (which can later be distributed to lenders, investors and taxing authorities) in relation to the assets that they have available to them. In more technical terms, RONA is a performance measure which is *independent* of the capital structure of the firm.

Turnover ratios

In general, turnover ratios are those which look at the number of times some measure of the firm's asset ownership generates some measure of the firm's income. Two are particularly important.

Net asset turnover (NAT) indicates the number of times annual sales are generated by the firm's net assets. It is defined by:

$$\textbf{Net asset turnover} = \frac{\textbf{Sales}}{\textbf{Net assets}}$$

In a similar manner, fixed asset turnover (FAT) indicates the number of times annual sales are generated by fixed assets:

$$\textbf{Fixed asset turnover} = \frac{\textbf{Sales}}{\textbf{Fixed assets}}$$

Financial status ratios

An investor is not only interested in the performance of the firm they have invested in but also in the *risk* that that investment entails. A key element of risk for the entrepreneurial venture is its ability to meet the liabilities it accepts given the revenues it generates. *Financial status ratios* can be used to gain an insight into the business's position with regard to its liabilities. Two sorts of financial status ratio are useful. *Solvency ratios* give an indication of the firm's general financial health and its ability to meet its long-term liabilities. *Liquidity ratios* give an indication of the firm's ability to meet its short-term liabilities where it is called upon to do so in a crisis.

Solvency ratios

The debt ratio represents the capital structure of the firm. It is the ratio of debt (that is money which has been borrowed at a fixed rate of interest) to equity (that is, money obtained from investors whose return will depend on the overall performance of the venture). It is defined as:

$$\textbf{Debt ratio} = \frac{\textbf{(Long-term debt} \times \textbf{100\%)}}{\textbf{Capital employed}}$$

where **Capital employed = (Long-term debt + called-up share capital + retained profits)**

A related ratio is called *gearing*.

$$\textbf{Gearing} = \frac{\textbf{(Long-term debt} \times \textbf{100\%)}}{\textbf{Shareholders' funds}}$$

where **Shareholders' funds = (Called-up share capital + Retained profits)**

Clearly, the debt ratio and gearing provide related information. The debt ratio is more frequently used in the UK whereas gearing (also referred to as leverage) tends to be quoted in the USA.

Interest cover is a ratio of profits to interest owed to those who lend money to the venture. It gives an indication of a firm's ability to pay interest on its debts. It is given by:

$$\textbf{Interest cover} = \frac{\textbf{Profit before interest and tax (PBIT)}}{\textbf{Interest on long-term debt}}$$

Liquidity ratios

Liquidity ratios are concerned with *short-term* liabilities. Two ratios are particularly important. The *current ratio* is the ratio of current assets to current liabilities.

$$\textbf{Current ratio} = \frac{\textbf{Current assets}}{\textbf{Current liabilities}}$$

where **Current liabilities are those short-term creditors who expect payment within one year.**

The *acid test* (or *quick ratio*) is a straight measure of a firm's ability to pay its short-term creditors immediately from its liquid assets. It is defined as:

$$\textbf{Acid test ratio} = \frac{\textbf{Liquid assets}}{\textbf{Current liabilities}}$$

Liquid assets are cash and short-term debtors (and therefore equal to current assets minus stock). An acid test of 1.0 or more indicates that the business is 'safe'. It would, if demanded, be able to pay off its short-term liabilities from the liquid assets it has in hand.

Stock market ratios

If the venture has issued shares and is floated on a stock market, then a number of ratios can be used to evaluate the performance of the business and investments in it. To calculate these ratios, the information given in financial reports must be supplemented with routine reports on share price performance. This information is provided daily by the *Financial Times* and is available via the Internet.

Earnings per share

Earnings per share (EPS) are the profits potentially available for each share that has been issued. Profits are measured after interest and taxation but normally before extraordinary items have been paid.

$$\textbf{Earnings per share} = \frac{\textbf{Profit after tax}}{\textbf{Number of shares issued}}$$

Note that if more than one type of share has been issued then the ratio usually refers to ordinary shares.

Price/earnings ratio

The price/earnings ratio (PE ratio) is the ratio of the price at which a share in the business is trading on the stock market to the earnings per share.

$$\text{Price/earnings ratio} = \frac{\text{Market price of share}}{\text{Earnings per share (EPS)}}$$

$$= \frac{\text{Market price of share} \times \text{Number of shares}}{\text{Profit after tax}}$$

The market price per share multiplied by the number of shares represents the market's valuation of the firm as a whole. It is sometimes referred to as the firm's *market capitalisation.*

The PE ratio is an indication of the market's confidence in the business, both in terms of the risk it represents and of its future growth potential. A relatively high price relative to earnings indicates that the market regards the investment as being of relatively low risk or that the value of the investment will increase in the future.

Dividend yield

The dividend yield represents the payment made to investors on each share as a proportion of the market value of the share.

$$\text{Dividend yield} = \frac{\text{Dividend per share}}{\text{Market price of share}}$$

The dividend yield will be dependent both on the total profits generated by the business and on the way in which management offer them back to investors or, alternatively, retain them for future investment. A young, high growth business may have a relatively low or even zero dividend yield. However, investors will still value their investment and hang on to it if they feel the venture has the potential to offer high rewards in the future.

Dividend cover

Dividend cover is another measure which indicates the division of available profits by management between passing them to shareholders and retaining them within the business for future investment. Dividend cover represents the number of times the management could, potentially, have paid the actual dividend offered out of the profits that were available to shareholders. It is defined by:

$$\text{Dividend cover} = \frac{\text{Earnings per share}}{\text{Dividend per share}}$$

Clearly, stock market ratios are dependent on share price which is adjusted constantly as new information (both on the business specifically and on the economy in general) reaches the market. This information can be followed in the *Finanacial Times* or on a variety of Internet sites. The annual financial report is an important factor in providing this information but it is far from its entirety. A share price is just an estimation by an investor of the value of their investment. This valuation responds to the way in which the entrepreneur (and other managers) communicate with, and the message that is sent to, investors.

20.3 Financial growth

KEY LEARNING OUTCOME
An understanding of how financial analysis provides a context for understanding the financial growth and development of the venture.

The report of the financial situation, that is, the balance sheet and the profit and loss account and the ratios that can be derived from these items provide those interested in the venture (the entrepreneur, other managers, investors and taxing authorities) with a wealth of information which provides a basis on which decisions may be made. However, decisions must be made within a broader context which needs to consider both the firm's performance *relative to its particular business sector* and the overall *trends* in the firm's performance.

There are no absolute measures of performance. The profit margin, return on investment (or any other performance measure) to be expected from a venture will depend on the sector in which the business operates. What matters is not so much the performance of the venture but its performance *relative* to key competitors and to market norms. Similarly, the expected financial status ratios will vary between different industry sectors. The factor which determines how investment capital is distributed between sectors offering different levels of return is, of course, *risk*. The way in which risk is anticipated by investors can be gleaned from a close examination of the stock market ratios of players within a particular sector.

An entrepreneurial venture is not static. It is undergoing constant growth and development. Investors and other decision makers will colour their decisions not just by reference to the indicators for the business at a single point in time but by evaluating the *trends* in its performance. This will be particularly important for investors who are not expecting immediate returns from the venture but who are willing to accept some risk for the promise of higher returns in the future. Investors' decision making (particularly the key decision of whether to hold or exit from their investment) will be influenced by four main factors.

The underlying performance (return on investment) of the venture

Investors will be interested in the performance of the venture not just in absolute terms but relative to their *expectations* of that performance. Their expectations will be a result of their knowledge of the business and the sector it operates in, and of the promises offered by the entrepreneur driving the venture.

The growth in the value of the venture

The *growth* of the venture can be qualified by a number of financial criteria. Growth in *income* (and by implication, *outgoings*), *assets* and *capital* are equally important. Some of the key indicators to follow include changes in turnover; changes in cash profits; changes in tangible assets; changes in total assets; and changes in shareholders' capital. Growth in these measures can be followed both in absolute terms and as a proportion of absolute values. Proportional changes can be indicated as an index or as a percentage. A *growth index* is calculated as:

$$\text{Growth index} = \frac{\text{Value of measure in year}}{\text{Value of measure in year previous year}}$$

Growth as a *percentage* is given by:

$$\text{Growth \%} = \frac{(\text{Value of measure in year} - \text{Value in previous year})}{\text{Value of measure in previous year}} \times 100\%$$

When making a comparison it is often useful to *discount* for general inflation in an economy. This enables the *real* growth of the venture to be measured. To discount for inflation the *nominal* growth calculated for the venture must be divided by the inflation index for the period under consideration.

$$\text{Real growth} = \frac{\text{Nominal growth}}{\text{Inflation index}}$$

Usually, the general retail price index is used but other more specialist inflation measures may be adopted. If inflation is quoted as a percentage it can be converted by the following formula:

$$\text{Inflation index} = \frac{[(\text{Inflation as \%}) + 100]}{100}$$

Growth by the venture is usually received positively. Expansion of the venture drives an increase in the underlying value of a shareholder's investment. Growth also indicates that the venture has a successful formula and so, *in general*, it signals a reduction in risk. Growth does not, however, come for free. It must be *paid for* and a high level of growth may make cash-flow tighter and so lead to less favourable financial status ratios. This may make the venture slightly more risky in the short-term, particularly if there is a crisis and short-term liabilities have to be met.

The trend in the risk of the venture

While growth tends to reduce risk overall, the specific level of risk faced by the business is, to a degree, under the control of the entrepreneur and other managers. An important factor is the debt ratio (or, alternatively, gearing) of the venture. Debt, on the whole, is cheaper than equity finance. However, debt must be repaid whatever the performance of the business. Debt repayment must take priority over the repayment of equity or dividends. Therefore a high debt ratio does expose the business (and that means its investors) to more risk.

No generalisation can be made about the optimum level of debt to equity. This is a complex issue and not only are interest rates and industry risk relevant, but taxation effects also have an influence. Comparison to industry norms can provide a rough and ready guide.

Financial status and (if the firm has floated shares) stock market ratios provide an insight into the overall risk status of the venture. In general, as the business grows, matures and stabilises investors will expect risk to be reduced. Having faced risk initially they become ready to enjoy the return they are owed.

The dividends yielded by the venture

At the end of the day, investors will wish to see a capital gain through their investment. This may take the form of them receiving dividend payments on the shares they hold or by selling those shares. These two approaches to liquidating investment differ in timing rather than substance. The buyer of the share does so in the expectation of a future flow of dividends. An independent market values the investment on the basis of the cash-flow it can generate.

Managers in the venture will make a decision about how much of the profits generated is to be passed on to the shareholders and how much is to be retained within the business for future investment. Shareholders will either agree to this split or will not. They will show their approval (or otherwise) either by direct interference in the firm or, if their investment is liquid, by buying or selling their shares thus raising or depressing the share price. In general, while investors may be willing to see managers recycle profits back into a young, fast-growing venture they will at some point expect to see a real cash reward for their investment. As the firm matures, it is likely that investors will expect a greater proportion of profits to be given back to them.

A general scheme for analysing the financial growth of an entrepreneurial venture is indicated in Fig. 20.3.

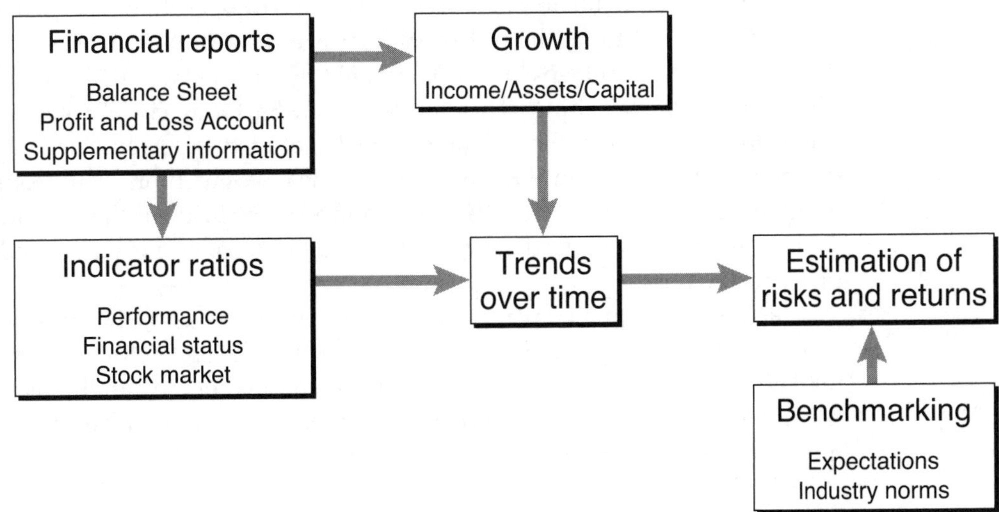

Fig. 20.3 A model of financial appraisal for the entrepreneurial venture

20.4 Strategic growth

KEY LEARNING OUTCOME

An understanding of the ways in which competitive advantage can be developed as the venture grows.

The strategic approach to organisational management regards the organisation as a single *coherent* entity which must be managed in its entirety. It locates the organisation conceptually in an *environment* from which it must draw resources and *add value* to them. The organisation must then distribute the new value created to its stakeholders. The strategic approach also recognises that the organisation is in *competition* with other organisations who also seek to attract and utilise those resources.

From a strategic perspective, the organisation is able to compete for resources by virtue of the *competitive advantages* it develops and maintains. Growth represents the business's success in drawing in resources from its environment. It is a sign that the business has been effective in competing in the marketplace. This suggests that the business has built up a competitive advantage and has managed to sustain it in the face of competitive pressure. However, a competitive advantage is not static. Sustaining an advantage simultaneously develops and enhances it.

All advantages are very sensitive to business growth. In general, expansion of the business can be used to enhance a competitive advantage. This will only occur, however, if the entrepreneur is sensitive to the nature of the competitive advantages that their venture enjoys and strives to actively manage that advantage as the business grows and develops.

Growth and cost advantages

The main source of cost advantages are experience effects. Practice in delivering the outputs leads to a reduction in cost (strictly, the cost of adding a particular amount of value). Costs tend to fall in an exponential way as output increases linearly. Hence, experience cost advantages are (usually) held by the business which has achieved the greatest cumulative output. This can lead to a 'virtuous circle' (see Fig. 20.4). Cost leadership means that the customer can be offered a lower price. This increases demand for the firm's outputs relative to those of competitors. This leads to the firm developing a volume output lead over competitors. In turn, this volume advantage leads to enhanced cost leadership and the ability to offer customers and even lower price, and so on.

Clearly, the entrepreneur can build in cost advantages as the business grows. Such a strategy offers the potential for a consistent and sustainable advantage in the marketplace. It is, however, a strategy which requires certain conditions to be met and it is not without risk. If the strategy is to work the entrepreneur must be sure of a number of features of the market they are developing.

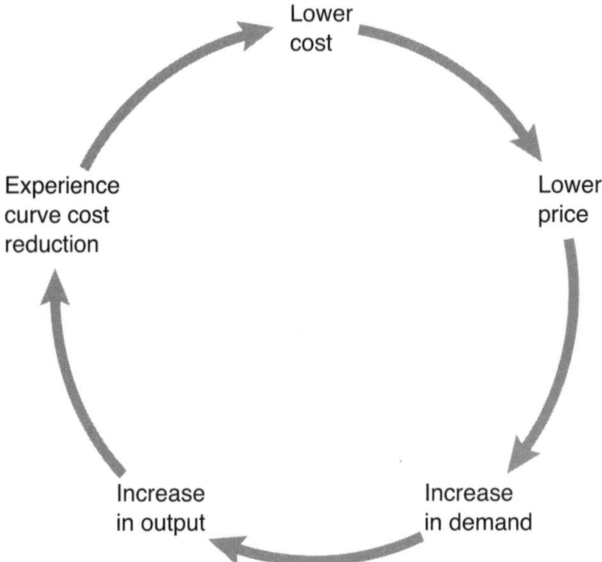

Fig. 20.4 The virtuous circle of cost leadership

Cost advantages have not already been established in the market

If cost advantages have already been established in the market, then the business will risk being a follower rather than a leader. If the venture's costs are not *genuinely* lower than those of the leading competitor then undercutting the leader to subsidise costs and offer the customer a lower price will demand a high level of investment. In some instances such 'undercutting' will be construed as anti-competitive by regulatory bodies. It is, in any case, always expensive.

In order to become a cost leader it is better if the entrepreneur is first into a market. In effect, what this means is that the innovation on which the venture is based is sufficiently different to constitute a 'new' market.

Potential volume outputs make entry into the market worthwhile

Experience curve cost reductions only become meaningful when the output volumes are quite high. Consequently a cost leadership strategy is not a realistic option for a small or even a medium-sized business serving a local market. Cost leadership really becomes a serious option for the business which is an industry maker and which aims to deliver its outputs to a wide (which increasingly today means *global*) market. This is not to say that price is not an important factor for smaller businesses or that they should not manage costs, rather that cost as the *mainstay* of competitive advantage is really the prerogative of the large player.

A corollary of this fact is that the entire market must be ready to accept a fairly homogeneous product. If too much specialisation is required at a local level then the extent to which production is repetitive will be lost and hence the possibility of cost-reducing experience will also be lost.

Sales of the product they are offering to the market are sensitive to price

Experience cost advantages are gained via volume output. The virtuous circle will only be followed if customers respond to lower prices by buying more of the price leader's offerings. This demands that the products offered are *price sensitive* which means that the firm's products must be *substitutable* with those of competitors. Substitutability implies that the products of different suppliers are pretty much equivalent (from the buyer's perspective) and can replace one another in use. To be substitutable, products must not only be similar in a technical sense but they must not have any switching costs associated with them; that is, there should be no additional expense for the customer when moving from one supplier to another.

If switching costs are present *and* the entrepreneur is the first to get customers on board then they may use these costs as the basis of a competitive advantage. Again, this emphasises the importance of innovation in entrepreneurial success.

The experience curve will be steep enough (but not too steep!)

An experience curve has a *gradient*. This is the rate at which increasing output reduces costs, that is, the speed at which learning takes place. The experience curve needs to be steep enough for the volume advantages that the pioneering entrepreneur can gain to lead to cost advantages which have a meaningful impact on prices in the marketplace. If, however, the curve is *too* steep then followers will find it easier to catch up, and any advantage gained initially will be quickly eroded.

Distribution can be maintained

A price advantage offered to the customer is only useful if the customer can get hold of the product. This implies that distribution can be readily achieved. If independent agencies are involved in the distribution process (e.g. wholesalers or retailers) then there is always the danger that a follower will, in some way or other, interfere with the cost-leader's ability to distribute. In effect, they will look towards distributors as the basis for developing a non-cost competitive advantage. If such a distributor 'lock out' occurs, then the leader will lose volume and any cost advantage can be rapidly lost. Often, such actions are restricted by anti-trust legislation. However, such legislation is difficult to enforce. If the business is multinational, then distributors may be tempted to favour local suppliers. Governments who have seen a 'strategic' advantage in supporting local producers have been known to resist pressure to open their markets by accusing global cost-leaders of 'dumping' (i.e. of selling below cost to establish their presence in a market). Even if such accusations are eventually disproved, volume sales may have been lost already. With a cost leadership strategy, time equals volume which means costs which equals money.

Technological innovation will not reset the experience curve

Experience is gained by repetitive utilisation of a particular operational technology to manufacture or deliver a service. If the technological basis of an industry changes then descent down a new experience curve begins. In cost terms, all bets are off! Innovation, both in the type of product offered to the customer and the means for its delivery, offers both an opportunity and a threat. It may be the means by which the entrepreneur first enters the market and gains an advantage over existing players, but, once they are established, and competitive advantage has been built on a particular technology, they are vulnerable to a new generation of innovators. This means that the entrepreneurial business, even if it is following a cost leadership strategy must still look towards maintaining innovation.

The entrepreneur (and financial backers) have patience!

Cost leadership is not a short-term strategy. The pay-offs are far from immediate. While competing on a price leadership basis, profit margins must be kept slim i.e. just sufficient to cover overhead costs. This is the only way in which the business can be sure that it is reflecting its cost advantage with the most competitive market price. However, it will be tempting to raise prices and to increase short-term profit margins. The entrepreneur may be looking for additional returns to invest in the growth of the business. Investors may be eager to see a positive return on their investment. The business may see a price increase as a viable option. It will be in a market-leading position (certainly in volume terms). It may have established a strong relationship with customers. Competitors may have found it hard to gain a foothold in the market. However, the temptation to increase prices must still be resisted!

All these advantages are a *consequence* of keeping prices low. They are the basis on which the business can gain a future reward for maintaining tight profit margins. If the business increases its prices too early then it can create a 'cost umbrella' under which less efficient competitors may shelter. It may be just the gap a competitor needs in order to gain a toe-hold in the market. If a cost leadership strategy is to be effective then the business pursuing it must keep its nerve and keep prices as low as possible for as long as possible. Optimally, prices should be kept to a minimum until market growth has stopped. After this the market will start to lose its attractiveness to new entrants as gaining market share will tend to require the conversion of existing customers rather than drawing new ones into the market. At this point the cost leading business can start to raise prices above costs, to increase profit margins and to harvest its investment.

Figure 20.5 shows how technological innovation and the creation of cost umbrellas both present risks for a cost leadership strategy.

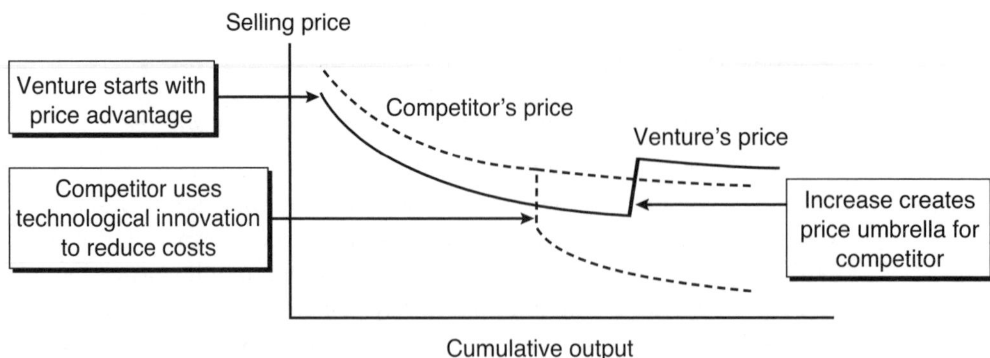

Fig. 20.5 Risks in a cost leadership strategy

Costs are actively managed

Even though costs often follow a mathematical relationship to output volume this does not mean that increasing output *automatically* drives down costs. Increasing output gives the firm's managers the *opportunity* to drive down costs but that is an opportunity they must grasp actively. The management of cost must become the focus of managerial activity. In fact, it must become the key criterion around which decisions are made.

Cost leadership is a strategy which has an impact on, and must be supported by, all the firm's stakeholders. As noted above, customers must be responsive to price and investors must be willing to play a long game. In addition, suppliers must recognise that they must be competitive in the price at which they offer inputs to the business. Further, employees will become aware (and if not managed properly, *acutely* aware) of the fact that they themselves are 'costs' as well as partners in the creation of the business. There is a danger that this will lead them to see their interests as being counter to that of the business. A focus on managing costs must be single-minded. It must also be implemented with sensitivity.

Growth and knowledge advantages

Knowledge advantages arise from knowing something about the customer, the market or the product offered that competitors do not know, which enables the business to offer something of value to the customer. The development of a knowledge-based advantage is dependent on two factors: the *significance* of the knowledge advantage and the rate at which it will be *eroded*.

How significant is the knowledge advantage?

How *valuable* is what is known? Is the knowledge sufficient in scope and does it have significance to enough customers in order to sustain the growth of the business? If so, what level of growth can it sustain?

How will the knowledge advantage be eroded?

How long will it take competitors to *gain* the knowledge and use it themselves? Can they discover it for themselves or through others? Will the venture's activities *signal* it to them?

Clearly, these two factors work against each other. The more valuable the knowledge, the more that competitors will be encouraged to get hold of it for themselves. Knowledge is difficult to protect. A particular piece of knowledge rarely offers more than a transient advantage. If the business aims not just to survive, but to *grow*, on the back of knowledge advantages, then it must be active in a process of constant re-discovery about what it is offering the market and why the market buys it.

To do this the business needs to position itself in a market where discovery and innovation are well received and rewarded. This is certainly the case in 'high-tech' markets where technological innovation is the norm. However, the market does not have to be high-tech. More generally, knowledge-based advantages can be gained in any market where customer expectations are in flux and they are likely to respond well to new offerings.

In order to respond to this the entrepreneurial business must ensure that two activities are given priority. First, it requires that resources are put into understanding the market and its customers. In a functional sense this means *market research*. More broadly, it means that the whole organisation must be attuned to new ideas and new initiatives. It particularly demands that the organisation be responsive to the signals sent out by customers about their needs and desires. Second, it requires that the organisation be active in creating, developing and offering new products and services to the customer. Product development activity must be supported by the processes and systems within the organisation. Indeed it must be *prioritised* by them. These systems must be given centre stage as the growth and development of the organisation is managed.

Growth and relationship advantages

Relationships exist between *people*, not just organisations. During its early stages, the business may be 'fronted' directly by the entrepreneur. He or she will be directly responsible for building productive relationships with the venture's stakeholders. Indeed, tying together and securing the threads of the network into which they have entered may be the entrepreneur's key role. Customers, suppliers, employees and investors will be drawn to the venture as a result of the positive relationship they develop with the entrepreneur. The question becomes how can the entrepreneur maintain relationship advantages as the business grows and develops? Further, how can the entrepreneur use such advantages to *drive* growth in the business?

This challenge is acute. In the first instance, the entrepreneur will be located at the centre of the web of relationships and will be in control of them all. As the organisation grows and develops then the web of relationships becomes much more complex. The entrepreneur can no longer represent the organisation to all the parties who have an interest in it. New individuals must develop the organisation's relationships on a specialist basis. For example, salespeople will make representation to customers.

Procurement and purchasing specialists must work with suppliers. At some stage it may even be necessary to have finance specialists to manage the venture's relationship with its investors.

To understand how relationship advantages may be maintained and developed as the business grows, it is necessary to have a deep understanding of the ways in which the relationships the business has with its stakeholders are *different* from those of competitor organisations; why that difference is important in offering *value* to those stakeholders; and why competitors find it hard to *imitate* those relationships. In particular the entrepreneur must ask the following questions.

Why are the relationships valuable?

What aspect of the relationship creates value for the stakeholder? Does the relationship provide trust which reduces the need for monitoring costs? Does the relationship offer benefits which satisfy social needs? Does the relationship promise the potential to satisfy self-developmental needs? Are these benefits carried as part of the product (say, through *branding*) or are they supplementary to it (say, through working in *association* with the business)?

What are the expectations of the relationships?

What matters in a relationship is not actual outcomes but outcomes in relation to *expectations*. If expectations are met (or even better, *exceeded*) then satisfaction will occur. If they are not met then disappointment will result. Human relationships are complex. The expectations they generate are multi-faceted. They may be manifest at economic, social and self-developmental levels. Often these interact with each other and the effective entrepreneur must manage relationships at each level.

What practices sustain the relationships?

Relationships are acted out. The parties to the relationship play *roles*. To a greater or lesser extent, relationships are *scripted*. Selling, for example, involves a series of reasonably well-defined steps: first approach, introduction, product presentation, close, etc. Internally, employee motivation may be sustained through appraisal and reward procedures. Not all the practices that sustain relationships are explicit. Some may not even be noticed until the practice is broken! Practices, even quite trivial ones, may almost become ritualised. In this, they are one of the building blocks out of which expectations are created. Changing a routine may have an impact on a relationship at a deep level.

By way of an example, consider an entrepreneur whose business is doing quite well. The venture's backers are very happy. Their expectations have been more than met. The entrepreneur provides the backers with a financial report every three months. After a while, this becomes routine. The backers, acknowledging that the business presents them with no concerns, stop examining the report in any detail. After a while the entrepreneur recognises this and decides that the report is 'a waste of time', so the entrepreneur, without informing the backers, stops sending it.

What are the backers to think? Should they be concerned? They contact the entrepreneur who informs them that they should not worry, that the business is still doing well and that the report was stopped because it was not giving them any new information and so the communication 'was not important'. How are the backers to likely to interpret the attitude of the entrepreneur towards them?

What relationship skills are required to maintain them?

Relationships must be managed and this management, like any other form of management, calls upon knowledge and skills. As discussed fully in section 3.3, the key skill areas that are important for managing the relationships in and around the entrepreneurial venture include *communication* skills, *selling* skills, *negotiating* skills and *motivational* skills.

What behaviour standards are demanded?

Behaviour standards (which are as much about what should *not* be done as what should be) are a critical dimension of relationships. A society will, in general, define the behavioural standards expected for business practice. This is only a minimum guide. The entrepreneur may always look for competitive advantage in accepting discretionary responsibilities that go *beyond* those normally expected for a business in the sector (see section 8.4).

Growth and structural advantages

Structural advantages arise when the business organises itself in a way which gives it more flexibility and responsiveness in the face of competitive pressures. This is often a key area of advantage for the entrepreneurial business. Lacking the cost and possibly the relationship advantages enjoyed by established businesses the entrepreneurial venture must prosper by being more acute to the market's needs and innovating to satisfy them.

The challenge to the entrepreneurial business is to retain this responsiveness and drive for innovation as the business grows and matures. The key to this is understanding the nature of the structural advantages the business has gained and designing the development of the business's structure and organisation so that these are sustained and encouraged to flourish. This important idea will be developed further in sections 20.5 and 20.6.

20.5 Structural growth

KEY LEARNING OUTCOME
An understanding of the factors which drive the structure of the organisation as it grows.

Every organisation has a unique *structure*. An understanding of this structure is best approached from a broad perspective. It has both static and dynamic aspects. At one level it is the framework of reporting relationships (who is responsible to whom) that describes the organisation. This is how the organisation is often depicted in hierarchical 'organograms'. This formal structure is however just a skeleton. The organisation gains its flesh from the way in which those reporting relationships are played out in terms of the *communications* that take place, the *roles* that must be performed and the *power structures* that define, support and confine those roles. Some of these are formal and explicit, others are informal and implicit but the entrepreneur must learn to manage all of them.

The structure of the organisation, and the way that structure develops as the organisation grows, is both a response to the circumstances in which the organisation finds itself and a reaction to the opportunities with which it is presented. One well-explored approach to understanding how the particular situation of an organisation defines its structure is provided by *contingency theory*. In essence, contingency theory regards the structure of an organisation as dependent on five 'contingencies', or types of factor. These are: the organisation's *size*, the operational *technology* it uses to create value, the *strategy* it adopts, the *environment* it is in, and the way *power* is utilised within it (see Fig. 20.6).

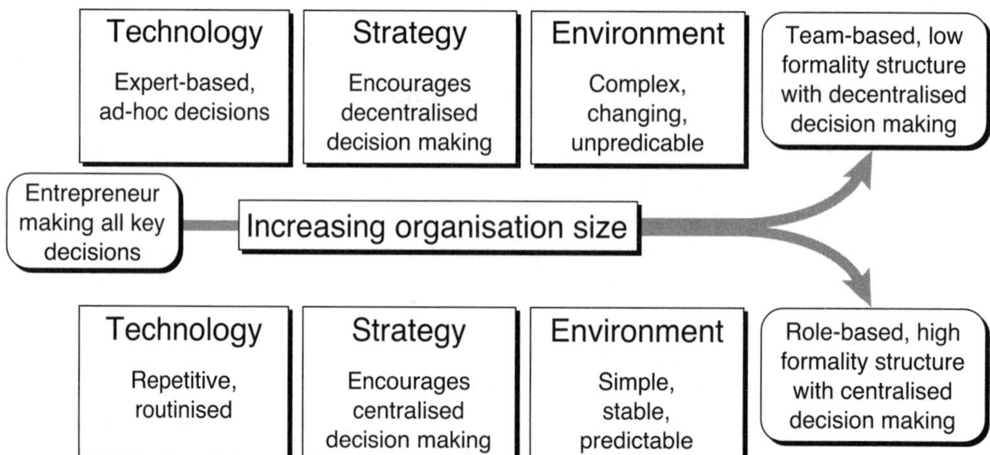

Fig. 20.6 Factors influencing organisational structure

Size

In general, the larger the organisation, the more complex its structure will be. A larger organisation provides more scope for tasks to be differentiated. As more information needs to be passed up to decision makers and more instructions passed back down again, there will be room for more layers of management. Once a certain size is reached, the complexity of the organisation may become so great that it is better to break it up into a series of sub-organisations (functions or departments) each reporting to a common centre.

Operational technology

In broad terms, an organisation's operational technology is simply the way it goes about performing its tasks. Some organisations are involved in repeating a series of relatively straightforward tasks. For example, McDonald's restaurants are involved in producing and retailing fast food through a large number of outlets. Others face tasks that are more complex but are still ultimately repetitive. For example, Easy Jet must transport air passengers from one place to another. On the other hand, some businesses, particularly 'high-tech' ones, undertake a small number of complex tasks, possibly with very few repetitive elements. An example here might be Microsoft's development of software packages.

Contingency theory predicts that organisations which undertake a large number of repetitive tasks will have a more formal structure with well-defined roles and responsibilities then an organisation undertaking less repetitive and predictable tasks which will tend to have a less formal structure. Individuals will tend to define their roles in relation to the demands of a particular project, rather than the expectation of a routine. In this case the organisation may develop expert roles and *ad-hoc* team structures.

Strategy

The strategy adopted by a business is the way it goes about competing for its customers' attention. It is, in essence, what it offers, to whom and the reasons it gives customers to buy. Some organisations, having established their business take up a defensive posture. They understand their products and the reasons why customers buy. They compete by being better at serving 'their' niche than anyone else and they only react to competitors when they move in on 'their' territory.

Other businesses – and entrepreneurs must be in this class – are more aggressive. They aim to grow their business by attacking entrenched competitors. They compete by offering the customer a new innovation which serves a need, or solves a problem, better than existing offerings. Some organisations may combine both these generic strategies: defending established business and using the resources gained to attack in other areas.

More specifically, the organisation's strategy is the way it goes about developing and sustaining competitive advantage, in particular *cost advantages*, *knowledge advantages*, *relationship advantages* and *structural advantages*.

There is no simple relationship between strategy and structure. The defining tension is the way in which decision making within the organisation drives the strategy. In short, if decision making can be centralised then a more regular, and formal structure should be expected. If, on the other hand, decision making must be 'pushed down' to lower levels of the organisation then a less formal, more flexible, structure might be expected. Organisations pursuing cost leadership (for example, the Japanese engineering conglomerate, Minebea) tend to centralise control in order to ensure that costs are managed. Retail organisations which depend on a strong brand presence (for example, The Body Shop) may also enact strong central control in order to ensure that the brand, and the products and services it endorses, are carefully managed.

Businesses based on knowledge advantages, especially where there is a lot of expertise involved, may avoid strong central control systems. Decision making may be localised. Actions may, however, be guided by a strong organisational culture. Team structures may be important as may informal mentoring of less experienced employees by more experienced. Many professional organisations with an entrepreneurial background (for example, Saatchi and Saatchi) have adopted this approach.

The environment

Organisations find themselves in an environment made up of macro-economic features, stakeholders, and competitors. This environment both offers resources and challenges their availability. Opportunities offer new possibilities whereas threats present the danger that what is enjoyed now may be lost in the future. The environment is defined by a number of factors. In particular: how *complex* it is (that is, how much information must be processed in order to understand it); how *fast* it is developing or changing; and how *predictable* those changes are. As with strategy, the influence of the environment on structure impacts through the way in which decision making is shaped. A known, slow-changing, predictable environment encourages centralised decision making. A new or fast-changing and unpredictable environment encourages decision making to be passed down to those at the cutting edge of the organisation who are 'in contact' with the environment.

Power, control and organisational politics

The structure of an organisation represents a response to the contingencies of size, technology, strategy and environment. But the extent to which it represents a controlled, deliberate and rational response depends on the extent to which, and the way in which, the entrepreneur can exert control over the organisation as it grows. A powerful central entrepreneur can be a great asset to a business. He or she can provide vision and leadership and keep the organisation focused on the opportunities with which it is presented. In the absence of this, the organisation may lack direction and so lose its momentum. Individuals, and informal coalitions of individuals, can begin to see their interests as being different to those of the organisation as a whole and the organisation can become *politicised*.

On the other hand, if the power the entrepreneur enjoys is misdirected, then the organisation may be led down the wrong path. Entrepreneurial power brings responsibility. It is important that the entrepreneur uses their position and power to create an organisational environment in which individuals are free to express, and act upon, their own analysis and decision-making skills. This is particularly important for the fast-growing, innovative business pursuing an aggressive strategy in a changing, unpredictable environment where localised decision making can offer an advantage. Even if the organisation can benefit from a degree of centralisation of decision making the entrepreneur will face practical limitations in the range and number of decisions he or she can make personally. Once the organisation reaches a certain size (and it need not be that large) the entrepreneur is well advised to call upon the skills of a supporting management team. A summary of the influence of contingency factors on structure is provided in Table 20.3.

Table 20.3 A summary of the influence of contingency factors on organisational structure

Contingency	Influence on organisational development
Size	Organisational complexity tends to increase with size; development of internal structure occurs. Roles and responsibilities become more specialised.
Technology	Structure driven by nature of organisation's tasks: are they repetitive, ad-hoc or based on expert judgement? Repetitive tasks tend to favour routinised activities and repeated unit structure with centralised decision making. Ad-hoc and expert tasks encourage de-localised decision making, perhaps within a strong 'organisational cultural' framework.
Environment	Well-understood, stable and predictable environment favours centralised decision making and formal, routinised structures. Poorly understood, unstable and unpredictable environment favours decentralised decision making and empowerment at low levels in the organisational hierarchy.
Strategy	Influence depends on how strategy is sustained through decision making. Does strategy adopted demand strong central control or does it favour decentralised decision making?
Power	Can entrepreneur impose strong central control? By what means?

20.6 Organisational growth

KEY LEARNING OUTCOME
An appreciation of how the resource requirements of the organisation can be used as a guide to its design.

The entrepreneur is faced with the task of designing and creating an organisation. Contingency theory provides a valuable insight into the variables that mould the organisation but it does not provide a detailed guide to shaping a particular organisation. A better approach is to consider the resource requirements of the organisation and to design its structure around them.

The 'traditional' path of development for an entrepreneurial venture is sometimes related as follows. At its inception, the business consists of just the entrepreneur and perhaps one or two others. The entrepreneur makes the decisions and undertakes the task of performing the business's activities, perhaps with a little delegation. In its early growth stages, as the business takes on more staff, the entrepreneur is freer to undertake the decision making and delegate more of the actual business generating activity. As growth continues, the entrepreneur may develop a management team to support his or her own decision making. In time, the members of this management team may act as the nucleus for more formal departments or business functions. As this process continues, the entrepreneur's role becomes that of the chief executive and the organisation settles down to maturity.

While this presents a plausible story for the growth of a business it is, at best, retrospective. Models (and there are many) which define the development of an organisation in terms of definite stages should be met with some caution. While they may provide an account of what *has* happened they have little power to predict what *will* happen. Even if particular stages of development do exist, an individual businesses will move through different stages at different rates and may miss out some stages altogether. Such models are of limited use as a guide to decision making. It is hard to say at a particular time exactly what stage a business has reached or when it can be expected to move on to the next stage.

For the decision maker attempting to design an organisation it is more profitable to ask what governs the structures a particular business should adopt given the (unique) situation with which it is faced. One option is to consider the *resource requirements* of the organisation.

The resource requirement approach

The nature of the resources available to the entrepreneur have been considered in Chapter 6. In essence, the entrepreneurial venture needs only three things: *information* from which an innovation can be developed, *capital* (money) for investment and *people* to make the venture happen. The initial resource requirements of an organisation are shown in Fig. 20.7. In practice, the venture will obtain these things through a variety of routes.

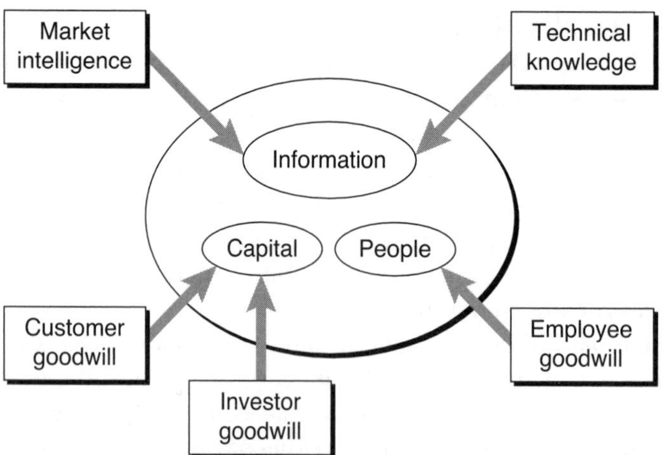

Fig. 20.7 The resource dependency model of organisation

Information

In the first instance, information will be obtained via the entrepreneur's experience within a particular business sector. As the business grows, market intelligence gathering will become increasingly important. As it develops further this may be supplemented by formal market research to provide market information and a research and development programme to provide information on products and technology.

Capital

The entrepreneur may use his or her own money to initiate the business. This may be supplemented by formal and/or informal investment capital. If the business is to be sustained, however, it must attract money from customers. This will, of course, be a result of the business selling its products to them. If this is to occur then the customer's interest and *goodwill* towards the business, and what it offers, is needed. If the business is to grow at a sustainable rate then additional capital may be needed from investors. Again, their interest and goodwill towards the venture is needed.

People

In the early stages of the business the entrepreneur may invite close associates to join in the venture. However, as the business grows more formal procedures for identifying and recruiting personnel and gaining their goodwill will be needed.

The structure adopted by a particular organisation can be thought of as a response to its requirements in relation to these three key resources. Particular functions appear within the organisation in order to manage the acquisition of these resources. The 'conventional' response for the large, mature organisation is to set up *departments* with specific responsibility for the acquisition of particular resources. Thus customer goodwill is captured by marketing and sales; investor goodwill by the finance department; market knowledge by the marketing research function (perhaps integrated into the marketing department); technical knowledge by the research and development function; and so on.

The complete organisation will include two additional functions. The operational system which actually produces the outputs of the business (i.e. production or service provision) is responsible for adding value to the inputs and a strategic control function co-ordinates the operation of the organisation as a whole.

The resource acquisition approach

This is, however, only *one* of a range of possible responses. It represents the limitation of the organisation as it reaches maturity. It also reflects a traditional environment in which different types of resource are independent and quite predictable in the way they may be acquired. It is this feature which allows them to be acquired by 'specialist' managers. The evolution of the entrepreneurial organisation can thus be thought of in terms of it developing internal structures to manage the acquisition of the resources it needs to undertake its business.

In its early stages, the entrepreneur will take a great deal of responsibility for attracting the critical inputs: customer, investor and employee goodwill as well as information. In other words he or she must be the marketing, sales, finance and development specialist rolled into one. The entrepreneur must also maintain strategic control over the business and may be responsible for undertaking operations as well. At this early stage, the entrepreneur's role is a challenging one!

As the business grows then tasks can be differentiated, and the role of the entrepreneur can become more distinct. Usually, he or she will relinquish participation in operational activities and concentrate on managing the business as a whole. As the business grows further, roles can become even more specialised. Individuals can focus their attention on obtaining critical resources. As a result, specific resource acquisition functions can start to emerge. The evolution of input acquiring functions in the development of the entrepreneurial business is shown in Fig. 20.8.

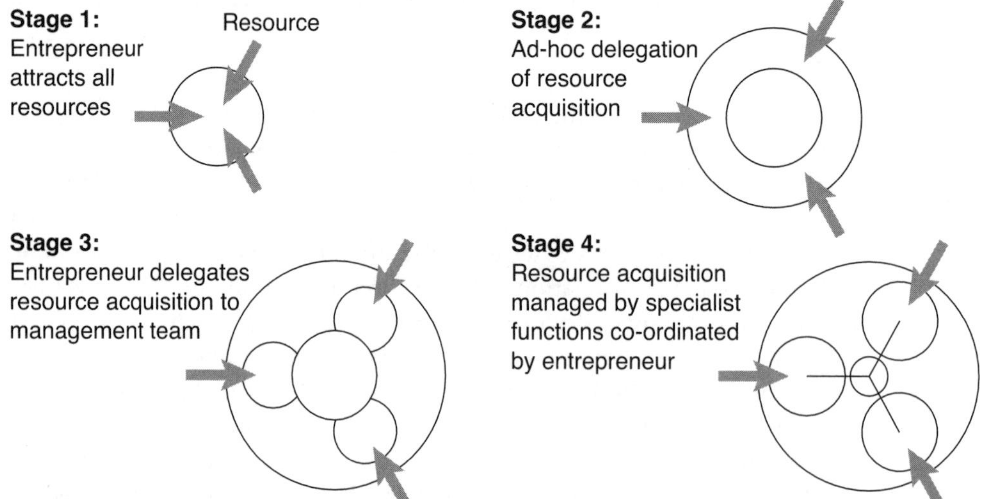

Fig. 20.8 The development of resource acquisition in the growing venture

This approach can be used as a guide for decision making about the structure the organisation should adopt. The key issues in relation to deciding on structure are:

1 *How large is the organisation?* How many people work for the organisation? How much latitude is there for individuals to take on specialist roles? To what extent is it possible to use outside specialists? (Consider here the points raised in section 16.3 in particular.
As a rule, tasks, roles and responsibilities should be specialised, if possible.

2 *What are the critical inputs?* All inputs are important. However, the acquisition of some will take priority at any one point and this will alter at different stages of development. The question is what matters *most* at this point in time: information on markets and product technology or investment capital or sales to customers or people? Is the lack of any one of these *in particular* responsible for limiting the venture's potential? To what extent is

it possible to dedicate available resources to the acquisition of a particular input? H. might this situation change in the near future?

As a rule, attention should be focused on critical inputs – but it is important not to neglect other inputs.

3. *What is the venture's skill profile?* What skills are available in order to be dedicated? How is the venture served for people with selling, marketing, financial negotiating and research skills, etc.? How might these be acquired (e.g. through training, new recruitment or external support)? What does this say about the venture's skill requirements for the future?

   As a rule, the venture's skill profile should be built up (but an awareness of fixed costs is important). The entrepreneur must be willing to call on outside help in the short term if necessary.

4. *What is the nature of the inputs needed?* The nature of inputs the venture needs will differ depending on the environment in which it finds itself. Are they well defined? (If the business is very innovative or if it is in a business environment which is not well developed then they might not be.) Are they easily obtainable? How intense is the competition for them? On what basis does competition take place?

   The key issue here is how *specialist* the task of managing the acquisition of a particular input needs to be in order to be successful. As a rule, the possibility of gaining competitive advantage by building in-house specialisation should be considered.

5. *How do different inputs interact?* Different inputs interact with each other. The acquisition of one cannot be considered in isolation since how one input is acquired affects how the others will be. Technical knowledge means little without consideration of what the market wants. The acquisition of investors' capital will be facilitated if the venture has a good knowledge of market conditions. Similarly the goodwill of employees will provide a strong platform on which to build a culture which attracts the goodwill of customers.

   This means that one input attracting function must communicate with the others. Those responsible for market research must talk to those responsible for development. The finance department must talk to those responsible for marketing. Inter-function communication is facilitated (or hindered) by organisational structure. If the acquisition of inputs can be considered largely in isolation of each other, then a structure which features dedicated specialist functions co-ordinated centrally (perhaps supplemented by informal inter-functional communication) may be suitable. On the other hand, if detailed co-ordination of input acquisition is necessary, then a matrix or a team structure may be more effective and offer a better route to developing a structural competitive advantage.

20.7 The venture as a theatre for human growth

KEY LEARNING OUTCOME

A recognition of the importance of the human dimension in organisational growth.

limensions of business growth

ısiness organisations are not just systems for generating wealth. They are the stages ı which human beings live their lives. Individuals use their organisational role to 'eate images of themselves. For many people, what you *do* is who you *are*. In building n organisation, an entrepreneur is not just generating employment opportunities but .lso creating a theatre in which people will play out the parts which are critical to their personal development. Organisations are the places where people meet and interact. The entrepreneur is offering not only economic rewards, but social and personal development ones as well.

Effective entrepreneurs will recognise this. They will understand that an individual working in the organisation is bringing a number of different expectations operating at different levels with them. Entrepreneurs should be aware of the meaning that the organisation offers to the people who are part of it and, critically, of how that meaning changes as the organisation grows.

The small, informal organisation will offer a different environment to the larger one where roles and relationships are more formal. Of course, there is a trade-off. The larger organisation offers more security and the possibility for employees to use and develop specialist skills whereas the smaller one may offer a more flexible and personal environment. The entrepreneur must recognise the balance of benefits from the perspective of the individual employee.

An entrepreneur, like any good manager, recognises that the development of the organisation is also the development of the people within it. Its growth offers them the potential for their growth. Developing and communicating vision means writing the story of how the organisation will develop, the roles that particular individuals will play in that development, and what those roles will mean for them.

In practice this means that the entrepreneur must discuss the changes that are taking place within the organisation with individuals, and use those discussions to develop an understanding of what those changes mean for the individuals. Presenting the future possibilities offered by, and removing the fear of, change is the platform on which motivation is built. Such discussions may be quite formal (for example, regular appraisals and objective setting) or informal chats with employees.

Understanding what the prospects and achievement of growth offer and the fears and apprehensions they create for the individual within the organisation is crucial since these are the platform on which the entrepreneur builds his or her leadership strategy.

Summary of key ideas

- The growth of the venture must be approached from a number of perspectives of which the key perspectives are: *financial*: growth in income, expenditure and profits; *strategic*: growth in market presence and competitive advantages; *structural*: growth in organisational form, process and structure; and *organisational*: growth in the organisation's culture and attitudes.
- Effective entrepreneurs recognise that the growth of the venture provides all of its stakeholders with an opportunity for personal growth and development.

Suggestions for further reading

Birley, S. and **Westhead, P.** (1990) 'Growth and performance contrasts between "types" of small firm', *Strategic Management Journal*, Vol. 11, pp. 535–57.

Brocklesby, J. and **Cummings, S.** (1996) 'Designing a viable organisational structure', *Long Range Planning*, Vol. 29, No. 1, pp. 49–57.

Gibb, A. and **Davies, L.** (1991) 'In pursuit of frameworks for the development of growth models of the small business', *International Small Business Journal*, Vol. 9, No. 1, pp. 15–31.

Glancey, K. (1998) 'Determinants of growth and profitability in small entrepreneurial firms', *International Journal of Entrepreneurial Behaviour and Research*, Vol. 4, No. 2, pp. 18–27.

Greiner, L.E. (1972) 'Evolution and revolution as organisations grow', *Harvard Business Review*, July-Aug, pp. 37–46.

Mintzberg, H. (1979) *The Structuring of Organisations: A Synthesis of the Research*, Englewood Cliffs, NJ, Prentice Hall.

Scott, M. and **Bruce, R.** (1987) 'Five stages of growth in small business', *Long Range Planning*, Vol. 20, No. 3, pp. 45–52.

Smallbone, D., Leigh, R. and **North, D.** (1995) 'The characteristics and strategies of high-growth SMEs', *International Journal of Entrepreneurial Behaviour and Research*, Vol. 1, No. 3, pp. 44–62.

van de Ven, A. and **Poole, M.S.** (1995) 'Explaining development and change in organisations', *Academy of Management Review*, Vol. 20, No. 3, pp. 510–40.

Selected case material

Challenge of going global

19 August 1999

The company has already been at the crossroads, it might be there again, says **Richard Rivlin**

Peter Brooke, chairman of Advent International and one of the founding fathers of private equity investing, looked out of his office window overlooking the Charles River in Boston and said: "I may be 70 but the older I get, the more interested I am in pioneering."

Mr Brooke's 36 years in private equity have ensured he is beyond chasing dollars. He can afford to think of his legacy more in terms of the business he leaves rather than in the number of greenbacks.

After discussing European history in general and Germany's doomed Weimar Republic in particular which he majored in at Harvard, Mr Brooke began to discuss his day job.

"To be in it just to make money is not sustainable. My vision is to create the pre-eminent global private equity operation," he says.

Advent International was formed out of TA Associates in 1984 and is not to be confused with Advent, a UK fund that focuses on more early stage businesses.

TA was one of the leading US operations of its day but reached a crossroads: it had to decide whether to invest to take its domestic operation on to the next level or to build an international brand. Resources were not available for both, which led Mr Brooke in 1984 to start afresh and create Advent International.

During the past 15 years it has made more than 400 investments – current ones include HMV Media, the UK books and music retailer, Dollar Express, a US discount store group, and Jazztel, a Spanish telecommunications start-up – but it is the group's international range that stands out.

The rise to globalism among US leveraged buy-out funds is not a new story. Each week the press is filled with stories of individuals and companies raising hundreds of millions of dollars, to rush headlong into Silicon Valley in California for pure venture capital and into Europe via London for more established business opportunities.

Both are old news for Advent. It opened in Menlo Park in Silicon Valley in 1988 and was in London a year later. Frankfurt and Milan followed in 1991 and then offices throughout the Far East, South America and central Europe.

Today it has 15 wholly owned offices and a further eight affiliates. Douglas Brown, the president and chief executive officer, says: "If you buy into the global theme it makes sense to have a network of funds to back the network of offices."

Its signature fund is the $1.3bn (£810m) Global Private Equity III fund which closed in 1997. It also has a $182m pool for investing in central Europe and a $250m fund for investing in Latin America. There is also a $70m media fund and $100m healthcare and life sciences fund which both target the early stage.

Consequently the group is poised to begin fundraising for its first general early stage and ventures fund later this year. (see panel)

Rivals respect Advent's strategy yet suggest it is close to facing another crossroads.

One says: "Their global fund is now dwarfed by more than half a dozen others so

: for the largest sized e this terrific interna- office in Bangkok and ely to provide tomor- ls but these may be at npeting for more tradi- tional deals ... US."

Focusing an increasing attention on pure ventures and emerging markets also requires the continued support of its investors. The demands to achieve higher returns from the higher risks will be fundamental to Advent's continued growth.

Mr Brown says: "Institutions normally want 18-20 per cent net rates of return. The private equity industry as a whole has been in the low 20s for the US and Europe. Institutional investors want significantly more than that for emerging markets."

Advent's strategy and longevity would appear to indicate that investors, which include Coca-Cola, General Motors, the Rockefeller Foundation and RJR Nabisco, appear satisfied with how the balance between old and new markets is being handled.

Ernest Bachrach, chief executive of the Latin America region, says: "To develop a private equity operation in a region without private equity history is not easy. Businesses in Brazil are being phoned by bankers suggesting they do a deal.

"The owner asks them if they have the money and they say no but they know people (private equity investors) who do. The owner will put the phone down on them because he thinks they are time wasting. But it makes our job easier when we phone them and show we do have the funds available."

This slow process has begun to pay dividends in Latin America, despite its choppy economies, where Advent has made nine investments. These include Aeroplaza de Mexico, which manages commercial and office space at the Puerto Vallarta and Guadalajara airport.

It is also in talks with a soccer club which would further catapult its name to prominence and may smooth its path in the region's business arena.

Building a brand and business on the global stage is expensive and time consuming but vital if Advent is to enjoy a sustained life.

Mr Brooke says: "The challenge for us is to improve our performance to raise more capital and to utilise our place in the market. I wish I had more years left for this."

A remark that led his PR man to point out that his performance on the tennis court suggested he would orchestrate many more deals yet.

Card player's healthy start

Nicki Brimicombe learns how a troubled vitamins group became an international company with more than 500 employees

2 December 1999

"Don't put it off, put it on" urges the credit card advertisement. In 1985 Terry Sadler took NatWest, Lloyds and Barclays at their word and borrowed to his limit to buy an ailing vitamins company.

Today he is chairman and chief executive of Bioglan Pharma, which recently entered the FTSE 350.

Mr Sadler began working in healthcare in 1969 and had diverse commercial roles in small, large, private and public companies. By 1981 he was a director of a privately owned skin care business and had despaired of finding a company which met his aspirations. "I realised the only solution was to create that company," he says.

"I resigned my directorship, and took a year to review the options. In 1982 I discovered Bioglan by chance. I was flicking through the index of manufacturers directory, MIMS, and I spotted Bioglan, which was based five miles away. I obtained their report and accounts from Companies House and made an offer through their accountants."

Menzies Sharp, an entrepreneur, founded Bioglan in 1932. His children inherited the business but it failed to thrive and by 1982 was "on its last legs – with three employees and a turnover of £94,000", recalls Mr Sadler. The asking price was £176,000. Mr Sadler mortgaged his house and borrowed as much as he could from the bank: but he was still £30,000 short. "So I put £10,000 each on my NatWest, Lloyds and Barclays gold cards and bought the company!"

"The strategy was simple," according to Mr Sadler. "We had to sell more of the existing product range and expand the portfolio. I also decided to start generic drug development. I chose this area because generics were relatively simple to develop, required smaller promotional expenditure compared with branded products, and they can be fast cash generators."

By 1988 Bioglan had made its first profit. "National Westminster Bank gave me some sensible guidance," comments Mr Sadler. But, he points out, "advisers are good at telling you how to avoid potholes but not how to grow the business – that's your job."

By 1989 generics were performing well and the company's other key focus area, dermatology, was also starting to pay off. Products had been acquired from large pharmaceutical companies, and internal research and development of dermatological products was also under way. Mr Sadler considers dermatology to be "somewhat of a Cinderella area, below the radar screen of the major pharmaceutical companies".

In 1994 the company added a third leg to its business, and diversified into drug delivery.

"Large pharmaceutical companies tend to concentrate on developing new chemical entities. Areas like drug delivery are good opportunities for medium-sized companies like Bioglan," says Mr Sadler.

Business blossomed, and by 1996 profits from organic growth were insufficient to support ambitious expansion plans. "We decided to go for a private placement to raise £10m," explains Mr Sadler. "We had a beauty parade of potential sponsors and chose Hoare Govett because they were very encouraging and supportive, liked our track record and we got on well with the people."

The £10m supported two years of growth by which time Mr Sadler felt ready to float the company. This time he chose to work with HSBC. "They had the breadth of capabilities to undertake the project, were able to move quickly, according to our timetable, and they gave us a realistic (although not the highest) valuation," he explains. Mr Sadler reflects that it is important not to be overawed by the City. "Recognise your company's worth and don't undersell yourself," he advises.

Bioglan floated last December. "The market was flat on its face but I never had second thoughts," he recalls. "You need enormous reserves of self-belief and commitment to make things happen." His confidence paid off: the issue was oversubscribed and the share price has doubled in a year. He admits that living with a share price creates extra work, but says the freedom to grow at a faster rate outweighs the downsides.

Today Bioglan is an international company employing more than 500 people. "You must recruit and retain the very best people," stresses Mr Sadler. "I stayed in touch with good people I met during my career and when appropriate I invited them to join Bioglan." Effective delegation is also important. "Get good people, set the framework for their role, trust them 100 per cent, and let them get on with it," he advises.

When expanding abroad Mr Sadler believes that recruiting a local national who understands the market is the ideal route. He also notes that "strong, experienced non-executive directors" rather than "expensive suits" are particularly important.

In terms of culture, Mr Sadler stresses the need to nip politics in the bud, support individual development and reward hard work. "Even when we were a private company all our employees owned shares," he comments.

Bioglan has been profitable in eight of the past 10 years, and in 1998 reported sales of £43m and pre-tax profits of £3.4m.

Mr Sadler wants to see Bioglan enter the FTSE 100. Growth will be driven by expanding into areas of medicine that require a modest-sized sales force, relatively low development costs and that are of significant size but of lesser interest to large pharmaceutical companies. The mergers and acquisitions route for growth is also under constant review.

The limits on Mr Sadler's credit cards have been increased since 1985. But he has big plans for Bioglan. The next time he looks for funds, "putting it on the plastic" may not be a realistic option.

Weighing up the funding options - the Terry Sadler model

Bank	Venture capitalist
- Great personal control	- Less personal control
- High personal risk	- Lower personal risk
- Difficult to raise substantial funds	- Easier to secure significant sums
- Ability to plan for the long term/retain full ownership/support organic growth	- Investors likely to require short-term exit route e.g. merger/float

Ruler of a ring of steel

Peter Marsh meets an Indian entrepreneur who is using global management techniques to transform an unglamorous industry

7 February 2000

Lakshmi Mittal likes high-tech companies. He has an investment fund of several hundred million dollars that holds stakes in several internet businesses, and has recently started up a global venture in pay television. What most excites his imagination, however, is the apparently unglamorous business of steelmaking.

Mr Mittal is the founder and majority owner of the LNM group, the world's fifth biggest steel producer and on most counts the most global, with production operations on four continents. Unlike virtually all steel companies worldwide, the group is run as an international, rather than regional, business.

But while the 49-year-old Indian is bringing a new management style to what is normally considered a rather old-fashioned industry, he also has time for other business interests. He owns a bank in Trinidad, copper mines in Zambia, a fleet of ships, and an unusual industrial empire in Kazakhstan that employs more than 58,000 people in activities from shoemaking to tram services. He hit the headlines recently through putting an undisclosed sum into B4U, a cable television venture that plans to channel Indian "Bollywood" films to homes in Britain, Canada and the Middle East.

In conversation, Mr Mittal comes across as a mixture of old-style industrial baron and new-age manager keen on the softer aspects of running a business. He is fond of highlighting his company's direct approach – for instance, it wastes little time in getting rid of underperforming managers – and clearly has a taste for the dramatic business gesture. He is attracted by the policies of Mannesmann, the German engineering-to-phones business which succumbed last week to a takeover bid by UK company Vodafone AirTouch. "They started off in steel and are now in telecoms – I wish I had thought of that," he says.

Yet this jet-setting businessman, who clocked up 750 hours in his company Gulf Stream last year visiting steel plants around the world, has another side to his personality. One of his main interests is yoga, and he tries to make time for a swim every day to help him relax.

He gets most animated, however, when the subject turns to steelmaking. "I find the industry exciting," he says. "What we've done shows that in this industry you can create value and provide growth. If you look at our share price it rose substantially (about 150 per cent) last year. That's no less than a lot of high-tech companies and we are making money at the same time."

On the subject of the share price, Mr Mittal is skating on thin ice. He is referring to the price of stock in Ispat, the publicly quoted part of LNM, which accounts for more than three-quarters of the group's total annual sales of some $6bn (£3.6bn) and which Mr Mittal floated on the New York and Amsterdam stock markets in 1997. At the same time, he retained a share of 80 per cent for himself. Ispat's annual results for 1999 are being announced today.

After initially attracting a premium price, the shares bombed shortly afterwards, partly due to the recession in the global steel industry – which has rebounded only in the past six months. Accordingly, Ispat's stock recovered much of its value last year; it is now quoted at about $16, compared with nearly $30 at the flotation and a low of $5 during 1998. Even with these gains, the share price fall wounded investors, and left many somewhat wary about Ispat and its founder.

Mr Mittal, however, shrugs off the problems, and says that the recent share price gains show he retains a following. With just a hint of insouciance, he says: "I love having shareholders: they keep me on my toes."

He would probably never have become interested in steel had his father not owned a steel business in India and put up money for his son in 1976 to take over, with a local partner, a steel company in Indonesia. This became the foundation of the LNM group.

Global expansion started in the late 1980s through Mr Mittal buying up mainly underperforming operations around the world, including Mexico, Canada, Belgium, Germany and Ireland. In 1998 he bought Inland Steel, a large US steelmaker, for $1.43bn, while last year he bought a large wire products business in France from Usinor, one of Europe's biggest steelmakers.

…de: Lakshmi Mittal

…lia, on June 15 1950. …'s College, Calcutta. …$2bn (£1.2bn) and …lon, Indonesia and Trinidad.

Management strategy: Reckons steelmaking has a lot to learn from sectors such as banking, pharmaceuticals and accounting, which in the past decade have increasingly put their operations on a global basis. He adds: "I don't want to run the biggest steel company in the world, but the most profitable."

Steely tactics: Has an outsider's approach to steelmaking, which has given him a reputation among some in the industry for having wild ideas. For instance, he annoyed some of the big producers of iron ore (the main component of steel) by trying to push them into agreeing prices quarterly, so creating leeway for price reductions, in place of the annual price agreements that have become the norm. However, others in the industry respect his fresh approach. "He's come up with a very interesting model for globalising the industry," says one analyst.

Family connections: His wife Usha is a member of Ispat's board and is responsible for the Indonesian part of his business empire. Mr Mittal's 24-year-old son Aditya is Ispat's head of mergers and acquisitions.

Going with the flow: He is keen on new ways to channel information around the far-flung corners of his business empire. For instance, employees swap production ideas and market information in marathon conference calls, presided over by Mr Mittal every Monday from one of Ispat's joint head offices in London, Chicago and Luxembourg.

Investors on their mettle: He is considering selling more of his personal stake in Ispat to improve the attractiveness of the company to investors, by making the shares more liquid. Certainly this is something that would make Mr Mittal a lot more popular in the investment community.

He acquired his interests in Kazakhstan in 1995, purchasing a large, formerly state-owned steel works. The deal stipulated that at the same time he had to take over a large part of the country's other industrial operations (including coal mines and a power station), which had all been run together with steel as one integrated heavy industrial group.

"We had previously thought about the kind of steel company we wanted to be, with operations in all the developed parts of the world," says Mr Mittal. "As part of this there was the need to acquire a business in the former Soviet Union. Kazakhstan fitted in; it had a good cost base, good technology and the potential to grow. Since acquiring it, we have doubled output to 4m tonnes a year and it now supplies to 65 countries."

With the exception of the Indonesia and Kazakhstan operations, all Mr Mittal's steelmaking interests remain in Ispat, which he runs as a hands-on chairman, aided by his number two, Johannes Sittard, an experienced German steelmaker who is president and chief operating officer. Even his critics concede that Mr Mittal has brought some new ideas into the industry. Although the weight and relatively low price of steel prevent it being shipped around the world to any great extent, with most steel markets being organised on a regional basis, Mr Mittal nevertheless believes this should not stop steel companies having a global approach to management.

Accordingly, senior people within both the Ispat and LNM groups meet regularly to exchange information on subjects such as new ways to optimise steel production or advances in information technology.

The top 240 managers in the company have their pay linked partly to commercial performance through US-style incentive schemes, while Mr Mittal has recently started a "career enhancement" programme within Ispat, under which 200 high-flyers receive special training to prepare them for top jobs. "As we run this business we can learn a lot from global industrial players such as General Electric or ABB," says Mr Mittal.

The company's working language is English while its international nature is underlined by its executive board members: there are six Indians, two Americans, two Germans and a French Canadian. Mr Mittal believes his Indian background helps him in running a group whose 74,000 employees (the total LNM payroll) come from a wide range of nationalities. "In India we have a very diversified culture. This provides a lot of flexibility in adapting to different ways of doing things, within a philosophy of working in a global environment and looking for growth opportunities."

On this score, Mr Mittal continues to monitor the steel industry for possible acquisitions, for instance in the US, Latin America and eastern Europe. With LNM's steel output running at 20m tonnes a year, he believes the optimum annual production of a company in this industry is 40m-50m tonnes, a lot higher than the current sector leader – Pohang Iron and Steel of South Korea, which makes 26m tonnes a year, or about 3 per cent of world production.

Could LNM reach the optimum level? "I think so, as and when it is opportune," he says. As he pursues his global ambitions, he clearly still has a lot to aim for.

Review questions

Compare and contrast the financial, strategic, structural and organisational aspects of growth for:

1 Advent International

2 Bioglan Pharma

3 the LNM Group.

21 Strategies for expansion

Chapter overview

Expanding the business means increasing the amount of trade it undertakes. Expansion from any base can be achieved in one of four ways, by ***increasing core market share****, by* ***launching new products****, by* ***entering new markets*** *and by* ***acquiring established businesses****. This chapter considers each of these generic strategies in turn and the decisions the entrepreneur must make in order to deliver them.*

21.1 Increasing market share

KEY LEARNING OUTCOME
An understanding of the decisions that need to be made when considering an expansion strategy based on increasing market share.

Expansion demands an increase in the volume of the venture's sales. These sales are made into a market. The impact of this increase in sales volume on the market depends on the dynamics of the market itself. If the market is enjoying rapid growth then the business may increase its sales even if its market share is static. On the other hand, if the market is mature and not increasing in volume, then an increase in sales implies an increase in market share. Sales growth, then, is a combination of overall market growth, and increase in the share of that market. As the American business academic, Ansoff pointed out in his seminal book, *Corporate Strategy* (1965), any expansion strategy must involve a decision as to whether to base expansion on existing products or to develop new ones, and whether to rely on established market presence or to enter new markets.

The attractiveness of a market depends on its rate of growth (see Fig. 21.1). Studies of business performance in a number of market areas has suggested that the most attractive type of market (defined as the one which offers the best return on investment) is one of moderate growth. This is rationalised as follows. In a low-growth market, increases in business can only be obtained at the expense of competitors. This makes the fight for market share expensive. Conversely, in a higher-growth market the business can be expanded by taking the 'new' business as it becomes available. This reduces competitive pressures. Competitors may not even realise each other's

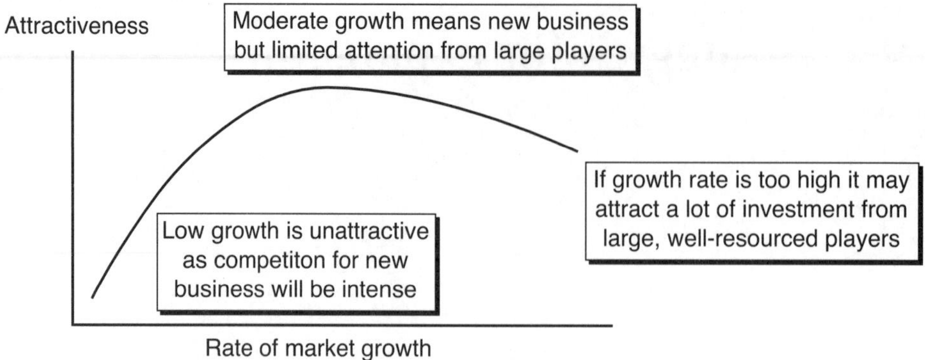

Fig. 21.1 Market attractiveness and rate of growth

presence. If the growth becomes very high, however, then the market may be seen as so attractive that the attentions of a large number of competitors may be aroused. Big players may invest heavily to gain control of the market. If this happens, then the cost of competing may increase again.

In practice, the simple formula of market growth versus share increase needs careful inspection. The dynamics of a market, and the share of a particular business within that market, are dependent on how the market is defined in the first place. A market represents the collection of goods which can be substituted for each other, but a variety of goods can be substituted in different ways. Some goods may make better substitutes than others. The situation is complicated further if the good in question serves a number of different needs.

For example, consider the jewellery that was marketed so successfully by Gerald Ratner in the 1980s. Clearly, the products were in competition with those on offer from other jewellery stores. However, jewellery is often purchased as a gift item and in this they were in competition with a whole host of other products which make interesting gifts such as books, CDS, flowers and so on. Ratner's target market was young people who bought the product to wear when they socialised with one another. With respect to this, the products were in competition with other fashion items that were bought for purposes of socialisation, particularly clothes. In a wider sense still, they were in competition with other areas in which young people could spend money in order to socialise such as meals out, attending concerts and so on. Thus a product sits in a number of markets depending on its pattern of substitution for other goods (see Fig. 21.2).

An entrepreneur must recognise that 'the' market in which their business operates is not a single thing at all, but a complex arena of overlapping market sectors. Whether or not a business is growing by increasing its share, or by capitalising on a growth market will depend on which sector of the market is under consideration. The business may, in fact, be doing both of these in different areas of the market at the same time.

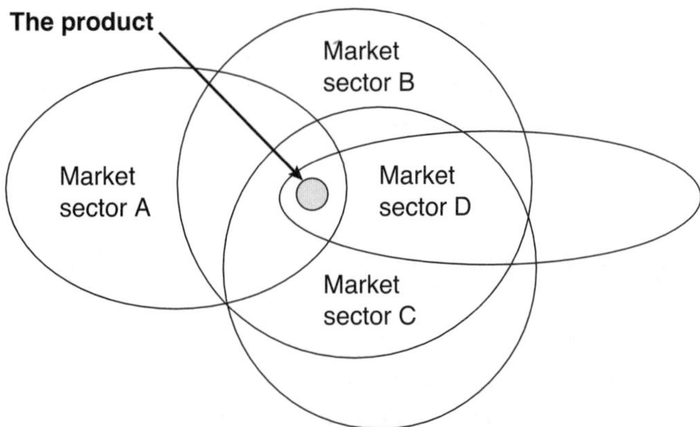

Fig. 21.2 The multi-market location of a product

This framework indicates the considerations the entrepreneur must have in view when developing a market share expansion strategy. These considerations have three parts:

1 *What market sectors are available into which expansion might take place?*
   - What product (or products) do the venture's offerings substitute? (What will people stop using if they buy the venture's products?)
   - In what ways does substitution take place? (Directly or indirectly?)
   - Who supplies the substitute products?
   - What benefits does the venture's product offer to the customer in each sector?

2 *What are the attractions of each sector?*
   - What is the volume potential within the sector?
   - What are the dynamics of market growth in each sector?
   - What are the competitive pressures (for example, the strength of competitors, the investment needed to build and sustain market share)?
   - How are competitors likely to react to the venture's actions? (Passively or aggressively?)
   - As a result, what is the likely return on investment?

3 *What are the venture's competitive advantages in a particular sector?*
   - How effectively can the offering be positioned in that sector?
   - What are the venture's competitive advantages in each sector in relation to costs, market knowledge, relationships, and structural factors?
   - How can competitive advantage be maintained within the sector?

In summary, even though an entrepreneurial venture sells its products into a competitive marketplace, and although increasing the size of the venture means taking competitors' business (and facing their reaction to this), the entrepreneur is free, to a degree at least, to decide which competitors they wish to confront and the way in which they wish to compete. The latitude which the entrepreneur has to do this is dependent on the potential to position the offering in different ways in different market sectors. The decision as to which sector, or indeed sectors, into which expansion will be directed is a feature of how attractive that sector is and the competitive advantages the venture enjoys within it.

21.2 Developing new products

KEY LEARNING OUTCOME
An understanding of the decisions that need to be made when considering a strategy of expansion through new product development.

Most businesses sell more than one product. Many offer hundreds, if not thousands, of lines. When it is initiated, the entrepreneurial venture is likely to have only one or at most only a few lines. Thus developing new products must be a critical factor in the venture's plans for expansion. New product development is not just about adding on new lines, though. No business can afford to stand still in a fast-moving marketplace. New products must be developed to replace existing ones and to keep ahead of competitors as the customer's expectations develop.

Product development covers a range of activities from minor modifications of existing products through the development of new variants and models, to the development of entirely new product concepts. Existing product development (EPD) and new product development (NPD) lie at opposite ends of a developmental spectrum.

The details of what existing and new product development mean for a particular business will depend on the nature of the products it is involved with. Clearly, advanced, technology-intensive products will require a different approach to 'simple' products based on established, well-understood technologies. Thus The Body Shop is involved constantly in developing new formulations and variants based on the ingredients that Anita Roddick collects on her world travels. The development of Windows 95 represented a major new product launch for Bill Gates and the Microsoft corporation. The satellite broadcasting channel, BSkyB, which was initially set up via Rupert Murdoch's News International Corporation, demanded the initiation of a whole new industry. Whatever the nature of the product, its complexity and the resources involved in its launch, the basic 'rules' of effective product development and the decisions that are involved in developing the strategy are similar.

The key is to remember that a product is not a thing in itself but a means to an *end*. The value of a product lies in the benefits it can bring to its users. The product is just a way of delivering an innovation to the market. The entrepreneur must apply the same market-orientated insights to the development of new products as were brought to the innovation on which the business was originally founded.

New product development is not just a technical process. It is something which cuts across every facet of the business. There will be a technical element to the actual creation of the product but product development must be considered in much broader terms than the purely technical. Some of the critical decision areas include the following.

Market positioning

What problems will the product solve? Why will it solve them better than existing products do? How will it be positioned in its marketplace? Against which competitors? How will it be priced relative to competitors?

Branding

Will the product be branded? If so, will it use its own branding or draw on corporate branding? Will it use an existing brand (i.e. a brand extension) or will it represent the establishment of a new brand identity?

Communication

How will the customer get to know about the product? How can it be promoted to them? What communication routes will be used? Will the customer need to be educated about the product? Will endorsement and professional recommendation be a factor in its position? What demands will promotion make on existing sales and promotional resources?

Distribution

How will the customer get hold of the product? Who will be involved in the distribution process? What support will be needed from distributors and other partners to promote the product?

Financial and operational forecasting

What is the anticipated demand for the product? What revenues are expected? Over what period? On what assumptions are these forecasts based? What are the risks if they are wrong?

Technical research and development

What technical challenges does the product present? How does its development fit with the venture's current technical competencies and skills base?

Production and operations

How will the product be manufactured (or the service delivered)? How does its production fit with existing competencies? Is production capacity adequate or must new capacity be established? What are the logistical implications (for example, in terms of storage)?

Supply issues

What factors are involved in producing and delivering the new product? Is it based on components which are currently supplied? Does it demand new components from existing suppliers or does it demand that new suppliers be brought on board? If so, how will they be identified and managed?

Resource implications

Does the business currently have the financial resources to fund such a strategy of expansion? Will it create cash-flow problems? Does the business have sufficient human capacity? Are sales resources sufficient to open and serve the new market sectors?

Strategic concerns of product development

Product development demands an investment. That investment must be considered in light of risk, possible alternatives and opportunity costs in the same way as any other investment within the business. This means that the development of new products must be considered strategically. The key questions in this consideration are as follows.

- How does the new product fit with the innovation on which the business was founded? Is it a way of presenting this innovation further or is it a diversification into a new area of innovation?
- How does the new product build on the venture's existing competitive advantages?
- How does the new product contribute to making those competitive advantages sustainable?
- How does the product fit into the venture's existing portfolio of products?
- What will be the resource demands (financial, operational and human) in developing the product?
- Over what period is the product to return the investment made in it? Does it represent a short- or long-term investment?
- What will be the implications of the product for the sales of existing products? (In particular will there be any 'cannibalisation' of existing sales?)

The success of a new product development expansion strategy does not depend solely on the success of the new products themselves. It also depends on the venture's ability to identify and deliver them. An ability to respond to customer demand through the capability of producing new products quickly and effectively is an important way of developing a structural competitive advantage.

21.3 Entering new markets

KEY LEARNING OUTCOME
An understanding of the decisions that need to be made when considering a strategy of expansion through entry into new markets.

When a new venture is initiated, its market scope is usually quite limited. This is only to be expected since the business's low resource base means that it is well advised to concentrate on serving defined and narrow sectors where it can gain an initial competitive advantage. Once this has been established, then the option of expanding the business by delivering the product or service on which it is based to a wider audience quickly becomes attractive.

The routes to expansion through new market entry are varied. To a great extent the options available will depend on the way in which the niche of the business is defined. The main options for new market expansion include the following possibilities.

New geographical areas

In its early stages, a business tends to serve a local geographic area. Therefore, expansion of the business into other geographical areas is an important option. Ultimately this might include expansion into the international arena through exporting, international marketing or even locating offices overseas. In fact, few businesses can now achieve any real size without taking on the international option.

New industry sectors

A new business will usually concentrate on marketing its products to a narrow range of customers. The composition of this customer base will reflect the entrepreneur's knowledge and experience in the application of their innovation. Again, this represents a sound move in terms of creating a defendable niche in the market. It is likely, however, that the innovation will be attractive to buyers with similar needs in other industry sectors. Developing a strategy to market the product to these groups is an important option for expansion.

New groups of consumers

A new product is often targeted at quite a narrow group of consumers. If it is particularly innovative then the nature of buyers will change over time. Initially, take-up will be led by *adopters*, that is, consumers who actively seek out innovations in the product area and greet them positively. *Non-adopters* will hold back until the innovation becomes more familiar. *Resistors* will reject the product out of hand. The product will also have a positioning which will make it more attractive to some groups of consumers (defined in demographic, sociographic or psychographic terms) than others.

Expanding the appeal of the product from the founding target groups to a wider audience demands careful consideration of how the product is communicated, promoted and distributed to different consumer groups. The option is often attractive but when developing the positioning to attract new groups care must be taken to ensure that core groups are not alienated.

The strategic issues which need to be considered in relation to new market entry parallel those that arise in relation to increase of market share and new product development strategies.

Positioning and branding

How does the competitive environment differ between the original sector and the new sectors? Can the positioning that has been developed for the product continue to be utilised as it is expanded into new sectors, or must a new positioning be developed? Can any branding that has been developed continue to be used or must a new branding, or sub-branding, be developed? Can the current pricing strategy continue or must it be changed?

Communication and promotion

What message must be sent to the new sector? How does this compare to the message that is being sent currently? What medium of communication must be used? What promotional tactics might be used in conjunction with the new sector? Can the current sales and selling strategy be used or must a new one be developed?

Distribution

What distribution routes are available to reach the new sectors? Do these demand that new distributors be used? Does this demand that a new *type* of distributor be used?

Resource implications

Does the business currently have the financial resources to fund such an expansion strategy or will it create cash-flow problems? Does the business have sufficient human capacity? Are sales resources sufficient to open and serve the new market sectors?

Product development and expansion into new market sectors

A strategy of expansion by entry into new market sectors can be adopted in conjunction with new product development strategy. Indeed modification of the product to make it more attractive may be an essential element of the strategy of expansion into new markets. A balance must be struck between ensuring that the offering is right for the sector at which it is aimed on the one hand and ensuring that the business does not lose its economies of scale and create logistical complexity by having a large number of low volume lines on the other.

21.4 Entrepreneurial exporting

KEY LEARNING OUTCOME
An understanding of the opportunities and challenges that exporting presents and the approach of entrepreneurial business to exporting.

If the entrepreneur has developed a significant innovation then the chances are there will be demand for it outside the local market into which the business first entered. If so, exporting can be a very attractive growth option for the venture. This is for a number of reasons. Exporting offers the possibility of:

- increasing demand for the firm's products or services resulting in greater income and an improved cash-flow position;
- more efficient utilisation of the firm's resources;

- reducing fixed costs;
- faster gains of experience curve cost savings;
- reducing the venture's overall risk, especially when there are significant demand fluctuations in local markets;
- an expanded strategic presence on a global stage.

All these things might be achieved with no, or only incremental, expansions in the business's capacity. Exporting can offer the possibility of gaining new income without the need for a significant and high-risk upfront investment. Exporting is increasingly being seen as an important platform for, and indicator of, an entrepreneurial business's success (Edmunds and Khoury, 1986; D'Souza and McDougall, 1989; Buckley *et al.*, 1990). However, being effective in an export market does make demands on the venture's existing knowledge base and its ability to acquire and manage new knowledge. In particular:

- knowledge of demand conditions in international markets;
- knowledge of customers, their needs and tastes in these markets;
- knowledge of why the offering will be attractive in these markets and why they will have an advantage over locally based and other exporting competitors;
- knowledge of the proper pricing levels in the export markets;
- knowledge of the distribution systems and partners who have access to the export market;
- knowledge of how the product or service might be promoted (either through advertising or direct selling) in the export markets.

In addition, the venture's managers must be aware of the political, economic, social, cultural and legal situation that might have a bearing on exporting activity. This is for both strategic reasons (assessing the risk of and prioritising the firm's exporting activity in relation to other growth opportunities) and tactical reasons (preparation by representatives of the venture before travelling out to meet with potential customers or partners). Leonidou and Adams-Florou (1999) review the exporting information management systems that are adopted by small businesses to acquire and use this knowledge.

Given the opportunity exporting offers, and the investment needed to exploit that opportunity it is evident that exporting is not just an adjunct to the entrepreneurial process; it is very much central to it. Exporting presents an opportunity. But it takes drive and initiative to take advantage of that opportunity.

There have been a number of studies into the exporting activity of small and entrepreneurial businesses. The findings are far from clear-cut. Recent studies by Bonaccoursi (1992), Calof (1994) and Westhead (1995) attempt to clarify the situation. The general picture that emerges is that:

- the larger the firm, the more likely it is to be an exporter;
- the older the firm, the more likely it is to be an exporter;
- manufacturers are more likely to export than service firms;
- there is no significant effect due to owner-managing on exporting propensity.

It must be said that these effects, when observed, are weak statistically. It is dangerous to generalise about any one particular firm given its size and age. Even just considering manufacturing firms, different studies have demonstrated great variation in exporting propensity within sectors, for example, from just 4 per cent actively exporting (manufacturers in Merseyside, England (Lloyd and Mason, 1984)) to 70 per cent ('high-tech manufacturers, south-east England' (Oakey and Cooper, 1989)).

A number of workers have proposed models of the process through which firms learn to export (e.g. Bilkey and Tesar, 1977; Joynt and Welch, 1985). Czinkota and Johnson (1981) suggest that a number of stages are involved including an 'unwilling' starting point, moving through 'experimenting' and finally moving on to 'experienced'. Many observers are keen to distinguish between none, sporadic and regular exporters (Samiee and Walters, 1991). Czinkota and Ursik (1991) have proposed a sales-growth matrix that can be used to classify exporting firms.

The reason usually given as to why manufacturers are more likely to be exporters is that it is easier to transport physical goods than it is to deliver services over a long distance. This may be so, but the Internet is changing the rules of service delivery and the future promises a lot more exporting opportunities for service firms in international markets.

A number of workers have examined the factors that encourage exporting. In a study of Australian very small enterprises (VSEs, firms with less than 10 employees and a turnover of less than Aus$1 million) Philp (1998) identified the following as important:

- a preparedness to invest and risk resources;
- a positive attitude towards exporting;
- a willingness to bring in outsiders with exporting expertise;
- having a product that is innovative and can be delivered price competitively into the export market.

Cavusgil and Kirpalani (1993) identified a distinct, but sympathetic, set of factors. These included:

- managerial commitment to exporting;
- export market entry strategy;
- choice of product range to export;
- product positioning in the export market;
- adaptation of the product to suit the export market.

Naidu and Kanti Prasad (1994) emphasise the importance of learning from sporadic export activity as an encourager of more regular, and strategic, exporting for small businesses. Axinn *et al.* (1995) also emphasise the importance of a positive managerial attitude towards exporting and the opportunities it presents. Networks are an important aspect of the entrepreneurial process. They provide the conduits through which resources and information flow to the venture (see Chapter 7). Holmlund and Koch (1999) found in a study of small Finnish firms that networking with overseas agents was a significant aspect of exporting activity. On the other hand, Chetty and

Hamilton (1996) found that many small businesses in New Zealand had low expectation about the rewards from, and were acutely aware of the obstacles to, exporting. Clearly, such beliefs limited exporting activity.

Exporting is usually the first stage of internationalisation for an entrepreneurial venture. The costs and rewards for, and managerial perception of, internationalisation are dependent on the global stage on which business takes place. The attractiveness of exporting can change quickly as a result of changes in international politics and economics. The growing pace of trade liberalisation is particularly important. Christensen (1993) suggests that the North American Free Trade Area (NAFTA) will create a host of new opportunities for entrepreneurial exporters. A study of trade liberalisation in Tanzania by Grenier *et al.* (1999) shows that many manufacturing firms had taken the opportunity liberalisation presents to become active exporters. Chhibber and Majumbar (1998) found that recent economic reforms in India had encouraged exporting and that those Indian firms that had taken the opportunity to do so were rewarded with growth and profitability. On the other hand, Filatotchev *et al.* (1999) found little evidence that the economic liberalisation had encouraged exporting for firms in the transition economies of eastern Europe. Smallbone *et al.* (1999) found that there was a great deal of variation in exporting propensity between different business sectors in transition economies.

Given its importance to success, both from the perspective of the specific entrepreneurial venture and national economies, and the rewards that can be gained from a successful exporting strategy it is not surprising that a number of agencies, both governmental and private, have emerged to support the small and entrepreneurial venture develop its exporting activity. Barrett (1990, 1992) has produced reviews of where SMEs can obtain information on help with exporting.

21.5 Acquisitions

KEY LEARNING OUTCOME

An understanding of the decisions that need to be made when considering a strategy of expansion through acquisition.

Success in the marketplace generates the financial resources which the entrepreneur can use to expand the business further. This money can either come from retained profits or be additional funds offered up by investors. This capital can be used to invest in increasing the market share of existing products, or to develop new products or to enter new market sectors. Such growth comes from 'within' the business and is sometimes referred to as *organic* growth. An alternative to organic growth is to acquire other businesses in their entirety and 'add' them onto the venture. This is referred to as growth by *acquisition*.

There are three sorts of acquisition. These differ in the way in which the integrated firm sits in relatin to the venture in the value addition chain. The first is *vertical integration*. This happens when the venture acquires a firm which is either above or below it in the value addition chain, i.e. it acquires a business which is a *customer* or a *supplier*. The acquisition of customers is referred to as *forward integration* and that of a supplier as *backward integration*. The second type of acquisition occurs when the venture integrates a business which is at the same level of value addition as itself, i.e. a business that is, ostensibly at least, a *competitor*. The third type of acquisition occurs in the remaining cases when the integrated business is not a supplier, nor a customer nor competitor. These might be referred to as *lateral* integrations. The various types of integration are shown in Fig. 21.3.

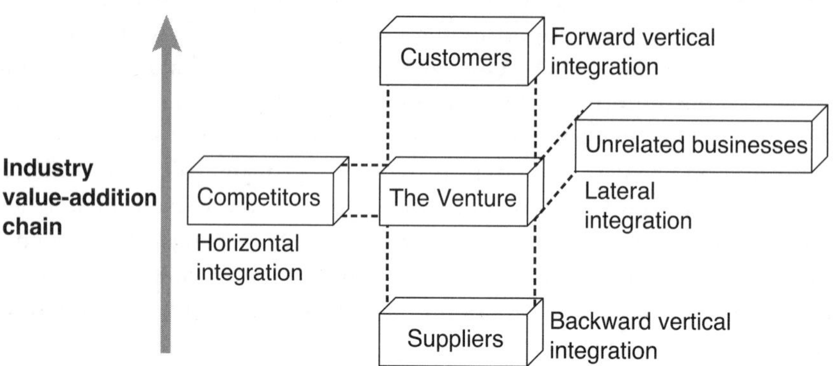

Fig. 21.3 Types of acquisition

Acquisitions are an attractive option for rapid growth because the only limitations on growth rate are the availability of targets and the funds to buy them. For example, Howard Hodgeson built up his funeral directing business from eighteen parlours to well over 500 over a three-year period solely by acquisition. Acquisitions do, however, represent a fundamentally different approach to growth than does organic expansion. With organic growth new resources are brought together by the entrepreneur in an innovative combination to create new value. An integrated business, on the other hand, represents resources which are *already combined*.

This means that an acquisition is not valuable in itself unless new value can be created from it. This demands that the acquiring venture must do something *different* with the business in order to make the acquisition worth while. In short, the entrepreneur must decide how they are going to add value through the acquisition; that is, what they can do, why that is valuable for the business's customers, and why the management of the acquired firm cannot do this on their own.

In strategic terms this means asking how acquisitions can be used to create and develop the venture's competitive advantage. There are four fundamental processes by which acquisitions can help in the development of competitive advantage:

1 *By reducing costs.* Does integration reduce overall costs? This may be achieved by eliminating some fixed or overhead costs. Alternatively, it may be gained by achieving some economy of scale in a key functional area. Production and sales are particularly important here. Existing production capacity may be used more

efficiently especially if there is some overcapacity. The sales team may find it relatively easy to add new items to the portfolio they are selling. They may also find it possible to serve additional customers in their area. (However, care needs to be taken to ensure that they can still develop a good understanding of the benefits offered by the things they are selling and that they can still give each customer the time they need in order to manage the supplier–buyer relationship.)

2 *By combining and creating knowledge.* Does integration increase the value of the knowledge held by the individual organisations? For example, can the acquired firm offer information on products, operational technology or markets that the acquiring entrepreneur can utilise in its own business area? Does the acquirer understand customers in a way which promises to make the selling of the acquired business's products more effective? Can the two organisations learn key skills from each other, for example, in R&D, or in marketing?

3 *By capitalising on relationships.* Does integration take advantage of the relationships enjoyed by one party? For example, does it allow the acquirer to use their brand (a relationship with the customer) on a wider range of products? Does the acquired business enjoy a particularly valuable relationship with suppliers or distributors? Does the acquired business have access to new geographical areas or to new customer groups?

   Of course, care must always be taken to ensure that the acquisition process itself does not upset established relationships.

4 *By developing organisational structure.* Does the integration allow the organisation as a whole to develop structural advantages? For example, does it make the processing of information on the market more effective? Does it make the business more responsive to customer needs? Does it allow the business to react more rapidly in producing new products? Does it enable the business to get its products into new areas or to new customer groups?

   It is important to note that these things do not happen just because the organisation becomes larger, but because it changes the way it does things, in particular because it differentiates tasks in a more effective manner.

In summary, an acquisition is not a way of adding value in itself. Two businesses added together are not automatically more valuable than two separate businesses. In fact, the reverse is often the case. An acquisition only creates value if it allows the venture to offer the customer something new and useful and allows the new venture to develop its competitive advantage in the marketplace.

Summary of key ideas

- The entrepreneurial venture is characterised by a potential for growth. After initiating the venture, the entrepreneur must develop a strategy to *expand* it.
- The *generic* options for growth are by increasing core market share; by developing new products; by entering new markets; and by acquiring existing businesses.

- The attractiveness of the first three of these options depends on the market characteristics, particularly *growth rate*.
- The attractiveness of the acquisition option depends on the ability of the entrepreneur to genuinely add value to acquired businesses.

Suggestions for further reading

Andersen, O. (1993) 'On the internationalization process of firms: A critical analysis', *Journal of International Business Studies*, Vol. 24, No. 2, pp. 209–31.

Ansoff, H.I. (1965) *Corporate Strategy*, New York: McGraw-Hill.

Axinn, N., Savitt, R., Sinkila, J.M. and **Thach, S.V.** (1995) 'Export intention, beliefs and behaviours in smaller industrial firms', *Journal of Business Research*, Vol. 32, No. 1, pp. 49–55.

Barrett, G.R. (1990) 'Where small and midsized companies can find export help; a number of government agencies have programmes to assist in all phases of exporting', *Journal of Accountancy*, Vol. 170, No. 3, pp. 46–50.

Barrett, G.R. (1992) 'Where small businesses can find export help', *Journal of Accountancy*, Vol. 174, No. 2, pp. 48–9.

Biggadike, R. (1979) 'The risky business of expansion', *Harvard Business Review*, May-June, pp. 103–11.

Bilkey, W.J. and **Tesar, G.** (1977) 'The export behavior of smaller-sized Wisconsin firms', *Journal of International Business Studies*, Vol. 8, pp. 71–8.

Bloom, P.N. and **Kotler, P.** (1978) 'Strategies for high market-share companies', *Harvard Business Review*, Nov-Dec, pp. 63–72.

Bonaccoursi, A. (1992) 'On the relationship between firm size and export intensity', *Journal of International Business Studies*, Vol. 23, pp. 605–35.

Bourantas, D. and **Mandes, Y.** (1987) 'Does market share lead to profitability?' *Long Range Planning*, Vol. 20, No. 5, pp. 102–8.

Buckley, P.J. and **Casson, M.** (1998) 'Analyzing foreign market entry strategies: Extending the internationalization approach', *Journal of International Business Studies*, Vol. 29, No. 3, pp. 539–61.

Buckley, P.J., Pass, C.L. and **Prescott, K.** (1990) 'Measures of international competitiveness: A critical review', *Journal of Marketing Management*, Vol. 4, pp. 175–200.

Calof, J.L. (1994) 'The relationship between firm size and export behaviour revisited', *Journal of International Business Studies*, Vol. 25, No. 2, pp. 367–87.

Cavusgil, S.T. and **Kirpalani, V.H.** (1993) 'Introducing products into export markets: Success factors', *Journal of Business Research*, Vol. 27, pp 1–15.

Chaney, P.K., Devinney, T.M. and **Winer, R.S.** (1991) 'The impact of new product introductions on the market value of firms', *Journal of Business*, Vol. 64, No. 4, pp. 573–610.

Chetty, S.K. and **Hamilton, R.T.** (1996) 'The process of exporting in owner-controlled firms', *International Small Business Journal*, Vol. 14, No. 2, pp. 12–25.

Chhibber, P.K. and **Majumdar, S.K.** (1998) 'Does it pay to venture abroad? Exporting behaviour and the performance of firms in Indian industry', *Managerial and Decision Economics*, Vol. 19, No. 2, pp. 121–6.

Christensen, S.L. (1993) 'Is there a role for the small business in the North American Free Trade Area?' *Business Forum*, Vol. 18, No. 1/2, pp. 44–6.

Cooper, R.G. (1994) 'New products: The factors that drive success', *International Marketing Review*, Vol. 11, No. 1, pp. 60–76.

Czinkota, M.R. and **Johnson, W.J.** (1981) 'Segmenting US firms for export development', *Journal of Business Research*, Vol. 9, pp. 353–65.

Czinkota, M.R. and **Ursik, M.** (1991) 'Classification of exporting firms according to sales and growth into a share matrix', *Journal of Business Research*, Vol. 22, No. 3, pp. 243–53.

D'Souza, D.E. and **McDougall, P.P.** (1989) 'Third world joint venturing: A strategic option for the smaller firm', *Entrepreneurship Theory and Practice*, Vol. 14, pp. 19–33.

Edmunds, S.E. and **Khoury, S.J.** (1986) 'Exports: A necessary ingredient in the growth of small business firms', *Journal of Small Business Management*, Vol. 24, pp. 54–65.

Filatotchev, I., Wright, M., Buck, T. and **Dyomina, N.** (1999) 'Exporting and restructuring in privatised firms from Russia, Ukraine and Belarus', *World Economy*, Vol. 22, No. 7, pp. 1013–14.

Grenier, L., McKay, A. and **Morrissey, O.** (1999) 'Exporting, ownership and confidence in Tanzanian enterprises', *World Economy*, Vol. 22, No. 7, p. 995.

Hamermesh, R.G., Anderson, Jr, M.J. and **Harris, J.E.** (1978) 'Strategies for low market share businesses', *Harvard Business Review*, May-June, pp. 95–102.

Holmlund, M. and **Koch, S.** (1999) 'Relationships and the internationalisation of Finnish small and medium-sized companies', *International Small Business Journal*, Vol. 16, No. 4, pp. 46–63.

Joynt, P. and **Welch, L.** (1985) 'A strategy for small business internationalisation', *International Marketing Review*, Vol. 2, pp. 64–73.

Leonidou, L.C. and **Adams-Florou, A.S.** (1999) 'Types and sources of export information: Insights from small business', *International Small Business Journal*, Vol. 17, No. 3, pp. 30–45.

Lloyd, P.E. and **Mason, C.M.** (1984) 'Spatial variations in new firm formation in the United Kingdom: comparative evidence from Merseyside, Greater Manchester and South Hampshire', *Regional Studies*, Vol. 18, pp. 207–20.

Naidu, G.M. and **Kanti Prasad, V.** (1994) 'Predictors of export strategy and performance of small- and medium-sized firms', *Journal of Business Research*, Vol. 31, No. 2/3, pp. 107–15.

Newton, J.K. (1981) 'Acquisitions: A directional policy matrix approach', *Long Range Planning*, Vol. 14, No. 6, pp. 51–7.

Oakey, R.P. and **Cooper, S.Y.** (1989) 'High technology industry, agglomeration and potential for peripherally sited small firms', *Regional Studies*, Vol. 22, pp. 347–60.

O'Farrell, P.N., Wood, P.A. and **Zheng, J.** (1998) 'Internationalisation by business service SMEs: An inter-industry analysis', *International Small Business Journal*, Vol. 16, No. 2, pp. 13–33.

Philp, N.E. (1998) 'The export propensity of the very small enterprise', *International Small Business Journal*, Vol. 16, No. 4, pp. 79–94.

Samiee, S. and **Walters, P.G.P.** (1991) 'Segmenting corporate exporting activities: sporadic versus regular exporters', *Journal of the Academy of Marketing Science*, Vol. 19, No. 2, pp. 94–104.

Schuster, C.P. and **Bodkin, C.D.** (1987) 'Market segmentation practises of exporting companies', *Industrial Marketing Management*, Vol. 16, No. 2, pp. 95–102.

Smallbone, D., Piasecki, B., Venessar, U., Toderov, K. and **Labrianidis, L.** (1999) 'Internationalisation and SME development in transition economies: An international comparison', *Journal of Small Business and Enterprise Development*, Vol. 5, No. 4, pp. 363–75.

Szymanski, D.M., Bharadwai, S.G. and **Varadarajan, P.R.** (1993) 'An analysis of the market share–profitability relationship', *Journal of Marketing*, Vol. 57, pp. 1–18.

Walters, P.G.P. (1991) 'Segmenting corporate exporting activities: sporadic versus regular exporters', *Journal of the Academy of Marketing Science*, Vol. 19, No. 2, pp. 93–104.

Westhead, P. (1995) 'Exporting and non-exporting firms in Great Britain', *International Journal of Entrepreneurial Behaviour and Research*, Vol. 1, No. 2, pp. 6–36.

Selected case material

Nice work for the Celtic tiger

4 November 1999

Irish magic has worked wonders in helping the Belfast-based recruitment consultants expand overseas, says **Elizabeth Robinson**

Ken Belshaw believes the Irish were put on earth to be recruitment consultants.

Certainly the expansion of Grafton Recruitment, the Belfast-based chain of employment agencies run by him and fellow Irishman James Kilbane since 1983, owes much to skilful playing of the Irish card.

In the past five years, Grafton has grown from a two-shop Northern Irish concern into a 31-strong network of agencies around the world. It holds the number one position in the Czech Republic and Hungary; has operations in Poland, Chile, New Zealand and South Africa; and has plans for US offices in Boston and San Francisco.

Grafton's Irish identity has made it easier to enter foreign markets, says Mr Belshaw. "Ireland is hot around the world, thanks to Riverdance and Guinness pubs. We can go anywhere and say we're Irish and we get that smile – there's instantly a friendship and a personality there."

Overseas operations now account for one-third of Grafton's profits, and Mr Kilbane, the quietly spoken half of the partnership, expects that to rise to 50 per cent by 2001. Since Grafton began its overseas operations in 1994, with the opening of an office in Prague, the company has seen year-on-year annual growth of 30 per cent, with global profits last year of £1.8m.

The partners are an unlikely double act, admits Mr Belshaw. "He's a southern Irish Catholic – a cultured boarding school guy and a university drop-out. I'm a Prod (Protestant) from east Belfast who failed the 11-plus, but I know the advantages of using Ireland around the world."

This straddling of both sides of the Irish border gives Grafton another advantage: at the parties to open its offices abroad, both Irish and British embassies, and therefore Irish and British companies, are represented. However, Grafton has no marketing department to mastermind such networking, relying instead on the charm – and blarney – of the two partners, although Mr Belshaw says: "James is your man for embassy dos."

Although the company is based in Northern Ireland, it relies on the myriad images that Ireland conjures up. This is helped by Irish staff in its overseas offices and by its name, which is taken from Dublin's most famous street. "Which is the stronger brand? General Motors or Ireland?" challenges Mr Belshaw. Ireland is a very strong brand, a welcoming brand – it's a tremendous image to be in the service industry – and we're a people industry."

This image has helped secure business from companies such as Philip Morris, Vodafone and Unilever in Grafton's overseas offices, but it has also facilitated migration by Irish workers back to their homeland.

The booming southern Irish economy – the "Celtic tiger" – has created a demand for skilled workers, with the Irish government estimating that it needs 20,000 immigrants in the next two years.

"To keep the Celtic tiger roaring, it's important to bring in immigrants," says Mr Belshaw. "I've spent 25 years exporting Paddys around the world – now the whole thing is reversed and we need them back."

The company has an agreement with the Irish government whereby Grafton brochures are provided with passports issued to immigrants. For example, 2,000 Irish passports sent to New Zealanders through the "grandparent rule" were accompanied by literature on Grafton. "When we bring people back to Dublin, they don't think of Dublin, they think of Ireland's west coast and diddlydee music at three in the morning. Why knock it?" asks Mr Belshaw.

It is not just the Irish abroad who are being wooed. "This week we're advertising for 50 butchers in Poland to come and work in meat lines in Ireland," says Mr Belshaw. The company also ships over short-term workers from employment blackspots in Wales.

The Irish card has also proved popular in central European countries, including the Czech Republic, Hungary and Poland. "Instead of going into Liverpool or Manchester we decided to leapfrog all that and get better value for our money. In fact, we leapfrogged the whole European Union," says Mr Belshaw.

Their timing was fortuitous. They set up in Prague just as the first crop of graduates after the country's Velvet Revolution were looking for work, and multinational companies were seeking to set up and recruit local talent, particularly in information technology.

The company's early lead in Prague has been maintained, despite rising competition, and spurred Grafton to enter Hungary and Poland.

In 1997 Mr Belshaw and Mr Kilbane decided to go even further afield.

"I'd been at a recruitment conference that said if an economy was growing by more than 2.2 per cent, then recruitment agencies should make money. I came away thinking the world was dead simple," says Mr Belshaw. They pinpointed Chile, where the economy was growing at 8 per cent, and set up an office in Santiago, which, curiously, soon found an Irish pub opening on the other side of the street.

However, it was in Chile that the company's overseas strategy had to be adjusted. Until then, Grafton had been primarily a temporary staff agency at home, but a permanent placement agency abroad, a combination it found the most lucrative.

"In Chile, however, recruitment was done on an old-boy network that would have put Northern Ireland in the 1950s to shame. We had to reposition ourselves into a temporary agency. But that's where we're lucky we're not a plc, because I would have got my ass kicked for dropping a quarter of a million pounds," says Mr Belshaw.

The partners considered plc status 18 months ago, but were persuaded that there was no appetite for such a small-cap company.

It is an aim that remains at the back of their minds, but in the meantime a strategic alliance or venture capital deal is more likely, especially to fund the opening of an office in Sydney next year and their desire to tap the Irish-American market.

Needless to say, wherever they go Mr Belshaw and Mr Kilbane fly the Irish flag, though sometimes unwittingly.

Mr Kilbane recounts how on a recent visit to Prague, he was sitting in the James Joyce pub when "in walks Mary McAleese (Ireland's president) with Vaclav Havel and she smacks me a big kiss on the lips." She lives near him, he explains.

"I thought, 'My God, you come all this way and you meet a neighbour in the pub.'"

"But where else would you meet them?" asks Mr Belshaw.

Lollipop name aims to stick

31 March 2000

Catalan sweet maker Chupa Chups wants to create a global brand on the back of its main product, writes **Ross Tieman**

It takes a certain Catalan creative confidence to build a global brand on the back of a lollipop. But that is what Chupa Chups, the Barcelona-based sweet maker, is trying to do.

With manufacturing sites in five countries, including China and Russia, and sales in 168 countries, Chupa Chups is already familiar to many of the world's children. Last year it sold 4bn of its lollipops.

But now a combination of fashion, government anti-smoking campaigns and cheeky, opportunistic marketing are building an adult customer base. And to exploit its "fun" appeal, the family-owned company is launching complementary ranges of toys, stationery, clothes, children's spectacles and sunglasses.

The resulting sales surge has been spectacular. Revenues have grown to Pta73.1bn (£264m) last year from Pta60.5bn in 1997. Xavier Bernat, the 46-year-old president and chief executive, says sales are forecast to reach Pta125bn by 2002, when he and his siblings plan to float the company on a European stock exchange.

"We see ourselves growing organically, but this does not mean that if we see something interesting we would not buy it," he says. "Globally, the confectionery market is very fragmented. There are a lot of family companies, especially in Europe, with owners who are ageing and where there are no clear succession plans."

All this is a far cry from 1954, when Mr Bernat's father, Enric, a small-time Barcelona confectioner, was asked to try to revive Granja Asturias, a flagging manufacturer of 200 products derived from apples.

Enric Bernat struck a deal by which he would own half the company if he turned it round. He succeeded, and in 1958 bought the rest of the shares and dropped the entire product range to concentrate on a single novelty that he had developed: the Chups lollipop.

From the outset, Enric Bernat knew the key to success was marketing and distribution. The lollipops were sold for Pta1 each in an eye-catching hedgehog display unit as near to the till as a squadron of salesmen could get it.

Soon, sales were extended to France. Encouraged by success, and with a new daisy logo designed in 1969 by the Catalan surrealist artist Salvador Dali, the renamed Chupa Chups mounted a big export push. Between 1970 and 1980 the proportion of sales outside Spain soared from 10 per cent to 90 per cent.

By the mid-1990s, Chupa Chups had established a global presence, with factories in Spain, France, Russia, China and another under development in Mexico. And the business had become a family affair, employing Enric's three sons.

Chupa Chups then attacked an unlikely new market: adults.

Johan Cruyff, then coach of Barcelona football club, was obliged to quit smoking. A present of Chupa Chups lollies was arranged, and images of Mr Cruyff sucking a lollipop on the trainer's bench were on prime-time television. The product caught on among a generation of young clubbers who spurned alcohol, but wanted a sugar-rush to keep them dancing all night.

The company's marketing has caught the *zeitgeist*. Photos of "celebrity suckers" have been published around the world. In Germany, previously a poor market for Chupa Chups, the slogan "lick me" caused sales to soar. Drag queens were recruited to dish out lollies at London Fashion week. Chupa Chups has promoted its products as innocent fun, a taste of childhood but also something a little *risqué* for the unconventional.

Its marketing campaigns have drawn a fine line between amusing and indecent. "We were a children's product, but we had a teenage spirit," says Xavier de Lame, communications manager.

But he admits the sensitivities of positioning such a product at the borders of respectability. "Xavier Bernat is very much a gambler," says Mr de Lame. "He is willing to take risks."

So far, the campaign has worked. The effect on sales has been astonishing. Last year, some 23 per cent of Chupa Chups were bought by teenagers and young adults.

In Britain, since the brand was relaunched four years ago, sales have risen 230 per cent to 150m a year. Chupa Chups are on sale in clubs, bars, even second-hand clothes shops. The core purchasers are now 12-14 year olds, and young adults account for between 15 and 20 per cent of sales. According to Sue McDermott, UK marketing manager: "Our purchasers aren't aware that we market to them – we just seem to turn up in the cool places where they hang out."

The company has courted older customers with new flavours. Alongside classics such as strawberry, chocolate-vanilla and cappuccino, Chupa Chups has launched highly coloured "tongue-painter" lollipops and extra-large ones filled with bubble-gum.

It has also diversified into sugar-free mints with its Smint range, and sweets-with-toys under the Crazy Planet banner.

The strength of the brand, its quality, and the absence of international competitors enables Chupa Chups to sell for twice the price of local rivals in most markets. As a confectionery company, Chupa Chups ranks number 25 worldwide, with a market share of just 0.9 per cent. If chocolate is excluded, it rises to number seven, behind Nestlé, Cadbury, Haribo, Warner Lambert, Storck and Mars. In lollipops, it is pre-eminent, with a 34 per cent share.

The challenge now is to capitalise on the rising recognition of its brand. Xavier Bernat's sister, Marta, has been appointed licensing director to do just that.

Last year, licensees sold 50,000 pairs of Chupa Chups spectacles for children at a price of £50 a pair for the frames alone. Working with reputed partners, the company has licensed its logo for use on children's and adult clothing, school stationery, and a growing range of lifestyle products.

Today, pre-tax profits are "in line with the industry average" of 10-12 per cent, and should improve as volumes rise, says Mr Bernat.

At the same time, Chupa Chups is open to more alliances in marketing, such as those with Dutch confectioner Van Melle in Germany or Britain's Cadbury in Australia.

But the main goal, it seems, is to ride the wave of fashion and use the adult market for lollipops to achieve the scale that will enable Chupa Chups to expand into a brand – and to stay true to its Catalan roots: creative and confident.

Review questions

Compare and contrast the expansion strategies being adopted by:

1 Grafton Recruitment

2 Chupa Chups.

22 Organisational growth and development

Chapter overview

This chapter is concerned with developing an understanding of how organisational growth and development present themselves as opportunities and challenges to the decision-making entrepreneur. The first section explores some of the metaphors that decision makers can draw upon to create a picture of organisational growth. Subsequent sections of the chapter deal with setting objectives for growth and then planning for and controlling it.

22.1 Conceptualising growth and organisational change

KEY LEARNING OUTCOME
An understanding of the metaphors used to describe organisational growth.

The idea that organisations and organising are best understood through the use of metaphor was introduced in section 7.1. The point was made that the way in which management is approached is dependent, to some extent, on the metaphor being used to provide an image of organisation by the entrepreneurial decision maker. As well as influencing the way in which organisation is perceived in a static sense, metaphors also influence the way in which organisational *growth* and *change* are seen to take place. Again, such metaphors provide a base for recognising the challenges the organisation faces and the approaches the entrepreneur might take to meet them.

Andrew van de Ven and Marshall Scott Poole have summarised the most important metaphors of organisational change. These are based on the notions of *life-cycle, evolution,* the *dialectic* and *teleology*. In addition, the metaphors of the trialectic and chaos complement the picture.

Life-cycle

The notion of life-cycle suggests that the organisation undergoes a pattern of growth and development much like a living organism does. Life for an organism consists of a series of different stages: it is born, grows, matures and eventually ages and dies (Fig. 22.1). This pattern is pre-programmed and the changes that take place are both unavoidable and irrevocable. Drawing on the experience of living things this metaphor accounts for the view that youthful entrepreneurial organisations are dynamic whereas older organisations are more sedate and sluggish and that this is a fate that will eventually befall the entrepreneurial venture as it matures itself. The metaphor does not give a definite lifespan, however; it does not say *when* this must happen.

This metaphor is limited in that it (falsely) suggests that organisational decline is inevitable. It does, however, serve to warn the entrepreneur against complacency as the venture becomes successful.

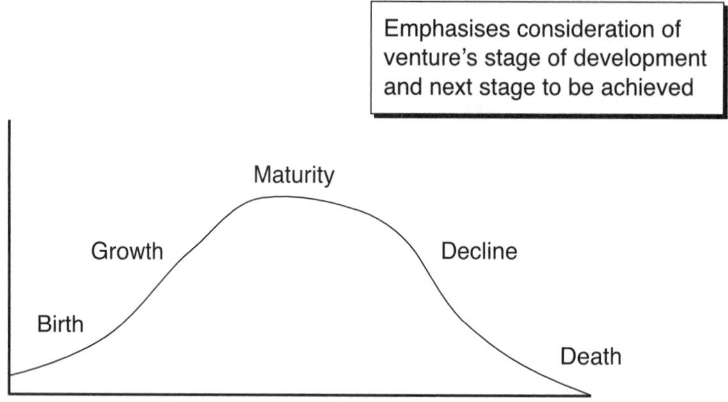

Fig. 22.1 Life-cycle growth metaphor

Evolution

Evolution is a theoretical scheme which explains changes over time of the morphology of biological populations. It is founded on the concepts of *competition*, *fitness*, *selection* and *survival*. This scheme has been co-opted from biological science to describe changes in populations of business firms (Fig. 22.2).

As a metaphor, evolution reminds the entrepreneur that they are operating in a competitive environment, that they must compete for scarce resources and that the venture must be efficient ('fit') in the tasks it undertakes. While evolution may conjure up an image of untrammelled competition – of a nature 'red in tooth and claw' in the words of Tennyson in his poem *In memoriam* – a more sophisticated reading reminds us that co-operation within and between species is also a feature of the natural world. This is similar to the entrepreneurial venture which not only competes, but also grows within a stakeholder network which may be supportive as well as competitive.

The dialectic

The dialectic is a concept which can be traced back to classical Greek philosophy. It has been extensively developed by thinkers such as Marx and Freud and is based on a notion of progression through conflict and resolution. A system is initially unified but,

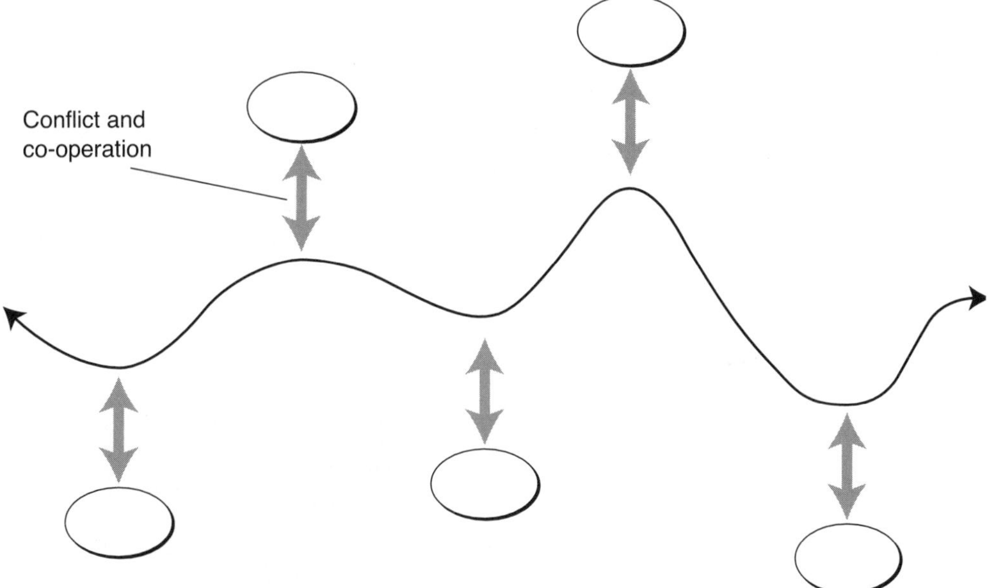

Fig. 22.2 Evolutionary growth

over time, distinct parts begin to distinguish themselves. These parts recognise that their interests conflict and so they begin to oppose each other. Neither part can actually win the conflict and what eventually emerges is a newly unified system in which both parts have been changed and reintegrated (Fig. 22.3).

As a metaphor of organisational development, the dialectic illuminates conflict and conflict resolution at a number of levels, for example between the entrepreneurial venture and competitor firms, between different stakeholder groups within the venture such as investors and employees, and within stakeholder groups. This latter level would include, for example, political manoeuvring by managerial factions within the business.

The importance of this metaphor for the entrepreneur is not so much its emphasis on the inevitability of conflict as in the idea that value can be created by resolving that conflict. The entrepreneur brings stakeholders (whose interests may differ) together in a way in which all benefit.

The trialectic

Jeffrey Ford and Laurie Ford (1994) have drawn upon a development of the dialectic to present a new metaphor for describing organisational growth. This is the *trialectic*. The dialectic suggests that a system separates into two conflicting parts. As its name suggests, the trialectic suggests that systems have a dynamic consisting of three parts.

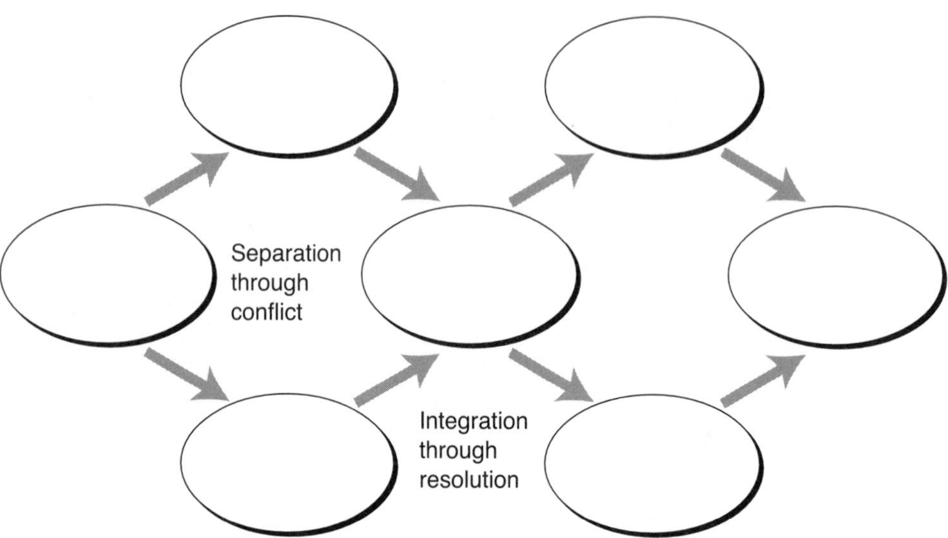

Fig. 22.3 Dialectical growth

However, the way that these three parts attract rather than conflict with each other is emphasised. Trialectics takes as its starting point the notion that all things are in a state of flux. This flux is the fundamental 'stuff' of the universe, not the objects we see. When we recognise objects or systems we only do so as a result of our seeking out transient 'resting points' or 'material manifestations'. The three aspects that are important to the growth of an organisation are its current state or 'manifestation' and two alternative possible futures or potential manifestations. These possible future states act to attract the venture and pull it forward. In pursuing these, the organisation creates new pairs of possible future states (Fig. 22.4). This process is ongoing, continuous and dynamic. Again, we only notice these states because we continually seek out the transient manifestations.

The metaphor of trialectical change calls upon some deep philosophical ideas. As a metaphor for growth in the entrepreneurial venture it does, however, emphasise the fact that change is not just an aspect of the organisation; it is fundamental to it. It also emphasises the possibility of choosing a number of different future states and the freedom the entrepreneur has to create his or her own entirely new world.

Teleology

Teleology suggests a process of change in which a system is progressing toward some future state or *teleos*. This future state both attracts the system or pulls it forward, and

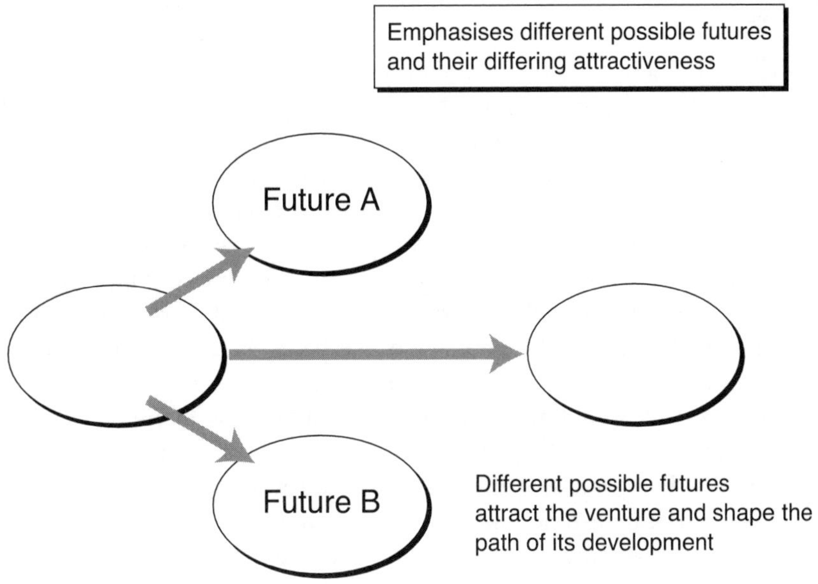

Emphasises different possible futures and their differing attractiveness

Future A

Future B

Different possible futures attract the venture and shape the path of its development

Fig. 22.4 Trialectical growth

defines the shape the system takes as it progresses (Fig. 22.5). More than any other metaphor, teleology introduces the notion of *purpose* to organisational change and growth. The entrepreneur can use his or her vision as the future state which pulls the organisation forward. It can be used to define goals and objectives and it is a critical element in leadership. Visionary leadership is a teleological process.

Emphasises role of entrepreneur's vision in shaping the venture's future

Vision of the future is constructed and used to draw the venture forward

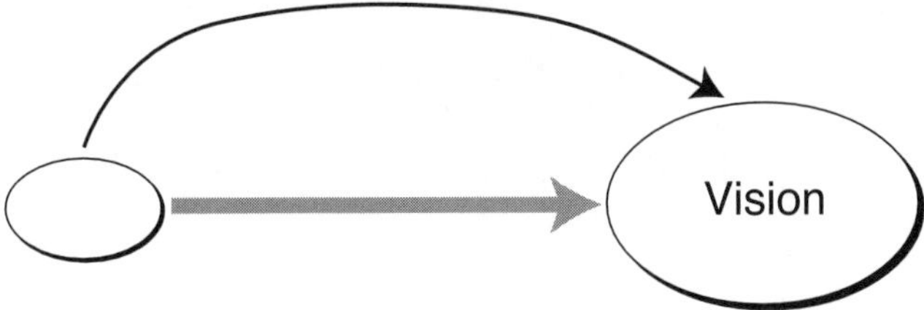

Fig. 22.5 Teleological growth

Chaos

In addition to these 'traditional' metaphors, a new perspective is becoming increasingly important in providing a context for understanding organisational change. This is based on the notions of *complexity* and *chaos*.

Complexity science has its origins in the physics of turbulent and far-from equilibrium systems. Its insights have escaped from the boundaries of these narrow concerns and they now inform thinking on a wide range of topics including biology, economics and organisation theory. The defining feature of complexity is its rejection of simple lines of causality which characterise traditional systems thinking. In a complex system a small cause may, in time, have a very large and unpredictable effect (Fig. 22.6). The beat of a butterfly's wing eventually causing a hurricane is a dramatic example. Systems theorists modelling the Earth's atmosphere discovered that a slight movement of air in one part of the world (say, from the beat of a butterfly's wing) could cause enough of a disturbance of the global atmospheric system to result in a large effect (such as a hurricane) some time later in a distant part of the world. The atmosphere is a chaotic system. A small cause leads to a large effect that cannot be predicted *ex ante*. Complex systems are not simply disorganised, however. They may show higher levels of form and order as a result of 'emergent' features which do not have a straightforward one-to-one relationship with lower levels of order. This is a perspective which has been developed extensively by Ralph Stacey in his book *Strategic Management and Organisational Dynamics* (2000).

The main question which complexity theory poses to management thinking is, if organisations are chaotic systems, can they be 'managed' at all? The answer usually leads not to a rejection of management but to demands to view it in a more sophisticated light. What is rejected is the idea that management can be reduced to a simple process of moving the venture to a pre-determined end point by a series of controlled steps.

The entrepreneurial venture is inherently unpredictable. By its very nature, it creates a future which is uncertain. Systems emerge to manage this uncertainty, for example the network of stakeholder relationships which define the venture, but they cannot eliminate it completely. The chaos metaphor reminds the entrepreneur that control and direction cannot be 'programmed' into the organisation. Events cannot be foreseen and each contingency must be responded to on its own terms. Entrepreneurial management is a *dynamic* process and it demands a 'hands on' approach. The future of the venture is not pre-determined by its present, rather it is actively shaped by the entrepreneur as new, unseen and often unseeable possibilities emerge.

As with metaphors of static organisation, the entrepreneur must learn to enrich their decision making by recognising the metaphors they are using and by drawing on as wide a variety of metaphors of organisational change as possible.

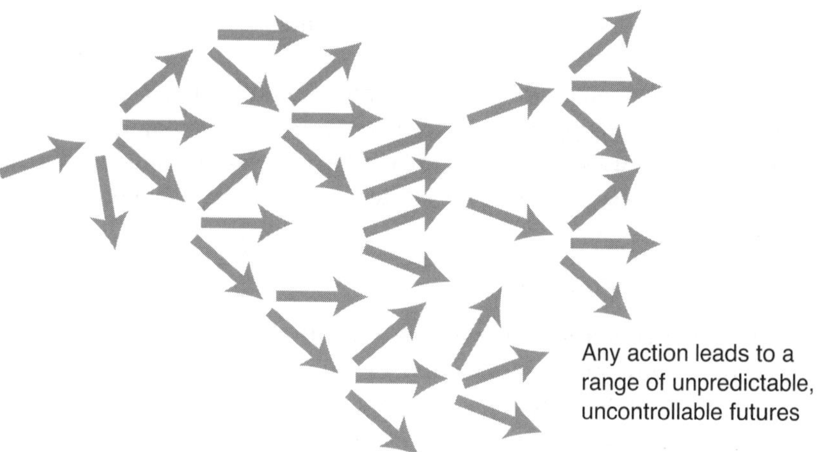

Fig. 22.6 Chaotic growth metaphor

22.2 Growth as an objective for the venture

KEY LEARNING OUTCOME

An appreciation of the issues associated with setting growth as an objective for the venture.

The entrepreneurial venture is characterised by its growth potential, but why might an entrepreneur wish to take advantage of that potential and grow their venture? There are a number of answers to this question. It might be the result of a desire to increase personal wealth but this is not usually the main motivation of an entrepreneur. More usually it relates to a sense of achievement. In a sense, the size of the venture is a way of 'keeping the score'. Entrepreneurs are also driven by a desire to make a difference to the world. And in general, the larger the venture they create, the bigger the difference they have made. Driving growth can also relate to the desire for personal control. The bigger the venture, the greater the domain over which the entrepreneur can express their power.

For these reasons growth is often an important objective for the venture. However, setting growth targets creates challenges in relation to the venture's strategy and resources and the risk to which it is exposed.

Growth and strategy

Growth has to be achieved. It must be delivered by obtaining a greater volume of business. Ultimately, it must be driven by increased sales. The venture must have a strategy in place to develop its sales base. As discussed in Chapter 20, such a strategy may be based on exploiting market growth, increasing market share, developing new products or entering new markets.

An expansion strategy must be consistent with the capabilities of the venture, it must draw upon and develop the venture's competitive advantages and be viable given the competitive situation it will have to face. Growth targets must be demanding but they must also be reasonable given the strategic constraints the venture faces.

Growth and resources

Growth is dependent on the venture's ability to attract new resources. The ultimate source of resources is customer money. Investment and loan capital can only be a means to the end of attracting customers.

Capital is not useful in itself. It must be converted into productive assets in terms of people and operating resources. Growth targets must take account of the resources the venture will be able to acquire. Consideration must be made not just of the ability to attract capital from customers, lenders and investors but also the ability of the venture to *use* that capital to bring in the people and specialist assets the venture depends on. If these are in short supply, then any limitations imposed on growth must be taken into account.

Growth and risk

There is a complex relationship between growth and risk. In general, the larger a firm, the less risk it is exposed to. There are two reasons for this. First, size reflects *success*. A large firm is successful which implies that it is good at what it does. Clearly, being effective in the marketplace is the best way to reduce risk. Second, the larger the firm, the more resources it will have. In particular, larger firms tend to have more 'slack' resources. These are resources that are not dedicated to specific projects and can be moved around quickly. The large business can use these resources to buffer themselves from short-term environmental shocks better than can the small firm.

However, growth carries some risk in itself. Growth implies developing new business which means venturing into the unknown. The degree of risk depends on the way in which the expansion draws upon the venture's capabilities, its knowledge of products and markets and the environment in which it competes. Using resources to fuel growth is an *investment* regardless of whether new investment capital is obtained or profits are reinvested rather than distributed back to shareholders. As an investment, growth must be judged like any other in light of the risks it presents, the returns it offers and the opportunity costs it imposes.

The growth objective for the venture must be set following consideration of these factors. It must define the growth of the venture in terms of increased sales, increased income (including new investment capital) and how these revenues will be converted to assets. Growth targets must be consistent with, and feasible from, a strategy to achieve that growth and they must be acceptable to the venture's stakeholders in terms of the risks this creates.

Not all entrepreneurs set out with high growth objectives in mind. When Anita Roddick established The Body Shop in Brighton she intended to start only a small business capable of providing an income for her and her family. However, once the potential of her innovation became evident, growth (particularly through franchising) became a strategic priority for the business.

22.3 Controlling and planning for growth

KEY LEARNING OUTCOME
A recognition of the ways in which growth can be controlled by the entrepreneur.

The fact that growth presents strategic, resource and investment decision-making issues to the entrepreneur means it is a process which must be both planned for and controlled. Indeed, the objective of growth, once it has been established, should lie at the heart of and drive forward the venture's planning and control process. The idea of controlling growth is critical to entrepreneurial success. It draws together a number of themes which have been developed in this book so far.

The *desirability* of growth must be reflected in the entrepreneur's vision (see Chapter 9). This vision must act as a force which co-ordinates and focuses the whole organisation on the tasks it faces. To do this, the vision must not only illuminate the *what* of growth but also the *why*, that is, not only what is in it for the organisation but why the stakeholder will gain from it.

The *potential* for growth must be recognised in the venture's mission (see Chapter 10). This mission should be reasonable given the venture's capabilities and competitive situation but it should also stretch the organisation to make maximum use of its capabilities and exploit its competitive potential.

The *direction* of growth must be indicated by the venture's strategy (see Chapter 11). This should indicate the products the business will offer, the markets it will operate in and the competitive advantages it will develop and exploit in order to serve the customer better than competitors in those markets.

The *management* of growth demands the management of resource flows within the organisation. It means designing the organisation so that appropriate resource-acquiring functions are in place to co-ordinate resource-acquiring activities effectively. This relates to the ideas developed in Chapter 20.

In summary, the *achievement* of growth is a result of the decision-making processes that go on within the venture. The entrepreneur must control these through their power and leadership strategies. The entrepreneur's need (and desire!) to impose their will on the organisation must always be tempered by the value to be gained from letting individuals use their own insights and initiative. This is a theme to be developed further in Chapter 24.

Summary of key ideas

- Organisational growth, like organisation itself, is best understood through *metaphors* of change.
- Growth is an important objective for the venture. The growth objective must be considered in the light of the venture's *market potential*, its *strategic capabilities*, its *resources* and the *risks* it wishes to undertake.
- Growth must be both planned for, and controlled by, the entrepreneur, both in terms of *rate* and *direction*.

Suggestions for further reading

Bitner, L.N. and **Powell, J.D.** (1987) 'Expansion planning for small retail firms', *Journal of Small Business Management*, Apr, pp. 47–54.

Ford, J.D. and **Ford, L.W.** (1994) 'Logics of identity, contradiction and attraction in change', *Academy of Management Review*, Vol. 19, No. 4, pp. 756–85.

Gaddis, P.O. (1997) 'Strategy under attack', *Long Range Planning*, Vol. 30, No.1, pp. 38–45.

Hunsdiek, D. (1985) 'Financing of start-up and growth of new technology based firms in West Germany', *International Small Business Journal*, Vol. 4, No. 2, pp. 10–24.

McKergow, M. (1996) 'Complexity science and management: What's in it for business?' *Long Range Planning*, Vol. 29, No. 5, pp. 721–7.

Oakley, R. (1991) 'High-technology small firms: Their potential for rapid industrial growth', *International Small Business Journal*, Vol. 9, No. 4, pp. 30–42.

Stacey, R. (1996) 'Emerging strategies for a chaotic environment', *Long Range Planning*, Vol. 29, No. 2, pp. 182–9.

Stacey, R. (2000) *Strategic Management and Organisational Dynamics* (3rd edn), London: Pitman Publishing.

Tuck, P. and **Hamilton, R.T.** (1993) 'Intra-industry size differences in founder controlled firms', *International Small Business Journal*, Vol. 12, No. 1, pp. 12–22.

Selected case material

The cult of gigantism

11 April 1998

Is size being pursued and celebrated for its own sake? ask **Richard Waters** and **Tracy Corrigan**

"I'm going to change the world." Thus Sandy Weill explaining to a friend last weekend the mammoth merger he was about to announce.

For the corporate world, at least, this is no exaggeration. The plan to combine Travelers and Citicorp, each of which is worth around \$80bn (£48bn), has left observers leafing through their dictionaries of superlatives. It would also put every other merger into the shade – until the next record-breaking deal comes along. These days, it seems big just keeps on getting bigger.

Phillip Purcell, who pulled off the merger that created Morgan Stanley Dean Witter last year, predicted as much in November. "We're about to go from \$20bn to \$100bn deals," he said. Why? Because companies and investors want to do business with financial institutions that can do anything, anywhere, anytime. Mr Purcell's own ground-breaking merger, which was seen at the time as likely to precipitate similar combinations among more financial institutions, suddenly seems to be in a minor league.

It is not only the likes of banks, insurance companies and stockbrokers who are thinking this way. Two giant drug companies, SmithKline Beecham and Glaxo, recently tried to merge but failed. Telecommunications companies are caught in a spiralling succession of deals that has already led to one enormous takeover, that of MCI Communications by WorldCom. Yesterday, Cable and Wireless and Telecom Italia confirmed they were in talks which could lead to the formation of the world's second largest international carrier. Yet more companies are now circling each other.

For example, London was recently swept by rumours that British Telecom was about to be bought by Bell Atlantic, or by Microsoft. After the merger of Citicorp and Travelers, is any deal, however outrageous it may have seemed a year ago, now possible?

Possible, perhaps. But the question is: would "any deal" be a good idea? Seen from one perspective, the search for size is a rational response to an accepted wisdom in the stock market – that big is beautiful. Wall Street's reaction to the Citicorp/Travelers announcement was euphoric: the combined market value of the two rose $30bn in a day, almost as much as the market capitalisation of Merrill Lynch.

Markets like large companies for their stable and predictable earnings and for their ability to ride out "little local difficulties" such as a crisis in Asia. Their shares generally outperform smaller rivals.

As John Kay, of Oxford University's business school, has suggested, one reason why this may be the case is not that big companies become successful, but rather that successful companies get big. Microsoft may soon overtake General Electric as the world's biggest company, at least by stock market value.

Some of the pressures that are frequently listed as reasons for companies to get bigger – globalisation, the cost of technology, the growing importance of global brands – are real enough.

But seen in another light, merger mania is just that – mania. "Putting together two five hundred pound gorillas to make a thousand pound gorilla does not necessarily make a stronger beast," says Sam Hayes, a professor of finance at Harvard Business School. In short, the cult of gigantism that has been emerging may not be particularly beneficial, either for the companies themselves or their customers.

Even investment bankers, who make their living from arranging such corporate marriages, seem to be beginning to wonder. "Is it being overdone? I don't think so, but it is closer to being overdone in financial services than other industries," says Steven Rattner, deputy chief executive of Lazard Freres in New York.

At times it looks as though a cult of gigantism has taken over and size is being pursued, and celebrated, for its own sake. The reaction to the Citicorp/Travelers announcement carried a message that will surely not have got lost on other chief executives. "Markets just like action – a dramatic gesture that looks positive," says Rosabeth Moss Kanter, a Harvard Business School professor, who expresses scepticism about some aspects of the combination.

This is bad if it forces other companies to undertake mergers themselves without adequate reason. Combinations like Citicorp and Travelers, or WorldCom and MCI, are widely expected to precipitate other combinations as rivals try to make up for perceived inadequacies stemming from their relative lack of scale. Copy-cat deals are often a disaster, even if the original succeeds.

There is also the rather disturbing fact that, while Wall Street seems to love big in all its guises, most management thinkers and consultants say that large mergers more often than not produce disappointing results – and that big and complex companies of the type Citicorp and Travelers are trying to create often fail to achieve the potential benefits claimed for them.

According to an analysis by Mercer Management Consulting, two out of every three mergers fail – that is, they underperform their peers in the years after the combination. Serial acquirers – companies which, like Travelers, do so many acquisitions that they get good at them – are more likely than most to succeed. However, a combination on the scale of that planned with Citicorp is an entirely new venture in which Travelers' previous experience will be of little use.

Also, Citicorp and Travelers seem to have fallen into another trap noted by Mercer.

"If there is a corporate indictment, it is the amount of deals that are based on a vision, without an aggressive and detailed plan at the time they are agreed for putting it into action," says James Quella, a vice chairman at the consulting firm. Simply having a big idea is not enough.

Even for companies that avoid the worst failings of most mergers, there is the awesome task of getting to grips with a vast and often complex business.

Bigness itself may not be the main problem here. According to Ms Kanter, some industries may be better suited than others to operating on a global scale: telecoms companies or airlines, for instance, generally benefit from extending their networks farther afield.

The problem, rather, stems from the difficulty of running a company spanning many different products – particularly if it tries to find the illusive synergies that mergers so often fail to achieve.

Ms Kanter, who made a study of some of the unsuccessful attempts to create giant financial supermarkets during the 1980s, says that Mr Weill and his counterpart at Citicorp, John Reed, will have their work cut out for them as they try to sell Travelers' insurance policies through Citicorp's bank branches or Citicorp's student loans through Travelers' sales channels. "I think they are brilliant men – but unless they are geniuses in human nature and organisation, then it's a myth, a fantasy."

Not all big and complex companies fail. John Gutfreund, a former head of Salomon Brothers, the investment bank that was recently absorbed by Travelers, calls General Electric "the exception to the rule". It has long been a big, successful and diversified company. But who knows whether even it will survive the eventual retirement of its chairman, Jack Welch, who is widely credited with creating the unusual conditions in which its disparate businesses have been able to thrive and produce its current bout of success.

Corporate history is littered with the corpses of once-great companies. ITT, a vast conglomerate that was formed in an earlier takeover boom, was finally wiped from the corporate map by a takeover last year after being progressively dismembered over a number of years. Corporate empires formed as recently as the 1980s, such as Hanson, are also being dismantled.

This latest boom in corporate bigness will also one day meet its antithesis. "Whether it's five years or 10 years from now, there will be a de-conglomeration," says Henry Kaufman, a Wall Street economist who also once worked at Salomon.

There seems little danger that the prospect of this future unbundling will stop the new mega-companies from being formed in the first place, though. As one Wall Street insider said of the reaction at her company to Mr Weill's show-stopping merger: "It's a male thing. They are all in a tizzy with this deal because now Sandy's is bigger than theirs'."

Review questions

1 Why do entrepreneurs seek their venture's growth? How might this support and come into conflict with the other goals the venture has?

2 In what ways might the merger between two large firms benefit from an entrepreneurial approach to management?

23 Leadership, power and motivation in the entrepreneurial venture

Chapter overview

Managing the human dimension of the venture is critical to entrepreneurial success. This chapter deals with the tools for managing human relationships within the venture: ***power, leadership*** *and* ***motivation*** *and the way in which they are interconnected.*

23.1 The human dimension: relating leadership, power and motivation

KEY LEARNING OUTCOME
An appreciation of the way in which the concepts of leadership, power and motivation are interrelated.

Entrepreneurs are managers, but they are not just any sort of manager. If we were to seek the one characteristic that distinguishes entrepreneurs from their more conventional colleagues it would most likely be found *not* in their strategic or analytical insights (though these are important) but in the *human dimension*: the way in which they use leadership and power and their ability to motivate those around them. Any discussion of entrepreneurship must, therefore, develop an insight into the ways in which leadership, power and motivation may be used as managerial tools.

An economic perspective suggests that human organisations exist to process resources. The differentiation of labour within them allows that processing to be carried out more efficiently. However, once those resources are processed they must be distributed to the stakeholders who make up the organisation. That distribution is rarely on an 'equal' basis. Further, organisations are not just rational orderings of activities but are also the stages upon which their members act out the roles which define them. Hence any discussion of leadership, power and motivation must be willing to take its cues from a variety of perspectives: *functional* ones which construe the organisation as a deterministic system, *interpretive* ones which explore human experience within organisations and *radical* ones which question the way in which different individuals benefit from organisational life.

In light of this, no one definition can possibly hope to fulfil the complete potential of any of these concepts. However, it is important to give the ideas some kind of conceptual location and basic definitions can be suggested as follows.

Leadership might be defined as the power to *focus* and *direct* the organisation.

Power might be defined as the ability to *influence the course of actions* within the organisation.

Motivation might be defined as the *process of encouraging* an individual to take particular courses of action.

Leadership, power and motivation are distinct concepts but clearly any discussion of one will usually draw in the others since they are different aspects of the overall process of control over the venture. It is useful to regard them as different aspects of the approach the entrepreneur takes to controlling the direction of the venture (see Fig. 23.1).

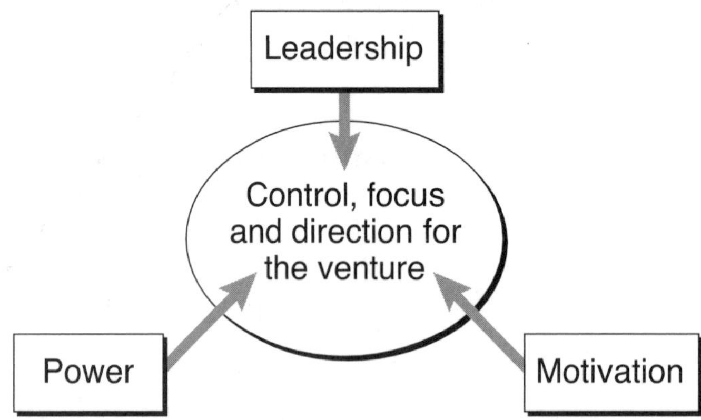

Fig. 23.1 The dynamics of entrepreneurial control: leadership, power and motivation

Leadership, power and motivation come together in the means the entrepreneur chooses to shape and drive their venture in the *direction they wish to take it*. They are tools the entrepreneur adopts in order to turn their vision into reality, and as such, they lie at the heart of their project to create an entire new world.

It is important to recognise that entrepreneurial leadership, power and motivation cannot be confined within the formal organisation. They must extend beyond it to draw *all* the venture's stakeholders (its investors, customers and suppliers as well as its employees) together.

23.2 Understanding leadership

KEY LEARNING OUTCOME
An understanding of the factors which underpin entrepreneurial leadership.

Leadership is one of the most essential ingredients for entrepreneurial success yet it is conceptually elusive. We recognise leadership when we see it but it is very hard to say *what* we are recognising. The way in which the concept has been used, and the framework for understanding it has evolved considerably over the time that leadership has been seen as a proper subject for investigation. The challenge is not just to understand leadership but also to provide recommendations on how leadership skills can be developed and used to enhance organisational performance.

Early approaches to leadership looked towards 'great men' to provide examples of how to behave. The main tool was the biography which detailed the life and exploits of appropriate leaders. A development of this approach was to try to distil out the personality traits which made great people 'great' and which underpinned their leadership. Both these approaches still inform a good deal of popular thinking on leadership but they are very limited because they make leadership inherent in an individual. They fail to recognise that leadership involves followers as much as leaders and that leadership takes place in a social setting.

Later modes of thinking looked towards *influence* (how leaders coax followers) and *behaviour* (what leaders actually *do* rather than who they *are*) in an attempt to minimise these limitations. An important avenue of exploration into leadership amalgamated all these approaches with an integration of behavioural, personality, situation and influence factors. This approach is known as contingency leadership theory.

A number of distinct approaches to leadership emerged in the aftermath of contingency leadership theory. The *transactional* approach emphasised the importance of the pattern of one-to-one relationships or 'dyads' the leader established with the followers. In this perspective the follower was seen to develop the leader as much as the leader developed the follower. The *culture* perspective emphasised that the leader is not solely managing one-to-one interactions or even groups, but is managing the culture of the organisation as a *whole*: that is, the set of expectations and assumptions that define what the organisation should do and should not do and how it should go about its tasks. These expectations and assumptions are often unarticulated and informal. This was the approach advocated by Tom Peters and Robert Waterman (1982) in their highly influential book *In Search of Excellence*. The *transformational* approach to understanding leadership develops the notion of the leader using his or her charisma and personal vision to transform individuals into followers. From this perspective, the process of leadership is both collective since the *whole* organisation is involved, and dynamic. Leadership is not so much about being a leader; it is about *leading*.

Thinking about leadership is developing rapidly. In some ways a new post-transformational integration which draws from the whole tradition on leadership thinking is emerging. By distilling this integration, entrepreneurial leadership can be thought of as having eight key elements (see Fig. 23.2).

1 *Personal vision.* The entrepreneur's vision is the driving force behind leadership. It is vision which transforms a disparate group of stakeholders into the people who will act to move the venture forward. Vision must be rationalised and communicated. As

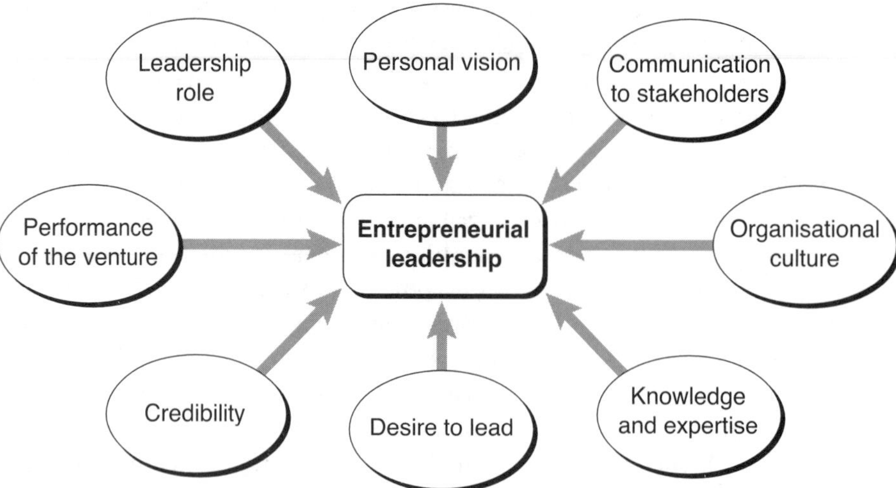

Fig. 23.2 Factors in entrepreneurial leadership

discussed in Chapter 10, it is critical that the entrepreneur turn their vision into a 'narrative' which provides the venture's stakeholders with roles and responsibilities and defines the rewards they will get for participating in the venture.

2 *Communication with stakeholders.* The entrepreneur must relate their vision to stakeholders through a variety of communication channels and forums, for example, one-to-one talks, meetings, formal presentations, sales pitches, business plans, etc. Such communication is not simply a passing of information, it is a *call to action*. What matters to the entrepreneurial leader is not so much what people know as a result of a particular communication but what they will *do* in response to it. The content of communication is not confined to what is said. *How* things are said is just as important. In face-to-face communication non-verbal aspects such as body language can have a great influence on how things are interpreted. Leadership is built on effective communication and the style of communication can be as important as content.

3 *Organisational culture.* An organisation's culture is the web of rules which define how it goes about its tasks. These rules are often unspoken. Culture is, in a sense, 'the way things are done round here'. The culture defines what is allowed, and what is not allowed, for both internal and external relationships. An organisation's culture is created along with the organisation itself. It is the entrepreneurial leader's role to shape that culture by setting standards and defining values for the organisation. It also becomes manifest through the objectives the entrepreneur sets for the venture and the rewards and sanctions used to manage outcomes and expectations for both individuals and groups. The relationship between leadership and culture is reciprocal. Leadership creates the organisation's culture and, in return, the organisation's culture creates a space to be filled by a leader.

4 *Knowledge and expertise.* Entrepreneurs are experts. This expertise may be in some specialist technology (for example, Bill Gates' knowledge of computing) or in the

particulars of an industry sector (for example, Rupert Murdoch's extensive knowledge of the newspaper business). In addition to this specialist knowledge there is the general sense of an entrepreneur being an 'expert' decision maker. Expertise provides a basis for leadership in that it offers authority for decision making.

5 *Credibility.* Credibility is critical for leadership. If credibility can be built up, then leadership (that is attracting followers) becomes easier. Conversely, if an entrepreneur loses credibility, then leadership is likely to be made more problematic if not lost altogether. Leadership offers the possibility of shaping the venture and directing it in a particular way. Leadership will only be accepted by followers if they are confident in the ability of the entrepreneur to take the venture in a direction that will benefit them.

6 *Performance of the venture.* Credibility comes, in the main, from being seen to make decisions which lead to successful outcomes. This is often an issue of association rather than causation. Decisions, not least those made at the higher levels of the organisation, usually lead to a cascade of further decisions. Causal chains can be hard to trace, especially when a good deal of latitude for decision making is allowed to subordinates. Further, success itself cannot be reduced simply to financial performance, it needs to be considered in the light of all the stakeholders' expectations (see Chapter 8).

If credibility comes from being associated with success, it is not *necessarily* true that credibility is automatically lost as a result of the occasional failure. Failure might have occurred for the 'right' reasons (a risky option was taken and it didn't pay off even though it was well thought out, the course was well managed and all parties involved were prepared for the possibility of failure). An ability to learn quickly and effectively from failure can, in fact, be a way to build credibility. One sure way to lose credibility, however, is to attempt to distance oneself from failure and to shirk responsibility when it is clear where responsibility lies!

7 *Leadership role.* The entrepreneur will usually be the most senior manager in the venture. They will be expected to take on a leadership role merely by virtue of being an entrepreneur. Entrepreneurship itself comes, as it were, with the option of taking the position of leader.

However, care must be taken here. Though being an entrepreneur presents the *possibility* of being a leader, it does not offer it as a matter of *right.* Setting up the venture provides authority, not power (a distinction to be developed in section 23.3). While people involved with the venture will look towards the entrepreneur for leadership, that is, they will set themselves up as followers, the entrepreneur must actively fulfil their expectations by exhibiting leadership behaviour. The entrepreneur must constantly use his or her position to reiterate the leader–follower relationship.

8 *Desire to lead.* The thing which ultimately underpins leadership is the desire to lead. No-one can be an effective leader unless they *really* want to take on the role of leader. Effective entrepreneurs recognise this in themselves. They accept positively the need they have to express their desire for power. The freedom to lead and use power is one of the great motivators driving many, if not all, entrepreneurs.

23.3 The basis of power and using power

KEY LEARNING OUTCOME
An appreciation of the nature and role of power within the entrepreneurial venture.

As with leadership, power is a concept which appears to be central to successful management which has resisted being reduced to a simple conceptual formula. To many people the term has a negative connotation. Power means power 'over' people. It suggests coercion and is something which must be curtailed.

Wilson (1975) drew on evolutionary concerns to define power as 'the assertion of one member of the group over another in acquiring access to a piece of food, a mate, a place to display, a sleeping site or any other requisite to the genetic fitness of the dominant individual'. Watson (1971) referred to a 'stable personality characteristic' that was functional in the emergence of dominant individuals in a group. Ray (1981) also considered power to be a consequence of genetic (unlearned) and environmental (learned) factors.

An alternative approach (e.g. Emerson, 1962; Hickson *et al.*, 1971, Thompson, 1967; Pffeffer and Salancik, 1978; Bacharach and Lawler, 1980) has risen to dominance, especially in management studies. This is the idea that power is not centred on an individual at all. It is a result of the structural factors that define how people work together and interact with each other. House (1988) offers a good review of the development of this idea.

However, if we define power as an ability to influence the course of actions within the organisation it becomes a necessary feature of organisational life. Power is a feature of situations in which resources are limited and outcomes are uncertain. Under these conditions actions *must* be influenced or the organisation would not be an organisation! In this respect power is an inevitability and, like the organisation itself, it can be made to work for good as well as ill. Certainly, entrepreneurs must recognise the basis for power within their organisation and learn to use it both positively and effectively. This is an approach taken by Jeffrey Pfeffer (1981) in his important study, *Power in Organizations*.

Power must be distinguished from *authority*. Authority presents a *right* to influence the course of actions due to the position the holder of that authority has within the organisation. This right is not the same as *ability*. The way in which authority translates into actual power depends on how the people who make up the organisation regard the holder's standing and the position they occupy. While one group may recognise the position, others may not do so. The entrepreneur may be given a high degree of ostensible authority by the social system in which they operate. The venture may 'belong' to them and be seen as the property of the individual entrepreneur. They will probably be seen as the chief executive, that is, the most senior decision maker. However, this in itself is no guarantee that they will actually have power over their venture. As with leadership, the entrepreneur's position *potentiates* power rather than provides it.

An important line of analysis sees power manifest itself as the control of different aspects of the venture. The relationship is reciprocal. Power gives access to control, and control provides a basis for power. Dimensions of control which are important for the development of the entrepreneur's power base are *resources, people, information, uncertainty, systems, symbols* and *vision*.

Control of resources

The fast-growing entrepreneurial venture is characterised by a constant influx of new resources. The decision as to how those resources will be used is one which must be addressed constantly. The entrepreneur, if not actually making those decisions, will normally be in a position to influence them greatly and to sanction those they oppose.

Control of people

The phrase 'control' of people sounds ominous and has authoritarian overtones. However, in the context of the entrepreneurial venture, the notion corresponds more to positive qualities of leadership (offering people a direction forward) and motivation (encouraging and supporting them in taking that direction) than it does to the negative aspects of coercion.

Control of information

Information informs decision making and makes it more effective. It has a critical role to play in establishing power structures. The entrepreneur is in a special position in relation to the information on which the venture is founded. In the early stages of the venture, he or she may actually be responsible for bringing in information on products, customers and finance. Later they will have control over what information is regarded as important and should be invested in. At every stage of development, it is the entrepreneur who has the unique position of viewing the venture from a strategic perspective.

Control of uncertainty

All stakeholders experience some uncertainties in relation to the entrepreneurial venture. Employees will be concerned about their remuneration and job security. Customers are often concerned about continuity of supply. Suppliers have an interest in the success of their customers, and investors are eager to ensure that their investments are sound ones. Managing this uncertainty provides a basis for power and the entrepreneur is in a unique position when it comes to managing this uncertainty. After all, it is the entrepreneur who will deliver the venture and ensure its success. As was discussed in section 8.1 the process of managing success is as much about controlling *expectations* as it is about delivering outcomes.

Control of systems

Once the organisation grows beyond a certain size it becomes impossible for the founding entrepreneur to make all resource allocation decisions. At this point a number of systems emerge to control the process of resource allocation. These take the form of routines, procedures and operating practices. As the organisation grows the entrepreneur can, and indeed must, develop their power base by shifting their attention from controlling resource allocation itself, to controlling the systems which guide resource allocation.

Control over symbols

Symbols are very important in organisational life. Symbols may be overt, like company names, logos or brand names, or they can be more covert, like the arrangement of office space. They may take the form of stories or 'myths'. A good example is the way the Disney Corporation has co-opted the story of its founding father, Walt Disney, as a defining force for the organisation. The entrepreneur can access power within the organisation by learning to use, and claiming the right to use, the venture's symbolic forms in the right way. This can be an important factor in managerial succession for the entrepreneurial venture (see section 25.4).

Control of vision

Vision, when properly used, is a powerful driving force for the entrepreneurial venture. However, there can only be one vision which dominates within the venture. There is no room for an alternative. Two or more visions offering different directions within the same organisation will inevitably come into conflict. An important, perhaps *the* most important, element in the power base of the entrepreneur is the ability to compose, articulate and control the elements of *the* vision that shapes and drives the venture as a whole.

Power brings responsibility. The right to exercise power brings with it the need to direct it in an appropriate way. Many entrepreneurs are seen to be motivated by power, but effective entrepreneurs are motivated not by power as an end in itself, but by using power as a tool to deliver the venture in a way which offers success to all its stakeholders. This is not only a positive use of power, it is, in the long run, the only way in which power can be sustained.

23.4 Approaches to understanding motivation

KEY LEARNING OUTCOME
An appreciation of the approaches that have been made to understanding the phenomenon of motivation and its importance to successful entrepreneurship.

Motivation, the condition that makes individuals undertake, or at least desire to undertake, certain courses of action is a subject that has received a lot of attention from psychologists over the past hundred years. Because of its impact on organisational performance, it is of great interest to management theorists and practitioners. A number of approaches to its understanding have been developed. These approaches are varied, emphasise different factors and generally supplement, though, at times, they do contradict, each other. They all offer unique insights. They differ in the impact they have had on the understanding that has been gained of managerial motivation in general and on entrepreneurial motivation in particular. A major dichotomy exists between those theories that regard motivation as an outward expression of inner drives and those that regard motivation as something directed towards achieving externally defined and rewarded goals. Some approaches attempt reconciliation between these two factors.

Historically, the most significant of the former is Freud's *psychoanalytic theory*, which regards behaviour as being driven by basic sexual and aggressive instincts. Despite its influence on psychology and psychotherapy, this theory has had relatively little impact on management thinking. This is mainly because the theory at one level attempts to explain the generalities of the human condition and, at another, account for the maladaptive behaviour of individual subjects. It has been less able to explain the adaptive behaviour of individuals and small groups in organisations. Though they are of great historical importance, Freud's ideas have come under increasing attack from more empirically minded psychologists.

Another drive-based conceptualisation of motivation is Hull's (1943) *experimental drive* theory. Hull explained motivation in terms of the drive to fulfil four basic, internalised, primarily physiological needs: *hunger*, *thirst*, *sex* and the *avoidance of pain*. In simple terms, behaviours that achieve the fulfilment of these drives are motivated. The weakness of this theory is in explaining how these generalised needs are manifest in the wide range of varied, complex and sophisticated actual behaviours exhibited by people in a social and managerial setting. From this perspective, it is difficult to say specifically why pursuing an entrepreneurial path is able to fulfil these needs better than, say, a career as a conventional manager.

The idea of human needs is a fundamental one and it has informed a number of approaches to understanding motivation. Lewin (1952) developed a theory in which motivation arose from a 'tension' in the perceived difference between actual states of being and desired states of being. According to this theory, these states cannot be resolved into components based on specific needs. Rather they are integrated wholes – that psychologists call *gestalts* – which are experienced holistically. Lewin's approach resonates with the idea of *entrepreneurial vision*; a picture of the state the entrepreneur wishes to create that acts as a driving force for them. (We have considered entrepreneurial vision earlier in Chapter 9.)

The idea of a series of needs that can be resolved into separate components was the basis for Maslow's (1943) well-known theory of need hierarchy in which physiological, security, social and self-development needs were satisfied in that order of priority. Maslow's ideas will be explored further below.

The role of 'achievement' in motivation has been studied extensively by McClelland (1961). In McClelland's view behaviour is directed towards an aspirational picture of delivering personal excellence. What constitutes this excellence may be derived from internally referenced considerations or it may be picked up from external signals. McClelland was particularly interested in achievement as a motivator for entrepreneurs. The goals that are set for people are also considered relevant in motivation theory. A number of studies suggest that individuals are motivated to achieve specific, well-defined goals. These suggest the way these goals stretch an individual, or team, are important. Goals that are too easy do not motivate. They are regarded as trivial and unimportant. Goals that are too ambitious also fail to motivate if they are seen to be unachievable. The most motivating goals are those that are demanding, but within the bounds of possibility: precisely the kind of goal a good entrepreneur sets for him- or herself.

A number of motivation theories take a cognitive approach in that they are concerned with motivation as a goal-directed phenomenon. In these explanations, behaviour that achieves an individual's goals is motivated; that which fails to deliver them is demotivated. The process is dynamic and iterative. Behaviour that delivers desired outcomes is *reinforced* – encouraged as the basis for future behaviour. Behaviour that does not deliver is discouraged. An important factor in behaviour is *expectation*, that is, the belief that a particular course of action will result in a particular outcome. The key thing is not so much that an action actually delivers, just that the actor believes it will. So, in this view, entrepreneurs become entrepreneurial because they expect it will deliver the set of financial, social and self-developmental conditions they desire. This conceptualisation of motivation is one that is readily quantified and can be expressed in mathematical form.

A particularly sophisticated development of expectancy theory is that of Vroom (1963). Vroom breaks motivation down into four components: *outcomes*, *valence*, *expectancy* and *instrumentality*. An *outcome* is the state of affairs that might be achieved as a result of some course of action. *Valence* is the desire that an actor has for a particular outcome, either in absolute terms or as a ranking of priorities from a set of outcomes from which one must be selected. *Expectancy* is the belief as to what outcomes are possible, that is, how likely it is that they might be achieved given the investment of time and effort in a particular course of action. *Instrumentality* is the perceived effectiveness of a particular course of action in achieving an outcome. Actors will, in part, chose between different courses of action based on how effective they will be in achieving what they want. Together these factors will define the *force* – the intensity – of the motivation to undertake particular actions.

Together, these approaches to understanding motivation add up to a general picture of what motivates the entrepreneur. Entrepreneurs, like everybody else, have basic economic needs that they aim to fulfil through their entrepreneurial careers. But entrepreneurial motivation goes beyond this. Entrepreneurs have a need to achieve and so gain social standing and effect personal development. They want to see their visions turned into reality. The course of action entrepreneurs adopt is based on the desire for these outcomes and a belief that certain actions will result in their delivery. Expectations are the things that link an entrepreneur's objectives to the effectiveness of the strategy they feel the venture should adopt in order to achieve them. The specific motivations of the individual entrepreneur are shaped by, and can be explained in terms of, this general framework.

23.5 Self-motivation and motivating others

KEY LEARNING OUTCOME

An insight into how entrepreneurs may motivate themselves and those around them.

People work best when they are motivated to do so. The entrepreneur cannot *demand* effort from someone; they must *support* the individual and encourage them to offer their efforts.

Self-motivation

The first person whose motivation the entrepreneur must address is his or her own! It is difficult, if not impossible, to motivate others if one's own motivation is lacking. This can be a challenge. The entrepreneurial course offers great rewards but it also demands resilience. The knocks are frequent and often hard. Failure, as well as success, must be managed with a positive response. Some important elements to address in terms of self-motivation are as follows.

Why am I doing this?

Good entrepreneurs know why they have chosen to be entrepreneurs. They constantly remind themselves why they have chosen the entrepreneurial path. The model developed in section 4.2 gives an insight into this process. The attractions of entrepreneurship can be understood in the way that the course fulfils economic, social and self-developmental needs better than alternative routes open to the entrepreneur. Self-motivation must be built on an understanding that the option taken is one which is desirable.

Learning from mistakes

Like any other manager, entrepreneurs make mistakes from time to time. Sales may not be made or investment propositions may be rejected. Personal interactions may be mismanaged. Entrepreneurs are, however, very sensitive to the mistakes they make. This is not just because the consequences of the mistakes are greater than those made by other managers (although they may be) but because entrepreneurs present themselves as experts in managing their venture and its associated uncertainty. Errors of judgement cut to the heart of this role. They can be a great blow to the entrepreneur's confidence.

Of course, mistakes are an inevitable part of any managerial career, not just the entrepreneurial one. Effective entrepreneurs try to avoid mistakes by thought and preparation before entering situations, but when mistakes do occur they are met positively. The good entrepreneur does not try to deny the mistake or pass off responsibility to others. Rather, mistakes are regarded as an opportunity to learn. This means that ego must be detached from the incident and a cold analytical eye used to view the situation to identify a way of avoiding a similar mistake in the future.

Enjoying the rewards

All too often the entrepreneur can become so involved in running the venture that they forget to enjoy its rewards. At one level, this could mean spending the money that has been made. However, this consumption can only be a narrow part of the rewards of entrepreneurship. Money is rarely a complete motivating force for the entrepreneur and, in any case, significant financial rewards may only be accrued a long way down the line. The main rewards lie in the job itself: the challenges it presents, the opportunity to develop and use new skills, the power to make changes, the satisfaction of leadership, and so on.

Learning to recognise these rewards and to savour them is a major factor in developing and sustaining self-motivation.

Motivation of others

Once self-motivation has been achieved the entrepreneur is in a strong position to start motivating others. Motivation is a behavioural phenomenon. Individuals are motivated (or demotivated) by the way people act towards them. This behaviour is an integral part of leadership. It is sensitive to personality and situation. As such, motivating behaviour is a complex process although some common patterns of motivating behaviour can be identified. Figure 23.3 shows a framework for managing individual motivation. Its key elements are:

- *Understanding personal drives* – Before someone can be motivated it is important to recognise what they want to gain from their situation. Management occurs in a social setting and the needs which individuals bring to a situation are a complex mix of financial, social and developmental ones. The effective entrepreneur lays the groundwork for motivating the people in the venture to undertake specific tasks by involving them in the vision that has been created for the venture. This is achieved by communicating the role they will play in this vision and what they will get out of it.
- *Setting goals* – People are not just motivated in an abstract sense. They are motivated to *do something,* i.e. motivation must lead somewhere. The entrepreneur is responsible for setting the goals that must be achieved. The degree to which these are specific objectives and the formality they take will be dependent on the situation, the entrepreneur's personal style and the cultural setting.

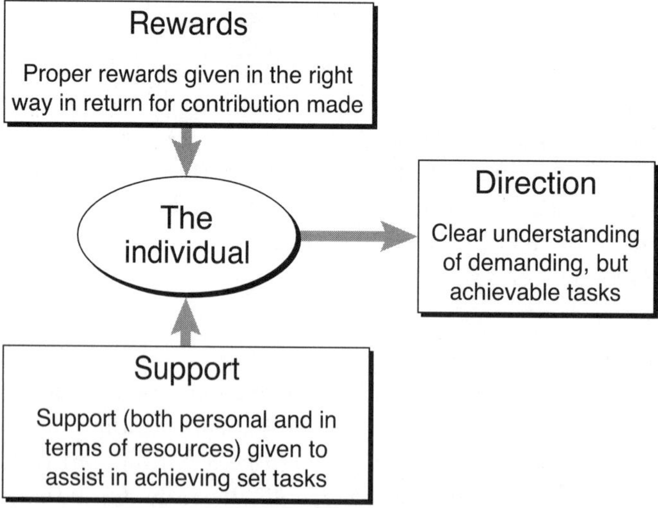

Fig. 23.3 A framework for individual motivation

Whatever their form, individuals must recognise their goals and be able to locate them in relation to the goals of the organisation as a whole. Such goals should stretch the individual but also be realistic. They should demand effort but must be achievable given the personal and organisational resources the individual commands.

- *Offering support* – Setting objectives is just the first step in motivating people. If people are to deliver, they require support. This can take the form of ongoing encouragement, advice, the provision of resources and influencing behind the scenes. The support offered should be commensurate with the level of the task and the demands on the person undertaking it. Effective motivation means giving people room to use their skills and insights but never letting them think that they are out on their own.
- *Using rewards* – Rewards take a wide variety of forms. In character, rewards are the means that satisfy an individual's economic, social or developmental needs. In scope, the term 'reward' covers everything from a simple nod of approval from the entrepreneur to a complex deal offering a share in the financial performance of the venture. Whatever the nature of the reward an entrepreneur who knows how to motivate understands how best to use it.

  First, rewards must be *appropriate* for the task undertaken. They must match the individual's expectations of what the reward should be. Second, their magnitude must be right: too small and they can lead to cynicism; too large and they can engender suspicion. Third, rewards must be used on the proper *occasions*. Rewards which are given too freely (and this includes simple things like comments of approval) become devalued. Fourth, they must be seen to be *equitable*. If the reward structure for different individuals and groups is seen to be unfair then jealousy and conflicts can result.
- *A positive approach to sanctioning* – The entrepreneur must occasionally resort to sanctioning individuals who fail to perform in an appropriate way. How this necessary task is handled is important, not just for maintaining the motivation of the individual, but for the signals it sends to the organisation as a whole. In general, a positive approach to sanctioning is to be advocated. The objective of the sanctioning must be seen to be one of helping the individual to deliver at the proper level, not just as a punishment. It should not (primarily) be about what was done wrong in the past, but about how performance can be improved in the future. This should also encourage a forum which allows the issues to be discussed while personality and ego are put to one side. Indeed, it can provide an opportunity for the entrepreneur to show his or her goodwill. All in all, sanctioning, so far as possible, should be seen as a positive experience.

Summary of key ideas

- *Leadership*, *power* and *motivation* are interrelated and interdependent tools which the entrepreneur can use to control the venture and give it direction.
- Leadership is the power to *focus* and *direct* the organisation. Entrepreneurial leadership is based on the communication of *vision*.

- Power is the ability to influence the *course of actions* within the organisation. Power is based on the control of *resources* and the *symbolic* dimensions of the organisation, particularly the vision which drives it.
- Motivation is the ability to *encourage* an individual to take a particular course of action. Motivation is based upon an understanding of drives and the ability to reward effort.

Suggestions for further reading

Bacharach, S.B. and **Lawler, E.J.** (1980) *Power and Politics in Organizations,* San Francisco, CA: Jossey-Bass Publishers.

Boyce, M.E. (1996) 'Organisational story and storytelling: A critical review', *Journal of Organisational Change Management,* Vol. 9, No. 5, pp. 5–26.

Cropanzano, R., James, K. and **Citera, M.** (1992) 'A goal hierarchy model of personality, motivation and leadership', *Research in Organisational Behavior,* Vol. 15, pp. 267–322.

Emerson, R.M. (1962) 'Power-dependent relationships', *American Sociological Review,* Vol. 27, pp. 31–41.

Hamilton, R. (1987) 'Motivations and aspirations of business founders', *International Small Business Journal,* Vol. 6, No. 1, pp. 70–8.

Hickson, D.J, Hinings, C.R., Lee, C.A., Schneck, R.J. and **Pennings, J.M.** (1971) 'A strategic contingencies' theory of intraorganizational power', *Administrative Science Quarterly,* Vol. 30, pp. 61–71.

Hofstede, G. (1980) 'Motivation, leadership and organisation: Do American theories apply abroad?' *Organisational Dynamics,* Summer, pp. 42–63.

House, R.J. (1988) 'Power and personality in complex organizations', *Research in Organizational Behaviour,* Vol. 10, pp. 305–57.

Hull, C.L. (1943) *Principles of Behaviour,* New York: Appleton-Century-Crofts.

Kuratko, D.F., Hornsby, J.S. and **Naffziger, D.W.** (1997) 'An examination of owner's goals in sustaining entrepreneurship', *Journal of Small Business Management,* Jan, pp. 24–33.

Lewin, A. (1952) 'Group decisions and social change', in Swanson, G.E. Newcombe, T.N. and Hartley, E.L. (eds) *Readings in Social Psychology* (rev. ed.), New York: Holt.

Maslow, A.H. (1943) 'A theory of human motivation', *Psychological Review,* July, pp. 370–96.

McClelland, D.C. (1961) *The Achieving Society,* Princeton, NJ: Van Nostrand.

Peters, T. and **Waterman, Jr, R.H.** (1982) *In Search of Excellence,* New York: Harper & Row.

Pfeffer, J. (1981) *Power in Organizations,* Cambridge, MA: Ballinger.

Pffeffer, J. and **Salancik, G.R.** (1978) *The External Control of Organizations: A Resource Dependent Perspective,* New York: Harper & Row.

Ray, J.J. (1981) 'Authoritarianism, dominance and assertiveness', *Journal of Personality Assessment,* Vol. 45, No. 4, pp. 390–7.

Seters, D.A. Van (1990) 'The evolution of leadership theory', *Journal of Organisational Change Management,* Vol. 3, No. 3, pp. 29–45.

Tait, R. (1996) 'The attributes of leadership', *Leadership and Organisational Development Journal,* Vol. 17, No. 1, pp. 27–31.

Taylor, B., Gilinsky, A., Hilmi, A., Hahn, D. and **Grab, U.** (1990) 'Strategy and leadership in growth companies', *Long Range Planning,* Vol. 23, No. 3, pp. 66–75.

Thompson, J.D. (1967) *Organizations in Action,* New York: McGraw-Hill.

Vroom, V.H. (1963) *Leadership and Decision-making*, Pittsburgh, PA: University of Pittsburgh.

Watson, D. (1971) 'Reinforcement theory of personality and social system: Dominance and position in a group power structure', *Journal of Personality and Social Psychology*, Vol. 20, pp. 180–5.

Wilson, E.O. (1975) *Sociobiology: The New Synthesis*, Cambridge, MA: Harvard University Press.

Zaleznik, A. (1977) 'Leaders and managers: Are they different?' *Harvard Business Review*, May-June, pp 67–78.

Selected case material

Lust for life, work and elections

7 April 2000

In the second of an occasional series about business people and what drives them, the chairman of research company MORI talks to **Alison Maitland**

Bob Worcester, Britain's best known pollster and expounder of trends, has headed MORI, the market research organisation, for 31 years. Last month he sold a 43 per cent stake to his management team and 3i, the venture capital firm, but at 66 remains executive chairman with 20 per cent of the shares. The deal will allow MORI to expand through acquisitions or mergers in Europe and North America, with several tie-ups already under negotiation. MORI is considering a public flotation in the future. Mr Worcester was born in Kansas City in 1933 and moved to the UK after working in advertising, journalism and as a McKinsey consultant. He is a visiting professor at the London School of Economics and City and Strathclyde universities.

"I've only fired two clients. One was Robert Maxwell, because he wanted to suppress the results, and the other was Sir James Goldsmith, because he wanted to write his own questions [about the Referendum party] and put my reputation behind them.

Maxwell said: 'I will want to look at the results and I will decide whether to publish them.' I said: 'That's your prerogative. But if you haven't published them within seven days of the anticipated date of publication, then I'm free to give them away and I lodge the results of all my public polls with the ESRC [Economic and Social Research Council] at the University of Essex.' He said: 'We'll have to agree to disagree' and I said: 'Thank you, goodbye.'

We've probably done more than 300 staff attitude surveys. One of the things I'm most personally interested in is being paid to systematically – and objectively – assist managements to understand what their most scarce resource believes and knows.

Managements' challenge is to stay ahead of rising expectations for more communications, more transparency, more integrity. The 'triple bottom line' is being driven as much by internal communications questions as by NGO [non-governmental organisation] pressure.

I am entirely in favour of wider share ownership and employee involvement. Thirty years ago we set aside 10 per cent of the profits on an annual basis and distributed them to staff. That was extremely unusual in this country then. In the re-organisation of the shares, we've brought in 116 members of staff [out of 250] who will be shareholders in MORI.

My chief job these days is quality control. We have a customer satisfaction monitor on every study we do and I look at every single one of those and follow up on them. I've got so much to learn and can always do things better. My life is so intertwined with Mori that I take more offence at criticism of MORI than I do of myself.

Enthusiasm is my strength. And good health, and energy and endeavour. I love what I do. It's just so interesting, it is new every day, exciting every day.

I work 364 days a year. The only day I don't work is Christmas Day, because it's my wife's birthday. I try to spend two months a year on holiday, in the Caribbean. I wake at about 4am, work until 8am, and I work maybe mid-morning a bit, and the rest of the day we swim and garden and play.

I've written eight or nine books down there and countless articles and speeches. The last book was explaining Labour's landslide [election victory in 1997]. I wrote 25,000 words in two weeks. General elections for political people are like having children for women. You have this post-natal or post-election depression. You're so involved in the experience you can't think or talk about anything else.

What are my weaknesses? Over-enthusiasm. I take on too much. I'm an atheist and I believe you pass this way but once. If you don't do everything you possibly can in your life, see everything, go everywhere, meet everybody and make as good a contribution as you can, you've missed it. I'm too open and I'm bitter when I'm betrayed. I expect other people to act as openly and as honestly as I do, and they don't do it. I'm constantly betrayed. I suppose I choose to be naive.

I have always felt very comfortable with journalists, even though one or two have turned round and bitten me in the backside – they've either got something wrong, or in one or two cases deliberately set me up, or quoted something that was told in confidence. Three journalists have been excluded from my life. They betrayed confidence and will never again darken my door.

I've lived with myself a long time and I recognise my many failings – arrogance, impetuousness, impatience. I suffer fools gladly but I don't suffer gladly very clever people who are lazy, who don't do their homework, who haven't read the papers, who come to a meeting and sound off and don't know what they're talking about.

I put down a list of things when I was 15 that I was going to do in my life. It included going round the world, writing a book, being in a movie, living in England. I haven't learned to fly and I haven't learned to speak French fluently. But other than that, everything on the list is done.

The movie was *Julia*, the Lillian Hellman story, with Jane Fonda, Vanessa Redgrave, Jason Robards and Bob Worcester. Don't you remember? I was the man walking down the gang-plank behind Jane Fonda when she was saying goodbye to Vanessa Redgrave. I'm in it for about three frames."

Branch line to success

21 February 2000

Khozem Merchant meets an Indian software tycoon who thinks a little craziness can help an optical networking entrepreneur go far

Gururaj Deshpande seemed the obvious choice for celebrity speaker at India's top information technology conference in Bombay recently. The theme was "creating wealth in the digital economy".

Mr Deshpande, a US-based software engineer turned serial start-up entrepreneur, came bearing ideas and the popular – but, he says, erroneous – title of "the richest Indian in the world".

"I guess I am just a crackpot who hit the jackpot," he told the audience, which could boast of a few jackpots of its own. But the businessmen in the audience had made their money in bricks-and-mortar, family-owned companies now struggling to compete in a liberalising home market.

Mr Deshpande is different. He founded Sycamore Networks in Boston two years ago to develop optical networking as a means of expanding the data-carrying capacity of bandwidth. These are the communication highways that carry millions of messages each second. Mr Deshpande says bigger bandwidths "will fuel the new information based economy for the next 25 years, just as oil powered the old economy".

Last year Sycamore listed on the Nasdaq. The initial public offering was priced at $38 (£24) and opened at $270 on the first day of trading before closing at $184.75. Mr Deshpande owns 21 per cent of the equity, currently valued at about $3.7bn.

For the assembled executives Mr Deshpande – or "Desh" as he is known – seemed too good to be true. He is both an Indian IT tycoon and the boss of a Nasdaq-listed company. He is a mirror held up to a world many Indian executives would like to inhabit.

Anand Mahindra, scion of one of India's most venerable business houses, admitted he made a special effort to attend his local business group's "Conversation with Desh".

"Like many Indians, I was fascinated by Deshpande's success, primarily because it has been in information technology. Deshpande is an exceptional manager – an appropriate business model for India in the new millennium."

Indians love to celebrate the overseas success of their compatriots. In the week Mr Deshpande was garlanded in Bombay, the World Economic Forum in Davos praised India's IT industry.

President Bill Clinton will see for himself the remarkable IT revolution when he visits India next month. His visit will highlight the country's extraordinary contribution to the US IT sector. Indian software exports are forecast to total $5.8bn this year, according to industry estimates, mostly to the US.

The IndUS Entrepreneurs, a powerful mentoring group started by Indians in Silicon Valley, says 30 per cent of software engineers in the valley are of Indian origin. Most were educated at India's renowned institutes of technology. These are the intellectual hothouses whose graduates – known as "IITians" – litter Silicon Valley. They include Rakesh Mathur, who with three friends founded Junglee.com (which in colloquial Hindi means mad), before selling to Amazon.com for $187m; and of course Mr Deshpande himself.

"You have to be slightly crazy to be an entrepreneur – you should only get into this game if you have passion," says the man now involved in his third and most ambitious IT start-up.

"Don't worry about failure: if you lose because of market conditions then another time someone will say 'Hey, this guy can make things happen. I'll back him'."

Mr Deshpande is in a hurry. He should be exhausted – 16-hour days are common in the industry – as he juggles business and the demands of an insatiable domestic audience. He thinks and speaks fast. Occasionally his glib assertions about best practice sound like plain common sense – for example: "Be focused, conviction is key."

But his advocacy carries the authority of a man who practises what he preaches. Mr Deshpande's rule of thumb for would-be entrepreneurs is simple. "First, believe in your idea and run with it. The IT sector is changing fast and time spent dithering is time wasted. Second, be broad in your outlook. Do not believe your idea will work simply because of technology. Try to garner skills in sales and banking and so on.

"Third, buy some insurance by installing the best people and plenty of capital. Empower your people (with stock options) but do not worry about losing your company: the pie is big enough for everyone."

Mr Deshpande's best practice has evolved during the 27 years he has lived in north America. He left his home town in Karnataka in southern India to study in Canada, where he gained his PhD in data communications. He joined a fast growing Motorola division in Canada. "I was head of engineering and as the company grew, I fell in love with start-ups."

But Canada offered little for the determined entrepreneur. He recalls, famously, that he finally left Canada because it had no venture capitalists. He transferred to a Motorola subsidiary in Boston where he gained expertise in sales, budgeting and marketing. He also met many venture capitalists.

Mr Deshpande's first start-up was Coral Network, where his experiences were par for a debutant. He raised $4m, went without a salary, struggled to support his family, and eventually parted from his business partner. "It was not an acrimonious split: we just disagreed on how to take the company to market."

Cascade Communications was the second and happier experience. Cascade made the switches which control most internet traffic. It grew from a two-man operation to a company with $500m in revenues and 900 employees, and was bought by Ascend Communications for $3.7bn in June 1997.

"With Cascade I felt I was running a 100-metre race. I just wanted to touch the finishing ribbon. So I sold. I spent the next eight months mentoring and chairing a couple of companies. But it was not much fun. I just wanted to jump back (to start-ups), but this time I wanted to run a marathon. I wanted my new start-up, Sycamore, to be something big and enduring."

At the heart of Sycamore is the development of optical networking "as a brand of technology that can really liberate the bandwidth potential of optical fibres". Expanding the capacity of bandwidth to satisfy the expansion in demand for connectivity and information will also change fundamentally the economics of this technology, he says.

"The last two years have seen huge changes in internet technology. In the US retail industry, every 55 cents in the dollar is spent on distribution. The net is overhauling distribution channels by allowing businesses to touch the consumer. Information is empowering the consumer like never before."

It is this potential that supports some of the extravagant valuations that starts-up, including Sycamore, attract, says Mr Deshpande. "It is difficult to find validation to support your idea . . . it is future potential, the trust of investors in your team and your gut conviction."

Essential Guide: Gururaj Deshpande

Education: Born Hubli, Karnataka, in southern India, in 1950. Educated at India Institute of Technology, Madras.

In 1973 went to Canada where he gained an ME in electrical engineering from the University of New Brunswick and a PhD in data communications from Queen's University.

He has attracted many accolades, including "Visionaries of the Industry" (Communications Week, 1996); and one of the Top 25 Technology Drivers (Network Computing, 1996).

Early career: Cut his teeth in Canada with Codex, a subsidiary of Motorola, where he caught the start-up fever.

Quit Canada "because there I just could not find a venture capitalist anywhere" for the US, where he found many VCs. First start-up flopped after disagreements with his partner; second start-up hit the jackpot.

Sycamore, the third and most recent start-up, is, he says, a long-term affair.

Management style: Empower your staff. "People, people, people" is his mantra. If you do not have the right staff, fire them, quickly. Be nimble and act on your convictions.

Work closely and don't let political cracks emerge as they will be exploited.

Definition of a well-run company: Where any three people within the organisation will give the same answer to a question on the company's mission statement. That reflects total coherency and a focused workforce, he says.

This may be one reason why Forbes named Cascade as one of the US's "Top 25 Very Cool Companies" in 1996.

Management gurus: Did not reveal who his mentor is, but Gururaj Deshpande is probably the best mentor for Gururaj Deshpande.

He admires N.R. Narayana Murthy, his brother-in-law and founder-chairman of Infosys Technologies, India's best-known IT company which listed on Nasdaq last year.

Outside interests: Likes to spend time with his family, which, like the business, is totally focused on IT; his wife is a computer science lecturer at Clark University, Boston, and his two teenage sons are nerds, says dad.

The future: Sycamore and bandwidth.

Mr Deshpande says he is "a broad-based kind of guy". By this he means he is as comfortable in the manager's chair as he is in the laboratory. He says he has an understanding of financial markets and other factors required to go to market because "a PhD isn't going to get your business running. In fact, a PhD will probably disqualify you."

His strong management principles are popular with venture capitalists looking for ideas and leadership. "You do not have to do complicated things to succeed. You simply have to have the confidence to know that you are doing your thing better than any other guy in the world." Venture capitalists like such demonstrations of utter self-belief.

Faith in tough targets

17 December 1998

Victoria Griffith finds that the chief executive of one of the US's fastest growing companies has an uncompromising approach

With his easy-going charm, Mike Ruettgers, chief executive of computer group EMC, does not seem like the boss from hell. Over coffee in his office, he jokes that his status as head of one of the most successful companies in the US doesn't bring him "respect" at home. "I still have to do the dishes," he laments, his demeanour implying that he does not put up much of a fight.

Yet beneath his soft-spoken manner lies a tough manager. "EMC can be a harsh environment for people who don't perform," he admits.

Given EMC's sales and stock price performance, his hard edge should come as no surprise. While few consumers recognise the EMC name, it is held in high esteem among its corporate clients. The group – the largest computer company in the high-tech region of New England following the takeover of Digital Equipment – sells storage capacity to corporations that need to manage vast amounts of data; airline and banking industries are heavy users of its products.

According to Kiplinger's Personal Finance Magazine in the US, EMC's share price rise this decade – with an astounding 21,085 per cent return on each dollar invested – has been second only to that of Dell Computer. Sales at the company stand at $4bn (£2.4bn) a year. Mr Ruettgers was named as one of the world's 25 best managers by BusinessWeek.

He refers to his own style as "results-oriented management". "There's no safety net here," says Rick Wojcik, vice-president of sales. "You're held accountable for what you do. It can be a hard environment, but for people with faith in their abilities, it can also be rewarding."

To his credit, Mr Ruettgers has tried to make his results-orientated approach as humane as possible. Objectivity, he says, is his greatest friend, and performance relative to a list of pre-set targets has become almost a religion at the company. Of 9,000 employees, 400 have a hefty part of their pay – at least 10 per cent – linked to quarterly goals. "Usually, you might see this kind of thing for the top 10 managers at a company, but we take it much deeper," he says.

Some of the goals are simply meeting sales targets. Others are more complex: boosting customer satisfaction as measured by client surveys, or improving the usability of the system. Many of the goals are cross-functional. "Engineering and customer service have to work together to improve client satisfaction," says Mr Ruettgers.

Each of 400 managers decides, with his or her immediate bosses, on four or five goals for the quarter. Before and after the quarter, Mr Ruettgers personally reviews at least 40 sets. Employees receive their full pay only if all goals are reached. If too many goals are missed, the worker risks being sacked.

Doesn't such a system discourage risk-taking? Probably for some employees, but not for most, insists Mr Ruettgers. "The goals are reasonable, but aggressive," he says. "People need to put themselves out a little if they are going to reach them." Moreover, Mr Ruettgers says he offers a kind of "amnesty" to a manager who tells him early on when something is going wrong. "Sometimes, events in the economy or markets just don't go your way, or sometimes you just make a mistake," he says. "If a manager tells us [senior executives] early enough, we can often help, by suggesting a different tactic or adjusting the goals."

The environment at EMC is so tough that a few years ago the company's annual staff turnover was 17 per cent. That was considered bad even by the standards of the computer industry, where companies can count on losing about 15 per cent of workers a year, on average. Low retention was hurting the company, Mr Ruettgers says, by adding to training costs and undermining morale.

Yet he felt lowering standards was the wrong way to go. Instead, it was decided the company needed to be more selective about the sort of employee it was hiring. "We used to think: hire smart people who work hard," Mr Ruettgers explains. "But we were bringing in people who had been extremely successful in other companies, and who failed here."

Again, he turned to objective standards to make sense of the process. Mr Ruettgers created a list of personality characteristics, or "competencies", for all job candidates at EMC. They included a sense of urgency, and an ability to adapt quickly to change.

During interviews, candidates are now grilled on these competencies. Mr Ruettgers usually asks applicants to describe a situation in which they had to make sweeping adjustments, and how they managed.

"You eventually get a feel for the people who are just telling you what you want to hear and those who really rose to the occasion," he says. "I also rely more on references these days to get a strong sense of what the candidate is like. We are not right all the time, but more often than we were before." Staff turnover has fallen to 10 per cent annually.

Mr Ruettgers is single-minded about strategy. EMC is focused on data storage, and he believes other businesses would be nothing but a distraction.

That is not to say EMC is a static company. The group developed a strong software capability when it became clear that clients wanted better ways to manage and store their data. But because the storage business is so profitable, and growing so rapidly, Mr Ruettgers is wary of getting into lower margin businesses.

The reluctance to slow EMC's momentum stopped the company buying Digital Equipment last year. Other managers would no doubt have been tempted by the sheer thrill of being able to purchase a former giant in the industry. Mr Ruettgers flirted briefly with the idea, but in the end rejected it.

"We would have had to put so much effort into fitting their culture in with ours," he says. "Why waste the time? I'd rather spend our time growing in the data storage business. It's much more fun, and it will give our shareholders better value."

Review questions

Compare and contrast the leadership styles of:

1 Bob Worcester

2 Gururaj Deshpande

3 Mike Ruettgers.

4 What benefits and problems might having two chief executives present to developing and implementing a growth strategy?

24 Consolidating the venture

Chapter overview

*The entrepreneurial venture is characterised by growth, but at some stage growth slows and the venture becomes a mature organisation. This chapter is concerned with describing the process of consolidation, how the rules of success change and how some of the entrepreneurial vigour of the venture might be retained through **intrapreneurship.***

24.1 What consolidation means

KEY LEARNING OUTCOME
A recognition that maturity is accompanied by significant changes in the way the venture functions at a financial, strategic, structural and organisational level.

No business can grow for ever. There must come a point at which its expansion slows. In the same way the entrepreneurial venture must *mature*. However, maturity is associated with more than a simple cessation of growth. As discussed in Chapter 20, the growth of a business is a complex and multi-faceted phenomenon. It has financial, strategic, structural and organisational dimensions. As the venture matures, the slowing of growth is associated with a number of changes in each of these aspects of the organisation. Together these changes are referred to as *consolidation*.

At the *financial* level, consolidation means that turnover (and profits) begin to plateau out. Turnover should still increase, at a rate not less than the overall expansion of the economy in which the business operates (which would imply a contraction in real terms), and it is not unreasonable to set growth objectives above this. But dramatic increases in turnover are not to be expected (unless, perhaps they are achieved through acquisitions). Growth in the assets supporting turnover will also slow to a similar level. New assets will tend to be a replacement for the depreciation of existing assets.

Consolidation means that *investment* in the growth of the business can be reduced. So it is at this point that financial backers will be looking for their returns. Shareholders will expect to receive a greater share of the profits and to see their dividends increase. Venture capitalists will look to exit and liquidate their investment.

Strategically, consolidation means that the venture has successfully defined its position in the market. The place it occupies in the industry value addition chain, the customer groups it serves and the technology it uses to serve will be *largely* established – only largely because there is always room for development of the strategic position through organic developments and acquisition. The business's attention will shift from aggressive strategies aimed at encroaching into competitors' territory to more defensive postures aimed at preventing competitors (including new entrepreneurial ones!) from taking business away.

In *structural* terms, consolidation means that the internal configuration of the business develops some permanence. During the growth phase organisational structures and the roles and responsibilities they define will tend to shift, merge and fragment as the business's complexity increases. Consolidation allows the venture to give key roles and responsibilities a longer-term definition. These roles and responsibilities will tend to be defined around the resource needs of the organisation with structures emerging to manage the acquisition of key inputs.

Alongside structural consolidation there will also be *organisational* consolidation. Growth means that the organisation's systems, procedures and operating practices must be in a state of constant flux. Maturity allows these systems to settle down into more permanent patterns of activity. Out of the complex interaction between the entrepreneur, the venture's stakeholders and the wider social world, the organisation's culture will take a final shape.

The prospects and rewards the business offers its employees will also change as it consolidates. Risks will be lowered and job security may be higher. The positions within the organisation will be better defined and career pathways will become more predictable. Change will be at a slower pace. On the other hand, some may miss the challenge that comes from managing rapid growth, including the day-to-day changes this brings and the excitement of not knowing, exactly, what the future might bring.

24.2 Building success into consolidation

KEY LEARNING OUTCOME
An appreciation of how the rules of success change as the venture matures.

The rules of success change as the entrepreneurial venture consolidates. The business becomes less concerned with making rapid strides forward and more concerned with progressing in a measured and sure-footed way. Success is measured not so much by what might be achieved tomorrow but by what is being achieved today. This is not to say that the mature business can afford to forget about the future. Far from it. All businesses must plan for an uncertain tomorrow and invest accordingly. It is to suggest, however, that the balance of interest shifts from the possibility of long-term returns towards the reality of short-term rewards.

In section 8.1 the success of the venture was defined in terms of the *stakeholders* with an interest in it, their *needs* and their *expectations* of what it will offer them. This framework provides an insight into how the terms of success change as the venture consolidates.

For investors, the main shift in their expectations is in relation to the risks and returns offered by the venture. After initiation, and while it is growing strongly, the entrepreneurial venture is offering the prospect of high returns for the investor at some point in the future. Returns cannot be offered immediately because any profits generated will need to be ploughed back into the business. In any case, profits are often low during growth. This is certainly the case if a cost leadership strategy is being pursued (as described in section 18.3). The future is uncertain: profits promised in the future carry a higher risk than those on offer today. The plan for the venture must be based on assumptions. Risk enters the equation because there must be some doubt about the validity of those assumptions.

Investors accept risk if the future returns, properly discounted, are attractive enough. There will come a point, however, when they will want to see those returns. Many investors hold a *portfolio* of investments. This portfolio mixes investments which are currently net generators of money (and are therefore low risk) with those demanding money on the basis of future return (high risk). The entrepreneurial venture starts as a high-risk absorber of capital. If it is to remain in the investor's portfolio long-term it must eventually move to be a lower-risk generator of capital (see Fig. 24.1).

From the perspective of the investor, the success of the venture stops being measured in terms of the way it is growing its sales and assets and establishing its position in its marketplace to the short-term return it is generating on the (investor's) capital it is using. The key measures of performance become the *profit margin* and *return on capital employed*.

Stakeholders other than investors also share in the risks taken on by the entrepreneurial venture. Employees who make a contribution to the venture in its early stages are called upon to make a special effort. The demands will be high. Roles and

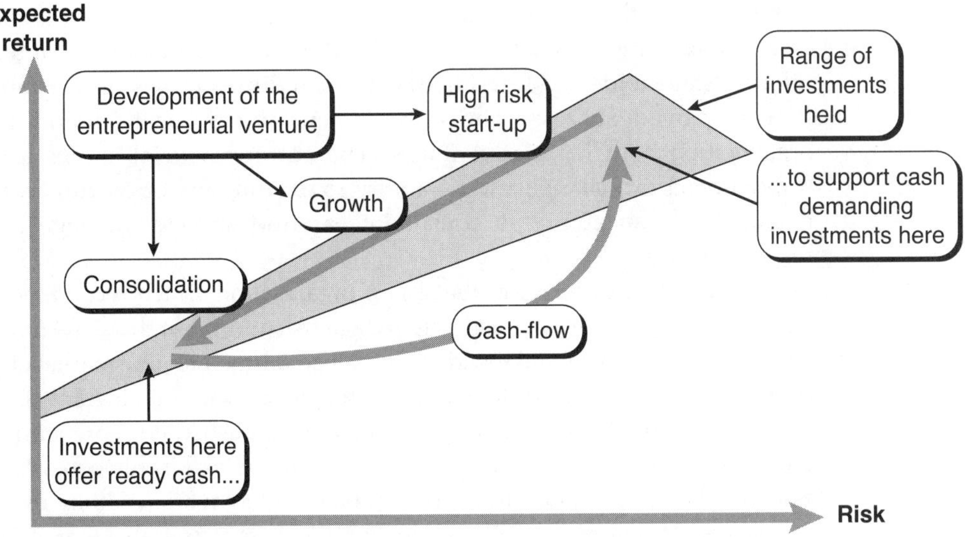

Fig. 24.1 The changing position of the entrepreneurial venture in the investor's portfolio

responsibilities may be poorly defined. Job security will be relatively low. The immediate financial rewards may be less than can be obtained elsewhere. In return for this commitment employees will, in general, expect an increase in remuneration, a well-defined role and an improvement in job security as the venture consolidates.

While the financial and security rewards of the entrepreneurial venture may be more limited than those offered by the established business, working with a fast-growing and dynamic organisation brings its own rewards at the social and personal development level. Some may perceive a loss in the way the organisation can satisfy these needs, as it consolidates. To such people, the venture's consolidation may signal an end to the sense of personal success it promises. They may feel it is time to move on to new entrepreneurial pastures.

Suppliers and customers may also have offered a commitment to the venture in its early stages. The turnover of the business will have been quite low. Many suppliers may nonetheless, have made a commitment to supplying it with a high level of customer service even though it may have cost more in real terms than they received. Customers may have taken on the business as a supplier even though switching costs had to be faced and continuity of supply was not assured. Such suppliers and customers will see the venture as successful if it returns this early commitment by operating within the business network as a fair, effective and rewarding customer / supplier itself.

24.3 Encouraging intrapreneurism

KEY LEARNING OUTCOME
An appreciation of the potential and limits to intrapreneurship in the consolidating organisation.

In recognising the power of the entrepreneurial organisation, it is important not to be too dismissive of what the established 'non-entrepreneurial' organisation has to offer its stakeholders. After all, an established business is only established because it has enjoyed success. The entrepreneurial organisation and the established organisation both have advantages. The entrepreneurial shows an acceptance of (even a need for) change and an ability to exploit new opportunity. The established demonstrates an ability to consolidate around success, manage risk and control resource flows.

A combination of the two, that is, an organisation which recognised the basis of its success and was able to manage it to reduce risk and yet at the same time was flexible to the shifting needs of its stakeholders, remained attuned to new market opportunities and responsive to the need for change, would suggest itself as an ideal type of business. The *intrapreneur* provides a means of achieving the established-entrepreneurial synthesis. The intrapreneur is a role defined by Gifford Pinchot (1985) in his book, *Intrapreneuring*. In essence, the intrapreneur is an entrepreneur who works within the confines of an established organisation. The intrapreneur's role would parallel that of the entrepreneur. In particular they would be responsible for developing and communicating organisational vision; identifying new opportunities for the organisation; generating innovative strategic options; creating and offering an organisation-wide perspective; facilitating and encouraging change within the organisation; challenging existing ways of doing things and breaking down bureaucratic inertia. This role has also been described as that of a 'change master' (Kanter, 1985).

Intrapreneurial activity can be directed at four levels within and outside the organisation. These differ in the impact they will have on the organisation and its surroundings, their effect on the venture's stakeholders, the resources they will require and the level of risk they entail.

- *The management of specific projects*. All businesses engage in new projects of some type. Projects such as new product development, the exploitation of a new market opportunity (perhaps international through exporting or strategic alliance), the integration of a new technology into the firm's operations or the acquiring of new funding are especially important to the maturing entrepreneurial venture that wants to keep its competitive edge. Such projects may be best managed in an entrepreneurial way that cuts across conventional organisational boundaries. They may be made the responsibility of a particular cross-disciplinary team that operates with intrapreneurial flair.
- *The setting up of new business units*. As the venture becomes larger, new and distinct business functions and units come into their own. A particular part of the business may operate best if it has a distinct character degree of independence. The setting up of new business units is a demanding project. Not only must the structural and external strategic issues be considered. There are also the resourcing issues (including human) and the relationship with the parent business to be taken into account. Again, an intrapreneurial team, the members of which may have a future role in the new unit, may best manage this sort of project.
- *Reinvigorating the whole organisation*. Entrepreneurship, and the success of entrepreneurial ventures, is largely based on their flexibility and responsiveness to new and unmet customer demands. Such flexibility can be lost as the business grows and its attention is drawn to internal concerns. Reintroducing the inventive spirit back into the business may be a radical process. Making the organisation entrepreneurial again is clearly an intrapreneurial project. An intrapreneur must lead such a project with entrepreneurial vision for the organisation's future, with an entrepreneurial approach to using power, leadership and motivation and an ability to overcome organisational resistance to change.
- *Reinventing the business's industry*. Entrepreneurs make a difference. The world is not the same after they have built their venture. The most successful entrepreneurs do not just enter a market: they reinvent the industry in which they operate by introducing new technology, delivering new products or operating in a new, more effective way. There is no reason why the maturing entrepreneurial venture should not hold on to this ambition. A business can win by playing to the rules well; but it can also win by changing the rules to suit itself. Clearly though, such a project is wide in its scope and challenging to implement. It demands an eye on the future, strategic vision, comfort with risk and an ability to lead people forward. It is at this level that intrapreneurship meets up with and becomes entrepreneurship.

Intrapreneurism offers an exciting option for the consolidating entrepreneurial venture. It promises a way to build on success while retaining the original dynamism of the venture. It suggests a way to reduce risk while still pursuing fleeting opportunities. However, any organisational form which promises such high rewards must also present some challenges. There are limitations to intrapreneurship.

Entrepreneur's comfort

Allowing a role for the intrapreneur to develop demands that the entrepreneur actually create space for the intrapreneur to operate. That means letting go of some degree of control. The entrepreneur, having brought the organisation to where it is by exerting control, may not feel comfortable with this. In effect, allowing the intrapreneur to operate means that the entrepreneur must share a part of his or her own role at a core rather than a peripheral level. After all, as Young (1999) points out, intrapreneurial management is about breaking rules. And this means the rules the entrepreneur has created.

Decision-making control

Entrepreneurs exist to challenge orthodoxies. They seek a better way of doing things. They must be dissatisfied with the status quo. This same dissatisfaction must also motivate the intrapreneur. Unlike the entrepreneur, however, the intrapreneur must operate within some sort of organisational decision-making control. If they were not, then they wouldn't actually be working for the organisation at all! The question here is to what extent the intrapreneur can be allowed to challenge existing decision-making procedures and to what extent they must be bound by them. A balance must be created between allowing the intrapreneur freedom to make their own moves and the need to keep the business on a constant strategic path.

Internal politics

The intrapreneur must question the existing order and drive change within the organisation. For many individuals and groups within the organisation such change will present a challenge. As a result the intrapreneur is likely to meet resistance, both active and passive, to the ideas they bring along. An ability to predict and understand that resistance, and developing the leadership skills necessary to overcome it, presents a considerable challenge to the manager. Intrapreneurs are a rare breed. Tom Peters (1989) has suggested that intrapreneurs must be able to 'thrive on chaos'.

Rewards for the intrapreneur

This point really results from the latter. The intrapreneur, if he or she is to be effective, must bring along the same type, and level, of skills that entrepreneurs themselves offer. The question is, can the organisation *really* offer the intrapreneur the rewards (economic, social and developmental) they might come to expect in return for using them? In short, if someone is an effective intrapreneur how long will it be before the temptation of full-blown entrepreneurship is felt and he or she moves off to start a venture of his or her own?

Clearly intrapreneurship presents itself as a spectrum which, as a style of management, acts to connect 'conventional' management with entrepreneurial management. It offers a way to bring the advantages of both types of management together. In this it is a compromise. The entrepreneur can only facilitate intrapreneurship within the business by recognising the nature of this compromise and making decisions in relation to it. The central question relates to how much latitude the venture's strategy gives individuals to make their own decisions. The question is not just strategic. An entrepreneur must decide to what extent he or she will be willing to accept dissent from the intrapreneur. Will it be received as a challenge? How does active dissent fit with the leadership strategy the entrepreneur has nurtured?

Entrepreneurs must also ask how the reward structure they have set up encourages and discourages individual decision making. What does the individual get in return for venturing on behalf of the business? What sanctions come into force if things go wrong? The entrepreneur must remember that such rewards and sanctions are not always formal and explicit. Further, the entrepreneur must recognise the level of resistance that agents driving change meet from the organisation and accept responsibility in helping the intrapreneur to overcome this. No less than any other member of the organisation, the intrapreneur needs support, encouragement and leadership.

Summary of key ideas

- As the venture matures, its rate of growth slows. This process is known as *consolidation*.
- Consolidation involves changes to the *financial, strategic, structural* and *organisational* dynamics of the venture.
- Consolidation offers the venture a chance to create a defendable competitive position in the marketplace. This offers the promise of rewarding the commitment stakeholders have shown towards the venture.
- *Intrapreneursim* is a form of management which, potentially, offers the venture a way of combining the flexibility and responsiveness of the entrepreneurial with the market power and reduced risk of the established organisation.

Suggestions for further reading

Kanter, R.M. (1985) *The Change Masters*, London: Unwin Hyman.

Osborne, R.L. (1991) 'The dark side of the entrepreneur', *Long Range Planning*, Vol 24, No. 3, pp. 26–31.

Osborne, R.L. (1992) 'Building an innovative organisation', *Long Range Planning*, Vol. 25, No. 6, pp. 56–62.

Peters, T. (1989) *Thriving on Chaos*, London: Macmillan.

Pinchot, III, G. (1985) *Intrapreneuring*, New York: Harper & Row.

Stopford, J.M. (1994) 'Creating corporate entrepreneurship', *Strategic Management Journal*, Vol. 15, pp. 521–36.

Vrakking, W.J. (1990) 'The innovative organization', *Long Range Planning*, Vol. 23, No. 2, pp. 94–102.

Weseley Morse, C. (1986) 'The delusion of intrapreneurship', *Long Range Planning*, Vol. 19, No. 6, pp. 92–5.

Young, A.P. (1999) 'Rule breaking and a new opportunistic managerialism', *Management Decision*, Vol. 37, No. 7, pp. 582–8.

Selected case material

Dealing in dynasties

15 March 1999

Despite its old-fashioned approach, the family-run conglomerate is one of Canada's most successful companies, writes **Edward Alden**

Power Corporation of Canada is that deeply unfashionable thing: a diversified holding run by two brothers in an age where both conglomerates and family-run businesses are out of favour.

Perhaps it is the exception that proves the rule. In Canada, where it has big insurance and mutual fund interests, Power Corp is often held up as a metaphor for the nation: its impact has been far out of proportion to its size, yet it is reluctant to boast of its accomplishments.

Paul Desmarais Sr acquired the holding company in 1968, and through a series of acquisitions and well-timed sales, market capitalisation grew from C$61m (£25.4m) to nearly C$8bn today. It is one of the largest corporations in Canada, with assets of more than C$120bn under its control in Europe, China and North America.

The only hint of the role played by Mr Desmarais Sr in opening China to Canadian investment is in the intimate dining room at Power Corp's headquarters in Montreal, where original prints from a 17th-century Chinese manuscript adorn the walls.

The prints were a gift from Bo Yibo, one of the "immortals" from China's Long March, and Chairman Mao's head of economic planning. Mr Bo spent a week at the Desmarais country estate near Quebec City in 1973, after falling ill on his way to Washington to brief Richard Nixon before his historic trip to China. Mr Nixon's visit is usually thought to have opened up diplomatic and commercial relations between China and the west. But before the US president set foot in Beijing, Pierre Trudeau, Canada's then premier, had already travelled to China. A few years later, Mr Desmarais, a legendary deal-maker, headed Canada's first trade delegation there.

The Desmarais clan is even more influential in national politics. After a separatist government first came to power in Quebec in 1976, Power Corp halted new investments in the province and strengthened its ties with the Quebec federalists who dominate the Canadian government.

No other Canadian company enjoys closer relations with the Liberal government of Prime Minister Jean Chrétien. Paul Martin, finance minister, made his fortune at Power Corp, and John Rae, Mr Chrétien's campaign manager, is among the company's top executives. In addition, André, one of Mr Desmarais's sons, is married to Mr Chrétien's daughter France.

Mr Desmarais Sr, now 73, handed over the day-to-day running of the company to his sons three year's ago. Paul Desmarais Jr, 44, and Andre, 42, became chairman and president respectively, and are co-chief executives. Their father, however, remains a significant influence behind the scenes. He still controls a majority of Power Corp's voting shares.

The challenge for Paul and André has been to keep shareholders happy with the company's complex holding structure and diverse portfolio of investments at a time when many investors want pure plays.

In Europe, where Power Corp began investing in the 1980s, investments are being pared down to four sectors: broadcasting, specialty minerals, utilities and oil.

Pargesa, a Swiss subsidiary jointly owned with Albert Frère, the Belgian financier, has acquired a 50 per cent stake in CLT-UFA, one of Europe's biggest broadcasting companies. It owns a majority of the French specialty minerals giant Imétal, which bought the UK-based English China Clays for £756m earlier this year.

Pargesa is also a big shareholder in the French utility Suez Lyonnaise des Eaux, and in TotalFina, the oil merger between Total of France and Belgium's Petrofina.

With no debt and C$3m in cash, Paul and André say they are eyeing further acquisitions in Europe.

Since taking the top jobs, the brothers have begun to put their mark on the company. In 1997, they engineered the C$2.9bn takeover of London Life, one of only two publicly quoted insurance companies in Canada, stealing the prize away from Royal Bank, the rival bidder. Canada and the US generate most of Power Corp's earnings through majority-owned subsidiaries Great-West Life, Canada's largest insurance group, and Investors Group, the largest mutual fund company.

The Desmarais approach is deceptively old-fashioned: the brothers buy large blocks in companies they think have excellent long-term growth prospects. Power Corp is an "active shareholder", says Paul Desmarais Jr: it chooses or influences the choice of top managers and shapes the strategic decisions of the companies it holds. The formula, he says, has produced steady returns with relatively low risk – compounded annual earnings have grown by 15 per cent a year over the past five years.

In addition to their investment philosophy is the Desmarais approach to business relationships, epitomised by the alliance with the Frère Group. The brothers believe in finding strong local partners and nurturing the relationship.

André Desmarais says: "An important thing for any family-controlled company is to be able to work through partnerships, because every culture is different. There are always things you have to learn and having partners is very helpful."

The search for the right partner in China partly explains why Power Corp took so long to invest there. While Power Corp has cultivated ties with top Chinese officials since the 1970s, it studied and rejected several investment opportunities before deciding last year on a joint venture with Bombardier and China's National Rail Company to build mass transit railcars in Qingdao.

André Desmarais says it took a long time

Essential Guide: Paul and André Desmarais

Groomed for the job: after education at McGill University in Montreal and the European Institute of Business Administration in France, Paul Jr became director of planning for Power in 1981, a vice-president in 1982, and chief operating officer in 1986. André was educated at Concordia in Montreal, became executive assistant to the chairman in 1981 and headed several Power subsidiaries before taking over from his brother as chief operating officer in 1991.

Family connections: the alliance between Power and the Belgian Frère Group, which formally extends to 2014, is cemented by more than just business interests. Albert Frère's son Gerald, heir to the Frère family empire, is a godfather to one of Paul Jr's children. André is married to Canadian prime minister Jean Chrétien's daughter France ("I knew when I married her 17 years ago that he would become prime minister," he quips.)

Sibling rivalry: most power sharing among chief executives falls on the sword of personal ambition, and brothers could be expected to cross swords more than usual. While the two are remarkably amicable, Paul Jr acknowledges that "the emotion factor is exponential" in a family company. But he says they have found a clever solution. André handles the China business and Paul is focused on Europe, so they rarely see each other.

to understand how to do business in China, but that patience has brought its rewards.

In Europe, Paul Desmarais Jr says the company has benefited immensely from its familiarity in both French and English-speaking cultures.

"In Canada we are bilingual, but more than bilingual, really bicultural, at ease with our British heritage and our French heritage," he says.

The brothers do not seem inclined to change their father's winning strategy, yet they are conscious that the record of family dynasties in Canada is dismal. Eaton's, once Canada's most successful department store chain, was driven to bankruptcy by the incompetence of Eaton heirs. The Southams, once the country's most powerful newspaper family, were bought out in 1996 by Conrad Black. And Edgar Bronfman, heir to the Seagram fortune, has been criticised for gambling his profitable liquor business on high-risk film and recording companies.

Paul and André will have to prove they have inherited their father's sense of timing – Mr Desmarais Sr sold his pulp and paper company, Consolidated-Bathurst, for a 50 per cent premium in 1989, just before the pulp market soured. And he disposed of Montreal Trust the same year, shortly before the entire trust industry collapsed in Canada.

Power Corp, like most holding companies, continues to trade at a discount to its underlying assets, reflecting shareholders' desire for more focused investments. Paul Desmarais Jr is sanguine, noting that the stock was briefly at a premium six months ago.

"We take a long-term view of this. If you're a long-term shareholder of Power Corp, do you really care? You will think about whether this company has sustainable earnings and sustainable franchise positions."

André Desmarais says the best insurance against a failed succession has been the careful way he and his brother have been eased into their jobs.

"This transition has been going on for a long time and the amount of responsibility given up by my father took a lot of courage," he says.

Paul and André concede that as long as their father remains the controlling shareholder, people will continue to believe he still calls the shots.

Paul Jr is good-humoured about his father being given credit for the London Life deal, even though he was then recovering from a heart operation. "My father joked: 'You know Paul, when I'm in heaven I'll still be doing the deals.' And you know something, he probably will."

Tightening Levi's belt

28 February 2000

Andrew Edgecliffe-Johnson meets the controversial brand builder who has been charged with restoring and dressing up the once iconic jeans label

Phil Marineau's wardrobe is "business appropriate" – turn-of-the-millennium jargon for casual office wear. Since Levi Strauss hired him from PepsiCo five months ago to run the company synonymous with denim, his collection of jeans has grown from two to 20 pairs, and he has yet to be spotted in a suit and tie.

"I'd taken a couple of company is dress-down before I came here," he says. "It's one of the easiest and most popular things you can do [as a boss]." His task at Levi, however, will be more difficult – to smarten up a brand that has worn through at the knees and frayed at the seams.

In past three years, Levi sales have slumped from $7.1bn (£4.5bn)to $5.1bn, poor distribution as allienated retailers, and once iconic brand is now seen by younger shoppers as "something you might put on if you're going to mend a leaking toilet", says Kurt Barnard, retail consultants. In the past decade, its market share has been cut in half, as the VF Corporations Wrangler and Lee brands, own-label offerings from Gap, and entrants such as Tommy Hilfiger have encroached on a market once dominated by Levi's 501 line.

As Levi is a private company, controlled by the descendants of its founder, Mr Marineau does not have a plunging stock price to worry about, nor does he have the comfort of a strong balance sheet. He arrived soon after Levi had breached its debt covenants, and has spent his first months renegotiating its bank loans, prompting rating agency downgrades and forcing Levi to use its prized trademark to secure new financing.

"We can restore Levi. I think it can be great, financially strong company again," he says. The 53-year-old forecasts that within two or three years sales growth will return, and cashflow haemorrhages resulting from costly restructurings will be stanched sooner.

"Businesses turn around in wide circles. They don't turn around in sharp angles." His plann is to restore financial disciplines without further disruptive restructurings, to tighten up Levis replenishment systems so retailer's shelves are not left empty, and finally to rethink Levi's portrayal of its brand.

The last goal may be a hardest to achieve. Martyn Shaw, Interbrand consultancy president, says: "Levi has not kept up with the brand's image of authenticity and rugged individualism." He argues that there are two aspects to any brand – its latent, long-term identity, and the way it is represented in the market. Of the first, he says: "The embers are still quite bright." As for market representation: "The brand is absolutely nowhere now."

Sitting in Levi's showroom in Manhattan's garment district, Mr Marineau says: "Levi jeans are a huge mass brand. Don't make them just for some 18-year-old with a ring through his or her nose. I want some 50-year-old fat guy sitting in a conference room in New York to wear them too."

Levi is launching Engineered Jeans, an aggressive modern range with skewed seams and a new, softer material, which it hopes will restore the brand's credibility with fashion-conscious 15-24-year-olds and create a "halo effect" for the entire brand. But Mr Marineau believes that Levi faltered because it veered too far towards fashion, and says its branding efforts should concentrate on the strengths of its core five-pocket product line.

"The advertising focused too much on being hip and cool, not on having a great product and then wrapping it in an attitude of youthfulness and sexiness," he says. "We are not selling attitude here, we are selling products."

His comments are heretical to some branding consultants, and Mr Straw is taken aback by Mr Marineau's plans. "[Emphasising] the quality of the jeans will absolutely take the brand the wrong way. The quality of Levi's product is good, but so is everybody else's. People buy jeans for attitude."

Instead, Mr Straw argues that Mr Marineau's priority should be to redefine what Levi brand stands for, even if that means applying it brand to other product lines such as fragrances, as Ralph Lauren and others have done. Such tactics have worked for once-lacklustre brands such as Oldsmobile cars and Gap's Banana Republic stores.

Mr Marineau's controversial branding ideas stem from his experience as head of Pepsi-Cola North America. On joining the cola company, his swiftly scrapped its "generation next" ads because he felt their focus on young customers was too narrow, and introduced the highly rated "joy of cola" campaign. "We went back to what Pepsi stood for – the product. Taste. A symbol of freedom of personal choice."

Just as he is seeking to use Engineered Jeans to bring some catchet back to Levis broader wardrobe, so he created a buzz around Pepsi with the launch of Pepsi One, it low-calorie drink. However, the fizz has gone out of Pepsi One in recent months and Mr Marineau concedes: "Getting your young to survive is really, really hard."

Mr Marineau earned his reputation as a brand builder during his 23 years with Quaker Oats. He took charge and Gatorade, an obscure sports drink, in 1984 and by the time he left Quaker in 1996 he expanded it to $1.2bn business.

During that period, Quaker also bought Snapple, another soft drink brand, which eventually sold a huge loss. Asked about the experience, he says: "Snapple was a great brand ... that was overpaid for. When people asked me was on the guy who bought Snapple, in an effort to be politically correct, I'd say "chief operating officers don't buy businesses". But I was the fall guy."

Barbara Pickens, a consumer industry recruiter with TMP Worldwide, who was known Mr Marineau since he was marketing cereal in the mid-1980s, says he has skills to revive Levi. "When he left Pepsi, people were as depressed as can be. This is a guy who leads and empowers people. He is consumer-orientated, idea-driven and he has incredibly rich, conceptual mind."

Mr Marineau marked his arrival Levi by holding one-to-one meetings with many of its employees "so people could only tell you what they feel". Ms Pickens recalls that at Quaker, "every once in a while he'd walk into his office, and say, "Throw out my in-tray – anything that's important will come to me face to face."

Such iconoclasm may go down well Levi's Californian headquarters, and Mr Marineau has already demonstrated an ability to go against the flow. As other apparel companies were pouring millions into e-commerce last year, he ceased sales over the Levi website because the effort was costing too much money.

The internet will be one of the great marketing tools of the next 20 years, he predicts, with unprecedented opportunities for marketing customised products are individually to customers, but "I wouldnt do a banner ad if my life depended on it".

If some of Mr Marineau's plans proved contentious, he will have to answer to the

Essential Guide: Phil Marineau

Education: A BA in history from Georgetown University and a MBA from Northwestern University.
Vietnam war: Headed for Saigon in 1971 "thinking I was going to be the last one out". A year later, returned to start work at Quaker Oats.
Early career: "I came out of the army on a Friday and started work on the Monday – poverty is a very motivating thing," he recalls. "Back in the 1970s, if you got a job in the packaged goods industry that was a very hot job."
Building a reputation: Within 10 years at Quaker, he was a cereal product director with a loyal following.

Barbara Pickens, a consumer industry headhunter, recalls: "When I was a recruiter in the early 1980s, the person I most wanted to meet was Phil Marineau because so many people were talking about him."

Success of Gatorade, the sports drink that has changed Quaker's focus from food to beverages, led to his promotion to chief operating officer in 1993.

Lured to Dean Foods in 1996, where he decided to persuade consumers to treat milk as a beverage in its own right rather than a food ingredient. Dean's stock doubled.
Cola wars: After only 10 months with Dean Foods, offered the role of president and chief operating officer of Pepsi-Cola North America. Improved Pepsi's relationshp with its bottlers and breathed new life into its battle with Coca-Cola.

His departure after 20 months caused consternation among some senior Pepsi executives. His friends say he preferred the idea of running his own show.
Outside interests: An opera enthusiast married to an artist. Has a house in Santa Fe, New Mexico, as well as a new property in California. Staring at his waistline, he complains that the past five months at Levi Strauss have give him little time for his other passions – hiking, biking and skiing.

Haas family, which controls Levi, rather than face the pressures the stock market places on most chief executives. "This is a great time to be a private company," he says. "It takes anywhere from 14-24 months to really figure out what our long-term strategy for growth should be, and sometimes a public markets don't give you that time."

He is confident he he will last longer at Levi Strauss than some of his predecessors. Having moved his family from mid-town Manhattan to San Francisco he says: "I'm never moving again. Off finish my career here."

Review questions

1 What are the consolidation issues present in the Power Corporation of Canada?

2 What benefits and problems might a succession buy-out present to consolidation of the venture?

3 Discuss Phil Marineau's project in terms of its intrapreneurial characteristics.

25 The changing role of the entrepreneur in the consolidated organisation

Chapter overview

This chapter is concerned with an exploration of the way in which the entrepreneur's role changes as the organisation's rate of growth slows and it consolidates its position in the marketplace. The role of the entrepreneur is compared and contrasted to that of the chief executive. It is considered why, despite its many strengths, entrepreneurial control may not always be right for the mature venture. The chapter concludes with a consideration of the responsibility of the entrepreneur in planning for passing on control to others after they have departed the organisation.

25.1 The entrepreneur versus the chief executive

KEY LEARNING OUTCOME
An appreciation of the differences between the roles of the entrepreneur and the Chief Executive Officer.

The vast majority of organisations offer a role for a single, most senior manager. This position has a number of titles. In for-profit businesses it is often the *managing director* or *president*. Generically, the role is referred to as the *chief executive officer* (CEO). while all organisations have a chief executive officer of some description, not all are led by someone we would recognise as an entrepreneur.

So while the entrepreneur *may* be a chief executive officer, the chief executive officer is not *necessarily* an entrepreneur. Clearly, both roles present considerable management challenges. Both demand vision, an ability to develop strategic insights and provide leadership. That said, the two roles are distinct in a number of ways.

Internal co-ordination versus external promotion

The resource-based view of the organisation presented in section 20.6 emphasises the role managers have in bringing in the resources that are critical to the success of the venture: capital, information, people and the goodwill of customers. The entrepreneur, especially when the venture is at an early stage and has limited management resources, will take on the responsibility for bringing in nearly all of these things. They will be the venture's salesperson, its finance expert, its recruitment specialist and so on.

The chief executive of even a moderately large organisation will not have direct responsibility for doing these things. He or she may not even have responsibility for *delegating* them, at least directly. What they will have responsibility for is setting up *management structures* within the organisation which will enable these tasks to be co-ordinated and carried out in a way that is effective and is responsive to the overall strategic direction chosen by the business. They may also recognise a need to manage the organisation's *culture*. The chief executive is not, primarily, responsible for acquiring resources so much as making sure that those which are acquired are used at a strategic level, in the best possible way.

In these terms, the entrepreneur provides a bridge between the small business manager and the chief executive of a large firm. In growing the venture, the entrapreneur transforms the role of acquiring resources into that of creating and maintaining structures to manage resources. The role changes from one of *external* promotion (that is, managing the venture in its wider *network*) to one of *internal* co-ordination.

Managing continuity versus driving change

As related in section 2.1 entrepreneurs are interested in driving change. So are chief executives. In a fast-changing world organisations must change if they are to survive and prosper. The management of change is now properly recognised as one of the key responsibilities of senior management, in whatever sector their organisation is operating. Entrepreneurs and chief executives are both interested in changing their organisations in response to the opportunities presented to them.

However, there is a difference in the *degree* of change entrepreneurs wish to see and that which chief executives would normally wish to occur. Entrepreneurs are interested in *radical* change. The entrepreneur's vision is created out of a tension between 'what is' and 'what might be'. For that vision to be powerful, the difference between what is and what might be achieved must be great. Chief executives, on the other hand, are more likely to be interested in slower and more measured *incremental* change. This is understandable. After all, their organisations have proved their success, at least historically. They must be doing something right! Incremental change can build on that success: strengths are managed in, while weaknesses are managed out. Radical change threatens to throw away the strengths as well as address the weaknesses.

Management by 'right' versus management by appointment

The third feature that distinguishes entrepreneurs from chief executives is the basis on which they obtain authority to manage the business and the influence this has on the power base they develop. As noted in section 23.3, *authority* and *power* are quite different things. Power is an ability to influence the course of actions within the organisation. Authority merely offers the potential to influence the organisation by virtue of a position within it. Authority is an *invitation* to power, not power itself.

Chief executives obtain their authority to run the business by virtue of appointment to the position. They may arrive at this position as a result of internal promotion or by being recruited into the organisation. The appointment process is governed by established organisational procedures. The views not only of internal managers but also of important investors may be sought. Once in this position, the power of the chief executive arises from the way they control resources and systems and the leadership they offer.

Entrepreneurs also gain authority from the position they occupy, their management of resources and systems, and the leadership they give to the organisation. However, an entrepreneur has an additional source of authority providing not only authority to run the business, but also a *right* to run it. While the chief executive is employed by the organisation, the organisation is perceived as 'belonging to' the entrepreneur. This perceived right can be derived from the entrepreneur's ownership of the business. However, owning the organisation they lead is not a necessary characteristic of the entrepreneur. The business is actually owned by those who invest in it. More important is the entrepreneur's historical relationship to founding the organisation and their association with *building* it up.

This difference is important not only for the way the entrepreneur actually manages the organisation but also for the way in which they are exposed as a result of its performance. While we would expect a chief executive to be ousted if the organisation he or she manages fails to perform, we can still be surprised when an entrepreneur who is seen to have created the organisation is greeted with the same fate.

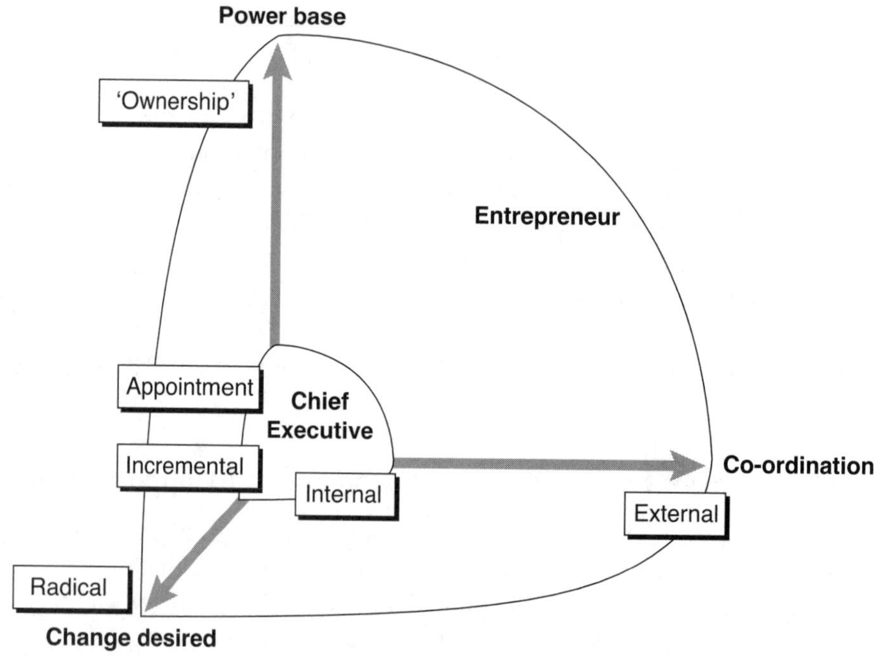

Fig. 25.1 The difference between an entrepreneur and a chief executive

Of course these three criteria do not create hard and fast categories. We are dealing with fuzzy concepts in the same way as we were when we discussed the distinction between the small business and the entrepreneurial venture in section 1.6. Whom we regard as an entrepreneur and whom we see as 'merely' a chief executive is a matter of judgement based on a consideration of the balance between all three criteria.

As with the distinction between the small business manager and the entrepreneur, we should not rush to make a judgement as to who is, or is not, an entrepreneur. We should not look towards the individual to assess whether they are an entrepreneur or not, rather we should look at what and how they manage in terms of the balance between internal and external co-ordination, the change they seek to create and the way authority is ascribed to them, i.e. the basis of their power (see Fig. 25.1).

25.2 The dangers of entrepreneurial control in the mature organisation

KEY LEARNING OUTCOME
An appreciation of some of the limitations of an entrepreneurial style of management in the mature venture.

Entrepreneurial management has a lot to offer. The entrepreneur's vision offers the potential for leadership. That vision and leadership can be used to give the venture direction. It provides an impetus for the changes that are necessary if a venture is to survive and prosper in a rapidly changing world. However, as a *style* of management, entrepreneurship is merely one style among many, and while entrepreneurship is a very powerful style of management it, like any other style, has its limitations.

Entrepreneurial management is concerned with the *whole* organisation. In the early stages of the venture this allows the entrepreneur to manage the organisation in an integrated way. The entrepreneur can put balanced emphasis on attracting all the resources the organisation requires: money, people, customers, and knowledge. Unfortunately, this may lead the entrepreneur to underestimate the value of the management of particular functions. They may be quite dismissive of the need for a dedicated approach to marketing or finance or human resource management as the venture grows and matures (relate this back to the heuristics described in Section 11.6). This can lead the entrepreneur to underestimate the contribution that specialists can make to the venture. Having made a success of the venture themselves they can become suspicious of the need for 'experts'. As a result, the entrepreneur may find it difficult to give specialist managers sufficient room to make the decisions they need to make.

Further, entrepreneurial management is concerned with driving change. This is a key and positive aspect of the entrepreneur's approach. It is only from change that new value can be created. However, it is often the case that the entrepreneur exhibits a greater desire for change than do other stakeholders. The entrepreneur may still be seeking new ways to push the venture forward while investors and employees seek consolidation and stability. As a result there may be a conflict over the type of investments undertaken by the mature venture. A number of high-profile run-ins occurred between highly successful entrepreneurs and institutional investors at the end of the 1980s in both the USA and the UK as the financial climate became more difficult. For example, both Anita and Gordon Roddick, founders of The Body Shop and Alan Sugar, founder of Amstrad, became involved in expensive share buy-backs to increase their personal control of their enterprises.

This touches on a wider issue. All organisations develop an *inertia* or resistance to change. Entrepreneurs and the organisations they create are not immune to this. While the entrepreneurial organisation is founded on an innovation there is no guarantee that it will be innovative in its innovation! Often, the innovation sets a pattern of strategic activity which the venture attempts to repeat in another sector. The initial success may not always translate to other sectors. Alan Sugar and his Amstrad venture were phenomenally successful with a formula which presented uncomplicated, easy-to-use and low cost hi-fi systems to the general public. However, the same formula was not repeated so successfully with business computers, a sector where the customer- buying criteria were quite different.

All in all, an entrepreneurial style of management has a great and valuable role to play in the mature organisation. However, it is essential that entrepreneurs recognise that the way they involve themselves with and apply their talents to the mature organisation differs from the way they did when the organisation was in a fast-growing state.

25.3 The role of the founding entrepreneur in the mature organisation

KEY LEARNING OUTCOME

An appreciation of the types of role the entrepreneur can undertake in the mature organisation.

The role of the entrepreneur must change as the venture develops. Growth offers founding entrepreneurs the same opportunity as it offers every other member of the organisation: the chance to develop and specialise the role they play within the organisation. Some of the more important types of specialisation are listed below (see also Fig. 25.2).

Chief executive

The most obvious role for the entrepreneur to play is that of chief executive. In this the entrepreneur has a clearly defined position at the head of the organisation. He or she retains the power to make and influence key decisions about the way the business should be conducted. The chief executive role is, of course, one which the entrepreneur can drift into by virtue of always being at the head of the business. However, the points made in the previous section about the differences between the way the entrepreneur leads the growing business and the chief executive manages the mature business must be considered here in relation to the evolution of that role.

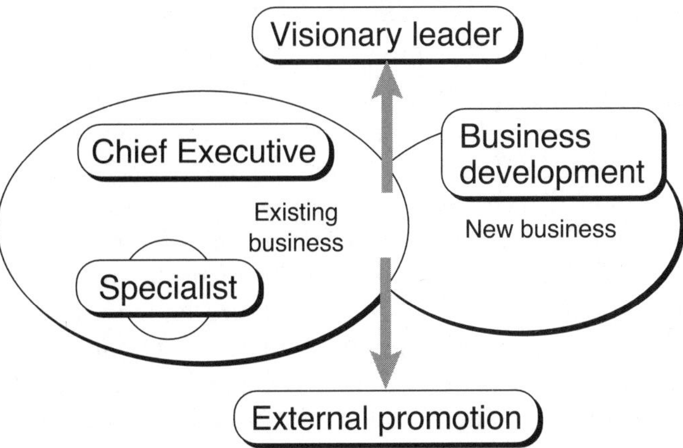

Fig. 25.2 The roles of the entrepreneur in the mature organisation

Visionary leader

As discussed in section 7.2 the entrepreneur has a variety of means at his or her disposal when it comes to influencing the direction the organisation takes and the way it manages its resources. Entrepreneurs do not have to direct every decision personally. They can use indirect means of communicating vision, directing strategy and controlling the organisation's culture. This means that the entrepreneur can specialise the role they play along the leadership dimension. By taking on the role of a visionary leader, the entrepreneur avoids making decisions personally. Rather they create an environment which brings out the best in the organisation's people by motivating them and giving them an overall sense of direction. This is the kind of role played by the Virgin chief, Richard Branson, who while providing leadership to his organisation leaves most of the decision making to his professional managers.

Manager of business development

Entrepreneurs sometimes find it difficult to let go of the entrepreneurial approach they have developed. They do not find the chief executive role a comfortable one. Yet they can still recognise the need for a consolidatory approach to the management of the mature venture. They may resolve this dilemma by concentrating on the development of new business, a task which is well suited to an entrepreneurial style. The entrepreneur then delegates management of the established business to another manager. If the business is made up of a number of independent business units then this arrangement can be made explicit. The entrepreneur can leave the running of the business units to their managers and can concentrate on making new acquisitions for example. On the other hand, if the business is a single coherent organisation then the arrangement may be more implicit and be based on internal delegation.

An example here might be Rupert Murdoch with his News International and BSkyB business ventures. While taking a very active interest in the established business, Murdoch is most active at the cutting edge of his growing empire.

Technical specialist

Sometimes the entrepreneur may decide to give up the chief executive position altogether and take on what, at face value, appears to be a subordinate role within the organisation. In this role they will specialise in some way, perhaps in managing product development or marketing. Though uncommon, this sometimes occurs in high-technology organisations which have been founded by technical experts. An example of this is Martin Woods, a physicist, who while based at the Cavendish Laboratories founded the successful Oxford Instruments Company, a major manufacturer of components for hospital scanners. Once the venture had passed the stage where product innovation was the most important thing, and marketing and financial management became of greater importance, Dr Woods passed on the day-to-day running of the company to marketing and finance professionals and moved back to the laboratory as the company's research and development director.

Promoter of the venture

The entrepreneurial venture must continue to attract the support of external stakeholders, not least customers and financial backers. The entrepreneur may take on the role of figurehead and work at promoting the organisation to these stakeholders. An important example of this kind of approach is that of Anita and Gordon Roddick and The Body Shop organisation. The conventional chief executive role is largely played by Gordon while Anita Roddick represents the organisation in the media, promotes it to existing and new franchise holders and seeks out new ingredient suppliers in the developing world.

Entrepreneur in an alternative venture

Entrepreneurs can, of course, decide that the consolidated organisation has little to offer them. They may decide to liquidate their holding and use the resources to start another venture. This is precisely what the serial entrepreneurs Howard Hodgeson of Hodgeson Holdings and James Dyson have done in the past.

25.4 Succession in the entrepreneurial business

KEY LEARNING OUTCOME
A recognition of the importance of managing leadership succession when the entrepreneur leaves the venture.

The average life of a business is probably about the same as the working life of a manager. However, this average can be misleading. It includes a lot of businesses which only last a few years, and a few who have existed for hundreds. The successful entrepreneurial venture should be expected to last a lot longer than the career span of the founding entrepreneur. This longevity raises the issue of *succession*.

Succession creates a number of issues for the venture. Even though the business has an existence independent of the entrepreneur, the entrepreneur is more than an 'optional extra'. He or she is an integral part of the organisation. The loss of the entrepreneur represents the loss of one of its key resources. The entrepreneur must be replaced. How the entrepreneur is to be replaced, by whom, when, and in what way, represent critical decision areas for the business.

As Harris and Ogbonna (1999) make clear, founding entrepreneurs leave a *strategic* as well as a personal legacy. Reuber and Fischer (1999) develop a perspective on founder contribution that emphasises that the founder's knowledge and experience is not so much a 'stock' but a continual 'stream' that flows into the organisation.

The need for continuity ...

All organisations need some continuity. The entrepreneur, especially if they are a motivating leader, offers a reference point about which the organisation can cohere. After the entrepreneur has gone that coherence may be lost. As a result the business risks losing focus and direction.

... and for change

On the other hand, all organisations must recognise the need for change in response to a rapidly changing environment. Founding entrepreneurs, while they may be effective managers of subsequent change, may also impart an inertia to the business which makes some changes difficult. Bringing a new leader presents an opportunity which, if used properly, offers the chance to effect necessary and beneficial changes in the way the business is run.

Choosing a successor

Change at the top is a contingency which may be planned for. The entrepreneur may not like to think in terms of ending their relationship with the venture but they owe it to all the other stakeholders to consider the possibility and prepare for it. A major part of this is identifying a successor. It is important here for the entrepreneur to recognise the opportunity for change. The business will have moved a long way from its foundation. The characteristics the entrepreneur originally brought to the venture may not be the same ones it needs from a chief executive now. In choosing a successor, the entrepreneur must look for someone who is right for the business, not someone who is a copy of themselves.

The entrepreneur should also look for advice in choosing a successor. The opinions of other managers and key outsiders (particularly investors) may be valuable and influential. A successor may be sought within the business or they may be brought from outside. There are a number of key questions that must be asked about any candidate for succession.

- Do they have the necessary technical knowledge of the business sector?
- Do they have the right business skills?
- Do they have the ability to manage and develop the relationships the entrepreneur has established?
- Do they have an ability to lead the business?
- How will the leadership style offered compare with that of the outgoing entrepreneur?

- Do they have the ability to take on the entrepreneur's vision and continue to communicate it?
- Do they have the ability to provide a sense of continuity?
- Yet are they also capable of offering a new perspective?
- Will they be acceptable to all the stakeholders in the venture?

A 1992 issue of the *Journal of Accountancy* (Vol. 174, No. 4, p.24) offers a comprehensive checklist for managing family succession. Fox *et al.* (1996) consider the management of these issues.

Mentoring

The entrepreneur may be replaced as the head of the business. However, this is only a transfer of title. Being made the new chief executive only offers a promise of *authority*, that is, the potential to create change, not *power* which is an ability to create change. (Consider the points made in section 23.3.) Exercising power demands not only a position but also influence over the organisation's resources. This means not just tangible resources, but also the intangibles of generating vision and control of the symbolic dimensions of organisational life.

Mentoring may offer a means by which these things may be transferred. The entrepreneur selects a successor well ahead of the time when succession actually need take place and the successor is then trained to take over. This process involves the transfer of knowledge, education and support and a passing on of power. The successor is made *visible* as a successor. The organisation is made to recognise the successor as its future leader. The entrepreneur educates his or her successor not only in the details of the business, but also in terms of how it may be led and controlled. The actual transfer of power may be gradual with the successor given responsibility for distinct aspects of the business over time.

Remember the business

Choosing a successor is not easy. It demands that the entrepreneur admit to being mortal. It may also be tempting for the entrepreneur to favour a relative as successor if a relative wishes to take over! Many do not wish to (see Stavrou (1999). Morris *et al.* (1996) detail some of the challenges family successors meet on taking over the business. While the offspring of entrepreneurs often show great business acumen and leadership ability, there is no reason why they *must* do so. Entrepreneurship is learnt, not inherited! Keeping a business within the family may be appropriate (especially if it is privately owned). However, the entrepreneur has a responsibility to *all* the organisation's stakeholders. The entrepreneur should always remember the business and select a successor who is able to manage it as effectively as they themselves could.

Succession is an important issue and it is one which good entrepreneurs address openly, rationally and honestly. Successful entrepreneurs build entire new worlds. There is no reason why that new world should not continue after they have left it. The businesses they leave are testaments to the differences they have made.

Good luck in making the difference you want to!

Summary of key ideas

- The roles of the entrepreneur and the chief executive are subtly different, although they overlap in many ways. The entrepreneur is more interested in creating change, and may be more willing to take risks than the role of chief executive properly calls for. This can expose the mature venture to unnecessary risk.
- Consolidation gives entrepreneurs an opportunity to specialise their roles within their organisations.
- Effective entrepreneurs manage the process of *succession* (the handing over of power within the venture) when it is time for them to move on.

Suggestions for further reading

Fox, M., Nilakant, V. and **Hamilton, R.T.** (1996) 'Managing succession in family-owned businesses', *International Small Business Journal,* Vol. 15, No. 1, pp. 15–25.

Gabarro, J.J. (1985) 'When a new manager takes charge', *Harvard Business Review,* May-June, pp. 110–23.

Harris, L.C. and **Ogbonna, E.** (1999) 'The strategic legacy of company founders', *Long Range Planning,* Vol. 32, No. 3, p. 333.

Kransdorff, A. (1996) 'Succession planning in a fast-changing world', *Management Decision,* Vol. 34, No. 2, pp. 30–4.

Morris, M.H., Williams, R.W. and **Nell, D.** (1996) 'Factors influencing family business succession', *International Journal of Entrepreneurial Behaviour and Research,* Vol. 2, No. 3, pp. 68–81.

Pearson, G.J. (1989) 'Promoting entrepreneurship in large companies', *Long Range Planning,* Vol. 22, No. 3, pp. 87–97.

Reuber, A.R. and **Fischer, E.** (1999) 'Understanding the consequences of founders' experience', *Journal of Small Business Management,* Vol. 37, No. 2, pp. 30–45.

Slatter, S., Ransley, R. and **Woods, E.** (1988) 'USM chief executives: Do they fit the entrepreneurial stereotype?' *International Small Business Journal,* Vol. 6. No. 3, pp. 10–23.

Stavrou, E.T. (1999) 'Succession in family businesses: Exploring the effects of demographic factors on offspring's intentions to join and take over the business', *Journal of Small Business Management,* Vol. 37, No. 3, pp. 43–61.

Wills, G. (1992) 'Enabling managerial growth and ownership succession', *Management Decision,* Vol. 30, No. 1, pp. 10–26.

Selected case material

Founders must learn when to step down

11 June 1998

Companies may benefit when a new manager with outside experience takes over at the top, says **Victoria Griffith**

Shortly after Ben & Jerry's, the ice-cream company, went public in 1985, Ben Cohen, co-founder and then chief executive officer, gave an interview to a publication called the Wall Street Transcript. Anyone reading the conversation might have guessed Mr Cohen's days as chief executive were numbered. When asked if he believed he could attain a 15 per cent increase in earnings each year for the next five years, Mr Cohen responded: "I got no idea." When questioned about capital spending, he replied: "I don't have any idea as to that either." Finally, the interviewer asked Mr Cohen about his hobbies. "Eating mostly," he replied. "Ping-pong."

Mr Cohen may have felt serious talk about financial statements would not fit his image as a free spirit and ice-cream man. But it is just as likely that Mr Cohen was genuinely uninterested. His skill and interest lie in creating ice-cream flavours and marketing the company, not in projecting profits. Soon after the company went public, he handed the day-to-day operations of the corporation to Fred "Chico" Lager in the first of a string of chief executive appointments. No businessman is more admired in the US than the successful entrepreneur. The idea of building something out of nothing appeals to Americans' sense of frontiersmanship. Yet the qualities that enchant the public may turn off investors who often see founders as people with good ideas but without the maturity to oversee a large operation.

At a time when the internet has turned a number of entrepreneurs into overnight millionaires, it is ironic that company founders are having a harder time maintaining control. In the past, it would have been unthinkable for anyone to ask Henry Ford to step down from running Ford Motor Company. These days, founders step aside almost routinely from the key management role in the companies they created.

"Silicon Valley is teeming with engineers with good ideas," says Mike Moritz, partner of Sequoia Capital, the venture capital firm that backed the internet search engine Yahoo!. "But to make it work, you need experienced managers with the advantage of having trained and participated in a marathon before."

In the new rush to form and build companies quickly, founders are under pressure to step aside early on. Netscape, the brain-child of Marc Andreessen and Jim Clark, was placed in the hands of seasoned manager Jim Barksdale shortly after its birth. Dave Dorman took over from founder Christopher Hassett at Pointcast, the internet news service, three years after it was formed.

Venture capitalists at Sequoia Capital in California took one look at baby-faced Jerry Yang and David Filo, founders of Yahoo! and told them they would need to pass the reins to a more experienced manager if they wanted to cut a deal. "We realised it was time to bring in an adult," joked Mr Yang during a presentation at Harvard Business School.

What has changed? Companies are more dependent on outside capital to grow and founders are likely to be scrutinised by investors and financial analysts before they have had much chance to prove themselves as managers. Theorists say markets are also shifting with such speed that many companies need a constant changing of the guard to keep pace.

"Founders are seldom the best people to manage the company in the long run," says Allan Cohen, professor of entrepreneurship at Babson College and author of a new book on leadership. "It's difficult for anyone to remain in power for more than a decade and continue to be effective."

The constant metamorphosis of industries means companies need ever-changing sets of skills to stay on top. "If your strength as head of a bookselling chain has been store location and the sector becomes internet-based, as seems to be happening, you may find yourself unable to provide the right leadership," says Mr Cohen.

The pressure may be strong in Silicon Valley. "We haven't got the luxury in this industry of letting managers learn on the job," said Mr Moritz of Sequoia Capital. "By the time they've got a lesson or two under their belts, the company's dead."

Corporate graveyards are filled with founders who overstayed their tenure. Ken Olsen, the creator of Digital Equipment Corporation, the computer giant, was exiled from the company in 1992 – too late say some, who believe the group had been run into the ground. Steve Jobs was criticised for not leaving his creation, Apple Computer, sooner, although as its current chief executive, he has been welcomed back as conquering hero. Paul Fireman, chief executive of Reebok, the athletic shoe company, has lingered at the company, in spite of promises to step down if he failed to stage a recovery.

The youth and inexperience of company founders can become apparent quickly, say managers. "Jerry and David are really smart, articulate and have a visceral sense of audience, but I brought in strong cash management right away," says Tim Koogle, chief executive of Yahoo!. "It's amazing how many start-ups forget about that. You can also get into some ego problems with the young. They want to control everything."

Dave Dorman, chief executive of Pointcast, says the danger of over-inflated egos has grown with the media attention lavished on young internet stars. "Marc Andreessen landed on the cover of Business Week, a spot that used to be reserved only for the executives of blue-chip companies," says Mr Dorman. "These guys are treated like rock stars and like new rock stars, they can get carried away with it all."

But writing founders out too quickly may do the company a disservice. In some cases, eccentric tinkerers have the ability to see their companies through many stages of development – Bill Gates and Richard Branson come to mind.

Even if their day-to-day management skills are lacking, founders can be powerful figureheads for companies, particularly in consumer industries. Much of the appeal of Ben & Jerry's has been the founders' personalities. Tom First and Tom Scott, founders of Nantucket Nectars, the drinks group, do most of the company's radio commercials and give the brand an effective folksy feel.

Is it possible for companies to have the best of both worlds – keeping founders on board while bringing in experienced management for day-to-day operations? Perhaps. Some question the extent of Mr Gates's involvement in Microsoft, seeing him as an ideas man largely keeping out of short-term strategy decisions.

Founders may yearn to step out of the spotlight, leaving behind big company management for the fun things they used to do when they started the company. At Ben &

Jerry's for instance, Mr Cohen continues to invent new ice-cream flavours.

Yet co-habitation is difficult to pull off. Few founders can take a back seat while new management takes their business in a direction they do not approve of. Bob Holland, chief executive of Ben & Jerry's, clashed so harshly with the company's founders that he was replaced.

"I see the company as my baby," says Jim Koch, founder and chief executive of Boston Beer, the maker of Sam Adams. "New management may take unnecessary risks. This is the last job I'll ever have, but if you bring in someone from outside, they may just be building their résumé."

While there are no easy solutions, the trend away from founder-managed companies looks likely to continue. For creators, the challenge becomes when to step down and how much involvement to maintain afterwards. For investors, the question is how much the corporation will gain and lose by the exit of its founders.

"Too many companies become the albatross around founders' necks," says William Sahlman, a professor at Harvard Business School. "They don't see any reason to leave when things are going well and can't bring themselves to leave when things go badly. For the ones who stay on, it usually ends up with the founders going out in a body bag after a palace revolt."

The importance of a smooth transition

7 October 1998

It's one of the toughest challenges facing family companies. **Katharine Campbell** looks at how one company successfully handed over the reins from one generation to another

Allan Willett, founder and chairman of Willett International, a manufacturer and distributor of coding and labelling systems, was already running his first business – importing plastics machinery – in his mid-20s.

So he is unconcerned by the relative youth of his 31-year-old son, Robert, to whom he has recently handed the reins. "By his age I had had my business for six years," he says. "Of course it wasn't the size of Willett [sales £74m in the year to March 31 1998]. But Robert has people around him to help. I didn't have that – my father was a farmer [in east India]." Managing succession is one of the toughest challenges facing family companies. But Mr Willett reckons that by planning the process over many years, and by allowing Robert to develop an independent career abroad first, he has assured a smooth transition and installed a boss with the right attributes for the next phase of the company's development.

Founded in 1983, business has grown rapidly. By retaining cash and not paying a dividend until four years ago, it has flourished without outside funding. It draws as much as 95 per cent of its revenue from outside the UK, and has subsidiaries in 25 countries.

Back in 1990, with turnover at £27m and growing fast, Mr Willett had already spotted the need for change. "I was just one heartbeat away from disaster. It was becoming more than one man could operate."

So, as a first step, he created what he dubbed the "tricom": a management committee of three. That meant opening up the decision-making process to include Alan Barrell, recruited from outside to bolster sales and marketing, and Chris May, a trusted insider in charge of finance and administration. Both in their late-50s, they were, however, not the people to take the business on, according to Mr Willett. Nor were his two daughters interested in the job.

Robert, meanwhile, had been "running his own career" in the US. Fed up with the "rigidity" of life at Radley, the public school, he had read comparative literature at Brown University and taken an MBA at Stanford.

The company lent rather than gave him the money for the latter, his father explains proudly.

Robert moved into business development at Pfizer, then into strategic planning in Unilever's North American detergents operation. "No one I worked with even knew there was a family business," he says in his mid-Atlantic accent.

It was at his father's 60th birthday, in August 1996, that he was confronted with the big decision. "We sat down and I said 'It's sort of now or never'," explains Mr Willett.

Robert admits to having agonised for months. He was reluctant to leave the career he had built in the US, and had also been toying with the idea of starting his own business.

"I decided in the end I was not a street-fighter" – unlike his father, whom he credits with "phenomenal business cunning".

Meanwhile the board met, without Mr Willett in the way. "Robert's appointment didn't just happen, they came back with questions. Their main concern was whether the chemistry worked."

They decided it did – and Robert says he was considerably influenced by four senior managers who took him aside at his father's birthday party and told him how much they wanted him to join. When he finally agreed, it was a huge relief. About the only other option had been to go public – but Mr Willett felt he was too old, and his staff were not keen. "When you see the gyrations our competitors go through every six months to make the figures work for the stock market, it rather puts you off."

Robert joined in January 1997 – as deputy chairman – and spent the first six months on a strategic review. The business was decentralised, and four regional general managers appointed.

"Creating a global business is like building a house. Did he give you my analogy?" Mr Willett asks. (The two had been interviewed for this article separately). Robert – who refers to his father as "Allan Willett" – had not used the analogy. "I told him, I have built the foundations, the roof is on. But the plumbing is not very good. The staircase is a bit rickety, the electricity needs fixing."

The industry was also changing. No longer driven purely by the provision of the right hardware, it was more about coming up with the right software solutions, and about good marketing. These were areas Robert understood, and he also possessed a more patient management style, according to his father.

"If you are taking 25 companies into systems integration, it has got to be carefully handled," says Willett senior.

The succession planning has involved the creation of a new trust – to stop fragmentation of the family shareholding that often happens as share ownership passes down the generations.

An advisory board is being established, with three, as yet unnamed, outside directors (two Americans and one Scandinavian), and three insiders, presently the two Willetts and Mr May.

"There has got to be a majority if (the family) wants to sell a single share or pay a dividend. I'm putting an anchor down so that my descendants can't just flog the business."

A new remuneration structure has also been set up – an idea Robert picked up from a fellow participant at a succession planning course he attended with his father at IMD, the Lausanne business school, last year.

The advisory board decides the split between retained cash (currently 70 per cent of after tax profits), the family's dividends, and senior managers' bonuses (split equally).

"We have taken out a whole area of potential conflict," claims Robert, who took the chief executive title in the summer.

His father is now "hands-off chairman" – spending half his time on his public policy roles, notably his chairmanship of the new south eastern regional development agency.

"Funnily enough, I don't have a problem with Robert running the business. The much tougher thing was sharing the decision-making with Chris and Alan."

So far there has only been one significant disagreement. He had been developing a particular business that Robert felt was a distraction from the company's focus. "I would have gone on, but that's me, the nature of the beast. He said no, he wanted to talk to the executive board. They agreed to dispose of it [which is happening now]. I respect that, I'm not going into the desert to sulk."

The new boss has plenty on his plate. The strength of the pound has already wiped some £16m off last year's sales, forcing a cut in the dividend, and a few redundancies – even if Mr Willett is adamant the company is holding "a steady course, doing exactly what we planned to do, as a private company can".

But Willett senior reckons his new appointee has already proved himself, not least by showing he is "not his father's son".

He is probably right. He certainly does not borrow his analogies.

Review questions

Outline the issues in, and suggest means to deal with the succession issues for:

1 Ben & Jerry's

2 Willet International.

Index